H. P. Zima (Ed.)

Parallel Computation

First International ACPC Conference
Salzburg, Austria, September 30 - October 2, 1991
Proceedings

Springer-Verlag
Berlin Heidelberg New York
London Paris Tokyo
Hong Kong Barcelona
Budapest

Series Editors

Gerhard Goos
Universität Karlsruhe
Postfach 69 80
Vincenz-Priessnitz-Straße 1
W-7500 Karlsruhe, FRG

Juris Hartmanis
Department of Computer Science
Cornell University
5148 Upson Hall
Ithaca, NY 14853, USA

Volume Editor

Hans P. Zima
University of Vienna, Dept. of Statistics and Computer Science
Brünner Str. 72, A-1210 Vienna, Austria

CR Subject Classification (1991): D.1.3, D.3.2, D.2.6, F.2.1-2

ISBN 3-540-55437-8 Springer-Verlag Berlin Heidelberg New York
ISBN 0-387-55437-8 Springer-Verlag New York Berlin Heidelberg

This work is subject to copyright. All rights are reserved, whether the whole or part of the material is concerned, specifically the rights of translation, reprinting, re-use of illustrations, recitation, broadcasting, reproduction on microfilms or in any other way, and storage in data banks. Duplication of this publication or parts thereof is permitted only under the provisions of the German Copyright Law of September 9, 1965, in its current version, and permission for use must always be obtained from Springer-Verlag. Violations are liable for prosecution under the German Copyright Law.

© Springer-Verlag Berlin Heidelberg 1992
Printed in Germany

Typesetting: Camera ready by author
Printing and binding: Druckhaus Beltz, Hemsbach/Bergstr.
45/3140-543210 - Printed on acid-free paper

Lecture Notes in Computer Science   591
Edited by G. Goos and J. Hartmanis

Advisory Board: W. Brauer   D. Gries   J. Stoer

Preface

The Austrian Center for Parallel Computation (ACPC) is a co-operative research organization founded in 1989 to promote research and education in the field of Software for Parallel Computer Systems. The areas in which the ACPC is active include algorithms, languages, compilers, programming environments, and applications for parallel and high-performance computing systems.

The partner institutions of the ACPC come from the University of Vienna, the Technical University of Vienna, and the Universities of Linz and Salzburg. They carry out joint research projects, share a pool of hardware resources, and offer a joint curriculum in Parallel Computation for graduate and postgraduate students.

The First International Conference of the ACPC took place in Salzburg, Austria, from September 30 through October 2, 1991. The conference attracted more than 130 participants from around the world. Authors from 15 countries submitted 66 papers, from which 28 were selected and presented at the conference. In addition, eight distinguished researchers presented invited papers. The papers from these presentations are contained in this proceedings volume. Based on the quality of the papers presented and the response of the participants, the ACPC has decided to organize a conference every other year. The Second Conference of the ACPC will take place in Vienna in June 1993.

The organization of the conference was the result of the dedicated work of a large number of individuals, not all of whom can be mentioned here. I would like, in particular, to acknowledge the efforts made by the members of the Program Committee, the referees, and the Local Arrangements Committee. The organizational and administrative support from Barbara Chapman, Irmgard Husinsky, Bernhard Knaus, Romana Schiller and Peter Zinterhof was exceptionally valuable.

Finally, we gratefully acknowledge the following organizations which have supported the conference:

The Austrian Ministry for Science and Research
The Austrian Science Foundation (FWF)
The Governor of the Province of Salzburg
The Mayor of the City of Salzburg
Amt der O.Ö. Landesregierung
Kulturabteilung des Amtes der Oberösterreichischen Landesregierung
Kammer der Gewerblichen Wirtschaft für Oberösterreich
Linzer Hochschulfonds
Vereinigung Österreichischer Industrieller Landesgruppe Oberösterreich
Digital Equipment Corporation GmbH (Vienna)

Digital Equipment Corporation GmbH Campusnahes Forschungszentrum (Vienna)
IBM Austria (Vienna)
Sony Austria GmbH (Anif, Salzburg)
MASPAR Distributor AG (Zürich-Oberengstringen, Switzerland)
Intel Corporation Ltd. (Swindon, UK)
nCUBE Deutschland GmbH (Munich)
Bacher Electronics GmbH (Vienna)
SiliconGraphics Computer Systems (Grasbrunn-Neukäferloh)
Cray Research GmbH (Munich)
Cray Research Inc.(USA)
Meiko Limited (Bristol, UK)
Parsytec (Aachen)
Floating Point System GmbH (Riemerling)
Convex GmbH (Frankfurt)
Control Data GmbH (Vienna)
Emco Maier and Co. (Hallein)

Vienna, March 1992   Hans P. Zima

Contents

Scalable Cache Coherence for Shared Memory Multiprocessors 1
M. Thapar, B.A. Delagi, M.J. Flynn

New Program Restructuring Technology 13
M. Wolfe

Data Parallel Program Design 37
T.G. Lewis, R. Currey, J. Liu

A Powerful High-Level Debugger for Parallel Programs 54
Ch. Caerts, R. Lauwereins, J.A. Peperstraete

The PCP/PFP Programming Models on the BBN TC2000 65
E.D. Brooks III, B.C. Gorda, K.H. Warren

Knowledge-Based Parallelization for Distributed Memory Systems 77
B.M. Chapman, H.M. Herbeck

Parallelization for Multiprocessors with Memory Hierarchies 89
M. Gerndt, H. Moritsch

Trace View: A Trace Visualization Tool 102
A.D. Malony, D.H. Hammerslag, D.J. Jablonowski

Parallel and Distributed Programming With ParMod-C 115
A. Weininger, Th. Schnekenburger, M. Friedrich

Code Generation for a Data Parallel SIMD Language 127
P. Brezány, V. Sipková

Data Structures for Optimizing Programs with Explicit Parallelism 139
M. Wolfe, H. Srinivasan

MODULA-S: A Language to Exploit Two Dimensional Parallelism . . . 157
W. Diestelkamp, H. Bi, A. Böttcher

MODULA-2* and Its Compilation 169
M. Philippsen, W.F. Tichy

ADAPTing Fortran 90 Array Programs for Distributed Memory Architectures . 184
J.H. Merlin

Evolution of Massive Parallel Compute Servers from a Research Object to a
Production Pool 201
M.H. Reymond

Processor Scheduling in Multiprocessor Systems 208
S.K. Tripathi, G. Serazzi, D. Ghosal

Multipacket Routing on Rings 226
F. Makedon, A. Simvonis

Massively Parallel Processing in High Energy Physics:
The CERN-MPPC Project 238
G. Vesztergombi, F. Rohrbach

A Heuristic Algorithm for Dynamic Task Allocation in
Highly Parallel Systems 252
H.-U. Heiss, R. Wiesenfarth

Analysis of Parallel Lisp Programs Based on a Trace Mechanism 266
H. Ilmberger, S. Thürmel

A Distributed Implementation of Flat Concurrent Prolog on
Multi-Transputer Environments 277
U. Glässer, G. Hannesen, M. Kärcher, G. Lehrenfeld

Negation in Conclog 289
J.-M. Jacquet

Symbolic Computation and Parallel Software 316
P.S. Wang

On the Parallelization of Characteristic-Set-Based Algorithms 338
D. Wang

Multiplication as Parallel as Possible 350
P. Lippitsch, K.C. Posch, R. Posch

On the Existence of an Efficient Parallel Algorithm for a
Graph Theoretic Problem 359
J. Zerovnik

On the Multi-Threaded Computation of Modular Polynomial
Greatest Common Divisors 369
W. Küchlin

A Buchberger Algorithm for Distributed Memory Multiprocessors 385
D.J. Hawley

Computational Biology on Massively Parallel Machines 391
K. Schulten

Time-Parallel Multigrid in an Extrapolation Method for Time-Dependent
Partial Differential Equations 401
G. Horton, R. Knirsch

Parallelization of Simulation Tasks: Methodology - Implementation - Application 412
F. Breitenecker, G. Schuster, I. Husinsky, J. Fritscher

Parallel Algorithms for Stress Analysis on Shared-Memory Multiprocessors 426
H. Adeli, O. Kamal

Elastic Load-Balancing for Image Processing Algorithms. 438
S. Miguet, Y. Robert

Scalable Cache Coherence for Shared Memory Multiprocessors

Manu Thapar
Digital Equipment
Corporation
and
Stanford University

Bruce A. Delagi
Sun Microsystems
and
Stanford University

Michael J. Flynn
Stanford University

701 Welch Road, Palo Alto, CA 94304, USA

Abstract

This paper presents a performance analysis of a new directory based cache coherence protocol. We compare the fully mapped centralized directory protocol with a distributed directory protocol developed by us. The distributed directory protocol is based on a linked list of caches and is more scalable in terms of cost and performance. It does not require the network to preserve the order of messages and allows adaptive routing so that network performance may be more robust. Simulation results show that the distributed directory protocol has better performance than the centralized directory protocol for the benchmarks we have analyzed.

1 Introduction

In a shared memory multiprocessor system, each processor usually has an associated cache. If these multiple caches are allowed to simultaneously have copies of a given memory location, a mechanism must exist to ensure that all copies remain consistent when the contents of that memory location are modified. This is known as the cache coherence problem, which is an important and well known problem in shared memory multiprocessors. "Snoopy" cache coherence protocols are well understood for bus-based shared memory architectures [2]. These protocols require that each cache watch all traffic on the bus and take appropriate action for addresses that are present in that cache. Addresses are, in effect, transmitted to each cache by global broadcast. The shared bus limits the number of processors to the number that can be connected to the bus without saturating it. To support *scalable* shared memory architectures, the cache coherence protocol must work in the absence of a global broadcast mechanism. Centralized directory based schemes [1, 4] are a possible solution in this environment. More recently, protocols based on a linked list of caches have been proposed [11, 8]. In this paper we compare the

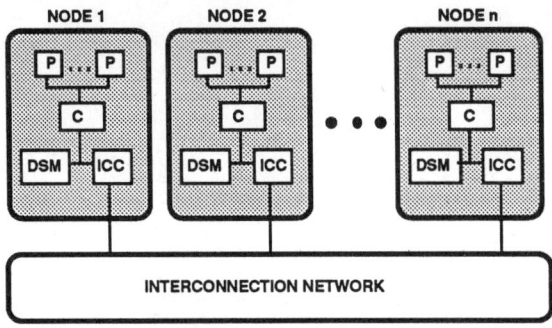

Figure 1: The basic architecture

fully mapped centralized directory protocol [4] with a distributed directory protocol [11] that we have developed.

In the distributed directory protocol, the information about which caches have copies of the data is decentralized and distributed among the cache lines. Our implementation, like the fully mapped centralized directory scheme, tracks any number of cache copies and never requires invalidates to be sent to all caches in the system. It is scalable to larger systems and has better performance than the fully mapped directory based coherence scheme. In the fully mapped scheme, the size of the memory required to hold the state information is $O(MN)$, where M is the size of main memory and N is the number of caches. In our scheme, on the other hand, the size of the memory required to hold the state information is only $O(M \log N)$. We do not assume that the interconnection network preserves the order of messages and thus allow adaptive routing. The protocol also allows an efficient implementation of locks [11].

2 Centralized Directory Protocols

We assume a very general computing system structure in our description of the protocols. Figure 1 describes this basic architecture. Each node consists of one or more processing elements (P), a cache (C), an interconnect controller (ICC) and part of the distributed shared memory (DSM). The DSM includes the directory.

In the directory based protocols there is a directory "tag" associated with each line in main memory. This directory is used to hold information about which caches have copies of the line. In the fully mapped centralized[1] directory scheme, the directory has N valid (or "present") bits per line, where N is the number of caches. The amount of storage needed for the directory in the fully mapped scheme is thus $O(MN)$, where M is the size

---

[1] We use the term *centralized* since the information about caches that have copies of a memory line is located at one place. The directory tags are an extension of the lines in the DSM and are located on the same node as the corresponding lines in main memory.

of main memory. If a cache has a copy of the line, the present bit corresponding to that cache is set. The directory also has a dirty bit. If the dirty bit is set, only one of the caches can have a copy of the line.

On a read miss, the directory is checked to see if the block is dirty in another cache. If so, consistency is maintained by copying the dirty block back to the memory before supplying the data. The reply is thus serialized through the directory. To ensure correct operation, the memory line has to be "locked" by the directory controller until the write-back signal is received from the cache with the dirty block. No other coherency related operations on this line may be undertaken while a line is locked. If the line is not dirty in another cache, then data is supplied from the main memory and the corresponding present bit is set in the directory.

On a write miss, the central directory is checked to determine the state of the line. If the line is dirty in another cache, then the line is first flushed from that cache before supplying the data. Again, the reply is serialized through the directory. The memory line is locked while this is being done. If the line is clean in other caches, invalidate signals are sent to the caches. The memory line is locked until acknowledgements are received from the caches. The data can then be supplied to the requesting cache. Thus, if the line is present in one other cache on a write miss, four network operations are required before the write can be considered to be complete. These include:

1. The miss signal that is sent to the main memory.

2. The invalidate or write-back signal that is sent to the cache that has the data in clean or dirty state respectively.

3. The invalidate-acknowledge or write-back-data signal that is sent from the cache that has the data in clean or dirty state respectively.

4. The write-miss-reply is sent from the main memory to the requesting cache.

The serialization of responses through the directory and the locking of lines by the directory controller impacts the performance of the cache coherence scheme. Requests that arrive while a line is locked have to be either buffered at the directory, or else bounced back to the source to be reissued at a later time. If the requests are buffered at the directory, the network traffic is lower. However, if the buffer overflows, the requests still have to be bounced back. Requiring transactions to be serialized through the centralized directory (and the locking of lines while servicing a request that requires a coherency-related transaction) could make the directory a bottleneck.

To reduce the amount of storage required, a number of modifications to the above scheme may be made [1]. However, these modifications either require the implementation of an efficient broadcast mechanism contradicting our assumption about scalable systems, or may generate excess network traffic along with performance penalties. For example, one simple modification is to have i pointers per line in the directory. Each pointer may point to a cache that has a copy of the line. If more than i caches have copies of the line, a broadcast has to be done to *all* caches to service a write miss. The memory line has to be locked until all caches acknowledge the invalidation. Another alternative is to allow at most i caches to have copies of a line at the same time. In the case where a read

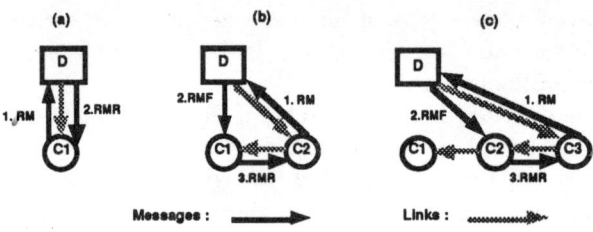

Figure 2: Linking of caches due to read misses

miss occurs when i caches have copies of the line, the directory has to invalidate one of the copies before the data can be supplied to the requesting cache. This might result in "thrashing" the line between caches.

The amount of memory required for the directory may also be reduced by caching the directory [7]. This technique may be used to further reduce the amount of memory required for the distributed directory protocol as well. In this paper we compare the distributed directory protocol with the fully mapped centralized directory protocol which has better performance than any of the centralized directory protocols that try to minimize the amount of memory required for the directory.

3 The Distributed Directory Protocol

In our distributed directory protocol, caches that share data are linked together in a list. Each line in the main memory and the cache has a cache-pointer field associated with it. This pointer can specify any cache in the system. The directory services a read or write miss request by changing the cache-pointer in the directory entry associated with the line to point to the requesting cache. A line in main memory is originally in state "absent" from all caches. Each request causes the value of the cache-pointer to be updated to point to the requesting cache. If the line is absent from all the caches, the main memory sends a reply. Otherwise the request is forwarded to the last cache to make a request for the same line.

In case of read misses, that cache replies to the requesting cache. The reply consists of the data and the address of the replying cache. The requesting cache sets its cache-pointer to point to the replying cache. A singly-linked list of caches that contain shared copies of the data is thus formed. Read misses require a maximum of three network operations regardless of the length of the linked list.

A line in cache memory is originally in state "invalid". A read or a write request from the processor causes the state to change to "writing-or-reading" and a read-miss or write-miss signal to be sent to the appropriate main memory module. On a read-miss-reply, the value of the cache-pointer is set to be the address of the object sending the reply. This causes a linked list of caches that contain the data in shared state to be formed. Figure 2 illustrates the process followed to set up the linked list. Consider the case where cache C1 has a read miss for a line followed by caches C2 and C3. As show in fig. 2(a), cache C1 sends a read-miss signal to the directory. The cache-pointer of the line in the directory

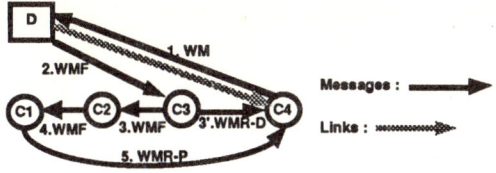

Figure 3: Invalidations due to write misses

is made to point to C1. Since no other cache has a copy of the line, the main memory sends a read-miss-reply to C1. When C1 receives the reply, the line is loaded into the cache in state "exclusive". Now, when cache C2 sends a read-miss to the directory, a read-miss-forward signal is sent to C1 as shown in fig. 2(b). The directory does not send a reply directly to C2 since C1 may have written to the line locally. The cache-pointer in the directory now points to C2. When C1 receives the forwarded signal, it changes its state to "shared" and sends a read-miss-reply to C2. The reply includes the data and the address of C1. When C2 receives the reply, it sets its cache-pointer to point to C1. Thus a linked list is formed. Fig. 2(c) shows how C3 gets linked into the list.

Write misses cause a write-miss signal to be sent to the directory. A line is allocated in the cache before the miss signal is sent. This line is used to buffer the write. Write buffering along with weak ordering [6] allows the processor to proceed immediately without stalling. A write is considered to be *issued* when a write-miss is sent by the cache. A write is considered to be *performed* when a write-miss-reply is received by the cache. A write-miss-reply may consist of two signals as in the example below. A *fence* [3] operation may be used to ensure that all writes that have been issued by a processor are performed before that processor is allowed to proceed. If a copy of the line is not present in any other cache, the main memory directly sends a reply. Otherwise, the copies of the line have to be invalidated before a reply can be sent.

Figure 3 shows the sequence of events that result when multiple caches have a copy of the line and C4 has a cache miss. The directory forwards the write miss signal to the old head (C3) pointed to by the cache-pointer and the cache-pointer is updated to point to C4. When C3 receives the write-miss-forward signal, it invalidates its copy and forwards the signal to C2. C3 also sends a write-miss-reply-data signal along with the requested data to the requesting cache C4. When C2 receives the write-miss-forward signal, it invalidates its copy and forwards the signal to C1. Since the cache-pointer of C1 points to the directory, it can be determined locally that C1 is the tail of the list and a write-miss-reply-performed signal is sent to C4 after the data in C1 is invalidated. C4 needs to receive both the write-miss-reply-data and the write-miss-reply-performed signals before the write can be considered to be performed.

In the distributed directory protocol, the information about which caches have copies of the data is distributed among the cache lines. The servicing of requests does not require any locking of lines as in the case of the centralized directory protocol. Direct cache-to-cache operations are used to send the replies and none of the replies have to be serialized through the main memory. The centralized bottleneck which is present in the centralized directory protocols is thus eliminated.

A cache line would be in state "writing-or-reading" after a read-miss or a write-miss has been generated and before a read-miss-reply or a write-miss-reply has been received. If the line in the cache is in state "writing-or-reading" and a read-miss-forward or a write-miss-forward signal is received, the forwarded signal is stored in the cache-pointer field of the cache line. The state is changed to note that a forwarded signal has been stored. Such signals that are stored are called *pending signals* and are serviced when the reply to the local read or write miss is received. If multiple transactions for the same line are pending, the caches form a *distributed queue* of pending signals. The requests are thus serviced in a pipelined manner rather than causing any bouncing of signals or contention at the directory as in the case of the centralized directory protocol. A more detailed description of the protocol may be found in [11].

The amount of memory required for the pointer is $\log N$ where N is the number of caches. The total amount of memory needed is thus $O(M \log N + Nc \log N)$ where M is the total size of main memory, N is the number of caches and c is the size of each cache. The above expression can be written as $O(M(1 + k) \log N)$ where k is Nc/Nm (m being the amount of memory per node). We interpret k as the ratio of the size of cache memory per node to the size of main memory per node.

Assuming a constant value of k for the machine, the amount of memory required for the distributed directory scheme is $O(M \log N)$. We can expect then that, using the same technology, the cost of implementing the distributed directory scheme is significantly less than the fully mapped scheme—which requires $O(MN)$ amount of memory.

4 Performance Evaluation

We used two benchmarks to compare the performance of the fully mapped centralized directory protocol and the distributed directory protocol. The benchmarks consisted of an explicit partial differential equation solver (explicit PDE)[2] and a gaussian elimination program (gauss). These algorithms were chosen since they are widely used in scientific and engineering communities in applications requiring high performance computation.

Weak ordering was used in all the applications. For example, in the PDE algorithm used, for each element in the data array, two writes may be buffered at each time step before a fence [3] operation is required.

The simulation models were built upon an event driven simulation environment. The simulator uses traces that are generated "on the fly", in response to actual conditions at each instant in the simulated system, in order to preserve proper temporal ordering between the processors [12].

A mesh topology with 32-bit bidirectional channels was used for the comparisons. The caches were assumed to be 128 KB 2-way associative with a line size of 64 bytes. The SRAM cache to DRAM main memory access ratio was assumed to be 1:10. The directories for both the protocols was assumed to be implemented in SRAM whose cycle time was taken to be 1 cycle.

---

[2]The explicit solver used has data access patterns similar to those found in SOR and polynomially preconditioned conjugate gradient methods and so, while simple, is likely representative of a wider class.

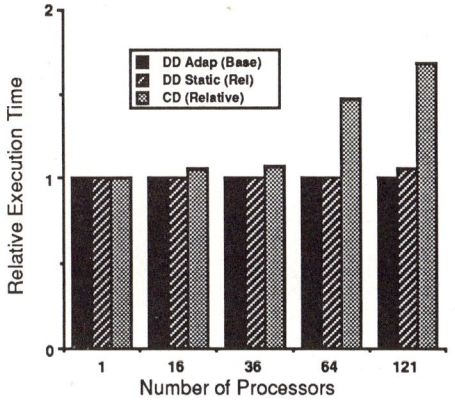
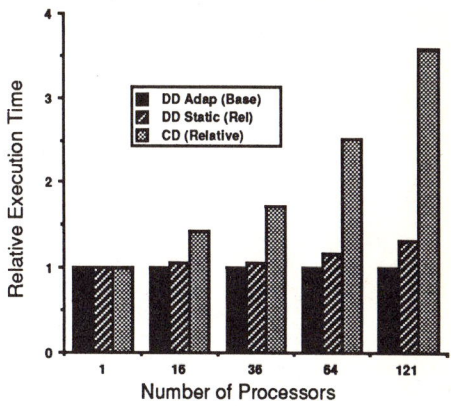

Figure 4: Explicit PDE with 1 network hop = 1 cycle

Figure 5: Explicit PDE with 1 network hop = 10 cycles

For one set of measurements, data was assumed to be transferred to a neighboring node (1 hop) in 1 cycle. This assumption would be true for systems using aggressive packaging techniques for the interconnection network. For another set of measurements, a slower network was assumed and data was assumed to be transferred to a neighboring node in 10 cycles.

Figures 4, 5, 6 and 7 compare the performance of the fully mapped centralized protocol and the distributed directory protocol (with and without adaptive routing) for the various cases. The execution time for the distributed directory protocol with adaptive routing was used as the base. The y-axis shows the relative execution time for the distributed directory protocol without adaptive routing and the centralized directory protocol as compared with the base. The x-axis shows the number of processors. The size of the input data set was kept constant.

For the explicit PDE solver the data was uniformly distributed among the nodes and the processes were randomly scheduled so as not to favor the distributed directory protocol. Figure 4 shows the relative execution time for a fast network which which requires one cycle for one hop. Figure 5 shows the relative execution time for a slow network which requires ten cycles for one hop. In the centralized directory protocol, the invalidations on a write can be done in parallel instead of sequentially as in the case of the distributed directory protocol. This can potentially cause the performance of the centralized directory protocol to be better if the number of caches that have to be invalidated is large, write buffering is ineffective, and the network is slow. However, for the explicit PDE benchmark, most of the communication is between two logical neighbors and the number of caches that have to be invalidated on a write is zero or one.

Figures 8 and 9 show a histogram for the number of readers between two successive writers for explicit PDE running on 64 and 121 processors respectively. The y-axis shows the percentage of times there were x number of readers between two successive writers,

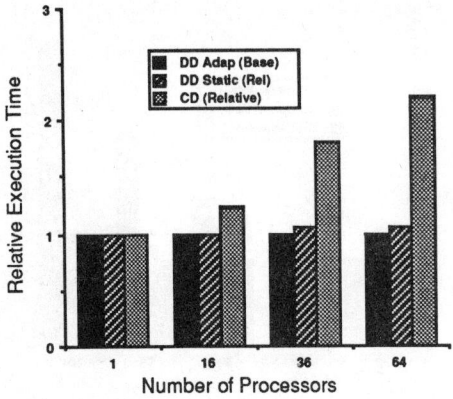
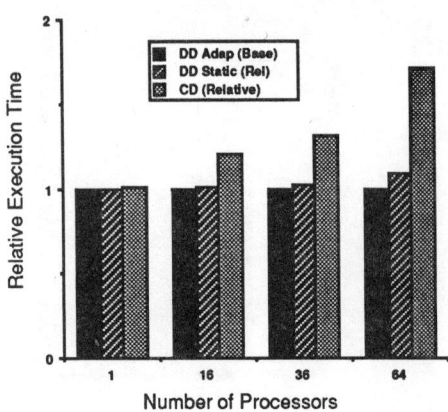

Figure 6: Gauss with 1 network hop = 1 cycle

Figure 7: Gauss with 1 network hop = 10 cycles

where x is the value shown on the x-axis.

These measurements were done using the centralized directory protocol. For x equal 0, the data was either obtained from the main memory directly, or it was present in the requesting cache but the processor did not have permission to write to the data, in which case permission had to be obtained from the main memory by sending a modify-request signal and receiving a modify-granted signal before the write could be considered to be performed. For x equal 1, the data was present in one other cache, in which case that cache had to be invalidated and the data obtained from that cache in case it was dirty, before the requesting cache could be given permission to write to the line. For x equal 2 or more, the data was present in two or more caches which had to be invalidated.

As shown in figures 8 and 9, the data was present in at most one other cache most of the time for explicit PDE. In the distributed directory protocol, most of the requests require three or less network operations. On a write, if the requesting cache is the only cache that has a copy of the data, it also has permission to write to the line. Permission to write does not have to be obtained from the main memory in this case as in the centralized directory protocol. If one other cache has a copy of the data, the miss request is forwarded by the main memory to that cache which invalidates its copy and sends a reply directly to the requesting cache instead of sending it through the main memory (as in the case of the centralized directory protocol described in section 2). In the centralized directory protocol most of the requests require 4 or less network operations.

Figure 5 shows that the relative execution time of the centralized directory protocol became worse when the network was slowed down by a factor of ten. There was not enough opportunity for the centralized directory protocol to take advantage of the parallel invalidations since the data was not shared by many caches at the same time. A slower network results in more contention for the centralized directory protocol.

The advantage due to adaptive routing increases as the network becomes slower. This is shown in figures 4 and 5 by the difference in the relative execution time for the distributed directory protocol with and without adaptive routing. Techniques for adaptive routing [5] that are better than the one used for the simulations would further improve the performance of the distributed directory protocol.

Figures 6 and 7 show the relative execution times for gauss. Again, the distributed directory protocol performed better than the centralized directory protocol. For the gauss benchmark, figures 10 and 11 show the number of readers between writes for 36 and 64 processors respectively. The synchronization was done using an algorithm similar to a software barrier [9]. The degree of the tree structure used for the synchronization was 2. This accounts for the higher proportion of 2 readers between writes. For the gauss benchmark also, the length of the list of caches that had to be invalidated on a write was never large.

For the applications we have analyzed, the length of the list of caches that has to be invalidated on a write is small. This length depends more on the application than on the size of the system. This characteristic is also common to a range of applications studied in [13]. Thus, it seems that the distributed directory protocol would have good performance for a wide range of applications.

The distributed directory protocol has better performance since most of the requests can be serviced in three or less network operations verses four or less network operations in the case of the centralized directory protocol; the resource utilization is more distributed and there is no centralized bottleneck; and adaptive routing can be used to improve the performance in the case of congested networks. The direct cache to cache transfers used in the distributed directory protocol allows the performance to be more robust for more cost effective choices in main memory technology [10].

5 Conclusions

We have shown that the distributed directory protocol has good performance. The implementation of the distributed directory protocol is more scalable to larger systems than the centralized directory protocol. Simulation results have show that the distributed directory protocol has better performance than the centralized directory protocol. The protocol provides an efficient implementation of locks at minimal cost [11]. The scalability of the distributed directory protocol in terms of both cost and performance, makes it an attractive solution for the cache coherence problem in large scale systems.

References

[1] Anant Agarwal, Richard Simoni, John Hennessy, and Mark Horowitz. An evaluation of directory schemes for cache coherence. In *Proceedings of the 15th International Symposium on Computer Architecture*, pages 281–289, 1988.

[2] James Archibald and Jean-Loup Baer. Cache coherence protocols: Evaluation using a multiprocessor simulation model. *ACM Transactions on Computer Systems*, 4(4):274–298, November 1986.

[3] W.C. Brantley, K.P. McAuliffe, and J. Weiss. RP3 processor-memory element. In *Proceedings of the 1985 International Conference on Parallel Processing*, pages 782–789, 1985.

[4] Lucien M. Censier and Paul Feautrier. A new solution to coherence problems in multicache systems. *IEEE Transactions on Computers*, c-27(12):1112–1118, December 1978.

[5] William J. Dally. Virtual-channel flow control. In *Proceedings of the 17th International Symposium on Computer Architecture*, pages 60–68, 1990.

[6] Michel Dubois and Christoph Scheurich. Memory access dependencies in shared-memory multiprocessors. *IEEE Transactions on Software Engineering*, 16(6):660–673, June 1990.

[7] Anoop Gupta, Wolf-Dietrich Weber, and Todd Mowry. Reducing memory and traffic requirements for scalable directory-based cache coherence schemes. In *Proceedings of the 1990 International Conference on Parallel Processing*, 1990.

[8] David V. James, Anthony T. Laundrie, Stein Gjessing, and Gurinder S. Sohi. Scalable coherent interface. *IEEE Computer*, 23(6):74–77, June 1990.

[9] Boris Lubachevsky. Synchronization barrier and related tools for shared memory parallel programming. In *1989 International Conference on Parallel Processing*, pages 175–179, 1989. Vol II.

[10] Manu Thapar and Bruce Delagi. Cache coherence for large scale shared memory multiprocessors. In *Proceedings of the 1990 ACM Symposium on Parallel Algorithms and Architectures*, 1990.

[11] Manu Thapar and Bruce Delagi. Stanford distributed-directory protocol. *IEEE Computer*, 23(6):78–80, June 1990.

[12] Manu Thapar and Bruce Delagi. Simulation of cache coherence protocols for shared memory multiprocessors. Technical Report KSL-91-01, Stanford University, January 1991. To appear in International Journal of Computer Simulation.

[13] Wolf-Dietrich Weber and Anoop Gupta. Analysis of cache invalidation patterns in multiprocessors. In *Proceedings of the Third International Conference on Architectural Support for Programming Languages and Operating Systems*, pages 243–256, 1989.

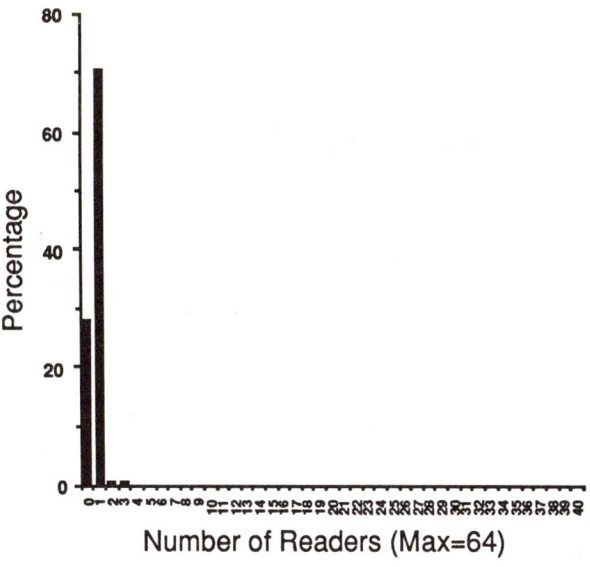

Figure 8: Explicit PDE, 64 processor system

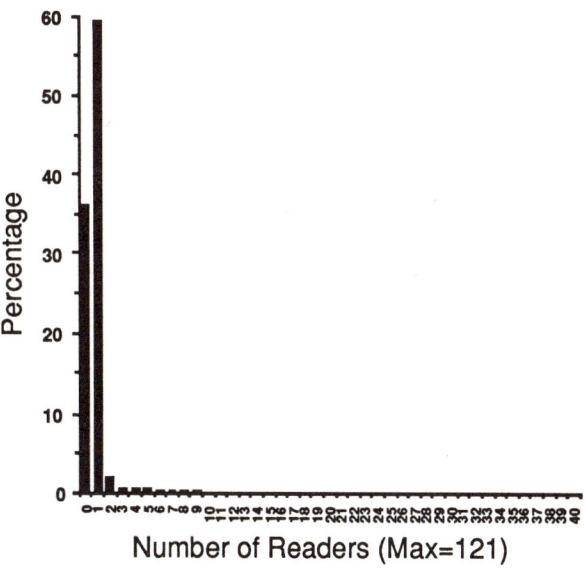

Figure 9: Explicit PDE, 121 processor system

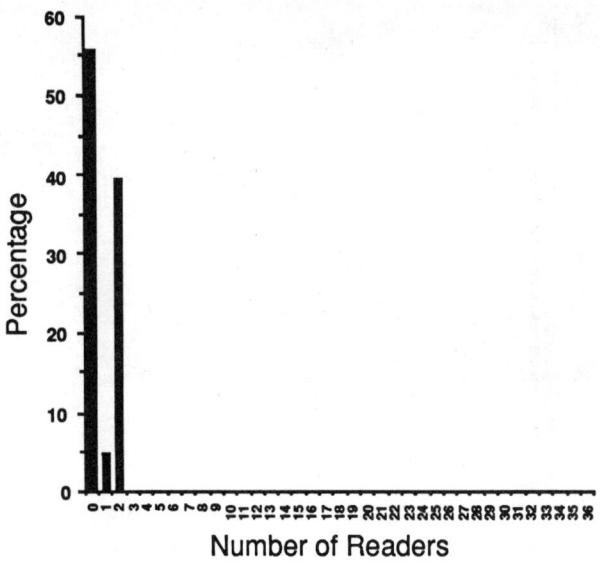

Figure 10: Gauss, 36 processor system

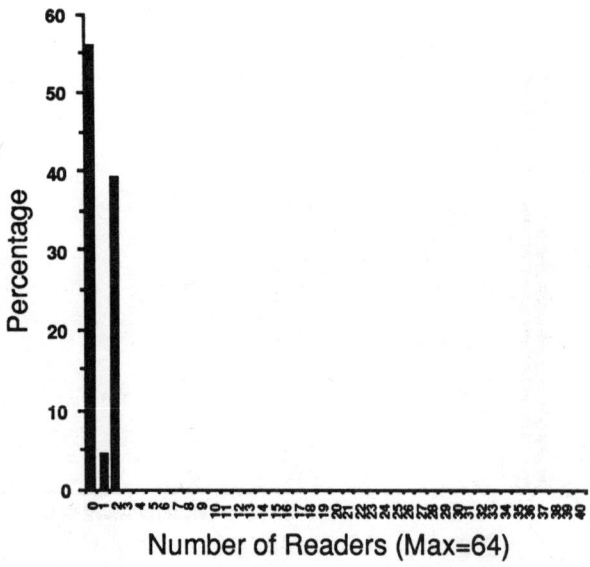

Figure 11: Gauss, 64 processor system

New Program Restructuring Technology

Michael Wolfe
Oregon Graduate Institute

Abstract

Compilers for vector and parallel computers advertise the ability to automatically detect the parallelism in sequential loops. Sometimes these compilers change the structure of nested loops, for instance by interchanging loops, to uncover more parallelism. The technology used for parallelism discovery can also be used to optimize nested loop algorithms for many other architectural characteristics, such as memory hierarchies, or limited interprocessor connection networks. While much of this technology has been successfully commercialized, recent research has discovered new technology and transformations. The potential for these new optimizations and how they will interface with users is discussed.

1 Prologue

Program restructuring, or more specifically, loop reindexing is used to optimize programs to take advantage of many architectural features, such as parallelism, memory hierarchies and multicomputer topologies. Precise analysis of the flow of data in a program is necessary to enable the restructuring transformations. In loops, data flow can be concisely encapsulated in a data dependence graph.

In this paper we quickly review several important program restructuring transformations, such as vectorization, parallelization, interchanging and the wavefront method. We show what kind of dependence information is necessary in each case to test that the transformation is legal, and propose several abstractions and annotations that capture this information. We propose representation schemes for each abstraction, and compare them in terms of precision and efficiency of access and space.

Next, we concentrate on the problem of finding the dependence information. We show how to formulate the dependence equation, and review several methods to solve it. Each method has strengths and weaknesses; some have been extended to extract the additional necessary information to annotate the dependence relations to test for various restructuring transformations.

Finally, we look to the future, when more complicated restructuring techniques will be explored and implemented. We try to see how well our data dependence abstractions fare against the problems posed by various advanced transformations.

2 Loop Reindexing

Nested loops define an *iteration space*, comprising a finite discrete Cartesian space with dimensionality equal to the loop nest level. For example, the loop below:

Program 2.1:
```
    for i = 1 to 5 do
        for j = 1 to 10 do
            A(i,j) = B(i,j) + C(i)*D(j)
        endfor
    endfor
```

defines a two-dimensional 5 × 10 iteration space:

```
        J=1 2 3 4 5 6 7 8 9 10
    I=1  o o o o o o o o o o
      2  o o o o o o o o o o
      3  o o o o o o o o o o
      4  o o o o o o o o o o
      5  o o o o o o o o o o
```

Each point in the iteration space represents the execution of one iteration of the nested loop. In imperative languages, the semantics of a serial loop define the order in which the points in the iteration space are visited:

```
J=1  2  3  4  5  6  7  8  9 10
I=1 o-o-o-o-o-o-o-o-o-o
    o-o-o-o-o-o-o-o-o-o
    o-o-o-o-o-o-o-o-o-o
    o-o-o-o-o-o-o-o-o-o
    o-o-o-o-o-o-o-o-o-o
```

There is no reason that the iteration space need be rectangular; many popular algorithms have inner loops whose limits depend on the values of outer loop indices. The iteration space for the loop below is triangular, suggesting the name triangular loop:

Program 2.2:
```
for i = 1 to 5 do
    for j = i to 5 do
        A(i,j) = B(i,j) + C(i)*D(j)
    endfor
endfor
```

```
    J=1  2  3  4  5
I=1  o   o  o  o  o
 2       o  o  o  o
 3          o  o  o
 4             o  o
 5                o
```

Other interesting iteration space shapes can be defined by nested loops, such as trapezoids, rhomboids, and so on; some of these shapes can be generated from each other via loop restructuring.

When a loop contains multiple statements, the iteration space can be extended by adding another dimension to explicitly express each individual statement; for instance, the extended iteration space for the loop:

Program 2.3:
```
        for i = 1 to 10 do
S₁:       A(i) = B(i) + C(i)*X
S₂:       B(i) = 0.0
        endfor
```

has a vertex for each statement in each iteration:

```
        I=1 2 3 4 5 6 7 8 9 10
    S₁   o  o o o o o o o o  o
    S₂   o  o o o o o o o o  o
```

Each point in the extended iteration space represents the execution of one iteration of a single statement in the loop. Nontrivial nested loops can give rise to interesting iteration space shapes, as in the nontightly nested loops below:

Program 2.4:
```
        for i = 1 to 5 do
S₁:       C(i) = C(i) / 2
          for j = i to 5 do
S₂:         A(i,j) = B(i,j) + C(i)*D(j)
          endfor
        endfor
```

```
              S₁   S₂
                  J=1 2 3 4 5
         I=1 o     o  o o o o
           2 o        o o o o
           3 o           o o o
           4 o              o o
           5 o                 o
```

2.1 Reindexing

The loop restructuring transformations presented here can all be defined as changing the order in which the nodes in the iteration space are traversed, or changing the shape of the iteration space itself. For instance, the sequential execution ordering of Program 2.3 is:

Distributing the loop produces the program:

Program 2.3a:
```
        for i = 1 to 10 do
S₁:         A(i) = B(i) + C(i)*X
        endfor
        for i = 1 to 10 do
S₂:         B(i) = 0.0
        endfor
```

the effect is to change the execution order in the extended iteration space to execute all iterations of each statement before executing any iterations of the next statement:

Vectorizing the loop corresponds to changing the execution order to execute all iterations of each statement in parallel:

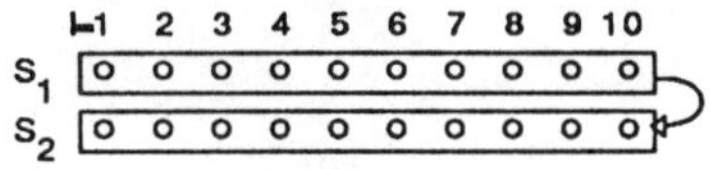

Distribution is essentially vectorization without the parallelism.

Contrast this to *parallelization* of a loop, which effectively removes any notion of ordering between different iterations. In the absence of explicit synchronization, any iteration can execute in parallel with any other iteration, though execution of the statements within an iteration is well ordered. Parallelization of the loop in Program 2.3 changes execution ordering of the iteration spacc to:

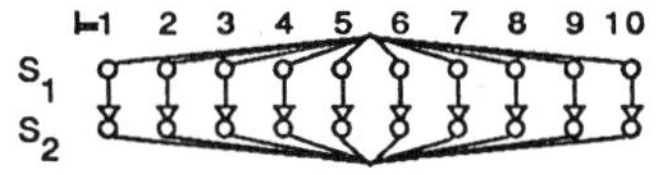

Parallelization can also be applied to non-inner loops. Parallelizing the inner loop of Program 2.1 gives the execution ordering:

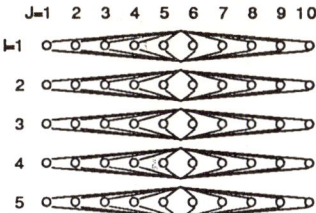

Notice the implicit *barrier* synchronization between every iteration of the outer loop. Parallelizing the outer loop of the same program gives the ordering:

No ordering between statements in different iterations of the outer loop can be guaranteed.

Interchanging the loops in Program 2.1 produces the program:

Program 2.1a:
```
for j = 1 to 10 do
    for i = 1 to 5 do
        A(i,j) = B(i,j) + C(i)*D(j)
    endfor
endfor
```

The effect in the iteration space is to run the loops the other way:

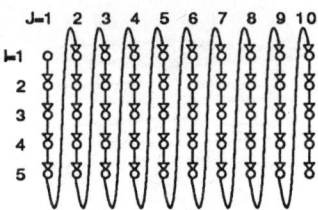

Skewing the loops in Program 2.1 corresponds to modifying the limits of the inner loop, as in:

Program 2.1b:
```
for i = 1 to 5 do
    for j = i+1 to i+10 do
        A(i,j-i) = B(i,j-i) + C(i)*D(j-i)
    endfor
endfor
```

While the order of execution of the iterations isn't changed by skewing, the shape of the iteration space is changed from a rectangle (for instance) to a parallelogram:

```
J=1  2  3  4  5  6  7  8  9 10 11 12 13 14 15
I=1  o  o  o  o  o  o  o  o  o  o
  2     o  o  o  o  o  o  o  o  o  o
  3        o  o  o  o  o  o  o  o  o  o
  4           o  o  o  o  o  o  o  o  o  o
  5              o  o  o  o  o  o  o  o  o  o
```

The point of most reindexing transformations is to change the order of execution of the iterations or statements; one may wonder what the point of skewing is, since it doesn't change this order. In fact, skewing by itself is not very interesting; however, interchanging the skewed loops gives a different index set traversal:

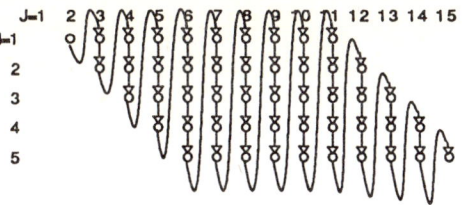

Other transformations can be and have been defined and implemented, but these are enough for our discussion.

3 Data Dependence

A transformation is *legal* if the restructured program will produce the same answer as the original program; in other words, the sequential loops and the statement ordering must satisfy all dependence relations. When compilers generate code for vector or parallel computers, there may be other means for satisfying dependence relations (such as interprocessor synchronization) which will allow the use of an otherwise 'illegal' transformation. Our definition ignores other potential problems, such as faulty programs which may generate a different sequence of exception conditions, restructured programs which may run out of memory due to extra temporary variables, or nonterminating programs which exhibit different behaviour.

In normal imperative languages, there are three essential kinds of data dependence. A *flow-dependence* relation occurs when the value assigned to a variable or array element in the execution of one *instance* of a statement is used by the subsequent execution of an instance of the same or another statement. The loop below has a flow dependence relation from statement S_1 to itself, since the value assigned to A(i+1) will be used on the next iteration of the loop, written $S_1 \,\delta\, S_1$.

Program 3.1:
```
       for i = 1 to N-1 do
S₁:    A(i+1) = A(i) + B(i)
       endfor
```

An *anti-dependence* relation occurs when the value read from a variable or array element in an instance of some statement is subsequently reassigned. In the loop below there is an anti-dependence relation from S_1 to S_2, since B(i,j+1) is used in S_1 and subsequently reassigned by S_2 in the next iteration of the j loop, written $S_1 \bar{\delta} S_2$.

Program 3.2:
```
        for i = 1 to N do
            for j = 1 to M-1 do
S₁:             A(i,j) = B(i,j+1) + 1
S₂:             B(i,j) = C(i) - 1
            endfor
        endfor
```

Finally, an *output dependence* relation occurs when some variable or array element is assigned in an instance of a statement and subsequently reassigned. An example of this is shown below where there is an potential output dependence relation from S_2 to S_1, since the variable B(i+1) assigned in S_2 may be reassigned in the next iteration of the loop by S_1, written $S_2 \delta^o S_1$. This also demonstrates that compilers must approximate the data dependence relations in a program; since a compilers do not know the paths that will be taken at run time, they must make conservative assumptions.

Program 3.3:
```
        for i = 1 to N-1 do
S₁:         if(A(i) > 0) B(i) = C(i)/A(i)
S₂:         B(i+1) = C(i) / 2
        endfor
```

3.1 Distance and Direction Vectors

In order to apply a wide variety of loop transformations, data dependence relations are annotated with information showing how they are affected by the enclosing loops; three such annotations are popular today. Many dependence relations have a constant distance in each dimension of the iteration space. When this is the case, a *distance vector* can be built where each element is a constant integer representing the dependence distances in the corresponding loop. For example, in the following program there is a data dependence relation in the iteration space as shown; each iteration (i, j) depends on the value computed in iteration $(i, j-1)$. The distances for this dependence relation are zero in the i loop and one in the j loop, written S_1 $\delta_{(0,1)}$ S_1.

Program 3.4:
```
        for i = 1 to N do
            for j = 2 to M do
S₁:             A(i,j) = A(i,j-1) + B(i,j)
            endfor
        endfor
```

Each distance vector will have n entries, where n is the nesting level of the loops surrounding the source and sink of the dependence. Since dependence distances are usually small, short words or perhaps even signed bytes could be used, reducing the storage requirements.

For many transformations, the magnitude of the distance is not needed as long as the sign is known; often the distance is not constant in the loop, even though it may always be positive (or always negative). As an example, in the loop:

Program 3.5:
```
        for i = 1 to N do
            for j = 1 to N do
S₁:             X(i+1,2*j) = X(i,j) + B(i)
            endfor
        endfor
```

the assignment to X(i+1,2*j) is used in some subsequent iteration of the i and j loops by the X(i,j) reference. Some of the dependence relations for this program are given in the table below:

	from		to		dependence
element	i	j	i	j	distance
X(2,2)	1	1	2	2	(1,1)
X(3,4)	2	2	3	4	(1,2)

The distance in the j loop for this dependence is always positive, but is not a constant. A common method to represent this is to save a vector of the signs of the dependence distances, called a *direction vector*. Each direction vector element will be one of $\{+, 0, -\}$ [Ban88]; for historical reasons, these are usually written $\{<, =, >\}$ [Wol78, WB87, Wol89]. In Program 3.5, the direction vector associated with the dependence relation is S_1 $\delta_{(<,<)}$ S_1; in Program 3.4, the dependence relation would be written S_1 $\delta_{(=,<)}$ S_1. A direction vector can be saved as a bit vector, with three bits for each loop.

Another popular data dependence annotation saves only the nest level of the outermost loop with a non-(=) direction (non-zero distance) [AK87]. The dependence relation for Program 3.4 has a zero distance in the outer loop, but a non-zero distance in the inner loop, so this dependence relation is *carried* by the inner j loop. Some dependence relations may not be carried by any loop, as below:

Program 3.6:
```
        for i = 1 to N do
            for j = 2 to M do
S₁:             A(i,j) = B(i,j) + C(i,j)
S₂:             D(i,j) = A(i,j) + 1
            endfor
        endfor
```

The references to A(i,j) produce a dependence relation from S_1 to S_2 with zero distance in both loops. This is written $S_1\ \delta_{(=,=)}\ S_2$ or $S_1\ \delta_{(0,0)}\ S_2$. Since it is carried by neither of the loops, it is a *loop independent dependence*. If the nest level of the outer loop is counted as level 1, then the *level* of a dependence relation is the nest level of the loop which carries that relation; the level of a loop independent dependence relation is infinity [AK87]. Loop levels can be represented with a single unsigned integer.

Distance vectors are the most precise of these three annotations; both direction vectors and dependence levels can be found if the distance vector is known. Dependence levels can also be found given the direction vector, and so are the least precise annotation, though dependence levels are perfectly adequate in some cases.

4 Legal Loop Reindexing

In order to determine whether a loop reindexing transformation is legal, we must know what effect the transformation has on the data dependence relations in the loop. In particular, if a transformation *preserves* all the dependence relations, then the transformation is legal. If any dependence relation is *violated*, then the transformation is illegal. We need data dependence tests which can tell whether a transformation will be legal; if we find what dependence relations will be violated by a transformation, then testing for those conditions will tell whether the transformation is legal.

4.1 Distribution

In a sequential program, there can be a dependence from any statement instance to any subsequent statement in the traversal of the extended iteration space. Dependence can be lexically forward (to a later statement) or lexically backward (to the same or an earlier statement); lexically backward dependence must be carried by a loop. The loop below has three dependence relations:

Program 4.1:
```
      for i = 1 to 10 do
S₁:     A(i) = A(i-1) + B(i-1)*X
S₂:     B(i) = A(i) + 1
      endfor
```

There is one lexically forward dependence: $S_1\ \delta_{(0)}\ S_2$; one self-dependence: $S_1\ \delta_{(1)}\ S_1$; and another lexically backward dependence: $S_2\ \delta_{(1)}\ S_1$. In the extended iteration space, the dependence relations are:

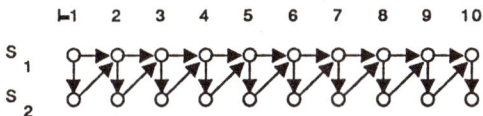

Distributing this loop changes the execution ordering:

Program 4.2:
```
      for i = 2 to 15 do
S₁:     A(i) = A(i-1) + B(i-1)*X
      endfor
      for i = 2 to 15 do
S₂:     B(i) = A(i) + 1
      endfor
```

The lexically backward dependence from S_2 to S_1 is violated. Lexically forward dependence relations and self-dependence relations are preserved; from this we have the rule that loop distribution violates strictly lexically backward dependence relations.

4.2 Vectorization

Vectorizing the same loop means executing all iterations of each statement in parallel. Vectorization will additionally violate the self-dependence from S_1 to itself; in fact, vectorization will violate any lexically backward dependence. In general, the nodes (statements) in any acyclic dependence graph can be reordered to change all dependence relations to lexically forward ones, allowing vectorization [AK87]. Both distribution and vectorization test only the lexical aspect of the dependence relation; neither transformation use the dependence distance or direction, and they do not distinguish between loop carried and loop independent dependence relations.

4.3 Parallelization

In contrast, parallelization of the same loop preserves only the loop independent dependence from S_1 to S_2. Any loop-carried dependence relation is violated by parallelization. In fact, parallelization tests only the dependence distance or direction; the relative lexical positions of the statements in the dependence relations are ignored [ACK87].

4.4 Nested Loops

Both vectorization and parallelization can be applied in cases with nested loops. When vectorizing an inner loop, any dependence relation that is carried by an outer loop can be ignored; this is due to the fact that sequential execution of the outer loop will preserve that dependence relation. For instance, the loop:

Program 4.3:
```
        for i = 2 to 10 do
          for j = 1 to 20 do
S₁:         A(i,j) = A(i-1,j) + C(i)*D(j)
          endfor
        endfor
```

has the dependence relation $S_1\ \delta_{(1,0)}\ S_1$; this relation is carried by the outer loop. In spite of the fact that the loop has a self-dependence and vectorization does not preserve self-dependences, vectorization of the inner loop is legal. In general, a sequential outer loop will preserve all dependence relations carried by that loop, regardless of any reindexing of inner loops; vectorization, parallelization, or other transformations can then ignore any dependence relations carried by outer loops.

Parallelization can itself be applied to outer loops. For instance, in the loop:

Program 4.4:
```
        for i = 2 to 10 do
            for j = 1 to 20 do
S₁:             A(i,j) = A(i-1,j) + C(i)*D(j)
S₂:             B(i,j) = B(i,j) + A(i,j-1)
            endfor
        endfor
```

there are two dependence relations, one at level 1 and one at level 2. Parallelization of the outer loop will violate the dependence carried by that loop (but will preserve the level 2 dependence).

Thus the vectorization of single loops requires only lexical information, while vectorization of a nested loops requires knowledge of dependence levels. Parallelization of loops requires knowledge only of dependence levels, even when applied to outer loops.

4.5 Interchanging

Loop interchanging effectively transposes the iteration space. As noted throughout the literature, interchanging two loops preserves loop independent dependence relations and dependence relations carried by the original inner loop. However, some dependence relations carried by the outer loop can be violated. Given the execution ordering of a two dimensional iteration space:

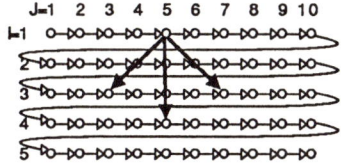

Interchanging the loops will violate the dependence relation to the lower left, which corresponds to a direction vector of $(<,>)$; interchanging preserves other dependence directions, such as $(<,=)$ or $(<,<)$ [Wol78, AK84]:

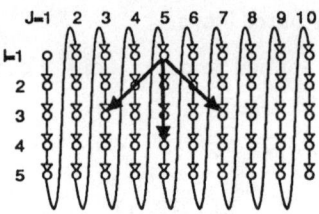

Thus, dependence levels are too coarse a test for loop interchanging; at least direction vectors are needed.

4.6 Skewing

As pointed out earlier, loop skewing is always legal since it does not change the order of execution of the loop iterations [Wol86]. However skewing does change the dependence direction vectors or distance vectors, thus allowing additional transformations or parallelism. For instance, in the standard wavefront example:

Program 4.5:
```
        for i = 2 to 89 do
            for j = 2 to 89 do
S₁:         A(i,j) = 0.25*(A(i-1,j) + A(i,j-1) + A(i+1,j) + A(i,j+1))
            endfor
        endfor
```

there are four dependence relations:

$$S_1 \; \delta_{(<,=)} \; S_1 \quad S_1 \; \delta_{(=,<)} \; S_1$$
$$S_1 \; \overline{\delta}_{(<,=)} \; S_1 \quad S_1 \; \overline{\delta}_{(=,<)} \; S_1$$

in the iteration space:

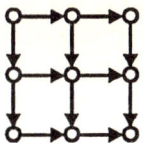

Since both loops carry a dependence relation, neither loop can be executed in parallel. Skewing the inner loop produces the program:

Program 4.5a:
```
        for i = 2 to 89 do
          for j = i+2 to i+89 do
S₁:         A(i,j-i) = 0.25*(A(i-1,j-i) + A(i,j-i-1)
                     + A(i+1,j-i) + A(i,j-i+1))
          endfor
        endfor
```

In this program, the data dependence direction vectors are modified to:

$$S_1\ \delta_{(<,<)}\ S_1 \qquad S_1\ \delta_{(=,<)}\ S_1$$
$$S_1\ \overline{\delta}_{(<,<)}\ S_1 \qquad S_1\ \overline{\delta}_{(=,<)}\ S_1$$

reflecting dependence in the modified iteration space:

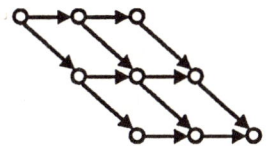

Now, interchanging the loops gives the program:

Program 4.5b:
```
         for j = 4 to 178 do
            for i = max(2,j-89) to min(89,j-2) do
S₁:            A(i,j-i) = 0.25*(A(i-1,j-i) + A(i,j-i-1)
                  + A(i+1,j-i) + A(i,j-i+1))
            endfor
         endfor
```

with the dependence relations:

$$S_1\ \delta_{(<,<)}\ S_1 \quad S_1\ \delta_{(<,=)}\ S_1$$
$$S_1\ \overline{\delta}_{(<,<)}\ S_1 \quad S_1\ \overline{\delta}_{(<,=)}\ S_1$$

After skewing and interchanging, all the dependence relations are carried by the outer loop (the j loop), and the inner loop can execute in parallel. For this transformation, again at least dependence direction vectors are required.

However, the effects of loop skewing can be improved with the more precise information in distance vectors. For instance, the program:

Program 4.6:
```
         for i = 2 to 89 do
            for j = 2 to 89 do
S₁:            A(i,j) = A(i-2,j+1) + 1.0
            endfor
         endfor
```

has the data dependence relation:

$$S_1\ \delta_{(2,-1)}\ S_1$$

Skewing a loop changes the direction of a dependence relation from (d_1, d_2) to (d_1, d_1+d_2); thus skewing the above loop changes the dependence relation to:

$$S_1\ \delta_{(2,1)}\ S_1$$

Notice that the skewed loops can be interchanged. With only have direction vectors, the sign as well as magnitude of $d_1 + d_2$ is unknown; we must assume the worst case. In this example, the original dependence relation would look like $S_1\ \delta_{(<,>)}\ S_1$; after skewing this becomes: $S_1\ \delta_{(<,*)}\ S_1$, where the $*$ direction means any direction could hold for this loop. Interchanging might be illegal after skewing. In fact, the dependence distance vector can be used to decide whether loop skewing is necessary and whether skewing by a larger factor will help.

5 Dependence Information

The following table gives the information used in each of the above transformations for maximum benefit.

Simple	Distribution	lexical
Simple	Vectorization	lexical
Simple	Parallelization	level
Nested	Distribution	lexical+level
Nested	Vectorization	lexical+level
Nested	Parallelization	level
	Interchanging	direction
	Skewing	distance

We will assume a data dependence data structure where each dependence relation is represented by a record (or object) holding the following information:

1. type of dependence (flow, anti, output)

2. source and destination of relation (lexical information)

3. relation to loop iteration (level, direction or distance)

Choosing whether to use dependence levels, directions or distances as a dependence abstraction involves a tradeoff between the space required to store the information, the time required to access the information, the precision of the information available, and the time required to generate the information.

The space required for distance or direction vectors depends on the nest level. We can use a fixed size direction vector by limiting the maximum nest level to be considered; a 32-bit word can store a direction vector for a loop nested 10 deep.

The access time of a dependence level is constant. The access time of a direction vector can also be constant; each direction vector test can be formulated as a bit vector test, involving some word-wide AND operations. The access time of a distance vector depends on the nest level for any test.

The distance vector appears to be the most expensive abstraction, but it is also the most precise:

		access	transformations enabled				
abstraction	space	time	Dist.	Vect.	Par.	Int.	Skew.
level	1	$O(1)$	yes	yes	yes		
direction	1	$O(1)$	yes	yes	yes	yes	some
distance	$O(n)$	$O(n)$	yes	yes	yes	yes	yes

6 Current Research

In recent research into program restructuring we have explored the robustness of the dependence abstractions and dependence tests. Here we present some examples of cases where current abstractions are inefficient.

6.1 Semantic Information

The data dependence relation for a reduction operation in an imperative language, such as:

```
         for i = 1 to N do
             for j = 1 to M do
S₁:          S(i) = S(i) + A(i,j)
             endfor
         endfor
```

is actually $S_1\ \delta_{(0,1)}\ S_1$; clearly the dependence relation is carried by the inner loop. There may be reasons to change the order of the summation. Vectorization of the summation loop will often change the order of the additions, changing the roundoff error accumulation and producing a (hopefully slightly) different answer. Strictly speaking, vectorizing this loop under those conditions will violate this dependence relation, but we realize that reductions like this are a special case and allow the transformation.

There are other transformations that sometimes make sense; for instance we may wish to execute the inner loop backwards. This will again change the order of the additions, but we assume the user will accept roundoff differences for reductions.

In a two dimensional reduction:

```
        for i = 1 to N do
            for j = 1 to M do
S₁:         S = S + A(i,j)
            endfor
        endfor
```

the dependence relations are $S_1\ \delta_{(0,1)}\ S_1$ (for dependence along the j loop) and $S_1\ \delta_{(1,>)}\ S_1$ (for dependence from iteration $[i, M]$ to iteration $[i+1, 1]$. This latter dependence distance prevents interchanging of the two loops, assuming there is some performance reason to interchange these loops (loop limits, memory strides, etc.).

The dependence abstractions used so far are inadequate to allow the types of transformations we wish to perform. In this case, the information needed to accept the transformation is semantic in nature - the dependence relation corresponds to an associative reduction. This can be represented by a new type of dependence arc (instead of flow-dependence), or by a new loop-level abstraction. We have proposed a new dependence direction, the reduction direction, to handle this case [Wol91].

6.2 Mixed Distances

We have explored more advanced restructuring transformations, such as interchanging non-tightly nested loops directly [Wol89, WT91]. An example is converting the KJI Gaussian Elimination (without pivoting) form:

```
        for k = 1 to n do
            for i = k+1 to n do
S₁:             A(i,k) = A(i,k) / A(k,k)
            endfor
            for j = k+1 to n do
                for i = k+1 to n do
S₂:                 A(i,j) = A(i,j) - A(k,j)*A(i,k)
                endfor
            endfor
        endfor
```

to the JKI form:

```
        for j = 1 to n do
          for k = 1 to j-1 do
            for i = k+1 to n do
S₂:         A(i,j) = A(i,j) - A(k,j)*A(i,k)
            endfor
          endfor
          for i = j+1 to n do
S₁:         A(i,j) = A(i,j) / A(j,j)
          endfor
        endfor
```

The dependence test for legality of this transformation requires verifying that there is no dependence from $S_1[k', i']$ to $S_2[k'', j'', i'']$ which satisfies both the conditions:

$$(c1) \quad k' < k''$$

$$(c2) \quad k' > j''$$

If there is such a dependence, then this interchanging will be illegal. The distance vector or direction vector will tell whether condition (c1) is a potential problem, however neither abstraction gives any information about condition (c2). Distance and direction vectors give information about relative values of the same loop variable in the statement instances involved in a dependence relation. By contrast, condition (c2) requires information about the relative value of different loop variables in a dependence relation. Some work has been done on computing this information, but no comprehensive abstractions have been proposed.

7 Summary

Program restructuring is an important capability for compilers and programming tools for complex computer architectures. It is one method to achieve improved performance on advanced computer architectures. Restructuring can never duplicate or surpass the benefits of finding an appropriate algorithm, but the ability to efficiently test for and perform many restructuring transformations will allow compilers to do a better job of mapping programs onto machines.

This paper reviews some important program restructuring transformations and the dependence information needed to test for their legality. We study data dependence abstractions and how they can be represented, used and computed. In our previous work we have focussed on data dependence direction vectors as the abstraction of choice, losing some precision but gaining space and access time efficiency. Now we look to the more advanced restructuring transformations, and see that the current dependence abstractions are incomplete.

We believe there is some important work to be done in finding an appropriate mechanism to represent data dependence information in programs. This will of course depend on the use to be made of the information. Today's simple vectorizing and parallelizing compilers may not need any more complexity than they already have; future more aggressive restructuring tools will need more precise and efficient abstractions to drive their optimizations.

References

[ACK87] Randy Allen, David Callahan, and Ken Kennedy. Automatic decomposition of scientific programs for parallel execution. In *Conf. Record 14th Annual ACM Symp. on Principles of Programming Languages*, pages 63–76, Munich, Germany, January 1987.

[AK84] John R. Allen and Ken Kennedy. Automatic loop interchange. In *Proc. SIGPLAN '84 Symp. on Compiler Construction*, pages 233–246, Montreal, Canada, June 1984.

[AK87] John R. Allen and Ken Kennedy. Automatic translation of Fortran programs to vector form. *ACM Trans. on Programming Languages and Systems*, 9(4):491–542, October 1987.

[Ban88] Utpal Banerjee. *Dependence Analysis for Supercomputing*. Kluwer Academic Publishers, Norwell, MA, 1988.

[WB87] Michael Wolfe and Utpal Banerjee. Data dependence and its application to parallel processing. *International J. Parallel Programming*, 16(2):137–178, April 1987.

[Wol78] Michael Wolfe. Techniques for improving the inherent parallelism in programs. M.S. thesis UIUCDCS-R-78-929, Univ. Illinois, Dept. Computer Science, July 1978.

[Wol86] Michael Wolfe. Loop skewing: The wavefront method revisited. *International J. Parallel Programming*, 15(4):279–294, August 1986.

[Wol89] Michael Wolfe. *Optimizing Supercompilers for Supercomputers*. Research Monographs in Parallel and Distributed Computing. Pitman Publishing, London, 1989. (also available from MIT Press).

[Wol91] Michael Wolfe. Data dependence and program restructuring. *J. Supercomputing*, 4(4):321–344, January 1991.

[WT91] Michael Wolfe and Chau-Wen Tseng. The power test for data dependence. *IEEE Trans. Parallel and Distributed Systems*, 1991. (accepted for publication).

This work was supported by NSF Grant CCR-8906909 and DARPA Grant MDA972-88-J-1004.

DATA PARALLEL PROGRAM DESIGN

T. G. Lewis, R. Currey, and Jie Liu
Oregon Advanced Computing Institute
Computer Science Department
Oregon State University, Corvallis, OR. 97331-3202, U.S.A.
lewis@cs.orst.edu

A *parallel programming support environment* is a coordinated collection of tools for automating part or all of the steps in writing a parallel program. In this paper, we present a parallel program support environment called PPSE (Parallel Programming Support Environment), which attempts to cover most of the steps of the programming lifecycle -- including design, coding, testing and tuning for improved performance. The major problem addressed in this paper is that of data parallel representation in high-level, machine-independent, graphical language such as used in PPSE. We show how PPSE tools can be extended to incorporate data parallel design and coding steps using three new graphical programming constructs: 1. stencil, 2. stream generator, and 3. replicator routines. While our initial results are somewhat limited at this stage, they do suggest that it is possible to design data parallel programs using graphical abstractions with little fore-knowledge of the target machine or the programming language that will be used during coding. However, the use of these new constructs also introduce design clutter, challenges to automatic code generation, and difficulties in optimizing message-passing in distributed-memory machines.

Parallel CASE

PPSE(Parallel Programming Support Environment) is a collection of tools for design, scheduling, generating, and measuring the performance of parallel programs for both shared and distributed-memory computers. In this paper we briefly describe PPSE and then propose an extension to PPSE that will allow it to represent data parallel designs.

Parallel programming tools have been proposed by a number of researchers, e.g. FAUST by Guarna et al., NOVIS by Glinert, PIE by Segall, POKER by Snyder, R^n/PTOOL by Kennedy et al., Start/Pat by Appelby et al., and a number of other researchers such as Zima, etc. The goal of all of these tools is to improve the quality and speed with which parallel programs can be designed, written, and debugged for a variety of parallel computers. We call these *parallel CASE* tools because of their similarity with computer-aided software engineering tools for serial programming.

The work leading up to our work with PPSE and most closely related to it is: ASPAR/EXPRESS by Ikudome et al. which does source code restructuring to map a serial program into a data parallel program; BUILD/SCHEDULE by Dongarra et al. which uses a task graph approach similar to PPSE's task grapher tool; Browne's CODE/ROPE which is based on a graphical design language similar to HIGHLAND by Meyer and PPSE's Parallax editor; the task scheduling work done by Wu et al. in HYPERTOOL; and the visualization tools in PICL/Paragraph by Heath et al.

The richness of previous research might suggest that the problem of designing a parallel CASE system is solved, but in fact significant problems remain. In particular, we address the problem of representing *data parallel* designs in a graphical high level design and coding environment. The advantages of such a system are portability across a variety of parallel computers, clarity of design, automatic analysis, and partially automatic program generation. For details on our general approach, see the references to the papers by Rudd et al., and El-Rewini et al.

In the next section we show that data parallel programming forces a different way of thinking about parallel program design and that current tools do not solve the problem of design representation of data parallelism. [We focus our attention on design as opposed to coding or debugging]. In the second section we propose an extension to PPSE that will permit flexible and expressive data parallel designs. Finally, we show how data parallel designs are mapped onto the interconnect topology of some target machine, and then suggest a number of unsolved problems to be addressed by follow-on research.

The Data Parallel Paradigm

A data parallel program is one in which multiple cpu's operate in parallel on different data. For example, matrix multiply might be performed in data parallel fashion by simultaneously computing inner products -- the cpus do the same thing at the same time, but on different vectors. Data parallel programming has been called SIMD programming, SPMD (Single Program, Multiple Data), and various other names. In essence, data parallel programming is a specialized programming paradigm in which a parallel program is constructed in two-phases :

1) *data partitioning* and *distribution*, and
2). *data parallel processing* respectively.

Data parallel matrix multiply uses two phases: 1). partition the matrices into columns and rows followed by distribution of the columns and rows to processors, and 2). simultaneaously compute inner products on rows and columns to produce the product matrix. If N^2 processors are available, N^2 inner products are computed simultaneously, otherwise, each processor is assigned one or more inner product routines to execute.

Although data parallelism seems rather restrictive, it abounds in scientific computing and offers a number of attractive advantages which are summarized below:

1. Scalable : Once a program is implemented in this style, scaling up the problem to finer grid sizes or smaller time increments is simple. Adding processors does not alter the program. Instead, a larger problem merely runs slower on a fixed-size machine, or faster on a more massive machine, see Figure 1.

2. Programming Ease : Data parallel programming is much easier to understand and do than general parallel programming. In some cases, parallelism can be detected and implemented by a compiler. In most cases, however, a modest change in the language and programming style is required.

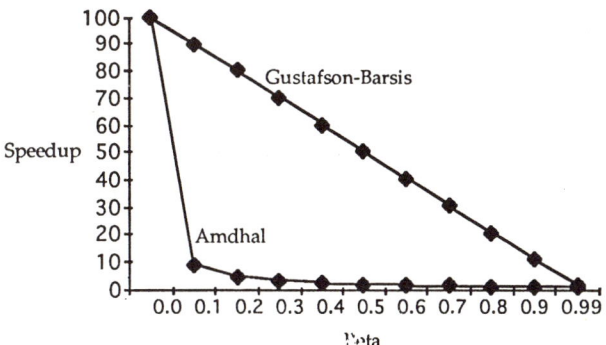

Figure 1. Speedup versus ß (Fraction of Program That Must Run Serially) For Amdhal's Law and Gustafson-Barsis Law Shows Greater Potential of Data Parallel Paradigm For Performance Improvements Due to Parallelism.

Because of the potential for tremendous speedup in processing, a number of manufacturers have designed machines to support data parallel programming in hardware:, e.g. the CM-2, MasPar MP-1, and WaveTracer DTC. But for software developers, the major disadvantages of the data parallel paradigm are

3. New algorithms and modifications of existing programming languages are needed to fully realize data parallelism. Speedup cannot be achieved without changes to current programming languages and programming style. This implies a change in the way we design parallel programs, and

4. Programmers must learn a new paradigm of programming, and therefore need new tools for analyzing parallel programs.

We propose an extension to PPSE to accommodate data parallel designs and therefore reduce the negative impact on programmers due to the disadvantages listed above. In this paper we describe how PPSE takes a high level graphical design of the parallel program, serial program routines, and target machine interconnection topology, and converts these into a running parallel program. Then we extend these semi-automatic tools to the data parallel paradigm using a combination of stencils, stream generators, and replicator routines. This is done by incorporating graphical constructs for representing the two-phases of data parallel programming listed above.

The purpose of this work is to advance the state of design representation as opposed to advancing the state of programming languages or coding techniques. Even though coding and debugging are important issues, we believe it is necessary to understand the design representation problem before addressing other issues. Therefore, this paper purposely focuses attention on design and analysis techniques for data parallel programs.

PPSE

PPSE is a parallel CASE toolset under development at Oregon Advanced Computing Institute (OACIS). Based on the well-known large-grain dataflow model proposed by Babb et al., and extended to incorporate hierarchy, PPSE consists of the techniques and tools snown in Figure 2, which are briefly described below.

1. pRETS : Parallel Reverse Engineering Tool System for converting an existing serial Fortran program into a database and then restructuring the database into a parallel Fortran program. We will not address this topic, here.

2. Parallax : A graphical design editor for viewing pRETS databases or entering new designs into the database. Parallax is a hierarchical dataflow design editor. We show how to extend the large-grain dataflow notation of Parallax to incorporate data parallel programming. This is the major contribution of this paper.

3. TaskGrapher : A graphical design editor and static scheduling tool that permits task graphs from Parallax to be analyzed and scheduled onto an arbitrary target machine. Parallax designs can be flattened and entered into Task Grapher where they are scheduled according to some optimal criteria. Scheduling data parallel designs remains a topic of continued research interest.

4. SuperGlue : A code generator which takes the optimal schedules produced by Task Grapher, and the code routines produced by Parallax, and generates a compilable source code application. C-LINDA and Strand are two of the languages supported by SuperGlue. Machine independence is a goal of SuperGlue, but this is achieved by constructing new code synthesizers for each target machine. We will not address this topic, here.

5. EPA : Execution Performance Analyzer which analyzes traces produced by the running application, and updates the program's design, based on the trace. We will not address this topic, here.

6. OREGAMI : A technique for designing regular communication structures. An OREGAMI design, along with the target machine interconnection network topology, can be used to arrive at an optimal mapping of tasks onto processors. Currently, OREGAMI is not integrated into PPSE, and so we show it as a separate tool within PPSE.

A feedback loop exists in Figure 2 whereby the actual timing values obtained by running the parallel program are fed back into the design. Each task in the design has an estimated execution time, and each data flow has an estimated communication time associated with it. These estimates may be initially wrong so it may be necessary to execute the program to obtain correct timing information. Once obtained from EPA, the accurate values are used in place of the early estimates, and a second iteration of the tools is necessary to produce a fully tuned version of the parallel program.

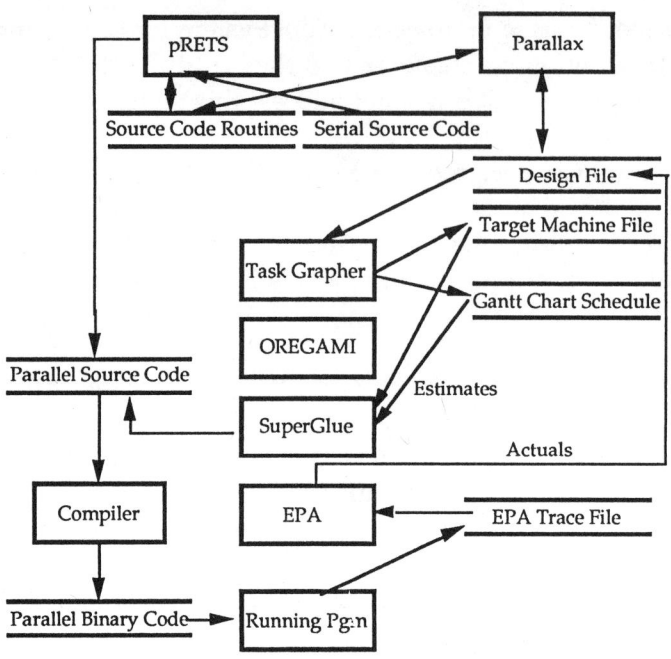

Figure 2. PPSE System Flow Diagram Showing Feedback via EPA.

PPSE produces code for any parallel computer that supports target languages C-LINDA, Strand, C, and Fortran. However, the system has only been used experimentally on Sequent shared memory, Intel, and NCUBE distributed memory machines.

Programming in PPSE

As an illustration of the Parallax design editor, we provide yet another program to calculate pi. Recall that pi can be estimated by numerical integration :

$$\int_0^1 \frac{4}{(1+x^2)} dx$$

The numerical quadrature algorithm divides the interval into strips, each strip area is computed by a processor, and the overall sum combined into the estimate. This is a perfect example of data parallel programming, where the intervals are distributed to different processors who perform exactly the same calculation, simultaneously.

The data parallel program design is shown in two levels in Figure 3. The top level design shows inputs and outputs as boxes, and a replicated component as a double-oval. The second level shows the decomposition of the replicated component plus the C source code for each parallel task.

Replicated tasks designated by "comps" in Figure 3(a) are controled by "myID, which is 0,1,2,3,... for each duplicate task. In short, the replication is enumerated to force many tasks to be created.

The source code in Figure 3(b) defines the actions of each task, but there are no explicit controls, synchronization, or target machine dependencies in the design. Instead, PPSE performs a series of mappings from the Parallax design down to running code. The mappings are shown in Figure 4, and described below.

1. Transformation of a hierarchical PPSE design into a flattened task graph, Figure 4(a)

2. Transformation of the flattened task graph into an execution schedule which defines not only which task is to run on what processor, but also when each task is to be activated, Figure 4(b)

3. Transformation of a schedule, and its source code fragments (procedures) into a compilable parallel program, shown in Figure 2. This step depends on an appropriate high level language compiler such as C-LINDA, Strand, or Fortran, on each target parallel computer. PPSE does not include compilers, linkers, or debuggers.

4. Monitoring of the running program by EPA, and then revising the program's design based on feedback from the EPA reports, per Figure 2.

Figure 4.(a) shows the first transformation performed automatically by PPSE. The hierarchical design of Parallax is flattened into a task graph. In this case, the replicated "comps" node of Figure 3(a) is flattened into six identical tasks which can be run in parallel.

In general, the number of replicates must be provided by the designer before the task graph is generated. This illustrates one of the shortcomings of PPSE. Because PPSE uses static scheduling of parallel tasks it is not possible to schedule the replicated tasks until the number of replications is known. In Figure 4.(a) we arbitrarily used 6 duplicates. In general, we might not know how many duplicates to use before the program executes.

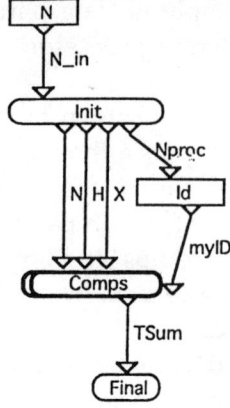

(a). Top Level Design of Pi Program in PPSE

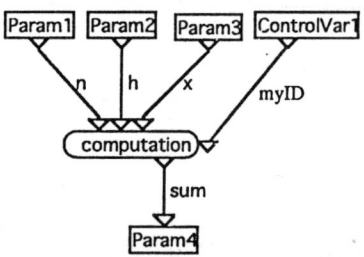

```
int i;
float y;
printf("computation %d start\n", myid);
*sum = 0.0;
for(i=myid;i<n;i+=nprocs){
  y=x+i*h;
  *sum+=(4.0/(1.0+y*y));
}
*sum= *sum/n;
}
```

(b). Level 2 Design and Code Fragment for Pi Design in PPSE

Figure 3. PPSE Parallax Design of Pi Problem

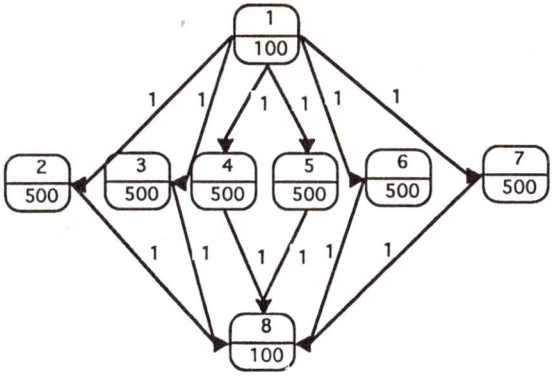

(a). Task Graph of Pi Design Created by PPSE

Task Graph : Task Graph 1
Topology : fullyConnected,   4 Processors
Heuristic : Rewini's Mapping Heuristic - MH

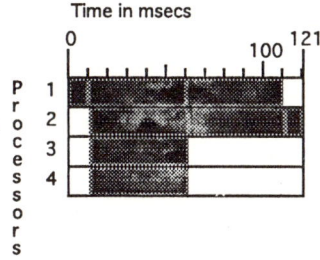

(b). Shortest Elapsed time Schedule of Pi Design

Figure 4. Task Graph and Schedule for Pi Problem

A second problem with this approach is the need to label the task graph with execution time estimates. We have estimated these to be 500 units for each duplicate, and 100 units each for the start and stop tasks. But, how do we know this? These are guesses at best, and we will not know the exact time estimates until after EPA reports actual execution times.

Similarly, we must estimate the time to communicate, start a task, and coordinate data flow between pairs of tasks. The estimates in Figure 4.(a) are once again guesses that will be changed after EPA results are known.

Figure 4.(b) shows one of many possible schedules of minimum execution time for the pi problem. Many factors go into scheduling. For example, we could have ignored inter-task communication time or not; include interconnection topology or not; include link contention or not; and trade memory for communication time by duplication of identical tasks across the entire set of parallel processors. Task Grapher consists of nine different scheduling heuristics. One for each case of potential interest.

The main problem addressed in this paper, however, is the problem of data parallel representation as a graphical design. In Figure 3-4, the replicated routine is not expressive enough to represent more elaborate designs, nor is it complete enough to automatically generate code from the design description. This problem is not restricted to PPSE, but rather it is a general problem of all graphical design languages. Accordingly, we propose an extension which overcomes this limitation in dataflow design representations used in PPSE and other similar systems.

Data Parallelism in PPSE

We propose three new constructs to be used by dataflow design tools for the purpose of representing data parallel computations: 1. stencil, 2. stream generator, and 3. replicator routines. These constructs are related to the stencil concept pioneered by Connection machine Fortran, stream generators found in functional languages, and replicators as originally proposed in CODE/ROPE and PPSE.

Data parallelism is realized in a PPSE design using a *stencil* for phase I representation, and a *replicator* for phase II representation within the data parallel paradigm. These constructs are illustrated by way of two revealing examples. Space does not permit a more formal definition.

A stencil is a filter routine that implements various data distribution patterns. A simple stencil might distribute the rows of a matrix across many processors, or alternately, it might insert a row into a matrix. Stencils are somewhat general, they can be used to broadcast, and then aggregate vectors, lists, matrices, and blocks of data. Stencil routines must be hand-crafted for each target architecture.

A stream is a consecutive sequence of values. A stream generator, or simply generator, is a routine which initially produces the first value of a stream, and subsequently produces each value in the sequence -- once each time the generator is activated. A generator for producing all integers from 1 to N in steps of 1 would produce the integer value 1, initially, followed by 2,3,4...,N in sequence.

A replicator is a computational routine that is copied onto each of N processors and executed in parallel. Replicators are distinguished from ordinary routines only in the way they are generated automatically from a design. That is, multiple replicates are generated from one manually constructed template. Replicates are expressed in a short-hand notation adapted from PPSE.

Generators and streams work together to create an expanded design as shown in Figure 5. A replicate routine is copied for each stream value, in sequence. The NEXT() generator produces a stream value each time it is activated.

In Figure 5, the two-level design of matrix multiply shows input values taken from matrices A and B and results fed back into matrix C. The inner product computation is shown at level two, and is replicated by the "Replicate" node at the top level.

The "ixj: Next(i,1,N,1,j,1,N,1)" stream generator produces all i and j values in cross-product order, e.g. i=1 to N in steps of 1; j=1 to N in steps of 1. The generator produces N*N replicates, each one labeled with an (i,j) ordered pair.

The stencils "Row", "Col", and "Element" filter the rows, columns and elements of each matrix, respectively. That is, the i-th row of A is filtered from matrix A and sent to the i-th replicate; the j-th column of B is sent to the j-th replicate, and the (i,j)-th element of C is updated with the sum returned as S.

The mapping from this data parallel design onto an 8-processor hypercube is shown in Figure 5(c-d). The replicated nodes are spread across the hypercube in a manner that minimizes communication delays. A full discussion of this technology is beyond the scope of this paper, but can be found in the references to El-Rewini et al. and Rudd et al.

The simple matrix multiply example does not reveal the full extent of design complexity that data parallel programmers encounter. On the surface, the use of stencils and replicators appear to cause minor modifications to the pure dataflow paradigm. In reality, the dataflow paradigm is in itself, insufficient to completely support the data parallel paradigm. The next example illustrates two major obstacles: one to do with stream generators, and the other to do with communication patterns among replicates. In fact, stencil routines may interact with replicators in complex ways as illustrated by the 5-point NEWS stencil for the well-known SOR algorithm, see Figure 6.

The SOR algorithm is used for solving Poisson's partial differential equation by discretizing and normalizing the surface to be computed over to fall into a unit square. Each point in the mesh is then computed by a weighted average of its current value and its neighbors in the mesh. For well behaved systems, the averages eventually converge to within a tolerence level.

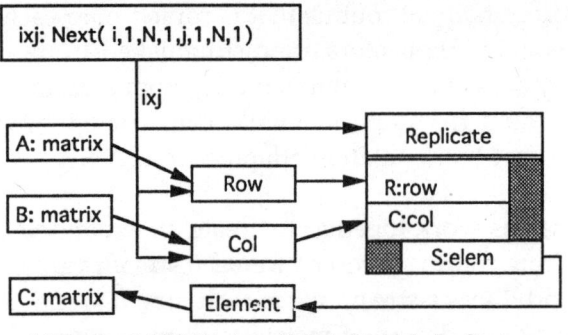

(a) Top-level PPSE Design of Matrix Multiply Replicator

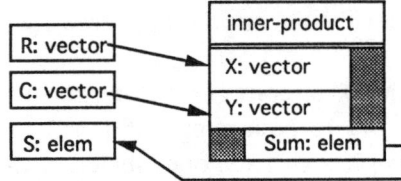

(b) Decomposition of Replicator Showing Inner Product Routine

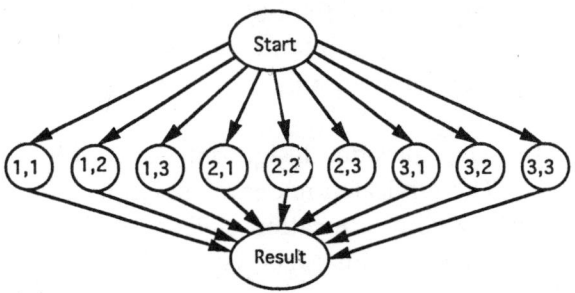

(c) Task Graph of Matrix Multiply for N=3

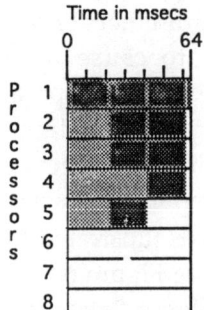

(d) Schedule of Matrix Multiply for N=3 on 8-node Hypercube

Figure 5. Example of Stencil/Replicator Constructs in Data Parallel Design of Matrix Multiply on an 8-processor Hypercube.

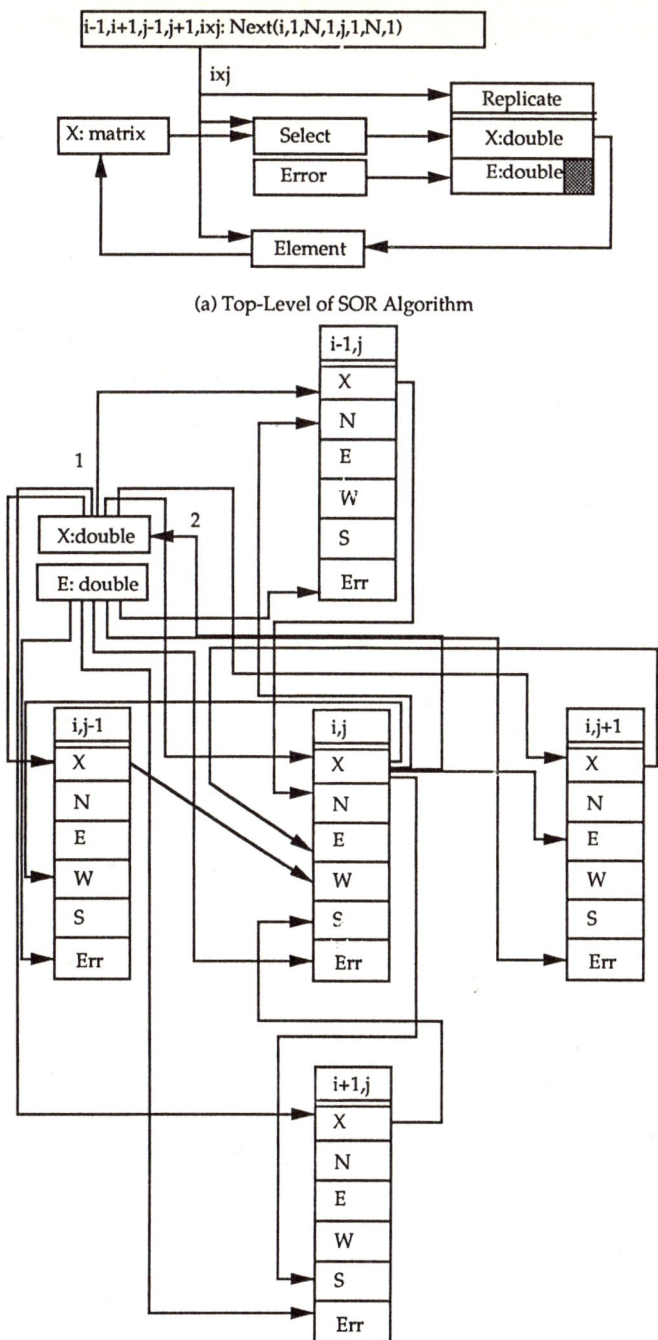

(a) Top-Level of SOR Algorithm

(b) SOR 5-Point Stencil and Replications of NEWS Average Routine

Figure 6. SOR (Successive Overrelaxation) Design.

SOR emphasizes several challenging problems for such graphical design languages, including:

1. The representation of a simple 5-point stencil is overly complex,

2. The dataflow patterns are not sufficient in themselves to determine the phases of distribution and calculation -- explicit sequencing is required, and

3. It is not clear how best to map such designs onto multiple processors, such that the greatest speed is achieved.

These problems constitute future research challenges for PPSE. A possible solution for problem 2 above, is to number the flows as shown in Figure 6. Thus, in this case we can generate the correct message-passing statements and insert the replicated code in the proper order. The code automatically produced from such a code generator is shown below. [We have simplified the code to make it readable without knowing the message-passing primitives of a certain machine].

```
repeat
  send( X, (i-1,j)); /* N */
  send( X, (i,j+1));/* E */
  send( X, (i,j-1));/* W */
  send( X, (i+1,j));/* S */

  receive( N, (i-1,j)); /* N */
  receive( E, (i,j+1));/* E */
  receive( W, (i,j-1));/* W */
  receive( S, (i+1,j));/* S */

  eps = X;
  X = (N+E+W+S)/4.0;
until ( abs(X-eps))<Error);
```

Clearly, this code can be optimized even further if we note that the send/receive pairs are indeed pairs, and so can be replaced by more efficient swaps. We can also gain greater performance if we combine swaps into blocks thus reducing the message-passing initiation time. To get the best possible performance from data parallel programming on a distributed memory machine, all of these optimizations must be performed. These and other problems remain to be solved.

Conclusions

We have shown how graphical languages such as CODE/ROPE and PPSE can be used to design SIMD or data parallel programs. The advantages of this approach are machine independence, design clarity, automated program analysis, and accelerated software development. The disadvantages are that many problems remain in this approach such as how to reduce design clutter, how to automate optimal processor mapping, and how to perform message-passing optimization. More work is needed before this approach can be used in the design of large-scale applications, but we believe the approach is promising. The main contribution is to show how the simple ideas of stencils, stream generators, and replicators can be used effectively to extend the classical dataflow design paradigm into the data parallel design paradigm. While more work is needed, these three ideas lead to greater expressiveness of design.

The PPSE toolset currently does much of the mapping, scheduling, and automatic code generation described in this paper. However, PPSE does not currently handle data parallel programming. Work is progressing toward a full implementation of these ideas. Even so, PPSE has been invaluable for performing a variety of what-if analyses on parallel programs. Insights have been gained with this approach that would not be possible with a purely textual representation of the parallel program.

References

Ahuja, S., Carriero, N., and D. Gelernter, "Linda and friends," Computer, 19, 8, (Aug 1986), 26-34.

Allan, R., Baumgartner, D., Kennedy, K., and Porterfield, A., PTOOL: A Semi-Automatic Parallel Programming Assistant, Proc. Int'l Conf. on Parallel Processing, August 1986, pp. 164-170.

Amdahl, G. M., "Validity of the Single-Processor Approach to Achieving Large-Scale Computing Capabilities", AFIPS Conference Proceedings 30, AFIPS Press, pp. 483-485 (1967).

Babb, R. G., Parallel Processing with Large Grain Data Flow Techniques, IEEE Computer, 17(7):55-61, July 1984.

Browne, J.C., Azam, M., and Sobek, S., CODE: A Unified Approach to Parallel Programming, IEEE Software, 6(4), July 1989, pp. 10-17.

Dongarra, J. J., and Sorensen D. C., SCHEDULE: Tools for Developing and Analyzing Parallel Fortran Programs, in The Characterstics of Parallel Algorithms, ed. L. H. Jamieson, D. B. Gannon, and R. J. Douglass, The MIT Press, Cambridge, Mass, 1987.

Dongarra, J., Karp, A., and Kennedy, K., "First Gordon Bell Awards Winners Achieve Speedup of 400", IEEE SOFTWARE, vol. 5, 3, (May 88), pp. 108-112.

El-Rewini, H., and Lewis, T.G., Scheduling Parallel Program Tasks onto Arbitrary Target Machines, *Journal of Parallel and Distributed Computing*, vol 9, pp. 138-153, (June 1990).

El-Rewini, H., Lewis, T. G., Fortner, J. Chu, and W. Su, Task Grapher: A Tool for Scheduling Parallel Program Tasks, *Proceedings of the 5th Distributed Memory Computing Conference*, April 1990, Charleston So. Carolina, pp. 1171-1178.

Evans, D. J., "Parallel S.O.R Iterative Methods", Parallel Computing, 1, pp. 3-18, (1984),
Glinert, E. P., Kopache, M. E., and McIntyre D. W., Exploring the General-Purpose Visual Alternative, Journal of Visual Languages and Computing, 1:3-39, March 1990.

Gustafson, J. L., "Reevaluating Amdahl's Law", Communications of the ACM, 31, 5, pp. 532-533 (1988).

Heath, M. T., Geist, G. A., Peyton, B. W., and Worley, P.H., A User's Guide to PICL. ORNL/TM-11616. Oak Ridge Nat'l Lab. Oak Ridge, TN. 37831. October 1990.

Ikudome, K., Fox, G.C., Kolawa, A., and Flower, J. W., An Automatic and Symbolic Parallelization System for Distributed Memory Parallel Computers, *Proceedings of the 5th Distributed Memory Computing Conference*, April 1990, Charleston So. Carolina, pp. 1105- 1114.

Muhlenbein, H., Kramer, O., Limburger, F., Mevenkamp, M., and Streitz, S., MUPPET: A Programming Environment for Message-Based Multiprocessors, Parallel Computing, vol 8, 1988, pp. 201-221.

Peir, J. K., Gajski, D. D., and Wu, M. Y., Programming Environments for Multiprocessors, Supercomputing, North-Holland, 1987, pp. 73-93.

Rudd, W. and Lewis, T. G., Architecture of the Parallel Programming support Environment, *Proc. CompCon'90*, San Francisco,CA., (Feb 26- Mar 2, 1990), pp. 589-594.

Snyder, L., Parallel Programming and the POKER Programming Environment, IEEE Computer, July 1984, pp. 27-36.

Wu, M. Y., and Gajski, D. D., Hypertool: A Programming Aid for Message-Passing Systems, IEEE Trans. Parallel and Distributed Systems, vol 1, no 3, July 1990, pp. 101-119.

Zima, H. P., Bast, H-J., and Gerndt, M., Superb: A Tool for Semi-Automatic MIMD/SIMD Parallelization, Parallel Computing, 6(1):1-18, Jan 1988.

A Powerful High-Level Debugger for Parallel Programs

Chris Caerts, Rudy Lauwereins[1] and J.A. Peperstraete
Katholieke Universiteit Leuven, E.S.A.T. Laboratory

Kard. Mercierlaan 94

B-3001 Heverlee, Belgium

ABSTRACT

The testing and debugging of complex programs has always been one of the most cost-determining factors in software design. This is even more true when parallel programs are considered. Debugging them is often based on a debugging cycle. First we make an assumption about the probable source of the bug, and next the validity of this assumption is verified. By repeatedly applying this technique, we try to limit the search-space until eventually the bug is resolved. There is a great need however for powerful high-level tools that enable the localization of bugs without indulging in this time-consuming error-prone debugging cycle. This paper describes such a high-level debugging tool, based on the animation of a program on its hierarchical-graphical representation.

Keywords : Parallel programs, high-level debugging, animation, graphical programming environment

1. INTRODUCTION

As computer hardware is getting less expensive every day, not longer the hardware cost, but the cost of the people developing software for these machines becomes determinant. Especially the testing and debugging of large complex programs is of the utmost importance, since it is one of the most time-consuming tasks in software development. This is especially true for parallel programs. Concurrency adds complexity which makes testing and debugging a difficult and

---

[1] **Senior Research Assistant at the Belgian National Fund for Scientific Research**

tedious task [1]. As parallel machines become more widespread every day, a lot of effort is made to assist in these tasks in order to increase efficiency of expensive man-power. Unfortunately, many parallel debuggers are little more than a parallel version of existing sequential debuggers, with little or no added functionality. As such they are geared towards low-level debugging : they assist in fixing the bug after having obtained a rough idea about its localization. There is a great need however for powerful high-level tools, which assist in the first debugging phase, when very little is known about the source of the bug.

In the second paragraph, a general picture of the classical sequential debugging methodology is given. Next we will discuss why this approach is not suited for the debugging of parallel programs. This will lead to a description of what the required functionality of an effective high-level debugger is, which is treated in paragraph four. In the fifth paragraph, the system we are developing at our laboratory will be described. Thereafter we will illustrate our debugging approach by resolving both a deadlock and a logical bug in a simple example program. And finally we will announce our future plans.

2. CLASSICAL SEQUENTIAL DEBUGGING METHODOLOGY

The debugging of classical sequential programs, however difficult it may be, is rather straightforward [2]. If a program does not behave the way it should, we make an assumption about what may have gone wrong by comparing the actual behaviour or result of the program with the expected one. This assumption is verified then, for instance by setting a breakpoint in the suspect code part. This allows us to examine the value of key variables or intermediate results or to step carefully through the code until the bug is spotted. When our assumption proves to be wrong, another one is made and checked in turn. This debugging cycle eventually leads to the fixing of the bug.

When it is difficult or impossible to make a good starting assumption, we try to get an idea about the whereabouts of the bug by patching our code with debugging statements (for instance 'printf' in a C program) to provide us with more information. The first location where erroneous results are observed is considered to be a practical point to start searching for the bug. Since there is only one single thread of control, it suffices to backtrack until the bug is reached (see figure 1). A drawback of this patching technique however is that it requires multiple recompilations and executions, and therefore is very time-consuming. It also relies heavily on the ability of the programmer in determining appropriate locations for inserting the debugging statements. Besides, it may not be possible when timing or memory constraints are imposed.

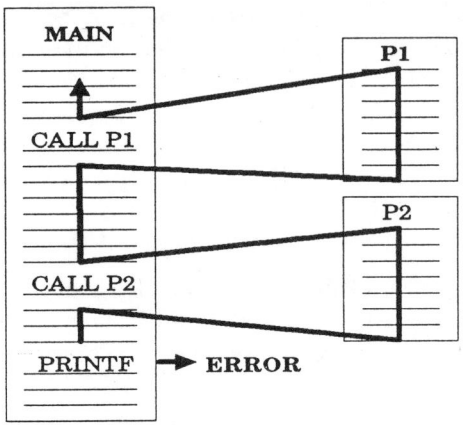

Figure 1 : Backtracking is an effective means for debugging sequential programs, since there is one single thread of control.

3. DEFICIENCIES OF THE CLASSICAL DEBUGGING TECHNIQUE

Parallel programs have added complexity when compared with sequential programs, which makes the classical debugging cycle not very effective [1][2]. The reason for this is that we have to deal now with multiple threads which are executing concurrently and which interact with each other. This makes it much more difficult to make a valid assumption about the source of the bug. Besides, the backtracking technique, which works very well for sequential programs, is completely ineffective.

Indeed, suppose that we manage to find a promising starting point. While backtracking, sooner or later we will reach a point where this thread is interacting with other ones. This means that we have to make a decision there : residing in the current thread or moving to the other one (see figure 2). It is clear that if this decision is to be made without relevant information, we can only decide by trial and error. In the worst case this forces us to exhaustively examine all threads. Only if we have a means to determine about the correctness of the exchanged data, we can make a wise decision here. By carefully observing the send-receive (or read-write) operations responsible for interprocess data exchange, it is possible to identify erroneous processes. Therefore the interaction points between concurrent threads are of key importance for high-level debugging [3].

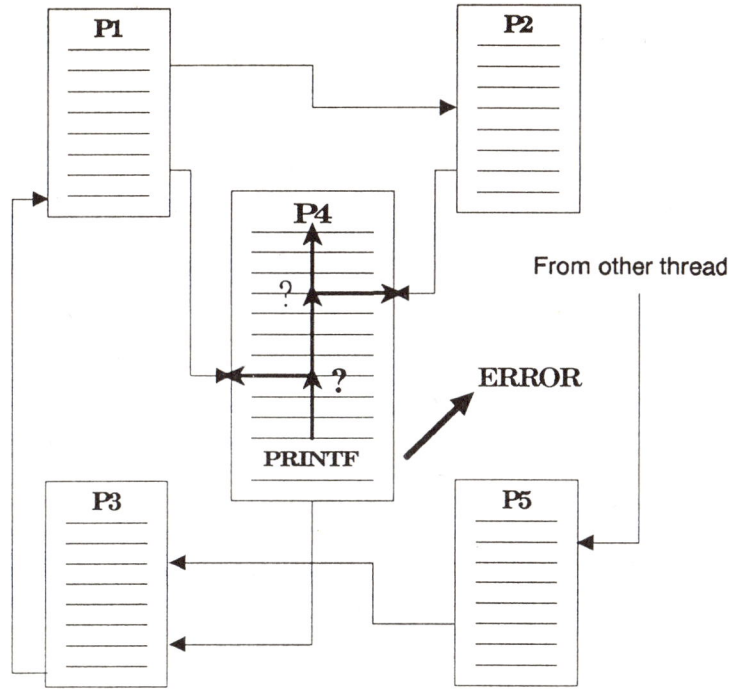

Figure 2 : Parallel Programs are difficult to backtrack. Interaction points between concurrent threads confront us with a search tree, which may require exhaustively exploring all branches.

Another problem is that the patching technique, heavily used in sequential debugging to give more information, is not liable to work properly. An obvious reason for this is that deadlocks can prevent debugging messages from reaching us, thus providing us with a heavily distorted, if not completely wrong, view of what is going on. This problem may be solved however by providing extra hardware to route debugmessages to the host. An example of this is the Supervisor Bus for the Meiko Computing Surface [13]. By using 'debugf' instead of 'printf', debugging messages are routed via the Supervisor Bus, so that deadlocks do not prevent them to reach the host. A more fundamental reason however is that parallel programs are often not deterministic. This means that the order in which key events are executed is not completely fixed. The key events that are of interest for debugging purposes have to do with interactions between concurrent threads, e.g. passing a message or accessing a shared resource [2]. Programs with such time-critical dependencies are subject to race-conditions, so that successive executions of the program may yield different results. In fact, this non-determinacy problem is very similar to the problem we are confronted with when debugging sequential programs dealing with asynchronisity. Non-determinacy may be, but is not necessarily, the bug we are looking for. Very often it is an innate aspect of the program, for instance in real-time systems dealing with asynchronous events [4]. But whether the non-the send-receive operations of all threads of a faulty program (see figure 3.a). It is clear that for all processes that have at least one faulty receive (e.g. a receive of erroneous data), it is impossible to decide about their correctness. In this particular example, this implies that we would be forced to examine three (P1, P3, P4) out of five processes in more detail (see figure 3.b). Introducing the time aspect however would reveal that process P1 is responsible for the occurrence of the first faulty argument (see figure 3.c). It is clear now that this process should be fixed first. This will reduce the number of faulty arguments, which in turn may reduce the number of suspect processes. By subsequently fixing all processes causing the next 'first faulty argument', we will evolve to an empty list of suspect processes by only examining the relevant one's. Therefore, we strongly believe in the effectiveness of animating the execution behaviour of the program. Also deadlocks can be spotted easily by means of animation, since it reveals clearly at which point interactions between processes come to a halt. Hence an event-driven animation, where an event is defined as an interaction between concurrent threads, clearly shows which processes or threads need closer examination. The programmer does not longer has to make assumptions, which may be wrong, but really sees what is going on. This technique leads to the bug first-time-right, without exhaustively examining all processes.

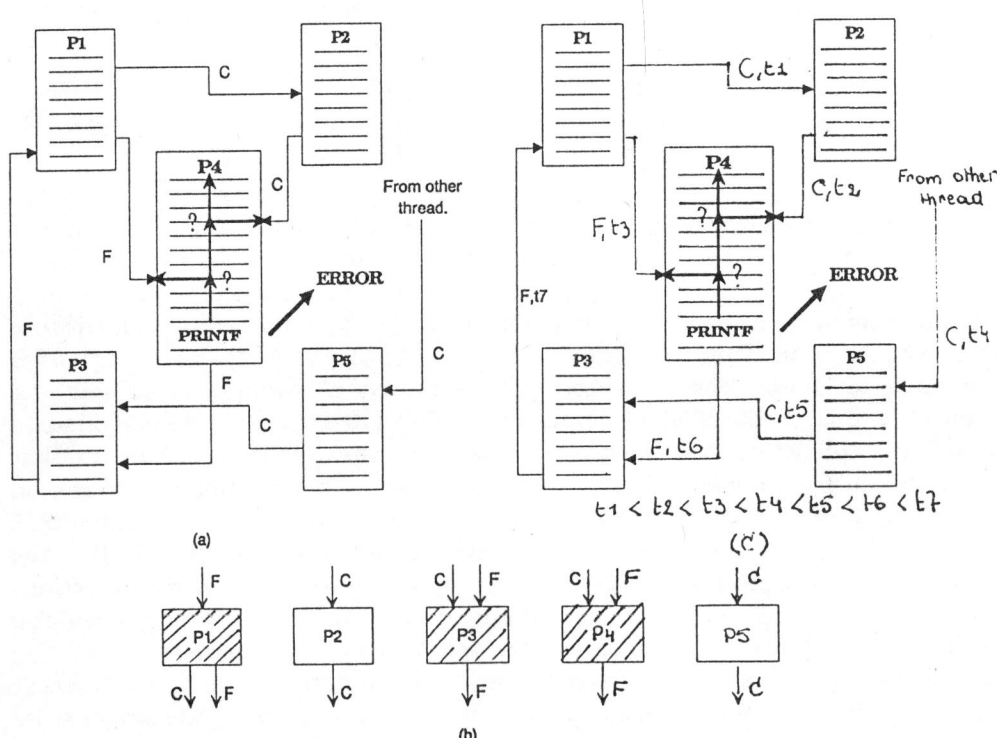

Figure 3 : By examining the input-output relationship of processes, it is possible to decide about their correctness. In general however, also the timing-relationship between the interactions must be taken into account.

Besides, a hierarchical view of the program should be provided to master the enormous complexity of parallel programs [7]. Hierarchy not only supports top-down program development, but also top-down debugging, hiding details when they are not needed. Hierarchical top-down debugging however requires multiple executions of the program. As mentioned earlier, this may be a problem when we are dealing with non-deterministic programs, since successive executions are not guaranteed to behave the same. Therefore, some kind of record-replay mechanism is needed [2][7][8][9]. During the original execution, one should record the order in which processes interact with each other, because these interactions may be responsible for non-deterministic behaviour. The same interaction sequence is then imposed during the following replays, ensuring deterministic behaviour. In fact it suffices to impose 'equivalent' re-executions, e.g. executions that behave the same as the original one, instead of identical replays. The actual data that are exchanged between threads need not be recorded during the original execution, thus minimizing overhead. They can be examined during the re-execution phase, since it is allowed then to set breakpoints or to step through code or to sprinkle it with debugging statements without the danger that this intrusion alters program behaviour. Indeed, the re-execution mechanism guarantees that, no matter what delays one introduces, the interactions between concurrent threads remain the same.

5. ANIMATING PARALLEL PROGRAMS IN GRAPE

At the moment we are integrating an animation tool for high-level debugging of parallel programs in GRAPE. This GRAphical Programming Environment has been developed in the ESAT laboratory at the Katholieke Universiteit Leuven and enables the effective top-down development of complex (parallel) programs in a hierarchical mixed graphical-textual manner [10].

At the highest abstraction level, a graphical representation of the program, consisting of coarse-grain interacting processes (or threads) is constructed. These coarse-grain processes are then more elaborated, using smaller grain building blocks. Only when the functionality of the processes becomes too small and the interactions between them so complex that a graphical representation becomes awkward, we switch to a textual representation of the task, using existing commercial editors. We decided to use a graphical representation on the higher levels because graphical views are very well suited to support in a natural way the hierarchical development of parallel programs [11]. A clear advantage of integrating the animation tool in the existing programming environment is that while debugging, the programmer can simply reuse the building blocks that he himself has defined during the specification phase. By doing so, only program-modules are used that are meaningful to him.

With this animation tool, the identification of erroneous processes is both fast and straightforward. Starting with an animation on a high-level representation of the program, e.g. consisting of high-level blocks (= threads) interacting with each other, we can actually see which processes are deadlocking, or which process is generating the first incorrect results. Next we focus attention on this erroneous process by zooming in on it, e.g. by going one abstraction level deeper. We continue zooming in repeatedly until we reach the lowest graphical level. Then, a commercially available debugger can be used to fix the bug. At each stage, there is no doubt about which process needs closer examination. The animation clearly shows which threads are ready to communicate but never do so because of a deadlock. Besides, the values that are exchanged between concurrent threads can be examined, therefore enabling the identification of modules that generate incorrect results for correct inputs [3]. By implementing a more sophisticated recording mechanism, it is even possible to trace user defined events such as the claiming and releasing of memory for instance.

Currently, we are incorporating a suitable tracing mechanism in a communication kernel for a transputer system. In RUN mode, only the relative order of message exchange will be recorded (e.g. the identification of the threads involved, together with a time-stamp), not the data associated with it. In order to reduce overhead, this trace is stored in local memory. In RE-EXECUTE mode then, the communication kernel will use this trace to impose the same relative order of interprocess interactions. This allows us to interfere with the application in an intrusive way now without changing global program behaviour. This means that it is possible to capture the actual exchanged data and to route them on-line to a host for animation purposes.

In the next paragraph, a short example will be given of the procedure to be followed in order to resolve both a deadlock and a logical bug.

6. EXAMPLE

In this paragraph, we will illustrate the high-level debugging methodology by fixing both a deadlock and a logical bug in a simple example.

When starting up the program, we are confronted with the fact that no results are produced. An animation on the highest hierarchical level reveals that although **Vkv** receives its inputs, it does not produces any outputs. This clearly shows that we should focus attention on **Vkv**, not on **Input** or **Output** which are irrelevant for the bug at hand (see figure 4.a). Zooming in on **Vkv**, the animation on this level shows that **Sqrtd** needs closer examination, since it gets its inputs but does not produce any outputs (see figure 4.b). When zooming in on **Sqrtd**, we see that **Sqrt_d** is of interest (see figure 4.c). By zooming in on **Sqrt_d**, we finally reach the lowest (textual) level. By examining the source code there, or possibly by switching to an traditional debugger, it is easy to spot the bug (see figure 4.d). At the end of process **Sqrt_d**, we mistakenly issued an input (?) instead of an output (!) command, causing our program to deadlock.

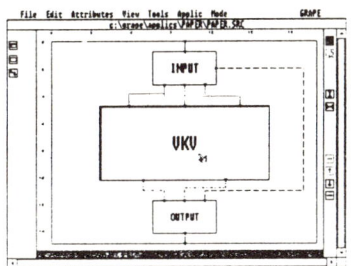
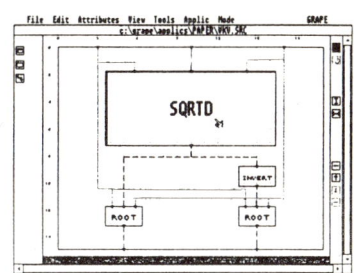

4.a : level 1 (top hierarchical level)   *4.b : level 2*

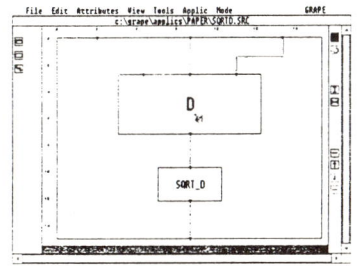

PROC Sqrt_d (CHAN OF REAL32
 chan_d, chan_sqrtd)

REAL32 d, sqrtd :

SEQ

    chan_d ? d

    sqrtd := SQR(d)

    chan_sqrtd ? sqrtd

:

4.c : level 3   *4.d : level 4 (bottom, textual, level)*

Figure 4 : Solving a program deadlock by using an animation on a hierarchical-graphical representation of the program .

Having this bug fixed, our program still does not behave the way it should. By examining the data exchanged between concurrent threads, we are able to locate the bug by zooming in subsequently on **Vkv**, **Sqrtd** and **Sqrt_d** (see figure 5.a-c). This eventually resolves the bug : we mistakenly called the function SQR instead of SQRT (see figure 5.d).

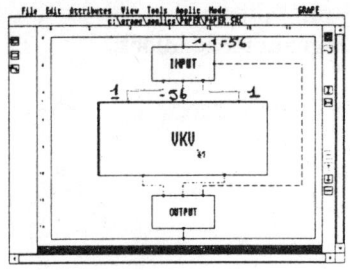
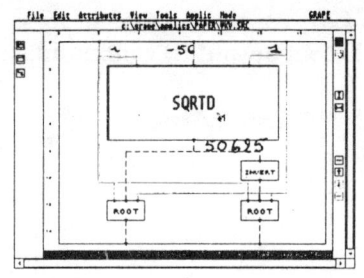

5.a : level 1 (top hierarchical level)   5.b : level 2

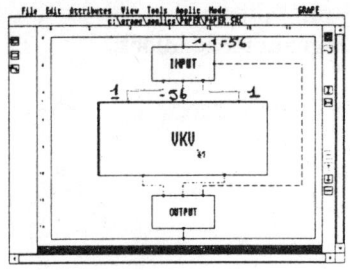

PROC Sqrt_d (CHAN OF REAL32
            chan_d, chan_sqrtd)
REAL32 d, sqrtd :
SEQ
    chan_d ? d
    sqrtd := SQR(d)
    chan_sqrtd ! sqrtd
:

5.c : level 3   5.d : level 4 (bottom, textual, level)

Figure 5 : Solving a logical bug by using an animation on a hierarchical-graphical representation of the program .

For both bugs, the animation clearly showed which processes were of interest for the bug at hand, removing the need to make a (wild) guess or to examine all processes exhaustively. The animation clearly pointed down the relevant processes, removing the need for making (erroneous) assumptions.

7. FUTURE WORK

Currently, tracing is done completely in software, without any hardware support. It is clear however that this may disturb the behaviour of the target program, therefore making it impossible to spot the bug [12]. Another problem arises when the trace buffer, which is stored in local memory, becomes full. We must choose then between either stopping tracing or emptying the trace buffer (by down-loading its content to the host) which causes considerable overhead. Therefore we would like to develop dedicated hardware to solve this problem. A possible solution for instance would be to implement the trace buffer as dual-ported RAM which can be emptied periodically by a (network of) control processor. The latter could also be used then for monitoring purposes.

We would also like to extend our tool, which use is limited currently to message passing systems, for shared memory systems. The above mentioned control processor could be used then to keep track of accesses to shared data, completely removing all interference with the application at hand. We assess that the needed hardware can be kept extremely simple if some compiler support can be provided, e.g. generation of an extra 'status' bit for these resources that are shared between multiple threads. It is important to stress at this point that also 'channels', used in message passing systems, can be viewed as a shared resource.

To resume, we intend to develop hardware to accomplish the tracing-task without intrusion. This is not only important for programs which are heavily non-deterministic, but also for real-time programs where timing constraints inhibit the use of software recording processes.

8. CONCLUSION

In this paper we described a powerful high-level debugger for complex parallel programs. Its distinctive feature is the fact that a hierarchical graphical representation of the program is utilised. By animating the execution behaviour of the program on successively lower abstraction levels, the search-space for the bug is increasingly restricted until the bug is found. The animation tool shows what is actually going on, therefore removing the need for errorprone assumptions. It clearly identifies erroneous processes, thus leading to the bug first-time-right. This speeds up the debugging task significantly.

REFERENCES

[1] W.H.Cheung, J.P. Black, E. Manning, "A Framework for Distributed Debugging", IEEE Software, January 1990, pp. 106-115.

[2] T.J. LeBlanc and J.M. Mellor-Crummey, "Debugging Parallel Programs with Instant Replay", IEEE Transactions on Computers, Vol.36(4), April 1987, pp. 471-482.

[3] C. Caerts, R. Lauwereins and J.A. Peperstraete, "A Powerful Monitor and Debugger for Multiprocessor Systems", Proc. of the ISMM International Symposium on Mini and Microcomputers and their Application, June 1990, pp. 281-284.

[4] P.A. Emrath and D.A. Padua, "Automatic Detection of Nondeterminacy in Parallel Programs", Proc. of the ACM SIGPLAN and SIGOPS Workshop on Parallel and Distributed Debugging, May 1988, pp. 89-99.

[5] J. Gait, "A Probe Effect in Concurrent Programs", Software - Practice and Experience, Vol.16(3), March 1986, pp. 225-233.

[6] Z. Aral and I. Gertner, "High-Level Debugging in Parasight", Proc. of the ACM SIGPLAN and SIGOPS Workshop on Parallel and Distributed Debugging", May 1988, pp. 151-160.

[7] C. Lin and R.J. LeBlanc, "Event-Based Debugging of Object/Action Programs", Proc. of the ACM SIGPLAN and SIGOPS Workshop on Parallel and Distributed Debugging, May 1988, pp. 23-34.

[8] I.J.P. Elshoff, "A Distributed Debugger for Amoeba", Proc. of the ACM SIGPLAN and SIGOPS Workshop on Parallel and Distributed Debugging, May 1988, pp. 1-10.

[9] S.H. Jones, R.H. Barkan and L.D. Wittie, "BUGNET : a Real Time Debugging System", Proc. Sixth Symp. Reliability in Distributed Software and Database Systems, CS Press, Los Alamitos, Calif., 1987, pp. 56-65..

[10] R. Lauwereins, M. Engels, J. Peperstraete, E. Steegmans, J. Van Ginderdeuren, "GRAPE : a CASE Tool for Digital Signal Parallel Processing", IEEE ASSP magazine, April 1990, pp. 32-43.

[11] G. Raeder, "A Survey of Current Graphical Programming Techniques", Computer, August 1985, pp. 11-25.

[12] F. Baiardi, N. De Francesco and G. Vaglini, "Development of a Debugger for a Concurrent Language", IEEE Transactions on Software Engineering, April 1986, pp. 547-553.

[13] Meiko Ltd., "Computing Surface : Hardware Reference Manual", 1989.

The PCP/PFP Programming Models on the BBN TC2000[*]

Eugene D. Brooks III, Brent C. Gorda, Karen H. Warren

Massively Parallel Computing Initiative

Lawrence Livermore National Laboratory

Livermore, California 94550

Abstract: We describe the PCP/PFP programming models which we are using on the BBN TC2000. The parallel programming models are implemented in a portable manner and will be useful on the scalable shared memory machines we expect to see in the future. We then describe the TC2000 machine architecture which is a scalable general purpose parallel architecture capable of efficiently supporting both shared memory and message passing programming paradigms. We also briefly describe a PCP implementation of the Gauss elimination algorithm which exploits the large local memories on the TC2000.

1 Introduction

Microprocessors have made incredible strides in performance in recent years and are beginning to overrun traditional supercomputer performance for scalar dominated application codes. It is anticipated that supercomputer class vector processing performance will appear in microprocessor form in the next few years. This development is enabling a new breed of supercomputers composed of hundreds, and in some cases thousands, of high performance microprocessors.

The BBN TC2000 is a scalable microprocessor based machine which provides a shared memory facility through a multi-staged interconnection network. It is similar to the IBM RP3 architecture [1] but is currently available commercially. Because the machine supports both high bandwidth interleaved shared memory and large local memories, it is well suited to supporting both shared memory and message passing programming models.

We have implemented FORTRAN and C versions of the *split-join* [2] parallel programming paradigm on the BBN TC2000 with the Parallel C Preprocessor (PCP) and the Parallel FORTRAN Preprocessor (PFP).

The split-join parallel programming model is highly portable because a full featured version is easily implemented with a preprocessor and relatively little back end compiler support. An earlier version of PCP has been used on a variety of machines, including Sequent Symmetry, Sequent Balance, Alliant FX/8, SGI, Stellar, and Cray multiprocessors. PFP was written specifically for the large base of FORTRAN users who are participating

---

[*]Work performed under the auspices of the U. S. Department of Energy by the Lawrence Livermore National Laboratory under contract No. W-7405-ENG-48.

in the Massively Parallel Computing Initiative at Lawrence Livermore National Laboratory. The PCP and PFP preprocessors have an option of generating efficient serial code, and this has been used to target both multiprocessors and uniprocessors with the same source code. We have found the split-join programming model to be a good match to the BBN TC2000 architecture. Users have found that one must exploit nested concurrency effectively in order to use successfully large numbers of processors on general purpose applications. The split-join programming model implemented in PCP and PFP provides the efficient means for exploiting nested concurrency effectively.

The sections of this paper are as follows. The split-join model and its memory model are described in Sections 2 and 3. Specifics on how the implementation of these models take advantage of the architecture are included. The synchronization primitives offered in PCP and PFP are discussed in Section 4. The actual PCP syntax is shown in Section 5. The BBN TC2000 hardware and capabilities are presented in Section 6. A PCP implementation of the Gauss Elimination algorithm which exploits the large local memories is discussed in Section 7.

2 The Split-join Model

In the traditional fork-join parallel programming model, a single processor starts the execution of the program and acquires more processors as concurrency is encountered in the code. Examples of this model are PCF [5] in which the system may utilize more processors for designated program sections if it desires, and the Cray autotasking model [6] which automatically distributes loop iterations to a number of multiple processors determined by the system and which itself obviously is not portable. The acquisition of more processors is generally an expensive operation. Nonetheless the fork-join programming model has been quite useful on tightly coupled shared memory machines with relatively few processors, and on some architectures such as the Alliant FX/8 and the Convex C2 which provide special hardware to make the dispatch of slave processors occur as quickly as possible. Scalable machine architectures are not as tightly coupled and the cost of communication between processors, heavily used in the process of dispatching processors in the fork-join model, is relatively high.

In the split-join paradigm we deal with the high cost of processor dispatch and the high cost of communication between processors by minimizing their occurrence in the fundamental constructs of the programming model. All of the processors the job will ever acquire are dispatched at the start of the program and are immediately placed under the control of the programmer. This set of processors which loosely follow each other through the code is referred to as a *team* of processors. At this level the split-join parallel programming model is very similar to Harry Jordan's Force [3] and the IBM SPMD [4] programming model, the most significant differences being the support for team splitting, the determinism which the user can establish with respect to which processors do what, and the arbitrary nesting of concurrency constructs.

The user is in complete control of the initial team of processors. Nested concurrency is exploited by the user through the notion of *team splitting*. In the static form of team splitting, the user explicitly marks off separate blocks of work which can be executed independently of each other (it is assumed that each block of work is itself a job consisting of subtasks which can be executed in parallel), and possibly indicates the relative total amount of work in each block of code. When the team encounters the split blocks, it divides into a number of subteams matching the number of blocks of code and tackles each block of work with new teams having smaller numbers of processors. If the user has provided accurate loading information controlling the relative number of processors in each subteam, the processors finish their work at the same time and join back up into the parent team nearly simultaneously. The total number of processors is conserved in the team splitting process; the processors merely become members of new subteams.

Splitting the size of the team into smaller subteams as nested concurrency is encountered is counter intuitive. The goal, however, in exploiting nested concurrency is to use a *fixed* number of processors more efficiently, not to use *more* processors. The split-join programming model is in some sense the *dual* of the fork-join model. One finds that one can usually accomplish the task at hand with either programming model. The advantage of the split-join programming model is its full featured, bottleneck free, implementation through a highly portable preprocessor.

3 The Memory Model

In the split-join programming paradigm, three types of memory are required to exploit fully the notion of team splitting. These are:

- memory which is private or local to a processor, *private* memory,
- memory which is shared among all processors, *shared* memory,
- and memory which is shared among the members of a given team or grouping of processors, but private to it, *teamprivate* memory.

Private, or local, memory is implemented on the processor which has access to it. Shared memory is implemented in the interleaved shared memory facility of the BBN TC2000, see Section 6. Teamprivate memory is allocated as an array in the interleaved shared memory, indexed by a *team descriptor* which is unique to the team.

Team splitting is handled in a block structured way. Each time a processor becomes a member of a new subteam, it computes a new team descriptor and its position in the new team without accessing any shared memory or synchronization resources. This leads to an efficient unrestricted implementation of team splitting, the cost of which is completely independent of the number of processors in the team. As the processor computes a new team descriptor, it pushes the old one on a private stack for recovery when it reaches the end of its share of the work in the split block. Since a processor carries the team descriptors of all its antecedent teams on a stack, it has access to the team private memory of a parent team. This can be very useful in a situation where the tasks in the split blocks are to compute some results required by all the members of the parent team, but for which the use of shared memory would pose an access hazard due to nested use of team splitting in a reentrant way.

4 Synchronization

Barrier synchronization and the notion of locks are provided in the PCP and PFP implementations of the split-join programming model. In barrier synchronization, all of the processors in a given team are forced to wait at the barrier until the last straggler has arrived. A bottleneck free software implementation [12] is used, requiring 30 to 40 microseconds to synchronize 32 processors. The execution time of the barrier scales as the log of the processor count. Each team has its own unique barrier.

The notion of a lock is also provided. A processor attempting to acquire a lock spin-waits until the lock is unlocked and then locks it. When done with the critical region the lock was being used to protect, it then unlocks the lock, making it available to others. Locks may be located in shared memory, or teamprivate memory, depending on the scope of the critical region which is being protected.

In addition to the use of barriers and locks, the user may implement an event by simply spin-waiting for a location in shared or teamprivate memory to change. On a machine supporting coherent shared memory caches this is particularly effective and has no negative impact. If the machine lacks this support, as is the case for the BBN TC2000, one must be careful about the possibility of generating adverse impact on available memory bandwidth through the introduction of a hot spot. If too many processors are waiting on a certain variable, one might *back off* in a random manner. Another efficient alternative is to allow the waiting processor to take on another task from a job queue. These alternatives to spin-waiting may be easily implemented in PCP and PFP.

5 PCP Syntax

A short summary of the PCP syntax follows. For more detailed specification, see the PCP user's manual [10]. The equivalent functionality exists for FORTRAN. For specific FORTRAN syntax, see the PFP user's manual [11].

5.1 Team State

Each member of a team carries in its local memory five variables which identify its current team state. PCP changes the team state by altering the three team state variables: team size, _TSIZE, the team index, _TINDEX, and the team descriptor, _TDESC. The old values are placed on a team state stack so that the original team state may be restored.

5.2 Variable Accessibility and Cachability Attributes

Variables may be declared with the accessibility attributes,

```
private
shared
teamprivate
```

depending on the type of memory in which they are to be located. They may also be declared with the cachability attributes,

```
writethru
copyback
uncached
```

which are translated to the appropriate machine dependent syntax.

5.3 master

Within the context of a specific team, that processor whose current team index is 0 executes the code delimited by a `master` block. Arbitrary PCP code may be enclosed by a `master` block. A `master` block is often used in the portion of the program that performs initialization as well as input/output and memory allocation. At a much smaller scale of granularity, `master` blocks are used to initialize shared data such as accumulators which all team members will access.

```
master {
  <declarations>
  <executable code>
}
```

5.4 forall

The `forall` loop is the PCP concurrent equivalent of the C language `for` loop. It achieves a fine-grained parallelism by dividing up the passes of the `for` loop among the members of the team:

```
forall (int i = <start>; <cond>; i += <step>)  {
    work(i)
}
```

The indices of the loop are interleaved among the members of the executing team. The loop index variable must be declared in the `forall` statement. We have borrowed this syntax from C++ to remind the user that the loop index is not defined after the closing brace of the loop body. The `<start>` and `<step>` expressions are currently restricted to simple constants or variables. The `<cond>` expression is unrestricted but not checked for sanity. `forall` loops may be nested arbitrarily. Inside the loop the processor team index is set to 0 and the team size to 1 to permit enclosed PCP constructs to work correctly.

5.5 barrier

The team of processors executing the code freely run through it unless explicit synchronization primitives are encountered. One basic and frequently used form of synchronization is the *barrier*:

```
barrier;
```

A barrier requires all members of the team to arrive *at the barrier* before any are allowed to continue. Each team has its own distinct barrier. A barrier is often used after a `master` block, or a `forall` loop, to ensure that the preceding work is complete before any processor is allowed to continue on. A fast barrier algorithm which has no hot spots or critical regions has been implemented for PCP runtime support.

5.6 `lock, unlock`

Concurrency must be inhibited in a statement that reads, modifies, and then writes a shared variable. To prevent team members from destructively interfering with each other, entrance to a critical section of a code must be restricted so that only one processor may execute it at a time. This is accomplished by using a lock.

PCP offers *spin wait* locks that are implemented by variables of the `lock` data type which has the two states `locked` and `unlocked`. A `lock` variable is a statically allocated and initialized C data type:

```
lock var = unlocked;
```

The functions that change the state of a lock are `lock()` and `unlock()` which take the pointer to the lock variable as an argument. A lock is used to protect a critical section in the following way:

```
lock(&var);

<critical section>

unlock(&var);
```

If the lock variable is shared, then the critical section is global. If the lock is declared `teamprivate`, then the critical section is local to the team.

5.7 `split`

To divide up a number of tasks, which is known at compile time, among subteams which are split from the parent team, one uses static team splitting:

```
split <weight1> {
    <task1>
}
and  <weight2>  {
    <task2>
}
...
and <weightn>  {
    <taskn>
}
```

The tasks may be executed in any order, including sequentially if the team encountering the split statement can not be split for some reason. If one task is much greater than another, one may assign weights to the blocks of work to achieve load balancing. The weights determine the fraction of the current team's processors which are used for each subteam.

5.8 splitall

The dynamic version of team splitting is the `splitall` loop:

```
splitall (int i = <start>; <cond>; i += <step>) {

    work(i)

}
```

When a team encounters a `splitall` loop, it disassociates into a number of subteams to which the indices of the loop are interleaved. The number of teams is determined at compile time or run time.

6 TC2000 Architecture

The BBN TC2000 [7] is a scalable multiprocessor architecture which can support up to 512 computational nodes. The Motorola 88100 microprocessor is used in conjunction with three Motorola MC88200 chips to provide for a 32K byte code cache and a 16K byte data cache. The data caches are under programmer control with no hardware assistance for maintaining the coherence of shared data.

The processors are operated at clock speed 20 MHZ, providing a manufacturer's rating of 17 MIPS and a peak single precision floating point speed of 20 MFLOPS. Double precision floating point computation runs at a peak speed of 10 MFLOPS because all data busses in the architecture are 32 bits wide. As is the case for other current microprocessor powered equipment, the difference between peak speed and actual realized speed is rather large. The size of the main memory on each computational node in our machine is 16 megabytes, although some earlier produced machines have only 4 megabytes.

The processors, with their 16 megabyte memories, are interconnected to each other in a PE-to-PE model by a variant of a multistage cube network [8] which BBN refers to as the "butterfly switch." In the TC2000, 8×8 switch nodes are used to construct the network. The 512 node configuration requires only three stages of switch nodes in the network, leading to a latency of about 2 microseconds for communication between arbitrary processors. This low latency is directly accessible to the programmer through the shared memory paradigm that the machine provides. The network connections are 8 bits wide and are clocked at 38 MHZ.

The BBN TC2000 supports local memory, shared memory wherein successive cache lines reside on one card, and interleaved shared memory wherein successive cache lines are placed on successive cards and wrap around the machine. The contribution of each node to the interleaved shared memory pool is made at boot time, set via device registers in the interface to the switch which connects the processors. Any number of processors can be configured to contribute to the interleaved shared memory pool and it is useful and convenient to set the number of contributing processors to a prime number to avoid hot spot problems. The rest of the memory in each node can be used for either local memory or non-interleaved shared memory. This division is enforced by the memory management unit attached to the processor and is set in a completely flexible way at the time an application is run.

As noted above, the data caches in the TC2000 are under programmer control. The cachability of sections of virtual address space can be adjusted at run time with system calls. System calls are also provided to flush regions of virtual address space from the data cache as required. This facility is used in the "data mover" routines of the message passing package to improve transfer rates, but the system call mechanism has too high an overhead to be used for fine grained concurrency control of specific variables. In general, local data is left cachable and shared data is left not cachable, with the possible exception of "write once - read many" variables (hot spots) that are efficiently handled as write through cachable shared memory variables.

Unlike the message passing and SIMD machines which tend to restrict the user to a single programming model, the BBN TC2000 offers a rich architectural structure presenting many possibilities for the language developer. In addition to the BBN supplied programming models, we have made a substantial effort to develop programming models which fit the TC2000 architecture well and have implemented them in a manner that preserves portability to the scalable architectures possessing shared memory that we expect to see in the future.

7 Gauss Elimination

The effective use of local memory is the key to good performance. To demonstrate this, we consider Gauss elimination without pivoting. Including pivoting can be done and does not qualitatively change the results but instead complicates the code examples given and reduces clarity of the discussion.

The Gauss elimination algorithm is composed of two parts. The first is referred to as the reduction wherein the matrix is reduced to an upper triangular form which exposes the last element of the unknown vector to direct solution. Reduction is done in n steps where n is the number of equations. In the $i'th$ step suitable multiples of the $i'th$ row, known as the pivot row, are subtracted from the rows below in order to zero out matrix coefficients. All of the operations on the rows below can be done in parallel, but each operation depends upon the pivot row.

In the second part, the backsolve, which is begun as soon as the matrix is brought to upper triangular form, elements, from n to 1, of the unknown solution are successively solved for and substituted into the remaining equations. These substitutions can also be done in parallel, as soon as a processor has provided the next element of the solution vector.

7.1 Simple Parallel Version

Assuming a shared memory machine, the easiest and most obvious way to design the Gauss elimination algorithm is to use parallel do loops in the reduction part, letting the processors work in parallel on the rows in shared memory. Similarly, for the backsolve part the processors work in parallel on the rows in shared memory. A barrier is used at the end of each reduction step and backsolve step to ensure that all of the calculations for that step have been completed before proceeding on to the next step. Implementing this version in PCP added or changed only seven lines of the original serial version. The PCP modifications are shown below in bold face.

```
void dgauss(double **a, double *b, int dim)
{
    /* reduction outer loop */
    for(int k = 0; k < dim; k += 1) {
        forall (int i = k+1; i < dim; i +=1) {
            double temp = a[i][k];
            if(temp == 0.0) continue;
            a[i][k] = 0.0;
            temp /= a[k][k];
            for(int j = k + 1; j < dim; j +=1) {
                a[i][j] - = a[k][j] * temp;
            }
            b[i] - = b[k] * temp;
        }
        barrier;
    }
    /* backsolve outer loop */
    for(int i = dim - 1; i >= 0; i - = 1) {
        master {
            b[i] /= a[i][i];
        }
        barrier;
        forall (int k = i-1; k >= 0; k - = 1) {
            b[k] - = a[k][i] * b[i];
        }
    }
    barrier;
}
```

This version of the code does not constrain the processors to perform repeated calculations on the same rows and uses excessively strong barrier synchronization on each step of the reduction and backsolve parts. If there is sufficient shared memory bandwidth to support the floating point operations, and the problem is large enough to amortize the cost of the barriers, good parallel performance is obtained.

The performance of this version of the code on the BBN TC2000, however, was disappointing. The use of 10 processors was required to reclaim the original serial program performance of one computational node. This arises from the number of clock cycles required to access a word in shared memory and the lack of shared memory coherent cache support. The BBN TC2000 is a realistic example of what one might expect in regard to scalable machine architectures. The latency of a cache hit on local memory is 3 clocks (pipelined at a rate of one per clock) where as the latency of a remote memory reference is roughly 40 clocks (not pipelined). If one must deal with a 40 clock latency for every memory reference required in the code used to dispatch processors, even an efficient spanning tree implementation can have substantial overhead. On this machine we must exploit local memories explicitly to reduce the adverse impact of slow memory accesses through the switch connecting the processors.

7.2 Explicit Local Memory Use

To exploit local memory on the BBN TC2000, the rows of the matrix which resides in shared memory are divided up and pulled in to local memory by the processors which will then perform the reduction and backsolve operations on those specific rows. There are two data dependencies to consider when optimizing the code. All operations for the $i'th$ reduction step must wait until the pivot row is ready and all calculations for a given row for a given step must wait for the previous calculations to have been completed. To avoid the use of time consuming barriers and to take care of the first dependency, the code was altered to use a *spin-wait* flag in shared memory to signal when a given pivot row is ready. The second dependency is taken care of by having all the calculations for a particular row being done by the same processor. Shared memory is now used only to communicate intermediate results such as pivot rows and newly solved elements of the solution vector between processors. On a scalable machine lacking coherent caches, read only hot spots, i.e., locations for which many processors are contending, become a serious problem, and such data needs also to reside in local memory. In our case, we avoid such hot spots by caching the pointers to the row matrices. Implementing this version required 106 lines of code, approximately 5 times more than the original serial version.

The results of this effort using 48 processors on the BBN TC2000 are shown in Table 1. n denotes the number of equations in the linear system, $MFLOPS$ is the overall speed of the code measured in millions of floating point operations per second, t_{sec} is the total execution time in seconds, t_r the reduction time, t_b the backsolve time and S the speedup. Speedups are relative to the original serial version of the code running in local memory.

n	MFLOPS	t_{sec}	t_r	t_b	S
100	3.40	0.20	0.16	0.04	2.6
200	10.47	0.52	0.46	0.06	7.7
300	18.85	0.96	0.88	0.08	13.7
400	27.65	1.55	1.44	0.11	19.8
500	31.34	2.68	2.48	0.20	22.2
600	38.32	3.78	3.61	0.17	28.0
700	42.25	5.43	5.25	0.18	33.0
800	44.75	7.66	7.46	0.19	35.0
900	46.96	10.38	10.16	0.23	36.7
1000	48.39	13.82	13.56	0.26	38.1

Table 1. Performance using local memory explicitly.

8 Discussion

We have described the BBN TC2000 architecture and the PCP/PFP programming models that we have developed for use on it by research staff participants in the Massively Parallel Computing Initiative at Lawrence Livermore National Laboratory. These programming models are routinely used by the research staff in a wide range of efforts in computational physics, chemistry, engineering, and graphics applications. The programming support is highly portable, having its roots in language support developed for earlier bus based shared memory multiprocessors such as the Sequent, Silicon Graphics, Stellar, and Alliant machines.

The key to high performance on the BBN TC2000, and any future scalable system supporting shared memory, is the efficient exploitation of data locality as demonstrated in our PCP implementation of the Gauss elimination algorithm. The split-join parallel programming paradigm implemented via PCP and PFP support the user in pursuing data locality by providing explicit local memory in the programming model and a predictable execution environment wherein processors can be tiled onto a data set in a way which makes maximum use of data locality.

References

[1] G. F. Pfister, et al, "The IBM Research Parallel Processor Prototype (RP3): Introduction and Architecture", *Proc. of the 1985 International Conference on Parallel Processing*, pp. 764-771, August 20-23, 1985.

[2] E. D. Brooks III, *PCP: A Parallel Extension of C that is 99% Fat Free*, UCRL-99673, Lawrence Livermore National Laboratory, 1988.

[3] H. F. Jordan, "The Force: A Highly Portable Parallel Programming Language", *Proceeding of the International Conference on Parallel Processing*, August, 1989.

[4] F. Darema, D. A. George, V. A. Norton and G. F. Pfister, "A single-program-multiple data computational model for EPEX/FORTRAN", *Parallel Computing*, April, 1988.

[5] A. H. Karp, "Programming for Parallelism", *Computer*, May 1987, pp. 43-57.

[6] Cray Research,Inc., *Autotasking User's Guide*, SN-2088, Cray Research Inc., Technical Publications, 1345 Northland Drive, Mendota Heights, Minnesota 55120

[7] BBN Advanced Computers Inc., *Inside the TC2000*, Cambridge, MA, 1989.

[8] H. J. Siegel, *Interconnection Networks for Large-Scale Parallel Processing*, 2nd edition, McGraw Hill, New York, 1990.

[9] BBN Advanced Computers Inc., *TC2000 Fortran Reference*, Cambridge, MA, 1989.

[10] Brent Gorda, Karen Warren, and Eugene D. Brooks III, *Programming in PCP*, UCRL-MA-107029, Lawrence Livermore National Laboratory, March, 1991.

[11] Karen Warren, Brent Gorda, and Eugene D. Brooks III, *Programming in PFP*, UCRL-MA-107028, Lawrence Livermore National Laboratory, March, 1991.

[12] D. Hensgen, R. Finkel, U. Manber, "Two Algorithms for Barrier Synchronization", *International Journal of Parallel Programming*, vol. 17(1), pp. 1-17, 1988.

Knowledge-Based Parallelization for Distributed Memory Systems*

Barbara M. Chapman
Heinz M. Herbeck
Department of Statistics and Computer Science
University of Vienna
Rathausstrasse 19/II/3
A-1010 Vienna AUSTRIA

Abstract

In current automatic parallelization systems for distributed-memory machines, the user must explicitly specify how the data domain of the sequential program is to be decomposed and distributed across the processors. In this paper, we outline the salient features of a new knowledge-based software tool that provides automatic support for data partitioning. The basic guidelines for the design of the tool are discussed, followed by a description of the adopted partitioning strategy.

Keywords: Automatic Parallelization, Data Partitioning, Knowledge-based Restructuring, Pattern Matching.

1 Introduction

While distributed-memory multiprocessing systems (DMS) are less expensive to build than shared-memory systems (SMS) and easily scalable to a large number of processors, the programming paradigm associated with SMS offers clear advantages by providing all processes with uniform access to a global shared memory. For a detailed discussion of this issue, see [ZiCh 90]. Various efforts have been made to bridge that gap by implementing a virtual shared memory on top of a DMS. This can be done either in hardware (as in the Myrias system, see [KVW 87]) or by appropriate software mechanisms. One important method for providing a virtual shared memory

---

*The work described in this paper is being carried out as part of the research project "Virtual Shared Memory for Multiprocessor Systems with Distributed Memory" funded by the Austrian Research Foundation (FWF) under the grant number P7576-TEC. The authors assume all responsibility for the contents.

for a DMS is automatic parallelization: in this approach, sequential programs (usually written in Fortran 77) are automatically transformed into explicitly parallel programs in a Fortran 77 superset, utilizing message-passing operations. During the last few years, the basic compilation techniques have been established, and a number of prototype systems were successfully implemented ([ZBG 88], [Gernd 89a], [CalKe 88], [GerZi 90],[RogPi 89]). In all these systems, parallelization is guided by data parallelism and based upon a user-provided specification of data partitioning. Data partitioning includes a decomposition of the sequential program's data domain into segments, and the mapping of these segments to the processors of the DMS. The task of the compiler then essentially consists of performing the complex clerical tasks implied by the specified data partition (in particular, inserting communication where necessary).

The specification of data partitioning is the crucial and most critical step in the parallelization process and requires detailed knowledge of the algorithm, the architecture, and the cost of communication in the transformed program. The penalty for a "wrong" decision may be quite high: excessive communication may be generated by the compiler, resulting in an inacceptable performance degradation of the target program. Thus a section of our paper is devoted to this topic.

In this paper, we describe a knowledge-based parallelizing tool that automatically determines an appropriate data partition whenever possible. This tool is currently being developed at the University of Vienna, based upon a second-generation version of the automatic parallelization system SUPERB ([ZBG 88]).

The paper is structured as follows: In Section 2, we outline the basic compilation model. The subsequent Section 3 describes the principal ideas underlying our system and the main features of the partitioning strategy. The paper closes with a discussion of related work.

2 Principles of Automatic Parallelization

In this section, we discuss the principles of automatic parallelization for DMS by outlining the salient characteristics of SUPERB, an automatic source-to-source parallelization system for distributed-memory systems. SUPERB is based upon a *Single-program-multiple-data (SPMD) model*, such that each process executes the same program, but is applied to different portions of the data domain.

The starting point is a Fortran 77 program Q, and a set of processes, P. Q is transformed into a parallelized program Q^* that is semantically equivalent to Q and exploits its inherent parallelism. Q^* is executed by the processes in P. The transformation process is controlled by a data partition which is specified by the user.

In the first step, the data domain of Q is partitioned by subdividing arrays into disjoint rectangular segments, and mapping the segments to processes. Standard partitioning schemes in SUPERB include (for two-dimensional arrays) *by row*, *by column*, and *by block*. A special case is the *trivial partition*, in which the array is subdivided into exactly one segment, the array itself. The set of all scalar variables is considered a trivially partitioned array.

Let A denote an array. A can be understood as a set of subscripted variables. Partitions can be formally described as total functions $\delta^A : P \to \mathcal{P}(\mathcal{A})$, which satisfy the condition $\delta^A(p) = \delta^A(p')$ for arbitrary processes p and p', whenever these two segments have at least one element in common. Trivially partitioned arrays are mapped to each individual process: the associated variables are called *replicated*.

The set of *local variables* of a process p then consists of all variables in the associated segments of non-trivially partitioned arrays, and all variables in trivially partitioned arrays. Each local variable of a process p is said to be *owned* by the process. Ownership implies two things: First, each variable v owned by a process p is allocated in the local address space of p; second, p is responsible for executing all assignments to v. In the course of evaluating the right-hand side of an assignment to a local variable, access to non-local variables may be required. The system automatically generates communication for these cases.

Q^* is an explicitly parallel program in a Fortran dialect containing explicit message passing operations SEND and RECEIVE. SUPERB does a large amount of work optimizing the target program, in particular combining individual communication statements (by vectorization and fusion) to reduce the effect of start-up delays [Gernd 89b, GerZi 90].

Data partitioning determines the process structure of the parallelized program. Parameters that influence the decision for a partition include, among other things, the size of the application, the ranges of do-loops, access patterns to arrays, and the structure of dependences among the statements of a loop.

3 The Design of a Knowledge-Based Tool for Automatic Data Partitioning

We begin this section by providing a very brief description of the elements of current parallelizers, and proceed by discussing why the current approach to designing parallelizing tools is not conducive to further automatization of the process of program restructuring. We identify reasons why a fundamentally different approach to their construction has to be taken, if we want such a tool to perform data partitioning in a modern parallel computing environment, and describe the main features of a knowledge-based tool to perform this task. Parallelizers need advanced analysis techniques: the analytic aspects of our approach and their overall role are explained in Section 3.4.

3.1 Major Components of Existing Parallelizing Tools

State-of-the-art parallelizing tools perform a detailed analysis of the program, including data and control flow analysis, dependence analysis, both in an inter- and intraprocedural sense. During program analysis, the program is converted into a standardized form to make the subsequent application of program transformations simpler and more efficient. The transformations provided for converting a program into another, equivalent form vary from one tool to another. Some are specific in their purpose (e.g. fusion of communication statements), whereas others (e.g. loop distribution, scalar forward substitution) may be useful under several different circumstances. Parallelizers must verify the existence of preconditions necessary for the valid application of transformations, as well as actually implementing them. A number of these transformations play a role in determining a good data partition, since they can convert parts of the program into a form which is better suited for exploiting locality (and are useful in pattern matching (cf. 3.3.3).

3.2 The Limitations of Current Parallelizers

3.2.1 The Knowledge Gap

A substantial amount of knowledge was required to build the current generation of parallelizing systems, and it has been incorporated into them. This knowledge is of several kinds. Most tools were constructed to handle the problem of parallelizing for a specific architecture or range of architectures, and knowledge about the relevant features of these machines was used to build the tool and decide what transformations to provide. Knowledge about the target system's software was also assumed to a varying degree, the restructured program was expected to conform to its major programming paradigm, which was thus implicitly known to the parallelizer, and a precise knowledge of the preconditions for valid program transformations was used to enable it to test for these and perform the appropriate transformation automatically when instructed to do so.

In contrast to the way in which parallelizers store the results of program analysis in data structures, providing an easily accessible base of information about the program, they do not explicitly store information about the target machine's hardware and software, or about programming methodology. Instead, this information is hardwired into the program, in a form which makes it inaccessible to the system and user alike.

3.2.2 There is No Guidance

Apart from certain pre-defined sequences of transformations for standardizing programs, current parallelizers require the user to specify which transformations are to be applied to the program and how and where to apply them. The Parafrase system developed at the University of Illinois, for example, requires the user to provide a so-called pass list, a fixed sequence of transformations which are applied to the program in precisely this order. The Superb system (University of Vienna) is a menu-based parallelizer that requires the user to interactively specify the transformations which are to be applied to the program. This approach provides a considerably larger degree of flexibility; however, it too requires almost complete manual control of the overall process.

But the crucial decisions involved are not of the kind that can be reached intuitively, even by an experienced programmer of parallel systems. Sometimes, details about the modalities of data transport may influence the performance effect of a transformation strategy, for example, and it is currently the user who is expected to know this. There are different, and sometimes conflicting, goals to be attained (e.g., load balancing vs. minimization of communication), and non-trivial trade-offs to be considered. The complexity of the restructuring problem and the number of details which must be managed mean that the average user will not be able to control the process effectively.

Existing parallelizing tools offer no form of guidance: not only do they not make the major decisions, they do not help the user to select certain regions of the program for transformation or further analysis, nor do they suggest a certain transformation or set of transformations for application. Further, they do not have facilities for evaluating the effect of transformations once they have been applied. As a result, restructuring for parallelization is currently a difficult process requiring expertise and an amount of trial and error in which it is hard to judge the outcome until the results are measured by simulation or at run-time.

3.2.3 There is No Advice

Parallelizers are programmed in such a way that they will recognize and transform certain kinds of statement forms and structures better than others. It is hard for them to deal adequately with unstructured programs, which may include large numbers of branches. So they may analyze and apply transformations to one program with relative ease, but perform poorly on a semantically equivalent program which makes extensive use of such programming practices.

Parallelizing tools are currently not able to advise the user about ways to improve the program to make it more amenable to automatic restructuring.

3.2.4 They are Hard to Modify

Parallel computing systems are in a constant state of development: not only are new architectures frequently introduced, existing machines are modified extensively to increase their overall performance, compilers are often updated, and better algorithms are being devised to solve larger problems more efficiently. Current parallelizers have not been designed with these kinds of change in mind: the implicit nature of the knowledge they embody makes them inflexible, and in general, any extension or modification required to adapt them to a changing computing environment will involve a major reprogramming effort. For the same reason, a system dedicated to one machine cannot be easily retargeted.

3.2.5 General limitations

There are other kinds of limitations inherent in the current generation of parallelizing tools: they know nothing about the problem that is to be restructured for parallel execution, so have no information about the functional specification realized by the program. The information that they gather about the program is of a low-level and local nature - but the task of parallelizing a program is also a global issue. They are not able to distinguish critical from relatively unimportant parts of the program, and thus cannot concentrate their efforts on the former.

To overcome these limitations, we base our design for a tool to partition data on two foundations: advanced program analysis and knowledge-based techniques, in particular the explicit representation and retrieval of knowledge, and pattern-matching facilities.

3.3 The Knowledge-Based Approach to Data Partitioning

In this section, we describe major design features of our data partitioning tool and identify those kinds of knowledge which need to be contained explicitly in an advanced program parallelization tool. Much of it is heuristic.

3.3.1 System Knowledge

Efficient parallel programming requires a significant amount of knowledge about the architecture of the machine being used and the actual configuration on which the program will run. Frequently, such programs are written for a specific number of processors, arranged in a specific topology, and make explicit use of any specialized processing units available.

If a parallelizer is to do the job of transforming a program adequately, it too will have to arrange for the efficient use of the available processors and their special features. Hence, it must have accurate information about the architecture of the machine, including details of its memory hierarchy and the time required for communicating data between different processors (latency, bandwidth, and the cost of routing between non-adjacent processors). If vector coprocessors are present, then it will be expected to produce vector code, for which information about the length of pipelines and the possibilities of chaining is required.

The tool must know about the different kinds of communication provided on the target machine, and have rules that tell it how and when to use them: The iPSC/2, for example, provides two kinds of message passing primitives for sending and receiving data. If the asynchronous send/receive primitives are used, it may be necessary for the receiving process to check that the message has arrived by calling msgwait(), and both participating processes must release message IDs explicitly. Special instructions, including broadcast facilities and block moves, are provided on some machines: the tool must be able to recognize code sequences where these can be used.

Architectural knowledge should be present in the form of facts: about the presence of certain features, the actual configuration, the performance for all kinds of communication and for computation operations. It is also present in the form of rules: in particular, about which code patterns to look for so that architectural features may be exploited.

Rules should also be present stating which language constructs to prefer, which order statements (or, within statements, operands) must be in for correct use of vector pipelines, where certain language constructs are required to use machine features, etc.

3.3.2 Problem Knowledge

A considerable number of researchers are currently engaged in analyzing a range of numerical problems and techniques, particularly those which are frequently used to model real-world problems, and are looking for the best ways to implement them on currently available parallel architectures. There is a growing body of knowledge about the performance of specific algorithms on certain machines, including new algorithmic formulations for standard problems designed to run on parallel machines.

This knowledge, which is generally formulated in terms of the problem size as well as the architecture, should be incorporated into the system in a form explicitly available to the user. If the tool can recognize that a particular program (or part of a program) implements an algorithm solving a specific problem, then we can use the information we have about how this problem is best coded to run on the target architecture to generate a suitably transformed program.

3.3.3 Program Knowledge and Pattern Matching

In order to be able to handle the task of transforming, the system must have a considerable amount of information about the source program. A good deal of this is gathered during the initial analysis phase. Furthermore, we require precise information about the data access patterns present in the program, and the relative frequency of their occurrence - this necessitates a simple kind of pattern matching. A more general pattern matching involving access patterns and statement patterns will be able to recognize code patterns within the program which are known to be implementations of certain standard problems, such as matrix-matrix multiplication, and for which the tool has precise implementation information.

For example, if we are able to detect the standard Jacobi form for two different arrays ARRAY1 and ARRAY2, then we have found an instance of the Jacobi relaxation:

```
DO I1 = 1, ITER
  DO I2 = 1, N
    DO I3 = 1, N
      ARRAY1(I3,I2) = CONST1 * (0.25* ( CONST2*CONST2*FUNC(I3,I2) +
        ARRAY2(I3-1,I2)+ ARRAY2(I3+1,I2) + ARRAY2(I3,I2-1) +
        ARRAY2(I3,I2+1)) + (1 - CONST1) * ARRAY2(I3,I2)
    ENDDO
  ENDDO
ENDDO
```

$\Longrightarrow$ JACOBI(ARRAY1,ARRAY2,N,ITER)
(pattern matching)

We then search our knowledge base for information on how to implement this code on the target architecture. Data partitioning information available will depend not only on the number of processors available, but also on the size of the values ITER and N.

A particular pattern can be described syntactically as a tree to which certain semantic predicates are attached, in much the same way that code patterns are handled for the purposes of code generation [ASU 86]. Program transformations can be used to convert some variants of a code pattern into an equivalent form which can be recognized by the pattern matching facility.

3.3.4 Strategic Knowledge

Strategic knowledge is, in this context, knowledge about how to go about transforming a program for a particular parallel machine. It specifies the goals to be reached, tells us in which order they are to be attempted and how to resolve conflicts if they arise. It is desirable to derive a general strategy for a reasonable proportion of numerical codes which goes beyond the task of partitioning data and creating process code. This is a subject for further research.

3.3.5 Interactivity

Our main devise for a parallelizer is that it must be as automatic as possible; it should also be as interactive as necessary.

The parallelizer may request certain kinds of information from the user which it cannot obtain statically (e.g. specifying the value of constants). It is also a source of knowledge for the user, who should be able to ask questions and obtain suitably displayed information about the program.

3.3.6 Modifiability

Since parallel computing systems are in a constant state of development and growth (cf. 3.2.4), it is an important criterion for the design of any parallelizing system that it be easily extended and adapted to meet changing demands. The use of explicit knowledge in the system will greatly facilitate this design goal.

3.4 Analytical Approach to Data Partitioning

It is the aim of the knowledge-based matching facility to recognize syntactic patterns in the code, and identify standard computations of numerical algorithms, such as matrix multiplication and matrix-vector operations. If we know what a sequence of statements does, we can derive all partitioning information from the knowledge base. Where this is not possible, distribution evaluation information is gathered in a bottom-up fashion and we employ low-level methods to calculate a partitioning scheme. The partitioning algorithm that performs this task concentrates on the program's loop nests. In the first step, we examine each statement inside a loop nest, to see whether arrays are referenced. Only statements containing array references are taken into account. For each such statement, we now determine a function taking a data partitioning scheme, the number of processors and the size of the arrays accessed in the statement as input parameters. This function calculates a measure of the communication penalty for the statement for each partitioning scheme taken into consideration. We restrict consideration to row-, column- and blockwise distributions, in both cyclic or contiguous form. If, for example, the appropriate partitioning scheme (incurring no communication) for a given statement were rowwise cyclic, the penalty function would have to yield the communication penalty for rowwise blocked, columnwise blocked / cyclic and blockwise distribution including replicating the array or assigning the entire array to a single processor. At this stage, the communication penalty may still be parameterized by the number of processors and domain size, i.e. the function result is a symbolic expression containing these parameters.

3.4.1 Pattern Matching

To determine a suitable partitioning scheme plus the corresponding functions for a single statement, we adopt a constraint-based approach similar to the one developed by Gupta and Banerjee (see [GupBan 90]). We will perform pattern matching on the index expressions occurring inside the statement and look up a suitable partitioning information in a knowledge base, from where we also retrieve the penalty function. This knowledge base contains a set of selected array index expressions which frequently occur in numerical programs. If the index expressions encountered in a statement can not be found in the knowledge base, we have to devise a partitioning scheme from scratch. This can be done by employing a stencil based approach as in [Hudak 90] or by using a matrix notation as proposed by Ramanujam and Sadayappan (see [RamSad 90]). We cannot, however, use these algorithms without modifications. It does not suffice to just calculate the appropriate partitioning for a statement, we also need the penalty function for the other - "wrong" - partitionings. These functions provide an integer result quantifying communication costs, as is the case in Hudak's algorithm which calculates communication weights for different partitionings for a given stencil and chooses the partitioning scheme with the lowest communication cost.

3.4.2 Alignment

Also at this - statement - level, we have to determine the alignment of dimensions of different arrays. The problem of alignment and its solution was described by Jingke Li and Marina Chen (see [LiChen 89]). Alignment and data partitioning strategy are different issues and therefore have to be treated separately. If, for example, we encounter the statement $A(i,j) = B(j,i)$ inside a loop nest with loop indices i and j, we can deduce a strong preference to align the first dimension of A with the second dimension of B and vice versa. On the other hand, this statement would give us no information at all about which partitioning scheme to choose for arrays A and B. Therefore, we have to determine a penalty function for the alignment of array dimensions too. Since the alignment problem has been proven to be NP-complete by Li and Chen, we either employ heuristic methods such as those they describe or resort to pattern matching methods associating an alignment function with specific array index expressions.

3.4.3 Finding a global solution

After we have determined a partitioning scheme as well as an alignment for each individual statement, together with the respective functions for quantifying communication, we now have to determine a suitable partitioning scheme and alignment for the entire loop nest. One step necessary to achieve this is to resolve the unknown parameters in the penalty functions, namely the number of processors (which may be solicited from the user or retrieved from a knowledge base characterizing the target machine) and the number of loop iterations, which, in most but not all cases, depends directly on the size of the arrays. We consider using a performance prediction tool which tries to determine the number of loop iterations, together with other information. By resolving the parameters in the communication penalty functions, all these functions now only take a partitioning strategy as argument and yield a (real or integer) number as result. (We assume that an appropriate machine and communication model exists, which gives the overhead associated with each communication primitive). Then the communication overhead for the entire loop nest can be found as the weighted sum of the individual penalty functions, for each single partitioning scheme taken into consideration. The weights mentioned have to be determined by the performance tool, which has to estimate the "importance", i.e. amount of runtime of each statement, basic block, loop nest and subroutine. Similarly, an alignment is computed for the loop nest, together with the penalty function.

From the technical point of view, the process of combining the solutions specific to individual statements is conducted using a tree obtained from the program flow graph. A node in this tree represents either a statement accessing an array or the beginning of a loop. Starting with the leaves and continuing upwards in the tree, partitioning information and an alignment are computed for each node. Whereever a node has more than one descendant, the solutions coming from either successor have to be combined, weighted according to some performance information, which assigns each branch a probability for being taken. A detailed discussion of this approach and the techniques employed is the topic of a forthcoming paper.

4 Related Work

Current research on automatic data partitioning by Ken Kennedy and Ulrich Kremer at Rice University, Houston, Texas has the goal of developing a tool based on the ParaScope system. They are constructing a tool for performance prediction to evaluate different partitioning schemes.

Jingke Li and Marina Chen at Yale University ([LiChen 89],[ChenChoLi 89], [LiChen 90]) have developed an alignment strategy for the functional language Crystal, based on an n-dimensional grid machine architecture.

For the Connection Machine, an SIMD computer, research on communication optimization by appropriate allocation of arrays was performed by Kathleen Knobe, Joan D. Lukas and Guy

L. Steele,jr. ([KnLuSt 90]).

In his Ph.D. thesis, Vasanth Balasundaram ([Balas 89]) presents a concept for analyzing and representing array accesses, the Data Access Descriptor (DAD). The DAD may be used to determine the way an array is accessed inside a nest of DO-loops and therefore find a good local partitioning scheme. By combining DADs, global information about how an array is accessed throughout the program can be derived.

David E. Hudak and Santosh G. Abraham at the University of Michigan ([Hudak 90]) have developed techniques for the automatic generation of partitions for sequentially iterated parallel loops based on the access patterns inside the loop.

Manish Gupta and Prithviraj Banerjee ([GupBan 90]) have developed the "constraint-based" approach, where pattern matching at statement level is used to derive a data decomposition and an alignment function, together with the goodness functions quantifying communication penalty.

J. Ramanujam and P. Sadayappan ([RamSad 90]) propose a matrix notation for computing a data partitioning scheme for DO-loops. Access patterns are represented in matrix form and the corresponding linear equation system is solved to yield the partitioning scheme.

Knowledge-based techniques have already been applied in several systems which restructure code for different machines. Vectorizers currently use pattern matching in a manner similar to our approach to recognize code sequences that can be vectorized, and even to detect common forms of data dependence. The expert adviser EAVE was developed to assist in the transformation of program for input to the IBM 3090 VF; it also looks for patterns within the code, and has rules telling it how code can be transformed to obtain an equivalent form that can be efficiently vectorized [Bose 88a, Bose 88b]. Wang and Gannon ([Wang85, WaGa89, Wang90]) are working on an expert system for the hierarchical parallelization of programs to run on different multi-processing architectures. PAT is a knowledge-based system being developed at the University of Illinois ([HarNi 90]), that matches syntactic patterns (with semantic predicates) to derive a program's underlying meaning.

References

[ASU 86] Alfred V. Aho, Ravi Sethi, Jeffrey D. Ullman: Compilers. Principles, Techniques and Tools
Addison-Wesley, 1986

[Bose 88a] Pradup Bose: Heuristic Rule-Based Program Transformations for Enhanced Vectorization
Proc. Int. Conf. on Parallel Processing, 1988

[Bose 88b] Pradup Bose: Interactive Program Improvement Via EAVE: An Expert Adviser for Vectorization
Proc. International Conference on Supercomputing, St. Malo, July 1988

[Balas 89] Vasanth Balasundaram: Interactive Parallelization of Numerical Scientific Programs
Rice COMP TR89-95, July 1989

[CalKe 88] D. Callahan and K. Kennedy: Compiling programs for distributed-memory multiprocessors
Journal of Supercomputing, 2(2), 151-69

[ChenChoLi 89] Marina Chen, Young-il Choo, and Jingke Li: Theory and Pragmatics of Compiling Efficient Parallel Code
  YALEU/DCS/TR-760 December 1989

[Fox 88] Fox, Johnson, Lyzenga, Otto, Salmon, Walker: Solving Problems On Concurrent Processors Vol. I
  1988 Prentice-Hall International, Inc.

[Gernd 89a] Gerndt,H.M.: Array Distribution in SUPERB
  Proc. ACM Int.Conf. on Supercomputing, Crete,164-174 (Jun 1989)

[Gernd 89b] H.M. Gerndt: Automatic Parallelization for Distributed-Memory Multiprocessing Systems
  Ph.D. Dissertation, University of Bonn, Technical Report Series ACPC/TR90-1, Austrian Center for Parallel Computation

[GerZi 90] Gerndt,H.M., Zima,H.: Optimizing Communication in SUPERB
  Technical Report Series ACPC/TR 90-3, Austrian Center for Parallel Computation (1990)

[GupBan 90] Manish Gupta, Prithviraj Banerjee: Automatic Data Partitioning on Distributed Memory Multiprocessors

[HarNi 90] Mehdi T. Harandi, Jim Q. Ning: Knowledge-Based Program Analysis
  IEEE Software, January 1990, 74-81

[Hudak 90] David E. Hudak and Santosh G. Abraham: Compiler Techniques for Data Partitioning of Sequentially Iterated Parallel Loops
  ACM Report 1990

[KnLuSt 90] Kathleen Knobe, Joan D. Lukas, Guy L. Steele: Data Optimization: Allocation of Arrays to Reduce Communication on SIMD Machines
  Journal of Parallel and Distributed Computing 8, 102-118 (1990)

[KVW 87] Kobos, VanKooten, Walker: The Myrias Computer System
  in Algorithms and Applications on Parallel and Vector Computers, 1987

[Lee 90] Fung F. Lee: Partitioning of Regular Computation on Multiprocessor Systems
  Journal of Parallel and Distributed Computing 9, 312-317 (1990)

[LiChen 89] Jingke Li, Marina Chen: Index Domain Alignment: Minimizing Cost of Cross-Referencing Between Distributed Arrays
  YALEU/DCS/TR-725 November 1989

[LiChen 90] Jingke Li and Marina Chen: Synthesis of Explicit Communication from Shared-Memory Program References
  YALEU/DCS/TR-755 May 1990

[RamSad 90] J.Ramanujam, P.Sadayappan: Compile-Time Techniques for Data Distribution in Distributed Memory Machines

[RogPi 89] Anne Rogers, Keshav Pingali: Process Decomposition Through Locality of Reference
SIGPLAN 1989

[Wang85] K. Wang: An Experiment in Parallel Programming Environment: The Expert Systems Approach
In: K.S. Fu (Ed.): Some Prototype Examples for Expert Systems, TR-EE-85-1, Electronic Engineering School, Purdue University, 1985, 591-624

[Wang90] K. Wang: A Framework for Intelligent Parallel Compilers
Tech. Report CSD-TR-1044, CER-90-52, Dept. Computer Science, Purdue University, November, 1990

[WaGa89] K. Wang and D. Gannon: Applying AI Techniques to Program Optimizations for Parallel Computers
In: K.Hwang and D. DeGroot (Eds.): Parallel Processing for Supercomputers and Artificial Intelligence, McGraw-Hill, 1989, 441-485

[ZBG 88] Zima H.P., Bast H.-J. and Gerndt H.M.: SUPERB - a tool for semi-automatic MIMD/SIMD parallelization.
Parallel Computing, 6, 1-18 (1988)

[ZiCh 90] Zima H.P., Chapman B.: Supercompilers for Parallel and Vector Computers
ACM Press Frontier Series, Addison-Wesley 1990

Parallelization for Multiprocessors with Memory Hierarchies *

Michael Gerndt   Hans Moritsch

University of Vienna
Institute for Statistics and Computer Science
Rathausstr. 19/II/3
A-1010 Vienna, Austria
EMAIL: A4424DAN@AWIUNI11.bitnet

Abstract:
Programming shared memory multiprocessors seems to be easier than developing programs for distributed memory systems. The reason is the existence of a global names space for parallel threads providing uniform access to all global data. This programming model seems to be inadequate for systems with a larger number of processors since memory hierarchies are integrated to eliminate the bottleneck of global memory access. Therefore programming these systems has to be done with respect to the distribution of data, thus to enforce the parallel processes exploiting locality of references. This paper describes an ongoing project in which we investigate the applicability of the distributed memory parallelization strategy for shared memory systems with memory hierarchies.

Keywords: shared memory multiprocessors, distributed memory multiprocessors, domain decomposition, program parallelization, program transformations

1 Introduction

In recent years a large number of parallel computers have become commercially available. These systems are of various architectures, including SIMD machines, e.g. DAP, Connection Machine, shared memory multiprocessors, e.g. Cray Y-MP, Alliant, Sequent, and distributed memory multiprocessors, e.g. transputer arrays, NCUBE, Intel iPSC, Suprenum.

Since the programming paradigm of SIMD machines, which is similar to that for vector computers, and the programming paradigm for shared memory systems (SMS) are

---
*The work described in this paper is being supported by IBM.

close to the standard sequential paradigm, these systems are more readily accepted by the users than the distributed memory systems (DMS). Furthermore, there are well-known techniques for parallelizing application programs for these types of systems [ZiCha 90].

The basic programming paradigm of DMS is significantly different from the sequential paradigm, since the user has to think in terms of processes exchanging messages. These systems become easier to use if a shared memory is emulated via the operating system [LiSch 89], the programming language, e.g. Linda [GelCar 86], or the compiler[ZBG 88, CaKen 88], but the loss of efficiency is an essential drawback of current implementations. In all these emulations it is very important to exploit data locality in the programs since communication is typically very slow, so that as few messages as possible should be exchanged between processes.

On the other hand, distributed memory systems, both SIMD and MIMD systems, have the advantage that they are in principle arbitrarily scalable. This is very important since a large number of applications, such as weather forecasting, need an almost unlimited amount of computer power, which only these systems will be able to deliver.

To overcome the bottleneck of limited memory bandwidth in SMS, these systems are often organized hierachically, e.g. an entire system is made up of a number of clusters, each of which contains a small number of processors. Corresponding to the hierarchy of processors there is a hierarchy of different memory levels. For example, processors may have their own local memory, they can access a global cluster memory and finally a memory global to all processors. Typically, access to *more local* memories is cheaper than access to *more global* memories. Examples for such systems are IBM RP3 [Pfist 85] and the CEDAR system [EHJP 90]. With this development on the hardware side, those systems become more scalable but lose the relative ease of programming and parallelization.

Efficient parallel programs for these systems have to take the distribution of data as well as the distribution of work into account. Data should be locally used in a single processor over long periods of the computation, so that data transfers between different levels of the memory hierarchy are minimized. Therefore, parallel loops which are the main source of parallelism on shared memory multiprocessors, have to be scheduled in such a way that data can be reused in a processor when executing another parallel loop.

This paper describes a project in which a parallelization tool for SMS with memory hierarchies is developed. The target system is the Advanced Computing Environment Machine (ACE) multiprocessor workstation from IBM [GarFF 89], which includes a two-level memory hierarchy consisting of processor-local memories and one system-wide global memory. The tool is designed for data parallel scientific applications and transforms Fortran 77 (F77) programs into programs written in PREFACE-1, a Fortran extension for shared memory parallel programming.

The parallelization strategy is based on domain decomposition (Sections 2 and 3) which makes it possible to exploit locality-of-reference in the computation during the parallel execution. A basic set of transformations for this strategy has been developed for DMS and are implemented in SUPERB [ZBG 88]. In addition to the existing techniques, new concepts and transformations have to be developed since SUPERB was designed for DMS only.

This paper is structured in the following way. Section 2 introduces the SPMD programming model for SMS and DMS. In Section 3 we outline the parallelization strategy for DMS. Section 4 presents the ACE workstation and the target programming language

PREFACE-1. In Section 5 we describe our concepts for effective parallelization of data parallel programs for the ACE. The Appendix contains a hand written example which illustrates the resulting code

2 The SPMD Programming Model for Parallel Scientific Applications

The widely accepted programming model for data parallel scientific applications on SMS as well as on DMS is the *Single-Program-Multiple-Data* (SPMD) model [DarNP 85, Karp 87]. A parallel program is executed by a number of processes which operate on different data. All processes are created once at the beginning of the parallel application.

In parallel codes for SMS, computational work that can be performed in parallel, e.g. loop iterations, are statically or dynamically distributed among the processes.

In the following, we describe the SPMD model for DMS. For DMS work distribution is determined according to a *Domain Decomposition* [Fox 88]. The data domain of the application is partitioned and distributed among the processes. Each process performs the computation on its own portion of data. In F77 programs the data domain is implemented via arrays. Thus, the SPMD model is extended for DMS by a *data distribution*.

The data distribution describes the mapping of the variables of the program to the processes. It determines individual distributions for some of the program's arrays. A *distribution* subdivides an array into disjoint rectangular segments which are assigned to individual processes. Elements of distributed arrays are called *distributed variables*. Scalar variables and elements of non-distributed arrays are assigned to each individual process. These variables are called *replicated variables*. In this way, the data distribution determines for each process a set of *local variables* which consists of (i) all distributed variables assigned to that process, and (ii) all replicated variables.

Each local variable of a process is said to be *owned* by that process. Ownership implies two things: First, each variable owned by a process is allocated in the local address space; second, the process is responsible for executing all assignments to that variable.

A process computing new values for its local variables may need values of local and non-local variables. Since a process cannot access non-local variables directly, their values have to be communicated. Communication is typically very expensive in DMS, so that it is crucial to minimize the number of messages exchanged.

3 Parallelization for DMS

The general idea for parallelizing scientific programs for DMS is to decompose the domain of the application and to assign the parts to individual processes. Each process then performs the computation only for its local part. In the SUPERB approach the data distribution is specified by the programmer. This strategy is also pursued by other groups working in the field of parallelization for DMS [CaKen 88, KoMeRo 88, PinRog 90, SCMB 90].

In the remainder of this section we outline the tranformation process implemented in SUPERB, a semi-automatic parallelization system for DMS transforming F77 programs into parallel programs written in the message passing fortran dialect of the target system. SUPERB provides special analysis services and transformations for automatic program

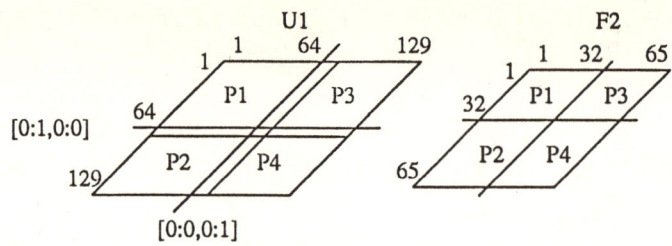

Figure 1: Distributions of U1 and F2 with Overlap Areas

restructuring guided by domain decomposition, including data partitioning, communication analysis, optimizing transformations and MIMD code generation. We illustrate the main transformations with the *restriction operation* of multigrid programs, which computes the right hand side (rhs) values of a partial differential equation on a coarser grid from the defect on the finer grid.

Let the rhs of the partial differential equation on the coarse grid be implemented via array F2(65,65) and the values of the solution on the fine grid via array U1(129,129). The code of the restriction operation is:

```
DO I=2,64
    DO J=2,64
        F2(I,J)= ...  - 4.0D0*U1(2*I,2*J)+U1(2*I-1,2*J)+U1(2*I,2*J-1)+
            U1(2*I+1,2*J)+U1(2*I,2*J+1)
    ENDDO
ENDDO
```

The parallelization is done in three steps:

1. Data Partitioning
2. Initial Adaptation
3. Optimization

In the following we explain these steps shortly in the context of our example.

Data Partitioning

The user specifies data distributions for some of the program's arrays interactively via commands. Each distribution characterizes the decomposition of an array into segments and the mapping of these segments to the processes. The arrays U1 and F2 of the program's data domain are distributed among 4 processes by the commands: *part U1(2,2)* and *part F2(2,2)*. The resulting distributions are shown in Figure 1.

Initial Adaptation

A process computes new values exclusively for local variables. This constraint is enforced in the system by determining an appropriate mask for each statement of the node program. The mask suppresses the execution of a statement in a process iff the written variables are non-local. If a process executes a statement, it may read local and non-local variables. For all references which may access a non-local variable a communication statement EXSR (EXchange Send Receive) is inserted which updates a copy of the variable if necessary.

```
DO I=2,64
    DO J=2,64
        EXSR (U1(2*I+1,2*J),[0:1,0:0])
        EXSR (U1(2*I,2*J+1),[0:0,0:1])
        owned(F2(I,J))→F2(I,J)= ...  - 4.0D0*U1(2*I,2*J)+U1(2*I-1,2*J)+
            U1(2*I,2*J-1)+U1(2*I+1,2*J)+U1(2*I,2*J+1)
    ENDDO
ENDDO
```

The communication statements are extended by an *Overlap Description*, e.g. [0:0,1:0]. This description determines for each process an *Overlap Area* which is a subset of the set of non-local variables. The resulting overlap areas of the example are shown in Figure 1. Only if the accessed variable belongs to the overlap area of a process, a copy is updated via communication. For example, if U1(2*I+1,2*J) in the first EXSR statement accesses U1(65,4) in iteration (i=32,j=2), P1 receives a new value for its copy of U1(65,4) since this variable belongs to its overlap area. In the same iteration P2 sends the value of U1(65,4) because the variable is local to P2 and in the overlap area of P1.

The overlap descriptions are computed from the mask of the statement and the accessing reference. The resulting overlap area of each process is a conservative estimation of the non-local variables which may be accessed in this process via the reference. The overlap analysis performed in SUPERB needs precise information about the distribution of the array in the mask and the array read.

Optimization

The initial masking and communication is usually not efficient. Thus the system tries to optimize the code. For example it may implement the masks by transforming the loop bounds. The communication is optimized by extracting communication from loops and thus combining messages.

```
EXSR (U1(*,*),[0:1,0:0])
EXSR (U1(*,*),[0:0,0:1])
DO I=max($L1,2),min($R1,64)
    DO J=max($L2,2),min($R2,64)
        F2(I,J)= ...  - 4.0D0*U1(2*I,2*J)+U1(2*I-1,2*J)+U1(2*I,2*J-1)+
            U1(2*I+1,2*J)+U1(2*I,2*J+1)
    ENDDO
ENDDO
```

The final code is parameterized according to the data distribution. The local segment of the executing process is F2($L1:$R1,$L2:$R2). The mask of the assignment is enforced in the loop bounds. Looking at process p1, for example, we see that it executes iterations 2 to 32 of the I- and J-loop. The EXSR statements describe all elements of the array as candidates for the updating. All of these variables which belong to the overlap area of a process are exchanged in a single large message. Combining messages is very important, since the start-up time for a message is typically high.

A more detailed description of these transformations can be found in [Gerndt 90].

4 ACE Multiprocessor Workstation

The ACE multiprocessor workstation consists of up to 8 processor nodes and up to 10 shared-memory modules. Each shared-memory module contains two interleaved banks of 4 MByte, so up to 80 MByte of shared memory are available. In addition, each processor node has 8 MByte of local memory.

Processor nodes, shared memory and high speed I/O devices are connected via a 32 Bit, 80 MByte/second inter-processor communication bus (IPC). Via the IPC-Bus a processor can access shared memory and another processor's local memory. A second Bus (IBM-AT Bus) connects the ACE with a host machine, an IBM RT-workstation. The RT-Host can access the local memory of the processor nodes to perform communication and I/O via the AT Bus.

The different physical memory types in the ACE-workstation establish a memory hierarchy, characterized by the different access times:

- local: 1 cycle
- shared: 4 cycles
- local memory of another processor: 8 cycles.

To gain faster access, data which is frequently used by a single processor can be placed in its local memory. The strategy of the operating system is to manage local memory as a cache of global memory, and the programmer's view is that of a shared memory model. Initially all data is held in shared memory. If a data object is referenced by a processor, the memory manager moves it to this processor local memory. If it will be used frequently by different processors, it will reside in shared memory.

The target language of our parallelization tool is PREFACE-1 which is an extension of Fortran77. PREFACE-1 implements the SPMD programming model. Work distribution among the processes is performed by splitting the code into different sections. There are three types of code sections:

- **Serial section**, which is executed by only one process and skipped by all others.
- **Parallel section**, which defines pieces of work (tasks), that are executed in parallel. Tasks can be iterations of a loop or arbitrary statement sequences. The processes cooperate in executing such a parallel section by asynchronously executing individual tasks. Processes can be synchronized at the end of a parallel section, i.e. none of the processes can continue execution until all tasks are executed.
- **Replicate section**, which is executed by each process.

Serial sections are enclosed within @SERBEG and @SEREND. A parallel section can be either a **parallel loop** or a **parallel segment**. Parallel loops are specified by @DO, @ENDO. Iterations of parallel loops can be assigned statically (*prescheduled*) or dynamically (*selfscheduled*) to the participating processes. The grain size of parallel tasks can be individual iterations or chunks of iterations. Furthermore, PREFACE-1 provides a mechanism to synchronize iterations of parallel loops.

Parallel segments are specified by @PARSEGM .. @SEGM .. @SEGM .. .. @END-PARSEGM. After the execution of a segment a process can be forced to wait until another segment has been executed. Parts of the program, which are neither serial nor parallel sections are implicitly defined as replicate sections.

Data can be **private** to a process or **shared**. Private data can be exclusively accessed by that process and is held in local memory. In PREFACE-1, *shared* data has to be explicitly declared as a FORTRAN common block, enclosed by the @SHARED and @ENDSHARED keywords, while *private* is the default. Each process has an own copy of private variables.

Synchronization of processes can be performed by barriers, critical sections and wait instructions. If a process encounters @BARRIER, it waits for all other processes to reach this point. Critical sections which are executed by at most one process at a time, can be specified with @LOCK and @ENDLOCK. In addition processes can be forced to wait for conditions or the termination of a previously defined serial or parallel section.

When starting a parallel program, the user can specify the number of processors executing it. This number is accessible in the program via the variable @NUMPROCS, whereas the variable @MYPROC keeps the identifier of the executing process. Detailed information about PREFACE-1 can be found in [BerSo 88].

5 Parallelization Strategy

The goal of this project is to translate FORTRAN 77 programs into efficient parallel code for the ACE workstation. Instead of parallelizing sequential code by transforming individual sequential loops into parallel loops as it is done in many existing shared memory parallelizers, we exploit coarse-grain parallelism by determining parallel processes executing large tasks[Carmo 89].

We generate code in PREFACE-1 according to the SPMD model. Data and work of the sequential program is statically assigned to individual processes so that at runtime the processes work mainly on their local data and thus access to shared memory is reduced.

This parallelization approach will be implemented with the techniques developed for DMS. In addition new transformations have to be defined and will be added. These new transformations combine both parallelization approaches, i.e. for DMS and SMS, so that the existence of a global shared memory can be exploited. They are applied in cases where reference patterns cannot be analyzed statically by the proposed tool, resulting in large overlap areas, or where non-local operations are executed.

5.1 Data Distribution

Our approach is guided by a user-specified *data distribution*. This data distribution determines the ownership of variables according to the SPMD Model for DMS. The ownership relation is fixed for the entire execution. In addition to the resulting sets of distributed and replicated variables, there is the set of *shared variables* at run-time. An *allocation attribute* determines for each variable to which set it belongs. A variable can move from the original set, either replicated or distributed, to the set of shared variables and return to its original set (Figure 2). For example, an array is usually distributed, if parallel computations are performed and shared, if it is output by a single process.

The change of the allocation attribute can be performed dynamically. For each reference in the source code it has to be known at compile time whether the variable at the time the reference is executed is distributed, replicated or shared. This knowledge is needed since different code has to be generated.

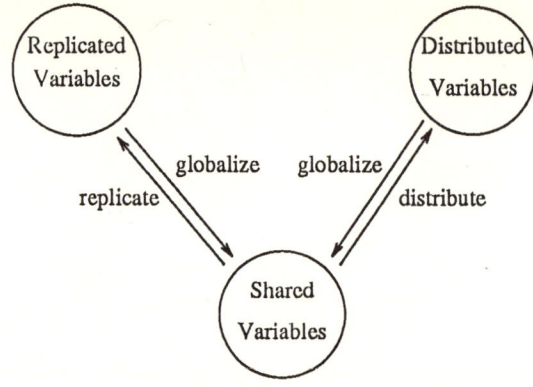

Figure 2: Variable Allocation

The change of the allocation attribute of a variable v is performed with the following operations:

- **globalize(v)**: Move from replicated or distributed to shared.
- **distribute(v)**: Move from shared to distributed.
- **replicate(v)**: Move from shared to replicated.

Globalize can only be applied to replicated or distributed variables. *Distribute* can only be applied to shared variables which are initially distributed. A variable is always distributed according to its initially specified distribution. *Replicate* can only be applied to shared variables which are initially replicated.

All three operations are synchronous, i.e. a barrier synchronization is executed at their start and the end. In the context of the project described here, the *distribute* and *replicate* operations could be combined in a single *localize* operation since the target set is determined by the user-specified data distribution. Our model is more flexible since in the future we plan to include the distribution of initially replicated variables and the redistribution of arrays according to a distribution different from that specified.

In this project, we develop a set of rules which implement a strategy for variable allocation. In addition, we intend to implement an interactive interface, which makes it possible for the user to influence the allocation attribute of variables.

Variables are allocated in the local memory of each process which owns that variable. If a process needs a variable that is neither owned by that process nor shared, a copy of that variable is allocated in the local adress space. In addition, there is a copy of a variable in the global memory iff this variable may belong to the set of shared variables at some time during the execution.

5.2 Work Distribution

Work distribution is guided in our approach by the data distribution according to the rule *"Compute iff local"*. This strategy is applied if the written variable is distributed or replicated. If it is shared, more flexible scheduling strategies can be applied.

Basically two alternatives exist in this case:

- **"Compute iff local"**: If this strategy is applied, it must be ensured that a value is computed for the shared variable by exactly one process. If a variable is owned by more than one process (this is true for initially replicated variables), a single process that owns that variable has to be selected to perform the computation.
- **standard loop-scheduling strategies**: Here we have to distinguish between two different scheduling strategies:
  - **compile-time scheduling**: If a static scheduling strategy is applied, the execution of an iteration is assigned at compile time to a specific process. In this situation the tool may be able to analyze which distributed variables are needed during the execution and to generate code to update private copies of these variables in the executing process.
  - **run-time scheduling**: A dynamic schedule can be implemented via parallel loops. If this scheduling strategy is applied, the compiler is not able to analyze access to non-local variables and thus all involved variables have to be shared too.

5.3 Generating Code for the ACE

In principle the generated code will be a replicate section. The assignment of work to different processes is done via masks as described in section 3. Parallel loops over distributed arrays - the most important source of parallelism - are implemented via parameterized sequential loops. Since these loops are included in a replicate section, they are executed in all processes. The parameters of these loops are the upper and lower bound, which depend on the distributions of the written variables. Thus, the iteration space of the original loop is usually statically spread among the processes and executed in parallel.

In a few exceptions, the code is not a replicate section.

- **serial section**: Code is contained in a serial section if it includes I/O, or dependences will cause an extensive synchronization overhead.
- **parallel sections**: These are used if run-time loop-scheduling policies should be applied in the case of write accesses to shared variables.

Variables are allocated as private variables of the processes and, if they are used as shared variables, additionally in the global memory. If variables are distributed, the necessary updating prior to non-local accesses is performed according to the *overlap concept*. Thus we allocate storage in the following way:

- **distributed variables**: Storage for the maximal segment assigned to a process and the variables in the maximal overlap area is allocated in the code as a single private variable.
- **replicated variables**: They are simply declared as private variables.
- **shared variables**: The entire variable is declared in the shared common block.

The example given in Appendix A outlines the resulting code which will be generated by the described tool. It illustrates storage allocation, work distribution among parallel threads and the implementation of overlap communication in a shared memory environment.

5.4 Conclusions and State of the Project

This paper outlines a parallelization technique for SMS with memory hierarchies which enforces local computation in parallel threads via special program transformations. The basic transformations have been originally developed for DMS where non-local data accesses of processes are very expensive. In SMS with memory hierarchies access to non-local data is also more expensive as access to local data. Thus parallelized code will benefit from the same techniques. In contrast to the distributed memory case parts of the code which are not well suited for our parallelization technique, e.g. where the parallelization tool is not able to detect the access pattern for distributed variables, can be handled by standard shared memory parallelization techniques. In these cases the hardware-supported shared memory provides more efficient access to non-local data than communication of those variables via messages. In addition, no copies of non-local variables are needed thus reducing the overall memory overhead.

In a first implementation phase we will develop strategies for dynamically changing the allocation strategy for distributed arrays in the context of individual loops and implement the code generation for the ACE. This prototype implementation will then be used as a testbed to investigate the relationship of shared memory and distributed memory parallelization in more detail especially in the context of virtual shared memory systems.

References

[BerSo 88] D. Bernstein, K.So, *Preface: A Fortran Preprocessor for Parallel Workstation Systems*, Research Report RC13600, IBM T.J.Watson Research Center, Yorktown Heights, March 1988

[CaKen 88] David Callahan, Ken Kennedy, *Compiling Progams for Distributed-Memory Multiprocessors*, J.Supercomputing, 2(2), 151-169,(Oct.1988)

[Carmo 89] Edward A. Carmona, *Parallelizing a Large Scientific Code - Methods, Issues, and Concerns*, ACM Proceedings Supercomputing 89, Reno, Nevada 89,21-31

[DarNP 85] F.Darema-Rogers, V.A. Norton, G.F. Pfister, *Using a Single-Program-Multiple-Data Computational Model for parallel Execution of Scientific Applications*, Research Report IBM Watson Research Center Yorktown Heights

[EHJP 90] R.Eigenmann, J.Hoeflinger, G.Jaxon, D.Padua, *Cedar Fortran and Its Compiler*, Proceedings of the CONPAR90, Zürich 1990, LNCS 457, pp.288-299

[Fox 88] Geoffrey C. Fox et al., *Solving Problems on Concurrent Processors*, Prentice Hall,Englewood Cliffs, 1988

[GarFF 89] A.Garcia, D.J.Foster, R.F.Freitas, *The Adavanced Computing Environment Multiprocessor Workstation*, Research Report RC 14491 IBM T.J.Watson Research Center, Yorktown Heights (Mar 1989)

[GelCar 86] D.Gelernter, N.Carriero, *Linda on hypercube multicomputers*, In: Proceedings of the 1985 SIAM Conference, Society for Industrial and Applied Mathematics, Philadelphia, 1986, 45-55

[Gerndt 90] H.M. Gerndt, *Updating Distributed Variables in Local Computations*, Concurrency: Practice and Experience, Vol.2(3), pp.171-193 (September 1990)

[Karp 87] Alan H. Karp, *Programming for Parallelism*, Computer 20(5): pp.43-57, May 1987

[KoMeRo 88] C.Koelbel, P.Mehrotra, J.Van Rosendale, *Semi-Automatic Process Partitioning for Parallel Computation*, International Journal of Parallel Programming, Vol.16, No.5,1987, 365-382
[LiSch 89]   Kai Li, Richard Schaefer, *A Hypercube Shared Virtual Memory System*, ICPP 1989, Vol I, pp. 125-132
[Pfist 85]   G.F. Pfister, *The IBM Research Parallel Processor Prototype (RP3): Inroduction and Architecture*, IEEE Proceedings COMPAR 85, pp.764-771
[PinRog 90] Keshav Pingali, Anne Rogers, *Compiler Parallelization of SIMPLE for a Distributed Memory Machine*, Technical Report, Department of Computer Science, Cornell University, No. TR90-1084
[SCMB 90]   Joel Saltz, Kathleen Crowley, Ravi Mirchandaney, Harry Berryman, *Run-Time Scheduling and Execution of Loops on Message Passing Machines*, Journal of Parallel and Distributed Computing 8, 303-312 (1990)
[ZBG 88]   H.P.Zima, H.-J. Bast, H.M.Gerndt, *SUPERB: A tool for semi-automatic MIMD/SIMD parallelization*, Parallel Computing 6, 1988, 1-18
[ZiCha 90]   H.P.Zima, B. Chapman, *Supercompilers for Parallel and Vector Computers*, Addison-Wesley, New York, 1990

Appendix A

This code is the SPMD Version of a sequential code, where the outer do-loops are transformed to parallel do-loops and I/O is included in a serial section. The arrays u and u1 have to be shared since their values have to be exchanged (u) or the array is written (u1).

```
        program relax
        parameter (N=80)

        @SHARED/sh1/u,u1
        real u(N,N), u1(N,N)              /* shared arrays          */
        @ENDSHARED

        integer i,j,k,l                   /* private variables      */

                                          /* initialization:        */
        @do i=1,N                         /* parallel loop with run-time */
          do 10 j=1,N                     /* scheduling             */
            u(i,j)=1000*i+j
10        continue
        @enddo
                                          /* computation:           */
        @do i=2,N-1
          do 20 j=2,N-1
            u1(i,j)= u(i,j)+u(i-1,j)
20        continue
        @enddo
```

```
        @SERBEG                                    /* serial section ensuring that */
        write(*,*) ((u1(k,l),l=1,N),k=11,12)       /* U1 is written by one process */
        @SEREND
        end
```

Both arrays, u and u1, are distributed among 8 processes. The computations are done locally on the copies of the local segment. The initialized values of the right boundary have to be communicated to the right neighbour prior to the computation in loop 20. This is performed via the updating operation. Copies of the overlap areas are contained in the global memory. In the updating operation these copies are written by the owning process and read by the neighbouring process. Barrier synchronization is used to guarantee that the correct values are communicated.

```
        program relax
        parameter (N=80,PROCS=8)

        @SHARED/sh1/u,u1                           /* overlap areas of U and copy */
        real u(PROCS,N), u1(N,N)                   /*    of U1 in shared memory   */
        @ENDSHARED

        integer i,j,k,l
        real lu1(N/PROCS,N)                        /* local segment of U1         */
        real lu((N/PROCS)+1,N)                     /* local segment plus overlap  */
                                                   /*    of U                     */
        integer SB(1,2),OB(1,2)                    /* local segment bounds        */

        call strt (SB,OB)                          /* compute local segment bounds */

        do 10 i=sb(1,1),sb(1,2)                    /* loop over local part        */
          do 11 j=1,N
            lu(i-ob(1,1)+1,j)=1000*i+j
11        continue
10      continue

        call update(lu,u,ob(1,1),sb(1,1),sb(1,2))  /* update local copies of non- */
                                                   /*    local variables (overlap) */
        do  20 i=max(SB(1,1),2),min(SB(1,2),N-1)
          do 21 j=2,N-1
            lu1(i-SB(1,1)+1,j)= lu(i-ob(1,1)+1,j)+lu(i-ob(1,1),j)
21        continue
20      continue

        call globalize(lu1,u1, SB(1,1),SB(1,2))    /* transfer local data to global*/
                                                   /*    memory                    */
        @SERBEG
        write(*,*) ((u1(k,l),l=1,N),k=11,12)
        @SEREND
        end
```

```
      subroutine strt(sb,ob)
      integer sb(1,2),ob(1,2)
      parameter(N=80,PROCS=8)

      sb(1,1)=(N/PROCS)*(@mynum-1)+1        /* compute local segment bounds  */
      sb(1,2)=(N/PROCS)*(@mynum)
      if (@mynum.gt.1) then
           ob(1,1)=sb(1,1)-1                /* compute bounds of overlap     */
      else                                  /*    area                       */
           ob(1,1)=sb(1,1)
      endif
      ob(1,2)=sb(1,2)
      end

      subroutine globalize(lu1,u1, lb,rb)
      parameter (N=80,PROCS=8)
      real u1(N,N)
      real lu1(N/PROCS,N)
      integer lb,rb

      do 10 i=lb,rb                         /* copy local data in LU1 to     */
         do 11 j=1,N                        /*   the shared array U1         */
            u1(i,j)=lu1(i-lb+1,j)
11       continue
10    continue
      @BARRIER
      end

      subroutine update(lu,u, lob,lb,ub)
      parameter (N=80,PROCS=8)
      real u(PROCS,N)
      real lu((N/PROCS)+1,N)
      integer lob,lb,ub

      @BARRIER
      if (@mynum.lt.PROCS) then             /* copy local data in last row   */
         do 10 j=1,N                        /*   to a copy in shared memory  */
            u(@mynum,j)=lu((ub-lob)+1,j)
10       continue
      endif
      @BARRIER
      if (@mynum.gt.1) then                 /* fetch values of non-local     */
         do 20 j=1,N                        /*   variables                   */
            lu(1,j)=u(@mynum-1,j)
20       continue
      endif
      end
```

TraceView: A Trace Visualization Tool*

Allen D. Malony[†]
Department of Computer and Information Science
University of Oregon, Eugene, Oregon 97403

David H. Hammerslag and David J. Jablonowski[‡]
Center for Supercomputing Research and Development
University of Illinois, Urbana, Illinois 61801

Although incorporating significant performance detail, the generation of large trace files poses problems for performance interpretation. The potential need to compare multiple traces, possibly produced by different means (e.g., measured execution or simulation), exacerbates the difficulties in building general trace analysis and display solutions. This paper describes a trace visualization tool, TraceView, that provides a convenient, general purpose environment for trace manipulation and display. TraceView manages trace visualization sessions that the user constructs, handling functions such as trace file I/O, view specification, and display selection. TraceView can be applied in several trace contexts. Examples are given using traces generated from measured application execution on a Cray X-MP and simulated application execution to determine maximum parallelism. The TraceView tool can be extended, particularly in the addition of new display methods.

1 Introduction

In order to measure the performance of a computer system, certain aspects of its behavior must be made observable. A computer system's operation can be regarded as a sequence of actions representing some significant physical or logical activity performed. In general, actions represent the computational parts of a program one wishes to analyze. The ability to observe time-dependent performance behavior requires some form of tracing

---

*An extended version of this paper will appear in IEEE Software, September, 1991.
[†]Supported in part by the National Science Foundation under Grants No. NSF MIP-88-07775 and No. NSF ASC 84-04556, and the NASA Ames Research Center Grant No. NCC-2-559. Work done while at Center for Supercomputing Research and Development, University of Illinois Urbana, Illinois 61801
[‡]Supported in part by the U. S. Air Force Office of Scientific Research under grant No. AFSOR 90-0044 and by the U.S. Department of Energy under grant No. DE-FG02-85ER25001.

measurement that captures actions during program execution. Unfortunately, tracing can quickly generate vast amounts of performance data, making analysis and interpretation difficult. The manual effort required to manipulate large trace files, including creating graphical presentations of the trace data, can be daunting, requiring some automatic support for trace analysis and visualization.

In many cases, a performance analyst can identify certain performance behaviors by just viewing a historical sequence of captured events (both system and application events) and their associated data. Whereas an analysis of the traced performance data could provide more in-depth statistical profiles of the execution, the visualization of event traces can lead to an intuitive understanding of the computation. This position is supported by recent work in integrated performance environments [8, 9, 10].

However, one problem associated with viewing performance behavior from event traces has been the availability of a generic, reusable visualization platform. Whereas several systems supporting performance visualization have been developed [3, 5, 6], most accept trace input of a specific type representing a particular execution paradigm within a certain system context; e.g, systems using message passing communication [3]. Additionally, the visual displays can be restrictive in their ability to show the time-dependent behavior of arbitrary data values that might be associated with different events [6]. Although trace-based performance tools have traditionally been developed around the semantic interpretation of a set of known events and, therefore, are limited in their general purpose application, there are common aspects of trace processing and display that could conceivably be incorporated into a reusable trace visualization system. However, the gains in the reusability of a general purpose trace visualization tool will be at the expense of specificity in trace data analysis precisely because of a necessarily simplified event interpretation model. The importance of this trade-off will depend on the trace visualization application.

In this paper, we discuss the design, development, and application of a general purpose trace visualization tool, *TraceView*. The fundamental goals of our work on *TraceView* are to understand those aspects of trace visualization that can be incorporated into a reusable tool and to evaluate the tradeoff in general purpose design versus semantically-based, detailed trace data analysis in the context of an existing tool as applied to real trace visualization applications. In §2, we describe the architecture on which *TraceView* is based and present the functional details of *TraceView*. A description of the *Gantt* display supplied in the initial *TraceView* prototype is described in §3. In §4, we show the effectiveness of *TraceView* for visualizing traces from application execution on a Cray X-MP and traces of maximum parallelism in a simulated application execution.

2 Architecture and Function of *TraceView*

An architecture to accommodate the requirements of a general purpose, trace visualization tool must be flexible enough to allow user selection of analysis and display alternatives, yet provide a rigid enough structure so that extensions to the base analysis and display methods can build on the existing conventions and resources of the tool. A trace visualization tool adopting such an architectural approach will not support all trace visualization models. At best, one would hope that the tool serves the purpose for a majority of trace visualization needs, particularly those simple visualization problems that occur most frequently, and that the mechanisms for extensibility will provide an easy customization path for more complex cases.

The *TraceView* architecture is based on the concept of a *trace visualization session*. Figure 1 shows the hierarchical, tree-structured nature of a *TraceView* session. A session consists of trace files, views, and displays. The topmost level of a session specifies a set of trace files to visualize. For each file, a set of *views* can be defined. A view defines a subregion of the trace by specifying a beginning location, an ending location, and event filtering. For each view, a set of *displays* can be created. Although the session paradigm precludes displays that combine data from multiple traces, it does support the notion of multiple displays being viewed simultaneously. Functionally, the *TraceView* architecture is composed of four components: the Session Manager, the Trace Manager, the View Manager, and the Display Manager.

2.1 Session Management

Session management provides support for the *TraceView* session model. It supports session configuration saving and restoring and coordinates trace, view, and display management. The current session configuration can be saved to external storage for later retrieval. The benefit of saving a session configuration is that one can return to the same visualization session environment when the configuration is restored. *TraceView* visualization sessions may be quite complex, with many trace files opened and many views defined on each trace. Restoring a saved session minimizes the work needed to recreate the visualization environment between sessions.

Session management is implemented by the Session Manager. At any point while *TraceView* is in use, the current session configuration is defined as the set of open trace files and set of defined views for each trace. However, the currently created displays on each view are not regarded of as part of the persistent session configuration but are transient, defined only for the particular *TraceView* invocation. Only enough information is saved in the file to reconstruct session state exclusive of the displays. For each open trace, the Session Manager saves the name of the file containing the trace data, the number of defined views, and the information necessary to reconstruct each view. The Session Manager assumes that a session configuration file is consistent with the data in the designated traces.

To the user, a session appears as shown in Figure 2. The open files are shown in the **FILES** sub-window, the defined views for the selected file in the **VIEWS** sub-window, and the created displays for the selected view in the **DISPLAYS** sub-window. When a trace file is selected from the open files list, *TraceView* automatically updates the views list to show the corresponding defined views. Similarly, selecting a view causes an automatic update of the displays list to show the view displays that have been created. This interaction provides the mechanism for positioning within the session tree. Files, views, and displays can be added or deleted at any time.

2.2 Trace Management

Before we discuss trace management it is useful to have a basic understanding of the trace file format. *TraceView* processes *event* traces. An event is a recorded instance of some logical action. We intentionally give only general descriptions of events because *TraceView* makes no semantic interpretation of the actions the events represent. Each event is assumed to be timestamped merely to establish an ordering relation (in most cases, a time ordering) among the events.

The trace file is divided into two parts: an ASCII header and binary trace data. The header describes several properties of the data, which are a time-sequenced list of trace events. Each event reflects the instance of some action taking place during the computation. This action is interpreted as a state transition by *TraceView*. Each event recorded in the trace includes encodings of the state being exited and the state being entered, an event type, and a timestamp. Each event may also include supplemental data fields. Events within a file are homogeneous in their format; that is, each one has the same number of data fields associated with it.[1] Each data field typically represents some numeric event metric.

The function of trace management is to support:

- opening trace files;
- interpreting the trace file header;
- calculating global trace statistics;
- reading events from open trace files; and
- closing trace files (and freeing any storage allocated when the trace was opened).

This functionality is implemented by the Trace Manager. In addition to supporting the various operations on traces, the Trace Manager also provides a graphical user interface.

---

[1] We are currently removing this restriction and will be allowing variable sized data fields dependent on the state.

The user selects traces to be opened through a standard dialog. The list of open files is presented to the user in the left-most subwindow of the main *Trace View* window as shown in Figure 2. Trace summary information is presented to the user in a separate window.

2.3 View Management

Recall that, in the *Trace View* session model, multiple views can be defined on each trace. View management must support the definition of these views and the creation of virtual traces. A view of a trace defines a virtual trace. A view consists of:

1. a starting time for the virtual trace,
2. an ending time for the virtual trace, and
3. a list of names of events to be excluded from the virtual trace.

The view management system must allow the user to define views on the trace and edit the definition of existing views.

The View Manager's second function is to apply a view definition to a trace to produce the virtual trace. A *virtual trace* is a derivative of an actual trace, produced by first discarding any events that occur before the view starting time or after the view ending time. The remaining events are filtered to remove the events specified for exclusion in the view definition. The goal of event filtering is to construct the virtual trace to simulate an execution where filtered events are not recorded. Removing the events that occur before the start or after the end of the view is trivial. Filtering out individual unwanted events is a bit more complicated. An event is removed from the trace if the *to* or the *from* designator matches an event name specified for exclusion.

2.4 Display Management

The final component of *Trace View* is the display management. At the lowest level of the session model (Figure 1) we have multiple displays defined for each view. The function of display management is to present the virtual trace constructed by the View Manager to the user in a graphical manner. Display management allows the user to select from among available display methods and creates a display window showing the data. It also supports the removal of defined displays.

Display management is implemented by the Display Manager. The Display Manager controls the right-most subwindow in Figure 2. The user is presented with a list of existing displays for the selected view. Closed displays can be reopened, existing displays destroyed, and new displays created. The Display Type option menu allows the user to select the type of display to be used. Presently only two types of displays are available: Gantt displays and Rate displays. Both of these use the Gantt Chart Widget which is the topic of the next section.

3 Display Methods

Although the *TraceView* architecture allows for multiple trace display methods, currently only displays using Gantt charts have been implemented. Gantt charts are line plot representations of time-sequenced performance data. *TraceView* uses a Gantt chart widget developed expressly for displaying trace data. The Gantt widget can be used in several different ways. In *TraceView*, Gantt charts are bundled together in a *display shell* which synchronizes a number of Gantt charts in a common display window. The display shell also provides the user interface to control the behavior and appearance of the individual Gantt charts.

3.1 The Gantt Chart Widget

The Gantt chart widget provides horizontal and vertical axes, axes labels, data display, density bars, and data averaging. Often, the number of points to be displayed in a Gantt chart greatly exceeds the pixel width of the x-axis of the Gantt. Based on our experiences, it is not uncommon for the ratio of data points to pixels to exceed 10:1. The Gantt chart widget offers two solutions to this "data density" problem: density bars and average curves; e.g., see Figure 3.

The display of a *density bar* on a chart is optional. If present, it is a band of color displayed above the Gantt's data display area. A density bar can represent either *value density* or *point density*. For the former case, the density bar color at pixel x represents the average of all the data points displayed at pixel x on the x-axis. In a point density bar the color at pixel x represents the number of data points represented at pixel x on the x-axis.

In addition to a density bar and the graphical data display, the Gantt chart widget also provides an *average curve*. To compute the average curve, the x-axis is divided into some number of intervals. For each interval an average value is computed, and these average values are connected to form the average curve which overlays the Gantt chart's data display. The average data point for location x along the x-axis is calculated using all the data points from the interval along the x-axis. If a point on the x-axis has no actual data points associated with it, it is assumed to have the same y-value of the most recent point preceding it on the x-axis.

3.2 The Display Shell

The display shell groups related Gantt charts together and provides a convenient user interface for interacting with the Gantt chart widgets. All the Gantt charts in a given display shell are derived from the same virtual trace, and the x-axis for all the charts is identical. Because of this, Gantt charts in a display are stacked horizontally and aligned such that a vertical line across the display shell will intersect all its charts at precisely the same point on the x-axis. The display shell also allows the user to manipulate all the Gantt charts together by adjusting the averaging interval and by zooming in on a region of the charts. To zoom in on a portion of the charts (recall that all charts displayed within one display shell have the same x-axis and distribution of points) the pointing device is first used to select a region of the chart. The user can then zoom in on that region in all the charts. Zooming can be undone stepwise or all at once.

3.3 Using Gantt Charts and the Display Shell in *TraceView*

In *TraceView*, we use the Gantt chart widget in conjunction with the display shell to present two different kinds of displays to the user: displays based on state transitions, and displays of the number of times a state is entered. We refer to the former simply as "Gantt displays" and the latter as "Rates displays." For the Gantt displays, the x-axis of the chart represents time. The Display Manager allows a Gantt chart for each state and each data field to be displayed in the same display shell. For these, the y-axis represents the state or data field values. Recall that because data are recorded only at state transitions, all the charts will have the same x-axis and the same distribution of data points. In the Rates display the user views metric data associated with a particular trace state. For the selected state the user can elect to have a chart for each of the data fields defined for the trace. In the Rates display, the x-axis represents ordinal instances of the state being entered. The y-axis represents the individual data field values.

4 *TraceView* Applications

The objective of a general purpose trace visualization tool is to be effective across a variety of applications. Using the standard features of the tool, traces from real or simulated systems should be equally convenient to process and visualize, and, by doing so, offer the potential for insight into important performance phenomena difficult to observe otherwise. The tool should allow input of trace data that coming from different performance levels (e.g., hardware, system software, application software) with different data appearing together in the trace. Finally, a trace visualization environment must allow multiple traces to be simultaneously visualized and compared.

To validate *TraceView* in respect to these practical objectives, we used *TraceView* to visualize traces encountered in our performance evaluation activities at the Center for Supercomputing Research and Development at the University of Illinois at Urbana-Champaign. One project requires *TraceView* to visualize program event transitions and associated hardware performance information from applications programs running on Cray supercomputers. Another project involves the determination via simulation of maximum parallelism within application executions. Here *TraceView* is used to show time-dependent levels of parallelism and corresponding system performance metrics. These two projects are described in more detail below. Other projects not discussed include the visualization of register and functional unit usage in traces from an instruction-level simulation of a single Cray X-MP processor.

4.1 Viewing Cray Applications Traces

Detailed data about the performance behavior of an application's execution on a machine can only be captured by tracing important application events and sampling relevant machine performance metrics. A tracing system has been developed for the Cray supercomputers [7] that can measure user program event transitions as well as store information about machine performance using the Cray hardware performance monitor (HPM) [4].[2] However, tracing application execution can quickly generate large amounts of trace data, and analyzing and presenting these data manually can be arduous. We have applied *TraceView* to the analysis and display of Cray application traces. The following describes a sample *TraceView* session where the trace from a vector execution of the Perfect benchmark [1] code, FLO52 (a multigrid fluid dynamics computation), is being viewed.

The session display in Figure 2 shows a snapshot of the session configuration used for the FLO52 traces. There are four open trace files from different vector executions of the FLO52 program. The file **ftrace** contains an events-only trace, while the other traces include HPM values with each event in the trace.[3]

Because the **ptrace** trace contains both event data and HPM data, it is important to be able to view event transitions and changes in HPM performance simultaneously. In this manner, different regions of the computation can be analyzed with respect to their effects on hardware performance behavior. The Gantts display allows the user to choose interactively which data will be shown. The Gantts display shown in Figure 3 shows the transitions between computational blocks of the FLO52 program during execution with the corresponding hardware behavior. The blocks here represent routines, and because this view selects all blocks for viewing, all entry and exit transitions between the FLO52 routines appear. All routines have been numbered and appear at their corresponding number level in the Events chart. The routine-to-number mapping can be brought up in another window for review. Each vertical line in the display represents a routine transition,

---

[2]Four different HPM counter groups can be accessed, covering different classes of hardware performance. Only one of the four groups is accessible at a time. See [4] or [7] for more information.

[3]The **ptrace** trace file contains the Group 0 counter values. The files **trace02** and **trace03** contain the Group 2 and Group 3 traces, respectively.

and each horizontal line indicates a period of time spent in the current routine. In this way, the user can identify the current routine at any point in the display. Thus, not only can we observe the relative pattern of routine occurrence, but differences in routine execution time can also be observed. For FLO52, the Events chart distinctly show the cyclic nature of the multigrid computation during one major phase of the entire execution as captured by the view region.

Corresponding to each routine transition we also see the values of the chosen hardware performance metrics. From these displays, one can see how hardware performance levels change between routines. It is also interesting to correlate performance across the different hardware metrics. We see the cyclic nature of the routine transitions in the displayed region of the FLO52 computation reflected in repetitive hardware behavior. This indicates relatively stable hardware performance behavior within and between the successive periods. We can zoom on the Gantts display for more visual detail.

We are continuing to use *TraceView* in the study of different versions of Cray applications, including FLO52. Because *TraceView* allows multiple trace files to be open simultaneously, traces from different executions can be viewed on the screen at the same time. This is of particular importance in the Cray work because multiple program executions must be performed in order to capture traces for all HPM counters. Additionally, we want to be able to compare the FLO52 traces of vector execution with those from scalar and concurrent executions to better understand the relative performance benefits of different compiler optimizations.

4.2 Viewing Maximum Parallelism

When evaluating the performance of a parallel computation, it is beneficial to know the maximum levels of parallelism that could be achieved during execution. Although the instantaneous parallelism will be limited in practice by the total processors available on the machine, a notion of peak parallelism can help in understanding execution efficiency. *MaxPar* [2] is a simulator for extracting the maximum theoretically attainable parallelism of a program. Based on the maximum parallelism levels, it is also possible to derive other operational statistics such the number of CPU memory references and floating point operations. *MaxPar* has been enhanced to generate extensive tracing information, roughly comparable to that produced by the Cray HPM tracing software. Event records are generated on each routine entry and exit, along with information on when the routine could have first been entered. In addition, performance profiling records when each instruction and arithmetic operation was ready to execute. Finally, a set of filters adapts this information to a format suitable for viewing by *TraceView*.

Once in *TraceView* format, the *MaxPar* profiles can be viewed side by side with Cray traces of the same program. This permits comparison of the potential peak parallelism, as generated by *MaxPar*, with the attained parallel performance from the Cray. Figure 4 shows a Gantts display for *MaxPar* performance data generated from FLO52. The Instructions Issued Gantt chart indicates the number of parallel instructions being executed. In comparison with a real traced execution, the *MaxPar* traces reveal the same phased, periodic behavior of the FLO52 computation. However, the levels of parallelism are significantly more enhanced and variable from phase to phase. The Instructions Issued levels in the measured Cray traces will be limited by the number of available processors and the vector register lengths.

As with a Cray execution trace, it is interesting to observe the side effects of instruction execution as related to the performance characteristics of the machine in the *MaxPar* case. The CPU Memory References chart can be used to observe the referencing demand on the memory system. A larger number of parallel instructions would be expected to generate a large number of simultaneous memory references, and this is can be seen quite clearly in the display. However, the performance variability also increases. Similarly, a larger number of floating point operations are expected at higher levels of parallelism. The Floating Point Adds chart shows this pattern.

5 Conclusion

TraceView provides a reusable platform for visualizing traces in various performance analysis applications. It implements trace management and I/O features that are commonly found in other special-purpose trace analysis systems while supporting a general, consistent framework for event interpretation that allows alternative display methods to made available. The *TraceView* architecture and the underlying event model are particularly suited to processing time-sequenced traces where each event has associated data values reflecting certain aspects of a system's state at the time the event occurred during execution. The Gantt-style of display is effective at viewing events and data histories during time periods as defined by the view specifications on a trace. Finally, the basic support for trace visualization sessions makes it possible to visually compare views from multiple traces at the same time.

The *TraceView* model will not apply for all trace visualization applications. However, it is expect that a majority of tracing applications will be able to make use of the tool. The principle shortcoming of the *TraceView* tool is in its semantic understanding of the trace events and data. The fundamental issue is whether by adding semantic knowledge to the tool, although potentially increasing its analysis capabilities, it will restrict the tool's general purpose nature.

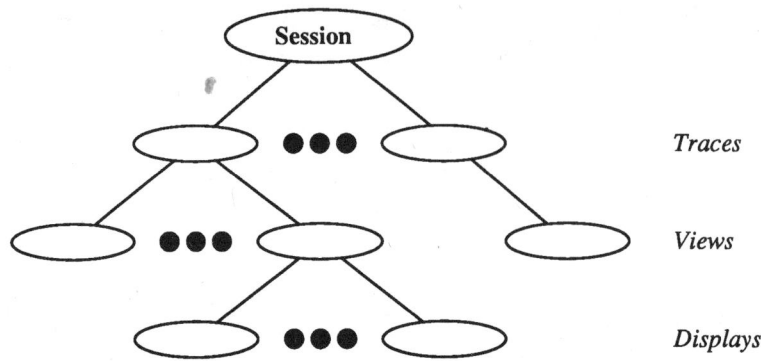

Figure 1: *TraceView* Session Model

References

[1] M. Berry. The Perfect Club Benchmarks: Effective performance evaluation of supercomputers. *The International Journal of Supercomputer Applications*, 3(3):5–40, Fall 1989.

[2] D. Chen. MaxPar: An Execution Drive Simulator for Studying Parallel Systems. Master's thesis, University of Illinois at Urbana-Champaign, Department of Computer Science, September 1990.

[3] M. Heath and J. Etheridge. Visualizing Performance of Parallel Programs. Technical Report ORNL/TM-11813, Oak Ridge National Laboratory, May 1991.

[4] J. Larson. Cray X-MP Hardware Performance Monitor. *Cray Channels*, 1985.

[5] T. LeBlanc, J. Mellor-Crummey, and R. Fowler. Analyzing Parallel Program Executions Using Multiple Views. *Journal of Parallel and Distributed Computing*, 9(6):203–217, June 1990.

[6] T. Lehr, Z. Segall, D. Vrsalovic, E. Caplan, A. Chung, and C. Fineman. Visualizing Performance Debugging. *IEEE Computer*, 22(10):38–51, October 1989.

[7] A. Malony, J. Larson, and D. Reed. Tracing Application Program Execution on the Cray X-MP and Cray 2. In *Proceedings of the 1990 Supercomputing Conference*, pages 60–73, November 1990.

[8] A. Malony, D. Reed, and D. Rudolph. Integrating Performance Data Collection, Analysis, and Visualization. In M. Simmons, R. Koskela, and I. Bucher, editors, *Parallel Computer Systems: Performance Instrumentation and Visualization*. ACM Press, 1990.

[9] B. Miller, M. Clark, S. Kierstead, and S. Lim. IPS-2: The Second Generation of a Parallel Program Measurement System. Technical Report CS-783, University of Wisconsin at Madison, Department of Computer Science, August 1988.

[10] D. Reed and D. Rudolph. The Intel iPSC/2: An Approach to Performance Instrumentation. *International Journal of High Speed Computing*, 1990.

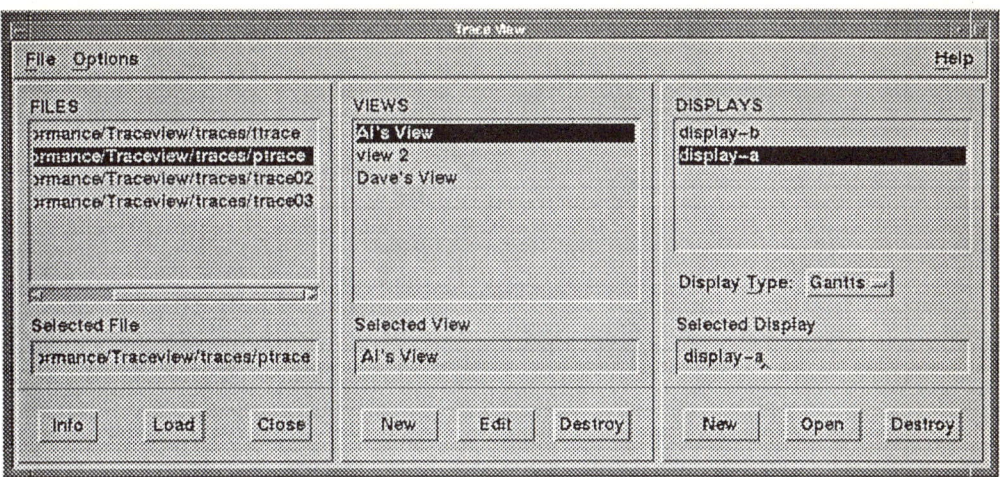

Figure 2: *TraceView* Main Session Window

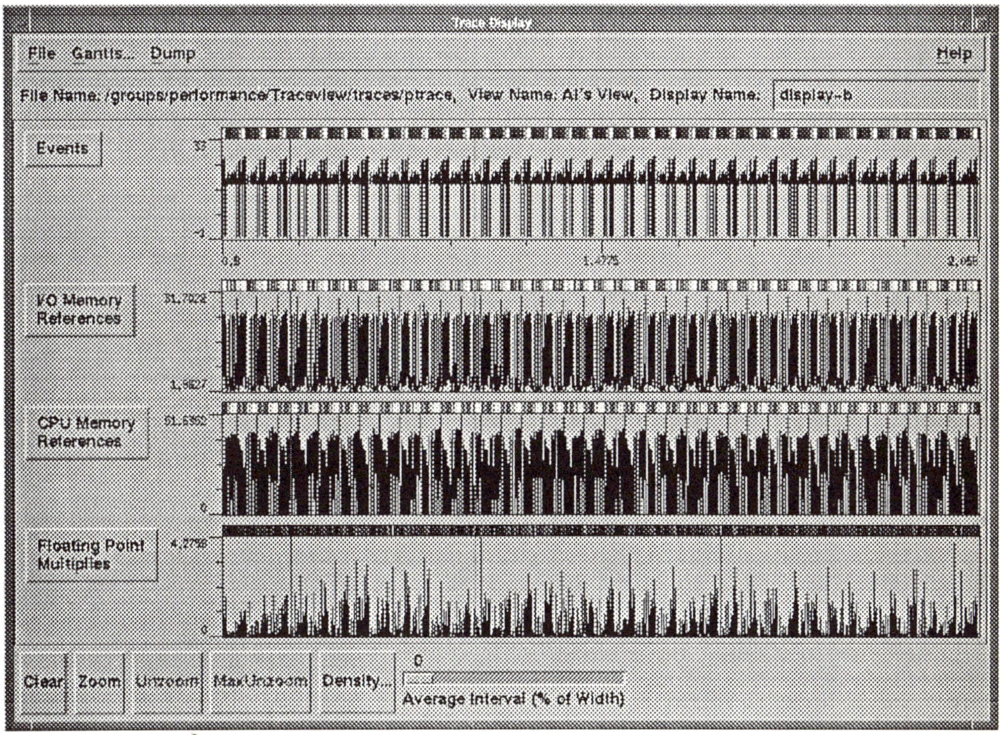

Figure 3: FLO52 Gantts Display (full range displayed)

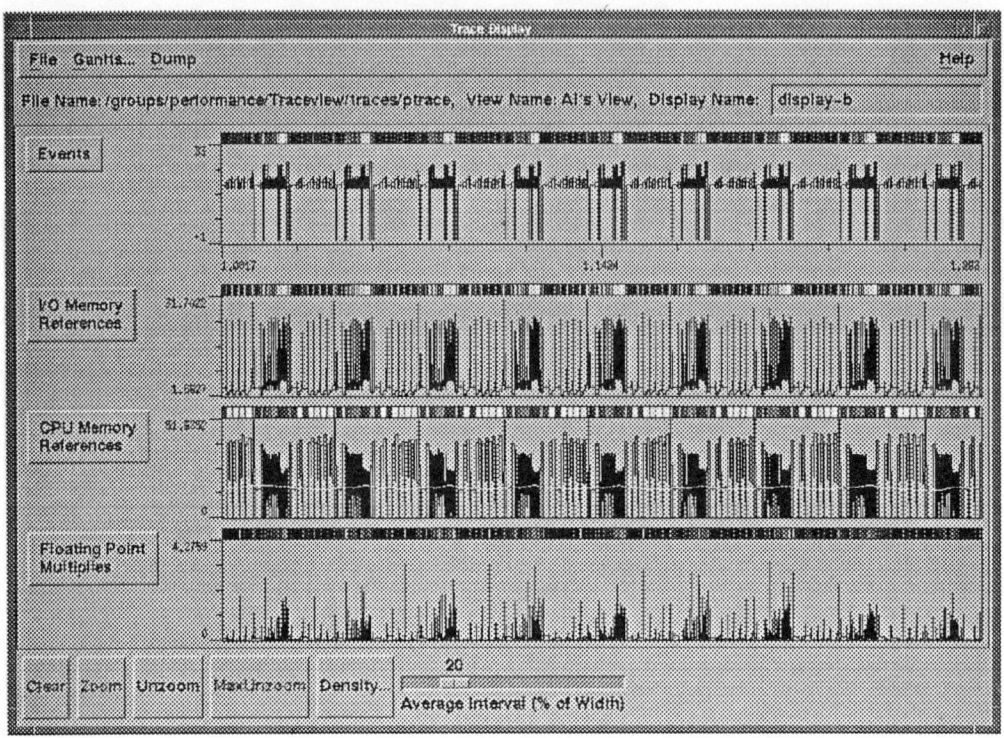

Figure 4: FLO52 Gantts Display (zoomed)

Parallel and Distributed Programming with ParMod–C

Andreas Weininger
Thomas Schnekenburger
Michael Friedrich

Institut für Informatik
Technische Universität München*

Abstract

ParMod is a set of language independent constructs for parallel and distributed programming. These constructs can be added to different sequential procedural programming languages. This paper describes an extension of the ParMod constructs. They are embedded in conventional C leading to the parallel and distributed programming language ParMod–C.

In addition, a new storage class concept is introduced, which is needed to improve the efficiency of ParMod–C implementations.

Several examples will demonstrate the usage of the ParMod–C language. We will also show how ParMod–C can be implemented on different hardware architectures.

1 Introduction

There exist a lot of approaches for the programming of parallel and distributed systems [BST89], [GM88]. Most parallel computers are programmed either in a sequential language like C or Fortran with the help of a special system specific synchronization and communication library[Sun90], or in a parallel language which is only efficient on a small subset of parallel and distributed architectures.

ParMod [Eic86], [Eic87] is a language independent concept for parallel and distributed programming which can be added to different sequential procedural programming languages. This has been done for instance for Pascal [Eic86] and will be done for Modula–2 [Tuf90], [Got90].

In this paper we will present an extension of the original ParMod incorporated in C. The resulting language is called ParMod–C.

The goals of of ParMod–C are

- to offer high level constructs for parallel and distributed programming which are efficiently implementable.
- to allow the user to easily specify a high degree of coarse–grain parallelism.
- to allow the reuse of sequential program parts and to minimize the effort for parallelizing existing sequential programs by preserving the spirit of C.

[Gre89] describes the first version of ParMod–C. The experiences made with this version yielded to the development of the ParMod–C versions described in [SW90] and this paper. The reasons for the extensions are

- to allow a more efficient implementa-

---
*This work was supported by Deutsche Forschungsgemeinschaft under contract number SFB 0342/B2

tion which forced us to introduce *storage classes*.

- improvements in the amount of communication which are one reason for new parameter passing mechanisms. Some examples are the introduction of out parameters in global procedure calls, which save one transfer of the parameter compared to inout parameters, and the introduction of dynamic length arrays as parameters (cf. section 2.3).
- improvements for the programmer's ease of use through a more obvious syntax
- to support data parallelization which resulted in replicated modules.

In the following section we will give an overview of the parallel language constructs in ParMod–C and how they are integrated in sequential C. The next section will present some examples to clarify the syntax and to show the usefulness and expressiveness of the constructs introduced in section two. Finally, we will show some current implementations and give a survey of future ParMod developments.

2 ParMod–C

A ParMod–C program is a finite non-empty set of several *ParMod–C modules* which are executed in parallel. A new feature in this version of ParMod–C is the possibility that each module may be replicated, i.e. there exist $n \geq 1$ instances from each module. The number of instances of each module is determined at program start from a special configuration file.

In the following text we will briefly write *module* instead of *module instance* if there is no danger of confusion. We define the parallelism among modules as *global parallelism*.

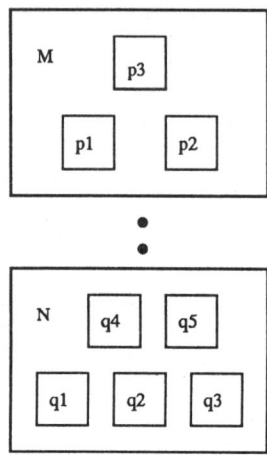

Figure 1: Structure of a ParMod–C program

A module contains local and global parallel procedures. The local parallel procedures, in the following named *parallel procedures*, can only be invoked within the module, in which they are defined.

The global parallel procedures, in the following named *global procedures* can be invoked from any module of the program. The mechanism of a global procedure call is not a synchronous *remote procedure call*, but an asynchronous *remote service invocation*[1]: The call of a global procedure always generates an activity in the module where the procedure is defined. This activity, called *task*, is a new incarnation of the procedure. The caller of a global procedure immediately proceeds. Calls of parallel procedures are asynchronous too. The parallelism within a module is called *local parallelism*.

Of course, in ParMod–C also exist usual C functions. A task which calls a function simply executes its code as in C.

Figure 1 shows an example for the static structure of a ParMod–C program. The pi and qi are the procedures defined in the modules M and N.

---

[1] a similiar mechanism is used in [AOC+86]

Figure 2 shows an example for the execution of a ParMod–C program. $M[i]$ denotes the instance i of the module M, $M[i].pj$ denotes an incarnation of the procedure pj in the i–th instance of M.

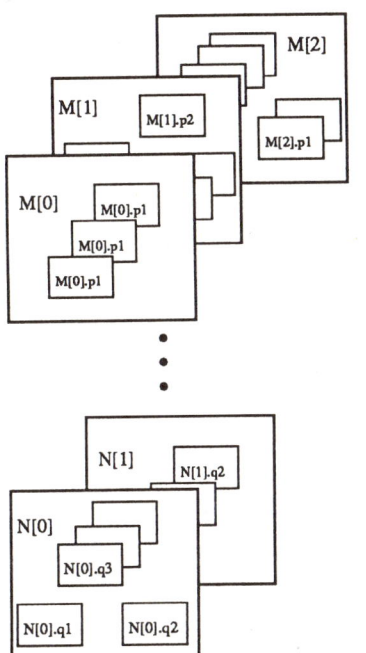

Figure 2: Execution of a ParMod–C program

The start of a ParMod–C program implies the start of all its modules. A ParMod–C program terminates if all modules terminate, i.e. all tasks and all calls of procedures are processed completely.

2.1 ParMod–C Modules

A ParMod–C module consists of several *compilation units*[2]. One of these must contain the clause:

module M;

which declares the module's name as M. A ParMod–C module may contain definitions

---

[2]in the same way as a C program consists of several compilation units.

and declarations of variables, global procedures, parallel procedures, functions and types. All these may be distributed over several compilation units as in sequential C.

A module must also contain declarations of the entities mentioned above if they are defined in other compilation units or – for global procedures – in other modules. The parallel procedures with the names *init* and *main* have special meanings. They may have the parameter list

int *argc*, **char** **argv[ ]*

and they are invoked automatically by the system. This means that at program start each module creates a task for the execution of its init procedure[3]. The variables *argc* and *argv* are initialized according to the arguments of the program call. As long as the init task is not terminated, no task will be created for a global procedure call in this module. After its termination the main procedure and the delayed global procedure calls are started in parallel.

The expression

lastmod M

returns the number of instances of the module M. The instances of each module are numbered from 0 to **lastmod** $M - 1$. The expression

mynumber()

returns the individual instance number of the executing module instance.

2.2 Variables

There don't exist any variables which can be accessed by different modules. The only way of inter–module communication is through global procedure calls. A feature which was not provided by the earlier versions of ParMod–C is the *storage class concept*, which splits up the variables of a ParMod–C program into three classes:

---

[3]if an init procedure exists

- The variables of the class *private* can be used only by the task, which defines them.

- The variables of the class *shared* can be used by different tasks of a module. The programmer should be careful about access conflicts on shared variables, because they may cause inconsistent states of these variables.

- The third class are *protected* variables. For these variables a task can request exclusive access, as we will describe later. Therefore this variables can be used for synchronization in contrast to shared variables.

For example

shared int x;

defines an integer variable in the class shared.

If the programmer specifies no storage class, then the predefined class of a variable is implicitly shared if the definition or declaration is external or if it is a definition or declaration of a static variable, otherwise the predefined class is private.

To guarantee the semantics of storage classes, casts between pointers to different storage classes are not permitted. It's also forbidden to define shared or protected pointers to the class private.

2.3 Global Procedures

The definition of a global procedure *GP* has the following syntax:

global *GP* (*ParDef*) { *Body* }

ParDef is the list of the formal parameters.

Pointers or structures with pointer members are not allowed as parameters of global procedures, because different modules have different address spaces. An exception are pointers to global procedures which can be passed between different modules because they are not represented as addresses, but as a program unique description of the global procedure. This allows to change the communication structure of ParMod–C programs dynamically.

In addition to the type of a parameter of a global procedure the programmer has to specify the parameter passing mechanism, which can be call–by–value (i.e. *in–parameters*), call–by–value–result (i.e. *inout–parameters*)[4] or call–by–result (i.e. *out–parameters*).

Private variables can't be used as out– or inout–parameters because this would violate the private–semantics.

The declaration of a global procedure has the following syntax:

extern *M* **global** *GP* (*ParDecl*);

M is the module which contains the definition of the global procedure *GP*. If *M* is missing then *GP* must be defined in the current module. *ParDecl* specifies the type of the parameters.

The syntax of a call of *GP* is

M [*InstNo*].*GP* (*Params*);

where *InstNo* is the number of the instance of *M* which is called. If [*InstNo*] is missing, this is equivalent to [0].

If a task t_1 in a module m_1 calls a procedure p_2 in the module m_2, the following actions are triggered:

- The values of the in– and inout–parameters are sent from m_1 to m_2, t_1 can proceed its work.

- A new task t_2 is generated in m_2 which runs parallel to all other tasks of m_2 and executes the code of p_2.

- If t_2 terminates, then all out– and inout–parameter values are returned to m_1 by a message from m_2 to m_1.

- If this message arrives at m_1, for each returned value a special task called *answer-task* is created in m_1 which

---

[4]This mechanism is called call-by-copy in [Tai82].

writes the returned value to the variable corresponding to the actual parameter in the call of p_2.

In addition, a global procedure can send result-values before its termination using the statement

answer *(ParList)*;

ParList is a list of the <u>names</u> of those out- or inout-parameters whose values have to be returned. If *ParList* is empty, then all not yet sent out- or inout-parameters are returned. It's not allowed to return the same parameter twice. Figure 3 shows an example of an invocation of a global procedure.

Older ParMod-C versions only offered the in- and inout-parameter mechanism for non-array variables, whereas arrays could only be used as inout-parameters. But this had drawbacks when for instance a global procedure computed an average value of an array of values or when a global procedure computed an array of values using only few input values, because two message transfers of large data blocks were necessary instead of one.

In addition to the in-, out- and inout-parameters, the new version of ParMod-C offers also the possibility of variable length arrays as parameters of global procedures. The size of the array must then be also a parameter of the procedure[5].

2.4 Parallel Procedures

The definition of a parallel procedure *PP* has the format:

parallel *PP (ParDef) { Body }*

A parallel procedure can be called only in the module in which it is defined. The parameter passing mechanisms are the same as for usual C functions. By this, it is allowed to pass pointers to parallel procedures. It is not allowed to pass pointers to

---
[5]cf. example in section 3.2

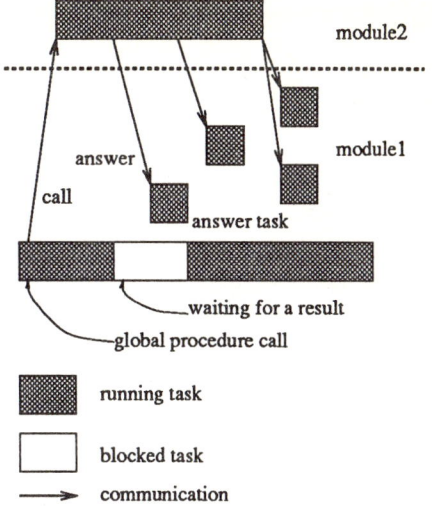

Figure 3: Call of a global procedure

private variables to parallel procedures.

2.5 Synchronization

For synchronization purposes ParMod-C offers the **await region** statement with the following syntax:

await *(await-condition)*
region *(region-list)*
region-body

await-condition must be an expression which yields an integer result. *region-list* may be a non-empty comma separated list[6] where each list element must have the storage class protected. *region-body* may be any ParMod-C statement. The semantics of this construct is similar to the conditional critical regions in [BH73]: Let t be the task executing the statement, A the *await-condition*, $r_0, ..., r_n$ the *region-list*, B the *region-body*:

1. evaluate $r_0, ..., r_n$ and map to storage ranges $s_0, ..., s_n$ where s_i is a pair (a_i, l_i) with the start address a_i and the length l_i of the storage range

---
[6]every element must be an l-expressions or an array

2. if there exists an s_i which is reserved by a task $t' \neq t$ then delay t until s_i is released and continue with step 2 afterwards, otherwise reserve $s_0, ..., s_n$ for task t

3. evaluate A; if this yields a value $\neq 0$ then start the execution of B, otherwise release $s_0, ..., s_n$ and goto step 2

4. when the execution of B has terminated then release all s_i reserved in this statement.

No other task may have write access to $s_0, ..., s_n$ during the execution of the region-body. We require that the assignment strategy for each storage range is fair [Eic86].

A missing await part is equivalent with **await** (1). If the region part is missing then the task which executes the statement waits until *await-condition* becomes $\neq 0$ and proceeds its work.

The compiler must generate implicit regions around each write access to a protected variable to assure mutual exclusion during write accesses.

The semantics for an assignment operation with assignment operator $AssOp$[7]

v *AssOp Expression*;

where v is protected, is equivalent to

h=*Expression*; **region** (v) v *AssOp* h;

where h is a private variable. "++v;" is equivalent to "v+ = 1". So it can be guaranteed, that v is incremented with 1.

A special operator **result** offers the possibility to test whether results have arrived. A task t, which executes the statement

result (*ResultExpression*)

where *ResultExpression* must be an l-expression or an array, gets the value 0 if and only if

- t has called a global procedure with an out- or inout-parameter p where the answer-task for p has not yet terminated and the storage range of p intersects the storage range of the *ResultExpression*, or

- t has called a parallel procedure with a pointer parameter to a storage range which intersects the storage range of the *ResultExpression* and this parallel procedure is not yet terminated.

In combination with the **await** statement a task is able to wait for results.

In addition to the explicit waiting there is an implicit waiting: A task which calls global or parallel procedures with some of its local variables as out- or inout-parameters resp. pointers to local variables has to wait for the answer resp. for the termination of the called procedure.

2.6 Usage of C Code

ParMod–C modules can be linked with conventional C compilation units. Functions in C compilation units can be declared in a ParMod–C program with the clause

linked *FuncDecl*;

where *FuncDecl* is a usual declaration of a function.

The keyword **linked** was introduced to allow the ParMod–C compiler additional checkings on calls of a linked C function.

Of course, the programmer can misuse this possibility and e.g. can break the cast restrictions for pointers or the region semantics. But since "trust the programmer" is a part of the spirit of C, the advantages of the linking facilities should outweigh the disadvantages.

---

[7] e.g. =, + =, * =, ...

3 Examples

In this chapter we give examples[8] for the ParMod–C syntax and the usage of the ParMod–C constructs. The horizontal dotted lines mark the borders between different modules. The emphasized phrases are pseudo–code. The functions *p_malloc()* resp. *s_malloc()* correspond to the C library function *malloc()* but are yielding pointers to an element of the storage class protected resp. shared.

3.1 Parallel Dining Philosophers

Our first example presents a parallel solution of the well–known problem of the dining philosophers [Dij71]. In our example the number of philosophers and forks is not fixed but is scanned from the standard input. Each philosopher is represented by an incarnation of the parallel procedure *philosopher*. The forks are represented by the dynamically allocated array *fork* in the storage class protected. This solution is free of deadlocks because at most ($n\_phils-1$) philosophers are waiting. The fairness requirements given in chapter 2.5 imply that the solution is starvation free.

Note again that external variables are implicitly shared and local variables and parameters are implicitly private.

module dining_philosophers;
linked scanf(char *,...);
extern protected char *
  p_malloc(unsigned int);
protected int in_room;
/* # philosophers in the room */
protected char * shared fork; /* the forks */
int n_phils; /* number of philosophers */
parallel philosopher(int i)
{

  for (;;) {
    think
    await (in_room<n_phils) region (in_room)
      ++in_room;
    enter the room
    region (fork[i])
      region (fork[(i+1)%n_phils]) {
        −−in_room; /* implicit region */
        eat using fork[i] and fork[(i+1)%n_phils]
      }
    return the forks, leave the room
  }
}
parallel main(void)
{
  int i;
  scanf("%d",&n_phils);
  fork=
    p_malloc(n_phils*sizeof(protected char));
  in_room=0;
  for (i=0; i<n_phils; ++i)
    philosopher(i);
}

3.2 Parallel Sorting

Now we show an implementation of a module which offers the global procedure *sort* to sort an integer array of variable length. The module uses a parallel position sort algorithm [9]: For every number in the array which has to be sorted, a task is generated which looks for the position of "its" number and then writes this number in the result array. The task generations are implemented by recursive calls of the parallel procedure *searchandset*. Note that the arrays need not be in the storage class protected, because the original array is only read and there are no write conflicts for the result–array. Because the arrays are local variables of the procedure sort, it automatically executes an implicit waiting for the termination of all searchandset tasks.

We also present a module which uses the sort procedure.

---

[8] Solutions in ParMod-Pascal for some of the examples are given in [Eic86]. Some of the examples are also used in a parallel programming course at the Technische Universität München.

[9] Of course, this algorithm is not very efficient.

module sort_server;

parallel searchandset(int n_start, int n_end,
                     int size, shared int f[],
                     shared int sf[])
{
    int myindex;
    int i,position=0;

    myindex=(n_start+n_end)/2;
    if (myindex>n_start)
        searchandset(n_start,myindex-1,size,f,sf);
    if (myindex<n_end)
        searchandset(myindex+1,n_end,size,f,sf);
    for (i=0; i<size; ++i)
        if (f[i]<f[myindex] ||
            (f[i]==f[myindex] && i<myindex))
            ++position;
    sf[position]=f[myindex];
    /* no implicit waiting ! */
}
global sort(in int size, in shared int f[size],
            out shared int sf[size])
{
    searchandset(0,size-1,size,f,sf);
    /* implicit waiting for all searchandsets ! */
}

....

module sort_user;

extern sort_server global sort (in int a_size,
        in int f[a_size], out int sf[a_size]);

parallel main(void)
{
    shared int * a, length;

    get storage for a and initialize a
    sort_server.sort(length,a,a);
    continue to work
    await (result (a));
    /* a is sorted */
}

3.3 Semaphore Manager

The next example implements a manager for counting semaphores. The module *semaphores* offers operations for initialisation of a new semaphore and the P and V operations for existing semaphores. The module *sema_user* shows the usage of these operations.

To get an unique object identifier which can be exchanged between modules, the C mechanism of the pointer difference from the NULL pointer which yields an integer value is used.

Note that the V-operation can be done asynchronously but the caller has to wait for the termination of the P- and init-Operations.

module semaphores;

extern protected char *
    p_malloc(unsigned int);
global init_sema(in int init_val,
        out int sema_result)
{
    protected int * sema_ptr;

    sema_ptr = (protected int *) p_malloc(
        sizeof(protected int));
    (*sema_ptr) = init_val;
    sema_result = sema_ptr −
        (protected int *)NULL;
}
global P(inout int sema_id)
{
    protected int * sema_ptr;

    sema_ptr = (protected int *)NULL +
        sema_id;
    await (*sema_ptr>0) region (*sema_ptr)
        −−*sema_ptr;
}
global V(in int sema_id)
{ ++ *((protected int *)NULL+sema_id); }

....

module semaphore_user;

extern semaphores global
init_sema(in int, out int);
extern semaphores global P(inout int);
extern semaphores global V(in int);

parallel main(void)
{
    int shared sem;

```
/* Initialisation of sem with value 12 */
semaphores.init_sema(12,&sem);
await (result (sem));

/* V-Operation on sem */
semaphores.V(sem);

/* P-Operation on sem */
semaphores.P(&sem);
await (result (sem));
}
```

3.4 Readers and Writers

The following modules show an implementation of the readers–writers problem given in [BH73] with a fair processing strategy (c.f. [Eic86]). A single resource is shared between concurrent read and write tasks, whereas each write task must have exclusive access to it. The module *readers_writers* represents the resource with the operations *read_resource* and *write_resource*.

```
module readers_writers;
typedef Data_Type Block[DATA_SIZE];
extern void read_data(Block);
extern void write_data(Block);
protected int readers,writers;
protected char next_access,writing;
global read_resource(out Block d)
{
  region (next_access)
    await (writers==0) region (readers,writers)
      ++readers;
  read_data(d);
  --readers;
}
global write_resource(in Block d)
{
  region (next_access)
    await (readers==0) region (readers,writers)
      ++writers;
  region (writing)
    write_data(d);
  --writers;
}
parallel init(void)
{
  readers=writers=0;
  initialize the resource
}
```
....
```
module user;
extern readers_writers
  global read_resource(out Block);
extern readers_writers   global
write_resource(in Block);
parallel main(void)
{
  Block block;
  readers_writers.read_resource(block);
  do something without the block
  await (result(block));
  block is read
  readers_writers.write_resource(block);
}
```

3.5 Distributed Dining Philosophers

This last example should demonstrate the usage of replicated modules. Again we solve the problem of the dining philosophers, but now the philosophers are represented by different instances of the module *dist_phils*. So the number of philosophers is given by the replication factor of the module *dist_phils*.

Each module instance manages one fork. The waiting for the $in\_room < n\_phils$ condition is replaced by a broadcast mechanism. A task which wants to *enter the room* has to get the permission from all module instances. By this, it can be guaranteed that at most $n\_phils-1$ philosophers are in the room.

The variable *myfork* is a flag to indicate that the fork of the module instance is free.

```
module dist_phils;
#define TRUE 1
```

```
#define FALSE 0
extern shared char * s_malloc(unsigned int);
protected int in_room, myfork;
global request(out int succ)
{
  region (in_room) {
    if (in_room<lastmod(dist_phils)-1)
      { ++in_room; succ=TRUE; }
    else succ=FALSE;
  }
}
global decrement(void) { --in_room; }
global takefork(out char f)
{
  await (myfork) region (myfork)
  myfork=FALSE;
}
global retfork(void) { myfork=TRUE; }
parallel init(void)
{ myfork=TRUE; in_room=0; }
parallel main(void)
{
  int i, succall;
  shared int * success;
  shared char fork1,fork2;

  success = (shared int *) s_malloc(
      lastmod(dist_phils) * sizeof(shared int));
  for (;;) {
    think
    do {
      for (i=0; i<lastmod(dist_phils); ++i)
        dist_phils[i].request(&(success[i]));
      await (result(success));
      succall=TRUE;
      i=0;
      while ((i<lastmod(dist_phils))
            && (succall &= success[i]))
        ++i;
      if (!succall) {
        for (i=0; i<lastmod(dist_phils); ++i)
          if (success[i]) dist_phils[i].decrement();
        wait for a random time
      }
    } while (!succall);
    enter the room
```

```
    dist_phils[ mynumber()].takefork(&fork1);
    dist_phils[(mynumber()+1) %
        lastmod(dist_phils)].takefork(&fork2);
    await (result(fork1,fork2));
    eat using fork mynumber() and
        (mynumber()+1)%lastmod(dist_phils)
    dist_phils[mynumber()].retfork();
    dist_phils[(mynumber()+1) %
        lastmod(dist_phils)].retfork();
    for (i=0; i<lastmod(dist_phils); ++i)
      dist_phils[i].decrement();
    return the forks and leave the room
  }
}
```

4 Implementations

ParMod–C is implemented on a system of several VAX computers connected by an Ethernet (cf. figure 4). Each module instance is executed by an UNIX process. The parallelism within a module is just simulated within the UNIX process.

The communication between different modules is managed by a *server*. Such a server exists on each workstation where the program runs. The server and the modules on the same workstation communicate via UNIX shared memory. The servers themselves communicate via sockets.

The same principle is used for implementations on DEC and SUN workstations.

In addition to the existing ParMod–C implementation on UNIX Workstations, we are implementing ParMod–C on an Intel iPSC/2 hypercube computer using the TOPSYS environment which was developed at the Institut für Informatik der Technischen Universität München [Beu91], [Bem88].

To use the parallelism within modules on a UNIX shared memory computer, each module instance can be mapped on several UNIX processes. All communications can be done via the shared memory. We will use this principle to implement ParMod–C on an Alliant FX/2800 supercomputer.

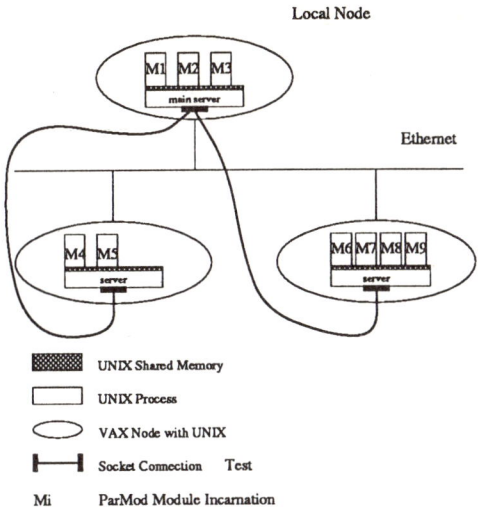

Figure 4: Workstation net implementation

5 Conclusions and Future Work

We gave a survey of the extended parallel and distributed language constructs of ParMod–C. The reasons for the extensions were improvements of the efficiency of ParMod–C implementations and improvements for the convenience of the programmer. Several examples showed the syntax, usage and expressiveness of the constructs. We also gave a short description of the current implementations of ParMod–C.

In the near future, we will investigate the usefulness of the new language constructs by implementing different applications, e.g. parallel and distributed implementations of relational database operators (sort, join, etc.). We will also use ParMod-C in a parallel programming course.

To test the suitability for parallelizing existing sequential programs, we will port the commercial database system TransBase [Tra88] to ParMod–C. TransBase is a relational multi–user database system[10] written in C. This is done in project B2 of Son-derforschungbereich 342 which is dealing with database systems for massively parallel computers.

To predict the runtime behavior of ParMod–C programs on further hardware architectures, we will implement a simulator for ParMod–C which is independent from the underlying hardware. This simulator will also be used to generate reproducible runs, which can be used for a deterministic debugging of ParMod–C programs.

References

[AOC+86] G.R. Andrews, R.A. Ollsson, M. Coffin, I. Elshoff, K. Nilson, Titus Purdin, and Gregg Townsend. An overview of the SR language and implementation. Technical Report TR 86-6c, Department of Compuer Science, The University of Arizona, Tucson, 1986.

[Bem88] T. Bemmerl. An integrated and portable tool environment for parallel computers. In *Proceedings of the IEEE International Conference on Parallel Processing*, pages 50-53. Pen. State University, St. Charles, USA, August 1988.

[Beu91] Beuter, T.: Implementierung der Programmiersprache ParMod-C auf einem Hypercube-Rechner. Master's thesis, Technische Universität München, 1991.

[BH73] P. Brinch Hansen. *Operating System Principles*. Prentice Hall, 1973.

[BST89] H.E. Bal, J.G. Steiner, and A.S. Tanenbaum. Programming languages for distributed computing systems. *ACM Computing Surveys*, 21(3):261–322, September 1989.

---
[10]with more than 80000 lines of code

[Dij71] E.W. Dijkstra. Hierarchical ordering of sequential processes. *Acta Informatica*, (1):115–138, 1971.

[Eic86] S. Eichholz. ParMod – A language for programming with parallel modules. Technical Report TUM-I8616, Technische Universität München, November 1986.

[Eic87] S. Eichholz. Parallel programming with ParMod. In *Proceedings of the 1987 International Conference on Parallel Processing*, pages 377–380. Pennsylvania State University Press, May 1987.

[GM88] N. Gehani and A.D. McGettrick, editors. *Concurrent Programming*. Addison–Wesley, 1988.

[Got90] Gottschalk, B.: Entwicklung eines freien Modulkonzepts für ParMod und dessen Integration in ParMod-2. Master's thesis, Technische Universität München, 1990.

[Gre89] Greverus, R.S.: Erweiterung der Sprache C um ParMod-Sprachkonstrukte und Implementierung auf einem VAX-Netz. Master's thesis, Technische Universität München, May 1989.

[Sun90] V.S. Sunderam. PVM: A framework for parallel distributed computing. *Concurrency: Practice and Experience*, 2(4):315–339, December 1990.

[SW90] Schnekenburger, T., Weininger, A.: Einführung in die parallele Programmiersprache ParMod-C. Internal report, Technische Universität München, Dezember 1990.

[Tai82] Kuo-Chnung Tai. Comments on parameter passing techniques in programming languages. *acm SIGPLAN Notices*, 17(2):24–27, Februar 1982.

[Tra88] TransAction Software GmbH. *TransBase Relational Database System, Version 3.0, TB/SQL Reference Manual*, 1988.

[Tuf90] Tuffentsammer, J.: Modifikation und Integration von ParMod-Sprachkonstrukten in die Sprache Modula-2. Master's thesis, Technische Universität München, 1990.

Code Generation for a
Data Parallel SIMD Language

Peter Brezány

Department of Statistics and Computer Science, University of Vienna
Rathausstrasse 19/II/3, A-1010 Vienna, AUSTRIA

Viera Šipková

Institute of Technical Cybernetics, Slovak Academy of Sciences
Dúbravska cesta 9, 84237 Bratislava, CSFR

Abstract: *A compiler for a Modula-2 based language M2PLUS is described. The M2PLUS has been designed and implemented for programming an existing associative array processor. The description of the compiler is concentrated on the techniques we have developed for compiling parallel expressions and parallel control statements.*

1. INTRODUCTION

Associative processors (APs) are a special class of SIMD array processors. They were originally intended for image and signal processing and for the fast search ordered retrieval of large files of records. However, APs have been found to be also well suited for grid or mesh type scientific problems in which the processing of data in regular patterns dominates. They are typically programmed in a data parallel style. For this type of applications high-level programming languages are required that enable definition of parallel data objects and specification of data parallel processing, which are still efficiently implementable on the given AP.
In this paper we describe characteristic features of the Modula-2 based data parallel programming language M2PLUS that has been designed and implemented for programming the real AP [Ric84]. The compiler transforms high-level minimal machine dependent language constructs into a form compatible with the target AP's architecture and generates corresponding machine instruction sequences. After describing the overal structure of

the compiler we will concentrate on code generation. The software runtime support enables the code generator to view the target architecture as an M2PLUS pseudo-machine. After the introduction of these machine principles, the compilation of parallel expressions and parallel control statements are explained.

2. TARGET ARCHITECTURE

The AP [Ric84] is a part of the parallel computer system (PCS SIMD) which can be viewed as a 2-processors system consisting of a commercial sequential computer and an associative processor (AP), both cross connected with a number of interconnection channels. Such a structure enables simultaneous running of scalar and vector processes, which can communicate with each other and synchronize their actions.

AP consists of the following major units: control memory, control unit and associative modules.
Control memory is used to store parallel programs and scalar data. The word length is 32 bits, each word has a 16-bit address. **Control unit** controls the execution of both scalar and parallel operations. In the control unit basic arithmetical and logical operations can be performed on scalar operands. **Associative modules** process vectors in parallel mode. Each module contains: an associative multidimensional access (MDA) memory, 256 one-bit processing elements (PEs), a flip network (FN), and a multiple match resolver (MMR). The MDA memory consists of memory pages organized as a square of 256 words by 256 bits. Data can be accessed in various modes, but always 256 bits in parallel. Alignment of 256-bit data in the MDA memory with PEs is accomplished by the FN, which also provides tools for mutual communication between PEs on the one hand and the PEs and MDA memory on the other hand. The memory organization along with the MMR allows to access data either by location (explicit address), or association based on their content. PEs act in unison upon instructions that are sent from the single control unit. Each PE comprises three one-bit registers X, Y, and M and an arithmetic-logical unit which supports all 16 functions of two logical variables. The MMR is connected to the Y register. The M fulfils the role of a mask register.

3. INPUT LANGUAGE

M2PLUS provides all scalar structured programming concepts of Modula-2. Most parallel constructs have been adopted from the language Actus

[Per79]. Here only some of the most important parallel features are described: parallel data structures and the statements for manipulating parallel data. For more details see [BreSip89].

The extent of parallelism (eop) is the central concept in the language. It specifies the subset of parallel array elements upon which operations are to be performed in parallel. The eop is associated with each of the parallel structures. Generally, it is set statically by an index set expression or it is yielded by a parallel control statement at run-time.

In M2PLUS it is possible to declare single-dimensional or multi-dimensional parallel arrays in which one dimension may be defined to be parallel. For example,

    VAR pa: ARRAY [0:999] OF INTEGER;

declares a 1000 element array which is to be processed in parallel.

Parallel arrays may appear in parallel assignment, WHILE, WHERE, CASE or USING statements.

For example, in the statement

    pa[!0:127!] := i

the scalar value of i is assigned in parallel to all elements referenced explicitly by the eop which is {0,1,2,...,127}.

The USING statement serves to construct an eop for the statements lying within its scope. This statement, for example,

    USING !64:255! DO pa[$] := pa[$] + 5 END

explicitly sets the eop to be {64,65,...,255} and references it by implication using the special symbol $.
The WHERE statement corresponds to the scalar IF statement. For example, in the construct, such as

    WHERE pa[!100:300!] > 0 DO pa[$] := 1 END

the eop is initially set to the values {100,101,...,300} and is used to index the array pa. All the index values of the elements of the array pa which do not satisfy the condition specified in the WHERE clause are removed from the eop, and this amended eop, if it is not empty, is then used by the statements that lie within the DO clause.

The USING and/or WHERE constructs can be nested (see Part 5.3). In such a situation, the eop is stacked as a new construct is encountered and then unstacked as the construct is exited. Then the symbol $ references the actual eop.

SEND and RECEIVE statements enable AP to communicate with the sequential part of the PCS SIMD.

4. PRINCIPLES OF THE COMPILATION SCHEMA

The M2PLUS compiler is implemented in the programming environment TopSpeed Modula-2 on IBM PC/AT computer. Many ideas have been taken from the multi-pass compiler for the Modula-2 [Gei82], [Jac83]. In the design and implementation of the M2PLUS compiler the standard techniques have been applied in several parts. The main difference lies in the code generation scheme. In this presentation we will concentrate only on the most important aspects concerning the parallel constructs.

The M2PLUS compiler is divided into several functional parts (see figure 1). Upon compilation of any compilation unit the source text of the compilation unit itself and the symbol files containing the interface information about the imported modules serve as an input. Symbol files are obtained by compiling definition modules giving the full description of all declared objects. Upon compilation of an implementation module the compiler writes the generated code with linker information on an object file. A set of object files can be linked together and loaded for execution.

As the syntax of the language does not exactly reflect the architecture, it is necessary that a M2PLUS program will undergo some machine dependent and some machine independent optimizing transformations. For this reason the graph representation of the symbolic unit representation of a compilation unit is constructed. On this structure the transformations are caried out and this is then passed to the code generator. In addition to the standard optimization techniques associated with sequential languages, special optimizations on parallel structures dictated by the

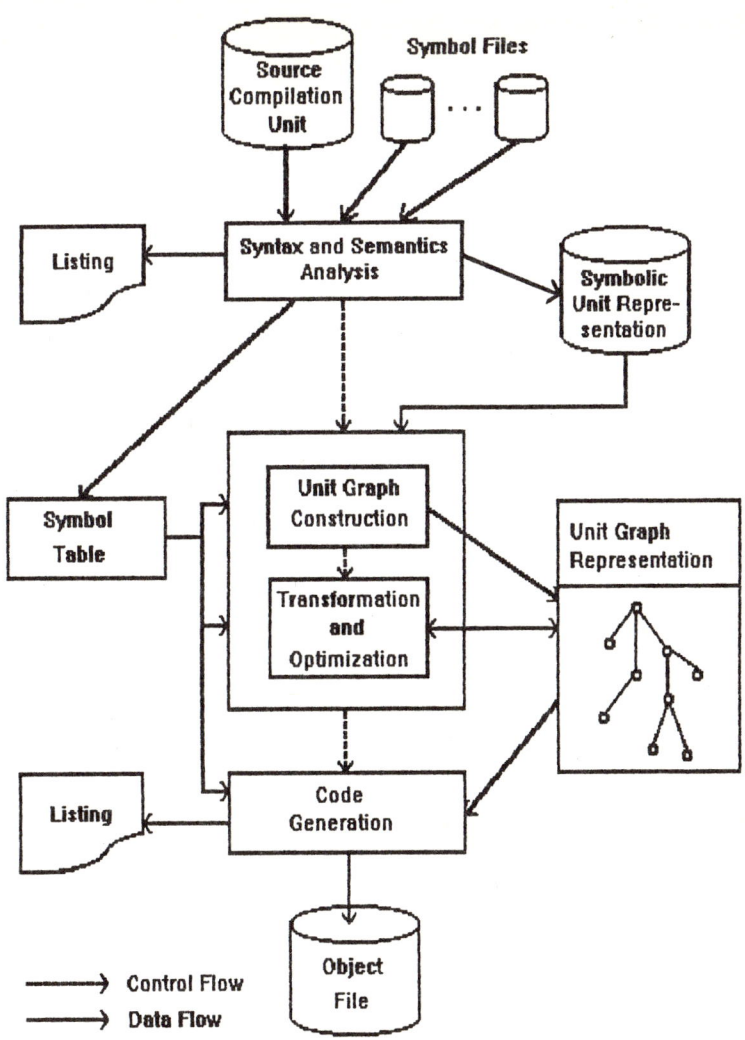

Figure 1 Compiling a Program and Implementation Module

hardware must be applied. For example, in M2PLUS there are several forms to set the eop. In the following statements

```
pa[!0:99!] := 10;     pb[!0:99!] := pa[!0:99!] * 10;
pb[105] := -20;       pa[!106:200!] := -10;
pb[!106:200!] := (pa[!106:200!] + pb[!106:200!]) DIV 2;
```

the eop is set explicitly and it is explicitly referenced on every use.
Each setting of the eop results in the mask generation which is a rather
complicated run-time process when considering an universal form of the
mask. To minimize these actions the statement sequence can be transformed into the following form:

```
   USING !0:99! DO   pa[$] := 10;   pb[$] := pa[$] * 10 END;
   pb[105] := -20;
   USING !106:200! DO
       pa[$] := -10;   pa[$] := (pa[$] + pb[$]) DIV 2
   END;
```

where the eop is set three times and is referenced by implication.

5. CODE GENERATION

The code generator scans the intermediate graph representation of a
program and produces the relocatable machine-language object file. Not
much can be said about the code generation without dealing with the
description of the particular machine. The software run-time support
enables the code generator to view the target architecture as a M2PLUS
pseudo-machine (m2p-machine).

5.1   Description of the M2PLUS pseudo-machine

In the description of the machine we will concentrate more on the
concepts related to the evaluation of parallel expressions and statements
and we shall leave out details about procedure entry and exit, parameter
passing mechanisms, etc.

The m2p-machine has several registers, uses five distinct memory areas
and contains scalar and vector operating units, as shown in figure 2. The
control unit of the AP contains several registers. Most of them are used
for fixed purposes; some of them must be held free to allow special
operations. In the m2p-machine this register set is modelled by the type
RegType. Type PRegType describes registers of associative modules.
Registers that may be utilized in conditional branch instructions are
modelled by the type BrRegType.
Program Memory holds the invariant machine code of the modules and its
procedures. A pointer pc points to the instruction that will be executed

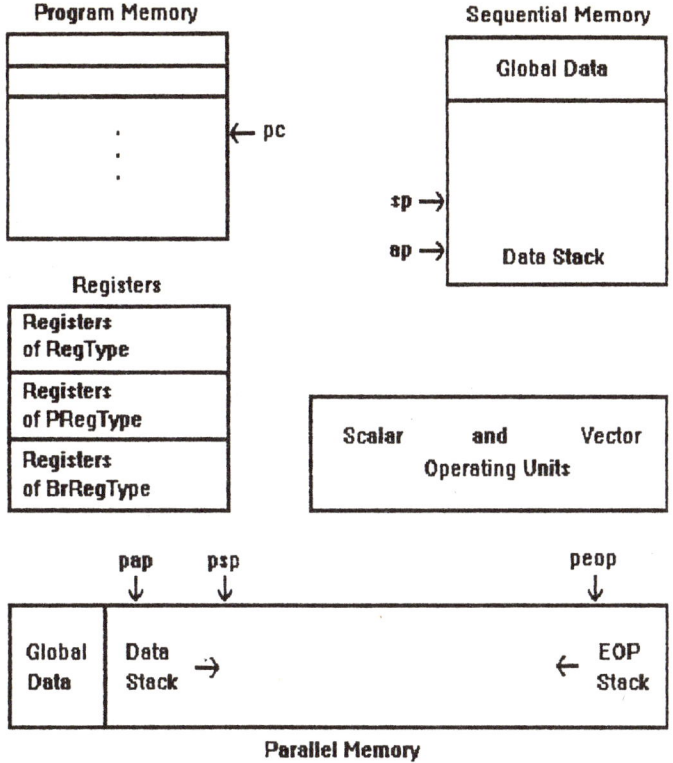

Figure 2   M2PLUS pseudo-machine

next. Global Data parts of Sequential and Parallel Memories contain all data declared at the M2PLUS module level. These parts are allocated statically. Data Stacks contain local data of activated procedures and temporaries. Pointers sp and psp point to the top-of-stacks elements and pointers ap and pap to the activation records of the currently executed procedure. Eops can be nested. The current eop is held in Mreg and the previous ones are stored in EOP Stack. The pointer eopp points to previous eop. Scalar and Vector Operating Units perform operations on scalar and vector operands due to the M2PLUS semantics.

In the implementation of the m2p-machine on the AP, Program Memory and Sequential Memory would be located in control memory and Parallel Memory in MDA memories of associative modules. The introduced pointers are held in registers or in dedicated memory locations of the sequential Global Data part.

The mapping technique for scalar and parallel data was chosen with respect to the loading and processing methods. All scalar data and scalar temporaries are allocated in Sequential Memory, all parallel data and parallel temporaries are allocated in Parallel Memory. A single-dimensional parallel array occupies a rectangle m-words by n-bits, where m is the number of array elements and n is the width of elements in bits. Multi-dimensional parallel arrays and parallel arrays with structured elements are broken up into a set of single-dimensional parallel arrays and these are in turn allocated in Parallel Memory. Information about the position and size of a parallel array is kept in its descriptor which is allocated in Sequential Memory and is initialized after being reserved the corresponding space in Parallel Memory. The elements which are to participate in an operation are specified by the current eop.

5.2 Compiling Parallel Expressions

Generating code for an expression requires that the compiler keeps track of the expression nature. It is possible to combine sequential and parallel objects in expressions as long as no type conflicts occur. An expression or part thereof which contains only scalar variables or constants results in a scalar value. An expression or part thereof which includes at least one parallel variable or constant results in a parallel value, unless the parallel variable is used as a parameter to a function that yields a scalar value.

The description of an expression is defined in terms of the Attribute record consisting of two essential components: a fixed part with a field which refers to the type structure of the object and a variant part which indicates the mode of the object. The different modes which an object can take are defined by the enumeration type AttrMode:
```
   AttrMode = (parraymode,pwrkmode,
               pYregmode,pXregmode,pMregmode,...);
```

The mode parraymode represents a parallel array, this is its descriptor by which a parallel array is referenced. The mode of the descriptor corresponds to the addressing modes of Sequential Memory. The mode pwrkmode represents a parallel array located in the Global Data part of Parallel Memory which holds intermediate results during evaluation of parallel arithmetic-logical expressions. The modes pYregmode, pXregmode, pMregmode are parallel register modes and are used during constructing and handling eops. The physical counterpart of the current eop are M-registers of associatives modules. So each eop calculations would lead to the execution of a run-time routine which sets the M-registers to the required values. The contents of registers M, Y, and X can be considered to be a parallel Boolean array, which is said to be TRUE when all bits are '1', FALSE when all bits are '0'; otherwise it is mixed. When starting the program all processing elements are enabled (this means the eop is set to TRUE values) then upon entry of any statement that may change the eop, the current eop is pushed onto the parallel stack and restored after the statement has been completed.

To generate code for expressions the procedure

    Expression(fnodp: NdPtr; VAR fat: Attribute)

is used, where the parameter fnodp holds the pointer to the root of the input graph structure corresponding to the expression, and the parameter fat is an Attribute variable which is being constituted during processing of the subtrees. Graph traversal starts at the root node and proceeds along a path from the left to the right subtrees until the terminal nodes (constant, name) are encountered. Code for arithmetic, logical and comparison operations between two Attribute variables is produced by procedures that can be subdivided into three groups according to the type of variables. For example, code for addition is generated by the following procedures:

    Addss(VAR fat1,fat2: Attribute)
    Addff(VAR fat1,fat2,fat3: Attribute)
    Addfs(VAR fat1,fat2,fat3: Attribute)

Procedure Addss generates code for addition of two scalar operands, fat1, fat2, and results in a scalar value which is always of register mode. There is only one register in which scalar arithmetic-logical operations can be carried out. So the compiler is forced to make this register free whenever a new request for arithmetic-logical operation is encountered. For the handling of register assignment several procedures are introduced.
Procedure Addff generates code for addition of two parallel arrays, fat1, fat2, and results in a parallel array fat3.
Procedure Addfs generates code for addition of a scalar operand fat1 and a parallel array fat2 and results in a parallel array fat3. The resulting parallel array fat3 is of the mode pwrkmode.

All operations on parallel arrays are accomplished in bit-serial and

word-parallel fashion. This level of processing is, however, not visible to the code generator. For a parallel operation the code generator produces an instruction sequence which includes instructions for loading the registers with data from corresponding descriptors and a 'jump into subroutine' instruction. The elements which participate in the operation at the same time are specified by the current eop that has to be set before the operation is executed. The subroutines which are responsible for performing the parallel operations are contained in the run-time support library. The M2PLUS run-time support library is implemented in assembly language and constitutes the absolute code part of the task. It involves the routines which perform the following functions:
parallel (arithmetical, logical, comparison) operations, scalar (arithmetical, logical, comparison) operations, stacks service operations, generating different types of masks (eops), data transferral between the control memory and MDA memory, communication between sequential and parallel program parts.

5.3 Compiling Parallel Control Statements

The control statements are translated in two phases. In the first phase the code for expression parts is generated, while in the second phase the code for statements is completed. Consider the following construct:

```
    USING !0:511! DO
       WHERE pa[$] < pb[$] DO
              pb[$] := pa[$] + s;    (* true-statements part  *)
       ELSE  pb[$] := pa[$];         (* false-statements part *)
       END
    END
```

The parallel Boolean expression in WHERE clause is used to calculate two new values of the eop, which are used when executing true-statements and false-statements. In general, in contrast to the corresponding scalar IF statement, both parts will be followed: in other words, both the true-statements and false-statements are executed, but on different data. The parallel Boolean expression yields a Boolean parallel array. The generation of optimized code for parallel Boolean expressions could be done in a very effective way. The resulting Boolean parallel array is held in Y-registers of associative modules. The contents of Y-registers are copied into M-registers and used as the eop for the true-statements. Then the complement of the Y-registers is done, copied into M-registers and used as the eop for the false-statements. In the case that the Boolean parallel array is FALSE (the eop is empty) the corresponding statements part is overjumped.

6. RELATED WORK

Compilers for Fortran, C, and Pascal based data parallel SIMD languages were developed for the Connection Machine ([Alb88],[RoSt86]), MasPar MP-1 (Compass compiler for a parallel Fortran) and DAP([AMT],[Per87]).

The M2PLUS project has been the first attempt to develop a compiler of a high-level data parallel language for an AP. The target AP has specific architectural features that are reflected in the data-layout, machine dependent transformations and especially in the target code generation techniques.

7. CONCLUSIONS

The AP architecture of the PCS SIMD has been designed without a high-level language and its compiler in mind, thus generating optimal code is a rather difficult challenge. In order to reduce complexity of the compiler some of the hardware features have not been taken into account. For example, the access mode utilized by the compiler in processing of parallel arrays is bit-serial and word-parallel. To utilize the entire spectrum of mixed access modes would require several data mappings in the MDA memory. One of the major problems encountered is that of handling the scalar data due to the inefficient scalar arithmetic-logical unit. Operations on parallel arrays, however, are able to be implemented in a very simple and efficient way. The only features that do not fit the architecture well are constructs which require data movements and communications among the associative modules.

Now, the compiler is able to generate code for all M2PLUS language constructs. However, a special linking program and the run-time support library are being implemented. The work has provided useful experience in the study of machine dependance with respect to a high-level parallel programming language.

REFERENCES

[Alb88] Albert E. et al.: Compiling Fortran 8x Array features for the Connection Machine Computer System. Proc. PPEALS 1988, ACM 1988.

[AMT] Introduction to FORTRAN_PLUS, AMT manual man001.04, Active Memory Technology Ltd., Reading, UK.

[BreSip89] Brezany P., Sipkova V.: M2PLUS - A Modula-2 based Parallel Programming Language and its Implementation. Proceedings of the First International Modula-2 Conference, Bled, Yugoslavia, 1989, pp.81-85.

[Gei83] Geissman L.B.: Separate Compilation in Modula-2 and the Structure of the Modula-2 Compiler on the Personal Computer Lilith. ETH Diss. Nr. 7286 Zurich, 1983.

[Jac82] Jacobi Ch.: Code Generation and the Lilith Architecture. ETH Diss. Nr. 7195 Zurich, 1982.

[Per79] Perrot R.H.: A language for array and vector processors. ACM Trans. Program. Lang. Syst., vol. 1, pp. 177-195, Oct. 1979.

[Per85] Perrot R.H. et al.: A compiler for an array and vector processing language. IEEE Trans. Softw. Eng., vol. 11, pp. 471-478, May 1985.

[Per87] Perrot R.H., Lyttle R.W., and Dhillon P.F.: The Design and Implementation of a Pascal-based Language for Array Processor Architectures. Jornal on Parallel and Distributed Computing, 4(3), pp. 266-287, 1987

[Ric84] Richter K.: Parallel Computer System SIMD. I. Plander (editor) Artificial Intelligence and Information-Control Systems of Robots, North-Holland, Amsterdam 1984, pp. 309-313.

DATA STRUCTURES FOR OPTIMIZING PROGRAMS WITH EXPLICIT PARALLELISM

Michael Wolfe, Harini Srinivasan
Oregon Graduate Institute of Science and Technology
Department of Computer Science and Engineering
19600 NW von Neumann Drive, Beaverton, OR, USA 97006

Abstract

When analyzing programs with parallel imperative constructs (e.g., cobegin/coend), standard computer intermediate representations are inadequate. This paper introduces a new relation called the *precedence relation* and new data structures called the *Parallel Control Flow Graph* and the *Parallel Precedence Graph* for programs with parallel constructs. We show how to report anomalies in parallel programs using *Parallel Precedence Graphs*. In sequential Control Flow Graphs, the precedence relation is represented by the dominance relation. With explicit parallelism, the dominance relation is not the same as the precedence relation; we discuss the significance of the precedence relation and the new data structures for analyzing programs with parallel constructs. These data structures form a concrete basis for the development of efficient algorithms for optimizing parallel programs.

1 Introduction

Parallel programming is becoming popular, and parallel extensions to programming languages are now available. For efficiency, compilers for languages with parallel constructs must still be able to perform classical code optimizations. To support this, it is important to establish an efficient compiler intermediate representation. Static Single Assignment form (SSA) is a powerful intermediate representation and an efficient platform for the optimization of sequential programs [CFR+89]. Extending SSA to parallel programs is a non-trivial task and requires the introduction of many new concepts.

We introduce Parallel Control Flow Graphs and Parallel Precedence Graphs and a new relation called the *precedence relation*. The dominance relation is the same as the precedence relation in sequential Control Flow Graphs; the two relations are not identical in Parallel Control Flow Graphs. We illustrate this using examples. We also define *parallel precedence frontiers*, the dominance frontiers for nodes in Parallel Control Flow Graphs.

Associated with Parallel Precedence Graphs are the *wait-dominance* relation and the wait-dominator tree, both of which are used in reporting anomalies in parallel programs.

Section 2 discusses Control Flow Graphs and dominance relations and defines dominance frontiers in the case of sequential programs. Section 3 describes the parallel construct considered in this paper. Section 4 illustrates the need to define the precedence relation and to redefine dominance frontiers. Section 5 defines the various new data structures introduced in this paper. Section 6 describes an application of Parallel Precedence Graphs.

2 Control Flow Graphs for sequential programs

A Control Flow Graph (CFG) is a directed graph that models program control flow. Nodes of a CFG represent the basic blocks of the program with two additional nodes, Entry and Exit. Edges in the CFG correspond to the transfers of control between basic blocks of the program. There is also an edge from Entry to any basic block where control enters the program and an edge to Exit from any basic block where control leaves the program.

Formally, we denote a Control Flow Graph as $G = \langle V, E, V_{entry}, V_{exit} \rangle$ where V denotes the nodes in the CFG, E denotes the edges and V_{entry} is the start node (in our case, Entry) and V_{exit} is the exit node (in our case Exit). Node Z is a successor of node Y if there is an edge Y → Z in the CFG. Node X is a predecessor of node Y if there is an edge X → Y in the CFG.

2.1 Dominance relation

Let G = <V, E, Entry, Exit> be a CFG with start node Entry and exit node Exit. A node X *dominates* another node Y (X dom Y) in G if every path from Entry to Y contains X. Note that Entry dominates all other nodes, and every node Y dominates itself. A node X *strictly dominates* node Y if X dom Y and X is not equal to Y.

Node W is the *immediate dominator* of Y if W dominates Y and every other strict dominator of Y also dominates W. Therefore, the immediate dominator of Y is the closest strict dominator of Y (denoted idom(Y)). In a sequential program, the immediate dominator is unique and the dominance relation can be represented by a tree rooted at Entry with an edge to every node from its immediate dominator.

```
v = 90
Parallel sections          (a)
Section A                  (a)
    v = 100                (a)
    u = 1                  (a)
    {stmt list}            (a)
Section B                  (a)
    u = 2                  (b)
    {stmt list}
Section C, Wait(A)         (c)
    {stmt list}            (d)
Section D, Wait(B,C)       (d)
    {stmt list}            (d)
Section E, Wait(D)
    {stmt list}            (e)
Section F, Wait(A)         (f)
    v = 120                (g)
    t = u                  (g)
    {stmt list}
end parallel sections      (h)
                           (i)
        (a)                (j)
                           (k)
                           (l)

                           (m)
                           (n)
                           (p)

                           (q)
                           (r)
                           (r)
                           (s)
                           (t)
                           (u)
```

```
begin
    F ← 1
    E ← 7
    G ← 0
    L ← 1
    K ← 5
    B ← 7
    Parallel sections
    Section
        if P then
            E ← F
            G ← G+1
            D(i) ← F−1
        else
            E ← F+G
            Parallel sections
            Section
                H ← E
            Section
                if Q then
                    G ← G+3
                endif
            end parallel section
        endif
    Section
        if R then
            L ← L× K
        endif
    Section
        if M then
            E ← D(j)
            D(j) ← B × 9
        endif
    end parallel section
    print B
end

        (b)
```

Figure 1: Example parallel programs

The *dominance frontier* of a node X, DF(X), is the set of all CFG nodes Z such that X dominates a predecessor of Z but does not strictly dominate Z. The rest of the paper refers to dominance frontiers as *sequential dominance frontiers*.

Lengauer and Tarjan [LET79] describe an $O(m\alpha(m,n))$ algorithm for finding dominators in a flowgraph [1].

Dominator trees are very useful data structures in code optimizations and also in developing efficient intermediate forms. Ferrante et al [FOW87] use dominators in the Reverse Control Flow Graph to find control dependences and Cytron et al [CFR+89] use dominator trees and dominance frontiers to find the Static Single Assignment intermediate form.

3 The parallel sections construct

The parallel sections construct [Par90] is similar to a cobegin-coend [BH73] or the parallel cases statement described by Allen et al [ABC+88]. The parallel sections construct is block structured and is used to specify parallel execution of identified sections of code. The parallel sections may also be nested. The sections of code must be data independent, except where an appropriate synchronization mechanism is used. If a variable is assigned in two different sections, the compiler may need to detect an anomaly. In the case of array variables, data dependence analysis is essential to report anomalies. Synchronization between parallel sections is realized using Wait clauses. An example of a parallel sections construct using Wait clauses is shown in figure 1.a. Each {stmt list} contains one or more statements and execution within a section is sequential.

Consider the parallel program in figure 1.a. Assuming that there are no other assignments to variables v and u in the program, the value of u used at section F is indeterminate. Since sections A and B execute in parallel, the variable u may be modified twice before section F starts execution. On the other hand, section F could execute before section B and the value of u used in F will then be the value of u assigned in section A, i.e., 1.

---

[1] $\alpha(i,j)$ is the functional inverse of Ackermann's function defined as follows:

$A(i,0) = 0;$

$A(0,j) = 2;$ for $j \geq 1$

$A(i,1) = A(i-1,2)$ for $i \geq 1$

$A(i,j) = A(i-1,A(i,j-1))$ for $i \geq 1, j \geq 2.$

```
X = 1                  X = 1
Y = 1                  Y = 1
if P then              Parallel sections
    X = 2              Section
else                       X = 2
    Y = 2              Section
endif                      Y = 2
Z = X+Y                end parallel sections

  2.(a)                   2.(b)
```

Figure 2: Example programs

To circumvent such non-determinism in the program, we follow *copy-in/copy-out* semantics in the following manner. When control flow enters a parallel block, every parallel section forked will get a local copy of the values of variables in memory. If there are no Wait clauses, then an update is done to the global copy at the coend node. Of course, if there are two assignments to the same variable within the parallel block, an anomaly should be reported. In the presence of Wait clauses, we need to propagate the modified local values to the *waiting* sections. Again, if a variable is assigned in more than one section for which another section is waiting, then it is an anomaly and should be reported.

4 Example

Consider the programs in figures 2.a and 2.b. The corresponding Control Flow Graphs are shown in figures 3.a and 3.b respectively. In figure 3.a, nodes c and d do not dominate node e. This is because nodes c and d do not always appear on the path from Entry to node e.

In the case of figure 3.b, nodes r and s do not dominate node t. However, we know that both r and s must precede node t in execution. Even though the dominance relation does not exist between nodes r and t and nodes s and t, there does exist a precedence relation.

Consider the parallel program in figure 1.b. The corresponding Control Flow Graph (using the definition in section 2) is given in figure 4. By definition of the dominance relation, nodes c, m and q do not dominate node t. This is because nodes c, m and q

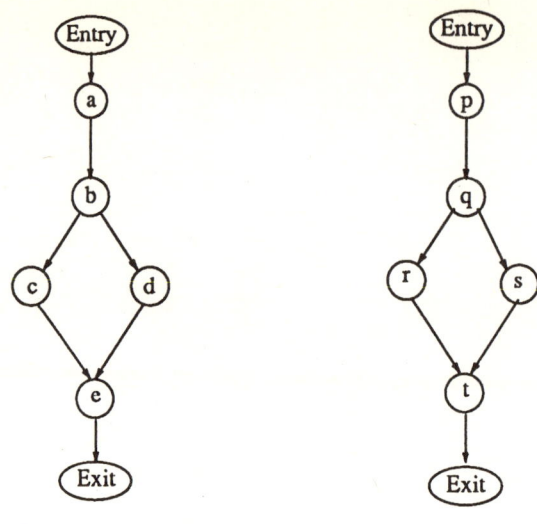

Figure 3.a   Figure 3.b

Figure 3: Control Flow Graphs for the programs in figures 2.a and 2.b

do not appear on all paths from Entry to node t. However, the semantics of the parallel construct considered here requires that nodes c, m and q *must all execute* before node t. In other words, the execution of c, m and q *must precede* node t.

Similarly, node l, p and s do not dominate node t, but *must precede* node t in execution. It is clear from the definitions in section 2.1 that a dominator tree cannot convey the precedence relation explained above.

Since we are interested in doing Static Single Assignment for parallel programs by extending the algorithms in [CFR+89], we find a need to compute dominance frontiers in programs having parallel constructs.

5 Parallel Control Flow Graphs and Parallel Precedence Graphs

A *Parallel Control Flow Graph* is a CFG which may have a new type of node called *supernode* or *parallel block*. A parallel block essentially represents the parallel construct

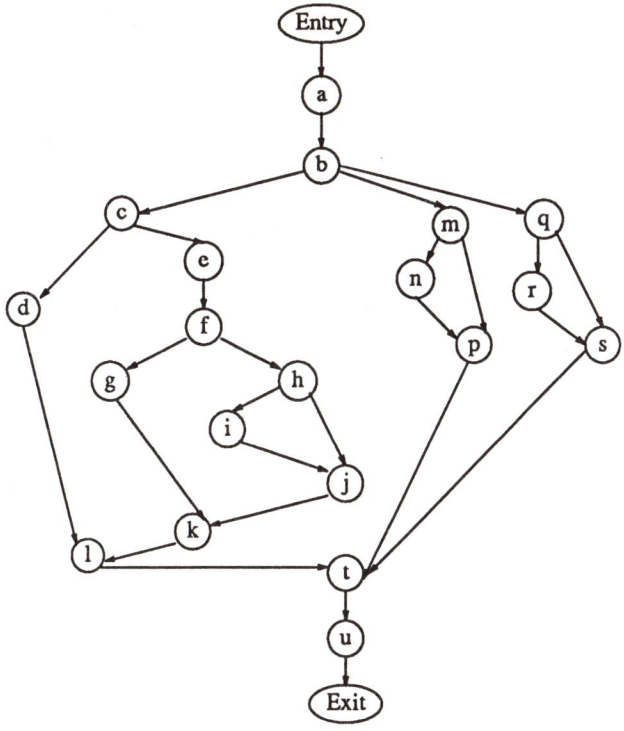

Figure 4: CFG for the parallel program in figure 1.b

described in Section 3.

A Wait clause in a parallel block imposes a dependence (called *wait-dependence*) between the waiting section and the sections specified in the wait clause. We introduce a new data structure called the *Parallel Precedence Graph* (PPG) that represents a parallel block. Nodes in the PPG represent the various sections in the parallel block with two additional nodes, cobegin and coend. The edges in the PPG (also called *wait-dependence arcs*) are those representing the Wait clauses. For example, the PPG for the program in figure 1.a in shown in figure 5. In the absence of any wait clause in the parallel block, we have a degenerate case where there are only two sets of wait-dependence arcs, one from the cobegin node to the sections in the parallel block and other from the different sections to the coend node.

Formally a PCFG is defined as the graph $G = \langle V, E, S_{entry}, S_{exit} \rangle$ where V, E, S_{entry} and S_{exit} are defined as follows :

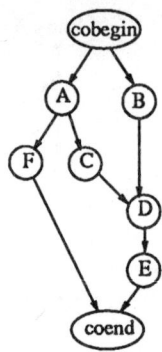

Figure 5: PPG for the program in figure 1.a

V = { a | a is either a basic block or a parallel block}

E = { a → b | a,b ∈ V }

Edges represent sequential flow of control in the parallel program.

$S_{entry} \in V$ is the start node of the PCFG.

$S_{exit} \in V$ is the exit node of the PCFG.

A parallel block is represented by a PPG, which is formally defined as a graph $G_p = \langle V_p, E_p, P_{entry}, P_{exit} \rangle$ where

V_p = {N | N is either the cobegin node, coend node or a section in the parallel block }

Each section in a PPG is again represented by a PCFG with entry node p_entry (marking the entry into that section) and exit node p_exit (marking the exit from that section).

E_p is the set of edges or wait-dependence arcs in the PPG.

$P_{entry} \in V_p$ is the cobegin node

$P_{exit} \in V_p$ is the coend node.

If the PCFG corresponds to a section in the parallel block, S_{entry} and S_{exit} are the p_entry and p_exit nodes respectively; otherwise, they are the Entry and Exit nodes. The PCFG of the parallel program in figure 1.b is shown in figure 6.

5.1 Precedence relations and parallel precedence frontiers

A node X precedes node Y (X and Y are both nodes in the same PCFG, nodes in distinct PCFG's or nodes in a PPG) if the execution of X precedes the execution of Y. The following observations can be made about the precedence relation:

- If X represents a basic block in a parallel block and Y represents a basic block after the parallel block, X and Y are nodes in disjoint graphs. Nonetheless, we want to be able to define a precedence relation between them.

- If a parallel block X precedes a node Y in the PCFG, not all the basic blocks within X must precede Y. For example, in figure 6, P2 precedes node l but node i within P2 does not precede l.

- Let X and Y be nodes in a PPG that represent two sections in a parallel construct. X precedes Y if the p_exit node in X must execute before the p_entry node in Y. This is true when there are Wait clauses in the parallel program. In the parallel program in figure 1.a, section A precedes section C because the p_exit for A in the PCFG of this program will execute before the p_entry node in C.

- In the case of sequential CFG's the dominance and precedence relations are the same. This is evident from the example in figure 2.a.

Definition

The **parallel precedence frontier** of a node X in a PCFG is defined as follows:

If X does not dominate p_exit (the exit node in the closest enclosing Parallel Control Glow Graph) then

$$PPF(X) = SDF(X)$$

If X dominates p_exit then

$$PPF(X) = SDF(X) \cup PPF(P_x)$$

where SDF(X) is the sequential dominance frontier of X, defined within the closest PCFG, G_x, enclosing X; SDF(X) is defined between nodes and supernodes in G_x and does not consider nodes within supernodes,

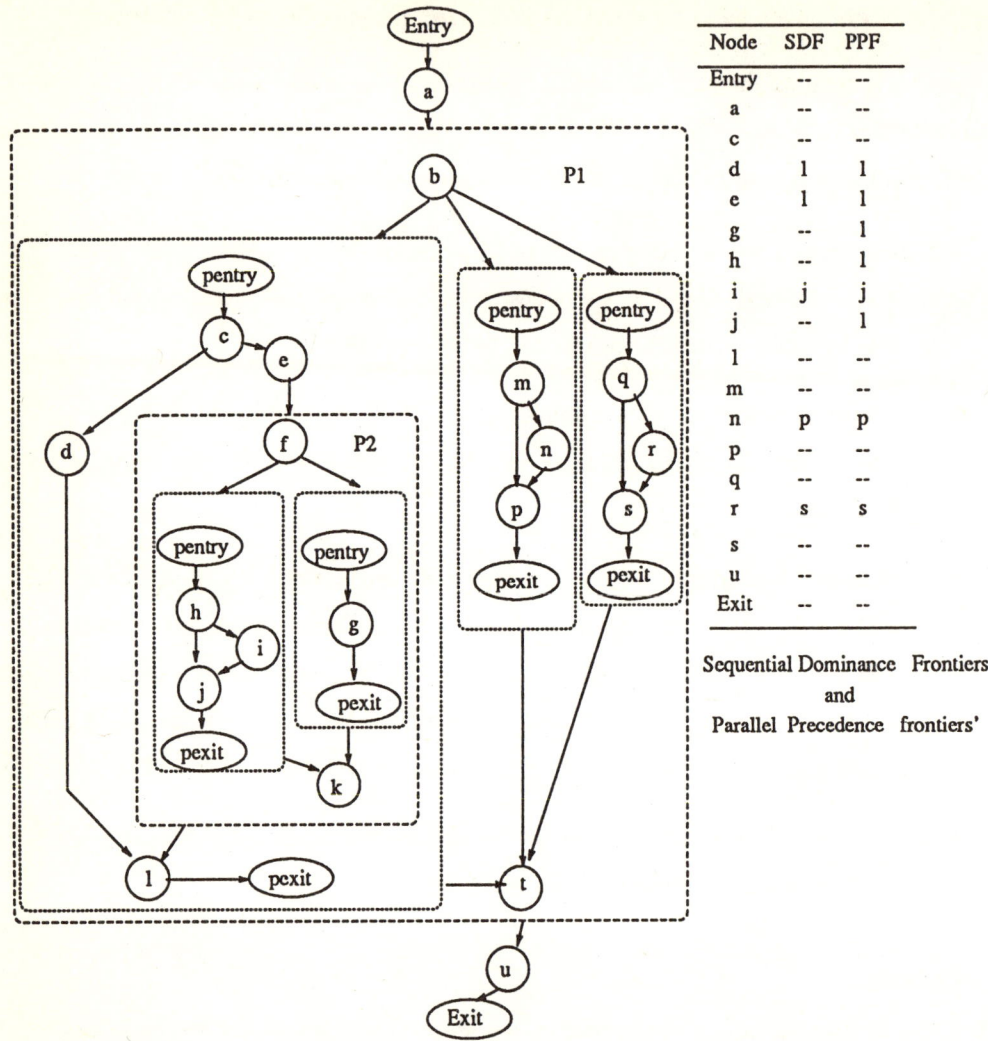

Figure 6: PCFG for the program in figure 1.b

and P_x is the closest parallel block enclosing the basic block represented by X.

For example, in figure 6, the sequential dominance frontier of node j, SDF(j), is ϕ. Since j dominates p_exit, the parallel precedence frontier of node j is PPF(j) = SDF(j) $\cup$ PPF(P2) = $\{l\}$. Similarly, the parallel dominance frontier of nodes l, p and s is the parallel precedence frontier of the enclosing parallel block, P1 ie., the empty set. This is because P1 is the outermost parallel block and PPF(P1) = SDF(P1) = ϕ.

The parallel precedence frontiers are used to do Static Single Assignment in parallel programs. We do not, however, discuss SSA here as it is the topic of a subsequent paper.

5.2 Wait-dominance

We define a new relation between the different nodes in a Parallel Precedence Graph called *wait-dominance*.

1. **Wait-dominance** – A node X in a PPG wait-dominates a node Y (X wdom Y) if X appears on all paths from the fork node to Y.

   The wait-dominance relation is reflexive and transitive. The *immediate wait-dominator* of Y in the PPG is the closest wait-dominator X of Y such that Y $\neq$ X.

   It is clear that wait-dominance is the dominance relation in the PPG; in the former we are considering sections of the parallel block. When there are no wait clauses, the wait-dominator tree is of depth one. Figure 7 gives the wait-dominator tree for the PPG in figure 5.

2. **Wait-dominance Frontier** – The wait-dominance frontier of a node X in the PPG is defined as follows

   $WDF(X) = \{Y \mid \exists P \ni (P \in Pred(Y) \wedge X \text{ wdom } P \wedge X \text{ does not strictly wdom } Y)\}$

   In our example in figure 7, the wait-dominance frontiers of C and B is $\{D\}$; the WDF's of D,E and F is $\{coend\}$; the WDF of A is $\{D, coend\}$.

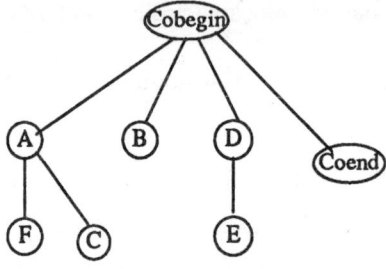

Figure 7: Wait dominator tree for the PPG in figure 5

6 Reporting anomalies in parallel programs

An application of Parallel Precedence Graphs is to report anomalies in parallel programs. When a variable is assigned in more than one branch of a parallel block, an anomaly should be reported because it is not clear which value assigned to the variable will reach the coend node. How do we detect such anomalies? This is discussed in this section with relevant examples.

ψ−functions : A ψ−function for a variable signifies the merge of potentially anomalous updates of the variable. Whenever a variable is assigned in more than one branch of a parallel block that can execute concurrently, a ψ−function is placed at the merge point. In the presence of Wait clauses, a ψ−function is placed for a variable at a node if the variable is assigned in more than one predecessor of this node in the PPG. A ψ−function is of the form $v_n = \psi(v_1, v_2, \ldots, v_{n-1})$ where each v_i is a variable and the number of arguments is the number of predecessors Y of the point where the ψ−function appears in the PPG such that Y contains an assignment to the variable v or propagates an assignment to variable v. The number of arguments is always greater than one.

For example, in figure 1.b, a ψ−function is required for variable E because it is assigned in more than one section of the outer parallel sections construct. A ψ−function is required for the array variable D. Since D is a subscripted variable, determining if the ψ−function corresponds to an anomalous update calls for data dependence analysis [BC86] [WB87]. Also, in figure 1.a, a ψ−function is required for variable v at the merge point, D.

6.1 Placement of ψ functions

Algorithm 1 (figure 8) places ψ functions using the concept of wait-dominance and wait-dominator trees defined in the previous section.

We use the following data structures in the algorithm to place ψ-functions:

$\mathcal{A}(V)$: nodes where variable V is assigned.

$\mathcal{W}(N)$: wait-dominance frontiers of node N.

$\mathcal{I}(V)$: accumulates iterated wait dominators.

hasalready(N) : a boolean array to tell if $\mathcal{W}(N)$ has been added to $\mathcal{I}(V)$.

$\mathcal{P}(V)$: Accumulates the pair-wise wait-dominance frontiers of all nodes where variable V is assigned.

Wait-dominance frontiers are computed using the same algorithm for computing dominance frontiers presented in [CFR+89].

Correctness and Complexity of Algorithm 1

A ψ-function for a variable is placed at all merge nodes in the PPG of the program where two or more definitions of the variable reach. A variable may be assigned in two nodes X and Y in the PPG whose wait-dominance frontiers do not intersect. However, the paths from X to coend and Y to coend must intersect at some point in the PPG, at least at the coend node. We are interested in the parallel merge nodes along such paths since such nodes are potential candidates for ψ-functions. $\mathcal{I}(V)$ for variable V, computed in the first while loop of Algorithm 1 gives the parallel merge nodes that propagate definitions of the same variable V.

We next prove that $\mathcal{P}(V)$ gives only the set of nodes where ψ-functions are required for variable V. $W(N_i)$ in the algorithm gives the wait dominance frontier of N_i where N_i is either a node where V is defined or a parallel merge node that propagates this definition. Therefore, the intersection of the wait-dominance frontiers of two distinct nodes N_i and N_j in $\mathcal{I}(V)$ gives the set of nodes (possibly empty) where two distinct definitions of V reach. These nodes are parallel merge nodes by definition of wait-dominance frontiers. Hence, a ψ-function can be placed here. Therefore, the set $\mathcal{P}(V)$ gives the nodes where ψ-functions must be placed.

```
for each variable V do
    hasalready(*) = 0
    ψ_complete = False
    $\mathcal{I}(V) = \mathcal{A}(V)$
    /* Compute iterated wait dominance frontier */
    while (ψ_complete = False) do
        ψ_complete = True
        for each $N_i \in \mathcal{I}(V) \ni$ hasalready($N_i$) = 0 do
            hasalready($N_i$) = 1
            if $\mathcal{W}(N_i) \not\subseteq \mathcal{I}(V)$ then
                add $\mathcal{W}(N_i)$ to $\mathcal{I}(V)$
                ψ_complete = False
            endif
        end
    end

    $\mathcal{P}(V) = \phi$
    for each $N_i, N_j \in \mathcal{I}(V)$ and $N_i \neq N_j$ do
        $\mathcal{P}(V) = \mathcal{P}(V) \cup (\mathcal{W}(N_i) \cap \mathcal{W}(N_j))$
    end
    Place ψ–function at all nodes in $\mathcal{P}(V)$
end
```

Figure 8: Algorithm 1

In order to show that $\mathcal{P}(V)$ gives exactly the set of nodes where ψ–functions are required for variable V, suppose there exists a node N such that $N \notin \mathcal{P}(V)$ and N is a parallel merge node where two or more distinct definitions of V reach. Since N is a parallel merge node where two or more distinct definitions of V reach, there should be two or more nodes $N_1, N_2 \ldots N_k$ such that V has distinct definitions in these nodes. Therefore, there have to be paths $p_1, p_2 \ldots p_k$ from $N_1, N_2 \ldots N_k$ to the coend node such that $p_1, p_2 \ldots p_k$ intersect at N. Therefore, by definition of $\mathcal{I}(V)$, either $N \in \mathcal{I}(V)$ or there are parallel merge nodes along this path which are in $\mathcal{I}(V)$. In either case, the pair-wise intersection of the wait-dominance frontiers of the nodes in $\mathcal{I}(V)$ must contain N. Hence N must be a node in $\mathcal{P}(V)$; a contradiction to the supposition.

For the algorithm to halt it is necessary that the while loop terminate. The while loop *will* eventually terminate because the wait-dominance frontier is a finite set of nodes.

Time Complexity

The time required to process a single variable using Algorithm 1 is proportional to the time to compute the iterated wait-dominance frontiers plus the time to compute the pairwise intersection of the wait-dominance frontiers. The former takes $O(N^2)$ time, where N is the number of nodes in the PPG, since adding nodes to I(V) is a union operation. The latter takes $O(N^2)$ time. Therefore, the overall algorithm takes $O(N^2)$ time.

Referring to figures 1.a and 5, $\mathcal{A}(u)$ is {A,B}, $\mathcal{I}(u)$ is {A,B,D,coend} and $\mathcal{P}(u)$ is {D,coend}.

7 Related Work

Though work has been done on parallelizing transformations in parallel programs [MPC90], little work has been done on classical optimizations for parallel code. Midkiff et al [MP90] discuss the issues in performing loop transformations and classical code optimizations on parallel programs. Analysis of the parallel program to report non-determinism uses an *instance level conflict graph* that has statement instances as nodes and directed program arcs and undirected conflict edges. The analysis proceeds by finding cycles in the graph that give rise to races. For analyzing loops, statement level conflict graphs are used. They, however, do not discuss a representation for performing classical code optimizations. The data structures defined in this paper are used to compute Static Single Assignment form which has been proved to be an efficient intermediate representation for performing classical code optimizations.

Extensive work has been done in detecting and reporting races in parallel programs. Race detection can either be done at compile time (static) or can be dynamic. Callahan et al [CKS90] use a data structure called *Synchronized Control Flow Graph* that has two kinds of sub-graphs; the Control Flow Graph and the Synchronized Flow Graph (SFG). The nodes in the SFG represent basic blocks with only one post and wait statement, and edges represent synchronization. Synchronization in the parallel programs considered is achieved using post and wait statements. The problem addressed in their paper is to statically verify which data-dependences in a parallel program are potential sources of non-determinism, in the presence of event variable synchronization. The paper assumes that a sequential execution of the program is defined and considers both parallel cases and parallel loops. Balasundaram and Kennedy [BK89] use a data structure similar to the Synchronized Control Flow Graph called the Program Execution Graph to detect potential races at compile time. The analysis proceeds by building a co-graph whose nodes represent races and there is an arc from node X to node Y iff there is no path between X and Y in the corresponding Program Execution Graph. *Data Windows* are used to detect races.

Dinning and Schonberg [DS90] describe an algorithm, called *trace cycling* for detecting *access anomalies*. The algorithm records read and write events in *access histories* that are associated with monitored variables. The trace cycling algorithm uses the *Partial Order Execution Graph* that captures Lamport's *happens before* relation [Lam78]. Their approach follows dynamic race detection technique since program execution is monitored to detect access anomalies.

Allen and Padua [AP87] use a combination of static and dynamic techniques. Their method of detecting races is done in three phases — compile time detection (static analysis) followed by run time *tracing* and *trace analysis*. The paper defines the "hides relation" that is used to indicate the possibility of one race hiding another race. The hides relation is represented by a *hides graph* which is used to direct the tracing.

Our work focusses on detecting anomalies (there are no races in the parallel programs we consider since we have assumed copy-in/copy-out semantics). Since we assume a very simple form of synchronization (we don't consider event synchronization),, the PPG is a DAG and the analysis used to detect anomalies is more simple and incomparable to the related work mentioned in the previous paragraphs.

8 Conclusion

The dominance relation is a very important concept used in code optimization algorithms and in developing efficient intermediate forms. We observe that the dominance relation does not convey the control flow properties of parallel programs as it does for sequential programs. The precedence relation is an important concept for analyzing parallel programs. We have not discussed SSA here. SSA is discussed in detail in [CFR+89] and we have extended dominance frontiers used in the algorithms to compute SSA to take parallel constructs into account. Parallel precedence frontiers have been implemented in our prototype compiler, **Nascent**. The implementation has been tested using many non-trivial explicitly parallel test programs. Experimental results, however, are not meaningful due to the lack of benchmarks for such programs.

Anomalies in parallel programs may be very common and it is desirable to report anomalies at compile time. We discuss an efficient method of reporting anomalies in parallel programs. Algorithm 1 is being implemented in **Nascent**.

References

[ABC+87] Frances Allen, Michael Burke, Philippe Charles, Ron Cytron, and Jeanne Ferrante. An overview of the PTRAN analysis system for multiprocessing. In Elias N. Houstis, Theodore S. Papatheodorou, and Constantine D. Polychronopoulos, editors, *Supercomputing: 1st International Conf.*, volume 297 of *Lecture Notes in Computer Science*, pages 194–211. Springer-Verlag, Berlin, 1987.

[ABC+88] Frances Allen, Michael Burke, Philippe Charles, Ron Cytron, and Jeanne Ferrante. An overview of the PTRAN analysis system for multiprocessing. *J. Parallel and Distributed Computing*, 5(5):617–640, October 1988. (update of [ABC+87]).

[AP87] Todd R. Allen and David A. Padua. Debugging Fortran on a shared memory machine. In Santaj K. Sahni, editor, *Proc. 1987 International Conf. on Parallel Processing*, pages 721–727, St. Charles, IL, August 1987.

[BC86] Michael Burke and Ron Cytron. Interprocedural dependence analysis and parallelization. In *Proc. SIGPLAN '86 Symp. on Compiler Construction*, pages 162–175, Palo Alto, CA, June 1986.

[BH73] Per Brinch Hansen. *Operating Systems Principles*, pages 57–59. Automatic Computation. Prentice-Hall, 1973.

[BK89] Vasanth Balasundaram and Ken Kennedy. Compile-time detection of race conditions in a parallel program. In *Proc. 3rd International Conference on Supercomputing*, pages 175–185, June 1989.

[CFR+89] Ron Cytron, Jeanne Ferrante, Barry K. Rosen, Mark N. Wegman, and Kenneth Zadeck. An efficient method of computing static single assignment form. In *Conf. Record 16th Annual ACM Symp. on Principles of Programming Languages*, pages 25–35, Austin, TX, January 1989.

[CKS90] David Callahan, Ken Kennedy, and Jaspal Subhlok. Analysis of event synchronization in a parallel programming tool. In *Second ACM SIGPLAN Symposium on Principles and Practice of Parallel Programming* [PPO90], pages 21–30.

[DS90]   Anne Dinning and Edith Schonberg. An empirical comparison of monitoring algorithms for access anomaly detection. In *Second ACM SIGPLAN Symposium on Principles and Practice of Parallel Programming* [PPO90], pages 1–10.

[FOW87]   Jeanne Ferrante, Karl J. Ottenstein, and Joe D. Warren. The program dependence graph and its use in optimization. *ACM Trans. on Programming Languages and Systems*, 9(3):319–349, July 1987.

[Lam78]   Leslie Lamport. Time, clocks and the ordering of events in a distributed system. *CACM*, 1(21):558–564, July 1978.

[LET79]   Thomas Lengauer and Robert Endre Tarjan. A fast algorithm for finding dominators in a flow graph. *ACM Trans. on Programming Languages and Systems*, 1(1):121–141, July 1979.

[MP90]   Samuel P. Midkiff and David A. Padua. Issues in the optimization of parallel programs. In David Padua, editor, *Proc. 1990 International Conf. on Parallel Processing*, volume II, pages 105–113, St. Charles, IL, August 1990. Penn State Press.

[MPC90]   Samuel P. Midkiff, David A. Padua, and Ron Cytron. Compiling programs with user parallelism. In David Gelernter, Alexandru Nicolau, and David A. Padua, editors, *Languages and Compilers for Parallel Computing*, Research Monographs in Parallel and Distributed Computing, pages 402–422. MIT Press, Boston, 1990.

[Par90]   Parallel Computing Forum. *PCF Fortran*, April 1990.

[PPO90]   *Second ACM SIGPLAN Symposium on Principles and Practice of Parallel Programming*, Seattle, Washington, March 1990. ACM Press.

[WB87]   Michael Wolfe and Utpal Banerjee. Data dependence and its application to parallel processing. *International J. Parallel Programming*, 16(2):137–178, April 1987.

MODULA-S

A Language to exploit two dimensional Parallelism [*]

W. Diestelkamp, H. Bi, A. Böttcher

GMD-TUB Research Center for Innovative Computer Systems and Technology

Hardenbergplatz 2

1000 Berlin 12, Germany

Abstract:

With the appearance of parallel and vector architectures in the late seventies, a growing need arose for means to efficiently program these machines to exploit the underlying parallelism. Two main streams tried to solve this problem: automatic parallelization or vectorization and new languages or language extensions, that can explicitly express parallelity. While the problem of automatic vectorization was partly solved in the last few years, automatic parallelization still remains a topic of current research. A few parallel languages were introduced recently, including FORTRAN-90, which support one dimensional parallelism. In many elementary numerical algorithms however, explicit parallelism is two-dimensional. MODULA-S was developed to exploit parallelism on n-dimensional structures by some sophisticated access patterns, that can be mapped to different hardwares very efficiently. MODULA-2 was extended by only a few, but very efficient constructs to overcome the limitations of sequential programming languages. The normal programming process of transforming a parallel algorithm into sequential code and then reparallelizing this program, probably with some loss, can be shortcut using our explicitly parallel language. The most striking disadvantage of using a new language, namely the need to reprogram existing programs, can be overcome by a source-to-source transformer, that even makes the detected parallelity of the algorithms visible and gives the programmer the opportunity, to enhance it by hand by producing readable source code.

1 Introduction

Most of the numerical algorithms exhibit a high degree of *explicit data structure parallelism*. Exploiting this parallelism in numerical applications led to the development of parallel architectures. Today's numerical programming languages are still sequential and cannot express the explicit parallelism of mathematical formulas and algorithms directly. Parallelity is mapped onto sequential control (loops), and must be retrieved to match a parallel architecture. An important progress in programming languages must follow the development of innovative parallel hardware architectures such as SIMD and MIMD systems.

1.1 Requirements of numerical applications.

Most of the important numerical methods exhibit a high degree of explicit parallelism: the algorithms for multigrid methods [STÜT82], Gauss eliminations and other solvers of linear equations are defined on matrices or even n-dimensional bodies, which are represented in the programming language as large, homogeneous, n-dimensional **data structures**. Similar calculations are performed on all elements of a structure or on a subset of it. The access to a

---

[*] This work was partly sponsored by the German Ministry for Research and Technology

structure or parts of it obey to regular functions, which e.g. select rows, columns, diagonals, rectangular and triangular submatrices or grids of an original matrix or other structure. Mostly the transformations on the elements of structures are independent, and are well suited for parallel execution on SIMD or MIMD computer architectures. We recognize that fact very clearly in the block-matrix algorithms where the elements of a matrix are matrices again [SCHRE]. The parallelism can be stated as one-dimensional and two-dimensional in most of these methods by the following principles [BI]:

(1) One-dimensional explicit parallelism can be found in operations on straight or diagonal subvectors with a stride from an n-dimensional array.

(2) Two-dimensional explicit parallelism can be found in operations on rectangular, triangular, and parallelogram submatrices from an n-dimensional array with the following variations:

- Submatrices may be accessed with a stride between the elements in a row or in a column;
- Submatrices may be formed by accessing a matrix not only in the row-major order but also in the column-major order.
- Submatrices may be formed by expanding a vector as a row or as a column.

2   Limitations of programming languages.

Even though most numerical algorithms are intrinsically parallel, the common programming languages are based on the Single Instruction - Single Data (SISD) principle of the classical von-Neumann computer architecture. All information about data independencies of data transformations and about the intrinsic parallelism is lost and often the structure information is destroyed by an early mapping of structures to the linear, one-dimensional storage scheme of the computer hardware.

There are two ways to resemble the change of computer architectures to the SIMD and MIMD principles. The first stems from the desire to keep up software continuity: numerical application programs are still written in FORTRAN, existing FORTRAN programs are still in use. To map these sequential programs to the new machines, big efforts had to be made in the construction of vectorizers and parallelizers which try to adapt the sequential programs to the new computer facilities [ABFC87,KKLW80,GERN89 etc.]. They have to recover the structure of data sets from variable declarations and must do elaborate dependency analysis on nested loop constructs and transformations of the program code to reextract existing implicit parallelism and to make it explicit for the underlying hardware architecture.

While state-of-the-art vectorizers appear to be doing a good work for a variety of program structures, parallelizers are but a topic of the current research work; very often it is necessary to modify sequential programs in order to give the compiler a chance to detect the underlying parallelism.

The other way to react on the new needs has been the development of new languages or language extensions which could express the parallelism of the underlying hardware concepts adequately.

Up to now very few languages are able to express parallelism by appropriate language constructs, e.g. APL, CLU, ALGOL68, ACTUS. FORTRAN-90 [METC,F8X] is the overdue approach to overcome the sequential programming style and will slowly change the 'sequential way of thinking' of application programmers. It introduces parallel facilities and will probably find a wide acceptance in future numerical programming.

Nevertheless FORTRAN-90 still is a one-dimensional approach: it does not support the requirements of two-dimensional parallel algorithms. With its language constructs it is impossible to select important substructures as diagonals, triangular matrices and others, without the use of sequential loops again.

3 Explicit Parallelism in Algorithms

Explicit parallelism is defined by [GIL87] as a transformation on a set of data such that (i) all data items are subjected to the same operation and (ii) by the very nature of the transformation there exist no data dependencies between the operations performed on the data items.

Parallelism is said to be n-dimensional explicitly parallel, if each operand of the explicitly parallel transformation forms an n-dimensional array.

For example in a two-dimensional array A[0 .. 99, 0 .. 99], the operation described by the following FOR statement

```
FOR I := 0 TO 99 DO
    A[1, I] := A[1, I] + 1;
END;
```

is one-dimensional whereas

```
FOR I := 0 TO 98 BY 2 DO
    FOR J := 0 TO 98 BY 2 DO
        A[I, J] := 1;
    END;
END;
```

is two-dimensional explicitly parallel.

By inspecting two typical numerical algorithms, we shall demonstrate the necessity of some of the different access patterns we propose later.

Our first example is the matrix multiplication. In MODULA-2, the standard algorithm for matrix multiplication is written as follows:

```
FOR I := 1 TO n DO
    FOR J := 1 TO n DO
        FOR K := 1 TO n DO
            C[I, J] := C[I, J] + A[I, K] * B[K, J];
        END;
    END;
END;
```

Clearly the inner loop must be executed sequentially because of data dependencies. If the loop over K is moved to the middle or even the outer position, more parallelism is exhibited:

```
FOR K := 1 TO n DO
    FOR I := 1 TO n DO
        FOR J := 1 TO n DO
            C[I, J] := C[I, J] + A[I, K] * B[K, J];
        END;
    END;
END;
```

In this code the two inner loops over I and J can be evaluated in parallel for all n^2 elements of C, where the operation is an element-by-element multiplication of an n*n matrix. Thus the algorithm is two-dimensional explicitly parallel.

To express this parallelism in a program we need to formulate patterns that multiply access a single row or a single column of a matrix.

In many applications matrix operations are performed on symmetric matrices. By performing operations only on lower or upper triangular matrices and yielding a symmetric result matrix, half of the operations can be saved.

The following fragment comes from a program to compute pressures and flow rates in a pipe network:

```
FOR I := 1 TO N DO
    FOR J := 1 TO I DO
        IF (I <> J) AND (NOT (INCID (I, J))) THEN
            T [I, J] := (P[I] - P[J]);
            Q[I, J] := T[I, J] / SQRT (C[I, J] * ABS (T[I, J]));
            Q[J, I] := - Q[I, J];
        END;
    END;
END;
```

The code could be executed in parallel under a condition mask over the I and J loops. The required access patterns are triangular submatrix in row-major and column-major order and triangular submatrices expanded from a vector as a row or column.

For an elaborate case study we refer the reader to [BI].

3.1 Access Patterns

Apart from the parallel operation on data explicit parallelism has the important feature of the data formation which is represented by the access patterns in array processing. Access patterns include subvectors, subvectors with stride or diagonal subvectors for one dimensional explicit parallelism, and rectangular submatrices, rectangular submatrices with stride, in column-major order, as expansion of a single row or column, triangular submatrices, and parallelogram matrices.

In regard to a given hardware, we can say that to implement a certain access pattern we need it to be able to "sample" the storage representation of an array in a certain mode.

In the following section we'll list 12 different sampling modes that can implement all the necessary access patterns.

3.2 Sampling Modes

The typical sampling modes are summarized as follows [GIL82, ERC]:

(1) **Indexing** selects those elements, whose indices are specified in an index vector,

(2) **Masking** selects those elements, whose corresponding bit in a bitvector is 1,

(3) **Sequence sampling** extracts a contiguous subsequence according to a specified start and length,

(4) **Stride sampling** selects a specified number of elements. It starts at a specified start index and chooses other elements equidistantly,

(5) **Multiple Sequence stride** selects elements sequence by sequence with a specified skip,

(6) **Incremental Sequence Sampling** selects elements sequence by sequence with incre-

ment in sequence lengths and decrement in skips between sequences,

(7) **Decremental Sequence sampling** selects elements sequence by sequence with decrement in sequence length and increment in skips between sequences,

(8) **Multiple Stride sampling** is defined as a combination of several Stride sampling modes, with a fixed skip between the stride sequences,

(9) **Incremental Stride sampling** is defined as a sampling of several stride sequences with increment in sequence length and decrement in skip between sequences,

```
Multiple-Stride( <   1   2   3   4   5
                     6   7   8   9  10
                    11  12  13  14  15 >,   start = 1, take = 2, stride = 2, step = 3, length = 6)
               = < 1 3 6 8 11 13 >.          (multiple columns)
Incremental-Sequence(<1   2   3   4   5
                      6   7   8   9  10
                     11  12  13  14  15 >,  start = 1, take = 1++, step = 5--, length = 6)
               = < 1 6 7 11 12 13 >.         (lower left triangular submatrix)
Decremental-Sequence (<1   2   3   4   5
                       6   7   8   9  10
                      10  12  13  14  15 >, start = 1, take = 5--, step = 2++, length = 12)
               = < 1 2 3 4 5 7 8 9 10 13 14 15 >  (upper right triangular submatrix)
Decremental-Unit(<   1   2   3   4   5
                     6   7   8   9  10
                    11  12  13  14  15>,    start = 1, take = 5--, step = 5, length = 9)
               = < 1 1 1 1 6 6 6 11 11 >     (multiple elements, decremented)
```

Figure 1. .Examples of sampling modes

(10) **Decremental Stride sampling** is defined as a a sampling of several strides with decrement in sequence lengths and increment in skips,

(11) **Incremental Unit sampling** consists of several sequences, each of which is formed by duplicating the same element, with increment in sequence length and a fixed skip between selected elements,

(12) **Decremental Unit sampling** consists of several sequences formed by duplication of one element, with decreasing length and fixed skip.

A partial relation can be setup among the sampling modes in the sense that mode A is a "submode" of mode B if mode A can be implemented by mode B. Figure 2. lists the relation among 10 sampling modes. Indexing and masking can be viewed as a "supermode" of all other modes, as by appropriate construction of index or bitvectors it is possible to implement any access pattern.

```
Sequence ⊂ Stride ⊂ Multiple-Sequence ⊂ Multiple-Stride
Incremental-Sequence ⊂ Incremental-Stride
Decremental-Sequence ⊂ Decremental-Stride
Incremental-Unit
```

Figure 2. Relations among Sampling modes

4 Design of MODULA-S

In our work, we tried to overcome the restrictions of other languages as stated above by introducing universal data-structure access patterns into a language. The language we used was MODULA-2 [WIRTH], partly because of its clear and well structured typing mechanism, partly because of practical reasons. Anyway, the concepts we introduced could as well be fitted into any other similar language like FORTRAN etc.

An important goal was to keep the strong static typing concept of MODULA-2. Any object in MODULA-2 has a type, and types of objects can be determined at compile-time; this guaranties, that no type-error can occur at runtime. This feature was to be preserved in order to keep an upward compatibility.

4.1 Structures and their Shapes

Stemming from the "occurrence equivalence" used for type compatibility checking in MODULA-2, it seems difficult to make arrays and subarrays compatible. For this and for the reason of expressing parallelism in MODULA-S explicitly, we introduce a new object attribute: Explicit parallelism in MODULA-S can only be exploited on *explicitly parallel arrays*, so called *Structures*. In addition to an object's type, the new concept of shape is introduced as follows:

- Any object of MODULA-2 has the shape <1> (or *scalar shape*),
- parallel arrays of rank 1 have the shape <length>
- parallel arrays of rank n have the shape
   <length-of-dimension-1, ... , length-of-dimension-n>

Note that by this definition, MODULA-2 arrays have the shape <1>.

Type compatibility in MODULA-S is the same as in MODULA-2, shape compatibility is defined as follows:

given two shapes s_1 = <$n_1, n_2, ... n_t$> and s_2 = <$m_1, m_2, ... m_s$> with rank (s_1) = t and rank (s_2) = s, s_1 and s_2 are shape compatible iff t = s and n_i = m_i for all i <= 1 <= t. In order to be compatible it is not only necessary for two objects to have the same type but also the same shape with one exception: Any structure is compatible to a scalar object of the same type[*].

4.2 Static parallel Arrays

A static parallel array is a structure whose shape is fixed. It is declared as

   StaticStructure =
   STRUCTURE "[" extent "]" { ", [" extent "]" } OF qualident.

   extent = integer.

"StaticStructure" declares a parallel array like a variable; its type is qualident, its shape is <extent, ..., extent>. The shape is thus statically determined.

4.3 Conformant parallel Arrays

A conformant structure is a palrallel array as a parameter or local object for some function

---

[*] In this case, the scalar will be expanded to fit the structures shape.

whose shape is determined by the shape of the actual parameters for this function:

ConformantStructure =
STRUCTURE "[" FormalExtent "]" { ", [" FormalExtent "]" } OF qualident.
FormalExtent = ident.

```
VAR A : STRUCTURE [10], [20] OF REAL;
VAR B : STRUCTURE [20], [10] OF REAL;
VAR C : STRUCTURE [10], [10] OF REAL;
PROCEDURE MatMul (
    X : STRUCTURE [I], [J] OF REAL;
    Y : STRUCTURE [J], [I] OF REAL) :
         STRUCTURE [I], [I] OF REAL;
VAR B : STRUCTURE [I], [I] OF REAL;
BEGIN
    ...
    RETURN (B);
END MatMul;
...
C := MatMul (A, B); ...
```

Figure 3. Examples for Structure Declarations

The conformant structure has the type "qualident" and a shape <FormalExtent, ... , FormalExtent>, where each formal extent is implicitly passed as the shape of the actual parameters; in a formal parameter list references can be made between different formal extents. Examples for declaration and use of structures are given in figure 3; by the declaration of the formal parameter X for MatMul, the identifiers I and J are implicitly created and used for conformance checks later; note that I and J are not variables that can be accessed as identifiers in statements[*]. The declaration of a structure object A implicitly creates special identifiers A_<n>, where n is a constant; A_<n> is the upper bound of A in the n-th dimension, while the lower bound is always 0.

4.4 Subarrays

Of any parallel array we can select subarrays as first class objects in MODULA-S, i.e. it is possible to use subarrays as parameters, as left hand assignment operators and as function return values just like any other objects.

Subarray selection can be done in two different ways, called inner and outer selection; any subarray selection is done by the means of index sequences as defined in the next section.

4.4.1 Index Sequences

Given the lower and upper bound for each dimension of a parallel array as defined in 4.3, an index sequence is a sequence of indices 0 <= i <= A_<n>, that can take three different forms:

---

[*] The accessibility of I and J in this context would destroy the feature of *implicit* conformance checking, as I and J could be reassigned by some statement.

> VAR A : STRUCTURE [10], [10] OF INTEGER;
> (a) A or A[,] selects the whole matrix, shape is <A_1, A_2>
> (b) A[I,] selects the I-th row of A, shape <A_2>
> (c) A[,J] selects the J-th column of a, shape <A_1>
> (d) A[I,J] selects the single I,J-th element of A, shape <1>

Figure 4. Outer Selection and Shapes

(1) a section a:b:c, with a being the start index, b the end index and c the skip between indices*,

(2) an index vector consisting of scalar integer expression i_k with $0 <= i_k <= A\_<n>$ is exactly the sequence of its

4.4.2 Outer Selection

A subarray can be selected from a scalar object A as outer selection (product selection) like A[IndexSeq$_1$, IndexSeq$_2$, ..., IndexSeq$_n$];

This selects all elements, whose subscripts are in the following set:

$\{<x_1(i_1), x_2(i_2), ..., x_n(i_n)> |$
$x_k(i_k) \in IndexSeq_k(i_k)\}$, for all $1 <= k <= n$, $1 <= i_k <= m_k$,

where m_j is the length of IndexSeq$_j$ for $1 <= j <= n$.

The shape of the resulting subarray is defined as follows:

(1) The rank is the total number of sections and index vectors it contains; if it contains no sections or index vectors, its shape is <1>,

(2) the length of each dimension is the length of the corresponding section or index vector.

Through the feature defined in (1), it is possible to access subarrays with a reduced rank, as shown in figure 4.

4.4.3 Inner Selection

An inner subarray selection (associate selection) can be used to select elements, whose indices correspond in some way in different dimensions. Inner selection is defined as

A[[IndexSeq$_1$, ..., IndexSeq$_n$]]

and selects all elements, whose subscripts are in the following set:

$\{<x_1(i), x_2(i), ..., x_n(i)> |$
$x_k(i) \in IndexSeq_k(i)\}$, for all $1 <= k <= n$, $1 <= i <= m$, where m is the length of the index sequences.

All index sequences have the same length, except any sequence of length 1, which is expanded to the length of the other sequences.

The new subarray has the type of A, the rank 1 and the shape <m>.

The inner selection mechanism is a unique feature in our language, that is not introduced by other languages including FORTRAN-90; yet it is necessary to express applications, as even

---

* There are two shorthands for sections: a:b denotes a:b:1, a blank section denotes 0:A_n:1

a simple thing like a diagonal subvector cannot be expressed through outer selection. Inner selection becomes particularly interesting in connection with **formindex** statement introduced in the next section.

```
...
VAR I, J : INDEXSEQ;
...
FORMINDEX
  I := < 0, m-1>;
  J := < 0, n-1>;
END;
```

Figure 5. Matrix Transposition by Inner Selection

4.5 The Formindex Statement

The FORMINDEX statement is a concise way to generate several dependent index sequences.

In the body of a formindex statement, multiple index sequences are assigned by a section each, where a section can be defined in terms of a previous index sequence.

FORMINDEX K := <1:4> ; J := <K:4> END;

will generate the index sequences K := < 1 1 1 1 2 2 2 3 3 4 > and J := < 1 2 3 4 1 2 3 1 2 1 >, which can access an upper right triangular matrix if used in the associate selection A[[K,J]], or the upper left in A [[J,K]].

4.6 Expressions and Assignments

The concept of shape is not only applied to parallel arrays and subarrays but also to any expressions; in this way it is easy to extend MODULA-2's compatibility rules to expressions.

All the standard operators are extended to parallel objects of compatible type; the operators are applied to all corresponding elements, with no order defined.

The rules for an operator op on two objects a and b are:

(1) if shape(a) = shape(b) = s => shape(a op b) = s

(2) if shape(a) = s and shape(b) = <1> => shape(a op b) = s

(3) if shape(a) = <1> and shape(b) = s => shape(a op b) = s.

Similarly, the shape compatibility rules for assignments (including parameter passing) can be extended; b is said to be assignment compatible to be (concerning shape) if one of two conditions holds:

(1) shape(a) = shape(b) or

(2) shape(b) = <1>.

Assignments, like operations, are evaluated in parallel; i.e. no order of elements is defined for the evaluation; like in MODULA-2, the right-hand expression is evaluated before the assignment takes place.

In any case - operation or assignment - if a scalar is used in combination with parallel arrays it will be expanded to fit the demanded shape.

4.7 Standard Procedures for Structures

Some architectures allow us to perform some array operations either particularly efficiently or get a result as a side effect of some other computation. The first class contains functions like the partial sum of a vector, the inner product, the maximum/minimum or the location of the maximum/minimum. Functions like 'ALL', 'ANY' or 'COUNT' fall into the second category.

As it is not always possible to express these functions as a standard array manipulation, some standard procedures are introduced that cover the two categories.

A third category of standard procedures was introduced to convert scalar arrays to parallel arrays and vice versus. These procedures are necessary to keep up the strict distinction between ordinary arrays and structures. They do not necessarily imply any actual conversion on the hardware level, but make clear the distinction between the two different object classes.

4.8 The Where Statement

The where statement known from FORTRAN-90 was included in MODULA-S to allow masked access to parallel arrays.

A condition expression is specified in the where statement, that controls the evaluation of the corresponding parallel arrays in the where body.

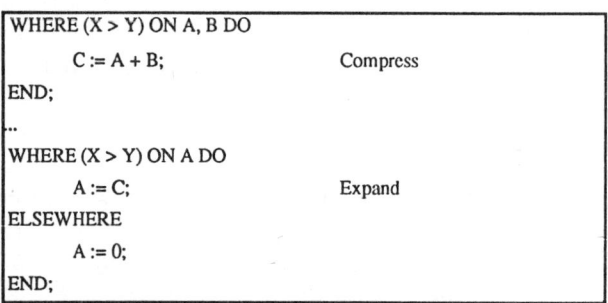

Figure 6. Compression and Decompression using the Where Statement

The ability to limit the application of the condition mask to only a part of the structures used in the body makes it possible, to operate and compress/decompress in a single operation as shown in figure 6, where A and B are added and compressed into C; X and Y have to have the same shape as A and B in the example.

5 Current Implementation

MODULA-S has been implemented for a dedicated vector hardware that directly supports most of the sampling modes; it was developed in the DATYPAR project [BOTT].

The intermediate language is an extension of a MODULA-2 intermediate language [SCHRO], which was enriched by the specific parallel features. It is a language, that describes the program in terms of an abstract architecture. Through our definition of this architecture it is on a level of abstraction, where no specific hardware, but, in its current state, a universal vector machine is described.

Through the intermediate language, that maps MODULA-S to the hardware using different levels of abstraction, it is easy, to implement MODULA-S on different architectures, parallel or superscalar; the sampling modes can always be either directly executed or emulated by the hardware.

6 Conclusions

Most of the elementary numerical algorithm exhibit explicit parallelism. Very often this parallelism is two-dimensional, but existing programming languages and vector architectures are not able to express and support this two-dimensionality. A large gap between the theoretical peak performance of a today's vector architecture and the sustained performance, which is realized in typical benchmark applications, stems from this insufficient correspondence between numerical requirements and the lack of expressiveness of existing programming languages.

MODULA-S implements parallelism by defining parallel objects and transformations on those objects. In this way, it is possibly to exploit most of the data parallelism or fine grain parallelism. It would be easy and was proposed in other languages to extend it towards large grain parallelism.

MODULA-S supports array accessing in completeness; any kind of subarray can be accessed by the powerful associative selection and formindex, while other languages like FORTRAN-90 do not allow e.g. such simple things like diagonals or triangular matrices.

Though at first glance it might seem unnecessary to develop parallel languages and instead use tools to parallelize sequential programs, there are a few reasons that strongly support our approach:

- Sequential programs often "hide" a lot of their parallelism; it is often necessary to rewrite sequential programs to have program structures that a particular parallelizer can detect,

- sequential programs can be subjected to a source-to-source parallelizer; so it is not necessary to find all parallelism automatically, the parallelizer yields parallel code as far as currently possible, the rest can be parallelized by hand,

- last but not least, we hope that programmers might slowly get away from the "von-Neumann-style" of programming, that implies sequential thinking.

We feel that - at least until parallelizers are maturing - effort put into explicitly parallel programming has a much greater effect than parallelization of sequential programs.

References

[ABFC] F. Allen, M. Burke, P. Charles, R. Cytron, J. Ferrante
"An Overview of the PTRAN Analysis System for Multiprocessing"
Journal of parallel and distributed computing, March 1987

[ALL] F. Allen et al. "A Framework for Determining Useful Parallelism"
1988 Intern. Conf. on Supercomputing.

[BAX] W.Baxter and H.R. Bauer III. "The program Dependence Graph and Vectorization",
16th ACM Symposium on Principles of Programming Languages, 1989.

[BI]   H. Bi. "Exploiting Two-dimensional Explicit Parallelism On Vector architectures."
Dissertation Draft, GMD, Feb. 1990.

[BOTT] A. Boettcher, "Strukturelle Unterstuetzung von mehrdimensionalem Parallelismus in der Computer-Architektur", Ph. D. Thesis in preparation, 1991

[DON] Dongarra, J. "Performance of Various Computers Using Standard Linear Equations in a Fortran Environment", Argonne National Laboratory, August 10, 1987

[ERC] M.D. Ercegovac and T.Lang "Vector Processing",
Supercomputers, Class VI Systems, Hardware and Software,
S. Fernbach (Editor), Elsevier Science Publishers B.V. (North-Holland), 1986

[F8X] ANSI FORTRAN Draft S8, Version 112 , S8 (X3.9-198x), 1989

[FEO] J.T.Feo "An analysis of the computational and parallel complexity
of the Livermore Loops", Parallel Computing, 7, 163-185, 1988

[GERN] H. M. Gerndt, "Automatic Parallelization for Distributed-Memory Multiprocessing Systems", Ph. D. Thesis, University of Bonn, Informatik Berichte 75, 1989

[GIL82] W. K. Giloi and R. Güth. "Concepts and Realization of a High-Performance Data Type Architecture", Int. Journal of Computer and Information Sciences 11, Jan. 1982.

[GIL84] W. K. Giloi, "Datenfluss-Architektur und Datenstruktur-Architektur", Fachberichte und Referate, Vol. 15, W. E. Proebster und R. Remshardt, (eds.), Oldenbourg, Apr. 1984.

[GIL87] W. K. Giloi. "Data Structure Architectures and Its Application",
in "Berichte der Deutsch-Chinesischen Elektronik Woche in Peking 1987", Teil 4, Data Processing. VDE Verlag, Offenbach, 1987.

[GIL87a] W. K. Giloi, "SUPRENUM - a Trendsetter in Modern Supercomputer Development", Proc. on second Symp. on Vector and Parallel Processors for scientific Computation, Rome, September 1987

[HAR] D.T. Harper and J.R. Jump "Vector Access Performance in Parallel Memories using a skewing storage scheme", IEEE Trans. on Computers, Vol C-36, n.12, Dec 1987

[HOSS] F.Hossfeld and P.Weidner "Parallele Algorithmen",
Informatik Spektrum, Vol. 6, pp. 142-154

[KEN81] K. Kennedy "Automatic Translation of Fortran Programs to Vector Form"
Rice Techn. Report 476-029-4, Dept. of Math. Sc., Rice Univ., Houston, TX, 10/1980

[KKLW] D. Kuck, R. Kuhn, B. Leasure, M. Wolfe
"The Structure of an advanced Vectorizer for pipelined Processors"
Proceedings COMPSAC'80, 1980

[ETC] M. Metcalf "Fortran-90 - A Summary"
Computing and Networks Division, CERN - CN /90/6

[RUSS] R.M. Russel "The CRAY-1 Computer System", Comm. ACM, 21, 63-78, 1978

[SCHRO] F.W. Schröer "An Intermediate Language for Portable Optimizing Compilers",
Techn. Report GMD-Karlsruhe, Germany

[SCHRE] R.Schreiber "Block Algorithms for Parallel Machines"
Martin Schulz (eds), Springer 1988

[STÜT82] K. Stüben, U. Trottenberg. "Multigrid methods: Fundamental algorithms". In W. Hackbusch, U. Trottenberg (eds.), Multigrid Methods. Lecture Notes in Mathematics, 960, Springer-Verlag, Berlin,1982

[WIRTH] N. Wirth "Programming in Modula-2", The third corrected edition, Springer 1985

Modula-2* and its Compilation

Michael Philippsen and Walter F. Tichy

Universität Karlsruhe
Fakultät für Informatik
D-7500 Karlsruhe, F.R.G.
email: philippsen@ira.uka.de

Abstract – Modula-2*, an extension of Modula-2, is a programming language for writing highly parallel programs in a machine-independent, problem-oriented way. The novel attributes of Modula-2* are that programs are independent of the number of processors, independent of whether memory is shared or distributed, and independent of the control modes (SIMD or MIMD) of a parallel machine.

This article briefly describes Modula-2* and discusses its major advantages over the data-parallel programming model. We also present the principles of translating Modula-2* programs to MIMD and SIMD machines and discuss the lessons learned from our first compiler, targeting the Connection Machine. We conclude with important architectural principles required of parallel computers to allow for efficient, compiled programs.

1 Introduction

Highly parallel machines with thousands and tens of thousands of processors are now being manufactured and used commercially. These machines are of rapidly growing importance for high-speed computation. They have also initiated a major shift within Computer Science from the sequential to the parallel computer. One of the major problems we face in the use of these new machines is programmability: How to write, with no more than ordinary effort, programs that bring the raw power of a parallel computer to bear on a problem.

Two major approaches to the programming problem can be distinguished: The first is to automatically parallelize sequential software. Although there is overwhelming economic justification for it, this approach will meet with only limited success in the short to medium term (see, for instance, [18]). The goal of automatically producing parallel programs can only, if ever, be achieved by program transformations that start with the problem specification and not with a sequential implementation. In a sequential program, too many opportunities for parallelism have been hidden or eliminated.

The second approach is to write programs that are explicitly parallel. We claim that only minor extensions of existing programming languages are required to express highly parallel programs. Thus, programmers will need only moderate additional training, mainly in the area of parallel algorithms and their analysis. This area, fortunately, is well developed; see for instance textbooks [1] and [5]. In compiler technology, however, new techniques must be found to map machine-independent programs to existing architectures, while at the same time parallel machine architecture must evolve to efficiently support the features that are required for problem-oriented programming styles.

We take the approach of expressing parallelism explicitly, but in a machine-independent way. In section 2 we analyze the problems that plague most parallel programming languages today. Section 3 then presents Modula-2*, an extension of Modula-2 [20], for the explicit formulation of highly parallel programs. The extension is small and easy to learn, but provides a programming model that is far more general and machine independent than other proposals. Next, we discuss compilation techniques for targeting MIMD and SIMD machines and report on experience with our first Modula-2* compiler [8] for the Connection Machine. We conclude with properties of parallel machine architectures that would improve the efficiency of high-level parallel programs.

2 Related Work

Most current programming languages for parallel and highly parallel machines, including *LISP, C*, MPL, VAL, Sisal, Occam, Ada, FORTRAN90, Blaze, Dino, and Kali [10, 9, 14, 19, 2, 12, 11, 15, 7] suffer from some or all of the following problems:

- Whereas the number of processors of a parallel machine is fixed, the problem size is not. Because most of the known parallel languages do not support the virtual processor concept, the programmer has to write explicit mappings for adapting the process structure of each program to the available processors. This is not only a tedious and repetitive task, but also one that makes programs non-portable.

- Co-locating data with the processors that operate upon the data is critical for the performance of distributed memory machines. Poor co-location results in high communication costs and poor performance. Good co-location is highly dependent on the topology of the communication network and must, at present, be programmed by hand. It is a primary source of machine dependence.

- All parallel machines provide facilities for inter-process communication; most of them by means of a message passing system. Nearly all parallel languages support only low level *send* and *get* communication commands. Programming communication with these primitives, especially if only nearest neighbor communication is available, is a time consuming and error prone task.

- There are several control modes for parallel machines, including MIMD, SIMD, data-flow, and systolic modes. Any extant, parallel language targets exactly one of those control modes. Whatever the choice, it severely limits portability as well as the space of solutions.

Modula-2* provides solutions to the basic problems mentioned above. The language abstracts from the memory organization and from the number of physical processors. Mapping of data to processors is performed by the compiler, optionally supported by high-level directives provided by the programmer. Communication is not directly visible.

Instead, reading and writing in a (virtually) shared address space subsumes communication. A shared memory, however, is not required. Parallelism is explicit, and the programmer can choose among synchronous and asynchronous execution mode at any level of granularity. Thus, programs can use SIMD-mode where proper synchronization is difficult, or use MIMD-mode where synchronization is simple or infrequent. The two modes can even be intermixed freely.

The data-parallel approach, discussed in [6] and exemplified in languages such as *LISP, C*, and MPL is currently quite successful, because it has reduced machine dependence of parallel programs. Data-parallelism extends a synchronous, SIMD model with a global name space, which obviates the need for explicit message passing between processing elements. It also makes the number of (virtual) processing elements a function of the problem size, rather than a function of the target machine.

The data-parallel approach has three major advantages: (1) It is a natural extension of sequential programming. The only parallel instruction, a synchronous **forall** statement, is a simple extension of the well known **for** statement and is easy to understand. (2) Debugging data-parallel programs is not much more difficult than debugging sequential programs. The reason is that there is only a single locus of control, which dramatically simplifies the state space of a program compared to that of an MIMD program with thousands of independent loci of control. (3) There is a wide range of data-parallel algorithms. Most parallel algorithms in textbooks are data-parallel (compare for instance [1, 5]). According to Fox [4], more than 80% of the 84 existing, parallel applications he examined fall in the class of synchronous, data-parallel programs. Furthermore, systolic algorithms as well as vector-algorithms are special cases of data-parallel algorithms.

But data-parallelism, at least as defined by current languages, has some drawbacks: (1) It is a synchronous model. Even if the problem is not amenable to a synchronous solution, there is no escape. In particular, parallel programs that interact with stochastic events are awkward to write and run inefficiently. (2) There is no nested parallelism. This means that once a parallel activity has started, the involved processes cannot start up additional, parallel activity. A parallel operation simply cannot expand itself and involve more processes. This property seriously limits parallel searches in irregular search spaces, for example. The effect is that data-parallel programs are strictly bimodal: They alternate between a sequential and a parallel mode, where the maximal degree of parallelism is fixed once the parallel mode is entered. To change the degree of parallelism, the program first has to stop all parallel activity and return to the sequential mode. (3) The use of procedures to structure a parallel program in a top-down fashion is severely limited. The problem here is that it is not possible to call a procedure in parallel mode, when the procedure itself invokes parallel operations (this is a consequence of (2)). Procedures cannot allocate local data and spawn data parallel operations on it, unless they are called from a sequential program. Thus, procedures can only be used in about half of the cases where they would be desirable. They also force the use of global data structures on the programmer.

When designing Modula-2*, we wanted to preserve the main advantages of data-parallel languages while avoiding the above drawbacks. The following list contains the main advances of Modula-2* over data-parallel languages.

- The programming model of Modula-2* is a strict superset of data-parallelism. It allows both synchronous and asynchronous parallel programs.

- Modula-2* is problem-oriented in the sense that the programmer can choose the degree of parallelism and mix the control mode (SIMD-like or MIMD-like) as needed by the intended algorithm.

- Parallelism may be nested at any level.

- Procedures may be called from sequential or parallel contexts and can generate parallel activity without any restrictions.

- Modula-2* is translatable effectively for both SIMD and MIMD architectures.

3 The Language Modula-2*

Modula-2 has been chosen as a base for a parallel language because of its simplicity. There are no reasons why similar extensions could not be added to other imperative languages such as FORTRAN or ADA. The necessary extensions were surprisingly small. They consist of synchronous and asynchronous versions of a **forall** statement, plus simple, optional declarations for mapping array data onto processors in a machine independent fashion. An interconnection network is not directly visible in the language. We assume a shared address space among all processors, though not necessarily shared memory. There are no explicit message passing instructions; instead, reading and writing locations in shared address space subsume message passing. This approach simplifies programming dramatically and assures network independence of programs. The burden of distinguishing between local and non-local references, and substituting explicit message passing code for the latter, is placed on an (optimizing) compiler. The programmer can influence the distribution of data with a few, simple declarations, but these are only hints to the compiler with no effect on the semantics of the program whatsoever.

3.1 Overview of the forall statement

The **forall** statement creates a set of processes that execute in parallel. In the asynchronous form, the individual processes operate concurrently, and are joined at the end of the **forall** statement. The asynchronous **forall** simply terminates when the last of the created processes terminates. In the synchronous form, the processes created by the **forall** operate in unison until they reach a branch point, such as an **if** or **case** statement. At branch points, the set of processes partitions into two or more subsets. Processes within a single subset continue to operate in unison, but the subsets are not synchronized with respect to each other. Thus, the union of the subsets operate in MSIMD[1] mode. A statement causing a partition into subsets terminates when all its subsets terminate, at which point the subsets rejoin to continue with the following statement.

Variants of both the synchronous and asynchronous form of the **forall** statement have been introduced by previously proposed languages, such as Blaze, C*, Occam, Sisal, VAL, *LISP [11, 17, 14, 9, 10, 16] and others [3]. Note also that vector instructions are simple instances of the synchronous **forall**.

---

[1]MSIMD: Multiple SIMD. Few but more than one instruction streams operate on many data streams. A compromise between SIMD and MIMD.

None of the languages mentioned above include *both* forms of the **forall** statement, even though both are necessary for writing readable and portable parallel programs. The synchronous form is often easier to handle than the asynchronous form, because it avoids synchronization hazards. However, the synchronous form may be overly constraining and may lead to poor machine utilization. The combination of synchronous and asynchronous forms in Modula-2* actually permits the full range of parallel programming styles between SIMD and MIMD.

The syntax of the **forall** is as follows.[2]

ForallStatement = FORALL ident ":" SimpleType IN (PARALLEL | SYNC)
       StatementSequence
  END.

The identifier introduced by the forall statement is local to the statement and serves as a run-time constant for every process created by the **forall**. *SimpleType* is an enumeration or a (sub-)range. The **forall** creates as many processes as there are elements in *SimpleType* and initializes the run-time constant of each process to a unique value in *SimpleType*. The created processes all execute the statements in *StatementSequence*.

3.2 The asynchronous forall

The created processes execute *StatementSequence* concurrently, without any implicit, intermediate synchronization. The execution of the **forall** terminates when all created processes have finished. Thus, the asynchronous **forall** contains only one synchronization point at the end. Any additional synchronization must be programmed explicitly with semaphores and the operations *WAIT* and *SIGNAL*.

In the following example, an asynchronous **forall** statement implements a vector addition.

```
FORALL i:[0..N-1] IN PARALLEL
    z[i] := x[i] + y[i]
END
```

Since no two processes created by the **forall** access the same vector element, no temporal ordering of the processes is necessary. The N processes may execute at whatever speed. The **forall** terminates when all processes created by it have terminated.

A more complicated example, illustrating recursive process creation, is the following. Procedure *ParSearch* searches a directed, possibly cyclic graph in parallel fashion. It can best be understood by comparing it with depth-first-search, except that *ParSearch* runs in parallel. It starts with a root of the graph and visits nodes in the graph in a parallel (and largely unpredictable) fashion.

---

[2] We use the EBNF syntax notation of the Modula-2 language definition, with keywords in upper case, | denoting alternation, [...] optionality, and (...) grouping of the enclosed sentential forms.

```
PROCEDURE ParSearch( v: NodePtr );
BEGIN
  IF Marked( v ) THEN RETURN END;
  FORALL s:[0..v^.successors-1] IN PARALLEL
    ParSearch( succ(v, s) )
  END;
  visit( v );
END ParSearch;
```

The procedure *ParSearch* simply creates as many processes as a given node has successors, and starts each process with an instance of *ParSearch*. Before visiting a node, *ParSearch* has to test whether the node has already been visited and marked. Since multiple processes may reach the same node simultaneously, testing and setting the mark is done in a critical section (implemented with a semaphore associated with each node) by the procedure *Marked*. If the graph is a tree, no marking is necessary.

3.3 The synchronous forall

The processes created by a synchronous **forall** execute every single statement of *StatementSequence* in unison. To illustrate this mode, its semantics for selected statements is described in some detail below:

- A statement sequence is executed in unison by executing all its statements in order and in unison.

- In the case of branching statements such as IF C THEN SS1 ELSE SS2 END, the set of participating processes divides into *disjoint* and *independently operating* subsets, each of which executes one of the branches (SS1 and SS2 in the example) in unison. Note that in contrast to other data-parallel languages, *no* assumption about the relative speeds or relative order of the branches may be made. The execution of the entire statement terminates when all processes of all subsets have finished.

- In the case of loop statements such as WHILE C DO SS END, the set of processes for any iteration divides into two disjoint subsets, namely the *active* and the *inactive* ones (with respect to the loop statement). Initially, all processes entering the loop are active. Every iteration starts with the synchronous evaluation of the loop condition C by all active processes. The processes for which C evaluates to FALSE become inactive. The rest forms the active subset which executes statement sequence SS in unison. The execution of the whole loop statement terminates when the subset of active processes becomes empty.

Hence, synchronous parallel operation closely resembles the lock-step operation of SIMD machines with an important generalization for parallel branches.

As an example, consider the computation of all postfix sums of a vector V of length N. The program should place into $V[i]$ the sum of all elements $V[i] \ldots V[N-1]$. A recursive doubling technique as in reference [6] computes all postfix sums in $O(\log N)$ time, where N is the length of the vector.

Figure 1 illustrates the process. The program operates by computing partial sums of length $s = 2^j$, where j counts the iterations. The inner **forall** creates N processes.

```
VAR V : ARRAY[0 .. N-1] OF REAL;
VAR s : CARDINAL;
BEGIN
    s := 1;
    WHILE s < N DO
        FORALL i:[0..N-1] IN SYNC
            IF (i+s)<N THEN
                V[i]:= V[i]+V[i+s]
            END
        END;
        s := s * 2
    END
END
```

Figure 1: Computing postfix sums of a vector

Note that there is a one-to-one mapping between process numbers and elements of the vector. In each iteration, the length of the partial sums is doubled by parallel summation of neighboring sums. The **if** statement inside the **forall** disables all processes that must not participate in the computation during a given iteration.

3.4 Allocation of array data

Co-location of data with the processors that access the data is important for parallel machines without uniform access time to memory locations. Poor alignment of data and processors may cause excessive communication overhead. We therefore provide a simple, machine-independent construct for controlling the allocation of array data. This construct is optional and does not change the meaning of a program; it affects only performance. A compiler for a machine with uniform memory access time may ignore the construct.

The allocation of array data to processors is controlled with one allocator per dimension. The modified declaration syntax for arrays is as follows:

ArrayType = **ARRAY** SimpleType [allocator]
            {"," SimpleType [allocator]} **OF** type.
allocator = LOCAL | SPREAD | CYCLE | RANDOM | SBLOCK | CBLOCK.

Array elements whose indices differ only in dimensions that are marked LOCAL are associated with the same processor. This facility is used to avoid distribution of data in a given dimension.

Dimensions with allocator SPREAD are divided into segments, one for each of the available processors. A vector with n elements is assigned to P processors by allocating a segment of length $\lceil n/P \rceil$ to each processor. While utilizing all available processors, it minimizes the cost of nearest-neighbor communication.

Dimensions with allocator CYCLE are distributed in a round-robin fashion over the available processors. Given P processors, the elements of a vector whose indices are identical modulo P are associated with the same processor. In contrast to SPREAD, CYCLE maximizes the cost of nearest-neighbor communication: neighboring array elements are

Once t is known, t stacks are created by assigning to each of p processors a segment of $\lceil t \div p \rceil$ stacks. This operations takes constant time and balances the load perfectly. Process termination also takes constant time, since there is no synchronization overhead. However, it may be necessary to provide each thread with some initial data (such as its number) during creation. Spreading this information takes again logarithmic time, but as demonstrated by the Connection Machine, special instructions for spreading data are so fast that, in practice, they can be regarded as constant.

What remains to be discussed is the scheduling of instructions. Since the asynchronous **forall** prescribes no scheduling of the threads at all, the compiler writer can choose one that works well on a given SIMD or MSIMD machine. We describe briefly the implementation we chose for the Connection Machine (CM). We assume initially, that the number of available processors equals the number of threads.

Activity Bits. The central idea of control flow on SIMD computers is deactivation and reactivation of processors, controlled by an activity bit associated with each processor. When the activity bit is off, the processor does not execute the instructions issued by the front-end. This facility is sufficient for simulating the usual control flow constructs in a parallel context. All that is needed is a stack of activity bits for each thread. The top of each activity stack is stored into the activity bit of a processor. Suitable manipulation of the activity bits turns threads on and off, as required by the instruction stream issuing from the front-end.

There are two small extensions of the usual control flow mechanism for SIMD machines. They are needed for recursion and for **exit** and **return** statements. First, consider parallel loops (i.e., loops within a **forall**). On a SIMD-machine, the front-end repeatedly issues the instructions for the loop body, until the termination conditions of all threads executing the loop are met. The usual technique is to evaluate a thread's termination condition directly into its activity bit. Before each iteration, the front-end tests whether there are any positive activity bits left. If not, the loop terminates. An **exit** statement may also terminate a loop, by turning off the activity bit of the corresponding thread. However, since an **exit** statement may be nested several levels deep within a loop, it must not only set the topmost activity bit to false, but all those that have been stacked since the last loop was entered. Similar considerations apply to the **return** statement.

Consider the following example.

```
FORALL i:[0..N-1] IN PARALLEL
    LOOP
        IF ODD(i) THEN EXIT END;
        SS
    END
END
```

When control flow reaches the **exit**, then two activity bits have been stacked for each thread: one for the **loop**, and one for the **if** statement. To prevent a thread that has already executed the **exit** from being reactivated after the **if**, its top *two* activity bits must be set to FALSE.

Recursion termination is similar to loop termination. If a recursive call occurs inside a parallel **if** or **case**, then the front-end must sense whether there is any active thread left in a branch. If not, then the branch terminates. Without this provision, unbounded recursion would ensue.

Parallel Procedure Call. Because procedures can be called from both sequential and parallel contexts, each procedure must be compiled twice: Once for executing entirely on the front-end in sequential mode and a second time for executing within a **forall** statement. The difference is that in the parallel version, the procedure call and return instructions are executed only on the front-end. Thus, we need two types of stacks: On the front-end, we stack return addresses. On the stacks associated with the parallel threads, we store parameters and local data. This division is a direct consequence of SIMD and would even occur if front-end and parallel processors had the same instruction set. On the CM, the instruction sets differ, and so the sequential and parallel versions are completely different.

Our compiler relies on a minor language restriction: Procedures may not be nested within each other. The reason is that up-level addressing is quite expensive. Since it is in general unpredictable in what context a procedure is called, each memory access would have to distinguish at run-time whether it references data on the front-end or the parallel processors.

Processor Virtualization. Simulating more threads than there are processors available is called *processor virtualization*. In SIMD mode, it is not possible to simply create new processes on demand and let the operating system schedule them. Instead, the front-end has to issue the instructions implementing the body of a **forall** in a loop. The number of iterations of this loop is given by the ratio of threads to available processors.

The PARIS instruction set of the CM provides automatic processor virtualization. This means that processor virtualization is transparent to the programmer. The firmware simulates as many threads as required. The maximum number of threads is only limited by the available memory, because the local memory of each processor must be shared out among the assigned threads.

Our Modula-2* compiler uses the automatic processor virtualization. However, this virtualization is quite expensive. The main reason is that the virtualization actually implements synchronous virtualization, which requires many temporary variables. In essence, this virtualization wraps every single instruction into a virtualizing loop, even though a loop around the entire body of a **forall** would suffice (since the asynchronous **forall** prescribes no scheduling of threads). The latter simulation would be obviously much more efficient.

4.2 Synchronous forall

4.2.1 Synchronous forall, MIMD implementation

The synchronous **forall** requires many more synchronization points than the asynchronous form. There must be a synchronization point between every two statements inside a **forall**, and in the case of the assignment, even within a single statement. A parallel assignment of the from L := R means that the value of R is evaluated synchronously and stored in a temporary. Similarly, the address represented by L is evaluated synchronously and stored in a temporary. Only after both of these parallel evaluations have completed can the assignment be made. Otherwise, interference is possible, as in the assignment `A[i] := A[i+1]`.

A synchronization point is implemented with a scheme similar to the one used to terminate an asynchronous **forall**, except that now the threads do not terminate, but wait for a signal to proceed. First, a logarithmic reduction informs the leader that all threads in the process have reached the synchronization point. Then a logarithmic doubling process sends signals back out to the threads to continue.

Clearly, synchronization points are expensive. We are currently investigating methods to eliminate them where possible. For instance, the synchronization point inside an assignment is not necessary if the left and right hand sides do not interfere. Furthermore, by scheduling processes in a certain fashion, the overlaps may be reduced greatly. Even synchronization points between statements can be eliminated if there are no dependencies. Much of the dependency analysis developed for parallelizing compilers applies here.

4.2.2 Synchronous forall, SIMD implementation

The SIMD implementation of the synchronous **forall** was simple on the CM: the built-in virtualization does the job. However, this virtualization cannot take advantage of the optimizations described above. Instead, it must make conservative assumptions. The resulting virtualization is far from efficient. An optimizing compiler could produce a much faster virtualization in the majority of cases. Consider the following example.

```
FORALL i: [0..N-1] IN SYNC
    A[i] := (A[i] + 1) / 2
END
```

Below are two possible virtualizations on p processors, expressed in Modula-2*.

```
s := CEILING(N, p)                          s := CEILING(N, p)
FORALL j : [0 .. p-1] IN PARALLEL           FORALL j : [0 .. p-1] IN PARALLEL
    FOR i:= j*s TO MIN((j+1)*s,N)-1             FOR i:= j*s TO MIN((j+1)*s,N)-1
    DO                                          DO
        TMP[i] := A[i] + 1;                         reg := A[i];
        TMP[i] := TMP[i] / 2                        reg := reg + 1;
    END                                             reg := reg / 2;
END                                                 A[i]:= reg
FORALL j : [0 .. p-1] IN PARALLEL               END
    FOR i:= j*s TO MIN((j+1)*s,N)-1         END
    DO
        A[i]   := TMP[i]
    END
END
```

The program on the left shows the conservative virtualization, as performed by PARIS. The optimized version on the right hand side exploits the fact that only one temporary location is required. By using a single register for it on every processor, the number of writes to memory are reduced to one third of the unoptimized version. Furthermore, no synchronization is necessary. On a SIMD machine, this means that the two loops can be merged; on a MIMD machine, we save the synchronization point. Furthermore, if the individual processors have a vector capability, the computation in each processor can even be interleaved.

While implementing the synchronous **forall** for the CM we have identified the main sources of optimization in compiling for massively parallel machines. We have started to include these optimizations in the next compilers for MasPar, CM, and Transputer, including the necessary data-dependence analysis.

5 Recommendations for Parallel Machine Architectures

The following list itemizes some broad requirements that parallel machine architectures should fulfill to allow for efficient, compiled programs. These requirements are likely to be encountered when designing the translation schemes for parallel, imperative languages.

- Hardware support for fast process creation and synchronization.

- Shared address space. All processors should be able to generate addresses for the entire memory on the system. In particular, the front-end's memory should be part of that address space. A source of great difficulty in our compiler were the many different types of addresses. The compiler has to distinguish between local addresses, global addresses, addresses in the front-end, general communication addresses, and communication addresses on a grid. Optimizing for all these cases is often impossible, even with detailed inter-procedural analysis. Furthermore, parallel pointers are quite expensive to implement without a shared address space – one basically has to simulate the shared address space in software.[3]

- Uniform communication mechanism. Most parallel machines today provide a set of instructions for accessing local memory, a second one for accessing memory in direct neighbors, and a third set for accessing distant memory units. The differences in speed are significant and therefore require that the compiler detect the faster cases. However, it is often impossible to know statically for which case to optimize. For instance, we found that in most cases it was impossible to determine in the compiler whether a procedure would access local or non-local memory. The generated code thus has to check all three cases at run-time. Such a simple and frequently repeated case analysis could be done much more efficiently in hardware.

- Autonomous addressing capability. An autonomous addressing capability means that each processor can generate its own address for accessing memory. The Connection Machine does not have such a facility – on the CM, each processor must use the same address. The lack of autonomous addressing not only makes many applications awkward to write, but also precludes certain optimizations in processor virtualization.

- Single instruction set. SIMD machines today typically have different instruction sets for front-end and parallel processors. This property implies that the code generator of the compiler has to be written twice. Also, each procedure has to be translated twice,

---
[3]A shared address space does not imply shared memory.

doubling code size. A speed differential between front-end and parallel processors, however, does not appear to be a major problem.

- Small instruction set. The CM offers about 400 PARIS instructions, only a few of which a compiler can actually generate. A study determining the most frequently used instructions in parallel programs is sorely needed.

6 Conclusion

Ease of programming as well as portability of programs will be of overwhelming importance for the acceptance of highly parallel machines. Modula-2* supports both: few extensions of a sequential programming language suffice for writing highly parallel, problem-oriented programs, and compilers that can generate efficient code for a wide range of parallel machines appear feasible. Improvements in hardware architecture, operating systems, programming languages and compiler technology should eventually render the current practice of machine dependent, parallel programming as obsolete as machine dependent, sequential programming.

References

[1] Selim G. Akl. *The Design and Analysis of Parallel Algorithms*. Prentice Hall, Englewood Cliffs, New Jersey, 1989.

[2] American National Standards Institute, Inc., Washington, D.C. *ANSI, Programming Language Fortran (Fortran90), Draft S8, Version 114 (X3.9-1990)*, January 1990.

[3] Henry E. Bal, Jennifer S. Steiner, and Andrew S. Tannenbaum. Programming Languages for Distributed Computing Systems. *ACM Computing Surveys*, 21(3):261–322, September 1989.

[4] Geoffrey C. Fox. What Have We Learnt from Using Real Parallel Machines to Solve Real Problems. In *Proc. of the Third Conf. on Hypercube Concurrent Computers and Applications*, pages 897–955. ACM Press, New York, February 26 – March 2 1988.

[5] Alan Gibbons and Wojciech Rytter. *Efficient Parallel Algorithms*. Cambridge University Press, 1988.

[6] W. Daniel Hillis and Guy L. Steele. Data Parallel Algorithms. *Communications of the ACM*, 29(12):1170–1183, December 1986.

[7] Charles Koelbel and Piyush Mehrotra. Supporting Shared Data Structures and Distributed Memory Architectures. In *Proc. of the 2nd ACM SIGPLAN Symposium on Principles and Practice of Parallel Programming*, pages 177–186, March 1990.

[8] Ralf Kretzschmar. Ein Modula-2* Übersetzer für die Connection Machine. Master's thesis, University of Karlsruhe, Department of Informatics, May 1991.

[9] James McGraw, Stephen Skedzielewski, Stephen Allan, Rod Oldehoeft, John Glauert, Chris Kirkham, Bill Noyce, and Robert Thomas. *SISAL Language Reference Manual.* Lawrence Livermore National Laboratory, March 1985.

[10] James R. McGraw. The VAL Language: Description and Analysis. *ACM Transactions on Programming Languages and Systems*, 4(1):44–82, January 1982.

[11] Piyush Mehrotra and John van Rosendale. The BLAZE language: A parallel language for scientific programming. *Parallel Computing*, 5:339–361, November 1987.

[12] Michael Metcalf and John Reid. *Fortran 90 Explained.* Oxford Science Publications, 1990.

[13] John K. Ousterhout, Donald A. Scelza, and Pradeep S. Sindhu. Medusa: An experiment in distributed operating system structure. *Communications of the ACM*, 23(2):92–205, February 1980.

[14] Prentice Hall, Englewood Cliffs, New Jersey. *INMOS Limited: Occam Programming Manual*, 1984.

[15] M. Rosing, R. Schnabel, and R. Weaver. Dino: Summary and Example. In *Proc. of the Third Conf. on Hypercube Concurrent Computers and Applications*, pages 472–481. ACM Press, New York, February 26 – March 2 1988.

[16] Thinking Machines Corporation, Cambridge, Massachusetts. **Lisp Reference Manual, Version 5.0*, 1988.

[17] Thinking Machines Corporation, Cambridge, Massachusetts. *C* Programming Guide, Version 6.0*, November 1990.

[18] Walter F. Tichy. Parallel Matrix Multiplication on the Connection Machine. *International Journal of High Speed Computing*, 1(2):247–262, 1989.

[19] U.S. Government, Ada Joint Program Office. *ANSI/MIL-Std 1815 A, Reference Manual for the Ada Programming Language*, January 1983.

[20] Niklaus Wirth. *Programming in Modula-2 (Third corrected Edition).* Springer-Verlag Berlin, Heidelberg, New York, London, Paris, Tokyo, 1985.

ADAPTing Fortran 90 Array Programs for Distributed Memory Architectures*

John H. Merlin,
Department of Electronics and Computer Science,
University of Southampton, Southampton S09 5NH, U.K.

Abstract

We describe a system that we are developing, whose purpose is to automatically transform data parallel Fortran 90 programs for execution on MIMD distributed memory architectures. The system is called ADAPT (for 'Array Distribution Automatic Parallelisation Tool'). Programs for the system should make full use of the array features of Fortran 90, as parallelism is automatically extracted from the array syntax. Parallelisation is by data-partitioning, guided by 'distribution' declarations that the user inserts in his program—these being the only additions required to standard Fortran 90 programs. This paper gives a brief overview of the array features of Fortran 90, describes the 'distribution' declarations required by ADAPT, and gives details of the parallelisation scheme.

1 Introduction

It is evident that distributed memory MIMD architectures have several advantages over shared memory and vector systems, among which are cost effectiveness, scaleability and, for suitable applications, high efficiency. The last property applies particularly to problems that have the potential for a large amount of data parallelism.

Currently, however, distributed memory architectures suffer a big disadvantage in terms of programmability. To program data parallel applications, for instance, it is necessary to explicitly decompose the data into a collection of pieces, each 'owned' by a single process, and specify all the data communications between the processes. This is a complicated and error-prone task, and the resulting programs are usually not portable and are hard to adapt. We are convinced that these deficiencies in *programmability* and *portability* must be overcome for distributed memory architectures to achieve widespread use.

This paper describes a system that we are developing with a view to addressing these issues for data parallel applications. The purpose of the system is to automatically transform data-parallel programs written in (a subset of)[1] Fortran 90, the new Fortran standard [1], so that they can be executed on distributed memory message-passing architectures. Programs for this system should make the fullest possible use of the array

---
*This research is funded by Esprit project 2701 (PUMA).
[1] See section 4.6

features of Fortran 90, as parallelism is automatically extracted from the array syntax. Parallelisation is achieved by distributing data arrays over a (logical) multi-dimensional array of processes, guided by 'distribution' declarations that the programmer inserts in his program—these being the only additions required to standard Fortran 90 programs.

The system is called ADAPT, for 'Array Distribution Automatic Parallelisation Tool'. It comprises two components: a *pre-processor* to transform the Fortran 90 program into a standard Fortran 77 program that constitutes a component process of the process array, and a *library* of communications procedures and Fortran 90 array intrinsic functions (generalised to handle both distributed and non-distributed data), that are called as necessary by the transformed Fortran program.

The current development of ADAPT is targetted to multi-transputer systems made of the next generation of Inmos transputer components, namely T9000 transputers and C104 switch chips [2]. The communications library is accordingly being written in occam for maximum efficiency. However, our techniques are applicable to all MIMD message-passing systems. Furthermore, our system can be ported to any distributed memory architecture by adapting just the library, as the library routines perform all of the message-passing and other machine-specific functions; the pre-processor need not be modified, as it generates standard Fortran 77 without machine-dependent extensions.

This paper is organised as follows. The next section gives a brief overview of the array features of Fortran 90, since they are central to the parallelisation system. Section 3 describes our data partitioning scheme and the associated partitioning declarations. Section 4 contains some details of ADAPT, including its execution and communications model, and the principal types of analysis and program transformation that it must perform to accomplish the parallelisation. Section 5 gives our conclusions.

2 Overview of Fortran 90 array features

We start by providing a brief overview of the array features of Fortran 90 on which the parallelisation system is based, for the benefit of readers who are unfamiliar with the new Fortran standard [1]. For a complete description of Fortran 90, the reader is referred to [3].

2.1 Array expressions and assignments

Fortran 90 introduces a new form of declaration, in which all of the attributes of a data object can appear together. Some typical array declarations are:

```
INTEGER, DIMENSION (10) :: I
REAL, DIMENSION (8, 8) :: A, B, C
REAL, DIMENSION (0:7, 0:7) :: D
```

It is useful to introduce some terminology for arrays. The number of dimensions of an array is called its *rank*. The total number of elements in a particular dimension is called the *extent* of that dimension, and the *shape* of an array is its vector of extents. For example, the last two declarations above both declare arrays with rank 2 and shape (8,8), although the subscript bounds differ in the two cases. Arrays with the same shape are said to *conform*, irrespective of their subscript bounds.

Arrays can appear in expressions and assignments just as scalar objects can, provided that all of the arrays conform. The correspondence between the elements of different arrays is by their position in the extents rather than by their subscript values, so arrays with the same shape can appear together in an expression or assignment even if their subscript bounds differ. A scalar can be used anywhere in an array expression, and is equivalent 'broadcasting' the scalar value to an array of the appropriate shape. For example, using the above declarations, the assignment:

```
A = 2.0 * D
```

is equivalent to:

```
A (1,1) = 2.0 * D (0,0)
A (1,2) = 2.0 * D (0,1)
...
A (8,8) = 2.0 * D (7,7)
```

Sections of arrays may be referenced by specifying a range of the form $[L] : [U] [: S]$ for one or more of the subscripts, where L, U and S are scalar integer expressions for the lower and upper bounds and the stride respectively. If L or U is omitted it defaults to the declared lower or upper bound, and if S is omitted the stride is 1. Negative strides are permitted, in which case a non-zero range is selected if $L \geq U$. Sections of zero size are allowed, which occur if $S > 0$ and $L > U$ or $S < 0$ and $L < U$ in any dimension. Examples of array sections, taken from an array A with dimensions (8,8), are:

```
A (1:6, 2:3)     ! array of rank 2;  shape (6,2).
A (1:6, 2)       ! array of rank 1 (i.e. a vector);  shape (6).
A (:, 5:1:-2)    ! rank 2; shape (8,3)
```

(! introduces a comment in Fortran 90!).

Irregular array sections can be formed by using one or more *vector* subscripts. For example, if I is the vector declared above and V is an integer vector whose elements are (/5,1,2/), then I(V) is a section containing the elements (/I(5),I(1),I(2)/). Incidentally, a list of expressions enclosed between (/.../) is an *array constructor*, that is, a vector whose elements are the given sequence of values.

Array sections may be used freely in expressions and assignments, provided only that they conform[2]. If overlapping sections of the same array appear on both sides of an assignment, the rule is that the expression is completely evaluated before the assignment takes place. For example:

```
I (2:3) = I (1:2)    ! new value of I is
                     ! (/I(1), I(1), I(2), I(4).../)
```

This is important for our purposes, as it implies that all of the elemental expressions that make up an array expression can be evaluated concurrently.

It is possible to *mask* an array assignment, so that it is performed only to certain elements of the array, by means of a WHERE statement. An example is:

```
WHERE (A > 0.0) B = 1.0 / A    ! A and B are conforming real arrays
```

which performs the expression evaluation and assignment only for those elements corresponding to elements of the mask expression (A > 0.0) that are TRUE. An equivalent WHERE *construct* is provided so that a single mask expression can mask a sequence of array assignments.

---

[2] There is just one restriction: if a section with a vector subscript appears as the variable in an assignment, all of its elements must be distinct.

2.2 Procedures

An *elemental function* is one that takes scalar arguments and produces a scalar result. Most of the Fortran 77 intrinsic functions are of this type. In Fortran 90 an elemental function may also be applied to conforming array arguments to produce a conforming array result, each element of which has the value that would have been obtained by applying the function to the corresponding elements of the arguments.

Functions can also have explicitly array-valued results, whose shape may be different from that of any of the arguments. We shall call these *array functions* to distinguish them from the elemental variety.

If a dummy argument of a procedure is an array, it can take its shape (though not its rank) from the actual argument rather than having it declared explicitly within the procedure. Such *assumed-shape* arrays are declared by omitting the upper bounds from the array declaration in the procedure. This allows the procedure to be called with array arguments of various shapes.

Fortran 90 also permits *automatic arrays* to be declared. These are *local* arrays, some or all of whose dimensions are functions of the procedure's dummy arguments. They may therefore have a different shape, and occupy a different amount of storage, each time the procedure is called. Intrinsic functions are provided to enquire about the extents and bounds of arrays, namely SIZE (ARRAY [,DIM]), LBOUND (ARRAY [,DIM]) and UBOUND (ARRAY [,DIM]).

In order to call either an array-valued function or a procedure that has assumed-shape dummy arguments, the calling procedure must know its *interface*, that is, the specifications of its dummy arguments and, in the case of a function, its result. This information is made available by declaring an 'INTERFACE block' within the calling procedure, which contains, for each of the procedures concerned, a copy of the procedure without its executable statements and with declarations that are unrelated to dummy arguments or function results optionally omitted. Interface blocks are also necessary in order to exploit some of the other useful new features of Fortran 90, such as optional and keyword-denoted arguments, and are in fact very useful generally, since they allow the compiler to check that the actual arguments of a procedure call match the dummy arguments.

An example of an array function that uses some of these features is shown below. The function performs a matrix × vector product. (Incidentally, Fortran 90 provides an intrinsic function MATMUL for this purpose).

```
FUNCTION MATVEC (MATRIX, VEC)
    ! Function to perform a matrix * vector product.

    REAL, DIMENSION (:,:) :: MATRIX
    REAL, DIMENSION (SIZE(MATRIX,2)) :: VEC
    REAL, DIMENSION (SIZE(MATRIX,1)) :: MATVEC

    DO I = 1,SIZE (MATVEC)
        MATVEC (I) = SUM (MATRIX (I,:) * VEC (:))
            ! SUM (ARRAY [,DIM]) is an array intrinsic function
    ENDDO
END FUNCTION MATVEC
```

Any procedure that called `MATVEC` would have to declare an interface block for it, because it is an array-valued function and also because it uses assumed-shape arguments.

Finally, Fortran 90 provides a rich set of intrinsic functions for performing operations on arrays, such as matrix multiplication, dotproduct, transpose, shifting, reduction operations, location enquiry, etc. The fact that they are part of the language is especially beneficial to the programmer in the present context, as the parallelisation system will automatically provide him with any distributed versions of these operations that his program requires (from the system library).

3 'Distributed Fortran 90'

The only modification required to standard Fortran 90 programs to enable them to be parallelised by ADAPT is to declare how the data arrays are to be partitioned over the process array[3]. We shall use the term *'Distributed Fortran 90'* to refer to the extended version of Fortran 90 that includes these data partitioning declarations.

The partitioning information is provided by declaring a `DISTRIBUTION` attribute for partitioned arrays. Its usage is similar to that of the standard `DIMENSION` attribute. The `DISTRIBUTION` keyword is followed by a comma-separated list of non-negative integers enclosed in parentheses, one for each dimension of the data array. A value $p > 0$ indicates that the corresponding data array dimension is mapped onto dimension p of the process array. The value 0 indicates that the array dimension is *not distributed*, i.e. that the whole dimension is held internally on each process.

For example, the declaration:

```
REAL, DIMENSION (8,8,8), DISTRIBUTION (2,0,1)  :: A
```

results in the following mapping of data dimensions to process array dimensions:

data array dimension	process array dimension
1	2
2	internal
3	1

If this program is executed on an array of 8 processes, logically configured as a 4×2 grid, each process is assigned a segment of the data array as shown in the following table:

	p_1	p_2
	0	1
0	(1:4, :, 1:2)	(5:8, :, 1:2)
1	(1:4, :, 3:4)	(5:8, :, 3:4)
2	(1:4, :, 5:6)	(5:8, :, 5:6)
3	(1:4, :, 7:8)	(5:8, :, 7:8)

The extent of a data array dimension does not need to be exactly divisible by the number of processes across which it is distributed. In general, if n elements are distributed across p processes, then $\lceil n/p \rceil$ elements are assigned to each of the first $n \backslash p$ processes

---

[3] We talk of *processes* rather than *processors* because some architectures (e.g. transputers) allow many processes to run concurrently on each processor.

and $\lfloor n/p \rfloor$ are assigned to each of the rest. ($\lceil x \rceil$ is the smallest integer $\geq x$, $\lfloor x \rfloor$ is the largest integer $\leq x$, and $n \backslash p$ is the remainder of $n \div p$).

Dummy argument arrays may take their distribution from the corresponding actual argument, rather than having it declared explicitly. This is analogous to the assumed-shape feature for dummy arrays, and is accordingly called *assumed-distribution*. It is denoted by omitting the integers in the DISTRIBUTION attribute (although the appropriate number of commas must be supplied). There will also be an extra intrinsic function, DISTRIB(ARRAY[,DIM]), that returns the distribution of an array, analogous to the standard intrinsic functions SIZE, LBOUND and UBOUND for dimension information. For example, the declarations in the function MATVEC of the last section could be extended as follows to include distribution information:

```
FUNCTION MATVEC (MATRIX, VEC)
    REAL, DIMENSION (:,:), DISTRIBUTION (,) :: MATRIX
    REAL, DIMENSION (SIZE (MATRIX,2)),                    &
        DISTRIBUTION (DISTRIB (MATRIX,2)) :: VEC
    REAL, DIMENSION (SIZE (MATRIX,1)),                    &
        DISTRIBUTION (DISTRIB (MATRIX,1)) :: MATVEC
```

(& at the end of a statement line indicates that the statement is continued).

Note that the size of the (logical) process grid is *not* declared in the program. This information is actually provided in an 'INCLUDE' file, as we shall describe later. To target the program to a process array of a different size it is only necessary to change the parameters in this file and re-compile the Fortran 77 program that was generated by the pre-processor; the Fortran 90 program does not need to be modified or pre-processed again.

Arrays need not be distributed, in which case no DISTRIBUTION declaration is necessary, or they may be distributed over a subset of the process grid dimensions. For instance, if a program is targetted to a 2-dimensional process grid, any vectors that it contains can only be distributed over one of the grid dimensions at most. Scalars and non-distributed arrays are *replicated*—a copy of the complete data object is kept on every process. Similarly, arrays that are distributed only over a subset of the process grid dimensions are replicated over the others. As we shall explain in the next section, the parallelisation scheme guarantees that data values are consistent over replicated dimensions, that is, all copies of a data item have the same value at any step of the program.

Obviously, the manner in which data is partitioned will only affect the performance of a program, not its logical behaviour: it will perform the same calculation steps and give the same results (modulo roundoff errors in the reduction functions) irrespective of the data distribution. However, an unsuitable distribution may seriously degrade the performance by increasing communications and/or decreasing the exploitation of potential data parallelism. Ultimately it is desirable to use automatic program analysis to determine a good data partitioning [4].

The distribution scheme presented here is obviously quite basic, and was chosen as a simple starting point. Many applications would benefit from allowing more general array distributions and alignments such as those in Fortran D [5] and CM Fortran [6, 7]. It is hoped that we will be able to exploit more flexible data mappings in future research.

4 The parallelisation system

The basic idea of the parallelisation scheme is that, given a pre-defined array partitioning, the potential for data parallelism, and the communications required to achieve it, are implicit in the semantics of array operations (array expressions, assignments and intrinsic functions), and can be detected and implemented automatically.

For example, given arrays A, B and C with identical shapes and distributions, the following operation can be performed concurrently by each process on its local segments of the arrays without communications:

```
A = 2.0 * B + SIN (C)
```

The following operations, however, all involve communications if acting on distributed data:

```
SUM (A)                    ! an array intrinsic function
A (2:2*N:2) = B (1:N)      ! a 'fan-out' operation
A (IVEC) = B               ! indirect addressing (gather/scatter)
```

(the SUM intrinsic function also involves calculation). As a final example, bearing in mind that scalar variables are *replicated*, the following assignment involves a broadcast communication if array A is distributed:

```
SCALAR = A (I)
```

As we have already mentioned, the ADAPT system comprises two components: a pre-processor and a communications library.

The pre-processor transforms a Distributed Fortran 90 program into a Fortran 77 program that constitutes a component process of a rectangular multi-dimensional grid of processes. It is equivalent to the original program, but with distributed array declarations transformed into declarations of the local segments of those arrays, operations on distributed arrays transformed into operations on the local segments, and calls to communications procedures from a purpose-built library inserted where necessary.

The reason for transforming the input into Fortran 77 rather than Fortran 90 is so that the resulting program can be compiled by currently available compilers. (In fact, the need to perform this language transformation greatly complicates the job of the pre-processor and makes it impractical to implement some of the new features of Fortran 90, as we mention in Section 4.6. When Fortran 90 compilers become available it will be beneficial to modify the pre-processor to produce standard Fortran 90 output).

The communications library contains routines for the Fortran 90 array intrinsic functions as well as procedures to perform all of the required communications.

The Fortran 90 array intrinsics are actually implemented as subroutines rather than functions, as they are called from Fortran 77, which does not support array-valued functions. Their arguments and result may have any distribution.

The communications procedures implement high-level, grid-based communication patterns, often involving all of the processes along one or more axes of the process grid (e.g. broadcasts, multicasts, shifts, gather-scatter operations, array reshaping, I/O of distributed arrays), rather than low-level point-to-point communications. In general, communications may occur in the following contexts:

- array expressions and assignments;
- array intrinsic functions;
- input/output.

Since the transformation scheme implements communications by invoking high-level communications procedures, it is insensitive to the underlying connectivity of the process grid—these details are left to the communications library. Our implementation of the library, which is targetted to networks of T9000 transputers, assumes that each process has a direct connection to all other processes on the same grid axes as itself [8]. For some systems it may be desirable to assume a fully connected network, whose higher connectivity may be useful for some of the communications procedures (e.g. I/O). However, the minimum connectivity required by the basic communications model of ADAPT is simply nearest neighbour connectivity in each of the process grid dimensions.

In general, communications are performed along axes of the process grid. The transformation scheme ensures that, if a library procedure has to communicate in direction μ of the process grid, it will be invoked by all of the processes along a given μ-directed grid axis. Likewise, if it involves communications in a pair of process grid dimensions (μ,ν), (e.g. transpose), it will be invoked identically by all of the processes in a given (μ,ν) plane. I/O procedures may potentially involve communications in any grid dimension, and so are called globally across the process grid. It is relatively straightforward to design communications procedures that are guaranteed to be deadlock-free under these assumptions. We shall not give details of the communications library in this paper; the base library on which the T9000 version is built is described in [8].

The rest of this section describes the principal program transformations that are performed by the pre-processor in order to accomplish the auto-parallelisation. This description will also clarify the execution model employed by the system.

In the following description, PROC_RANK is the rank of the logical process array to which the program is targetted, and PROC_SIZE_I is its extent in dimension I (I=1,2,..., RANK_PROC). These parameter names are referenced in the output program, which accesses their values from an 'INCLUDE file'.

4.1 Array declarations

Every array declaration in the Fortran 90 input program is transformed into a declaration of the 'local segment' of the array. This means that a dimension I that is distributed over process grid dimension J has its declared bounds, LI:UI say, replaced by an extent EI, given by:

    EI = (UI - LI + PROC_SIZE_J) / PROC_SIZE_J

This is actually the *largest* extent of a local segment in that dimension, bearing in mind that the total number of elements in a dimension may not be exactly divisible by the number of processes over which it is distributed. Because of the Fortran 77 requirement for static memory allocation, the size of the largest segment must be declared in all processes.

In addition to this transformation, every array has an 'attribute vector' declared and initialised for it. The attribute vector contains the following information:

```
INTEGER :: TYPE, LEN, RANK
INTEGER, DIMENSION (RANK) :: SHAPE, DISTR, LOC_SHAPE, LOC_USED,      &
                             LOC_LB, SECT_SHAPE, SECT_LB, STRIDE
INTEGER, DIMENSION (PROC_RANK) :: STEP_PROC

ATTRIB = (/ TYPE, LEN, RANK, SHAPE, DISTR, LOC_SHAPE, LOC_USED,      &
            LOC_LB, STEP_PROC, SECT_SHAPE, SECT_LB, STRIDE /)
```

`TYPE`, `LEN` and `RANK` are respectively the data-type of the array, the total number of elements of the *local* segment, and the rank. `SHAPE` is the shape of the *whole* array, and `DISTR` its distribution, as specified in the `DISTRIBUTION` attribute. `LOC_SHAPE` is the shape of the *local segment*, i.e. the vector of extents EI, where EI is as above for distributed dimensions and is the total extent for undistributed dimensions. The *used* local segment may be smaller than this for the reason given above, and its shape is given by `LOC_USED`. `LOC_LB` is the vector of lower bounds of the local segment. `STEP_PROC` is a vector that specifies, for each dimension of the logical process array, the coordinate of the first process on which the size of the *used* local segment is (EI-1) rather than EI. (The last four attributes that we have described are in fact redundant, as they can be computed from `SHAPE` and `DISTR`, but they are stored to avoid frequent re-computation.) The three remaining vectors, `SECT_SHAPE`, `SECT_LB` and `STRIDE`, allow a regular section such as `A(L:U:S)` of the parent array to be specified. Notice that in general the elements of a regular array section are not stored contiguously, and may reside in a subset of the processes. This parameterisation allows the section to be passed into a procedure by passing the parent array and the section parameters, avoiding the need to copy the section into a temporary array that is contiguous and uniformly distributed, and copy back the result on return, thus saving communication as well as storage.

For the declaration of a static array most of the attribute vector can be initialised at compile-time, but the `LOC_USED` and `LOC_LB` attributes must be initialised dynamically as their values depend on the coordinates of the local process. For automatic arrays, most of the attribute vector must be initialised dynamically. (Automatic arrays cannot be declared as such in the output program, as Fortran 77 requires all local arrays to be statically dimensioned. They are implemented by a simple stack memory management scheme, which we shall briefly describe later.)

All array arguments of procedures are accompanied by their attribute vectors. They contain all the information necessary for assumed-shape and -distribution dummy arrays (which are transformed into Fortran 77 adjustable arrays), as well as all of the information required by library procedures in order to organise the communications. The reason for storing the `TYPE` and `RANK` of an array in its attribute vector is so that generic communications procedures can be used that handle arrays of any data type and rank.

4.2 Array expressions and assignments

The transformation of array expressions and assignments is the hardest part of the program restructuring, and is the core of the auto-parallelisation procedure. In general, data referenced in an array expression may have to be re-distributed so that they are 'co-distributed' with the array variable that is being assigned to (which means that corresponding elements of the array variable and expression are stored in the same process).

Array expressions can of course occur in contexts other than assignment statements (e.g. as procedure arguments, items in an output list or as the mask expression in a WHERE construct). In these cases, the result of the array expression must be assigned to a temporary array variable, and the same considerations apply as for assignment statements. For simplicity the temporary array can be taken to have the same distribution as the first term of the expression, though this is not necessarily the optimal choice.

The following analysis and transformation is required for each array assignment:

1. Firstly, a check is made that all of the subscripts are in range and that all of the arrays conform. If the shape of an array assignment is found to contain a zero extent, the assignment is skipped.

2. Array-valued functions in the expression, both user-defined and intrinsic, are transformed into calls to equivalent subroutines and the results returned via temporary arrays. This is necessary because Fortran 77 does not support array-valued functions. Note, however, that this transformation does not apply to elemental functions.

3. Now it may be necessary to re-distribute some of the array primaries so that they are co-distributed with the assignment variable. This re-distribution is performed in two stages.

    First it is necessary to check, for each array primary, whether the mapping of its dimensions onto the process array dimensions matches that of the assignment variable. If not, it must be 're-distributed' into a temporary array with the correct distribution (or possibly directly into the assignment variable). We refer to this re-mapping of the data dimensions onto the process array dimensions as 'dimensional redistribution', to distinguish it from re-mapping the distribution of data elements *within* a process array dimension.

    A 'distribution vector' $\underline{\mu}$ is defined for each array or array section, containing the sequence of process array dimensions μ_i onto which the corresponding data dimensions i are mapped. It is thus the same as the declared DISTRIBUTION vector of the array, except that dimensions with just a single element selected are omitted *if they are internal*—they must still be included if they are distributed. The latter case is equivalent to augmenting the shape of the array section with an additional dimension of extent 1, so, to ensure that conformance is maintained with the other array sections, it may be necessary to augment their shape vectors with a 1 and their distribution vectors with a 0 in the same position—this makes no difference to the semantics of the array sections. Now, the distribution of an array section in the expression, $\underline{\mu}$, matches that of the assignment variable, $\underline{\nu}$, if $\mu_i = \nu_i$ or 0 for each data dimension i—the latter case is allowed because a replicated array can be assigned to a distributed array without communication.

    If $\underline{\mu}$ does not match $\underline{\nu}$, the array section in the expression must be re-distributed. To economise on storage and communication, we achieve the required target distribution by distributing rather than replicating dimensions wherever possible (i.e. by setting μ_i to ν_i rather than 0). Dimensional redistribution is performed by two communication functions: 'TRANSPOSE', which interchanges the mapping of two, not necessarily consecutive, data dimensions (e.g. to change distribution (1,2) into (2,1) or (1,0) into (0,1)), and 'BROADCAST' (e.g. to change distribution (1) into (0) or (2)). These communications may need to be performed several times to achieve the required distribution. A certain amount of analysis is required to ensure that they are performed in an optimal order.

4. The second phase of re-distribution involves checking the *distributed dimensions* only, to ensure that corresponding elements of each array or array section are co-distributed (i.e. reside in the same process). If not, then elements must be redistributed *within* a process array dimension, which we call 'elemental redistribution'. If the distributed dimension has a vector subscript, a 'GATHER_SCATTER' communication procedure is called to rearrange the elements appropriately. A pair of regular array sections are co-distributed if the total extents of the distributed dimensions are the same and the sections have identical strides and offsets from the lower bound (this is actually the simplest case: in fact a less restrictive condition can be formulated). If not, elements are re-arranged by the communications procedures 'SHIFT' and 'FAN'.

5. At this stage, all of the array function references and communications arising from the array expression have been implemented by subroutine calls that are placed ahead of the array assignment. These subroutines return their results to temporary arrays that are referenced in the transformed array expression. The resulting array assignment contains only regular array sections (of the form A(L:U:S)) and elemental functions of such sections, and all of these sections are co-distributed.

The array assignment is now transformed into an equivalent elemental assignment enclosed in DO-loops over array subscripts, as Fortran 77 does not support array operations. As a result of this transformation, array arguments of elemental functions become standard scalar arguments.

Before this transformation is performed, however, a check is made to ensure that there is no overlap between the assignment variable and any of the array sections in the expression. If there is, the rule is that the expression is fully evaluated before the assignment takes place. Thus, if a straightforward expansion to DO-loops would result in a true dependence (i.e. assigning to an element that is referenced in a subsequent iteration), then the result of the expression must be assigned to an intermediate temporary array.

Obviously, a DO-loop over a distributed dimension must only select the *local* elements of the array section. For example, the DO-loop corresponding to a distributed array section A(L:U:S), where S is positive and LB and USED are the lower bound and used extent of the local segment, is as follows:

```
DO I = MAX (L+1-LB, 1+MOD(S+MOD(L-LB,S),S))), MIN (U+1-LB, USED), S
   A (I)
ENDDO
```

It is evident that replicated data will remain coherent, because the same assignments will be executed on all processes over the replicated dimensions. Assignments can only differ between processes as a result of process-selecting DO-loops like the one above, and these apply only to distributed data dimensions. This, together with the correct redistribution of data in steps 3 and 4 above, and the correct behaviour of the input routines, is sufficient to guarantee coherence.

Much of the above analysis must be performed dynamically if any of the array sections are automatic, adjustable, assumed-shape or assumed-distribution. For arrays with assumed-distribution, the generated Fortran 77 program executes step 3 by calling a general-purpose 'dimensional redistribution' procedure, which tests the distributions dynamically and invokes the communication primitives as necessary. Similarly a general-purpose 'elemental redistribution' procedure is used for assumed-shape and automatic arrays.

Our discussion has implied that terms in the array expression are redistributed to align with the assignment variable *before* the expression is evaluated. This corresponds to the 'owner-computes' rule that is commonly applied in distributed memory auto-parallelisation. However, a considerable optimisation may be achieved in some instances by evaluating the expression or a sub-expression *in situ*, if its primaries are co-distributed with each other but not the assignment variable. We believe that it should not be too difficult to implement this optimisation in our system. Hopefully this will be a topic for future research.

4.3 Scalar assignments and DO-loops

As one would expect, assignments to single array elements are just a special case of array assignments, and the same sequence of transformations is performed as above. For example, if vectors A and B are the same size and are distributed in grid dimension 1, then:

```
A (I) = B (I+1)
```

is transformed into something like:

```
CALL SHIFT (TEMP, B, DIM=1, SHIFT=1...)   ! some arguments omitted !
!
! Now the required assignment is  A (I) = TEMP (I)
!
DO I$ = MAX (1, I+1-LB_A), MIN (USED_A, I+1-LB_A)
    A (I$) = TEMP (I$)
ENDDO
```

The call to SHIFT shifts the distributed vector B by one element into array TEMP (which obviously involves communicating data between processes), so that TEMP and A are co-distributed. The subsequent loop performs a single iteration in the process that stores element I.

Some of the above analysis is also relevant for assignments to scalar variables, namely steps 1 and 3 (conformance checking and dimensional redistribution). Obviously, the expression evaluation and assignment is now performed in all processes, as required, since the process-selecting DO-loops that may be introduced by step 5 no longer apply. If the expression involves elements of distributed arrays, they are broadcast globally in the dimensional redistribution phase.

No transformation is performed on DO-loops appearing in the original Fortran 90 program, that is, every process executes every iteration of the loop. This is usually the desired behaviour, as the array programming style normally uses loops for sequential iteration rather than for iteration over array elements. Nevertheless, it is still of some interest to consider the behaviour of loops over array element assignments. The rule is that if the assignment involves communications in a subset of the process grid dimensions, then its iterations will be sequentialised over the corresponding data dimensions. This is because a communication synchronises all of the processes that are involved. For example, consider the previous elemental assignment, this time enclosed in a loop over elements.

```
DO I = 1,N-1
    A (I) = B (I+1)
ENDDO
```

The assignment is transformed exactly as before:

```
DO I = 1,N-1
    CALL SHIFT (TEMP, B, DIM=1, SHIFT=1...)
    DO I$ = MAX (1, I+1-LB_A), MIN (USED_A, I+1-LB_A)
        A (I$) = TEMP (I$)
    ENDDO
ENDDO
```

Now every process executes every iteration of the outer loop. In each one there is a call to SHIFT which sequentialises the iterations. To make this execute concurrently it must be written as an array operation:

```
A (1:N-1) = B (2:N)
```

which results in only a single call to SHIFT before the loop over single element assignments:

```
CALL SHIFT (TEMP, B, DIM=1, SHIFT=1...)
DO I$ = MAX (1, 2-LB_A), MIN (USED_A, N-LB_A)
    A (I$) = TEMP (I$)
ENDDO
```

In this case, therefore, each process executes its portion of the assignment loop concurrently.

However, if the loop iterates over distributed data dimensions that do *not* involve communications, then it can execute concurrently over those dimensions. For instance, altering the above example slightly so that the source and destination are co-distributed:

```
DO I = 1,N-1
    A (I) = B (I)
ENDDO
```

results in a similar transformation to the one above but without the call to SHIFT (and the transformed assignment becomes A(I$)=B(I$)). Now each process can execute its particular iterations of the inner loop concurrently (assuming that the time to cycle through the remaining empty iterations did not dominate the total time, as they might do in this simple example!).

4.4 Input and output

Input, output and operations on external files are implemented by communications procedures that communicate with a 'server' running on the host processor (which is also provided as part of the ADAPT library). These procedures are called globally across the process array to avoid the possibility of deadlock. For I/O, firstly the specification list (including the unit number and format specification) is sent to the server, then the data is communicated, and finally a terminating token is sent to the server to signal that the I/O is complete. Obviously, the I/O procedures must be designed to work properly with distributed and replicated data—for instance, input to replicated variables must ensure that all copies of the data are updated.

The use of a server running on the host process avoids the need for program 'splitting', as implemented in the Superb system [9], whereby the input program is transformed into a 'worker' program and a 'host' program that performs only I/O. This transformation is potentially very difficult as the I/O may be embedded in control constructs whose execution depends on the results of calculation. Another advantage of using a server is that it avoids the possibility of the host processor having to buffer a lot of data.

4.5 Temporary and automatic arrays

The pre-processor must perform a host of other transformations simply in order to implement in Fortran 77 some of the many new features of Fortran 90. We shall only describe the implementation of one such feature, namely dynamically-sized arrays.

In Fortran 77 all non-dummy arrays must be declared with constant bounds. However, Fortran 90 provides automatic arrays, which have variable bounds and exist for the duration of a procedure. Additionally, the process of transforming Distributed Fortran 90 to Fortran 77 often introduces variable-size temporary arrays. Both types of array require a stack memory management scheme to be simulated in the Fortran 77 program.

This is quite straightforward to implement. It is done by introducing a common block that contains a large vector for use as temporary storage (which we call the 'stack' vector), and the subscript of the current 'top-of-stack' element. The common block is declared in every procedure, and the stack vector is equivalenced to every data type. Temporary and automatic arrays are taken from the stack vector. Each has two variables associated with it, which store the subscript (with respect to the stack vector) of its first element, and its total length. As arrays are allocated or de-allocated from the stack vector, the 'top-of-stack' subscript is incremented or decremented accordingly. A small drawback is that all such arrays must be referenced as one-dimensional vectors, even if they are logically multi-dimensional arrays.

Temporary arrays introduced by the pre-processor are only allocated for the duration of their useful lifetime, which is usually a single assignment statement in the original Fortran 90 program. This helps to economise on memory usage.

4.6 Limitations of the current version

Because of time constraints and the limitations of translation to Fortran 77, some features of Fortran 90 will *not* be implemented by the first version of ADAPT, namely pointers, derived types and operators, allocatable arrays, internal subroutines and modules. The pre-processor will be able to parse programs that use these features, but will give error messages reporting that they are not supported.

5 Discussion and conclusions

Currently the programming of distributed memory MIMD architectures is hindered by the lack of support for a high level, shared memory programming style, and by the lack of program portability. The research presented here is an attempt to address these issues, in the field of data parallel programming, by designing and developing a system that will implement Fortran 90 array programs with minimal modifications on distributed memory architectures.

Fortran 90 is an attractive language for such a system for a variety of reasons. Its array features provide a natural and concise programming style for data parallel applications, and facilitate distributed memory implementation. It provides basic linear algebra and a rich set of array operations as intrinsic functions, which in the present context means that distributed versions of these operations will be automatically available as part of the system. Equally important, programs written in this language will be portable (modulo the distribution declarations) across a wide spectrum of architectures when Fortran 90 compilers become available. Indeed, the array features are already supported as extensions to Fortran 77 by many compilers for shared memory and vector systems and SIMD processor arrays (e.g. [7]).

The modular design of the system should make it easier to port to other distributed memory MIMD machines. The pre-processor converts the input program into standard Fortran 77, with no message-passing or other extensions, so it can be used without modification on any target system that provides a Fortran 77 compiler.

All of the machine-specific features are localised in the library. Since all of the communications and array intrinsic functions are performed by library procedures, they could potentially be highly optimised, just as Fortran 77 compilers normally provide highly optimised implementations of the standard intrinsic functions. Also, since the SPMD (Single Processor Multiple Data [10]) model is such a common programming paradigm for distributed memory architectures, the procedures provided by the library would be very useful outside of the context of ADAPT, and it is arguable that they should be provided as part of a standard library on any distributed memory system.

Other approaches to supporting a virtual shared memory programming style on distributed memory architectures are being researched elsewhere. For imperative language programming, they fall into the following categories:

- Automatic parallelisation of conventional sequential languages, especially Fortran 77 and C, with processor topology and data mapping specified interactively or by program annotations (e.g. Superb [9], Parascope [11] and Pandore C [12]).

- Extensions to conventional languages to explicitly express data parallel execution as well as the processor topology and data mapping, but without explicit message passing. Examples include Kali [13], Fortran D [5] and C* [14].

- New languages designed for efficient transformation to SPMD code on both shared and distributed memory architectures, such as Blaze [15] and Booster [16].

The motivation for the first approach is in providing a migration aid for existing software. However, this task is made very difficult by the unnecessary sequentialisation (DO-loops) introduced by conventional sequential languages, and, in the case of Fortran at least, by the many features that hinder distributed memory implementation (such as aliasing, equivalencing, reshaping of arrays across procedure boundaries).

In contrast, the aim of this project is to exploit and promote *new* language features that can assist in distributed memory auto-parallelisation while preserving portability to other architectures. Several features introduced into Fortran by the new standard are helpful in this respect, apart from the obvious one of the implicit parallelism of the array operations. For example, the provision of explicit procedure interfaces removes the need for interprocedural analysis, permits checking, and in our case allows the partitioning of array parameters to be assumed. The provision of dynamically sized automatic arrays allows a simpler implementation of problems such as the multigrid method, which in turn simplifies the parallelisation (cf. the complications that arise from allocating arrays from a single workspace vector [17]). In the spirit of our approach, we also restrict the use of features that inhibit parallelisation, such as automatic reshaping of arrays across procedure boundaries and passing single elements as actual arguments to dummy arrays.

The design of new languages such as Booster and Blaze that can be efficiently implemented on parallel architectures is obviously attractive for a number of reasons. The only significant advantages of Fortran 90 over this approach are the obvious ones of greater familiarity and greater certainty of program portability.

Currently a first version of ADAPT is being developed, targetted to networks of T9000 transputers. In this initial development stage, effort has concentrated on designing and implementing the basic methodology; little attention has been paid to optimisation issues. As we have indicated in the paper, there are many issues to be addressed in terms of increasing the efficiency and utility of the basic system presented here. Among the more obvious ones are improving its memory and communications efficiency (which are to some extent mutually exclusive), relaxing the 'owner computes' rule, allowing more flexible data partitioning schemes, and investigating the possibility of dynamic features.

Acknowledgements

The author would like to thank Bryan Carpenter for useful discussions and for providing the core of the T9000 communications library, and David Gee for providing some of the array intrinsic functions.

References

[1] ANSI X3J3/S8.115. Fortran 90, June 1990.

[2] D. Pountain. Virtual channels: the next generation of transputers, *Byte*, April 1990, p55.

[3] M. Metcalf and J. Reid. 'Fortran 90 Explained', Oxford Science publications, OUP, ISBN 0-19-853772-7, 1990.

[4] V. Balasundaram, G. Fox, K. Kennedy and U. Kremer. An interactive environment for data partitioning and distribution, *Proc. 5th Distributed Memory Computing Conf.*, Charleston, SC, April 1990.
K. Ikudome, G. Fox, A. Kolawa and J. Flower. An automatic and symbolic parallelization system for distributed memory parallel computers, *ibid*.

[5] G. Fox, S. Hiranandani, K. Kennedy, C. Koelbel, U. Kremer, C.-W. Tseng and M.-Y. Wu. Fortran D language specification, Technical report TR90-141, Dept. of Comp. Sci., Rice Univ., Dec. 1990.

[6] Thinking Machines Corp., Cambridge, MA. CM Fortran reference manual, version 5.2-0.6, Sept. 1989.

[7] E. Albert, K. Knobe, J. Lukas and G. Steele. Compiling Fortran 8x array features for the Connection Machine computer system, *Symposium on Parallel Programming: Experience with Applications, Languages and Systems*, New Haven, CT, July 1988.

[8] D. B. Carpenter. Array communication library: user guide and reference manual, Esprit-II project P2701 (PUMA) deliverable report 5.1.1.2, Univ. of Southampton, May 1991.

[9] H. Zima, H.-J. Bast and M. Gerndt. SUPERB, a tool for semi-automatic MIMD / SIMD parallelisation, *Parallel Computing*, 6, 1-18, 1988.

[10] A.H. Karp. Programming for Parallelism, *IEEE Computer*, May 1987, pp. 43-57.

[11] D. Callahan and K. Kennedy. Compiling programs for distributed-memory multi-processors, *Jnl. of Supercomputing*, 2, 151-169, 1988.

[12] F. André, J.-L. Pazat and H. Thomas. PANDORE: a system to manage data distribution, *Proc. Int. Conf. on Supercomputing*, 380-88, June 1990.

[13] C. Koelbel, P. Mehrotra and J. Van Rosendale. Supporting shared data structures on distributed memory architectures, *Proc. 2nd ACM SIGPLAN Symposium on Principles and Practice of Parallel Programming*, pp 177-86, March 1990.

[14] P.J. Hatcher, M.J. Quinn, A.J. Lapadula, R.J. Jones and R.J. Anderson. A production quality C* compiler for a hypercube multicomputer. Report from Parallel Computing Lab., Dept. of Comp. Sci., Univ. of New Hampshire, Durham, NH 03824, U.S.A.

[15] P. Mehrotra and J. Van Rosendale. The BLAZE language: a parallel language for scientific programming, *Parallel Computing*, 5, 339-361, 1987.

[16] E.M.R.M. Paalvast and H.J. Sips. A high-level language for the description of parallel algorithms, *Proc. of Parallel Computing '89*, Aug 1989, Leiden, The Netherlands, North Holland Publ. Co.

[17] M. Gerndt. Parallelisation of multigrid programs in SUPERB, *Proc. Int. Workshop on Compilers for Parallel Computers*, 213-223, eds. P. Feautrier and F. Irigoin, Ecole des Mines de Paris, Dec 3-5 1990.

EVOLUTION OF MASSIVE PARALLEL COMPUTE SERVERS FROM A RESEARCH OBJECT TO A PRODUCTION TOOL

Michel H. Reymond, Director of Scientific Computing Center,
EPFL Federal Institute of Technology, Lausanne

Abtract:

Massive parallel systems built from microprocessors have caught up with conventional supercomputers in performance and are expected to far exceed the conventional supercomputers in the current decade. Programmer productivity and deliverable, scalable performance are important requirements that must be met before massively parallel systems can achieve broader acceptance for scientific computing. However this will not be enough to compete on that market and generate profits as a production tool: potential customers in advanced sciences keep lots of proprietary know-how in form of existing software with no chance of rewriting, unless to loose their competitive edge by missing the time-window to market their products. Except for projects starting from scratch, the solution to MPP may depend on the ability to deliver enough sustained performance to somewhat modified existing application software thus keeping the customers competitive in their own market.

INTRODUCTION

Parallel processing has become a commonplace in the industry in the past decade, with even high-end workstations and PC's employing multiple CPU's. Symmetric multiprocessing under UNIX along with shared memory has been the approach for parallel OS kernels. Most of these architectures are bus-based or cross-bar, limiting the scalability of the architectures to tens of processors: bus-based architectures suffer from fixed band-width, while cross-bar architectures become economically unfeasable due to its price increase to the square of the number of ports. The term of 'MPP massive parallel processing' will thus apply to parallel architectures including the following characteristics:

1. High performance (RISC) microprocessors.
2. Large number of processors (64 and up)
3. Scalable interconnect and bandwith of distributed/shared memory
4. Advanced system software and programmer productivity tools

Most of trend analysis concerning MPP show a bright outlook for those architectures within this decade:

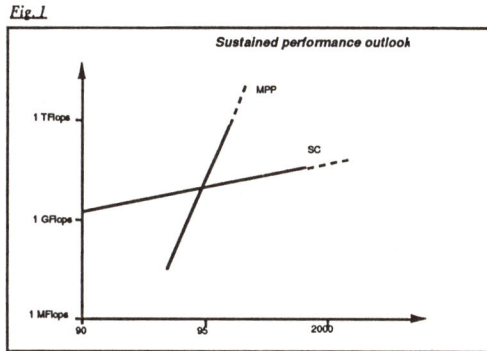

Fig.1 Sustained performance outlook

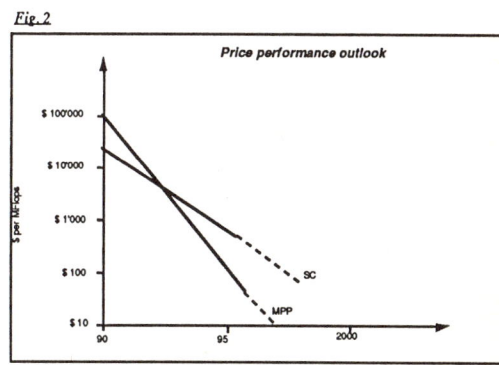

Fig.2 Price performance outlook

ummac32/10.9.1991

Unfortunately the roaring success is yet to come, except in some areas as image processing, VLSI-routing and simulation, data-base applications, etc. all of them written from scratch.

What is still holding MPP systems back?

DELIVERED PERFORMANCE

The conventional wisdom concerning MPP systems would be to acknowledge that many problems are naturally parallel and map readily to parallel architectures. However this will often yield to a complete change of data-structures and algorithms. Therefore many MPP software designers have proposed new languages capable of describing those parallel algorithms and mapping them directly to MPP systems. The delivered performance shows a good ratio vs. peak performance. OCCAM, STRAND, SISAL are a number of languages which have gained some significance in this context.

This approach to MPP programming will remain the best solution for a maximum delivered performance ratio, however a significant investment will be necessary to improve this kind of programmer productivity tools in the long term to gain acceptance:

- Package Object Oriented Programming (OOP) with many features needed for scientific computing:

    Visualisation, data-structure design, algorithms, mesh, elements, data-entry, software-engineering, data-base features, security, image-processing, visual programming, GUI, documentation, multi-media, performance monitoring etc.

- Portability, protection of software investment, standards

The availability of such programmer productivity environments in the near term is questionable due to the heavy development investment required to implement these tools. In addition, only a full blown feature environment will be enough to trigger the use of this tool for MPP programming.

Until such time, less elaborate solutions seem to be required to assure a fair level of delivered performance to MPP users!

THE FIVE SACRED FACTS OF SCIENTIFIC PROGRAMMING

Unlike the workstation and low end market, some facts can be observed for top scientific computing in research and very much in industry:

1. Scientists still love FORTRAN.
   80 % of todays top scientific code is still written in that 'Fatal Disease' (Dijkstra about Fortran)!

2. Top scientific code is not accessible.
   Most top scientific code is company proprietary and considered a trade secret,
   and thus unavailable for re-writing by outside parties!

3. Top scientific code is biased by history.
   Often such code has a 20 years history, biased by a number of machine architectures.
   Much code is serial, at most vectorized for Cray.
   Top scientific code is very large, often undocumented and in 'spaghetti'-quality.

4. Scientific programmers have a notorious resistance to change.

5. Owners of top scientific code have the money to invest, but no time!

Given those facts one can identify a number of alternatives:

THE GOOD, THE BAD AND THE UGLY (thanks to Sergio Leone)

THE GOOD:

The OOP approach as outlined above has to be encouraged by all means in the long term. A number of scientific applications could be re-written in man-months instead of man-years, provided the tools are bright enough!

However the wait time for elaborate 'GOOD' OOP programmer productivity tools & environments may be beyond the mid 90's, too late to fit the extremely performant MPP hardware becoming available within 2-3 years!

Obviously partial OOP productivity tools & environments will prevent their accepance!

A number of Algorithms in FEM, CFD and other areas of interest could be prioritized to be adapted to MPP architectures. Not to mention all other undergoing algorithmic work currently associated to MPP.

THE BAD:

Stick to serial code, use superscalar architectures at best, and forget MPP! Obviously this 'BAD' alternative is for sure a valid one for a number of existing applications.

THE UGLY:

Ask for a minor investment in the order of a few man-months in reprogramming of existing top scientific code and look for the MPP system that delivers the best performance.

Under that asumption, the least ugly of the common denominators to fit the sacred facts of scientific programming seems to be FORTRAN 90, which has been or is in the process of implementation by a number of manufacturers of present or future MPP systems: MASPAR, THINKING-MACHINES, CRAY, and others, as well as workstation vendors.

F90 allows to take advantage of some of the MPP architecural capabilities and yet to protect the software investment by retaining the portability of codes.

The F90 language extensions include following major features & highlights:

goodies:

- longer identifiers
- in-line comments and multistatement lines
- symbolic relational operators (e.g., < instead of .LT.)
- use of include statement
- optional free form
- utilities such as DATE and TIME

and new features which may be used by MPP resources:

- a variety of array operations
- control structure enhancements, including DO WHILE, DO (forever) and CASE statements
- new data types - including pointers, character strings, and those derived from others, as in Pascal
- bit operations similar to those in C
- nested scoping of procedures (a procedure can include one internal procedure)
- recursive procedures

- optional IN and OUT procedure parameters as in ADA
- modules containing both data types and procedures, with both PUBLIC and PRIVATE levels of access
- improved I/O, especially for database records

A promising evolution under these 'UGLY' circumstances may well be to closely couple conventional supercomputing architectures or alternatively forthcoming superscalar parallel RISC architectures with massive parallel processing subsystems sharing state of the art technology for maximum memory-bandwith, interconnect networks, packaging, cooling, and the system software environment. As an example Cray Research has announced a project in that direction using the Cray Y–MP as platform fot their MPP MIMD subsystem. Some indications from Japan show that Fujitsu among others have some activities undergoing in that direction.

UGLY, BUT HOPE TO DELIVER PERFORMANCE

Example:

A Maspar MPP system at the EPFL, using CFD Euler fluid dynamics code, itself written in a subset of F90 and optimized for vector computer and good size mesh, the following preliminary performance figures can be quoted:

Cray-2, 4 processors, 256 MWords: Normalized to 1.

Maspar MP1, 4096 processors   0.3 to 0.5 vs. Cray-2, still very depending on code options, accidents with 0.0001 can occur, but are trackable.

                                       30 to 50 vs. Cray-2 as above, same but performance/price and single use of system (3 to 5, if multiple-MPP systems).

The Maspar MPP system currently uses 4 bit processing elements for floating point computation, which is a limiting factor that will be improved in future releases of hardware implementing larger processing elements.

These figures have been obtained without big efforts and using the standard Maspar program productivity environment.

The analysis of behaviour of CFD codes on different MPP architectures is currently undertaken as a research project by IMHEF: Hydraulic Machines and Fluid Mechanics Institute, at EPFL, which will present a paper in due time.

This example yields to the conulsion that an interesting degree of delivered performance can be expected from the 'UGLY' case in the first half of the 1990's, even for shared MPP systems.

CONNECTING THE MPP PRODUCTION TOOL TO THE WORLD

Beside programmer productivity tools, and sharing equal importance, is network integration which is a conditio sin equa non for MPP systems to become a production tool.

Integrating the MPP resource as an element of a networked computing grid with high-speed links using a defined logical and physical interface is todays vision of EPFL regarding connecting topology.

Fig 3: EPFL networked computing topology block diagramm : see next page

Fig 4: EPFL networked computing topology : see next page

Fig. 3 : Topology of Networking resources at EPFL (1991-1993) :

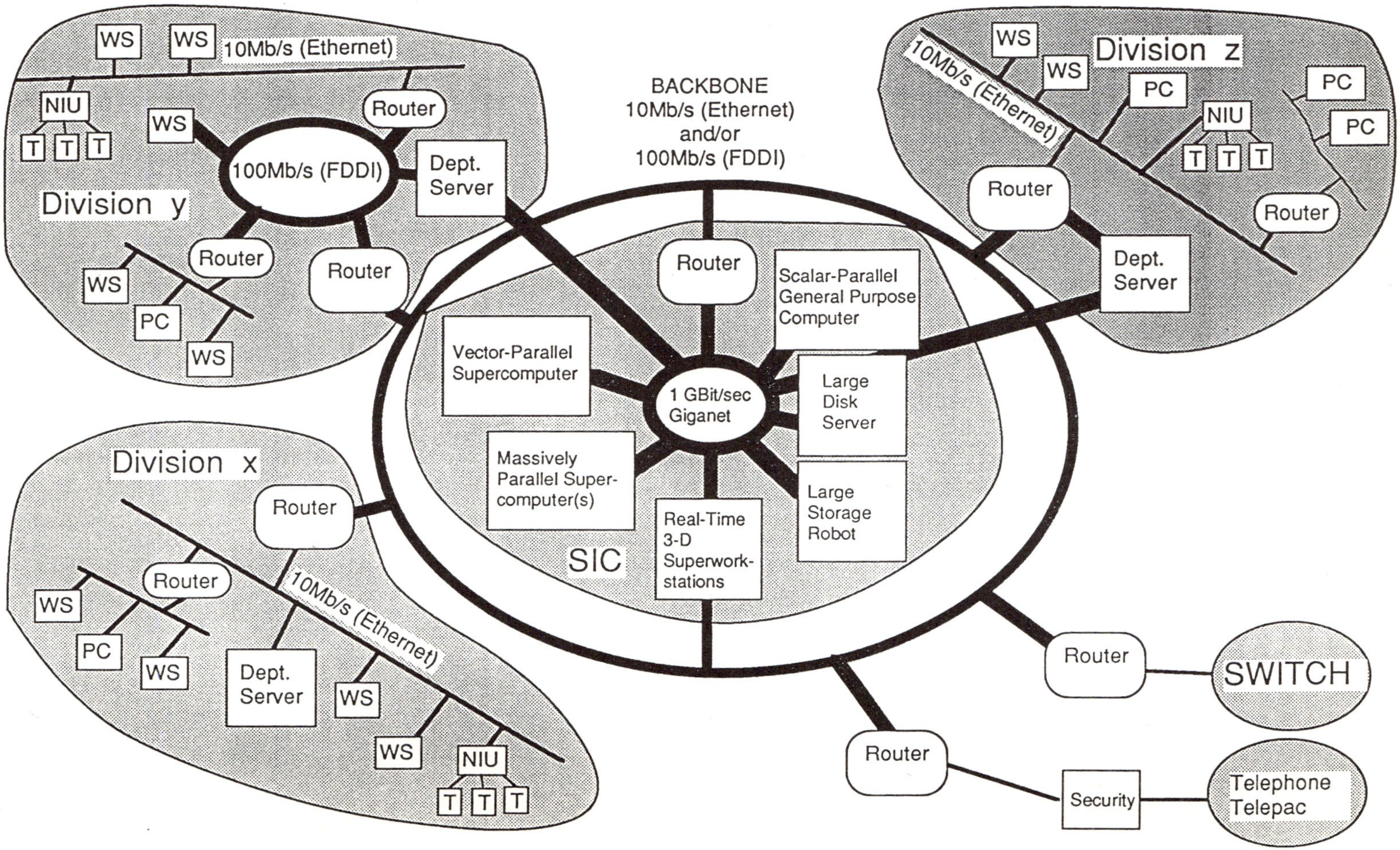

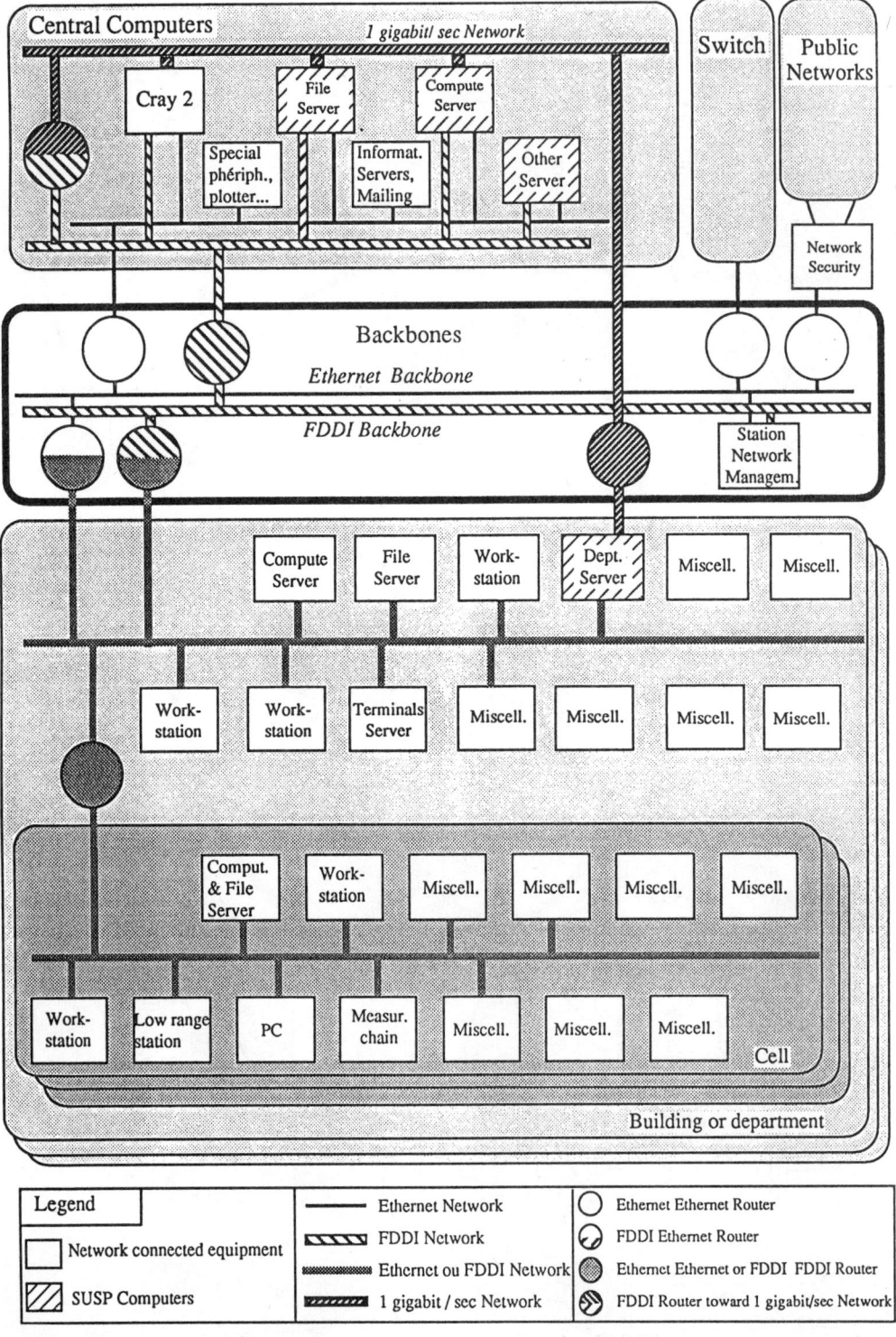

Fig. 4 : Topology of EPFL's Networks

Current EPFL NCS interface criteria (code name SUSP criteria: Système Universel à Services Partagés):

Compute Server:	File Server:
HiPPI/FDDI/Ethernet	HiPPI/FDDI/Ethernet
TCP/IP & applications:	TCP/IP & applications:
FTP, Telnet, SMTP, DNS client,	FTP, Telnet, SMTP, DNS client,
SUN RPC/XDR	SUN RPC/XDR
Client&Host NFS 4.0 and up	Host NFS 4.0 and up, Data Migration Facility
Client&Host DFS 1.0 (AFS) committed	Host DFS 1.0 (AFS), Data Migration Facility committed
OSI committment GOSIP V1.0	OSI committment GOSIP V1.0
(required for multiple redundant networks)	
B2 Security	B2 Security
From DCE 1.0:	From DCE 1.0:
-Time-Server	-Time-Server
-Name-Server	-Name Server
-Kerberos (NFS,DFS,FTP,FTAM,.), ACL's	-Kerberos (NFS,DFS,FTP,FTAM,.), ACL's
-RPC's (NCS)	-RPC's (NCS)
NQS	
X 11 R4 up	
LPR / LPD	

This table of EPFL interface criteria will be updated as necessary, and is a requirement to central resources and departemental servers.

CONCLUDING REMARKS

MPP will gain a broad acceptance as a production tool in the first half of the 1990's, provided the MPP vendors deliver elaborate programmer productivity environments for Fortran 90 which deliver sustained performance on the forthcoming hardware. Sharing the MPP resource among multiple users respecting standards and network computing facilities are a prerequisite. Ideally the MPP programming environment should be made available on major workstation platforms.

The development of OOP progamming tools & environments remains highly desirable for new applications or re-coded old ones. The issue of portability may be an inhibitor to its acceptance, because the new investments in application software need long-term protection.

The sacred facts on scientific computing may last a little longer!

Processor Scheduling in Multiprocessor Systems [1]

Satish K. Tripathi [2]　　Giuseppe Serazzi [3]　　Dipak Ghosal [4]

Abstract

Processor scheduling in multiprocessor systems can be divided into two steps. The first step, referred to as the *processor allocation problem*, is to determine the number of processors to be allocated to a job so as to maximize the system throughput and processor utilization. This depends both on the load on the system and on certain inherent characteristics of the job - most importantly how efficiently the job can utilize a given number of processors. The second step, referred to as the *processor assignment problem*, assigns processors to the parallel tasks in a job so as to minimize the execution time on the allocated processors. The processor assignment depends on the number of processor allocated, the processor interconnection structure, and the precedence relationship among the tasks in the job. This paper reviews the various issues in the above two steps of the processor scheduling.

1 Introduction

Considering the fact that parallel architectures with 64K processors [5] are now available commercially, it is not unreasonable to expect even larger machines with millions of processors to be built in the near future. Increase in the number of processors is not the only dimension of growth; one can also expect to see the basic building blocks of future systems to be more complex and powerful as well. Examples of two architectures in this path of evolution are the Connection Machine (CM) [5] and the MASPAR [11]. The processing units in the CM are 1-bit processors while those in the MASPAR are 4-bit processors. Evolution in these two dimensions will result in large parallel machines which will form the platform for both general purpose and special purpose computing.

Clearly, the one important architectural feature that must govern the development of these parallel machines is that they must be modular so that they can be easily scaled. Scalability must be transparent to the user and his programming environment similar to

---

[1] This research was partially supported in part by the Italian CNR "Progetto Finalizzato Sistemi Informatici e Calcolo Parallelo" under Grant 89.00055.69, by the MURST 40 % Project, and by the National Science Foundation grant CCR-9002351.

[2] Department of Computer Science, University of Maryland, College Park, MD 20742.

[3] Dipartimento di Scienze dell'Informazione, Universita di Milano, 20133 Milano, Italy.

[4] Bell Communications Research, Red Bank, NJ 07701.

memory systems in general uniprocessor machines today. This necessitates that these machines be distributed memory architectures. Shared memory architectures have their advantages but cannot be effectively scaled to construct massively parallel machines. From the performance viewpoint, the interconnection structure is a key factor in the design of these machines. The interconnection structure must not only be regular for modularity purposes but must also have a low diameter and a small number of connections. Hypercube topology [14] and its variants are very popular and have been used in many of the massively parallel computers which are available today [5] [11]. The diameter of a hypercube with N nodes is $O(\log_2 N)$ and so is the degree. The fact that the degree is not constant is one shortcoming of the hypercube topology.

The key resources in a parallel architecture are the processors, the internal communication bandwidth and the input/output bandwidth. In order to achieve high utilization and throughput from these multiprocessor systems it is necessary to efficiently allocate these resources among competing jobs. Availability of a large number of processors makes the task of processor scheduling even more critical. One can draw a parallel here with memory allocation in uniprocessor systems. It is well known that even with a large amount of memory, a poor allocation strategy can result in thrashing leading to a decrease in throughput [2].

The task of processor scheduling is viewed as a two-step process. In the first step, referred to as the *processor allocation problem*, the goal is to determine the number of processors that must be allocated to a job. The objectives in this step are to maximize the throughput of the system and the processor utilization. The second step, referred to as the *processor assignment problem*, deals with the assignment of the allocated processors to the parallel tasks in the job and the goal is to minimize the total execution time for the job. In the next section, a hierarchical model of the multiprocessor system is described and the two phases in processor scheduling are defined with respect to this model.

In order to develop a good processor allocation strategy, it is necessary to get an *a priori* estimate of the workload associated with the job. The workload here refers to the computation and communication requirements are functions of the number of processors on which the job is executed. This interdependence necessitates highly robust characterization schemes. The various parameters which are used to characterize the workload are discussed in Section 3. The other key issue in the processor allocation problem is load dependence. Specifically, a good processor allocation strategy must adapt to the load. However, there are inherent overheads associated with such dynamic schemes which can become significant especially when one considers massively parallel systems. These issues, along with certain architecture specific issues which must be taken into consideration during the processor allocation phase, are discussed in Section 4.

The processor assignment problem must account for the communication cost in the underlying architecture and the precedence relationship among the tasks in the job. Random assignment of tasks to processors is the simplest scheme. However, for large problem sizes, (i.e., with a large number of tasks) and for a large number of processors, the communication overhead may significantly increase the total execution time. Reduction in execution time can be achieved by properly assigning the parallel tasks in the job to the allocated processors. The cost of performing an optimal assignment, however, increases

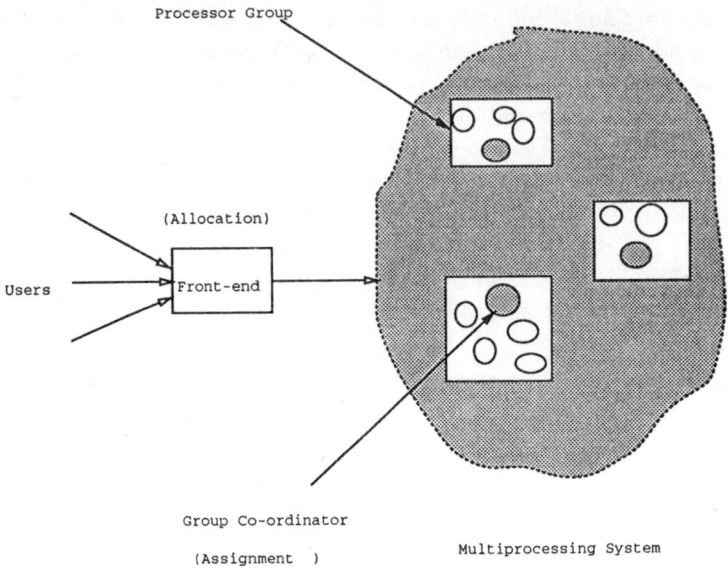

Figure 1: A hierarchical model of the multiprocessing architecture.

with the problem size and the number of processors. In general, the assignment problem is NP-complete. Thus, except for very special cases, the goal is to develop heuristics which yield good sub-optimal assignments without being computationally expensive. Some of the approaches are discussed in Section 5.

Finally, Section 6 concludes this paper with a list of promising research directions.

2 Processor Scheduling

From the viewpoint of processor scheduling, the multiprocessor architecture can be logically viewed as a hierarchical structure with two levels of control. At the top level the multiprocessor is controlled by a front-end system which serves as the interface to the user. At the lower level, associated with any particular group of processors, one can define a specific processor which other than performing computation, also coordinates the activity of the group. Figure 1 shows the hierarchical model of the multiprocessor architecture. The following points are noteworthy here.

1. The processors are viewed to be contained in a pool from which groups can be formed. Whether these groups can be of arbitrary size is an architectural issue which must be taken into consideration during the various stages of processor scheduling.

2. Once a group is formed, the above model assumes that one processor is selected to be the coordinator of the group. This choice of the coordinator can be done once a

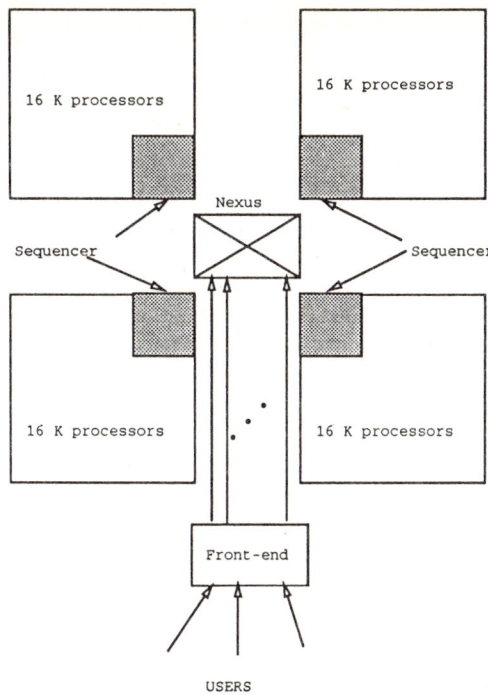

Figure 2: The organization of the Connection Machine.

job is allocated to that group or can be decided *a priori*.

3. Shared memory architectures are classified as uniform memory access (UMA) machines and non-uniform memory access (NUMA) machines. Parallel architectures which do not have shared memory and communicate via message passing (referred to in this paper as distributed memory architectures or message passing machines) can be similarly classified as UA (Uniform Access) and NUA (Non-Uniform Access) machines, where access refers to the distance between any two pairs of processors. Example of UA machines are distributed memory architectures with a multistage interconnection network. Message passing architectures based on the hypercube topology are examples of NUA architectures. These different architectural styles have different impact on the various stages of processor scheduling.

To illustrate the above model, Figure 2 shows the overall organization of the Connection Machine (CM) which is a massively parallel architecture with up to 64K processors [5]. The *Nexus* is a crossbar switch which connects the 4 partitions of the CM with the front-end. The front-end is the interface to the users and provides the programming environment. Each section of the CM has a *sequencer* which broadcasts the instructions to the processors. Note that the CM is an SIMD architecture and all processors controlled by a sequencer execute in a lock step fashion.

It is easy to draw similarities between the model and the CM. The front-end corresponds to the front-end of the model and the sequencer corresponds to the group coordinator. The major difference, however, is in the *granularity of control*. The model under consideration is geared towards an asynchronous parallel MIMD architecture. This implies that rather than having controllers coordinating a large number of processors, each processor is independent or belongs to a small group of processors coordinated by a controller. The two phases of processor scheduling can be easily identified with respect to the above model. The front-end performs processor allocation by appropriately partitioning the processors among the competing jobs. The processor assignment is performed by the group coordinator which assigns the tasks within a job to the processors in the group in a manner which minimizes the execution time. The following sections review the various issues involved in these two phases of processor scheduling.

3 Workload Representation

Many scheduling strategies for uniprocessor systems require some *a priori* information about parameters which characterize the various resource requirements of a job. The fact that this information may not be available in a real system does not diminish the importance of the workload characterization studies or the applicability of these scheduling strategies. Even a crude estimate of the workload can significantly improve the system performance [2]. It seems reasonable to assume the same to hold true for multiprocessor systems as well. However, workload characterization is much more difficult in parallel architectures than in uniprocessor systems. This is primarily due to the large number of parallel architectures available today which differ in many respects including the the control structure, the memory organization, the interconnection network and the I/O. The various schemes which have been proposed to characterize parallel program workload can be classified into two groups; one based on the execution signature and the other based on the parallelism profile.

The execution signature plots the execution time of a parallel algorithm for different numbers of processors. The execution time $T(p)$ with p processors can be decomposed into two components [4]:

$$T(p) = T_{comp}(p) + T_{comm}(p) \qquad (1)$$

where $T_{comp}(p)$ pertains to the computation part and $T_{comm}(p)$ is the communication overhead. Typically, $T_{comp}(p)$ is a monotonically decreasing function whereas $T_{comm}(p)$ is at best constant but, in general, an increasing function of p. Figure 3 shows the execution time of a matrix multiplication algorithm as a function of number of processors varying from 1 to 16 [4]. Processor allocation policies based on *a priori* knowledge of the execution signature have been studied in [3], [8], [13] and [4]. Based on the execution signature, the concept of *processor working set (pws)* is introduced in [4] to characterize the parallel program behavior when it is executed in a particular architecture.

The *pws* of a parallel program is defined in the following manner [4]. Let $C(p)$ denote a

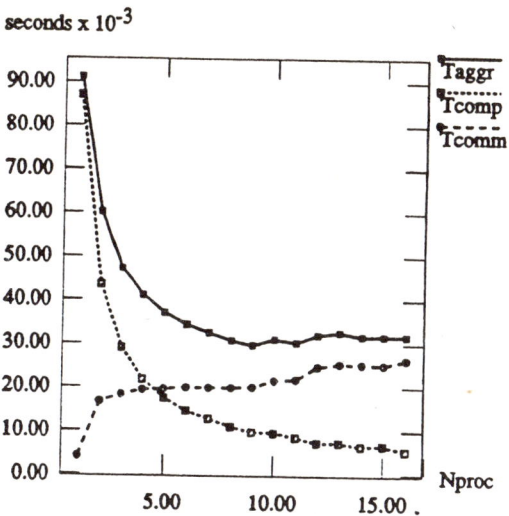

Figure 3: The execution signature of a matrix multiplication algorithm on a transputer machine [4].

cost function which is defined as

$$C(p) = p\frac{T(p)}{T(1)} = \frac{p}{S(p)} \qquad (2)$$

Note that if the speedup is linear, i.e., $S(p) = p$, then the cost of using more processors is small (equal to 1). On the other hand, if the speedup is small, then the cost is proportionately higher. Based on $C(p)$, the measure *efficacy*, $\eta(p)$, is defined as as the speedup per unit cost which yields

$$\eta(p) = \frac{S^2(p)}{p} \qquad (3)$$

The *pws* is defined as the minimum number of processors which maximizes $\eta(p)$. The robustness of *pws* as a single parameter characterization of the workload is addressed in [4]. Based on the experiments carried on a transputer machine it is shown that the *pws* is a good single parameter characterization of the parallel program behavior when executed in a specific architecture. The parameter is sensitive to both the changes in the algorithm and the architecture. Figure 4 shows $S(p)$ and $\eta(p)$ for the inner product algorithm. It can be observed that the maximum of $\eta(p)$ and $S(p)$ are obtained for different values of p. Allocation strategies based on *pws* have been studied in [4] and some of the salient features are discussed in the following section.

The other scheme for characterizing the parallel program behavior is based on the *parallelism profile*. This gives the number of busy processors as a function of time and is obtained by executing the parallel algorithm in an idealized machine with an unbounded number of processors and zero overhead [1], [6]. From the parallelism profile a number of

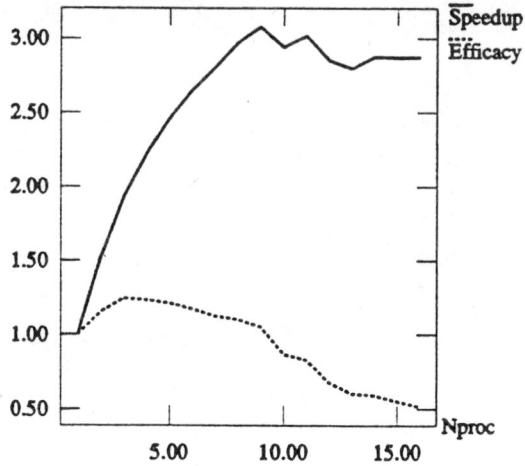

Figure 4: The plot of $S(p)$ and $\eta(p)$ for the matrix multiplication algorithm [4].

other measures can be derived. One example is the average parallelism A which is defined as

$$A = \frac{T(1)}{T(\infty)} \qquad (4)$$

where $T(1)$ is the execution time with one processor and $T(\infty)$ is the execution time with an unbounded number of processors. The parallelism profile and other derived measures have been used to study processor allocation strategies in [15] and to obtain bounds on speedup and efficiency in [1]. In the above definition the communication overhead is not included in the parallelism profile. One could obtain the parallelism profile for a specific architecture and a particular number of processors as shown in Figure 5 [4]. Another simpler representation is the *shape* which is derived from the parallelism profile. The shape is a cumulative plot of the fraction of the time a certain number of processors is busy [15].

The processor assignment problem requires information about the precedence relationship among the tasks in the job. This information is typically represented in form of a directed acyclic graph (DAG) where the nodes represent the computation and the arcs represent the precedence relationship among the tasks. The arcs can have weights representing the amount of data that needs to be transferred between the corresponding nodes. Most assignment schemes assume knowledge of the task graph and the processor interconnection structure.

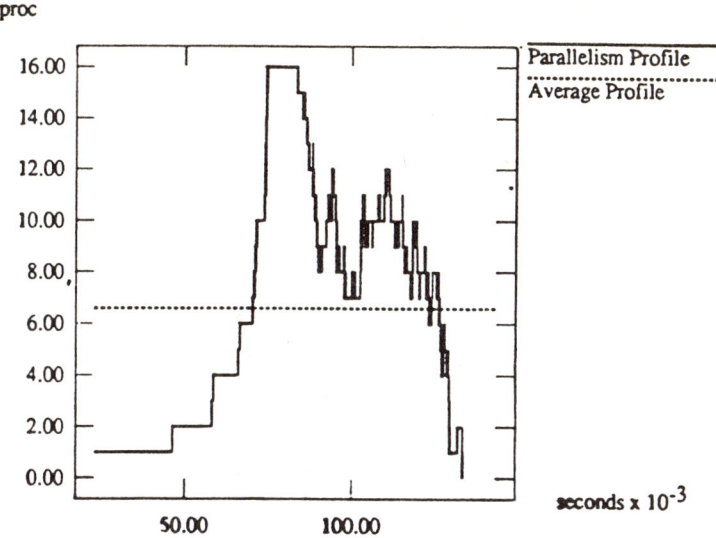

Figure 5: The parallelism profile for the quicksort algorithm on the transputer based machine [4].

4 Processor Allocation Strategies

The processor allocation problem deals with determining how the processors should be partitioned among the competing jobs. There are two primary approaches to the processor allocation problem. In *static processor allocation* schemes, a fixed number of processors are allocated to a job for its entire execution time. In the *dynamic processor allocation* schemes, the number of processors allocated to a job varies with time according to the changes in the number of executable tasks in each job.

4.1 Static Schemes

A number of different static processor allocation schemes have been proposed in the literature. In this section, rather than enumerating all the different policies, we review some of the key issues that have emerged. The details of policies can be found in the cited references.

Knowledge of Job Characteristics
In a uniprocessor system, any *a priori* information about the job significantly aids the scheduling and consequently impacts the performance of the systems. For multiprocessor scheduling this issue has been addressed in a number of studies [12], [15], [8]. The main conclusion of these studies is that the performance of allocation policies which take into account the knowledge of the job characteristic perform better than those which do not. In [12], it has been shown that simple strategies such as FCFS (First Come First Served) or RR (Round Robin) policies which are independent of the job characteristics perform

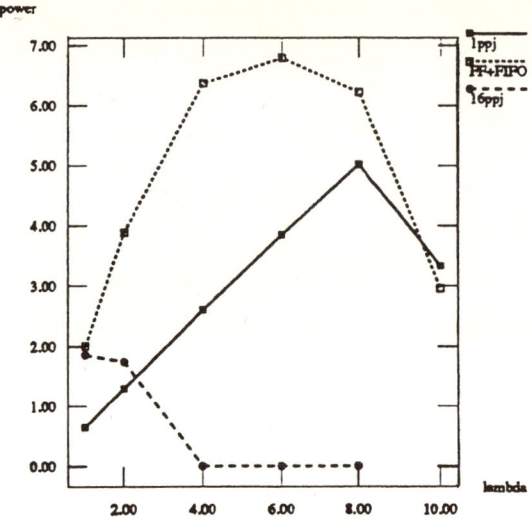

Figure 6: Performance comparison of different allocation policies [4].

inferior than SNPF (Shortest Number of Processes First) and SCDF (Shortest Cumulative Demand First) allocation policies which require information about the number of parallel tasks in a job and the cumulative service demands of the tasks, respectively. In [15], the jobs were characterized by their parallelism profile and derived measures such as the average parallelism and the maximum/minimum parallelism were used in the allocation policies. It was concluded that policies based on multiple parameter characterization performed superior than those based on single parameter characterization. Although the basic observation is intuitively clear, the important question is the amount of information that should be used. One can expect that there is a point of diminishing returns where the cost of additional information is not commensurate with the improvement in performance.

Effect of System Load

The manner in which the allocation policy should react to the system load (e.g., the mean number of jobs in the system) has been addressed in [15], [16], and [4]. Clearly, when the load is low, i.e., there is only one job in the system at a time, the allocation policy should allocate all the processors to the job or the number of processors requested by the job. The latter, typically, corresponds to the number of processors which maximizes the speedup. However, under high load, i.e., when there are jobs waiting for execution, the best policy is to allocate only a few processors per job [15]. Since parallel programs typically have sub-linear speedup characteristics, this policy maximizes the processor utilization and consequently maximizes throughput. A detailed study of this load dependent feature using a class of allocation strategies based on *pws* is reported in [4]. The multiprocessor with 16 processors is modeled as a multi-server queue to which jobs arrive from a Poisson point source. Associated with the queue is a window from which the scheduler selects jobs to schedule on the free processors. Figure 6 plots the power (ratio of the throughput to the response time) as a function of the job arrival rate for the following three policies

[4] :

1. FF (First Fit) : In this strategy the scheduler looks into the window of waiting jobs and finds the first job whose *pws* can fit into the available processors. Since jobs are allocated only their *pws*, no more or no less, this policy is not work conserving, in other word there may be free processors while jobs are waiting in the queue.

2. FF + FIFO : This is a work conserving policy, and a job can be allocated at most its *pws*. The scheduler looks in the window and finds the first job that can be allocated its *pws*. Once this is done any remaining processors, if any, are allocated to the first job in the queue.

3. Processor Partitioning : This policy equally partitions the processors into a fixed number of groups, one group with 16 processors i.e., 16ppj (16 processors per job) or 16 groups each with 1 processor (i.e., 1ppj). Jobs are allocated to one partition irrespective of their *pws*.

The results are shown for the $FF+FIFO$ policy and the fixed static processor partitioning policies. The overall performance is best for $FF + FIFO$. This policy allocates each processor its *pws* at low load and one processor per job at high load. Similar results have been demonstrated for the ASP (Adaptive Static Partitioning) policy [34] and the RTC (Run to Completion) policy [16]. These have the same load dependent behavior.

Time-Slicing (Round Robin Policies)

The main problem with run-to-completion policies such as RTC [16] and those based on *pws* [4] deals with the notion of fairness. In these policies, short jobs can have long waiting times while long jobs hold up the processors. Fairness can be achieved by allocating fixed time-slices to all the waiting jobs using a round robin policy. Allocation policies based on time-slicing were first studied in [27]. In this policy, referred to as *co-scheduling*, the processes of all jobs are maintained in a single shared process queue. Scheduling is done by moving a window of length equal to the number of processor over the queue. Each process in the window gets a quantum of service on a processor. At the end of a quantum, the window is moved down the queue until the first slot of the window covers the first process that was not scheduled in the previous quantum. In [7], a variant of this policy in which the round robin policy is performed at the job level has been studied. In this policy, all the processors are allocated to the processes of the same job for a quantum of time and the jobs are chosen in a round robin fashion. This policy is referred to as *gang scheduling* [28]. The performance effect of such time-sliced policies have been addressed in [12], [16], [28]. In [16] it has been shown that round robin policies are not as robust as RTC (run to completion) policies. First, the round robin policies do not have the load dependent feature of the RTC policy or those based on the *pws* [4]. Also, the context switch overhead at the end of each time slice and the cache misses for the new processes at the start of a new time-slice degrade the performance of the round robin policies.

Effect of Preemption

In uniprocessor systems, job preemption has been shown to be effective in improving system performance and ensuring fairness. The effects of preemption in multiprocessor systems were addressed in [12]. High priority was given to jobs with lower cumulative service demands. Similar to uniprocessor systems, it was observed that the effect of preemption is significant only when the coefficient of variation of the service demand is high. The study reported in [28] show two two key features which impact performance. First, preempting processes involved in synchronization can result in very high performance penalties. Second, the cache misses associated with the starting of new processes has a negative impact on performance. Improved scheduler based on smart thread packages [31] and *affinity scheduling* [32] have been proposed to minimize these performance penalties. Still, unlike in uniprocessor systems, much more in-depth analysis is required to implement preemption in multiprocessor systems.

Resource Contention

As mentioned in the introduction, the two main resources in a parallel system, other than the processors, are the interconnection network and I/O bandwidth. The contention for these resources and the corresponding effect on performance for different scheduling strategies have not been addressed.

Another key resource for many allocation strategies is the shared queue which is accessed by the processors to get tasks/jobs. The contention for this shared queue which can have detrimental effects on the performance of the system, has been modeled in [9]. Two approaches have been proposed to solve this problem and these are referred to as *autonomous scheduling* and *cooperative scheduling* policies. In autonomous scheduling, every time a processor finishes a task, it accesses the single shared queue and grabs a number of tasks. The number of tasks a processor gets each time is load dependent so as to ensure that processors are properly load balanced. At low load, a processor gets only a few tasks while at high load it grabs more.

In cooperative scheduling, one processor is responsible for performing task allocation to the processors. Each processor has its own queue. When a job arrives with a certain number of tasks, the scheduling processor schedules a batch of tasks following the join-the-shortest-queue policy, where again the size of the batch is dynamically adapted to the load on the system. These policies have the same load dependent behavior as the run-to-completion policies such as the RTC [16] and the those based on *pws* [4]. At low load a job will be allocated to many processors while at high load each job will get only a few processors. Results show that these policies perform significantly better than single shared process queue scheduling policies.

4.2 Dynamic Schemes

Dynamic schemes allow processors to be allocated and deallocated during the execution of the job. If a job is not using all its processors the local dispatcher will release some of them to other jobs. Similarly, if a job requires more processors, the systems will try to allocate more processors. Few studies on dynamic allocation policies have been reported in the literature.

In [13], dynamic allocation schemes have been studied for a two program workload model. When there is only one job in the system all the processors are allocated to it. Arrival of the second job initiates a re-partitioning of the processors depending on the execution

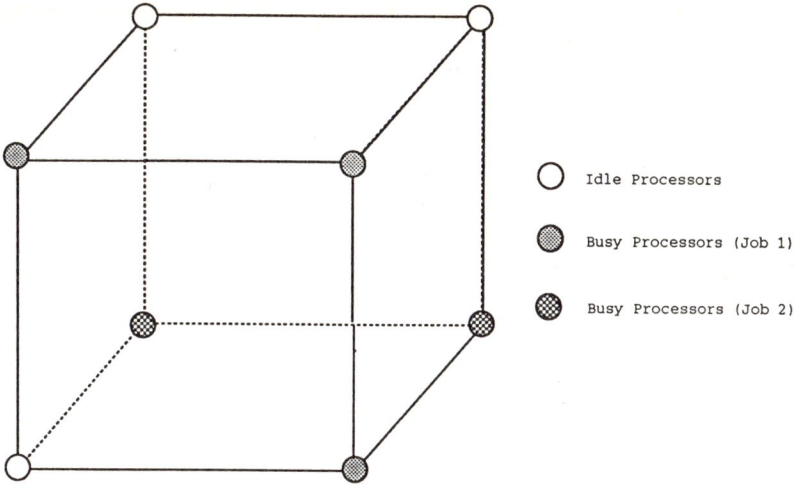

Figure 7: The allocation problem in NUMA/NUA architectures.

signature of the two jobs. The objective is to maximize the throughput. The dynamic re-partitioning scheme was also studied on a real system using a real workload in [29].

There are two key factors of dynamic policies. One is the re-partitioning overhead and the other is the rate at which the re-partitioning occurs. The former is an architectural issue and deals with the transfer of code and data between the processors. The latter depends on the policy. Clearly, these two factors determine the performance of the dynamic allocation policy. In [16] it is shown that for UMA architectures when the re-partitioning overhead is small, the dynamic schemes perform better than static schemes.

4.3 Architectural Issues

As mentioned in Section 2, shared memory architectures can be classified as uniform memory access (UMA) machines and non-uniform memory access machines (NUMA). Similarly, message passing machines can be classified as uniform access (UA) architectures and non-uniform access (NUA) architectures. These architectures impose different constraints on the applicability of various scheduling strategies. Most studies on processor allocation have been carried out on UMA architectures. It is evident the processor allocation problem is much more difficult in NUA/NUMA architectures. The key factor is due to the location dependent communication cost. Consider a hypercube with 8 processors as shown in Figure 7. The shaded nodes correspond to busy processors executing other jobs. Suppose a new job arrives with a request for three processors. From the figure it can be observed that only two processors are adjacent while the third processor is at a distance of two from nearest free processor. Depending on the communication cost, it may be better to allocate only the two adjacent processors instead of the three processors requested by the job. From the above example one can observe that for NUMA/NUA architectures, the processor allocation problem becomes closely linked with the processor assignment problem.

Another important architectural issue in NUA/NUMA architectures relates to the *granularity of control*. Associated with the granularity of control is the notion of *allocatable unit* which refers to the number of processors that must be allocated at a time. Fine granularity implies that the allocatable unit is small and in the limit each processor can be scheduled separately. Coarse granularity implies that the allocatable unit consists of a large number of processors. The issues which determine the size of the allocatable unit are in some part similar to the issues related to determining the page size in the memory organization of a uniprocessor system. Fine granularity of control would correspond to higher scheduling overhead at the front end specifically to maintain the status of a large number of allocatable units.

Another consideration is the effect of *external fragmentation* which corresponds to the situation where free allocatable units are separated by large distances and thus cannot be allocated together to the same job. Compaction algorithms can be developed to take care of external fragmentation. However, there is overhead associated with such schemes. Also, such compaction algorithms are difficult to design since they have to be load dependent. At high load the compaction is not required since each job will be allocated one unit. The compaction algorithm must be performed for low to medium loads. Finally, coarse granularity has low scheduling overhead but suffers from the problem of *internal fragmentation* as all processors in an allocatable unit may not be efficiently utilized by the job.

These are some of the issues which are related to the underlying architecture which must be addressed particularly with respect to the NUMA/NUA architectures.

5 Processor Assignment

The key issue in the processor assignment problem is to map the parallel tasks in a job on to the allocated processors such that the communication cost is minimized. Since UMA/UA machines have location independent communication cost, the processor assignment problem is relevant only in NUMA/NUA architectures. As mentioned in Section 2, most processor assignment schemes assume knowledge of the task graph and the processor interconnection structure. The assignment problem in a multiprocessing system is NP-complete when no constraints are placed on task processing times, the number of processors, the structure of the task graph, and the interconnection structure among the processors [24]. As a result, except for special cases, the general approach is to find heuristic strategies that give good sub-optimal solutions.

There are two major approaches in solving the assignment problem - *graph matching* and *priority listing*. In graph matching, algorithms both the architecture and the algorithm are represented as graphs (referred to as the system graph and the task graph, respectively) [23] [22] [21]. A node in the system graph represents a processing element (PE) and an edge represents a direct communication link between two PEs. In the graph matching approach it is assumed that there is little or no precedence relationship among the tasks. The objective is to obtain a mapping which minimizes the sum of the computation time and the communication time. A survey of different graph matching techniques appears in [20]. The key idea is to assign the adjacent nodes in the task graph to the same or adjacent nodes in the system graph so that the communication cost is minimized. Because the graph matching problem is NP-complete [20], heuristic algorithms have been developed.

Priority listing of tasks is the other approach for solving the assignment problem [19], [17]. Priority listing considers precedence relations of tasks and uses heuristic algorithms to generate task priority lists for every *executable set*, i.e., tasks which can be executed simultaneously. Tasks which are bottlenecks get high priorities in the executable set. PEs are assigned to tasks according to task priorities and task sizes in such a way that execution time is minimized. Usually, communication among tasks is ignored in this approach. This is a shortcoming of the priority listing approach which can make the scheduling algorithm very unstable when the amount of communication varies from computation to computation [18].

Optimal assignments have been found either for a specific class of task graphs or for a limited class of architectures or both. For a two processor system and an arbitrary task graph, optimal assignment can be easily computed when the task processing times are equal [2]. For an arbitrary number of processors the optimal assignment is only known for tree structured precedence task graphs with equal task processing times [25]. These assignment schemes do not take into account the topology of the interconnection network and the associated communication cost. For a linear array and an arbitrary fixed degree tree, assignment can be computed which is optimal upto a factor of $\log N$ where N is the number of tasks [30].

The general approach for the processor assignment problem is to obtain sub-optimal solutions taking into consideration the precedence relationship among the tasks, the number of PEs and the processor interconnection structure. The next section briefly discusses a search based heuristic for the processor assignment problem.

5.1 A Search Based Assignment Scheme

In [26], the underlying architecture is assumed to be a hypercube. The problem of minimizing the execution time is decomposed into two parts; 1) minimizing the processing time for every set of tasks which can be executed simultaneously, denoted as the *executable set* and 2) minimizing the communication time corresponding to the outgoing edges of the executable sets. Minimization of the processing time depends only on how many processors are allocated to a specific task in the executable set. This assignment of processors is done using the priority listing approach reported in [17], [19]. This step yields a mapping of the tasks to the n logical processing elements [26]. Note that the topology of the processor interconnection structure and the structure of the task graph is not considered in this step. Based on the above mapping an MPE (Multistage Processing Element) model is created. The MPE model of the task graph consists of l stages corresponding to the l executable sets. The stages in the MPE model are interconnected by arcs which represents the the precedence relation between the tasks in the original task graph.

The minimization of the total communication time is achieved by minimizing the communication time between every stage in the MPE model. This is done in the following manner [26]. Suppose the logical PEs in stage $i-1$ have been assigned physical ids. To assign physical processors to logical PEs in stage i, first a preference list is created for each logical PE in stage i. The preference list is based on the notion of *least common perfect set* and *candidate set*. The idea is as follows. Consider the generation of preference list for lpe_i^j, i.e., the jth logical PE in stage i. Let B be the set of logical PEs in stage $i-1$ which must send data to lpe_i^j. Let A be the set of physical processors which have been assigned to the the logical PEs in B. Now the common perfect set with parameter d, denoted as $pcs(d)$, is the set of processors which can be reached by *all* the processors in A in d routing steps. The least common perfect set is the non-empty perfect common set with the smallest d. The idea is that the best assignment of lpe_i^j is to a processor which belongs to the least common perfect set of A. Since the computation of least common perfect set may be expensive, the candidate set is generated by requiring that some majority of the processors in A can send data to the processors in the candidate set in the minimum number of routing steps.

Once the preference list for every logical PE in the MPE model is computed, a Least Cost Branch and Bound with Implicit Depth First (LCBB/IDF) search technique is used to find the best assignment. The details of the lower bound estimation technique to efficiently prune the search space are discussed in [26]. The results show that the pruning technique works very well and in most cases the resulting assignment is near optimal.

The processor assignment problem is difficult and for general task graphs, any reasonable assignment scheme will be computationally expensive. Integration of any assignment scheme in a general purpose processor scheduling strategy should take into account the dynamic state of the system. If the load on the system is high then only a few processors will be allocated to each job. In such a case, the benefits of performing a good assignment may be very small and thus a simple random scheme may be appropriate.

6 Conclusion

In this paper, processor scheduling in multiprocessor systems is considered in two phases, namely, the processor allocation phase and the processor assignment phase. The processor allocation phase determines how the processors should be partitioned among the competing jobs so as to maximize the system throughput and the processor utilization. Static processor allocation schemes have been proposed for UMA architectures. The one common result that has emerged out of these studies relates to the load dependent behavior of the static schemes. A good static scheme must adapt to the system load. At low load each job should be given the requested number of processors but at high load the best policy is to allocate only a few processors to each job. The effect of contention for I/O and interconnection network bandwidth and the corresponding impact on the performance of allocation strategies need to be addressed in case of UMA architectures.

Processor allocation is significantly more difficult in NUA/NUMA architectures. Since future large parallel architectures are likely to be NUA architectures, it is important to address processor allocation schemes for these architectures. A number of architectural issues which impact processor allocation were identified in Section 4. The interdependence between the design of the parallel architecture and processor allocation strategy and the impact on the system performance need to be addressed in depth. Finally, simpler assignment heuristics which yield good sub-optimal solution without being computationally expensive are required for processor assignment in NUMA/NUA architectures. Efficient processor scheduling is needed to exploit the potential processing power of parallel architectures.

References

[1] D. L. Eager, J. Zahorjan, and E. D. Lazowska, Speedup versus Efficiency in Parallel Systems, *IEEE Transactions on Computers*, Volume 38, Number 3, March 1989, pp.408-423.

[2] E. G. Coffman and P. J. Denning, *Operating System Theory*, Prentice-Hall Inc., 1973.

[3] L. W. Dowdy, On the Partitioning of Multiprocessor Systems, *Technical Report*, Department of Computer Science, Vanderbilt University, March 1988.

[4] D. Ghosal, G. Serazzi, and S. K. Tripathi, Processor Working Set and Its Use in Scheduling Multiprocessor Systems, *IEEE Transactions on Software Engg.* May, 1991.

[5] W. D. Hillis, *The Connection Machine*, MIT Press, Cambridge, Mass., 1985.

[6] M. Kumar, Measuring parallelism in computation intensive scientific / engineering applications, *IEEE Transactions on Computers* Volume 37, Number 9, September 1988, pp. 1088-1098.

[7] S. T. Leutenegger and M. K. Vernon, The Performance of Multiprogrammed Multiprocessor Scheduling Policies, *Proc. 1990 ACM SIGMETRICS Conf.*, May 1990.

[8] M. R. Leuze, L. W. Dowdy and K. H. Park, Multiprogramming a Distributed-Memory Multiprocessor, *Journal of Concurrency & Practice*, 1989.

[9] R. D. Nelson and M. S. Squillante, Analysis of Contention in Multiprocessor Scheduling, *IBM Technical Report*, 109.7, November 1989.

[10] R. D. Nelson and D. Towsley, A Performance Evaluation of Several Priority Policies for Parallel Processing Systems, *IBM Technical Report*, November 1989.

[11] MASPAR - The massively parallel architecture, MASPAR Inc. 1990.

[12] S. Majumdar, D. L. Eager, and R. Bunt, Scheduling in Multiprogrammed Parallel Systems, *ACM SIGMETRICS*, 1988, pp. 104-113.

[13] K. H. Park and L. W. Dowdy, Dynamic Partitioning of Multiprocessor Systems, *International Journal of Parallel Programming*, 1, 1989.

[14] Y. Saad and M. H. Schultz, Topological Properties of Hypercubes, *IEEE Transactions on Computers*, Vol. 37, No.7, July 1988, pp. 867-872.

[15] K. C. Sevcik, Characterization of Parallelism in Applications and Their Use in Scheduling, *ACM SIGMETRICS*, 1989, pp. 171-180.

[16] J. Zahorjan and Cathy McCann, Priority Scheduling in Shared Memory Multiprocesors, *Proc. 1990 ACM SIGMETRICS Conf.*, May 1990.

[17] C. D. Polychronopoulos and U. Banerjee, Processor Allocation for Horizontal and Vertical Parallelism and Related Speedup Bounds, *IEEE Transactions on Computers*, c-36(4), pp. 410-420, April 1987.

[18] S. P. Lo and V. D. Gligor, Properties of Multiprocessor Scheduling Algorithms, *Proc. of Int'l Conf. on Parallel Processing*, pp. 867-870, August 1987.

[19] H. Kasahara and S. Narit, Practical Multiprocessor Scheduling Algorithms for Efficient Parallel Processing, *IEEE Transactions on Computers*, c-33(11), Nov. 1984, pp. 1023-1029.

[20] W. H. Tsai, Graphic Matching Problems : A Survey and Tutorial. *Proceedings of the 1st Conference on Computer Algorithm*, Hinschu, Taiwan R.O.C, July 1982, pp. 16.1-16.66.

[21] S. Y. Lee and J. K. Aggarwal, A Mapping Strategy for Parallel Processing, *IEEE Transactions on Computers*, c-36(4), April 1987, pp. 433-442.

[22] C. C. Shen and W. H. Tsai, A Graph Matching Approach to Optimal Task Assignment in Distributed COmputing Systems Using a Minmax Criterion, *IEEE Transactions on Computers*, c-34(3), March 1985, pp. 197-203.

[23] S. H. Bokhari, On the Mapping Problem, *IEEE Transactions on Computers*, c-30(3), March 1981, pp. 550-557.

[24] M. R. Garey and D. S. Johnson, *Computers and Intractability : A Guide to Theory of NP-Completeness*. San Francisco, CA, Freeman Publishing Co., 1979.

[25] T. C. Hu. Parallel Sequencing and Assembly Line Problem, *Operations Research*, Vol. 9, Nov. 1961, pp. 841-848.

[26] Win-Tsung Lo, D. Ghosal and S. K. Tripathi, Task Allocation on Hypercube Multiprocessor, *High Performance Computer Architecture*, France, 1990.

[27] J. K. Ousterhout, Scheduling techniques for concurrent systems. In *Third International Conference on Distributed Computing Systems*, 1982, pp.22-30.

[28] A. Tucker and A. Gupta, Process control and scheduling issues for multiprogrammed shared memory multiprocessors, In *Proceedings of the 12th ACM Symposium on Operating Systems Principle*, 1989, pp. 159-166.

[29] K. Dussa, B. Carslon, L. Dowdy, and K-H. Park, Dynamic Partitioning in a Transputer Environment, *ACM SIGMETRICS Conference*, May 1990.

[30] D. Ghosal, A. Mukherjee, R. Thurimella, and Y. Yesha, Mapping Task Trees onto a Linear Array, *1991 Int'l Conference on Parallel Processing*, August 1991.

[31] J. Zahorjan, E. D. Lazaowska, and D. L. Eager, Spinning versus blocking in parallel systems with uncertainty, *Technical Report 88-03-01*, Department of Computer Science, University of Washington, 1988.

[32] E. D. Lazowska, M. Squillante, Using processor-cache affinity in shared memory multiprocessor scheduling, *technical Report*, Department of Computer Science, University of Washington, Seattle, June 1989.

[33] E. Gelenbe, D. Ghosal and S. K. Tripathi, Analysis of processor allocation in large multiprocessor systems. In *Proc. of the Intl. Conf. on the Performance of Distributed Systems and Integrated Communication Networks*, Kyoto, Japan, September 1991.

[34] S. Setia and S. K. Tripathi, An analysis of several processor partitioning policies for parallel computers, *Technical Report, CS-TR-2684*, University of Maryland, College Park, MD 20741.

Multipacket Routing on Rings

Fillia Makedon[1]
Computer Science Program
University of Texas at Dallas
P.O. Box 830688, MP 3.1
Richardson, TX75083 − 0688
makedon@utdallas.edu

Adonios Simvonis
Basser Department of Computer Science
University of Sydney
N.S.W 2006
Australia
simvonis@cs.su.oz.au

Abstract. We study multipacket routing problems. We divide the multipacket routing problem into two classes, namely, distance limited and bisection limited routing problems. Then, we concentrate on rings of processors. Having a full understanding of the multipacket routing problem on rings is essential before trying to attack the problem for the more general case of r-dimensional meshes and tori. We prove a new lower bound of $\frac{2n}{3}$ routing steps for the case of distance limited routing problems. We also give an algorithm that tightens this lower bound. For bisection limited problems, we present an algorithm that completes the routing in near optimal time.

1 Introduction

A great deal of work has been devoted to the study of the packet routing problem [1, 2, 3, 4, 5, 6, 7, 8, 9, 10, 11, 12]. This is because the packet routing problem is closely related to parallel computation. Through the routing of messages (packets) we are able to emulate shared memory [11]. More generally, for a parallel computer to be computationally effective, it must be able to route messages from their origin processors to their destination processors fast and with small, preferably constant size queues. These queues are created while two or more packets are waiting to cross the same communication channel.

In this paper, we consider two types of packet routing problems, namely, *distance limited* and *bisection limited* routing problems, a distinction which is based on the number of packets each processor has to route. We concentrate on permutation problems on a ring of processors. The reason for doing so, is because, before trying to attack the problem for the more general case of r-dimensional meshes and tori, we must have a full understanding of the problem in its simplest form. We prove a new lower bound for distance limited problems on rings and we give an algorithm that matches the lower bound. For the case of bisection limited routing problems, we present an algorithm that

---
[1] Currently at Computer Science Department, Dartmouth College, Hanover, NH 03755

routes the packets in near optimal time.

A *ring of processors* is defined to be a graph $G = (V, E)$ where, $V = \{i | i = 0, 1, 2, ..., n-1\}$ and an edge $e = (i, j)$ belongs to E if $|j - i| = 1$ or $|j - i| = n - 1$. At any step, each processor can communicate with both of its neighbors.

We define the *distance along the shortest path* between processors $P_1 = i$ and $P_2 = j$, denoted $D_s(P_1, P_2)$, to be the minimum number of links that a packet has to traverse starting from processor P_1 and destined for processor P_2. Obviously, $D_s(P_1, P_2) = D_s(P_2, P_1)$. Formally, for processors $P_1 = i$ and $P_2 = j$, $j > i$, we define $D_s(P_1, P_2) = \min\{(j - i), n - (j - i)\}$.

In a *permutation routing problem* each processor has one packet to transmit to any other processor. At the end, each processor receives exactly one packet. In the *multi-packet permutation problem* each processor has k packets all of which are destined for the same processor. At the end, each processor receives exactly k packets. This problem arises when a single packet in the permutation routing problem consists of k flits. Some work has already been done on square meshes for this case: Simvonis and Makedon [8] treated the k flits as an unbreakable "snake", while Kunde and Tensi [4] routed the flits of a packet independently. Up to now, however, no work has been done on rings.

The remainder of the paper is organized into sections as follows. In Section 2, we define the classes of distance limited and bisection limited routing problems. In Section 3, we concentrate on distance limited problems on rings of n processors. We present a lower bound of $\frac{2n}{3}$ steps, and we give an algorithm that matches that bound. In Section 4, we investigate the bisection limited problem on a ring of n processors. The known lower bound for this problem is $\frac{kn}{4}$ routing steps. We present an algorithm that routes any problem in at most $\frac{kn}{4} + \frac{5n}{2}$ routing steps. Finally, in Section 5, we discuss further work that has to be done in this area.

2 Two Types of Routing Problems

We obtain lower bounds on the number of steps required to solve a routing problem using two different arguments. The first one is a lower bound based on the maximum distance a packet has to travel (*distance bound*). The second one is based on the *bisection bound* of the network used. Then, the lower bound is *max(distance bound, bisection bound)*. For the case of r-dimensional meshes of side-length n, the distance bound is $r(n-1)$ and the bisection bound is $\frac{nk}{2}$, where k is the number of packets each processor holds. Thus, the lower bound on the number of steps required to solve the multipacket permutation routing problem on the r-dimensional mesh is $\max\{r(n-1), \frac{nk}{2}\}$. Similarly, for the torus, the lower bound is $\max\{\frac{r(n-1)}{2}, \frac{nk}{4}\}$.

It is clear from the above that we can divide the routing problems into two categories: the *bisection-limited problems* and the *distance-limited problems*. A problem is bisection-limited if the bisection lower bound is greater than the distance lower bound. Otherwise, we say that the problem is distance-limited. For r-dimensional meshes and tori, we obtain that a problem is distance-limited if the number of packets per processor is $k \leq 2r$. Otherwise it is bisection-limited.

It should be pointed out that the division of the routing problems into the two categories is based on worst case scenarios. Thus, there are problems that, according to the above distinction, are bisection limited, ($k > 2$ for rings), and still can be solved in less time than that indicated by the distance limit. One such trivial example is when all processors have to route their packets to the processor immediately after them in the clockwise direction. Obviously, this routing problem can be solved in k steps.

In the rest of the paper we will concentrate on rings of processors. For a ring ($r = 1$) the problem is distance limited if $k \leq 2$ and bisection limited otherwise.

3 Distance Limited Routing Problem on a Ring

In what follows, we demonstrate a better lower bound for the case of distance limited routing problems on rings. The channel utilization of the network is taken into consideration in order to obtain the new lower bound. Then, we give an algorithm that matches the lower bound.

3.1 Lower Bound on a Ring of Processors

Let us assume that we have a ring of n processors and we want to route a multipacket permutation on it. Each processor has two packets that will be routed independently. Consider the following situation: Initially, any processor i contains 2 packets destined for processor $(i + \frac{n}{3})$ mod n. Processors are numbered from $0...n - 1$ in the clockwise direction (CW) (Figure 1).

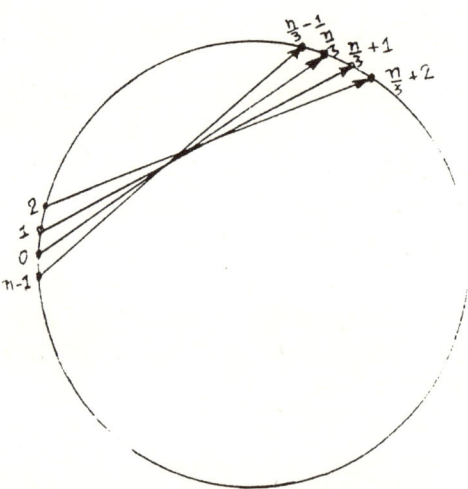

Figure 1. The instance of the permutation routing problem that requires $\frac{2n}{3}$ steps.

Hence, in the counter-clockwise direction (CCW), each packet has to travel distance $\frac{2n}{3}$. If some packet decides to move in the CCW direction, then at least $\frac{2n}{3}$ steps are required, since the distance between origin and destination is exactly $\frac{2n}{3}$ in the CCW direction. So, if we want to achieve a better routing time, we have to send all packets in the CW direction. In this case, each of a total of $2n$ packets will travel for $\frac{n}{3}$ steps. Then, the total movement (number of wire crossings) is $\frac{2n^2}{3}$. Since all packets are moving in the same direction, only n communication links are used. Hence, this movement requires at least $\frac{2n}{3}$ routing steps to be accomplished. Thus, we have:

Theorem 1. There is a distance limited routing problem on a ring of n processors that requires $\frac{2n}{3}$ routing steps for its solution.

3.2 An Algorithm that Tightens the Lower Bound

An algorithm that tightens the lower bound given in Theorem 1 is the following:

Algorithm *Route_on_a_Ring_1*

At step 1 Each processor determines the minimum distance its packets have to travel, say s, where $0 \leq s \leq \frac{n}{2}$. It also determines the direction in which the packets have to travel so that their distance to the destination is s. Let this direction be denoted by K (CW or CCW).

- If $s \leq \frac{n}{3}$, then both packets are send in direction K.
- If $\frac{n}{3} < s \leq \frac{n}{2}$, then the processor sends one packet in the CW direction and one in the CCW direction.

at step $i, i > 1$ Each processor transmits a packet toward its destination, if it has one.

A processor never changes the direction of a packet.

The packet that has to go further in a given direction has higher priority.

Lemma 1. At any time t, using Algorithm *Route_on_a_Ring_1*, a processor has at most 2 packets that want to move in the same direction.

Proof. The Lemma is obvious, since: i) each processor transmits a packet toward a given direction, if it has one, ii) at any step, it can receive at most one packet that must be sent in that direction, and, iii) the initial load of each processor is at most 2 packets that want to travel in the same direction. ∎

Lemma 2. Using Algorithm *Route_on_a_Ring_1*, there are at most $\frac{2n}{3}$ packets that want to cross any "cut" in the same direction.

Proof. W.l.o.g., we assume a "cut" after processor $n-1$, and we will examine packets moving only in the CW direction. The proof for the CCW movement is symmetric. Let processors $P_{\frac{n}{3}}, ..., P_{\frac{2n}{3}-1}$ constitute segment A of the ring, and processors $P_{\frac{2n}{3}}, ..., P_{n-1}$ constitute segment B of the ring (Figure 2).

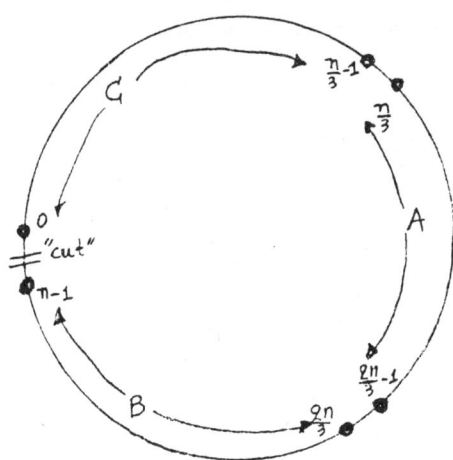

Figure 2. The ring is divided into three sections that are used in the proof of Lemma 2.

Initially, each processor in segment A has at most 1 packet that wants to move in the CW direction and also wants to cross the "cut". Assume that the number of packets in segment A that want to cross the "cut" is m, $0 \leq m \leq \frac{n}{3}$. Then, these packets must be destined for segment C, where processors $P_0, ..., P_{\frac{n}{3}-1}$ constitute segment C. Since we are examining permutation routing, for any packet in segment A that wants to cross the "cut" in the CW direction, there must exist a unique destination in segment C. This means that, there exist m positions in segment C, none of which can be the destination of a packet that is initially in segment B. Thus, in segment B, there must exist m processors that initially have no packets that want to cross the "cut" and are also a distance $d \leq \frac{n}{3}$ from the "cut". (Note that these processors might have only one packet that wants to cross the "cut"). So, the total number of packets which are initially in segment B and want to cross the "cut" is at most $(\frac{2n}{3} - k)$. This implies that the total number of packets that want to cross the "cut" in CW direction is at most $(\frac{2n}{3} - m) + m = \frac{2n}{3}$. ∎

Theorem 2. Using Algorithm *Route_on_a_Ring_1*, a distance limited permutation problem on a ring of processors can be solved in $\frac{2n}{3}$ steps.

Proof. In order to prove this, we need to show that all packets that want to cross any "cut" in a given direction, will have done so after $\frac{2n}{3}$ steps. W.l.o.g, let us assume the "cut" is after processor $\frac{2n}{3}$ in the CW direction. We simulate the routing process as follows: Assume we have two tapes, tape A and B. Tape A has $\frac{2n}{3}$ cells and can move to the right. Tape B has $\frac{n}{3}$ cells, is not allowed to move, and is placed, initially, on top of the $\frac{n}{3}$ rightmost cells of tape A. Each cell of a tape can hold at most one "pebble". A pebble represents a packet that wants to cross the "cut" in the CW direction. If a pebble is placed on a cell of tape B, then a pebble must also exist on the underlying cell of tape A. We now observe that, initially, we have the following situation: If k pebbles are on tape B, then at least k cells in the $\frac{n}{3}$ leftmost positions of tape A are empty. We associate the ith pebble of tape B, $0 \leq i < \frac{2n}{3}$, where we count from left to right, with the ith empty cell ("hole") of tape A, where we count from right to left (Figure 3). This is a 1-1 relation.

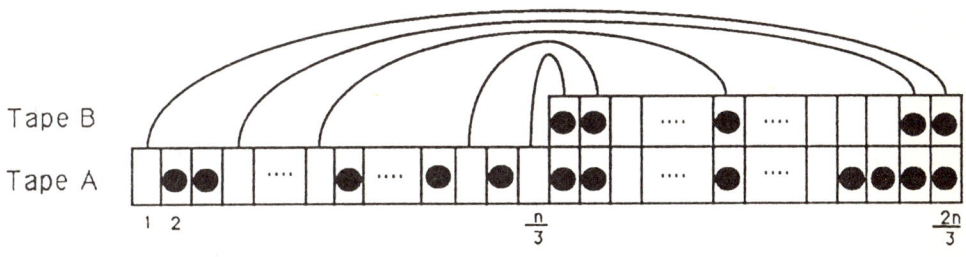

Figure 3. The simulation of the routing by two tapes as used in the proof of Theorem 2.

Now, we start moving tape A to the right. In the worst case, each pebble in tape B will drop into its corresponding "hole" in tape A. Since the whole tape A will cross the "cut" after exactly $\frac{2n}{3}$ steps, all pebbles cross the "cut" in at most $\frac{2n}{3}$ steps. Thus, all packets that want to cross the "cut" can do so in $\frac{2n}{3}$ steps. ∎

4 Bisection Limited Routing Problem on a Ring

In this section, we consider bisection limited problems on rings of n processors. Recall, from Section 2, that a problem is bisection limited for rings when k, the number of packets per processor, is greater than 2. The lower bound based on the bisection of the ring is $\frac{kn}{4}$. We give an algorithm that completes the routing in $\frac{kn}{4} + \frac{5n}{2}$ steps. The trivial greedy algorithm that routes each packet along the shortest path to its destination takes, in the worst case $\frac{kn}{2}$ steps.

4.1 The Algorithm

Before we proceed with the description of the algorithm, we need to give some definitions for certain variables that we use: Let S_i denote the distance that the packets initially located at processor P_i have to travel along the shortest path to their destination. S_i can be written as $S_i = \lambda_i n$, $0 \leq \lambda_i \leq \frac{1}{2}$, where λ_i is a coefficient used in our algorithm. Our algorithm routes a fraction of the packets which are initially at processor P_i along the shortest path to their destination, and routes the remaining packets along the longest path. The number of packets that are routed along the shortest path and are originated at processor P_i is denoted by σ_i.

Algorithm *Route_on_a_Ring_2*

At step 1 Each processor P_i determines the number of packets σ_i it will send along the shortest path using the following rule:

$$\sigma_i = k - \lfloor \lambda_i k \rfloor$$

It then adds σ_i of the k packets to a queue associated with the link on the shortest path, and the remaining packets to the queue associated with the other link.

The packets at the front of the queues are transmitted.

at step $i, i > 1$ Each processor transmits a packet toward its destination, if it has one.

A processor never changes the direction of a packet.

The packets are transmitted using a FIFO policy.

Our efforts to analyze Algorithm *Route_on_a_Ring_2* in a way similar to the analysis of Algorithm *Route_on_a_Ring_1* were not successful. In particular, we were not able to introduce in a proof of that kind the fact that the routing problem is a permutation. So, we proceed with a totally different approach. Again, we consider the number of packets that cross any "cut" in any direction. But now, we prove that the given routing problem is "easier" to be solved than a special kind of routing problem for which we can make statements regarding its complexity. In what follows we assume that the ring consists of an even number of processors.

Definition Let a ring be divided by a diameter into two sections. Each section consists of $\frac{n}{2}$ processors. A multipacket routing problem in which all packets from one section are destined for the other is called a *symmetric multipacket routing problem*. All other multipacket routing problems are *asymmetric*.

Lemma 3 Assume any "cut" in any direction. Using Algorithm *Route_on_a_Ring_2*, an asymmetric multipacket routing problem with initial load of k packets at each processor sends at most as many packets to cross the "cut" in the given direction as a symmetric one with load of $k+1$ packets per processor where, the extra packet is routed towards the "cut".

Proof. Without loss of generality, assume a ring of n processors, and a "cut" between processors P_0 and P_{n-1}. We will concentrate in the number of packets that cross the "cut" in the CW direction. A diameter that passes through the "cut" divides the ring into two sections. Section A consists from processors $P_0, P_1, ..., P_{\frac{n}{2}-1}$ and Section B consists of processors $P_{\frac{n}{2}}, P_{\frac{n}{2}+1}, ..., P_{n-1}$. We will show how to transform any asymmetric multipacket routing problem with initial load of k packets to a symmetric problem with initial load of $k+1$ packets. Furthermore, the solution of the new routing problem will require greater or equal number of routing steps. (Both problems are solved by Algorithm *Route_on_a_Ring_2*.) First observe that if there is a processor in section A that has packets destined for section A, then, there exist a processor in section B that has packets destined for section B. The above observation follows from the pigeonhole principle.

Our transformation consists by picking two processors, one in each section, that have packets destined for the sections they belong. Then, the destinations will be switched. By performing the above transformation for at most $\frac{n}{2}$ times, we will get a symmetric multipacket routing problem. Now it remains to prove that if we load each processor at the new problem with one additional packet, the new problem is at least as hard as the initial one. We distinguish four cases.

Case 1

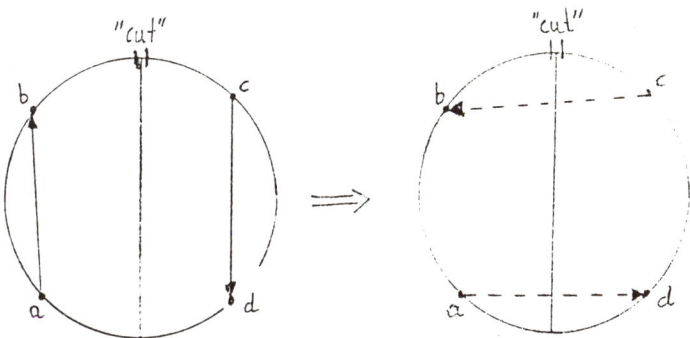

The packets at processor a are destined for processor b. Also, the packets at processor c are destined for processor d. After the switch of the destinations, the packets at processor a are destined for processor d and the packets at processor c are destined for processor b. Observe that before the switch no packet wants to cross the "cut". After the switch a portion of the packets located at processor a might cross the "cut" in the CW direction. So, the new problem is of greater or equal difficulty with the original one.

Case 2

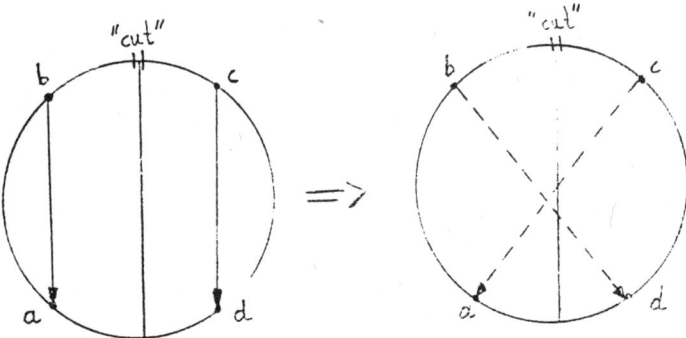

The packets at processor b are destined for processor a. Also, the packets at processor c are destined for processor d. After the switch of the destinations, the packets at processor b are destined for processor d and the packets at processor c are destined for processor a. Observe that before and after the switch only packets that are initially located at processor b will cross the "cut" in the CW direction. After the switch, at least the same number of packets will cross the "cut" in the CW direction since the distance the packets have to travel in the CW direction is reduced.

Case 3

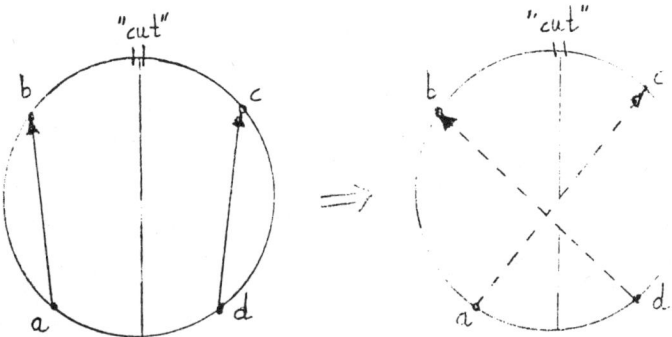

The packets at processor a are destined for processor b. Also, the packets at processor d are destined for processor c. After the switch of the destinations, the packets at processor a are destined for processor c and the packets at processor d are destined for processor b. Before the switch only packets initially located at processor d will cross the "cut" in the CW direction. After the switch only packets located at processor a will cross the "cut" in the CW direction. But the number of packets that cross the "cut" now, is at least as large as before. This is because the distance the packet which cross the "cut" have to travel is reduced.

Case 4

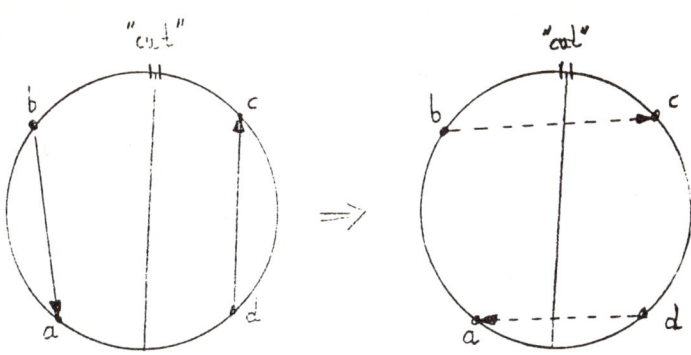

The packets at processor b are destined for processor a. Also, the packets at processor d are destined for processor c. After the switch of the destinations, the packets at processor b are destined for processor c and the packets at processor d are destined for processor a. This is the most interesting case. Before the switch packets from both origins want to cross the "cut" while, after the switch, only packets initially located at processor d want to do so. Before the switch, processor b sends at most $\frac{k}{n}(ab)_{cw}$ packets towards the "cut". Processor d sends at most $\frac{k}{n}(cd)_{cw}$ packets towards the "cut". Thus, before the switch, at most $\frac{k}{n}((ab)_{cw} + (cd)_{cw})$ packets cross the "cut" in the CW direction. After the switch at least $\frac{k}{n}(cb)_{cw} - 1$ packets will cross the "cut" in the CW direction. But $(cb)_{cw} \geq (ab)_{cw} + (cd)_{cw}$. Thus, if we load processor b with one extra packet and we force it to cross the "cut" in the CW direction, the new problem is of equal or greater difficulty.

The observation that all of the transformations needed to convert an asymmetric multipacket problem into a symmetric one might be of that described in case 4 proves the lemma. ∎

Lemma 4 Assume a symmetric multipacket routing problem with initial load of k packets per processor around a given "cut". Also assume that its solution by Algorithm *Route_on_a_Ring_2* causes X to cross the "cut" in a given direction. Then, the symmetric multipacket routing problem where the packets at any processor are destined after $\frac{n}{2}$ positions in the given direction, causes at least $X - \frac{3n}{2}$ packets to cross the "cut" in the direction under consideration.
Proof Omitted.

Lemma 5 Using Algorithm *Route_on_a_Ring_2*, there are at most $\frac{kn}{4} + \frac{5n}{2}$ packets that want to cross any "cut" in the same direction.
Proof Lemmata 3 and 4 imply that a routing problem that is symmetric, and has initial load of $k + 4$ packets per processor destined for the processor located after $\frac{n}{2}$ positions in the CW direction, is harder than any other multipacket routing problem with initial load k packets per processor. (The 4 extra packets will be routed in the CW direction.)

Algorithm $Route\_on\_a\_Ring\_2$ will send at most $\frac{kn}{4} + \frac{n}{2}$ packets to cross the "cut". The routing of the 4 extra packets per processor will contribute $2n$ more packets to that number. ∎

Theorem 3 Using Algorithm $Route\_on\_a\_Ring\_2$, a bisection limited permutation problem on a ring of processors can be solved in $\frac{kn}{4} + \frac{5n}{2}$ routing steps.

Proof. The theorem is implied from Lemma 5. If at every step of the algorithm one packet wants to cross the "cut", the theorem is obviously true. In the case where there is a period during the execution of the routing algorithm that no packet crosses the "cut", say μ steps, then there are μ processors that do not have any packets that want to cross the "cut". Thus, the number claimed at Lemma 5 was overestimated by at least μ. So, the theorem holds. ∎

5 Conclusions - Further work

In this paper, we have examined multipacket routing problems on rings. We divided these problems into two categories, distance limited and bisection limited routing problems. We presented a new lower bound for the case of distance limited problems and we gave an algorithm that tightens the lower bound. For the case of bisection limited problems, we presented an algorithm that solves any problem within $\frac{kn}{4} + \frac{5n}{2}$ routing steps. We believe that the number of routing steps that Algorithm $Route\_on\_a\_Ring\_2$ actually requires is at most $\frac{kn}{4} + n$, and we are working on improving our proofs. No matter if our conjecture is true, we have succeed to present an algorithm that approximates within an additive factor the number of routing steps required in the worst case.

References

[1] B. Aielo, F.T. Leighton, B. Maggs, M. Newman, "Fast Algorithms for Bit-Serial Routing on a Hypercube", Proceedings of the 2nd Annual ACM Symposium on Parallel Algorithms and Architectures, SPAA '90, July 2-6, 1990, Crete, Greece.

[2] D. Krizanc, S. Rajasekaran, Th. Tsantilas, "Optimal Routing Algorithms for Mesh-Connected Processor Arrays", VLSI Algorithms and Architectures (AWOC'88), J. Reif, editor, Lecture Notes in Computer Science 319, 1988, pp. 411-422.

[3] M. Kunde, "Routing and Sorting on Mesh-Connected Arrays", VLSI Algorithms and Architectures (AWOC'88), J. Reif, editor, Lecture Notes in Computer Science 319, 1988, pp. 423-433.

[4] M. Kunde, T. Tensi, "Multi-Packet Routing on Mesh Connected Arrays", Proceedings of ACM Symposium on Parallel Algorithms and Architectures, SPAA'89, June 1989, pp. 336-343.

[5] F.T. Leighton, "Average Case Analysis of Greedy Routing Algorithms on Arrays", Proceedings of the 2nd Annual ACM Symposium on Parallel Algorithms and Architectures, SPAA '90, July 2-6, 1990, Crete, Greece.

[6] F.T. Leighton, F. Makedon, I.G. Tollis, "A 2n-2 Algorithm for Routing in an $n \times n$ Array With Constant Size Queues", Proceedings of ACM Symposium on Parallel Algorithms and Architectures, SPAA'89, June 1989, pp. 328-335.

[7] F. Makedon, A. Simvonis, "Fast Parallel Communication on Mesh Connected Machines with Low Buffer Requirements", Proceedings of the 1990 IEEE International Conference on Computer Design (ICCD '90).

[8] F. Makedon, A. Simvonis, "On Bit-Serial Packet Routing for the Mesh and the Torus", Proceedings of the 3rd Symposium on the Frontiers of Massively Parallel Computation, October 8-10 1990, pp. 294-302.

[9] J.Y. Ngai, C.L. Seitz, "A Framework for Adaptive Routing in Multicomputer Networks", Proceedings of ACM Symposium on Parallel Algorithms and Architectures, SPAA'89, June 1989, pp. 1-9.

[10] S. Rajasekaran, R. Overholt, "Constant Queue Routing on a Mesh", to appear in the Journal of Parallel and Distributed Computing.

[11] A.G. Ranade, "How to Emulate Shared Memory", Proceedings of the 28th IEEE Symposium on Foundation of Computer Science, 1987, pp. 185-194.

[12] L.G. Valiant, G.J. Brebner, "Universal Schemes for Parallel Communication", Proceedings of the 13th Annual ACM Symposium on the Theory of Computing, May 1981, pp. 263-277.

MASSIVELY PARALLEL PROCECESSING IN HIGH ENERGY PHYSICS
THE CERN-MPPC PROJECT

G. Vesztergombi
Central Research Institute for Physics (KFKI)
H-1525 Budapest 114, POB 49, Hungary

Francois Rohrbach
CERN, CH-1211 Geneva 23, Switzerland

Abstract

The next generation of high luminosity hadronic colliders (LHC and SSC) requires novel detectors, both highly time-sensitive and selective. The high selectivity will require devices which must allow to take on-line decisions (at $\sim$ 100 kHz) of a complexity comparable to what is today done in off-line analysis. Such decisions will be based on local or global fine-grain data (many Megabytes), and will require the on-line execution of algorithms in extremely fast computer-like devices. In order to solve this difficult task a Research and Development programme "The MPPC Project" has been launched at CERN which includes ASPEX (UK), CEA/CEN-Saclay (F), CERN (CH), EPFL-Lausanne (CH),CNRS/IN2P3-LAL-Orsay (F), CRIP/KFKI Budapest (H), University of Brunel (UK), University of Geneva (CH) and Thomson-TMS (F). The MPPC collaboration concentrates its effort on the development of machines based on massive parallelism with thousands of integrated processing elements, arranged in string: the ASP (Associative String Processor), a new flexible and scalable architecture endowed with an intelligent and powerful communication network. The present goal of the project is to evaluate the ASP architecture on real time test benches. For this purpose, four 16K-APE (Associative Processing Element) machines are under construction. The basic element is a hybrid module (1K APE) based on an existing and fully tested 64 APE chip. The four 16K could be combined into a single 64K-APE machine, specially suited for on-line image processing. Seven applications are under detailed studies within the collaboration: three for LHC, one for SSC, two for fixed target high energy physics at CERN and one for HDTV. Preliminary results are presented. They show that the objectives should be reached with the use of the ASP architecture.

1. Introduction

High luminosity hadronic colliders (LHC & SSC) will require novel detectors, both highly time-sensitive and selective. Potentially, Megabytes data will be produced at rates (66 MHz at LHC) that are beyond performance of today modern transmission and recording technology. From this huge amount of information, however, only a tiny fraction is possessing any real interest. The required high selectivity is assumed to be achieved by a two steps procedure. A first-level decision based on simple "hard-wired" logics can provide significant rate reduction, it leaves, however, for the second-level decision so complex patterns which require a detailed analysis similar to what is done today in off-line programmes, but with an event frequency of typically 100 kHz. Such decisions, based on a huge number (10 to 100 Mbytes) of digitised local or global data coming in a narrow time window, will require the fast execution of precisely tuned algorithms in extremely fast computer-like devices. A potential match has been identified between the needs of executing algorithms on data from future detectors, and industrial efforts to solve much more general classes of computing problems in other domains. The very general base for obtaining the necessary speed of execution is parallelism, i.e. the simultaneous execution of different instructions, or of the same instructions on different data (MIMD, respectively SIMD machines). Industry and computer science make serious efforts in this field. The MPPC (Massively Parallel Processing Collaboration) is concentrated on problems that are likely to benefit from massive parallelism of SIMD type. Such massively parallel machines operate with thousands of processing elements, all highly integrated and controlled under a single controller. The key elements of the SIMD processor architecture are the data flow (I/O rate) and the data communication between processors. Taking advantage of the application needs and of the coincidence between technological opportunities - the development of a new kind of SIMD machine by ASPEX Microsystems (UK): the ASP (Associative String Processor [1]) and the continuous improvement in silicon integration (VLSI/WSI) - a Research and Development programme "The MPPC Project" has been launched [2-5] between ASPEX (UK), CERN (CH), CEA/CEN-Saclay and CNRS/IN2P3-LAL-Orsay (F), as main partners, and EPFL-Lausanne (CH), University of Brunel (UK), University of Geneva (CH), CRIP/KFKI Budapest (H) and Thomson-TMS (F), as associated partners. In the MPPC collaboration, the overall architecture is defined and implemented by a group consisting of both application-oriented physicists and computer scientists. The applications are dominated by but not exclusively driven by the problem of triggering events in HEP; EPFL, as MPPC partner, is indeed working on a first application in image processing for HDTV. More generally, it can be expected that the same basic processing elements will find their way into quite different application fields. Indeed, the almost infinite scalability of the ASP architecture[1] and its impressive performance targets (in terms of cost, power and achieved density) will attract other suitably parallelized projects (e.g. relational data processing, simulation, computer vision, cellular automata, neural networks) in applications such as, high-definition TV, autonomous guiding vehicles, artificial intelligence, medicine, space science, meteorology, plasma physics, etc.

2. The ASP architecture

The choice of the ASP, as a R & D platform for the Collaboration, was based on the exceptional potentialities offered by this new architecture which allows a wide range of applications.

The main hardware task is to build four ASP machines, one for each main partner, with 16384 APE array, referred to as the "MPPC array". It is based on the existing VASP-64 VLSI ASP chip used for the TRAX-1 machine, another ASP project dedicated for off-line image processing [6,7]. The MPPC-array design allows for maximum processor element density and maximum direct parallel interfacing via conventional electronics to the readout of particle detectors. For this task, dense packages of ASP must be constructed. This is based on a modular design, using hybridation on insulators of the VASP-64 chips. These modules are built by PolyCon (USA) ; they contain a string of 1024 APEs (16 chips) with two parallel I/O per module. These modules will be installed on boards to make 8K strings. Two ASP boards and a low level controller (LAC) in extended VME standard (in order to be compatible with existing industrial modules) are under construction for each 16-K MPPC-Array machine.

2.1 Associativity and string features

The ASP consists of associative processing elements (APE) working as SIMD machines. The string can be arranged in a loop: the architecture is reconfigurable by programmation. Each APE is an associative memory cell with processing capability. Synchronous and asynchronous communication between APEs is provided through an inter-APE communications network dynamically reconfigurable. APEs are addressed by content through a common bus, which minimises data movement. Parallel processing is performed on active APEs selected at a given step of the programme. The architecture is scalable up to hundred of thousands APEs, due to high integration (VLSI/WSI) and low power consumption ($\sim$ mW/APE). The low target cost (below 5.- SFr per APE) is leading, together with the low power and high integration capability, to the possibility of massive integration. The system has maximum application flexibility and computational efficiency. It is fault tolerant: blocks of faulty APEs may be disactivated without breaking the string. The MPPC-Array machines will have Parallel I/O capabilities (10 Gbit/s). ASP application programmes can be written in any block-structured language (Modula 2 is the commonly used language). An introductory course to ASP, provided by ASPEX, is useful to reach a good level on the learning curve in parallel algorithms.

2.2 ASP chip and module

The basic chip for the construction of the compact hybrid MPPC modules (HASP) consists of a programmable VLSI SIMD parallel processing device, incorporating 64 associative processing elements (APE, see fig.1 and 2): the Aspex Microsystems Limited VASP VLSI ASP chip presently manufactured with $2\mu m$ technology at ES2 (F).

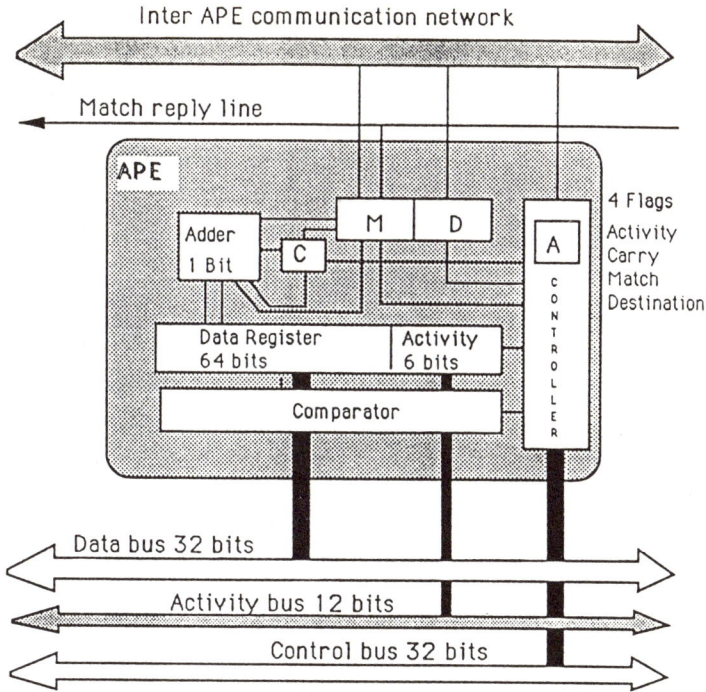

Fig. 1 - Schematic of the associative processing element

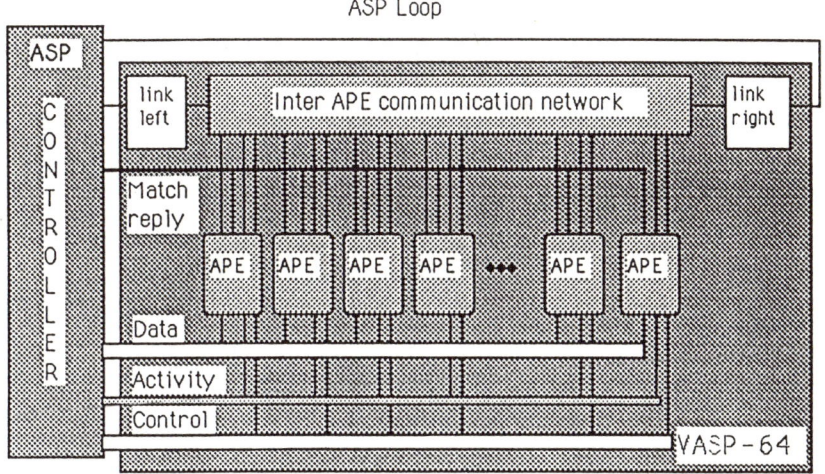

Fig. 2 - The basic Associative String Processor

This chip, although slower than expected, is suitable for making the first prototype hybrid HASP module (fig.3). This module is under development at ASPEX for the MPPC-Arrays and is to be manufactured by the sub-contractor Polycon Inc. (USA). For second-level triggering experiments a faster device will be required. It will use a 1.2μm SOS (silicon-on-sapphire) device in order to achieve a fully working 25ns VASP chip in the summer of 1991 (a high performance ASP chip presently developed by ASPEX and Hughes Company). It will be the basic stone for the final hybrid ASP module for MPPC-arrays: the HASP/P1. This 1K APE module, using 16 dice, has a bypass of 64 and 256 APE blocks and 2 I/O ports which can be configured as 2 x 512 APE substrings or a 1K substring with a LAC interface and an ADB (ASP data buffer) interface. The design is targeted to a standard 184 pin package (3" x 3" with leads). A thermal analysis of the HASP design has shown that a reasonable airflow (200 linear feet per minute) across the surface of the HASP will hold the device junction temperature below 70 degrees C.

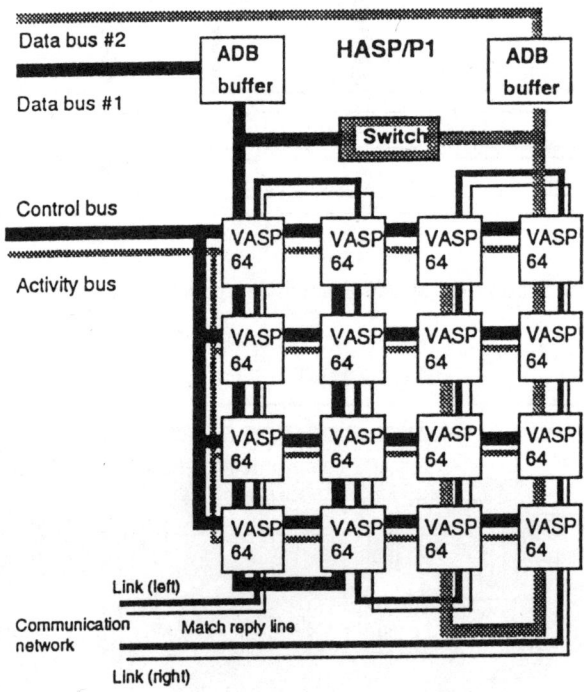

Fig. 3 - The HASP, Hybrid ASP module organisation

The operating system and programming tools are ready for a test using the controller (LAC prototype) under construction at Saclay.

2.3 Machine architecture

Each MPPC-Array will be composed by one LAC and two ASP boards giving a 16 K machine. In concentrating all ASP boards in the same machine we will have the

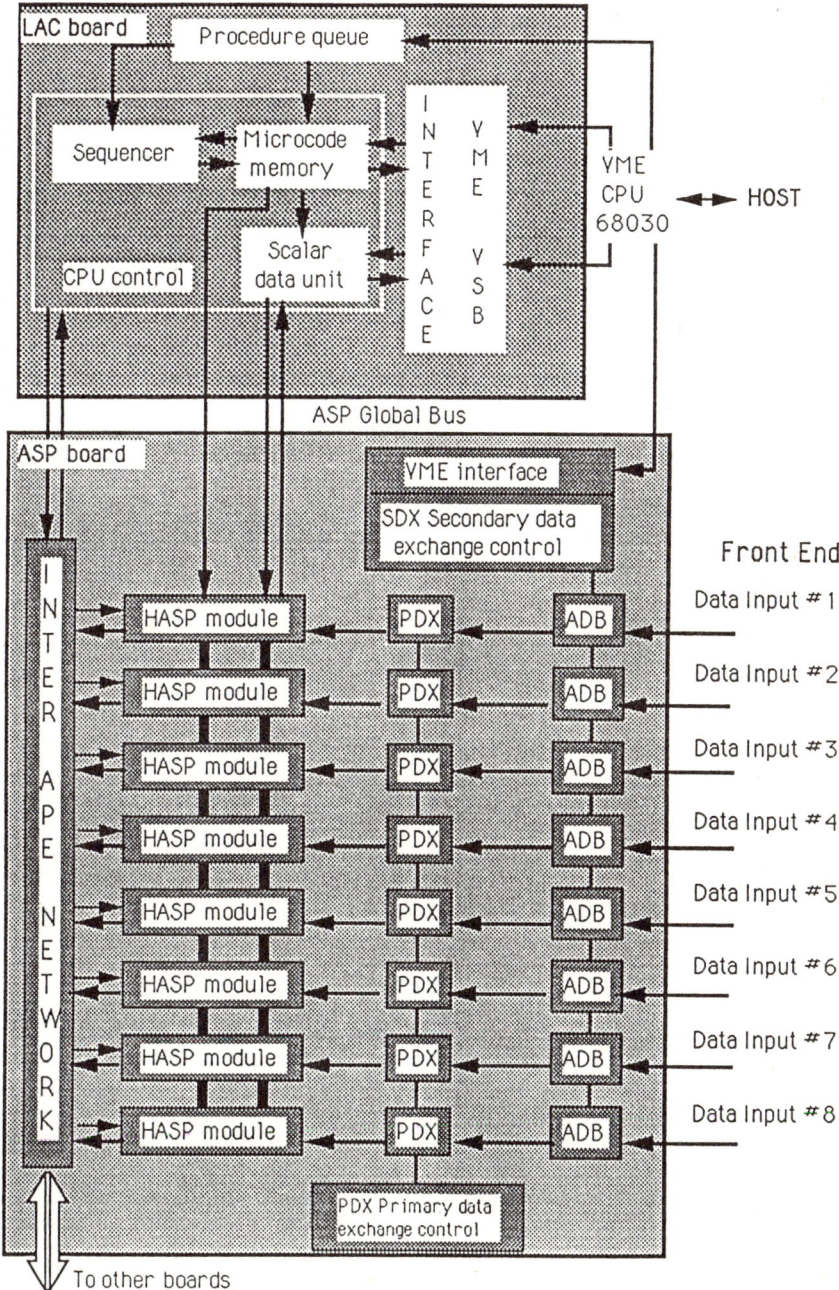

Fig. 4 - MPPC-array machine architecture

possibility to evaluate the power of a 65536 processors compact machine (50 GOPS for 12-bit addition). The ASP board (fig.4) will use the hybrid modules. Each ASP board will contain 8 modules giving a number of 8192 APE per board. Each module will have its own data exchange and ADB double port memory to allow a faster feed for data; 8 connectors will give the possibility to connect external data acquisition hardware (5 Gbit/s I/O per ASP board). ADB memory is large enough to store more than one event and can be fed with the next event during the process of the previous one. Results are stored in an output data buffer to be read out by the data acquisition host through the VME interface. In some applications, the match reply line could be used as a fast trigger.

2.4 The controller

The Low level ASP Controller card (LAC in fig.4) provides the environment to execute ASP application programme on one or more associate ASP boards. The LAC is controlled by higher level ASP controllers. The major parts are a CPU formed by a high speed sequencer and a microprogramme memory to store the LAC operating system and the low level procedures used in application programmes. Most of the glue logic is done with Xlinx PGA. The LAC is in its final construction at Saclay in close collaboration with ASPEX.

3. Applications: status and first results

As previously stated, seven applications are studied: three LHC oriented, one SSC oriented, two for fixed target physics at CERN and one for HDTV.

3.1 Muon selection at LHC (CERN)

At LHC, on a technical side, a trigger on muons is an advantage: compared to using other particle species, it can be performed after thick absorbers reducing the particle flux. On the physics side, single and multi-muon triggers will play a crucial role in particular for Higgs search through its four leptons decay. An analog first-level muon trigger is expected to cut down the single particle rate below 10^5 Hz. In order to identify the muons, a more sophisticated second-level trigger is further required. By identification we mean triggering: the decision is taken by performing an on-line analysis of all the charged particles, curved in the solenoidal magnetic field of the LHC detector. This includes momentum determination, charge assignment and counting all the tracks which are above a given cutoff momentum. This task must be achieved in less than $\sim 20\mu s$ in order to cope with the rate of the first-level trigger. ASP architecture is well adapted for solving this kind of problem. The solution which is under study proposes to divide the triggering procedure (fig.5) into three phases: the loading of the hit information coming from the muon detector (detector mapping into the ASP), the preprocessing of the data (determination of the best hit positions: the "Master point determination") and the tracking (track finding, charge signature and p_T determination).

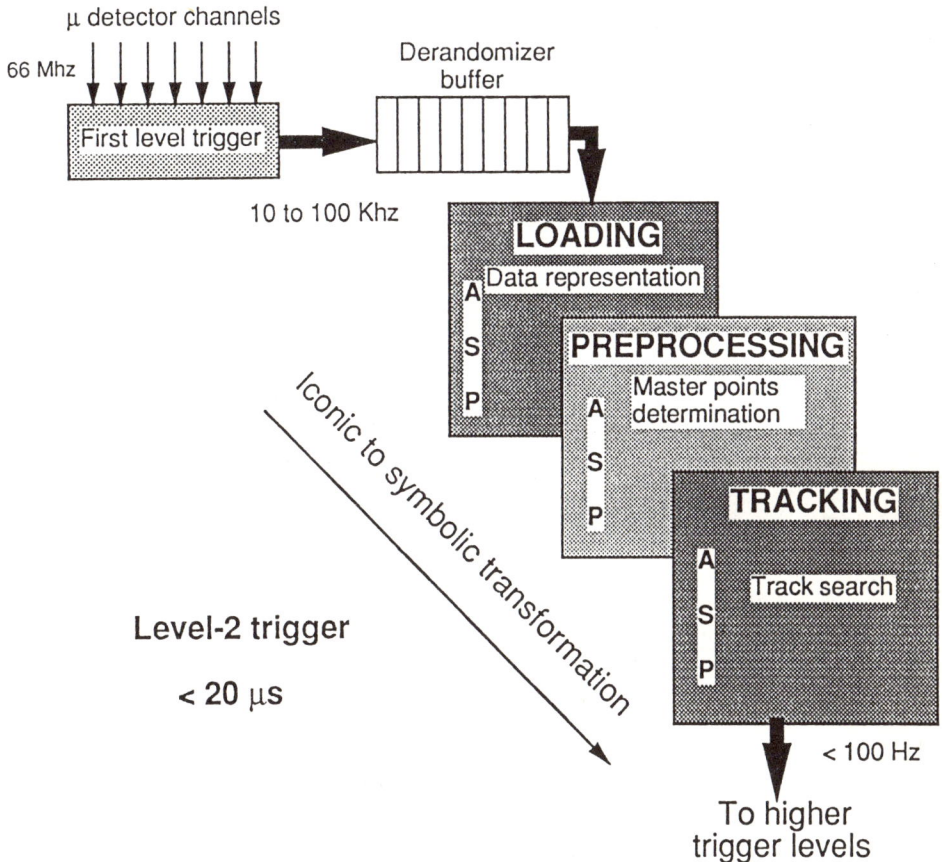

Fig. 5 ASP Muon trigger scheme

Taking advantage of the rotational symmetry of the CMS detector model [8], a (r, ϕ) mapping of the fine-grain muon detector can efficiently be done in the ASP [9]. A track is defined in the central plane of projection (plane of deflection perpendicular to the beam axis) by the vertex of the interaction, positioned with high precision, and by the muon trajectory detected at five radii with multi-layer detectors (fig. 6). The mapping is done in a way which associates one APE to each $\Delta\phi$: this allow to identify in a single search all the high p_T tracks. The granularity $\Delta\phi$ (typically in the mrad range) is a parameter dictated by the size of the Coulomb-scattering. As long as $\Delta\phi$ is above its minimum physical detector pitch value, the mapping is reconfigurable according to the chosen triggering p_T threshold.

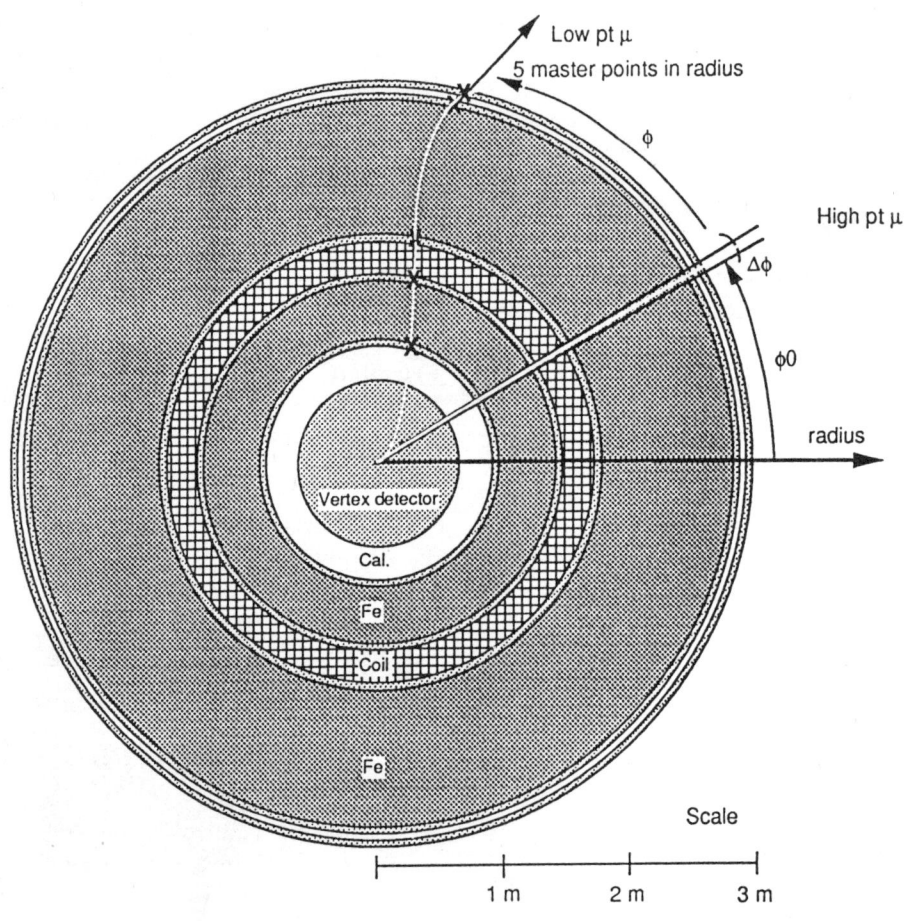

Fig. 6 - Muon tracking simulation modelling

Only the active cells are loaded into the ASP, preserving the topology of the detector which provides the so-called "iconic mapping". Then, a "master-point" is calculated from the multi-layer detector hits, taking into account detector inefficiency and possible multiple hits in one or more layers. This preprocessing is done using a fast "iconic average" using data shifting and bit-logic operations across the APEs. For the third step of the triggering scheme, the tracking, iconic algorithms use bit representation of the image of tracks and the image processing can be done bit parallel in the ASP machine. The five consecutive values of the azimuthal angle ϕ relative to the innermost ϕ_0 value, expressed in unit of $\Delta\phi$ is used for calculating a "track-code". The track-code is a unique representation of a given charged particle trajectory through the muon detector. A preliminary study was to construct track codes from the Geant Monte Carlo data and to explore the feasibility and efficiency of triggering by the proposed iconic algorithm. It consists of looking for all hits at the same time for a fit between master points configuration and all possibilities of track-codes. The number of track-codes depends on the ϕ binning. This number determines the muon search execution time. On the contrary, the triggering time will not depend upon the muon multiplicity because the search is done in parallel over all ϕ_0 and ϕ values. For triggering purpose ($p_T \geq p_T$ threshold) a momentum is determined for each track, by assigning to each track-code a maximum p_T value using a simple look-up table. The preliminary results of the simulation show that the trigger can be worked out within about 20 μs: 5 μs for loading, 5 μs for preprocessing and 10 μs for tracking. This timing fits the requirements imposed by the expected first level trigger rate at LHC.

3.2 TRD electron selection at LHC (CERN)

An integrated transition radiation detector (TRD) and charged particle tracker has been proposed for a LHC detector in order to improve the identification of electrons beyond the level of electromagnetic calorimetry[10]. The TRD tracker will have about 500 000 channels (straws) put inside a cylinder installed around the beam axis (the Halo model). Electron candidates will be tagged by a surrounding calorimeter and the information will be used to define planes cutting the tracker detector and defining candidate roads inside the TRD. One assumes limits on both, the number of candidates (no more than four per event) and the rate of candidate occurrence (not more frequently than every 10 μs average). The basis of discriminating electrons from hadrons in the TRD tracker lies in the statistical analysis of pulse heights of all digitising belonging to a track candidate. This allows to measure the probability of TRD X-ray emission (and detection), which is strongly enhanced for electrons due to their very high γ values. As for the muons, the trigger procedure can also be divided into three phases, but each of them is being implemented on a different type of hardware for optimising the running of the dedicated algorithms.

The first phase is the data distribution. At the input side, the full data rate will be $\sim$ 100 Gbit/s. Due to the limitations in transmission rate and to the simplicity of the selection mechanism, the ASP is not considered for this phase. The second phase is the low-level feature extraction of the track candidates. For that purpose, simultaneously and within all the candidate planes determined by the first level-trigger, all the possible road combinations are scanned (histogramming) in parallel. This will transform the track finding in a peak finding problem. This work is particularly well adapted for the ASP. Then comes the third phase, which is the decision taking. The hits inside the best peaks found in phase two are analysed in pulse heights for electron signature. The number of peaks will be low (no more than 64) and consequently the analysis will likely be better achieved, after transfer from ASP, into fast dedicated processors (RISCs or transputer-like nodes, programmed under C in a real-time operating system environment).

3.3 LHC calorimetry, jets and shower detection (Orsay)

The use of ASP at the second-level trigger of a barrel calorimeter model for LHC is under detailed study using the ASP simulator. It is assumed that the event buffering at that level should not exceed 100 μs on average. Special care is put on the study of the mapping of the calorimeter cells into the ASP (patching optimisation). The basic procedure is to associate one APE to each cell. The loading time will be of the order of 10 to 15 μs. If the Vector Data Buffer feature (VDB: a word parallel, bit serial ASP loading under development at ASPEX) becomes available on the chip, most of this time will be overlapped with the processing of the previous event, and the real cost of loading will only be 1 μs. A fast rejection of each event detected inside the calorimeter should be done in an average time of 50 μs. Jet energy, isolated electrons, missing energy, shower shape and position are the essential event feature extracted from the calorimetry. Various selection algorithms are under detailed study. They are based on the analysis of the energy deposited in neighbouring cells, making correlations between the information coming from the electromagnetic and hadronic parts of the calorimeter. The possible use of preshower detector is also considered. As a result, 20 to 30 μs processing time is obtained. The work is still very preliminary, but already it gives evidence that isolated electrons, jets and shower determination can be implemented in an ASP based second-level trigger for LHC.

3.4 Possible use of ASP for SSC/SDC detector (Saclay)

At SSC, the measurement of jet energies is essential for the detection of neutrinos and others unseen particles. The SDC (Solenoidal Detector Collaboration) detector [11] is based on a (ϕ, η) tower segmentation where ϕ is the azimuth angle and η the pseudo-rapidity ($\eta = -\ln \tan \Theta/2$ where Θ is the polar angle). Each tower is logically divided into five layers providing the symbolic information which will give the necessary event topology and e/h/μ particle identification used for triggering. Starting from the vertex, the five layers of detectors give the following information: tracking (hits/track), answer for isolated electron, number of electron clusters, number of hadron jets and muon hits. In the calorimeter, an isolated electron pixel is characterised by an electromagnetic energy value greater than an e.m.-threshold, a hadronic energy value lower than a hadronic-threshold, and no direct neighbouring cell with e.m.-energy greater than an other e.m.-threshold. The basic principle of using ASP in a second-level trigger is to associate one APE for each calorimeter cell and to load into this APE all the information about the five layers contained within a corresponding (ϕ, η) tower. Inside each APE, the 64 bit data register is enough for storing all this information. For the detection of missing energy, the calculation of the transverse energy E_t is done by summing $E_{sin\Theta}$, calculated simultaneously in the APEs for each cell. Preliminary results of algorithms simulation using the VASP-Simulator give 7 μs for the detection of isolated electrons and $\sim$ 20 μs average time for missing energy (dependent on clusters number and geometry). These results are very encouraging. More work for optimising parallel algorithms and system integration are pursued.

3.5 A K_0 trigger for NA48, a fixed target physics experiment at CERN (Saclay)

The NA48 experiment is an experiment aiming to perform, in 1994-96, a high precision measurement of the ϵ'/ϵ parameter in order to have a better understanding of CP violation [12]. This parameter is determined from the measurement of charged ($\pi^+\pi^-$) and neutral ($2\pi^0$) decays of K_0^S or K_0^L, concurrently. The target is to obtain on-line a very good signature of $2\pi^0$ candidates in less than 10 μs, taking as inputs the energy deposits in the 12000 cells of an electromagnetic calorimeter array. Candidates should give exactly four photon shower clusters in the detector. Physics constraints from the K_0 decay are used for validating good triggers: the transverse momentum conservation implies zero value for the first moment of the energy distribution (relative to the centre of the calorimeter) and, from the K_0 mass constraint, the vertex position can be calculated by using second moment of the energy distribution and total energy of the clusters. These calculations should be invalidated if an accidental hit occurred in the calorimeter in the sensitive time window. Processing time was evaluated for the ASP and for digital signal processors (DSPs). ASP is better suited for the topological processing tasks (find clusters and count them, find accidentals and locate them relative to the normal signal timing), while DSPs are better on the fast, high accuracy, stream arithmetics required in the energy balance and vertex calculations. This application is an example of the use of ASPs in prompt trigger systems, where real time response performance, and fast parallel loading capability is of prime importance. The result of this study shows that combining ASP and DSP processors in the fast neutral NA48 trigger system is currently sufficient to fulfil the NA48 requirements: an efficient $2\pi^0$ trigger can be performed in less than 10 μs.

3.6 ASP tracking with CCD on-line camera in WA93, a fixed target heavy ios physics experiment at CERN (U. of GENEVA)

A heavy ion experiment (WA93) is scheduled at CERN with the aim to study Bose-Einstein correlations among charged pions. The reconstruction of the pion momenta with a large acceptance will be done with a tracking system consisting of a spectrometer magnet and new type of light emitting multistep avalanche chambers[13]. The passage of a charged particle through the chamber is detected as a cluster of light registered by Megapixel CCD cameras. The analysis implies various stages: image preprocessing (back ground reduction and subtraction, optical distortions) then actual image processing (cluster analysis) and finally tracking and momenta correlation . The use of ASP for these tasks looks very promising as they are well adapted for massively parallel image processing. Bose-Einstein correlation requires computation of four-momentum difference for all pairs of tracks which means that many TFLOPS of computing power will be required for only a few days of running ($\sim 10^6$ events).

3.7 Image sequence coding, data compaction for HDTV (EPFL)

At the signal processing laboratory (LTS) in EPFL, the image sequence coding group has developed number of techniques for image sequence compression reaching very high compression ratios. For real time processing at video rate of large images, a parallel computation approach is necessary. This is why the use of ASPs is studied using two different methods: the parallel implementation of the Gabor compression algorithm [14] and the parallel implementation of artificial neural networks on the ASP [15]. In the Gabor compression algorithm, the image is decomposed in elementary Gabor functions basis. The use of such a decomposition is motivated by the fact that Gabor functions have optimal localisation in both spatial and frequency domains. The realisation of this algorithm requires the study of efficient parallel algorithms for matrix computation, particularly large matrix multiplication (typically 256x256). Several algorithms for matrix multiplication on ASP are under study. At this time, two programmes for integer computation have been developed, one using 8 bits and one 16 bits. The best results have been obtained with an algorithm called outer product [14]. The initial results obtained with the ASP simulator in function of the matrix dimension for 8 and 16 bits integers are very encouraging in view of video rate compression up to 200:1 ratio.

4. Conclusion

From the applications under detailed studies for high energy physics at the future hadron colliders LHC, SSC and for SPS fixed target experiments at CERN, preliminary results obtained from simulations, based on the use of ASP machines developed in the MPPC project, can be summarised as follows:

- a second level muon trigger at LHC is feasible and could be done within about 20 μs.

- a second level trigger for calorimetry at SSC and at LHC would require something like 50 μs,

- for the NA48 fixed target experiment, a $K^0 \rightarrow 2\pi^0$ trigger could be achieved in less than 10 μs.

All these results are encouraging and could fulfil the ambitious objectives of these applications. In another domain, for HDTV and videophone applications, preliminary results for compression and restoration of images show that using ASPs could open the possibility of working algorithms at video rates. Real time tests for the seven applications studied at present should be possible in about a year, when the four MPPC-array machines become available.

References

[1] ASP: A cost effective Parallel Microcomputer, R.M. Lea, IEEE Micro, October 1988.

[2] The Massively Parallel Processing Collaboration, The MPPC project MPPC/89-1, CERN, 30 June 1989, Proc. of a Meeting held at EPFL Lausanne 9 June 1989.

[3] Proposal- The MPPC Project, MPPC / 89 - 2, CERN, 28 July 1989.

[4] Memorandum of Understanding for the Execution of the MPPC Project, CERN/EF/FR/fr, 16 March 1990.

[5] MPPC -1990 Status Report, CERN/DRDC/90-76, DRDC/M4-Rev., 18 January 1991.

[6] TRAX-1 proposal, Proposal to develop a physics image processing workstation for Megabytes per event data based on fine and medium grained parallel processors, A. Sandoval et al., CERN, 27 April 1988.

[7] CERN-LAA/89-1, 15 September 1989, section II.6, p.267.

[8] Study of muon triggers and momentum reconstruction in a strong magnetic field for a muon detector at LHC, CERN/DRDC/90-36, DRDC/P7, 30 August, 1990.

[9] Second-Level Muon trigger for the Large Hadron Collider, G. Odor, F. Rohrbach, G. Vesztergombi, CERN/ECP 90-20, 21 December 1990. Aachen LHC Workshop Proceedings CERN 90-10, vol.III. p.136.

[10] Integrated High-Rate Radiation Detector and Tracking Chamber for the LHC, Proposal, B.Dolgoshein, spokesman, CERN - DRDC/90-38.

[11] SDC, Letter of intent SSC/LOI-0001, 30 November 1990

[12] Proposal for a precision measurement of ϵ'/ϵ in CP violation $K^0 \to 2\pi^0$ decays CERN/SPSC/90-22 SPSC/P253, 20 July 1990.

[13] Proposal for a Light Universal Detector for the Study of Correlation between Photons and Charged Particles CERN/SPSC 90-14 May, 1990 and CERN/SPSC 90-32 October, 1990.

[14] T. Ebrahimi, T.R. Reed, M. Kunt, Video coding using pyramidal Gabor expansion, SPIE, Vol 1360, Visual Communications and Image Processing 90, p. 489-501.

[15] G.W. Cottrel, P. Munro, D. Zipser, Image compression by back propagation: an example of extensional programming, ICS report 8702, February 1987, UCSD.

A Heuristic Algorithm for Dynamic Task Allocation in Highly Parallel Systems

Hans-Ulrich Heiss
Rainer Wiesenfarth

Faculty for Informatics, University of Karlsruhe,
P.O.Box 6980, 7500 Karlsruhe 1, Germany
heiss@ira.uka.de

Abstract: We consider the task allocation problem for a homogeneous, multiprogrammed MIMD multicomputer system. Programs arrive in a Poisson stream, and are given as so-called phase graphs. Each phase is described by a task interaction graph. We propose an $O(n^2)$ heuristic allocation algorithm where n is the number of tasks. The algorithm has two parts, the first independent of, the second dependent on the topology of the multicomputer. The first part performs a linear hierarchic clustering of the tasks which is used by the second part to map clusters of suitable size onto free parts of the processor graph. The algorithm is evaluated by simulation for a binary tree topology.

Keywords: task allocation, mapping problem, highly parallel systems, distributed systems

1 Introduction and Problem Description

Highly parallel systems are currently the most promising architectures to further increase computer performance. Although many of these systems are already in use - at least in research institutions - the problem to exploit the parallelism in both an efficient and comfortable way is still not satisfactorily solved. Part of this exploitation problem is the question of how parallel programs should be mapped onto a highly parallel architecture. We refer to this question as the *processor allocation problem* [Hei91]. As we will see below, a solution to this problem depends on various parameters. It is useful to classify these parameters by regarding the problem as being composed of four parts,
- a machine model M,
- a load model L,
- an allocation relation R, and
- an allocation goal G

Hence, an allocation problem is a quadruple (M,L,R,G).

1.1 Machine Model

According to Flynn´s classification scheme, today available highly parallel systems are either of SIMD (single instruction stream - multiple data stream) or of MIMD (multiple instruction stream - multiple data stream) type. In this paper, we consider the mapping problem for homogeneous MIMD multicomputer systems. We assume a large set of processor elements (PEs), each consisting of a processor and a dedicated local memory. Because no shared memory is available, communication between the PEs is done by *message passing*. To that end, the PEs are interconnected through a mostly regular network. Typical structures are e.g. tree, mesh, torus, or hypercube. The common property of these networks is that the number of direct links of each node to other nodes is relatively small compared to the total number of nodes. Hence, communication between two arbitrary nodes usually involves message transport through other, intermediate nodes. The time needed for a message transport is therefore a monotonically increasing function of the distance between the communicating PEs. The actual time needed depends further on the message size, the bandwidth of the links, and some transmission delay at each intermediate node. A natural way to model those architectures is the usage of a weighted graph with the PEs as nodes and the direct links as the edges weighted by the time it needs to transport a data unit over that link. This graph is called the *processor connection graph* (PCG) an example of which is depicted in figure 1. It may be directed or undirected.

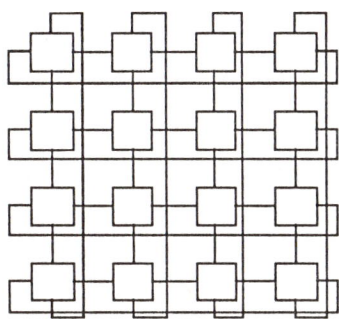

Figure 1: Processor connection graph (2D-Torus)

More formally, a parallel machine is given as a PCG = (P, E^P) with

P	set of processor elements
E^P	set of processor connections (links)
μ	the uniform processor speed (instructions per time unit)
β	the uniform processor transmission rate
γ	the uniform link bandwidth

1.2 Load Model

A parallel program is assumed to consist of a set of *tasks* or *threads* that can be run concurrently. To perform their function, these tasks have to communicate with each other by sending messages. Sometimes, the program requires that one task may not start before another task has finished. This leads to a precedence relation on the set of tasks which forms a partial order. Both aspects, the communication and the precedence relation can be modeled as a graph with the tasks as the nodes. In the former case, the edges that may be directed or not indicate communication between the tasks and can be weighted with the communication intensity leading to the so-called *task interaction graph* (TIG) shown in figure 2a. The latter case is modeled by the *task precedence graph* (TPG) which is necessarily a directed one without any edge weights (figure 2b). The two graph models emphasize different aspects.

The problem usually associated with the TIG is the search for a mapping that minimizes the resulting communication costs. In its purest form, the problem is equivalent to the graph isomorphy problem, i.e. the question whether there is a one to one correspondence between the elements of the TIG and of the PCG. This problem is known to be NP-hard [GJ79]. On the other hand, the TPG addresses the classical scheduling problem [Cof75] that asks for a schedule of task executions satisfying the precedence relation and needing minimal total execution time. This problem is in its general case also NP-hard [GJ79].

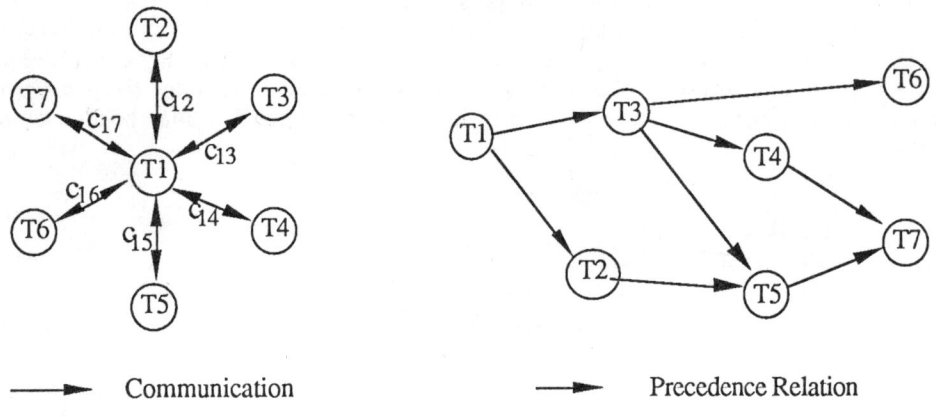

Figure 2a: Task interaction graph (TIG) (TPG)

Figure 2b: Task precedence graph

Generally speaking, the problem of allocating processors to tasks or, conversely, mapping tasks onto processors has two aspects, a spatial one and a temporal one. The TIG associated problems are focussing on the spatial aspect, i.e. *where* the tasks are executed. The TPG related problems, on the other hand, are concerned with the temporal aspect, i.e. *when* the tasks are executed, producing a (partial) order of task executions. To put it another way, the TIG problems are concerned with the aspect of *information flow*, the TPG problems are concerned with the aspect of *control flow*.

In our phase model of parallel programs, both aspects are considered. We assume a program to consist of many phases, each of which can be modeled as one TIG. That means, within a phase, the number of tasks and the communication relationships among them are constant. After having finished one phase, the program enters another one with possibly totally different structure. The phases are not necessarily forming a linear sequence, the program regarded on the phase level is rather similar to a sequential program, allowing branches and loops (figure 3).The branching can be described by branching probabilities p_{ij}. Starting with a single initial phase (S1), the program proceeds through different phases and ends in one of the final phases (S7 or S8).

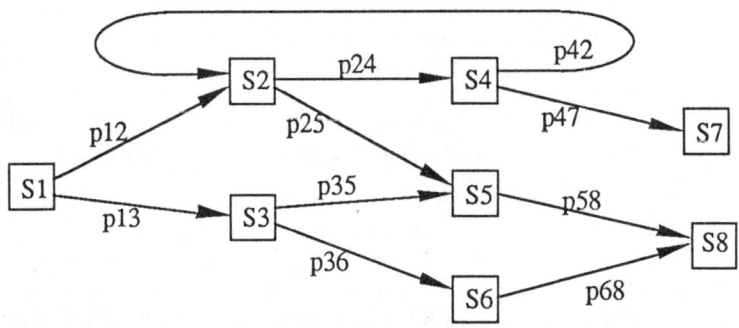

Figure 3: Phase graph (PPG) of a parallel program

Formally, each of these phases consists of a set of concurrent tasks described by a TIG=(T, E^T) with

T	the set of tasks
E^T	communication links
(c_{ij})	communication intensity (number of data items) between T_i and T_j
(b_i)	length of each process (e.g. no. of instructions)

Each parallel program PP is described as a directed program phase graph PPG=(S, E^S) with

S	the set of phases
E^S	phase transitions
(p_{ij})	phase transition probabilities

Having an operating system research background we are interested in allocation problems a general purpose operating system controlling a multicomputer may be faced with. We are convinced that highly parallel systems will become the prevalent architecture even for general purpose computers, and that the programs running on these systems will also be increasingly parallel. We therefore assume a multiprogramming environment where several parallel programs are running in parallel. We further assume that the parallel programs are not given as a set in a static way but arrive at and leave the system in a stochastic manner. This means that we consider the *dynamic case*, where the programs may change their demand for processors at (almost) any time, and where the load to be processed by the computer system is given as a stream of arriving parallel programs forming a Poisson process with parameter λ.

1.3 Allocation Relation

Generally, an allocation between tasks and processors can be described as a relation $R \subseteq T \times P$. Because it raraly makes sense to allocate a task to more than one processor at a time, the relation is usually a mapping $\pi: T \rightarrow P$.

Given that the relation is a mapping, it may be either *injective* (i.e. to each processor at most one task is allocated) or *contractive* (i.e. more than one task may be allocated to a processor). In this paper, we assume the allocation relation to be an *injective mapping*.

The dynamic case that we consider here is characterized by a sequence of releases (programs or phases are finished) and requests (new phases start). Hence, the situation our allocation mechanism sees is a partially allocated processor set. An allocation takes place every time a phase of a program is beginning and is constant until the phase is finished. (With respect to that, one may call this allocation scheme also *semi-dynamic* instead of *dynamic*). There is no migration and no preemption. So at each step, we actually perform a mapping of a TIG onto a fragmented processor set. The tasks of a phase are either allocated completely or all tasks have to wait until a sufficient number of processors is available. However, if there are enough free processors, the allocation will be performed (even if the tasks are spread over the entire network).

1.4 Allocation Goals

With the allocation of processors one pursues a specific goal, e.g. efficient usage of hardware resources or user specified performance requirements. These goals come in two types: *restrictions* and *optimizations*. When the goal type is optimization, an objective function has to be defined which has to be minimized (or maximized) by the mapping π. Here, we use as our goal the minimization of the communication overhead:

$$\sum_{i=1}^{|T|} \sum_{j=1}^{|T|} c_{ij} \, \delta(\pi(i), \pi(j)) \rightarrow \min \quad \text{with} \quad \delta: P \times P \rightarrow \mathbb{R}$$

where $\delta(p,q)$ indicates the transportation cost for one data unit from processor p to processor q. This cost function may include load-dependent routing and communication delays at links and intermediate nodes.

1.5 Algorithm requirements

As already mentioned, the aim of our work was to design an algorithm that is suited for dynamic allocation as part of a general purpose operating system (GPOS). This implies several requirements:

- *Portability:* A GPOS and therefore all its algorithms should be largely independent of the architecture of the underlying parallel machine. If there is an unavoidable dependency, the dependent part should be clearly separated from the independent one to increase portability.

- *Speed:* Because it is performed at program load time, it should be fast. This naturally excludes optimal algorithms which are known to be NP-hard. The alternative is the use of heuristics which can also be fairly costly. Our requirement was that its asymptotic complexity should not exceed $O(n^2)$ where *n* is the number of tasks.

- *Use of information:* Information about the programs to be allocated is hard to obtain. In the worst case, the actual structure of the program (TIG) depends on input data and cannot be determined in advance. The same is true for the intertask communication intensities. We assume that the TIG needed by the algorithm is an estimate from the compiler (maybe improved by some hints from the programmer or user). It is also possible that the operating system has taken measurements from previous executions of the program. Because these estimates have to be considered rather inaccurate, we require the algorithm to be robust with regard to the accuracy of the information provided.

1.6 Related Work

In recent years there has been a great many contributions to the task allocation problem in parallel or distributed systems. Some algorithms are distributed [BK90], most of them are centralized. They all differ from each other concerning one or more aspects and therefore actually address different specific variants of the assignment problem. In many cases, the mapping problem to minimize some cost function is formulated as a *static* one [KM88, BP89, CCL89, Lo88]. *Dynamic* allocation problems are either restricted to the *partitioning* problem, i.e. how many processors should be given to a parallel program [Bok88, Sevc89, DCDP90], or are specific to a particular processor topology such as hypercube [GIB90, KDL89, ERS90]. Because of the clustering used, the work by Sadayappan et al. [SER90] is similar to our approach. Unlike our work, however, they address the static problem and consider a *contractive* mapping. With contractive mapping, there is the additional problem of *load balancing* that we don´t have. With regard to the efficiency, the heuristic algorithms proposed for these problems have - as far as they are mentioned in the papers - a complexity higher than $O(n^2)$.

2 The Algorithm

The idea behind our heuristic algorithm is the following simple intuition: Suppose you have a program phase consisting of three tasks two of which are communicating heavily with each other, the third having only little communication. Suppose further that you have three processors available, two of which are adjoining, the third apart. In this situation it is reasonable to map the first two tasks onto the neighbouring processors and the third onto the remote one. To make the resulting algorithm largely adjustable to different architectures and load situations, the mapping problem is divided into two steps or parts. In the first part, the concurrent tasks of a phase are combined to clusters (or the TIG is decomposed into clusters, respectively) in a hierarchical way independent of any target hardware structure or load situation. In the second part, clusters of different levels and sizes are allocated to free processor subnets trying to minimize communication delays.

2.1 Part one: Linear Hierarchical Decomposition (LHD)

To illustrate the working of our algorithm, we use the following TIG as our running example (Fig. 4):

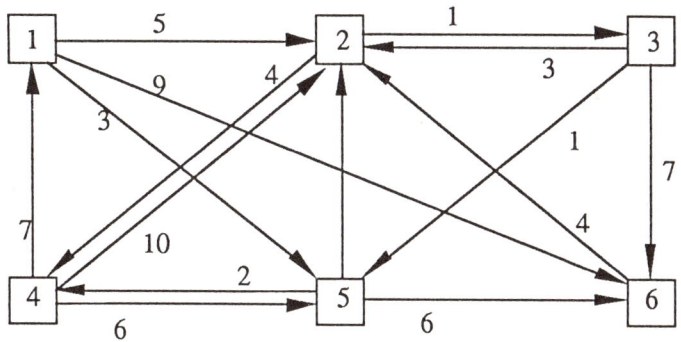

Figure 4: TIG of the running example

The hierarchical linear decomposition is itself built of several substeps which are described in the following. For each step, the asymptotic complexity is given in brackets, where n is the number of nodes in the TIG, and k is the node degree.

Step 1: Calculating the number of the neighbours (node degree) $[O(nk)]$: In this step, the degree of each node is determined by counting outgoing and incoming edges. For our example, we obtain the following list:

Node	# neighbours
1	4
2	7
3	4
4	5
5	6
6	4

Step 2: Building the neighbour lists [O(nk)]: For each node, a list of all incoming and outgoing edges with their respective weights is built.

Node   neighbour, *communication intensity*

1	6, 9	4, 7	2, 5	5, 3			
2	5, 5	3, 1	6, 4	4, 10	1, 5	3, 3	4, 4
3	2, 3	2, 1	6, 7	5, 1			
4	1, 7	2, 4	5, 2	5, 6	2, 10		
5	1, 3	3, 1	4, 6	2, 5	6, 6	4, 2	
6	3, 7	1, 9	5, 6	2, 4			

Figure 5: Neighbour list

Step 3: Removing duplicates [O(nk)]: Now parallel edges are cumulated so that we have no more duplicates in the lists.

Step 4: Sorting [O(nk log n)]: The lists are then sorted by decreasing edge weights. For our example, the cumulated and sorted neighbour list is shown in Figure 6.

Node   neighbour, *modified communication intensity* (sorted)

1	6, 9	4, 7	2, 5	5, 3	
2	4, 14	5, 5	1, 5	3, 4	6, 4
3	6, 7	2 4	5, 1		
4	2, 14	5, 8	1, 7		
5	4, 8	6, 6	2, 5	1, 3	3, 1
6	1, 9	3, 7	5, 6	2, 4	

Figure 6: Neighbour list after cumulation and sorting

Step 5: Generating the cohesion list [O(n^2 + nk)]: The generation of the cohesion list is the most costly step in the algorithm:

It starts with an arbitrary node (e.g. no.1) that is put into the empty list. Of all tasks not yet in the list we pick that one that has the highest edge weight to a node already in the list. This node is put next into the list and the edge weight is used to describe the cohesion to the former sublist. If no such node can be found which is the case when we have isolated subgraphs, we pick an arbitrary node. The cohesion in this case is 0. We stop when all nodes are in the list.

Figure 7 shows from left to right the gradually generated list, the sublists and the cohesion to the newly included node. The dotted lines indicate which node in the sublist is responsible for that cohesion.

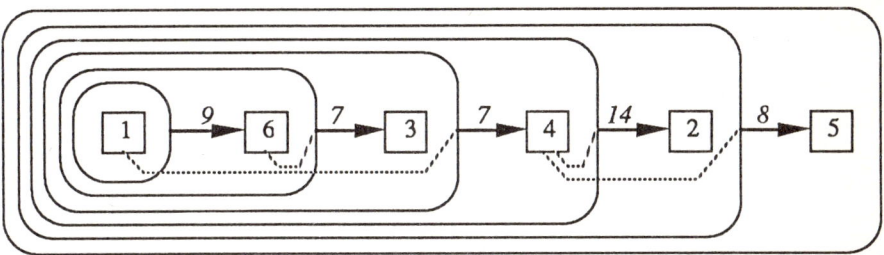

Figure 7: Construction of the cohesion list

Step 6: Stepwise decomposition $[O(n \log n)]$: This last step determines in which order the list should be broken down into sublists to cope with fragmented processor networks. These cuts are obtained by sorting the cohesion edges by increasing weights (Figure 8).

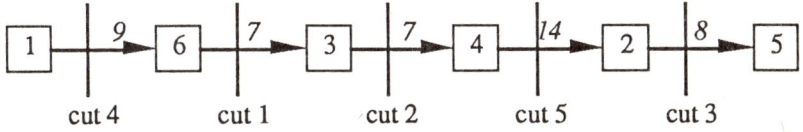

Figure 8: Sequence of cuts applied to the cohesion list

This leads to the following stepwise decomposition of the node list (Figure 9)

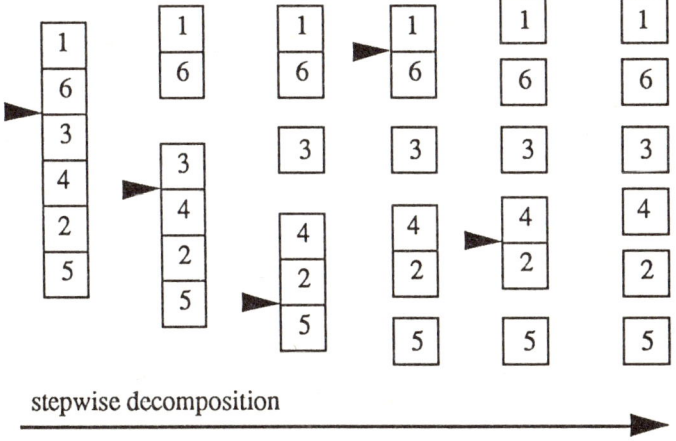

Figure 9: Stepwise decomposition according to the cuts shown in Figure 8.

The overall complexity of this part totals to $O(n^2 + nk \log k)$. Assuming that k, the number of communication channels per task, has an upper bound, we end up with a complexity of $O(n^2)$.

2.2 Part Two: Mapping onto target machine

In the second part, the mapping onto the actual target machine under the restrictions of the present allocation situation is performed. This part can also be broken down into several steps:

- selection of the processor set
- mapping the tasks onto that set
- routing for intertask communication

The basic idea behind this part of the algorithm is to find the smallest processor-subnet (i.e. subtree in a tree, subcube in a hypercube, rectangle in 2D-torus) that fits the requirements (at least n processors for n tasks). If no such subnet can be found, the task set to be allocated is broken down into two subsets according to the order of cuts in the cohesion list. Then we try to find matching processor subnets for these task-subsets, and so forth until all tasks are allocated.

We have worked out these steps for four different topologies, i.e. binary tree, 2D-torus, hypercube, and ring. In this paper, we only describe the case of a binary tree, the interested reader may refer to [Wie90] for the other cases. For hypercubes, for instance, we use the allocation mechanism described in [KDL89].

Step 1: Processor selection: We simply search for the root of a subtree that has a sufficient number of free processors. Of all these subtrees we pick that one with the smallest number of free processors (*best fit*). To that end, with each node i, a variable $F[i]$ is associated that indicates the number of free processors in its subtree. Let n be the number of processors needed, then k, the number of the root of the selected subtree satisfies

$$k \in \{i \mid F[i] \geq n \wedge \forall j, F[j] \geq n: F[j] \geq F[i]\}$$

Step 2: Mapping: Suppose we have found a suitable subtree with root k. We first try to fill the left subtree and the root, and then put the rest into the right subtree. We start with the entire cohesion list:

- Let l be the number of free nodes in the left subtree, and r the number of remaining tasks that have to be placed in the right subtree. Set $r = n-l-1$ if the root is free, otherwise set $r = n-l$.

- At each time, there is a sequence of sublists that is executed sequentially. Let i be the length of such a sublist. One of the following conditions must hold:

    $i > l \wedge i > r \wedge i = 1$: allocate to the root
    $i \leq l \wedge (l \leq r \vee i > r)$: allocate to left subtree
    $i \leq r \wedge (r \leq l \vee i > l)$: allocate to right subtree
    $i > l \wedge i > r \wedge i > 1$: no allocation is possible, break down the list into two sublists and try for the sublists. Repeat this step until all sublists are allocated.

- This function is recursively called for the right and the left subtree.

Step 2 has a complexity linear in n, the number of tasks. Applied to our running example and a free seven-node tree it results in an allocation as depicted in figure 10.

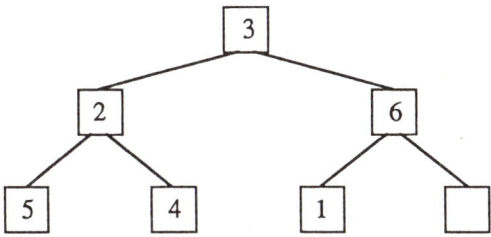

Figure 10: Example program allocated on a tree.

Step 3: Routing: While in other topologies routing can be a problem (see [Wie90] for discussion), in the case of binary tree there is no choice: there is only one path between two nodes.

3 Simulation Results

To evaluate the behavior of the proposed algorithm, we implemented it in a simulation model (Figure 11) The simulation program which is currently being expanded to become a more general algorithm testbed has the following features:

Machine model:
    It allows the selection of different usual regular processor networks (e.g. hypercube, tree, torus) of almost arbitrary size. The processor speed is unity. Communication delays are governed by two parameters:
- bandwidth of the links   [1000]
- transmission rate of the processors.   [10000]

Load model:
    Programs are described by random program phase graphs (PPG) which are automatically generated according to the following parameters
- arrival rate (generation rate of new programs)   [15]
- number of phases (nodes in PPG) per program   [12]
- number of final phases (sink nodes in the PPG) per program   [2]
- number of transitions (node degree in the PPG)   [4]
- task execution time (length of a task)   [15]
- parallelism (number of nodes in the TIG)   [25]
- channels (node degree in the TIG)   [4]
- messages (edge weights in the TIG)   [10]

All these parameters are the mean values of random variables which are described by their respective distribution. In our simulations, except for the interarrival time which is exponentially distributed, we used a uniform distribution with varying dispersion.

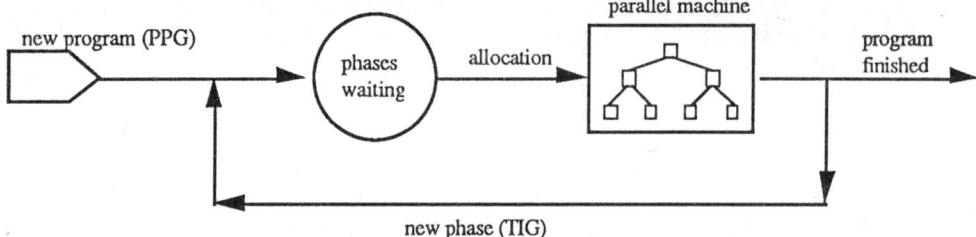

Figure 11: Overall structure of the simulation model

We report the results for a series of simulation runs with a 127 node tree as the machine model. Almost any parameter was varied in its mean as well as its dispersion. Variation of one parameter means keeping all others constant at their basic values. These basic values are indicated in brackets in the above parameter list. As evaluation of the allocation chosen by the algorithm, we used the communication overhead in percent of the execution time. It consists of all delays caused by transmission over the network at links and intermediate nodes. To have a yardstick for the performance of the allocation algorithm we compared its results with that of a random allocation scheme.

Some parameters (e.g. arrival rate, # phases, task execution time) only affected the utilization of the system. It is obvious that high utilization leads to higher communication overhead for both, our algorithm and the random allocation.

Figure 12 shows the impact of an increase in parallelism on the communication overhead. The percentage values on the vertical axis indicate that communication intensity was rather low compared to execution, i.e. for our parameter set, communication was no bottleneck.

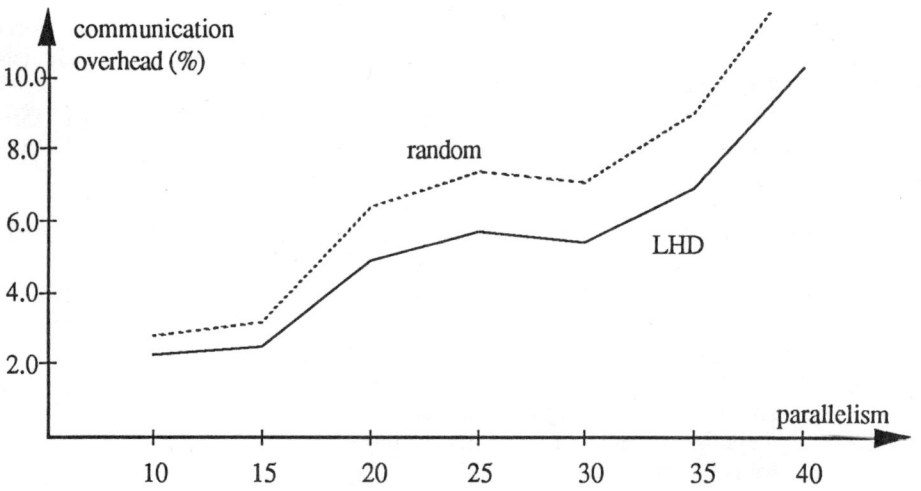

Figure 12: Communication overhead as a function of the degree of parallelism

The gain achieved by our algorithm was in the 25% range. It was a surprising result that this improvement over the random scheme was unaffected by almost all parameter variations. The only parameter with a strong impact on it was the number of channels (Figure 13). For a low number which means a scarcely interconnected TIG structure, the gain was largest (Figure 14). This is due to the fact that the algorithm uses a linear list to represent the cohesion of the tasks. The correspondence between this list representation and the TIG is best if the TIG is actually a linear list. The more the TIG departs from this structure, the more inappropriate is the cohesion list as description of the TIG´s actual cohesion. However, many parallel programming models suggest rather scarcely interconnected TIGs.

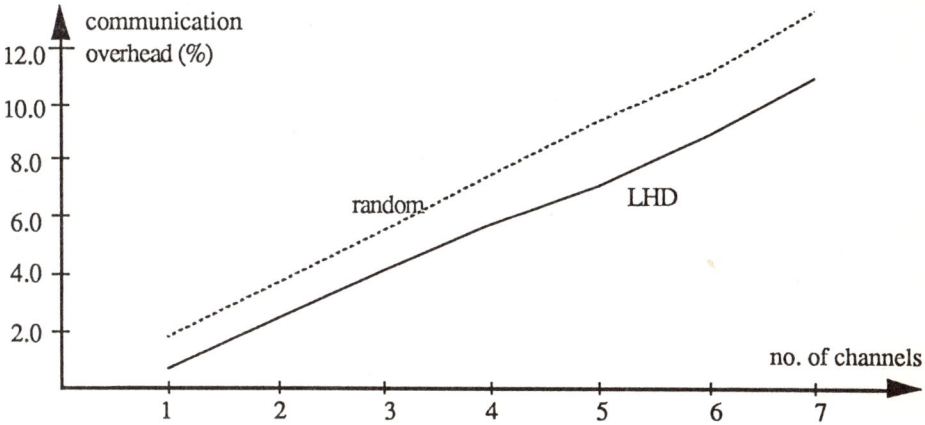

Figure 13: Communication overhead as a function of the no. of channels

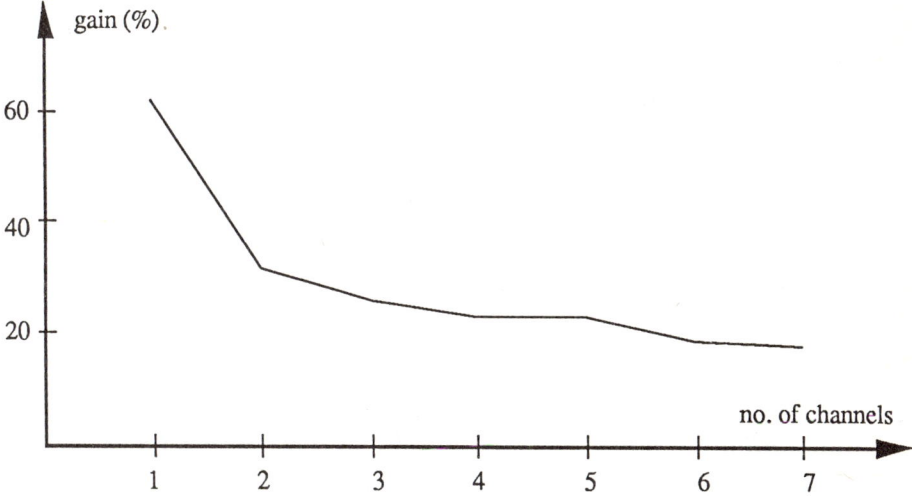

Figure 14: Gain achieved by the algorithm as a function of the no. channels

The simulation model was implemented in C++ and runs on a Sun Sparc-station. The average time the LHD-algorithm needed for the mapping was between one and two milliseconds (for the above parameter set) and by that almost of the same order of magnitude as the random placement that needed 0.2 - 0.4 milliseconds.

4 Conclusion

We proposed a simple heuristic algorithm for the dynamic task allocation problem in multiprogrammed multicomputer systems. The algorithm is based on the information provided by the task interaction graph (TIG) and on the current allocation situation. It consists of two parts: The first part, independent of the machine topology, builds the so-called cohesion list which provides a linear hierarchic decomposition (LHD) of the TIG. What is actually needed by the LHD is just an ordering of the edge weights, not the edge weights themselves. This is what makes the LHD robust with regard to inaccurate estimates of the communication intensities. The complexity for that part is $O(n^2)$ with n as the number of tasks. If all information for building the TIG is already available, this part may be performed at compile time. The actual mapping is done in the second step which is dedicated to the respective topology and dependent on the current load situation. The basic idea of the mapping step can be described as a *hierarchic best fit*. Simulations performed for the case of a 127-node binary tree multicomputer showed significant improvement over a random placement, while the cost for the mapping algorithm was remarkably low. Even in cases unfavorable for our LHD algorithm, we measured an improvement of 25% of the communication overhead.

References:

[ABPV88] Antonelli,S.; Baiardi,F.; Pelagatti,S.; Vanneschi,M.: A Static Approach to Process Mapping in Massively Parallel Systems. Parallel Processing (1988) pp.319-332.

[BP89] Baxter,J.; Patel,J.H.: The LAST Algorithm: A Heuristic-Based Static Task Allocation Algorithm. Proc. 1989 Int. Conf. on Parallel Processing, pp.II-217 - II-222.

[Bok88] Bokhari,S.H.: Partitioning Problems in Parallel, Pipelined, and Distributed Computing. IEEE TOC Vol.37,1 (Jan. 1988), pp. 48-57.

[BK90] Boillat, J.E.; Kropf,P.G.: A Fast Distributed Mapping Algorithm. CONPAR 90, pp.405-416.

[CCL89] Chern,M.-S.; Chen,G.H.; Liu,P.: An LC Branch-and-Bound Algorithm for the Module Assignment Problem. Information Processing Letters 32 (1989) pp.61-71.

[Cof76] Coffman,E.G.: Computer and Job-Shop-Scheduling Theory. John Wiley & Sons, New York, 1976.

[DCDP90] Dussa,K.; Carlson,B.; Dowdy,L.; Park,K.-H.: Dynamic Partitioning in a Transputer Environment. ACM SIGMETRICS Conf. 1990, pp.203-213.

[ERS90] Ercal,F.; Ramanujam,J.; Sadayappan,P.: Task Allocation onto a Hypercube by Recursive Bipartitioning. Journal of Parallel and Distributed Computing 10 (1990) pp.35-44.

[GJ79] Garey,M.R.; Johnson,D.S.: Computers and Intractability: A Guide to the Theory of NP-Completeness. Freeman, San Francisco (1979).

[GIB90] Gulati, S.; Iyengar,S.S.; Barhen,J.: The Pebble Crunching Model for Fault-tolerant Load Balancing in Hypercube Ensembles. The Computer Journal 33,3 (1990) pp. 204-214.

[Hei91] Heiss, H.-U.: Classification of Task Assignment Problems in Parallel Systems. Internal Report No. 7/91, Faculty for Informatics, University of Karlsruhe, June 1991.

[KDL89] Kim,J.; Das,C.R.; Lin,W.: A Processor Allocation Scheme for Hypercube Computers. Proc. 1989 Int. Conf. on Parallel Processing, pp.II-231 - II-238.

[KM88]   Krämer,O.; Mühlenbein,H.: Mapping Strategies in Message-Based Multiprocessor Systems. Parallel Computing 9 (1988/89), pp. 213-225.
[Lo88]   Lo, V.M.: Heuristic Algorithms for Task Assignment in Distributed Systems. IEEE TOC Vol.37, No.11 (Nov. 1988) pp. 1384-1397.
[SER90]   Sadayappan,P.; Ercal,F.; Ramanujam,J.: Cluster partitioning approaches to mapping parallel programs onto a hypercube. Parallel Computing, Vol.13 (1990), pp. 1-16.
[Sev89]   Sevcik,K.: Characterizations of Parallelisms in Applications and Their Use in Scheduling. ACM SIGMETRICS Conf., Berkeley, 1989.
[Wie90]   Wiesenfarth, R.: Design and Analysis of a Heuristic Algorithm for Dynamic Process Allocation in Highly Parallel Systems. Diploma thesis, University of Karlsruhe, Faculty for Informatics, 1990 (in German)
[Wil90]   Williams,S.A.: Programming Models for Parallel Systems. John Wiley & Sons, Chichester, 1990.

Analysis of Parallel Lisp Programs Based on a Trace Mechanism

Hermann Ilmberger, Sabine Thürmel
*EDS Project**
Siemens AG, ZFE IS SOF 22
Otto-Hahn-Ring 6
D-8000 München 83
Germany
e-mail: thuermel@ztivax.uucp, hermann%km21@ztivax.uucp

Abstract

This paper introduces a parallel debugging environment for parallel Lisp programs. The toolkit is part of the ESPRIT-II project 2025 EDS (European Declarative System). It consists among others of tools for visualization of runtime behavior and replay. It may easily be extended by new tools. The basis to all these debugging components is a parallel tracer.

1 Motivation

The trace based analysis and debugging environment for parallel Lisp programs is part of the ESPRIT-II project 2025 EDS (European Declarative System). The project will produce the prototype of a homogeneous distributed machine supporting parallel versions of Extended SQL, ElipSys, a logical language, and Lisp (EDS Lisp). EDS Lisp is intended to support large knowledge based systems, for example for natural language translation or VLSI chip design [EDS89]. This paper describes the concepts of a toolkit for the debugging and the visualization of EDS Lisp programs. The toolkit is currently under implementation.

The paper starts with an overview of EDS Lisp and a short characterization of the EDS Machine. In chapter 3 our concept of trace-based analysis and debugging is outlined. The trace-mechanism for EDS Lisp is introduced. It is shown how the user can benefit from a set of complementary trace-based analysis and debugging tools. In chapters 4 to 6 three exemplary trace-based analysis and

---

* The EDS-Project (European Declarative System) is partially sponsored by the European Community under ESPRIT-II 2025.

debugging aids are described in detail. A comparison to related concepts is made in chapter 7.

2 EDS Lisp and the EDS Machine

EDS Lisp is an extension of Common Lisp [Steele 84]. Common Lisp has been chosen as the base language because one goal of the project is to port real life applications to the EDS system. Using a clean and more functional dialect like Scheme would have avoided many problems inherent to Common Lisp and would have facilitated debugging, but in fact we cannot expect to find many real applications written in a Lisp dialect like Scheme.

EDS Lisp offers explicit parallelism. New processes are spawned by the future construct which may be used most profitable for coarse grain parallelism in the envisaged class of target machines. The Lisp processes may communicate via mailboxes (many to many) or via access to shared variables within critical regions.

EDS Lisp is developed for the EDS Machine, a homogeneous distributed multiprocessor, supporting up to 255 processing elements. A prototype will consist of 63 processing elements and a diagnostic node. During the test phase the latter will serve as an interface between the 63 node EDS machine and the user's workstation. The Process and Store Model of EDS Lisp is described in detail in [HaHe90]. We won't refer to it in this paper because our debugging concepts are intentionally independent of the EDS system. So our ideas are also applicable to similar architectures.

3 Traced based Debugging of Parallel Lisp Programs

During the run of an EDS Lisp program a minimal trace is logged automatically and kept in a file. It consists mainly of parallel events as process spawning, synchronization and communication. This minimal trace can be used by several debugging and analyzing tools to debug, visualize, replay and tune the program.

Our debugging toolkit is constructed like a compiler, the minimal tracer being the frontend (considered the minimal trace being the generated intermediate language) and for example the visualizer and the replayer being backends (fig. 1). Other backends can easily be added. The intermediate language generated by the minimal tracer represents the program run like a wire frame where the nodes are basic parallel events and the edges indicate the partial order of the events.

Since in general only the programmer knows additional interesting events in a program, the minimal trace can be extended by user defined events using a user-oriented tracer.

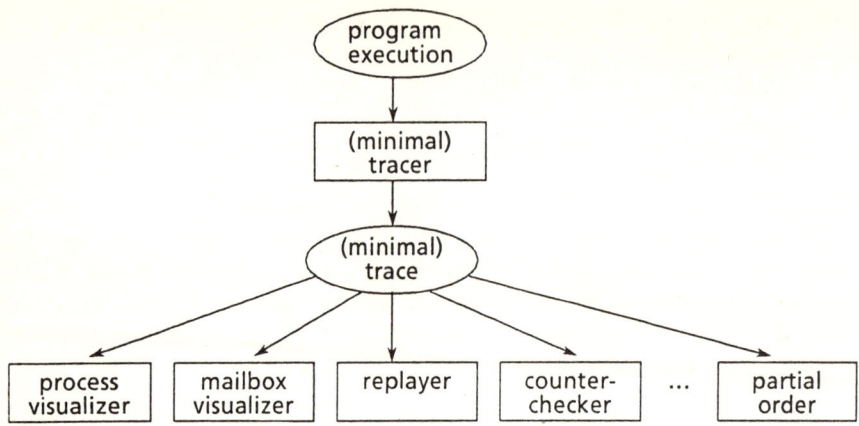

fig. 1: Minimal trace as intermediate language for trace based analysis and debugging

3.1 Benefits from Trace based Debugging

Before describing our system in detail we want to motivate why complementary (trace-based) analysis and debugging tools are essential in parallel debugging.

In parallel debugging at least a visualizer of the program behaviour is vital for the exact location and analysis of errors. It gives the programmer assistance in getting an overview of the current program state. In addition it allows him/her to make efficient use of the user-oriented tracer (see below) and the break-mode debugger (the latter being a straightforward extension of a classical Lisp break-mode debugger).

After the occurrence of an error it is very useful to be able to replay a program exactly in order to see how the error came into being. Replay techniques are an ideal approach to reproducing program executions ([LeBl87], [Mill88]). We adapt this technique so that the execution of EDS Lisp programs communicating by message passing or via critical sections can be replayed.

The trace allows inspecting process specific events. In combination with its basic (system) characteristics displayed by the visualizer, granularity analysis may be performed by the user. Making use of the parallel EDS Lisp constructs s/he may then tune the program on source code level.

3.2 The Trace Mechanism

The tracer consists of two components: a user-oriented tracer and a system-oriented tracer.

User-oriented Tracing

The user-oriented tracer provides the user with the opportunity of tracing and interactively redefining functions for debugging purposes without their recompilation (as in sequential case e.g. in the advice-facility of [Inter85]). The thus defined trace information is displayed during program execution and discarded afterwards.

Parallel processes are traced independently, the output is directed to separate windows on the user's workstation. To avoid a confusing display when many processes produce trace output, the user can control the window action via a graphical representation of the tree of the spawned processes. Fig. 2 shows an

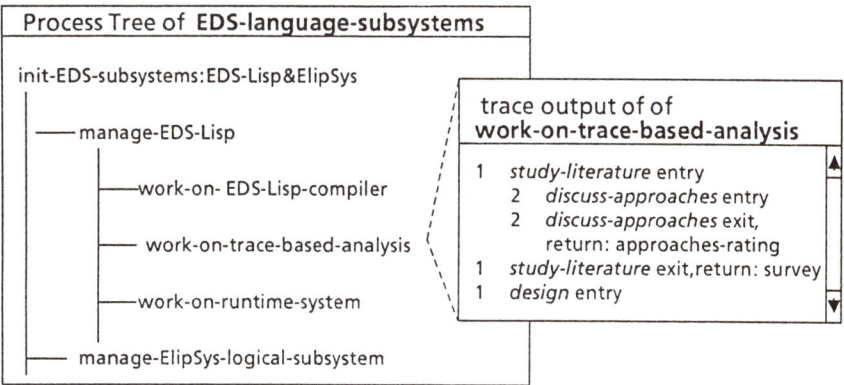

fig. 2: A sample process-tree and output of user-oriented tracer.

example: The EDS Lisp program's process tree is printed in linearized form, the nodes representing the processes. If trace-output is available for a process, this is indicated at the corresponding node. The user can decide which processes are of interest and can open the respective window. Trace output of other processes can be discarded.

System-oriented Tracing

The system-oriented tracer records for every program execution a minimal trace, consisting of basic parallel events. These comprise process spawning, waiting for process termination, sending and receiving of messages, entering and exiting a critical section. Together with the event type some basic event specific data is stored. Since we are talking about coarse grain parallel programs, the overhead for the permanent recording of the basic events can be kept low.

Since in general only the programmer knows additional interesting events in a program, the minimal trace can be extended by user defined events using the user-oriented tracer. These events can even be defined during runtime. This feature is specifically useful for a language like Lisp which is highly dynamic and allows code changes during runtime.

The minimal trace is the basis for example for visualization and reproduction of runtime behaviour. In the following chapters we describe three of the trace based tools (the "backends") we want to implement.

4 Visualization of the Runtime Behaviour

4.1 Process Observation and Control

For the exact location and analysis of errors the programmer needs assistance in getting an overview of the general program state (e.g. which processes are active, what is their status). In addition the user would like to control the amount of trace information to be displayed (there will be times when the user simply wants to discard trace output). Also it is helpful if broken processes can be continued individually after being inspected. Thus a mechanism for the observation and control of processes is necessary. It is based on a graphical representation of the program's process tree as logged in the minimal trace.

A process tree for the execution of an EDS Lisp program shows the spawning structure of the EDS Lisp processes generated during the execution. This is exemplified in fig. 2 and fig. 3. To navigate these displays, horizontal and vertical scrollbars are provided allowing depth first and breadth first search. For the hiding/unhiding of processes and their descendents appropriate operators are supported.

The behaviour of trace and debugger windows is controlled via the tree (see fig.3).

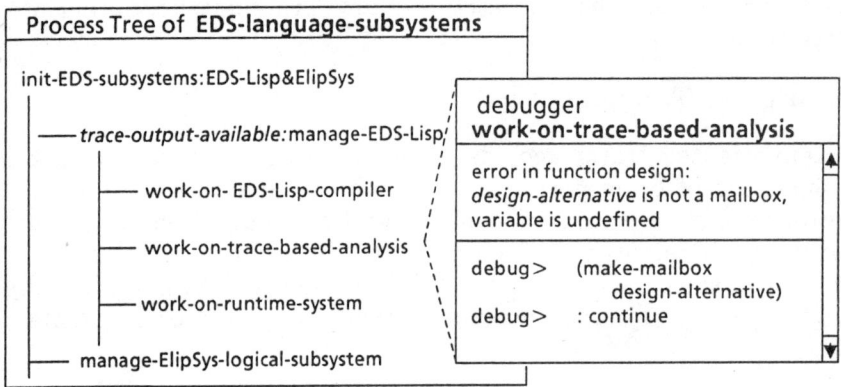

fig. 3: A sample process-tree and debugger invokation

The process tree is attributed with process specific runtime characteristics as average idle time, average number of remote accesses etc. This information supports the user in the granularity analysis (see ch. 6) and in the optimization of the EDS Lisp code.

To produce such views, the minimal trace is evaluated at the user's workstation. Displays are generated upon request. Even the minimal trace itself can be displayed for analysis. Since the graphical representations are built offline, the delay of the program execution caused by the visualizer is minimal.

4.2 Mailbox Communication

To assist the user in the detection of inappropriate communication structures in the EDS Lisp program we provide a view on the use of EDS Lisp mailboxes. Similar to [BuMil89] we want to display all send and receives to and from any user selected mailbox. By clicking on a specific access counter value in the display the corresponding message respective waiting queue is displayed (see fig. 4).

Comparing the waiting queues of different mailboxes when all processes are broken or killed makes deadlock detection feasible. Upon request the representations of the processes involved in the traffic at a specific mailbox will be highlighted in the corresponding process tree. After detecting a disadvantageous communication structure in the mailbox display, the process specific traces of the process tree will help to improve it.

Displays similar to the representation of mailboxes may be used for visualising the access to critical sections.

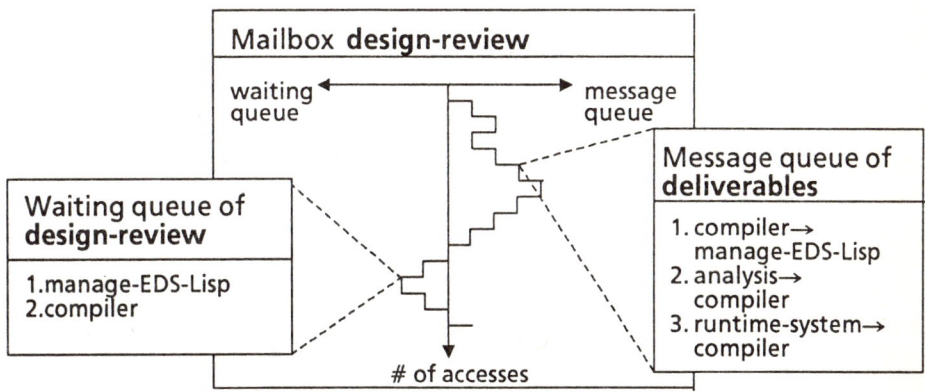

fig. 4: A sample communication at a mailbox

5 Replay

Typical EDS Lisp programs will consist of multiple asynchronous processes that communicate by message passing or synchronized access to shared variables in critical sections.

The sequence of messages arriving at a mailbox can vary in different program runs because of races between processes. An error in a program may occur only for a specific message sequence. A similar statement holds for accesses to critical sections.

So in general cyclic (iterative) debugging is not possible as in sequential programs. If an erroneous parallel program is started again with the same input and some breakpoints the error may not show up any more.

The instant replay technique [LeBl87] is an ideal approach to reproduce the program execution in such a case.

After an error the parallel program is started again in a supervised mode. The supervisor forces the execution to reproduce the former trace. To achieve this goal, the mailbox messages and critical section calls are numbered separately for each mailbox and critical section. If in the replay run a message arrives in a differing sequence, its sending process (which was too fast this run) is stopped until the message with the correct sequence number arrives.

It has to be stated that replay only works if each process alone is deterministic.

6 Performance Tuning on Source Code Level

The visualizer assists in the granularity analysis of parallel Lisp programs and supports the detection of inappropriate communication structures in an EDS Lisp program.

For every process the user-oriented tracer allows inspecting process specific events. By making use of the language independent performance monitor [HeNa90] basic (system) characteristics are available for every process. Upon request for example the process specific active and idle time and number of remote accesses may be displayed.

Based on this information granularity analysis may be performed by the user:
An extremely short active time will indicate that the process should be evaluated inline (locally) rather than in parallel.

Long idle times in combination with a large amount of remote accesses may be a hint to look for inappropriate variable bindings.

Long idle times in combination with few mailbox accesses are typical for inappropriate communication structures. By making use of the source code oriented mailbox displays (see 4.2) the user may restructure the mailbox communication adequately.

Thus this display may help the programmer to tune the performance on the EDS Lisp level.

7 Additional Trace Based Tools

Counterchecks:

The sequence of arrival of messages in a mailbox which collects the results of a distributed computation is usually unimportant. But for some applications the sequence may have to be fixed.
A counterchecker is helpful in such a situation. It takes as input two or more minimal traces kept during several runs of the same program. The counterchecker then compares the traces and finds out places of nondeterminacy. Countercheck sessions can only be of assistance in finding nondeterminacy.
It is self-evident that it does not provide a technique to prove the absence of nondeterminacy.

Partial Order:

The events in a parallel program usually cannot be ordered totally. A traced based tool could compute this partial order which can be a valuable information in debugging for checking the synchronisation structure.

8 Related Work

Traditional debugging toolkits exist for a variety of parallel Lisp dialects ([TopL90], [Allen87], [Miller87]). More advanced toolkits are provided by MUL-T [KrHaMo89] and Allegro CliP [CliP90]. All these debuggers concentrate on process oriented debugging. Recently for Multilisp a replay [HaKr91] and a visualization [HaKrSo91] facility have been implemented.
In addition to the already cited literature several approaches to replay are known for imperative languages (e.g. [Mazzeo90], [Wittie88], [Leu90]).
Most visualizers (as [Stone88], [Bag89], [HaKrSo91]) represent processes as horizontal bands with arrows between the processes indicating interactions. Such systems are limited in the size of an application they can deal with.

9 Current Status

At the moment the design phase is completed. We started implementing our approach this spring. A first protoype of the debugging environment will be available by the end of this year. With respect to symbolic debugging we will provide a functional superset of standard Lisp debuggers (e.g. [Inter85]). The stepper supports the concurrent single-stepping of processes with the user controlling their relative progress separately for each process. There is a separate break-mode debugger for each broken process. All debuggers can be remotely controlled from any other via the nonlocal command facility (communicating sequential debuggers), see [IlmThü90].

10 Conclusion

With its symbolic debugging tools, its visualizers and the replay the debugging environment contains flexible debugging tools that allow the programmer to focus on details as well as to get a general overview of a program execution. Its components are constructed like a compiler, the minimal trace being the frontend and the visualizer and the replay tool being backends. Other backends can easily be added. Our approach is not limited to parallel Lisp dialects on shared or distributed memory machines. It may be easily adapted to similar languages.

References

[Allen87] D. Allen, S. Steinberg, L. Stabile
Recent Developments in Butterfly Lisp, AAAI 87, Seattle, July 1987, pp. 2-6

[Bag89] Laura Bagnell
ParVis: A Program Visualization Tool for Multilisp, S.M. thesis, MIT E.E.C.S. Dept., Cambridge, Ma., Feb. 1989

[BuMil89] Helmar Burkhart, Roland Millen
Performance-Measurement Tools in a Multiprocessor Environment, IEEE Transactions on Computers, Vol.38, No. 5, May 1989

[CLiP90] Franz Inc.:Allegro Common Lisp in Parallel (Allgro CliP) - Product Information, July. 90

[EDS89] Carsten Hammer et al.
Volume 5 (Part 2) Language Subsystems The Lisp Subsystem, ESPRITII EP2025, Document:EDS.DD.5S.0001, Dez. 1989

[HaHe90] Carsten Hammer, Thomas Henties
Parallel Lisp for a Distributed Memory Machine, Proc. of the EUROPAL workshop on "High Performance and Parallel Computing in Lisp", Nov. 1990, Twickenham, UK

[HaKr91] Robert H. Halstead Jr., David A. Kranz
A Replay Mechanism for Mostly Functional Parallel Programs, Int. Symposium on Shared Memory Multiprocessing, Tokyo, Japan, April 1991; to be published by M.I.T. Press

[HaKrSo91]   Robert H. Halstead Jr., David A. Kranz, Patrick G. Sobalvarro
             MULTVISION: A Tool for Visualizing Parallel Program
             Executions,
             Proc. of the ACM/ONR Workshop on Parallel and Distributed
             Debugging, May 1991, Santa Cruz, California, pp. 237-239

[HeNa90]   Martin Herdieckerhoff, Klaus Nagel
             Performance Monitor and Implementation Strategy, ESPRIT-II
             EP 2025, Document: EDS:WP:8S:0013, Nov. 90

[IlmThü90]   Hermann Ilmberger, Sabine Thürmel
             Delphi: A Toolkit for Debugging Parallel Lisp Programs, Proc. of
             the EUROPAL workshop on "High Performance and Parallel
             Computing in Lisp", Nov. 1990, Twickenham, UK

[Inter85]   Xerox Cooporation
             Interlisp-D Reference Manual I-III, Okt.1985

[KrHaMo89]   David A. Kranz, Robert H. Halstead Jr., Eric Mohr
             Mul-T: A High-Performance Parallel Lisp, SIGPLAN 1989
             Symposium on Programming Language Design and
             Implementation, Portland, Oregon, June 1989

[LeBl87]   Thomas J. LeBlanc, John M. Mellor-Crummey
             Debugging Parallel Programs with Instant Replay, IEEE
             Transactions on Computers, Vol.C-36(4), April 1987, pp. 471-482

[Leu90]   Eric Leu, André Schiper, Abdelwahab Zramdini
             Execution Replay on Distributed Memory Architectures, Proc. of
             the Second IEEE Symposium on Parallel and Distributed
             Processing, Dallas, Texas, USA, Dec. 1990

[Miller87]   J. Miller
             MultiScheme: A Parallel Processing System Based on MIT
             Scheme, Ph.D. Thesis, M.I.T. E.E.C.S. Dept., Cambridge, Mass.,
             August 1987

[Mill88]   Barton P. Miller, Jong-Deok Choi
             A Mechanism for Efficient Debugging of Parallel Programs,
             Proceedings of the SIGPLAN '88 Conference on Programming
             Language Design and Implementation, Atlanta, Georgia, USA,
             June 22-24, 1988, pp. 135-144

[Mazzeo90]   A. Mazzeo, C. Savy, Giorgio Ventre
             A High Level Monitor for Parallel Systems, Proc. of the
             International Conf. on Parallel Computing, Capri, Italy, June
             1990

[Stee84]   Guy Steele
              Common LISP: The Language, Digital Press, 1984

[Stone88]   Janice Stone
              A Graphical Representation of Concurrent Processes,
              Proceedings of the ACM SIGPLAN and SIGOPS Workshop on
              Parallel and Distributed Debugging, Madison, WI, USA, May 5-
              6, 1988, pp. 226-235

[ToLe90]   Top Level, Inc.:Top Level Common Lisp - Product Information,
              Jan. 90

[Wittie88]   Larry D. Wittie
              Debugging Distributed C Programs by Real Time Replay, Proc.
              of the ACM SIGPLAN and SIGOPS Workshop on Parallel and
              Distributed Debugging, Madison, Wisconsin, USA, May 1988

A Distributed Implementation of Flat Concurrent Prolog on Multi-Transputer Environments

U. Glässer   G. Hannesen   M. Kärcher   G. Lehrenfeld
Department of Mathematics & Computer Science
University of Paderborn, D-4790 Paderborn, FRG

Abstract

FCP is a general purpose concurrent logic programming language. We describe a distributed implementation of FCP on a multi-transputer environment based on the design of a parallel FCP machine.

Substantial design issues including the applied distributed reduction algorithm as well as the integration of the different communication models – the one for the application language and the one for the target architecture – are considered in detail. From our prototype implementation running on a Parsytec Supercluster multi-transputer system, we present some performance results.

1 Introduction

Flat Concurrent Prolog (FCP) is a general purpose logic programming language designed for concurrent programming and parallel execution. FCP was developed at the Weizmann Institute of Science in 1985 [6]. A uniprocessor version of an FCP compiler has been used for implementing the Logix programming system [9]. The computational model of FCP is based on the process interpretation of logic programs. Its basic control mechanisms are data-flow synchronization and guarded-command indeterminacy. From an application point of view, FCP is representative for a whole class of concurrent logic programming languages all based on stream-parallel execution [8, 10, 13].

Our objective is to investigate the possibilities of embedding a concurrent logic application language into a multi-transputer hardware environment. We chose FCP as an implementation candidate as it provides an example with considerable communication demands. Essentially, we are concerned in the question on how features inherent to the language can be matched with those inherent to transputer architectures in order to utilize a maximum of parallelism.

An issue particularly being addressed is the concept for integrating two different communication models. Asynchronous communication via shared logical variables, as applied in FCP, has to be embedded on a synchronous communications architecture. The language's basic primitives for interprocess communication and synchronization thus has to be transformed into corresponding primitives for the transputer. The later ones are defined by the message passing model of CSP [4].

Parallel execution of FCP programs on transputer networks basically requires a *distributed reduction algorithm* to be combined with a *dynamic load balancing policy*. The algorithm we present rests upon a distributed representation scheme for shared logical variables, as it is embodied in the design of our parallel FCP machine architecture.

The whole machine is organized as a network of asynchronously communicating *reduction units*. An additional *host unit* takes the role of a central supervisor for performing I/O operations, deadlock detection, termination detection, etc. A reduction unit represents some extension of a sequentially operating FCP machine in such a way as it has additional capabilities for performing distributed computations in co-operation with other FCP machines.

A reduction unit's sequential machine component executes compiled FCP code. The applied machine model follows the concept of Warren's *Abstract Prolog Machine* [14]. Any interaction between reduction units, as required in order to communicate data and synchronize process reductions, is controlled by message passing protocols.

The overall machine design is oriented towards scalability, i.e. the total number of reduction units n that build up the network remains a free parameter. A minimal network configuration thereby consists of the host unit and a single reduction unit ($n = 1$). The maximum value for n, however, is a restriction placed by the underlying hardware system. Moreover, we do not assume any particular network topology such as a hypercube, a torus, etc. In fact, the machine runs on arbitrary network topologies provided that the network is connected.

A most important issue in the design of the sequential FCP machine component was to maintain uniprocessor performance as far as possible. In contrast to a purely sequential FCP machine, a reduction unit's FCP machine component needs to handle only a single additional data object in order to represent remote variables; i.e. variables residing on remote reduction units.

A prototype of the parallel machine has been implemented on a *Parsytec Supercluster* multi-transputer system using the parallel programming language Par.C [7]. The system is composed of T800 transputers with 4 MByte local RAM on each transputer. Several application examples have been tested with different network topologies and network sizes up to 256 transputer nodes.

Closely related to our work is a distributed implementation of FCP on an iPSC Hypercube which has been developed at the Weizmann Institute [11, 12]. However, this approach is different to ours in several ways. Beside using a different distributed representation scheme for globally shared logical variables, the reduction algorithm is more complex due to a variable locking mechanism it applies. Moreover, as the target architecture offers asynchronous communication, there is no need to cope with the integration of different communication models. Although using a highly optimizing compiler, the performance results presented in [12] are comparable to ours. Unfortunately, these results are only given for limited network sizes up to 16 processing nodes.

Another concurrent logic programming language that has also been implemented on transputer networks is Strand [2]. Compared to FCP, this language has several substantial restrictions leading to a completely different programming approach. As it lacks for the ability to perform automatic load balancing, the programmer has to specify all activities concerning dynamic load balancing explicitly in the program. This includes the partitioning of process networks as well as the mapping of processes to processors. As a consequence, programs are always written with a certain hardware configuration (network topology) in mind. In the language FCP dynamic load balancing is transparent for the programmer; in particular, it does not dependent on the applied network topology.

The remaining part of this paper is organized in 6 sections. Following the introduction, section 2 briefly introduces the computational model of FCP. Section 3 explains the distributed representation scheme for shared logical variables and the fundamentals of the distributed reduction algorithm. Livelock and deadlock prevention is discussed in section 4, while section 5 presents the parallel FCP machine architecture. Section 6 shows the performance results of two simple test programs. Some general conclusions are given in section 7.

2 Flat Concurrent Prolog

Formally, an FCP program $\mathcal{P}$ is represented by a finite set of universally quantified Horn clauses of the form:

$$\underbrace{H}_{Head} \leftarrow \underbrace{G_1, G_2, ..., G_m}_{Guard} \mid \underbrace{B_1, B_2, ..., B_n}_{Body}. \quad (m, n \geq 0)$$

With respect to a process oriented program interpretation, FCP clauses specify *process behaviour*. A process thereby corresponds to a unit of computation which is represented by an individual goal atom of the form $p(A_1, A_2, ..., A_k)$. The goal atom's predicate symbol p/k, where k denotes the arity of p, identifies the process *program state*; the list of terms in the argument of p/k is interpreted as a collection of process registers reflecting the current process *data state*. The computation goal as a whole forms a dynamic network of asynchronous processes communicating via shared logical variables.

The guard part consists of a conjunction of primitive test predicates $G_1, G_2, ..., G_m$ controlling clause selection. Guard test predicates state conditions referring to the process arguments. The reduction of a process A using a clause C from Program $\mathcal{P}$, $C = A' \leftarrow G_1, ..., G_m \mid B_1, ..., B_n$, is *enabled* if the goal atom of A unifies with the clause's head A' and the guard test predicates are fulfilled, all at once.

The body part consists of a collection of atoms $B_1, B_2, ..., B_n$ defining a set of concurrent subprocesses. As a result of a successful reduction step, these subprocesses spawn a local subnetwork replacing the reduced process within the global process network. Due to unification of respective variables in the environment of the process A and the newly created subprocesses data-flow is maintained.

In case several clauses become applicable, at a time, clause selection proceeds under control of the commit operator "|". Upon successful head unification and guard evaluation, a clause is definitively chosen for reduction after processing its commit operator. At the same moment, all alternative choices concurrently being regarded are discarded. The resulting behaviour is called *guarded-command indeterminacy*, or *don't-care non-determinism* which is in contrast to *don't-know non-determinism* of conventional Prolog. [8, 13]

Asynchronous interprocess communication via shared logical variables is controlled using the *read-only operator* '?' as a data-flow synchronization primitive. A process reduction that would affect the read-only counterpart 'X?' of a write-enabled variable 'X' thereby is delayed until 'X?' becomes instantiated as the result of instantiating 'X'. Such a reduction respectively the process is called *suspended*.

A computation $\mathcal{C}$ of a logic program $\mathcal{P}$ on a given input data set proceeds as a sequence of process reduction operations. At any time t, the resolvent $\mathcal{R}(\mathcal{C}^t)$ represents the current state of computation. Starting from the initial state $\mathcal{R}(\mathcal{C}^0)$, on performing a finite number s of process reduction steps, a computation may reach one of two possible terminal states; each of which corresponds to a situation where no reducible process is left in the resolvent $\mathcal{R}(\mathcal{C}^s)$.

In case $\mathcal{R}(\mathcal{C}^s)$ is empty, the computation was *successful*. Otherwise, if $\mathcal{R}(\mathcal{C}^s)$ is nonempty, but all remaining processes are suspended, the computation is *deadlocked*. A deadlock indicates that a result does not exist.

For a detailed description of FCP, we refer to [9]. An excellent general introduction to concurrent logic programming languages – including FCP – is presented in [8].

3 The Distributed Reduction Algorithm

When performing a distributed computation, at any time t, the global resolvent $\mathcal{R}(\mathcal{C}^t)$ is partitioned into n local subresolvents $\mathcal{R}_0(\mathcal{C}^t), \mathcal{R}_1(\mathcal{C}^t), ..., \mathcal{R}_{n-1}(\mathcal{C}^t)$ residing on reduction units $RU_0, RU_1, ..., RU_{n-1}$. These reduction units concurrently operate on a common set of logical variables; i.e. multiple occurrences of the same variable may be distributed over several reduction units.

The distributed reduction algorithm is based on a *distributed representation scheme* for globally shared variables. In combination with a set of rules controlling access to writable variables, evaluation of read-only variables, and the propagation of variable values within a distributed environment, the applied representation scheme must guarantee the following behaviour:

- Multiple occurrences of the same variable also when residing on different reduction units must not cause any inconsistent variable bindings.

- When a variable becomes instantiated to a value all its related read-only variables, including those on remote reduction units, also have to be instantiated accordingly. Processes being suspended on these variables need to be woken up.

In addition, the execution of the reduction algorithm must ensure that process reductions are carried out as *atomic actions*. That is, if a process reduction requires instantiation of more than one logical variable at a time, it either must instantiate the variables all at once or it must instantiate none of it.

In the approach being described, the representation scheme for a shared logical variable 'X' corresponds to a *directed acyclic graph* $G_X = (V, E, attr)$. To each node of G_X an attribute is attached using the function $attr : V \longrightarrow \{local, remote, read\text{-}only\}$.

Definition. Let $G_X = (V, E, attr)$ specify the *distributed representation scheme* of a shared logical variable $'X'$. For some subset of nodes $\{v_1, v_2, ..., v_k\} \subseteq V$ let $v_1 \stackrel{x}{\leadsto} v_k$, $x \in \{remote, read\text{-}only\}$, denote a path $v_1 \to v_2 \to ... \to v_k$ in G_X, such that $\forall\, 1 \leq i \leq k-1 : (v_i, v_{i+1}) \in E$ and $attr(v_i) = attr(v_k) = x$.

A legal representation scheme must satisfy the following three conditions, simultaneously:

1. $(\exists! \hat{u})\, \hat{u} \in V : attr(\hat{u}) = local \quad (\Rightarrow (\forall v)\, v \in V - \{\hat{u}\} : attr(v) \neq local\,)$.

2. $(\forall v)\, v \in V - \{\hat{u}\} : attr(v) = remote \Rightarrow (\exists v')\, v' \in V : v \stackrel{remote}{\leadsto} v' \to \hat{u}$ is a path in G_X.

3. $(\forall v)\, v \in V - \{\hat{u}\} : attr(v) = read\text{-}only \Rightarrow (\exists v')\, v' \in V : \hat{u} \to v' \stackrel{read-only}{\leadsto} v$ is a path in G_X.

The node with the attribute *local* represents the unique writable variable. Additional writable occurrences, which are identified by *remote* nodes, actually are remote references pointing to the variable location. With respect to the defined variable representation scheme, the following notion applies to reduction units. For a variable X a reduction unit that holds a writable variable occurrence corresponding to the local node is called the *variable owner*, whereas reduction units that hold writable occurrences corresponding to remote nodes are denoted as *variable members*.

Using the owner/member relationship conflicts caused from simultaneous writing on multiple occurrences of the same logical variable in a distributed environment can be avoided if the variable owner and the variable members operate in different access modes, respectively. Direct access to a variable, in order to bind it with another variable or to instantiate it to a non-variable term, solely is permitted to the variable owner. Any attempt to write on a variable when reducing a process results in an immediate process suspension if the reduction unit which tries to reduce that process is a variable member.

Variable Migration

A variable member must not change its member relationship into an owner relationship on its own, but it may do so under control of the current variable owner. The operation is initiated by sending a request upon ownership to the variable owner. As a consequence of the variable representation scheme, there always exists a path along remote references from each variable member RU_j to the current variable owner RU_i. Variable requests thus can be forwarded accordingly. A successful operation transferring variable membership into variable ownership is denoted as *variable migration*.

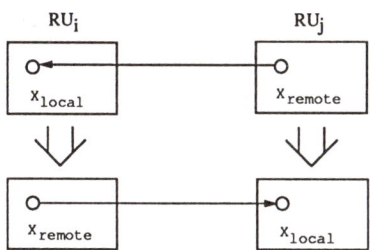

Figure 1: Exchange of owner/member relationship

Receiving a variable request for variable X from reduction unit RU_j, the reaction of reduction unit RU_i, being the current variable owner, depends on the actual state of X. This state is referred by $value_i(X)$. If X is yet an unbound variable then $value_i(X)$ represents a pointer to possible read-only occurrences belonging to X. That means, $value_i(X)$ either identifies the location of some read-only occurrence $X?$ or $value_i(X) = NIL$ in case read-only occurrences do not exist.

An unbound variable X causes RU_i to return $value_i(X)$ to RU_j. Now, RU_j replaces its remote reference $value_j(X)$ with the read-only variable pointer $value_i(X)$. On the other hand, RU_i substitutes $value_i(X)$ by a remote reference pointing on the current location of X on RU_j. At the same time, RU_i and RU_j respectively change the attributes of X from *local* to *remote* and vice versa. As a consequence, RU_j effectively becomes the new owner of variable X (Figure 1).

Otherwise, if X has already been bound to a non-variable term, RU_i returns a copy of this term in order to replace the remote reference on RU_j. Since the term itself may contain variables, in the structure being copied each of this variables has to be replaced by a corresponding remote reference.

Instantiation of remote variable occurrences follows the approach of data distribution by demand-driven structure copying. Instead of copying complex terms as a whole, the natural hierarchical embedding of nested data structures allows to copy just k layers. Substructures thereby are replaced by remote references pointing to their locations and are copied on request, only.

The applied variable representation scheme in combination with the different access modes for the variable owner and the variable members, respectively, ensures mutual exclusive variable write access.

Process Synchronization

With regard to the general structure of a guarded Horn clause and the typical data manipulation operations in processing it, a *process reduction cycle* consists of a number of clause try operations. Each clause try operation logically divides into two subsequent phases. The first phase handles *head unification* as well as *guard evaluation* prior to commitment; the second phase spawns new subprocesses as defined in the clause's body.

When performing a process reduction cycle, a reduction unit must not be interrupted before one of the following stable states is reached. It either has completed the second phase of a successful clause try operation or it has restored its old data state by releasing any computed variable bindings in case the process becomes suspended. This feature must be ensured by the implementation of the process reduction mechanism.

During the first phase of a reduction cycle variables are affected only within a reduction unit's local environment. If a clause try fails, these effects can easily be undone using a trail stack. The trail stack identifies all writable and read-only variables that have been modified during a reduction attempt. For each of this variables there is a trail stack entry containing the type, the pointer value, and the location of the variable.

In fact, a reduction unit is able to affect a variable, only if it is the current variable owner; otherwise, the reduction would be aborted and the process suspended. A successful clause try reaching the commit operator thus requires the reduction unit to be owner of all variables being involved in the reduction. At the same time, no other reduction unit can become owner of any of these variables, since the reduction cannot be interrupted. As a result, a reduction globally modifies all involved variables in case it succeeds, while it does not affect any variable neither globally nor locally when a suspension occurs; hence, it is *atomic*.

When a writable variable occurrence X becomes instantiated, $value(X)$ is propagated to all related read-only occurrences $X?$. Due to the variable representation scheme, there always exists a path along references from the location of X on the owner reduction unit RU_i to each occurrence $X?$ residing on reduction units $RU_{j_1}, RU_{j_2}, ..., RU_{j_k}$ (not necessarily being member units).

With each $X?$ we associate a list of so-called *process suspension notes*. A *suspension note list (snl)* is attached to a read-only variable occurrence $X?$ by storing a pointer on $snl(X?)$ in $value(X?)$. Each entry in $snl(X?)$ respectively identifies a process which has been suspended on $X?$. Evaluation of the process suspension notes then allows to wake up these processes.

Just the same way as for read-only occurrences, suspension notes are used in combination with remote references. Since a variable request should be started only for the first process attempting to write a remote reference, its value field thereafter becomes available to store a suspension note list address. Additional suspension notes can be included if necessary. When a remote reference is changed into a local variable, evaluation of the attached suspension note list activates processes that have been suspended on it.

Furthermore, suspension note lists also provide a mean to handle *remote instantiations*, i.e. to wake up processes outside a local environment. Remote instantiations become necessary when instantiating a variable which owns read-only occurrences outside the local environment. For that reason, so called *remote suspension notes* identify related read-only occurrences in the environment of remote reduction units. Remote suspension notes are simply included into suspension note lists together with local suspension notes.

The evaluation of a remote suspension note S causes a message transfer. If S occurs in the suspension note list of a read-only variable $X?$ residing on RU_i while referring to another occurrence of $X?$ on some RU_j, a message containing $value(X)$ is sent from RU_i to RU_j. On receiving this message, RU_j instantiates $X?$ and in turn starts evaluation of the attached suspension note list.

The example shown in Figure 2 illustrates the configuration for a single shared variable X with multiple writable and read-only occurrences residing on reduction units RU_1, RU_2, and RU_3.

4   Livelock and Deadlock Prevention

Livelock and deadlock prevention is a most important issue in distributed implementations of concurrent logic languages. Deadlocks as well as livelocks both may occur only in programs allowing several processes to write upon the same variables.

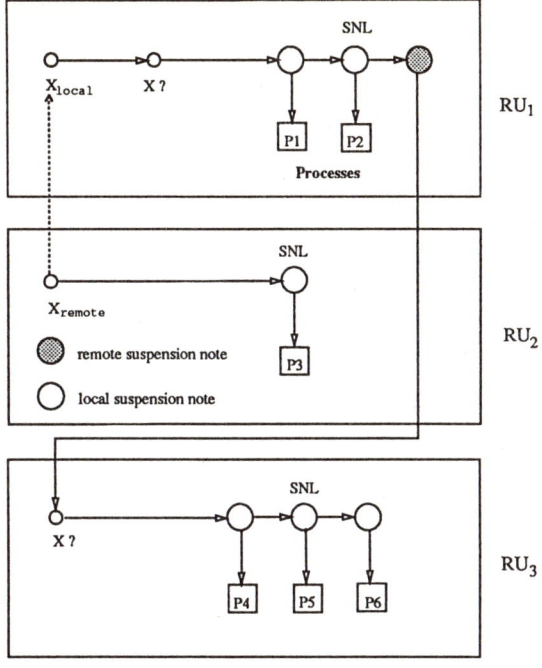

Figure 2: Representation of shared variables in a distributed environment

A livelock corresponds to a situation where two or more reduction units perform some kind of circular 'variable stealing.' As none of the reduction units achieves simultaneous ownership of all the variables it requires in a certain reduction, they are iterating the same sequence of variable migration operations to infinity. In order to resolve livelocks, a mechanism for locking variables against migration is needed.

Unfortunately, an implementation of variable migration using variable locking usually results in rather complex protocols in order to avoid deadlocks. On the other hand, livelock detection is relatively simple. A livelock can be detected by monitoring variable requests. As a consequence of a livelock, the same sequence of requests is produced, infinitely often. In a computation which is free of livelocks there appear only a small number of variable requests on the same remote reference location. Usually, there is just a single request.

As livelocks do not occur very frequently and it is possible to detect them, we propose to attack the problem by means of a two-phase algorithm. The first phase operates without variable locking but it ensures a livelock to be detected.

If a livelock occurs, the algorithm switches to the second phase. Now it operates in a mode allowing reduction units to lock variables. Attaching different priorities to each reduction unit guarantees that at least one reduction unit will be enabled to perform reductions. Thereby, a reduction unit always obtains ownership of variables being locked if the priority of the requesting unit is higher than that of the current variable owner. Upon successfully instantiating the variables that have been involved in the livelock, the reduction units again operate in the non-locking mode.

The advantage of the two-phase algorithm rests upon the fact, that the overhead paid for livelock detection is relatively small compared to a deadlock prevention algorithm. The maximum number of variable requests on the same remote reference that would not switch the algorithm from the first to the second phase, should be chosen carefully.

5 Parallel FCP Machine Architecture

Abstract System Architecture. With exception of a dedicated host unit, a single reduction unit essentially consists of three basic subunits, namely: *a reducer, a distributor,* and *a router*. The host unit, in addition, is supplied with special components for controlling I/O operations as well as arbiter functions for termination detection, deadlock detection, etc. The distributed termination detection algorithm currently being implemented was adopted from Dijkstra et al. [1].

Reducer, distributor, and router are implemented as concurrently operating sequential processes. The router acts as network interface unit. It is required for sending, receiving, and forwarding messages. Using a routing matrix in combination with unique unit identifiers, messages are routed along shortest paths. The reducer essentially performs the function of a sequentially operating FCP machine, which is extended by additional facilities to handle remote references. However, the reducer has no direct internetwork communication facilities.

Communication with other reduction units is under control of the distributor. Running the desired network protocols for the reducer, the distributor also needs to access the reducer data. Possible conflicts are avoided by explicitly synchronizing both units. In addition to reducer initiated communication activities, the distributor units in conjunction with the host unit perform utilities for termination detection, deadlock detection, and dynamic work load distribution. The reduction unit architecture is shown in Figure 3. A more detailed description of it can be found in [3].

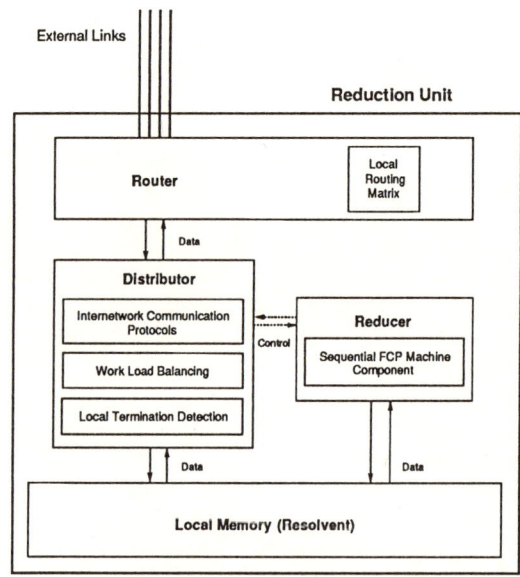

Figure 3: Reduction Unit Architecture

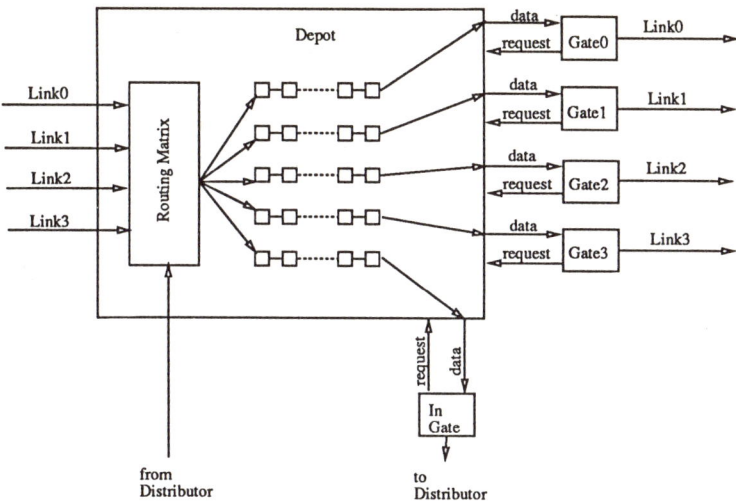

Figure 4: Router Structure

Integration of Communication Models. Implementing FCP on a synchronous communication architecture requires an efficient transformation of asynchronous communication behaviour into synchronous communication behaviour. Within a reduction unit the basic facilities for inter-network communication management are embedded in the routor. The router thus provides the interface where this transformation has to be done. The router function therefore is realized by a set of parallel processes.

Beside two internal ports to the reduction unit's distributor there are eight external ports connecting the router to a maximum of four neighbour reduction units (Figure 4). A single *depot process* receives all messages either incoming on one of the external input ports *Link0,...,Link3* or delivered by the local distributor. By means of a routing matrix in combination with unique unit identifiers, the depot process determines a corresponding output FIFO-queue to enqueue the message.

From the output queues the messages, one by one, are passed to *gate processes Gate0,...,Gate3* controlling the output ports. The gate processes then perform the actual send operation handling one process at a time. Upon completion of a send operation, a gate process explicitly requests the next message by sending a signal to the depot process via the request channel. The depot process performs a dequeue and delivers the resulting message to the gate process via the data channel.

While the gate processes are sending outgoing messages, the depot process may concurrently process new incoming messages. Due to the functional separation into a receiving process (depot) and several sending processes (gates) and the use of buffers, the asynchronous communication behaviour is realized.

An additional aspect in the design of the router is *fairness*. Both, fairness with respect to the order in which incoming messages are processed as well as the way in which gate requests are served should be taken into consideration. In the current version of the router this is achieved as the depot process serves the input ports and output ports, respectively, in a round robin fashion.

6 Implementation

The prototype implementation of our parallel machine comprises about 12,000 lines of Par.C code. It has been tested using several smaller example programs on a Parsytec Supercluster multi-transputer system with up to 256 processors. The resulting speed-up behaviour using a local-search-local-distribution load balancing strategy for the example programs *matrix-multiplication* and *towers of Hanoi* are presented in the diagrams below.

Speed-up here is defined as the runtime being required on a single processor network divided by the runtime being required on an n processor network ($n > 1$). The diagrams show this relationship for different problem sizes in contrast to different network sizes. For each test the network topology for *matrix-multiplication* has been a twisted torus of the appropriate dimension, while *towers of Hanoi* has been tested using DeBruijn networks of the appropriate dimension.

```
Towers of Hanoi:

hanoi(N,From,To,(Before,(From,To),After)) <-
  N>1 |
  sub(N,1,N1),
  free(From,To,Free),
  hanoi(N1,From,Free?,Before),
  hanoi(N1,Free?,To,After).

hanoi(1,From,To,(From,To)).

free(a,b,c).
free(a,c,b).
free(b,a,c).
free(c,a,b).
free(b,c,a).
free(c,b,a).
```

Towers of Hanoi

Matrix Multiplication

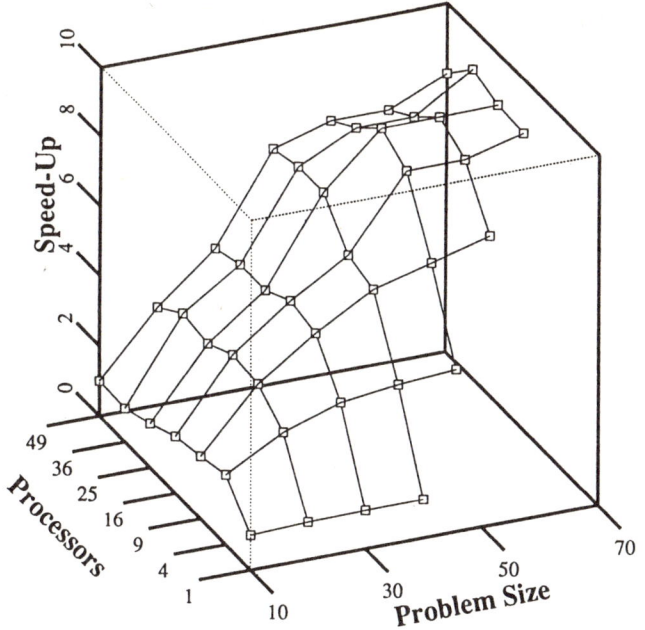

```
Matrix-Multiplication:

mm([Xv|Xm],Ym,[Zv|Zm]) <-
    vm(Xv,Ym,Zv),
    mm(Xm,Ym,Zm).
mm([],_,[]).

vm(Xv,[Yv|Ym],[Z|Zv]) <-
    ip(Xv,Yv,0,Z),
    vm(Xv,Ym,Zv).
vm(_,[],[]).

ip([X|Xs],[Y|Ys],P,S) <-
    P1 := P+X*Y,
    ip(Xs,Ys,P1?,S).
ip([],[],P,P).
```

7 Conclusions

We have presented a concept for a distributed implementation of the concurrent logic programming language FCP on a multi-transputer environment. A most important aspect in the design of our parallel FCP machine is scalability with respect to the network size and network topology. Its functional architecture is oriented towards an efficient integration of the different communication models for the application language and the transputer hardware.

Though the current prototype implementation has not been highly optimized, it already demonstrates the suitability of transputer systems as a target architecture for concurrent logic programming languages. An additional aspect encouraging this approach is the enhancement of transputer communication facilities due to new technologies and further developments [5]. Automatic routing facilities, support of virtual links, and a general increase in communication speed will match the communication demands of our design.

An important issue we have dropped here, is the dynamic load balancing algorithm. Applying different load balancing policies, several algorithms have been implemented but none of it was really satisfying. Main activities for optimizing the prototype implementation currently concentrate on the development of an improved load balancing algorithm.

References

[1] DIJKSTRA, E. W., FEIJEN, W. H. J., AND VAN GASTEREN, A. J. M. 1983. Derivation of a Termination Detection Algorithm for Distributed Computations. In *Information Processing Letters, Vol. 16*, pp. 217-219.

[2] FOSTER, I., AND TAYLOR, S. 1990. Strand, New Concepts in Parallel Programming. Prentice-Hall.

[3] GLÄSSER, U., AND LEHRENFELD, G. 1990. A distributed implementation of Flat Concurrent Prolog on Transputer architectures. In *Proceedings of the UNESCO Conference on Parallel Computing in Engeneering and Engeneering Education*, Paris, pp. 181-185.

[4] HOARE, C. A. R. 1978. Communicating Sequential Processes. In *Communications of the ACM, Vol. 21 (8)*, pp. 666-677.

[5] MAY, D. 1990. Future Directions in Transputer Technology. In *Proceedings of UNESCO Conference on Parallel Computing in Engineering and Engineering Education*, Paris, pp. 193-203.

[6] MIEROWSKY, C., TAYLOR, S., SHAPIRO, E., LEVY, J., AND SAFR A, S. 1985. The design an implementation of Flat Concurrent Prolog. Tech. Rep. CS85-9, Dept. of Computer Science, The Weizmann Institute of Science, Rehovot, Israel.

[7] PARSEC 1989. Par.C System: User's Manual and Library Reference Version 1.22. Parsec Developments, Leiden, The Netherlands.

[8] SHAPIRO, E. 1989. The Family of Concurrent Logic Programming Languages. In *ACM Computing Surveys, Vol. 21 (3)*, pp. 413-510.

[9] SILVERMAN, W., HIRSCH, M., HOURI, A., AND SHAPIRO, E. 1987. The Logix system user manual Version 1.21. In *Concurrent Prolog : Collected Papers, Vol. 2*, E. Shapiro, Ed. MIT Press, Cambridge, Mass., pp. 46-77.

[10] TAKEUCHI, A., AND FURUKAWA, K. 1987. Parallel Logic Programming Languages. In *Proceedings of the 3rd International Conference on Logic Programming*, Lecture Notes in Computer Science, Vol 225, Springer-Verlag, New York, pp. 242-254

[11] TAYLOR, S., SAFRA, S., AND SHAPIRO, E. 1987. A Parallel Implementation of Flat Concurrent Prolog. In *International Journal of Parallel Programming, Vol. 15, No. 3*, pp. 245-275

[12] TAYLOR, S. 1989. Parallel Logic Programming Techniques. Prentice-Hall.

[13] UEDA, K. 1989. Parallelism in Logic Programming. In Proceedings of the IFIP Congress, North-Holland Amsterdam, pp. 957-964.

[14] WARREN, D. H. D. 1983. An Abstract Prolog Instruction Set. Technical Note 309, Artificial Intelligence Center, SRI.

Negation in Conclog

J.-M. Jacquet
Center for Mathematics and Computer Science
P.O. Box 4079, 1009 AB Amsterdam, The Netherlands

Abstract

This paper presents a new constructive form of the negation-as-failure rule dedicated to concurrent executions and, based on it, a parallel execution model of general Horn clauses. Referring to the completion understanding of the programs, this model has been proved sound and as complete as possible when the resolution rule and the negation-as-failure rule are used. Furthermore, it does not suffer from the floundering problem : in contrast, negative literals can be used to produce computed answers as the positive literals can.

This new form of negation is based on an equational framework. It introduces generalizations of substitutions, terms and related concepts of instantiation and unification. A theory of such concepts is also presented in the paper.

Keywords : constructive negation, parallel logic programming, parallel language, theory of substitutions and terms.

1 Introduction

Although it is theoretically not necessary ([Tarnlund, 1977]), negation is one of the very desirable features of any logic programming language. Theoretically, it can take three places : in the head of clauses, in the body of clauses and in queries. Negation in the head of clauses provides the full power of first order logic and, consequently, needs a much more expensive form of resolution than the SLD one. One attractive feature of Horn clauses with SLD-resolution is precisely that it can be implemented very efficiently. Hence, the only places where not predicates are usually allowed to take place are in queries and in body of clauses. As a result, there is no means left to derive negative information so that the following trick is generally added to SLD-resolution. It consists of solving not(p) by first solving p and then inverting the answers, thus stating the provability of not(p) if p is found unprovable and vice-versa. This is known as negation as failure. Its great advantage is the possibility to implement it with essentially no extra-cost to the resolution system. Its main drawback is that it is not real negation. More specifically, variables have to be carefully manipulated, the result generally depending of the clause and the goal selection strategies. For instance, with Prolog depth first search strategy and with regards to the one clause program

p(a).

the reduction of not(p(X)) fails whereas that of not(p(b)) succeeds. In fact, with Prolog depth first search, the goal not(p($\vec{X}$)), with $\vec{X}$ the variables occurring in p, is interpreted as $\neg(\exists \vec{X} p(\vec{X}))$ whereas the expected interpretation is $\exists \vec{X}(\neg p(\vec{X}))$. These two interpretations are, of course, not always the same. To force the equality, it is of current and safe practice to reduce negative literals only when they are ground. They can thus be used only as tests and not to produce answers, as the reduction of positive literals does. Furthermore, one problem - known as the floundering problem - occurs when the reduction has to select one subgoal in a conjunction composed only of non-ground negative literals.

Recently, a new form of the negation-as-failure rule, called constructive negation ([Chan, 1988], [Chan, 1989]), has been proposed to remedy this situation. An alternative form dedicated to concurrent executions is presented in this paper. It is also constructive and, consequently, avoids the floundering problem. It issues from the design of a concurrent logic programming language, named Conclog, but is not dedicated to it. It rests on an equational perception of the computation and has induced the generalization of several basic concepts. All of these generalized forms have been extensively studied in [Jacquet, 1989]. They are used here only as a basis for the paper and are just sketched. Their reason for existence may be motivated as follows. Interpreting the executions in equational terms, it is not difficult to imagine that handling negation leads to negate some equations and, therefore, to solve systems composed of equations and inequations. In general, the set of solutions of these systems cannot be represented by a finite number of substitutions. Our remedy to this situation is to introduce negative information in the substitutions. This produces constructs of the form $(\theta, \text{not } \omega)$ where θ is a substitution and ω is a set of bindings presented in a normal form with respect to θ. Such constructs are called n-substitutions. In a symmetric way, negative information has also been introduced in terms. This results in so-called extended terms, of the form (t,Ω) where Ω is a set of "not ω" constructs, just introduced but normalized here with respect to t. Related concepts of unification and instantiation have then been extended to these new terms and substitutions.

Given these extended concepts, our constructive approach to negation basically consists of the following. Let, for any n-substitution $v=(\{X_1/t_1,...,X_p/t_p\},\text{not}\{Y_1/u_1,...,Y_q/u_q\})$, eq(v) be

$X_1=t_1 \wedge ... \wedge X_p=t_p \wedge Y_1 \neq u_1 \wedge ... \wedge Y_q \neq u_q$.

Assume the reduction of G has $v_1, ..., v_m$ as computed n-substitutions. Then return as computed answer n-substitutions to not(G) the n-substitutions $\mu_1, ..., \mu_n$ such that the negation of $eq(v_1) \vee ... \vee eq(v_m)$ is equivalent to $eq(\mu_1) \vee ... \vee eq(\mu_n)$. Of course, this basic scheme is slightly adapted to cope correctly with the quantification of the variables.

A parallel execution model of general Horn clauses based on the above features is also presented in the paper. Referring to the completion understanding of the programs, it has been proved sound and as complete as possible when the resolution principle and the negation-as-failure rule are employed. As a snapshot, it essentially rests on and-parallelism, or-parallelism and on the constructive negation introduced above. Reconciliation of n-substitutions is introduced as a means of combining n-substitutions issued from conjoined subgoals in order to produce n-substitutions for the whole goal. Negative information and extended unification are furthermore used to constrain the reduction process. Any computation under the model can thus be basically seen as the construction of the and/or/not search tree associated with the query and the program under consideration. However, this tree is not constructed in its pure form but slice by slice. At the end of the construction of each slice, branches that are detected useless are killed and some n-substitutions are published in order to avoid, in a "a priori" way, the production of such useless branches. The creation of the branches is, of course, made concurrent and independent so that n-substitutions might be delivered as answers to queries whereas others are still under computation. This parallel execution model corresponds to the second phase of the design of a concurrent logic programming language, named Conclog, where extra-logical features such as sequentialization, commit operators, guarded constructs are introduced in a third step to ensure efficiency and practicability.

The main originalities of our work are best presented by comparing it with related negations and execution models. Negation by complex solutions ([Khabaza, 1984]) also tackles negation in a parallel context by means of a reconciliation calculus. It does not use n-substitutions but more complex constructs, called complex solutions, of the form $\{P, \sim N_1, ..., \sim N_m\}$ where P and the N_i's are sets of bindings. Although the negated sets $\sim N_i$ can be viewed as negative pieces of information associated with the positive one P, no negative information has been coupled with the terms and the notions of instantiation and unification have not been extended to cope with it. As a result, some derivations that are removed in our model of execution are performed in Khabaza's model. Another major difference is that negation by complex solutions does not take into account sets of variables, intended to represent variables differently quantified, whereas we will do. The consequence is that the Conclog model is sound and is complete in some situations whereas the model of [Khabaza, 1984] is neither sound nor complete.

Negation by constraints ([Wallace, 1987]) uses directly the completed definition of the procedures to reduce the negative literals. This results in handling first order formulae which are far more complex than our extended terms. As another difference, negation by constraints take place in a sequential context and thus does not provide any counterpart for reconciliation and binding publication. Finally, negative information plays also a role in the deduction by means of so-called constraint sets but those are structured in a way that suits well the sequential executions but does not fit the parallel ones.

The SLD-CNF rule ([Chan, 1988], [Chan, 1989]) is another constructive form of the negation as failure rule. It consists of an extension of the SLD-resolution rule whose main feature is to reduce any negative literal, say not(Q),

(i) by reducing Q to an normalized conjunctive formula F involving equalities, inequalities and unreduced subgoals

(ii) and by negating F in a backtracking spirit.

This rule has first been presented in a sequential framework and has then been extended in [Chan, 1989] in an incremental version of constructive negation applied to co-routining.

A first difference with our work is that, although equations and inequations take a great place and although normalized formulas are introduced, there is, in [Chan, 1988] and [Chan, 1989], no counterpart for our theory of n-substitutions and extended terms, unification and instantiation. As a symptom, negative information plays no role during the reductions whereas it does in ours. Also, inequalities are treated in a more uniform way in our model: there is, in our work, no need to look for satisfiability or validity. Finally, no concurrent model is treated in [Chan, 1988] and the model presented in [Chan, 1989] does not tackle and-parallelism and or-parallelism. There is thus no concept of reconciliation and of communication of bindings between subtrees. It is here furthermore worth noting that incremental constructive negation can also be achieved in our Conclog model by means of the construction slice by slice of the and/or/not search tree and that co-routining can also be simulated in the same way by fixing the depth of the slices to 1.

The SLSC-resolution rule ([Przymusinski, 1989]) is a theoretical adaptation of the SLD-CNF resolution rule associating infinite derivation with failed derivation and making reference to the perfect model semantics instead of the completion interpretation of the programs. These two latter points make already two differences with the Conclog model. Other comparison points result from the above comparison with the SLD-CNF-resolution.

Negation by failure substitutions ([Maluszynski and Näslund, 1989]) is an extension of the negation-as-failure principle based on the idea that if γ is a substitution such that the query $\leftarrow G\gamma$ has a finitely failed SLD-tree then, by soundness of the negation as failure rule, $\forall \neg G\gamma$ is a logical consequence of the completion of the program under consideration. Reducing negative literals can thus be achieved by finding all such substitutions γ, called failed substitutions. Only the maximal substitutions need, of course, to be found. This is indeed performed in [Maluszynski and Näslund, 1989]. Concepts of constrained substitutions and constrained terms, adding inequalities of terms to substitutions and terms, respectively, are introduced for this purpose. Our n-substitutions and extended terms share some similarities with them. The major differences is that n-substitutions and extended terms are always presented in a normalized form and that n-substitutions may have the empty substitution as positive part θ. Furthermore, our theory of n-substitutions and extended terms is more elaborated than that of [Maluszynski and Näslund, 1989], where the concept of composition of substitutions is just extended.

Another difference with our work is that negation by failed substitutions only tackles the sequential compositions. It does not provide any counterpart for our concept of reconciliation of n-substitutions, our parallel form of negation or our concept of publication of n-substitutions.

Another way of handling negation consists of deriving from a Horn clause program P, a new set of predicates computing the negation of the predicates of P. This approach has been first proposed in [Sato and Tamaki, 1984] and has been improved in [Barbuti et al., 1987] and [Barbuti et al., 1990]. One attractive feature of those pieces of work is certainly that negation is tackled without extending the terms and the substitutions with negative information while negative literals can compute substitutions as the positive literals do. Another advantadge is that the resulting negation is complete. The drawbacks are that the derived procedures may be quite verbose and that the computed substitutions may suffer from conciseness problems. Furthermore, the treatment of negation requires both a new form of negation introduced by the synthesized predicates and the negation as failure rule, used to compute s-goals of the form $\forall Y\ r(X,Y)$.

The ENF deduction procedure ([Lugiez, 1989]) is a deduction procedure for first order programs which subsumes SLDNF-resolution and which improves the handling of the latter goals. It presents several similarities with our work in that negative information is also combined with the positive one to sum up solutions. In fact, the employed substitutions are quite close to our n-substitutions. However, no theory of such substitutions is proposed and negative information is not employed to constrain the reduction process. Moreover, as parallel executions are not tackled, there is also no counterpart for our reconciliation concept. Another major departure with our work is that first order formulae are handled by the ENF procedure. It is thus computationally more expensive than the Conclog one. Finally, the verbosity and conciseness problems of the above transformational approach to negation have not been solved in [Lugiez, 1989].

The Conclog execution model can be seen as an extension to incorporate negation of parallel execution models of Horn clauses ([Pollard, 1981], [Conery, 1983], [Li and Martin, 1986], [Kalé, 1987]). Besides the introduction of negation, the last three pieces of work take another approach to and-parallelism. Given a conjunction of subgoals that share variables, they do not allow those subgoals to be reduced concurrently but avoid the generation of conflicting bindings by designating a producer process for each shared variable. Unfortunately, the designation of the right producer is undecidable. Moreover, we strongly believe that it is impossible to find a sufficiently general class of programs for which it would be decidable. The practical consequence is that any algorithm computing this determination does not work properly on some goals. In view of this, we prefer to tackle the determination of dataflows at a programming level by means of annotations. Another difference with the Conclog model is that the models of [Conery, 1983] and [Li and Martin, 1986] are not complete whereas the Conclog model is when it is restricted to Horn clauses. Finally, all the three models suffer from the rigidity of the dataflow they determine : the unproductive derivations of the producer processes cannot be removed in view of the consumer ones and back communication cannot be performed. In contrast, this is possible in Conclog.

The Conclog model share the reconciliation approach with that of [Pollard, 1981] but differs in the way it manages the computed and/or search trees. In Conclog, every aspect is treated in a simpler and more uniform framework based on equation manipulation whereas a lot of concepts and principles are introduced in Pollard's approach. Moreover, this approach does not publish bindings, which prevents the Conclog model from developing useless branches.

As a final comparative remark, it is worth noting that, although systems of equations and inequations have already been studied and although extended substitutions have already been proposed (see e.g. [Khabaza, 1984], [Maluszynski and Näslund, 1989], [Turi, 1991]), no work has elaborated, to our extent, a theory generalizing, to a negative constructive framework, that of the basic notions of logic programming, namely terms and substitutions.

The remainder of this paper is organized in 5 Sections. Section 2 sketches our theory of n-substitutions, extended terms, extended instantiation and extended unification and introduces the basic mechanisms of our constructive negation. Section 3 presents the Conclog execution model of general Horn clauses including our constructive negation and sketches its main properties. Section 4 gives our conclusions. Finally, Sections 5 and 6 present our acknowledgments and references.

Lack of space prevents us to give proofs of the claimed results. All of them have however been established in [Jacquet, 1989], to which we refer the reader for more information. He is also assumed to be familiar with logic programming. We shall essentially use the conventional Edinburgh syntax (see e.g. [Clocksin and Mellish, 1981]) and the conventional logic programming terminology (see e.g. [Lloyd, 1987] and [Apt, 1990]). Our only particular notation is to denote the identity substitution by {}. We shall furthermore use the abbreviation s-goal to denote any subgoal (either positive or negative literal) of a conjunction and the qualification ps-goal and ns-goal to denote the positive and the negative s-goals, respectively. Finally, from now on, we assume that the language under consideration has an infinite number of variables, constants and function symbols and define the Herbrand universe with respect to the language rather than the programs under consideration.

2 Towards a theory of n-substitutions and extended terms

2.1 Intuition

In order to provide the reader with an intuitive support, it is worth presenting the underlying ideas having lead to our subsequent theory of n-substitutions and extended terms.

The ideal of concurrent logic programming is to use both or-parallelism and and-parallelism. In this ideal world, the sequential reduction of subgoals of goals is thus replaced by the concurrent reduction of the subgoals, even if they do share variables. It follows that the traditional composition of substitutions returned by the successive reductions of subgoals needs to be replaced by a concurrent composition of substitutions, devoted to combining the (possibly conflicting) substitutions issued from the concurrent reductions of the subgoals. It has been provided, independently, in [Jacquet, 1989] and [Palamidessi, 1990] under the name of reconciliation of substitutions and parallel composition of substitutions, respectively. In both cases, the basic idea is to interpret substitutions equationally and to combine them by solving the system of equations associated with the substitutions. This equational interpretation has been shown, in both references, to be quite intuitive and very simple. Nevertheless, it induces one restriction : unifiers and mgus should be taken as idempotent. Curiously, however, this restriction turns out to simplify the theory rather than to complicate it. It is furthermore worth noting that the restriction to idempotent substitutions is not of importance both from a theoretical and a practical point of view. Indeed, on the one hand, any pair of unifiable terms have an idempotent mgu . On the other hand, most unification algorithms report an idempotent mgu. Finally, the classical objection that the composition of two idempotent substitutions is not necessarily an idempotent substitution cannot be retained in our parallel context : reconciliation of idempotent substitutions delivers an idempotent substitution and the only compositions that are needed may be proved to deliver idempotent substitutions.

The equational interpretation of substitutions has another merit of suggesting a very simple way of dealing with negation. Let, for any substitution $\theta=\{X_1/t_1,...,X_m/t_m\}$, $eq(\theta)$ be the formula
$$X_1=t_1 \wedge ... \wedge X_m=t_m$$
Let not(G) be the negative literal under consideration and $\theta_1, ..., \theta_p$ be all the substitutions returned by the reduction of G. Then, the substitutions to be returned by the reduction of not(G) could be the substitutions $\mu_1, ..., \mu_q$ such that the formula $\neg(eq(\theta_1) \vee ... \vee eq(\theta_p))$ is equivalent to the formula $eq(\mu_1) \vee ... \vee eq(\mu_q)$. This basic idea needs however to be refined in two ways.

1° First, substitutions are, in general, not sufficient to ensure the above equivalence. In fact, keeping some negative information is necessary. This fact has lead us to generalize substitutions in so-called n-substitutions. As an additional consequence, reconciliation has to be extended to n-substitutions, or, restated in other terms, systems of equations and inequations have to be manipulated instead of just systems of equations.

2° Second, care must be taken to the quantification of the variables. This has lead us to introduce the concept of consistency of n-substitutions.

These notions have suggested us to extend other classical notions (such as composition, idempotence, ...) to n-substitutions. In particular, a natural notion to generalize is that of the instantiation of a term by an n-substitution. The concepts of extended term, and related ones of extended unification and instantiation, have followed.

All these extensions have been conflated in a theory of n-substitutions and extended terms. We will only describe here the part necessary to make the paper as self-contained as possible. The interested reader is referred to [Jacquet, 1989] for more details.

The remainder of this section is organized in three subsections. The first one discusses the systems of equations and inequations, introduces the concepts of unifier, mgu for such systems and the related notion of n-substitution. The second subsection generalizes, to n-substitutions, the classical concepts of composition, reconciliation, restriction of substitutions and the partial order $\leq$ on substitutions. It also introduces the concepts of negation and consistency of n-substitutions. Finally, the third subsection discusses the extended terms, extended unification and extended instantiation.

2.2 Systems of equations and inequations

For the ease of discussion, let us first adopt the following terminology.

Definition 2.1 We subsequently call *h-system* any system of equations and inequations over terms of the Herbrand universe. Given an h-system S, the system of the equations (resp. of the inequations) of S is subsequently denoted by S^+ (resp. S^-). A *solution* of S is a grounding substitution α verifying the three following properties :
  (i)   its domain, $dom(\alpha)$, consists of the variables of S,
  (ii) for any equation t=u of S^+, $t\theta$ and $u\theta$ are syntactically identical

(iii) for any inequation v≠w of $\dot{S}^-$, vθ and wθ are syntactically distinct.

The set of solutions of S is denoted by *Sol(S)*. The h-system S is said to be *solvable* iff the set Sol(S) is not empty. ♦

Domain restriction of solutions makes a solution of a system not necessarily a solution of an intuitively equivalent system. For instance, the solution {X/a,Y/b} of the h-system

$$\begin{cases} Y=Y \\ X \neq b \end{cases}$$

is not a solution of the h-system composed of the only inequation

X≠b.

It is however desirable to define, as equivalent, h-systems that are intuitively equivalent. This is achieved through the notion of solution-weaker systems.

Definition 2.2 The h-system S is *solution-weaker* than the h-system T iff for any solution σ of S, for any grounding substitution γ for the variables of var(T)\var(S), the restriction of σγ to the variables of T is a solution of T. This denoted by $T \supset_{sol} S$. The h-systems S and T are *equivalent* iff any of them is solution-weaker than the other. This is denoted by $S \approx T$. ♦

Notation 2.3 It will be convenient to extend the operand of the $\supset_{sol}$ and ≈ relations to "disjunctions" of h-systems. We write

$(T_1 \vee ... \vee T_n) \supset_{sol} (S_1 \vee ... \vee S_m)$

to denote the following property : for any i∈ {1,...,m}, for any solution σ of S_i, there is a j∈ {1,...,n} such that for any grounding substitution α for the variables of var(S_i)\var(T_j), the restriction of σα to the variables of T_j is a solution of T_j. The notation

$(T_1 \vee ... \vee T_n) \approx (S_1 \vee ... \vee S_m)$

is then employed to sum up the two inclusions

$(T_1 \vee ... \vee T_n) \supset_{sol} (S_1 \vee ... \vee S_m)$

$(S_1 \vee ... \vee S_m) \supset_{sol} (T_1 \vee ... \vee T_n)$. ♦

We are now in position to substantiate our need for explicitly coupling negative information to substitutions and, consequently, to generalize substitutions to n-substitutions. The following proposition, due to [Lassez et al., 1988], proves that, in general, one substitution and even a finite number of them are not sufficient to represent the set of solutions of a h-system. The above need results therefrom.

Proposition 2.4 ([Lassez et al., 1988]) Let S be a solvable h-system. Suppose S^- is not redundant with S^+ that is $S^+ \approx S$ does not hold. Then, there is no finite set of substitutions {$θ_1,...,θ_m$}, such that for any solution α of S, one has $θ_i \leq α$ for some i∈ {1,...,m}.

Substitutions are generalized to n-substitutions as follows.

Definition 2.5 An *n-substitution* ν is a pair of the form

({$X_1/t_1,...,X_m/t_m$},not{$Y_1/u_1,...,Y_n/u_n$})

where {$X_1/t_1,...,X_m/t_m$} is a substitution and {$Y_1/u_1,...,Y_n/u_n$} is a set of bindings such that

(i)   var({$t_1,...,t_m$}) ⊃ {$X_1,...,X_m$}∩{$Y_1,...,Y_n$},

(ii) var({$t_1,...,t_m$}) ⊃ {$X_1,...,X_m$} ∩ var({$u_1,...,u_n$}),

(iii) $u_i \notin$ {$X_1,...,X_m$}, for all i∈ {1,...,n}.

The two components are called the *positive part* and the *negative part* of ν, respectively. They are denoted by $ν^+$ and $ν^-$, respectively. An n-substitution whose positive part is empty is called an *en-substitution*. It is subsequently represented by its negative part, namely as not$\{Y_1/u_1,...,Y_n/u_n\}$. ♦

The interpretation of the n-substitutions is as follows : $X_1, ..., X_m$ have $t_1, ..., t_m$ as respective values with the constraint that each Y_i must differ from u_i ($1 \leq i \leq n$). Conditions (i), (ii) and (iii) further force the n-substitutions to be presented in a normal form. Basically, conditions (i) and (ii) express the fact that the inequations cannot directly constrain the X_i's but must do this indirectly through their bindings. This has the interesting consequence that no X_i occurs in the negative part of n-substitutions whose positive part is idempotent. Condition (iii) states a weaker property in the general case: the u_i's cannot be used to negate the X_i's.

Given the equational interpretation of n-substitutions, it will be useful to associate a h-system to any n-substitution. This is achieved as follows.

Definition 2.6 Let $\nu = (\{X_1/t_1,...,X_m/t_m\}, \text{not}\{Y_1/u_1,...,Y_n/u_n\})$ be a n-substitution. The *h-system associated with* ν, denoted by $hsyst(\nu)$, is the h-system composed of the following equations and inequations : $X_1 = t_1, ..., X_m = t_m, Y_1 \neq u_1, ..., Y_n \neq u_n$. The h-system associated with the n-substitutions $\nu_1, ..., \nu_m$ is the h-system composed of the equations and inequations of the h-systems $hsyst(\nu_1), ..., hsyst(\nu_m)$. It is denoted by $hsyst(\nu_1,...,\nu_m)$. ♦

The concepts of unifier and mgu are extended to h-systems by means of solutions. It is here worth noting that one n-substitution is, in general, not sufficient to sum up all the solutions of a h-system, as proved by the following h-system

$$\begin{cases} X = f(Y,Z) \\ X \neq f(a,b) \end{cases}$$

However, solving the positive part S^+, injecting the values in the negative part S^- and simplifying the resulting inequations make possible to represent the solutions of any h-system S by a finite number of n-substitutions. As a consequence, n-mgu's are not defined subsequently as n-substitutions but instead as finite sets of n-substitutions

Definition 2.7 An *n-unifier* of a h-system is an n-substitution ν that verifies $S \supset_{sol} hsyst(\nu)$. An *n-mgu* of S is a set of n-substitutions $\{\nu_1,...,\nu_m\}$ that verifies $S \approx hsyst(\nu_1) \vee ... \vee hsyst(\nu_m)$. ♦

Definition 2.8 Some n-mgu's have the property that their n-substitutions share the same positive part. They are called *elementary n-mgu* or *en-mgu*, for short. They are denoted as $\theta \oplus \{\omega_1,...,\omega_m\}$ where θ is the common positive part and $\omega_1, ..., \omega_m$ are the negative parts of the n-substitutions. Sets of this form are, more generally, called *elementary sets of n-substitutions* or *es-nsubst*, for short. ♦

2.3 The space of n-substitutions

A. The partial order $\leq$

We now show how the theory of substitutions can be extended to n-substitutions. As a first extension, the partial ordering $\leq$ on substitutions is extended by means of their associated system.

Definition 2.9
1) The n-substitution ν is *more general than* the n-substitution μ iff the inclusion hsyst(ν) $\supset_{sol}$ hsyst(μ) holds. This is denoted by $\nu \le \mu$. Similarly, the set of n-substitutions $M=\{\nu_1,...,\nu_m\}$ is more general than the set of n-substitutions $N=\{\mu_1,...,\mu_n\}$ iff hsyst(ν_1) $\vee$ ... $\vee$ hsyst(ν_m) $\supset_{sol}$ hsyst(μ_1) $\vee$ ... $\vee$ hsyst(μ_n) holds. This is denoted by M≤N, too.
2) The n-substitutions ν and μ are *variants* iff they verify the inequalities $\nu\le\mu$ and $\mu\le\nu$. Similarly, the sets of n-substitutions $M=\{\nu_1,...,\nu_m\}$ and $N=\{\mu_1,...,\mu_n\}$ are variants iff they verify the inequalities M≤N and N≤M. ♦

Note that, as a direct consequence of this definition, n-mgus of h-systems are still variants from one another.

B. Composition of n-substitutions

N-substitutions are composed in the following way.

Definition 2.10 The composition of the n-substitution
$$\nu=(\{X_1/t_1,...,X_m/t_m\},\text{not}\{Y_1/u_1,...,Y_n/u_n\})$$
by the n-substitution
$$\mu=(\{Z_1/v_1,...,Z_p/v_p\},\text{not}\{T_1/w_1,...,T_q/w_q\})$$
is the set of n-mgu's of the h-system obtained from the equalities and inequalitites
$$X_1 = t_1\mu^+, ..., X_m = t_m\mu^+, Y_1\mu^+ \ne u_1\mu^+, ..., Y_n\mu^+ \ne u_n\mu^+,$$
$$Z_1 = v_1, ..., Z_p = v_p, T_1 \ne w_1, ..., T_q \ne w_q$$
by removing any equality $Z_i = v_i$ for which $Z_i \in \{X_1,...,X_m\}$. It is subsequently referred to as Ncomp(ν,μ). The notation $\nu \,\tilde{o}\, \mu$ is furthermore used to refer to an arbitrary n-mgu of Ncomp(ν,μ). ♦

C. Idempotence

The notion of the composition of n-substitutions provides us with the possibility of introducing the notion of idempotent n-substitution.

Definition 2.11 An n-substitution ν is idempotent iff it verifies $\{\nu\} \in$ Ncomp(ν,ν). ♦

The following proposition gives a worth noting characterization of idempotent n-substitutions in terms of their positive part.

Proposition 2.12 ([Jacquet, 1989]) An n-substitution is idempotent iff its positive part is idempotent. ♦

Given a set of n-substitutions, we subsequently call it idempotent if all its n-substitutions are idempotent. The algorithm sketched for introducing n-mgus (see Definition 2.7) allows us to claim that any solvable h-system has an idempotent en-mgu. Thanks to this property, all subsequent notions defined from n-mgu's of h-systems have an idempotent instance. For example, n-substitutions admit an idempotent n-reconciliation when they are n-reconcilable; extended terms admit an idempotent n-mgu if they are unifiable in an extended sense.

D. Reconciliation of n-substitutions

Following our equational interpretation, reconciliation is generalized to n-substitutions as follows.

Definition 2.13 The n-substitutions $v_1, \ldots, v_m$ are *n-reconcilable* iff the h-system hsyst($v_1,\ldots,v_m$) is solvable. In this case, any n-mgu of this h-system is called an *n-reconciliation* of $v_1, \ldots, v_m$. It is called an *en-reconciliation* if it is of the es-nsubst form.

Reconciliation is extended to sets of n-substitutions as follows.

Definition 2.14 The sets of n-substitutions $\Theta = \{\theta_1,\ldots,\theta_m\}$, $\Psi = \{\psi_1,\ldots,\psi_n\}$, ..., $\Omega = \{\omega_1,\ldots,\omega_p\}$ are n-reconcilable iff at least one of the h-systems

$$\text{hsyst}(\theta_i, \psi_j, \ldots, \omega_k) \quad (1 \leq i \leq m, \ 1 \leq j \leq n, \ \ldots, \ 1 \leq k \leq p)$$

is solvable. In this case, let S be the set of tuples $(\theta, \psi, \ldots, \omega)$ of n-reconcilable n-substitutions of $\Theta \times \Psi \times \ldots \times \Omega$. An n-reconciliation of Θ, Ψ, ..., Ω consists of one union

$$\bigcup_{(\theta, \psi, \ldots, \omega) \in S} \rho_N(\theta, \psi, \ldots, \omega)$$

where, for any $(\theta, \psi, \ldots, \omega) \in S$, $\rho_N(\theta, \psi, \ldots, \omega)$ denotes an n-reconciliation of $\theta, \psi, \ldots, \omega$.

E. Consistency

Reconciliation of n-substitutions is quite intuitive but is still too weak to handle negation correctly, as shown by the following example.

Example 2.1 Consider the query ←not(p(X)),q(X) and the program
p(f(Y)).
q(f(3)).
Reduce the s-goals not(p(X)) and q(X) independently. The n-substitutions ({},not{X/f(Y)}) and ({X/f(3)},not{}) are produced respectively. They n-reconcile - with n-reconciliation { ({X/f(3)},not{Y/3}) } - although the query is manifestly not satisfiable! ♦

In fact, simple resolution of h-systems does not take into account the way in which variables are implicitly quantified. In the above example, the n-substitution ({},not{X/f(Y)}) reports the fact that X must be different from the term f(Y) whatever Y stands for. However, the reconciliation with ({X/f(3)},not{}) only tests whether there is some value of Y such that X=f(3) and X≠f(Y). Safe introduction of negation thus requires to fix some way of quantifying variables in n-substitutions. We adopt the following one.

Definition 2.15 Let $v = (\{X_1/t_1, \ldots, X_m/t_m\}, \text{not}\{Y_1/u_1, \ldots, Y_n/u_n\})$ be a n-substitution. Let furthermore Svars be a set of variables. The notation

Form(v;Svars)

denotes the formula

$$\exists Z_1 \ldots \exists Z_p \ \forall V_1 \ldots \forall V_q : (X_1 = t_1 \wedge \ldots \wedge X_m = t_m \wedge Y_1 \neq u_1 \wedge \ldots \wedge Y_n \neq u_n)$$

where
- $Z_1, \ldots, Z_p$ are the variables occurring in v^+ and not in Svars
- $V_1, \ldots, V_q$ are the variables occurring in v^- but neither in v^+ nor in Svars.

In particular, it is reduced to the empty conjunction (interpreted as true) if v is ({},not{}). ♦

The set of variables Svars is used to further postpone the quantification of some variables. This allows the Form interpretation to be used with different quantifications of those variables. For instance, assuming v is the only n-substitution computed by $p(X)$, the question

Is there X such that $\leftarrow p(X)$?

can be answered by answering the equivalent question using the interpretation $Form(v;\{X\})$:

Is there X such that $Ax_= \models \exists X\, Form(v;\{X\})$ holds

where $Ax_=$ denotes the usual axioms of equality. Moreover, the request

Find all X such that $p(X)$

can be equivalently treated by handling the query

Find all terms t for X such that $Ax_= \models \forall (\, Form(v;\{X\})\{X/t\}\,)$. [1]

Safety of the quantification of variables in n-substitutions is handled through the notion of consistency.

Definition 2.16 An n-substitution v is *consistent with respect to (wrt) a set of variables* Svars iff any binding Y/u of v^- verifies the following properties :

(i) Y is a variable of Svars or of v^+;

(ii) if u is a variable then u is a variable of Svars or of v^+. ♦

The following theorem relates the consistency notion and the Form interpretation.

Proposition 2.17 ([Jacquet, 1989]) Let Svars be a set of variables and v be an idempotent n-substitution. Then v is consistent wrt Svars iff the relation $Ax_= \models \exists_{Svars}(Form(v;Svars))$ holds. ♦

One desired property is that consistency is simultaneously achieved by variant n-substitutions. This is indeed the case for idempotent n-substitutions.

Proposition 2.18 ([Jacquet, 1989]) Let Svars be a set of variables. All variant idempotent n-substitutions are simultaneously consistent wrt Svars.

As n-reconciliation manipulate sets of n-substitutions, it is interesting to extend the above Form interpretation and consistency notions to sets of n-substitutions. This is achieved as follows.

Definition 2.19 A set of n-substitutions $\{v_1,...,v_m\}$ is *consistent wrt a set of variables* Svars iff, at least, one v_i is consistent wrt Svars. ♦

Proposition 2.20 ([Jacquet, 1989]) Let Svars be a set of variables and $\theta \oplus \{\omega_1,...,\omega_m\}$ be an idempotent es-nsubst. Then $\theta \oplus \{\omega_1,...,\omega_m\}$ is consistent wrt Svars iff the relation

$Ax_= \models \exists_{Svars}\, [\, Form((\theta,\omega_1);Svars) \vee ... \vee Form((\theta,\omega_m);Svars\,]$

holds. ♦

Proposition 2.21 ([Jacquet, 1989]) Let Svars be a set of variables. All variants idempotent en-subst's are simultaneously consistent wrt Svars. ♦

---

[1] The notation $\exists_{Set}$ (F) (resp. $\forall_{Set}$ (F)) is used as a shorthand to denote the formula $(\exists X_1...\exists X_m)$ (F) (resp. $(\forall X_1...\forall X_m)$ (F)), where $X_1, ..., X_m$ are the variables of Set. The notation $\exists$(F) (resp. $\forall$(F)) is used to denote the existential (resp. universal) closure of the formula F.

F. Quantified reconciliation

Example 2.1 shows that quantification of the variables must be introduced in the reconciliation process. This is achieved as follows.

Definition 2.22 Let Svars be a set of variables. The n-substitutions $v_1, ..., v_m$ are *qn-reconcilable wrt Svars* iff
- (i) they are n-reconcilable
- (ii) any idempotent en-reconciliation is consistent wrt Svars.

In this case, any such en-reconciliation, simplified from the n-substitutions that are not consistent with respect to Svars, is called a *qn-reconciliation* of $v_1, ..., v_m$ wrt Svars. Qn-reconciliation is extended to sets of n-substitutions by analogy to the n-reconciliation of Definition 2.14 ♦

It is worth noting that Proposition 2.21 ensures that all idempotent en-reconciliations simultaneously verify condition (ii) if one of them does. The consistency test can thus only be performed on one of them.

Example 2.2 Returning to the Example 2.1, it is worth noting that the n-substitutions $(\{\},not\{X/f(Y)\})$ and $(\{X/f(3)\},not\{\})$ are not qn-reconcilable wrt $\{X\}$. ♦

G. Negation of n-substitutions

Reducing negative literals constructively requires to negate n-substitutions in some way. This is performed according to their equational interpretation.

Definition 2.23 The *negation of the n-substitution*
$$v=(\{X_1/t_1,...,X_m/t_m\},not\{Y_1/u_1,...,Y_n/u_n\})$$
is the set of n-substitutions obtained by associating
- the n-substitution $(\{\},not\{X_i/t_i\})$ with each binding X_i/t_i, $1 \le i \le m$,
- the n-substitution $(\{X_1/t_1,...,X_m/t_m\} \circ \{Y_j/u_j\},not\{\})$ with each binding Y_j/u_j, $1 \le j \le n$.

It is denoted by *neg(v)*. ♦

Appealing to our equational interpretation of n-substitutions, it might seem quite natural to define the negation of the n-substitution $(\{X_1/t_1,...,X_m/t_m\},not\{Y_1/u_1,...,Y_n/u_n\})$ as the set of n-substitutions
$$\{ (\{\},not\{X_1/t_1\}), ..., (\{\},not\{X_m/t_m\}), (\{Y_1/u_1\},not\{\}), ..., (\{Y_n/u_n\},not\{\}) \}.$$
Once again, this does completely ignore the quantification of variables. Consider, for instance, the n-substitution $v=(\{X/f(Y)\},not\{Y/3\})$ of the first query $\leftarrow p(X)$ of Example 2.1. Its associated Form(v;$\{X\}$) interpretation is
$$\exists Y : X=f(Y) \wedge Y \ne 3.$$

Negating this n-substitution as above would lead to the two n-substitutions $(\{\},not\{X/f(Y)\})$ and $(\{Y/3\},not\{\})$ with the interpretation
$$\forall Y : X \ne f(Y),$$
$$\exists Y : Y=3,$$
respectively. Assigning the value f(2) to X would thus verify the negation of
$$\neg\ (\exists Y : X=f(Y) \wedge Y \ne 3)\ !$$

The problem is that the variable Y has lost its relation with X in the second n-substitution. This is circumvented by composing the positive part with each binding of the negative part (as achieved in Definition 2.23).

Following this remark, it may then be strange to find out that the variables $X_1, ..., X_m$ receive no special treatment. This is not necessary for our purposes since we can manage (and we do in fact) so that the quantification of the X_i's is always out of the scope of the considered n-substitutions.

Ns-goals will generally have to negate sets of n-substitutions rather than single n-substitutions. Negation should thus be extended to sets of n-substitutions. This is achieved by considering n-substitutions of sets as as many alternatives. Any set of n-substitutions is then negated by negating each n-substitution separately and by combining the resulting n-substitutions. The last operation implies reconciliation. This induces two possible acceptations according as quantification is taken into account or not. We could then have defined two negations, one involving quantification and the other not. The latter is however useless for our purposes. We will thus only describe the former.

Definition 2.24 A set of n-substitutions $\{v_1, ..., v_m\}$ is *negatable wrt the set of variables Svars* iff one of the two following conditions holds :
- the set is empty
- the set is not empty and the sets of n-substitutions $neg(v_1), ..., neg(v_m)$ are qn-reconcilable wrt Svars.

In the first case, the n-substitution $(\{\}, not\{\})$ is called the *negation* of the empty set. In the last case, any qn-reconciliation is called a *negation of $\{v_1, ..., v_m\}$ wrt Svars*. ♦

H. Restrictions of n-substitutions

Restriction of substitutions is finally extended to the n-substitutions. This is achieved subsequently in two ways. A first restriction, called equational restriction, rests on our equational interpretation of n-substitutions. It is however too strong to subsume the usual restriction of substitutions. To that end, another restriction, named functional restriction, is proposed. It rests on a functional perception of the substitutions (from which the usual restriction of substitutions issues).

Definition 2.25 Let $v = (\{X_1/t_1, ..., X_m/t_m\}, not\{Y_1/u_1, ..., Y_n/u_n\})$ be an n-substitution and Svars be a set of variables.

1) The equational restriction $v/_e Svars$ of v to Svars is the n-substitution μ
   - whose positive part μ^+ is obtained from $\{X_1/t_1, ..., X_m/t_m\}$
     1. by removing any binding X_i/t_i such that $X_i \notin Svars$,
     2. by removing any binding X_i/t_i such that $X_i \in Svars$ and t_i is a variable not in Svars,
     3. by replacing any occurrence of any t_i pointed out in 2 by one of the X_j such that X_j/t_i is of the form pointed out in 2.

- whose negative part μ^- is obtained from the version of $\{Y_1/u_1,...,Y_n/u_n\}$, updated as indicated in 3. above, by removing any binding Y_i/u_i that verifies one of the two following conditions [1]:
  (i) $Y_i \notin$ Svars, $Y_i \notin$ varcod(μ^+)
  (ii) u_i is a variable, $u_i \notin$ Svars, $u_i \notin$ varcod(μ^+).

2) The *functional restriction* $v \mid_f Svars$ of v to Svars is the n-substitution μ
  - whose positive part μ^+ is obtained from $\{X_1/t_1,...,X_m/t_m\}$ by removing any binding X_i/t_i such that $X_i \notin$ Svars;
  - whose negative part μ^- is obtained from $\{Y_1/u_1,...,Y_n/u_n\}$ by removing any binding Y_i/u_i that verifies one of the two following conditions :
    (i) $Y_i \notin$ Svars, $Y_i \notin$ varcod(μ^+)
    (ii) u_i is a variable, $u_i \notin$ Svars, $u_i \notin$ varcod(μ^+). ♦

Example 2.3 The strength of the equational restriction over the functional one can be illustrated by the following example. Let v be
  $(\{X_1/f(Z), X_2/Y_1, X_3/g(Y_1), X_4/h(Y_2)\}, not\{Y_1/1, Y_2/2\})$
and Svars be $\{X_2, X_3, X_4, Z\}$. The equational restriction $v\mid_e Svars$ is
  $(\{X_3/g(X_2), X_4/h(Y_2)\}, not\{X_2/1, Y_2/2\})$.
whereas the functional restriction $v\mid_f Svars$ is
  $(\{X_2/Y_1, X_3/g(Y_1), X_4/h(Y_2)\}, not\{Y_1/1, Y_2/2\})$.
The former results manifestly from a stronger restriction than the latter. Discarding the negative part, this example also shows that the equational restriction is too strong to be a generalization of the usual restriction of substitution. The functional restriction corresponds in fact to that restriction. ♦

Definition 2.25 is extended to sets of n-substitutions in a straightforward manner.

Definition 2.26 The equational (resp. functional) restriction of the set of n-substitutions Θ to the set of variables Svars is the set of the equational (resp. functional) restriction of the n-substitutions of Θ to Svars. ♦

2.4 Extending terms, unification and instantiation

The instantiation of a term by a n-substitution could be defined in two ways :
  - by ignoring the negative part of the n-substitution and by calling instantiation of the term its usual instantiation by the positive part of the n-substitution;
  - by keeping the negative part and by calling instantiation of the term the above instantiation coupled with the negative part of the n-substitution.

The second solution is adopted hereafter in order to conserve as much information as possible. It will be useful, in the execution model, in order to detect useless reductions as early as possible. It has two consequences :
  - any expression must be coupled with negative information;
  - unification and instantiation must be extended to such a generalized expression.

---

[1] Given a substitution θ, the notation varcod(θ) is used to denote the set of the variables of the codomain of θ.

Definition 2.27 On a point of terminology, the association (E,Ω) of an expression E with a set of en-substitutions Ω verifying the following property P is called an *extended expression*:

P : any Y/u of any en-substitution of Ω verifies the following conditions
    i) Y occurs in E,
    ii) if u is a variable then it should appear in E ♦

The intuition behind extended expressions $(E,\{\omega_1,...,\omega_m\})$ is to constrain E to at least one ω_i, with the variables of ω_i not in E universally quantified. For instance, $(h(X,Y),\{not\{X/f(Y)\},not(X/g(Z)\})$ represents the term $h(X,Y)$ restricted by one of the following constraints :
    i)   X differs from $f(Y)$ (i.e. $X \neq f(Y)$)
    ii) X differs from a 1-ary term which functor is f (i.e. $X \neq f(Z)$, $\forall Z$)

It is furthermore worth noting that, as for n-substitutions, the condition P is used to force the extended expressions to be presented in a normalized form.

Unification is generalized to extended expression by means of the classical unification and the qn-reconciliation.

Definition 2.28 Two extended expressions (E,Θ) and (F,Ψ) are said to be unifiable iff the two following conditions hold :
- E and F are unifiable, say with the idempotent mgu θ,
- the sets of n-substitutions $\{(\theta,not\{\})\}$, Θ and Ψ are qn-reconciliable wrt the variables of E and F.

Any resulting qn-reconciliation, if any, is called an *n-mgu* of (E,Θ) and (F,Ψ). As Θ and Ψ are composed of en-substitutions, one of them can be expressed in the form $\theta \oplus \Omega$ where Ω is a finite set of en-substitutions. Let Ω_r be the functional restriction of Ω to the variables of $E\theta$. The term $(E\theta,\Omega_r)$ is defined as the *most general common instance* of (E,Θ) and (F,Ψ) wrt the n-mgu $\theta \oplus \Omega$. Finally, this unification is called *extended unification*. The extended unifiability character can be proved independent from the choice of the idempotent mgu θ. ♦

Finally, the instantiation concept is defined for extended expressions and n-substitutions by means of qn-reconciliation. Some auxiliary set of variables is here taken into account in the aim of allowing some variables to be considered as existentially quantified. Note that, in contrast with the usual instantiation, the extended instantiation does not always succeed. Note also that the result, when it exists, is an extended expression. There is thus no need to introduce new expressions generalizing, in their turn, the extended expressions, and, consequently, there is no need to generalize once more the extended instantiation and unification.

Definition 2.29 An extended expression (E,Ω) is said to be *instantiable by an n-substitution* ν wrt a set of variables Svars iff the sets Ω and $\{\nu\}$ are qn-reconcilable wrt the variables of E and Svars. In this case, any resulting qn-reconciliation is called an instantiation n-substitution. Let $\psi \oplus \Psi$ be one of them and let Ψ_r be the set of the following restriction φ_r of the en-substitution φ of Ψ : for any $\varphi \in \Psi$, the corresponding restriction φ_r is defined from φ by removing any binding Y/u that verifies one of the following properties :
    i) Y is not a variable of $E\psi$
    ii) Y is a variable of $E\psi$, u contains one variable of Svars not occurring in $E\psi$.

Then, the extended expression $(E\psi, \Psi_r)$ is defined as *the instance of (E,Ω) by v wrt the instantiation n-substitution $\psi \oplus \Psi$ and the set of variables Svars*. Given, some set Ψ of en-substitutions, some (non-extended) expression E and some set of variables Svars, the set Ψ_r determined as above, but by taking E instead of $E\psi$, is called the term restriction of Ψ to E wrt to Svars. ♦

3 A parallel execution model with constructive negation

We are now in a position to show how the concepts of Section 2 can be used to design a parallel execution model of general Horn clauses. This model has, in its turn, been employed in the design of a concurrent logic programming language, named Conclog ([Jacquet, 1989]). To understand our motivations and the resulting model, it is worth spending a few words on it.

The Conclog language has been created with the aim of expressing concurrent executions in the conventional logic programming framework while standing as close as possible to the ideal of logic programming. Soundness and completeness properties have been ensured as much as possible. Multi-directional and multi-solution procedures are also supported. Nevertheless, efficient procedures can be coded thanks to the introduction of control annotations. To get such properties, the Conclog language has been designed in three steps. A parallel execution model of Horn clauses has first been conceived. It is sound and complete. Negation has then been integrated so as to preserve these properties as much as possible. Finally, annotations and built-in primitives have been introduced for purposes of optimization and practicability, respectively. We report hereafter the result of the second design phase. For the sake of space, the conceptual features are only presented. The reader is referred to [Jacquet, 1989] for more implementation details as well as for more information about the language.

3.1 Overview

As a snapshot, the main characteristics of the Conclog model are as follows. It uses both or-parallelism and and-parallelism in essentially an unrestricted way. Hence, all the clauses unifiable with a ps-goal are used simultaneously to reduce the ps-goal. Furthermore, conjoined s-goals are evaluated in parallel even if they do share variables. Quantified reconciliation is then employed to combine the produced n-substitutions.

The reconciliation calculus is also used intermittently to restore consistency in the deductions as well as to propagate bindings from subtrees to others. In operational terms, this means that the generation induced by the or- and and-parallelism is stopped after some amount of reduction steps and resumed on a purified version of these reductions. The purpose of this operation is to prevent the computation from useless reductions as soon as possible.

Negation is introduced by means of the not(.) predicate. Its argument is defined as a goal in order to conserve the alternation of goals and s-goals in the reductions. Its evaluation is performed according to Definition 2.24 and with respect to the variables of the ns-goal under consideration and the set of n-substitutions returned by the reduction of the associated goal.

As a final major characteristic, extended literals, extended unification and extended instantiation are used to avoid useless computations as early as possible.

The Conclog execution model of general Horn clauses is most easily further explained by using two complementary views, called the tree view and the process view. They are complementary in the sense that the former depicts the computation from a global perspective in terms of trees whereas the latter gives a more detailed and more dynamic view of the computation in terms of the behavior of processes.

3.2 The tree view

In the tree view, any computation is seen as the progressive construction, slice by slice, of the and/or/not search tree induced by the query and the program under consideration. This is achieved by means of a sequence of cycles, each one composed of one generation phase followed by one reconciliation phase. The aim of the generation phase is to extend the already constructed part from one slice. The aim of the reconciliation phase is twofold :
- to produce newly constructed solutions (i.e. n-substitutions corresponding to successful derivations of the general model, newly ended),
- to prevent the execution from useless computations by
    - cutting off branches that are detected to participate to no solution subtree (i.e. subtrees corresponding to the successful derivation of the general model),
    - communicating bindings (including negative ones) from one subtree to another.

The last operation is called *binding publication*.

The computation then consists of starting this sequence of cycles with the and/or/not search tree reduced to its query-node and of ending it when the and/or/not search tree is completely constructed.

The depth of the slices constitutes a parameter of the model. Precisely, it indicates the number of reduction steps that the reduction of any node of the slice can engender. (In this number, the reduction of an ns-goal to its positive goal is counted as one derivation step). A family of execution models is thus in fact defined. All of them have been proved sound and as complete as possible ([Jacquet, 1989]).

3.3 The process view

The real computation is far more dynamic. It is captured more closely by the process perception of the computations. According to it, the computation is described in terms of the behavior of processes, associated with nodes of the and/or/not search tree in a one-to-one mapping. The life of a process basically consists of creating its children as concurrent processes, of waiting for them to report sets of n-substitutions[1], of performing some reconciliation procedure (based on the qn-reconciliation) and of sending incrementally the set of the resulting substitutions to its father process or, for the process associated with the query, delivering them as computed answer substitutions.

---

[1] By abuse of language, we also say that the processes send n-substitutions instead of sets of n-substitutions.

Processes associated with the tips of one slice or of the whole tree make exception. They do not create children but directly report the following result :
   i)   processes associated with the last step of a failed derivation report failure by sending the empty set of n-substitutions;
   ii) processes associated with other tip nodes report (the set composed of) the restriction, to the variables of their father, of their associated en-mgu.

Tip processes associated with non completed reductions are re-activated to resume their process creation once the process associated with the query has completely performed its reconciliation procedure.

To complete the scheme, let us briefly comment on process creation, process reconciliation, process killing and binding publication. As a point of terminology, we will, from now on, call ps-goal-processes, ns-goal-processes, s-goal-processes, goal-processes and query-process the processes associated with ps-goals, ns-goals, s-goals, goals and the query, respectively.

A. Process creation

Process creation is performed in order to achieve and-parallelism, or-parallelism and the constructive form of negation. It reflects rules (E_1) to (C_2) above. Any goal-process thus creates a process for each of its subgoals, as restricted by rule (C_1). All of them are launched as concurrent processes. Ps-goal-processes search for unifiable clauses (in the extended sense) and create, for each of them, a process for the induced instance of the body. All these processes behave also concurrently. Furthermore, they register the associated en-mgu and the variables introduced at this point in the execution. Finally, any ns-goal-process, say associated with the ns-goal not(G), creates a goal-process for its argument G.

B. The reconciliation procedure

The reconciliation procedure of tip processes is performed according to points i) and ii) above. The reconciliation procedure of non-tip processes is as follows. It essentially rephrase rules (E_1) to (C_2) but deviates in making the restriction and composition in a slightly different way, of ordering the killing of some process and of publishing some bindings. N-substitutions are furthermore not transmitted alone but in so-called R-triplets. Such a R-triplet consist of a triplet composed of an n-substitution, of a label of value either "completed" or "incompleted", stating that the n-substitution is associated with a completed or incompleted derivation, and of a set of the tip-processes associated with the derivation. The label and set of processes information associated with n-substitutions issued from tip-processes is determined straightforwardly from this characterization. With respect to other processes, it is determined as indicated below.

1) Reconciliation procedure of ps-goal-processes

The reconciliation procedure of a ps-goal-process is performed with the intuition that its children represent alternative ways of reducing its associated ps-goal. It thus simply transmit the R-triplet sent by those children.

2) Reconciliation procedure of ns-goal-processes

The reconciliation procedure of an ns-goal is performed according to its intuitive understanding of negator. Any ns-goal-process first collects all the n-substitutions sent by its goal-process child and then negate the set of those corresponding to completely constructed subtrees (the negation is performed wrt the variables of its associated ns-goal). Two particular cases are worth noting :
1) if one of the reported n-substitutions is ({},not{}) then the empty set of n-substitutions is reported. In this case, failure is thus reported by the ns-goal-process.
2) if no n-substitution is reported (i.e. if the child goal-process fails) then the only ({},not{}) n-substitution is reported. In this case, the ns-goal-process succeeds.

N-substitutions are also sent in R-triplets. The auxiliary information attached to the μ_i's is as follows :
- the set of process identifiers part reduces to the ns-goal-process under consideration, say Proc.
- the label part is "completed" if the subtree engendered by Proc is completely constructed. It is "incompleted" otherwise.

Note that the set of n-substitutions sent by the ns-goal cannot be incrementally constructed as the n-substitutions are received from its goal-process child. Those latter n-substitutions are thus in fact collected by the ns-goal-process before being negated. However, in case the ({},not{}) n-substitution is received together with the complete label, failure can be reported directly without waiting for other n-substitutions. This is indeed achieved as an optimization in Conclog. Finally, partial information cannot be taken into account and is eliminated from the negation process. As a convincing argument of this rejection, consider a derivation with partial result ({},not{}) for one prefix that fails in a subsequent prefix.

3) Reconciliation procedure of a goal-process not associated with the query

Goal-processes not associated with the query form (incrementally) the cartesian product of the sets of n-substitutions sent by their children and for each tuple try to qn-reconcile them wrt to the variables of the goal. For any successful qn-reconciliation, the following n-substitution is sent. Let T be the considered tuple, ν be the substitution resulting from the reconciliation, $\theta \oplus \Theta$ be the en-mgu associated with the treated goal-process and Vars be the set of variables of the s-goal associated with the father process[1]. Then the equational restriction of the composition $\theta \, \tilde{o} \, \nu$ to the variables of Vars is sent. The label and set of nodes accompanying it are as follows. The label is "completed" if the n-substitution of T are associated with a "completed" label; it is "incompleted", otherwise. The set of nodes is just the union of the set of nodes appearing in T.

For the ease of the discussion, the n-substitutions ν resulting from the reconciliation of tuples are subsequently called n-reconciliation-substitutions.

---

[1] This set can be determined thanks to the set of variables associated with the goal-processes or more simply by the a suitable naming of variables.

N-reconciliation of distinct tuples may deliver the same results. Repetitions are avoided by eliminating those duplicates as follows : any goal-process records the R-triplets sent by its children. R-triplets are registered only if they do not correspond to an already sent R-triplet.

Finally, when all n-substitutions sent by all children have been registered, the goal-process order the killing of the children processes that are registered in one received R-triplet but participate to no sent R-triplet. It also orders the publication of the n-substitution
- whose positive part collects the bindings X_i/t_i that verify the following properties :
  - they are common to the positive part of all the n-reconciliation-substitutions
  - their LHS variable X_i is a variable introduced in the reduction at the goal-process or afterwards
  - their RHS term t_i is a non-variable term.
- whose negative part collects the bindings Y_j/u_j that verify the following properties :
  - they or their inversion u_j/Y_j are common to the negative part of the n-reconciliation-substitutions
  - their LHS variable Y_j is a variable introduced in the reduction at the goal-process or afterwards
  - they are not registered with their inversion i.e. there are no bindings Y_p/u_p and Y_q/u_q such that $Y_p=u_q$ and $u_p=Y_q$.

For the correctness of subsequent instantiation, the published n-substitution is sent together with the set of variables of the goal under consideration. The binding publication order is progressively transmitted from father processes to their children processes. What this induced is made precise in a moment.

4) Reconciliation procedure of the query-process

The query-process reconciles the n-substitutions from their children in the same way but delivers n-substitutions in a slightly different way. N-reconciliation-substitutions whose associated label are all "completed" only engender answer n-substitutions. They consist of their equational restriction to the variables of the query. Duplicates due to reconciliation are here avoided directly by memorizing the corresponding R-triplets and by discarding newly computed R-triplets already registered.

Binding publication and process killing are furthermore ordered in the same way as goal-processes by the query-process once it has completely treated all the R-triplets sent by its children. Finally, tip-processes corresponding to unreduced goals are woken up for a new generation phase.

C. Binding publication

Binding publication consists essentially of transmitting, in a given subtree, bindings (even negated ones) that are known to be verified by any answer n-substitution issued from the subtree. It acts in two ways : by constraining subsequent reductions that are incompatible with the published bindings and by killing some reduction whose prefix is incompatible with the published bindings. This incompatibility may have two sources :
- the extended instantiation of the goal or s-goal by the published n-substitution does not succeed;

- the published n-substitution is not consistent with the associated en-mgu.

Precisely, binding publication is operated as follows. Let ν be the n-substitution made public, Svars be its associated set of variables and P be the process receiving the publication message.
- If P is a(n) (extended) goal-process then the two following tests are operated. Let G be the goal associated with P.
    - The n-substitution ν is tested for qn-reconciliation with the en-mgu of P wrt to the variables of G and of Svars,
    - Each s-goal of G is tested for instantiability with ν with respect to the variables of Svars.
  Two different behaviors arise from the issues of the tests.
    - In case the two tests succeeds then G is replaced by the induced instantiation. The publication is passed thereafter to the child processes of P.
    - In case one of the tests fails, then a failure message is reported to the father process of P. Process P then orders the killing of its child processes and commits suicide.
- If P is a(n) (extended) s-goal-process then instantiation of its (extended) s-goal with ν is ensured by the previous instantiation of its father process. The s-goal is then replaced by the corresponding instantiation and the instantiation message is transmitted to the child processes of P.

D. Handling process killing and failure messages

Lack of space prevents us from describing the handling of failure messages and of process killing in all details. However the following rough description should be sufficient. Roughly speaking, process killing implies the real killing of the process as well as the following actions. There are, in fact, two types of killing. One involves the descendants and ancestors of the process to kill; the other involves the descendants only. The former is called all_killing (or a_killing, for short) and the other is called desc_killing (or d_killing, for short). Killing, ordered as a consequence of reconciliation (see point 3 above), is of the first kind whereas killing induced by failure messages or binding publication is of the second kind.

All_killing is handled as follows :
- the query-process reports failure of the computation if one of its children is killed and d_kills other children,
- when it is told of the killing of one of its children, any other goal-process commits suicide, d_kills its other children and reports its killing to its father,
- any ps-goal-process collects the killing reports of its children; when all children have been killed, it commits suicide and reports this killing to its father,
- report of a killing message has not to be defined for ns-goal-processes since it can be proved that, thanks to their reconciliation procedure, ns-goal-processes never receive them.

Desc_killing is handled as follows : when it is ordered to d_kill, the process just commits suicide and orders its children to d_kill. Finally, failure messages are treated as follows :
- any ns-goal-process treats failure report by reporting definite success,

- the query-process reports failure of the computation as a report of the failure of one child,
- any other goal-process reports failure in answer to the report of failure and d_kills all child processes,
- any ps-goal-process collects the failure reports and just reports failure when all its children did,
- any ns-goal-process treats failure report by reporting definite success.

To conclude, it is worth pointing out that because of process killing, some subtree may move from the incompletely constructed state to the completely constructed ones. Transmission of special messages are provided in Conclog for that purpose. Lack of space prevents us from detailing that point here. We refer the interested reader to [Jacquet, 1989] for more information.

3.4 Properties

The Conclog parallel execution model just presented has been proved sound with respect to the completion understanding of the programs in [Jacquet, 1989]. Assuming that all the derivations issued from the involved negative literals are finite, it has also been proved complete there. As this hypothesis on the negative literals is the more general situation where the negation as failure rule can be proved complete, the Conclog model can thus be said as complete as possible when the negation as failure rule and the resolution rule are used. Retricted to Horn clause programs, it has also been proved sound and complete (with respect to the classical first order models of the program).

Constructiveness of the negation is another major characteristic. In the Conclog model, the negative literals compute n-substitutions and thus act symmetrically to the positive literals. Consequently, the floundering problem is of no concern in Conclog.

It is also worth pointing out that, although they have been introduced for theoretical purposes (see Proposition 2.4), n-substitutions turn out to be very elegant and very intuitive. As an illustration, let us consider the efface procedure ([Deville, 1990]) :

efface(X,[X|L],L).
efface(X,[H|L],[H|L_eff]) ← not(X=H), efface(X,L,L_eff).

The relation it computes is defined as follows : efface(X,L,L_eff) holds iff X occurs in L and L_eff is L where the first occurrence of X has been removed. Consider the query efface(X,L,[1,2]). Intuitively, the answers are

L=[X,1,2],
L=[1,X,2] with X≠1,
L=[1,2,X] with X≠1, X≠2.

They are indeed found through the n-substitutions :

({L/[X,1,2]},not{ }),
({L/[1,X,2]},not{X/1}),
({L/[1,2,X]},not{X/1,X/2}).

Note that, in contrast, Prolog systems have a very poor behavior for such a query. They indeed only produce the first answer. Most of them - Prolog, in particular - fails in evaluating the negative literal not(X=H) because X is a variable. Then, the reduction of X=H succeeds and implies the failure of not(X=H). Other dialects such that Nu-Prolog ([Naish, 1985]) or Prolog II ([Giannessini et al., 1986]) suspends infinitely that reduction until X becomes non-variable.

The interest of the slice by slice construction of the and/or/not search tree and its parameterization in the Conclog model should finally be stressed. Fixing this parameter to 1 allows to simulate co-routining. Fixing it to a finite value allows to make an incremental form of constructive negation. Fixing it to the infinite value delivers a model where no intermittent restoring of consistency take place. Besides this modelling quality, the essential advantage of the slice by slice construction is to lighten the execution from the computation of useless branches. Its drawback is however to add some extra computation, issued from the reconciliation phases. An interpreter has been made for the Conclog model which allows to perform some tests. However, the optimal value of the depth parameter remains to be determined.

4 Conclusion and future work

A new constructive form of the negation-failure-rule related to concurrent logic programming has been presented. Based on it, a parallel execution model of general Horn clauses has also been exposed. It is sound wrt the completion understanding of the programs and as complete as possible when the resolution rule and the negation-as-failure rule are used. Restricted to Horn clauses, it is both sound and complete. Thanks to its constructiveness character, negative literals are reduced even if they are not ground. Furthermore, their reduction computes bindings for variables as the reduction of positive literals does. Hence, computations cannot flounder.

This new form of negation and this execution model take profit of a reconciliation-approach to concurrency and are based on an equational interpretation of substitutions. A generalization of substitutions, called n-substitutions, has resulted from the natural requirement of representing solutions of systems of equations and inequations in finite terms. They consist of coupling negative information with the substitutions. Despite their theoretical introduction, they have been argued to be quite intuitive and to provide a quite elegant representation of answers to queries. A generalization of the theory of substitutions to n-substitutions has been sketched in this paper.

In a symmetric way, negative information has been coupled with terms. The related notions of unification and instantiation have then also been extended.

The work presented in this paper issued from the second step of the design of a concurrent logic programming language, named Conclog. In addition to the language design purpose, we believe that the execution model has also a theoretical interest arising from their truly concurrent and constructive nature. Our future research will reflect these dual aspects of practicability and theory. They will include further developments of the theory sketched above, semantics of concurrent logic programming languages including this new constructive form of negation and practical issues of implementation of the Conclog language, in particular of the parallel execution model of general Horn clauses.

We refer the reader to the introductory Section 1 for a comparison of our work with related one.

5 Acknowledgements

I wish to acknowledge A. van Lamsweerde for having initiated my research in concurrent logic programming and for his valuable remarks on earlier versions of this work. I also thank the so many people at the University of Namur and at the Centre for Mathematics and Computer Science as well as the anonymous referees for their interest and comments on it. Finally, I like also to thank the Belgian National Fund for Scientific Research and the Centre for Mathematics and Computer Science for having supported this research.

6 References

[Apt, 1990]
> APT K.P., *Introduction to Logic Programming*, in : J. van Leuwen (editor), Handbook of Theoretical Computer Science, volume B : Formal Models and Semantics, Elsevier and The MIT Press, 1990, pp. 493-574.

[Barbuti et al., 1987]
> BARBUTI R., MANCARELLA P., PEDRESCHI D., TURINI F., *Intensional Negation in Logic Programs : Examples and Implementation Techniques*, Proc. TAPSOFT '87, LNCS 250, 1987, pp. 96-110.

[Barbuti et al., 1990]
> BARBUTI R., MANCARELLA P., PEDRESCHI D., TURINI F., *A Transformational Approach to Negation in Logic Programming*, Journal of Logic Programming 8, 1990, pp. 201-228.

[Chan, 1988]
> CHAN D., *Constructive Negation Based on the Completed Database*, Proc. 5th Conf. on Logic Programming, 1988, pp. 111-125.

[Chan, 1989]
> CHAN D., *An Extension of Constructive Negation and its Application in Coroutining*, Proc. of the North American Conference on Logic Programming, 1989, pp. 477-496.

[Clocksin and Mellish, 1981]
> CLOCKSIN W.F., MELLISH C.S., *Programming in Prolog*, Springer Verlag, 1981.

[Conery, 1983]
> CONERY J.S., *The And/Or Process Model for Parallel Interpretation of Logic Programs*, Ph.D. thesis, University of California, 1983.

[Deville, 1990]
> DEVILLE Y., *Logic Programming : Systematic Program Development*, Addison-Wesley, 1990.

[Eder, 1985]
> EDER E., *Properties of Substitutions and Unifications*, Journal of Symbolic Computation, 1, 1985, pp. 31-46.

[Giannesini et al., 1986]
> GIANNESINI F., KANOUI H., PASSERO R., VAN CANEGHEM M., *Prolog*, Intereditions, 1986.

[Jacquet, 1989]
  JACQUET J.-M., *Conclog : a Methodological Approach to Concurrent Logic Programming*, Ph.D. thesis, University of Namur, Belgium, November 1989, to appear as Lecture Notes in Computer Science, Springer-Verlag.

[Kalé, 1987]
  KALE L.V., *Parallel Execution of Logic Programs : the REDUCE-OR Process Model*, Proc. 4th Int. Conf. on Logic Programming, May 1987, pp. 616-632.

[Khabaza, 1984]
  KHABAZA T., *Negation as Failure and Parallelism*, Proc. Int. Conf. on Logic Programming, 1984, pp. 70-75.

[Lassez et al., 1988]
  LASSEZ J.L., MAHER M.J., MARRIOT K., *Unification revisited*, In Minker J. (editor), Foundations of deductive databses and logic programming, Morgan Kaufmann, Los Altos, 1988, pp. 587-626.

[Li and Martin, 1986]
  LI P.P., MARTIN A.J., *The Sync Model : A Parallel Execution Method for Logic Programming*, Proc. Symp. on Logic Programming, 1986, pp 223-235.

[Lloyd, 1987]
  LLOYD J.W., *Foundation of Logic Programming*, Springer Verlag, 1987.

[Lugiez, 1989]
  LUGIEZ D., *A Deduction Procedure for First Order Programs*, Proc. 6th Int. Conf. on Logic Programming, 1989, pp. 585-599.

[Maluszynski and Näslund, 1989]
  MALUSZINSKI J., NASLUND T., *Fail Substitutions for Negation as Failure*, Proc. of the North American Conference on Logic Programming, 1989, pp. 461-476.

[Martelli and Montanari, 1982]
  MARTELLI A., MONTANARI U., *An Efficient Unification Algorithm*, TOPLAS, vol. 4, No. 2, April 1982, pp. 258-282.

[Naish, 1985]
  NAISH L., *Negation and Control in Prolog*, Ph.D. Thesis, University of Melbourne, Australia, 1985.

[Palamidessi, 1990]
  PALAMIDESSI C., *Algebraic Properties of Idempotent Substitutions*, Proc. of the 17th ICALP, 1990, pp. 386-399.

[Pollard, 1981]
  POLLARD G.H., *Parallel Execution of Horn Clause Programs*, Ph. D. thesis, Dept. of Computing, Imperial College, London, 1981.

[Przymusinski, 1989]
  PRZYMUSINSKI T., *On Constructive Negation in Logic Programming*, Proc. of the North American Conference on Logic Programming, 1989.

[Sato and Tamaki, 1984]
  SATO T., TAMAKI H., *Transformational Logic Program Synthesis*, Proc. of FGCS, 1984, pp. 195-201.

[Tarnlund, 1977]
>TARNLUND S.A., *Horn clause computability*, BIT 17, pp. 215-226, 1977.

[Turi, 1991]
>TURI D., *Extending S-Models to Logic Programs with Negation*, to appear in Proc. 8th Int. Conf. on Logic Programming, 1991.

[Wallace, 1987]
>WALLACE M., *Negation By Constraints : a Sound and Efficient Implementation of Negation in Deductive Databases*, Proc. Int. Symp. on Logic Programming, 1987, pp. 253-263.

SYMBOLIC COMPUTATION AND PARALLEL SOFTWARE

Paul S. Wang[1]

Department of Mathematics and Computer Science

Kent State University, Kent, Ohio 44242-0001

Abstract

Two aspects of parallelism as related to symbolic computing are presented: (1) the implementation of parallel programs for the factorization of polynomials, and (2) the automatic derivation and generation of parallel codes for finite element analysis. The former illustrates the use of parallel programming to speed up symbolic manipulation. The latter shows how symbolic systems can help create parallel software for scientific computation. Through these two case studies, the promise of parallelism in symbolic computation is demonstrated.

1. Introduction

Significant development in parallel processing hardware have taken place in recent years. There are a wide variety of parallel architectures. A number of parallel processors are now available commercially at different price ranges. These parallel systems include message passing computers, shared-memory multiprocessors, systolic arrays, massive SIMD machines, as well as multiprocessing supercomputers. Together they promise to further speed up computations, especially through explicit parallel programming. However, the full potential of such systems can not be realized without similar advances in parallel software.

At Kent we have been interested in symbolic computation and in applying parallelism to realistic problems. Here, we will examine two such efforts: parallel polynomial factorization, and automatic generation of parallel programs for finite element analysis. By these two case studies, we hope to show that parallelism can speed up symbolic computations and, on the other hand, symbolic computing techniques can help create parallel software. More details can be found in [16] and [17], respectively.

---

[1]Work reported herein has been supported in part by the National Science Foundation under Grant CCR-8714836 and by the Army Research Office under Grant DAAL03-91-G-0149

Our presentation focuses on work at Kent. However, the application of parallelism is a very active research area within the symbolic computation community. The reader is referred to the proceedings of the International Workshop on Computer Algebra and Parallelism for more information [6].

2. Parallel Factoring

2.1 Strategy Outline

Consider factoring a univariate polynomial $U(x)$ of degree $n > 0$ with integer coefficients into irreducible factors over the integers **Z**. Without loss of generality, we assume that $U(x)$ is primitive (gcd of coefficients is 1) and squarefree (no repeated factors) [14]. $U(x)$ is NOT assumed monic and applying a *monic* transformation on $U(x)$ is not advisable. Instead, leading coefficient handling techniques are applied. This speeds up considerably the factoring of non-monic polynomials which occur often in practice, especially when univariate factoring is used as a sub-algorithm for multivariate factorization.

The polynomial $U(x)$ is first factored modulo a suitably selected small prime p.

$$U(x) = u_1(x) \, u_2(x) \ldots u_r(x) \quad mod \ p \tag{1}$$

where $u_i(x)$ are distinct irreducible polynomials over $\mathbf{Z}_p$. We know that $r \geq t$, the number of irreducible factors of $U(x)$ over **Z**. If $U(x)$ is irreducible mod p, i.e. $r = 1$, than it is irreducible over **Z**. If $r > 1$, the factors of $U(x)$ mod p are *lifted* to factors of $U(x)$ mod p^e for e sufficiently large. The actual factors of $U(x)$ over **Z** can then be derived from these lifted factors.

If $r > t$ then there are *extraneous* factors mod p that do not correspond to factors over **Z**. Extraneous factors complicate and slow down the lifting process and the recovery of actual factors.

It is advisable to use a prime that gives a value of r as close to t as possible. The fastest sequential implementation uses several primes to reduce r. We suggest to compute (1) for several primes in parallel and to use the information obtained to reduce the number of factors for the later stages of the factoring process. Factorization modulo each different prime is also parallelized by using a parallel Berlekamp algorithm.

Once (1) is computed, we go into the parallel EEZ lifting algorithm using multiple processes to compute the *correction coefficients* and to update all factors. Early detection of true factors will be included with correct handling of the leading coefficient. When processes are available, the polynomial arithmetic operations required in parallel EEZ lifting can also be parallelized. After lifting, actual factors can be found in parallel by simultaneous test divisions and grouping of extraneous factors.

A parallel package called PFACTOR has been implemented in C. PFACTOR takes an arbitrary univariate polynomial with integer coefficients of any size and produces

- A prime p

- A set of irreducible factors $u_i(x)$ mod p

- Information on grouping of extraneous factors for lifting

The output is much simpler if $U(x)$ is found to be irreducible.

To illustrate the parallel operations, the parallel extraction of factors through gcd operations in the parallel Berlekamp algorithm is presented. Timing data obtained on the Sequent Balance are also presented. But before we can do that, a few words on the parallel machines used are in order.

2.2 Shared-Memory Multiprocessors

The PFACTOR package has been implemented on the shared-memory multiprocessor (SMP) Encore Multimax and later ported to the SMP Sequent Balance. Performance tests and timing experiments have been conducted on both parallel computers. These SMPs are relatively common and should be familiar to most students of parallel systems. Therefore, we will describe them only briefly.

The Encore Multimax at Kent consists of 12 National Semiconductor NS32032 processing elements, each a 32-bit processor capable of executing 0.75 MIPS. The main memory of 32 MB is shared by all processors. The Multimax has architectural features for fast memory access and for avoiding bus contention. The Sequent Balance is very similar but offers 26 processors.

The Multimax runs under the Umax 4.2 operating system which is compatible with Berkeley 4.2bsd (and most of 4.3bsd). In addition to all the usual UNIX facilities, Umax provides multiprocessing, employing all the CPUs available to support concurrent processes by running up to 12 (in our case) of them simultaneously. The processors are shared by all system and user processes.

The C language is extended with parallel features [18] and augmented by parallel library routines. Programming primitives for allocating shared memory, synchronization and timing of parallel processes are provided. An interactive debugger dealing with multiple processes also exists. The Sequent Balance runs under Dynix, a dual-universe operating system combining Berkeley 4.2bsd and AT&T system V. The Balance operates under the same principles while providing a somewhat different set of parallel library functions.

For both SMPs, parallel activities are initiated in a program by creating *child processes* that execute independently but simultaneously with the *parent process*. Each process is essentially a separately running program. Communication among a group of cooperating parallel processes is achieved through *shared memory*. Data stored in shared memory by one process are accessible by all related processes with the same shared address space (Fig. 1). A program can generate many child processes. But if they are going to be executed in parallel, the total number of processes is limited to the total available CPU's.

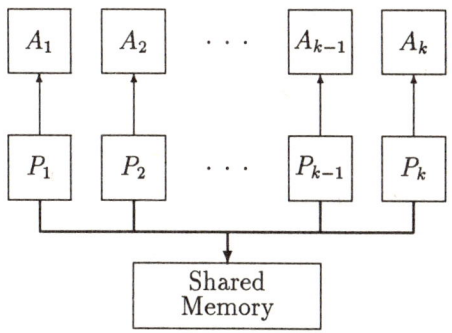

Figure 1: Private and Shared Address Spaces

2.3 Parallel Factoring Modulo Different Primes

To obtain factors modulo an appropriate prime in preparation for the EEZ lifting stage, PFACTOR uses several different primes and performs the following three major parallel steps in sequence. The output of PFACTOR is the shortest list of factors modulo the largest prime used.

1. Parallel choice of small primes and load balancing

2. Parallel Berlekamp algorithm on each prime simultaneously

3. Parallel reconciliation of factors

PFACTOR keeps a list of small primes from which several are chosen in parallel to satisfy two conditions: (i) the prime does not divide the leading coefficient of $U(x)$ and (ii) $U(x)$ stays squarefree modulo the prime. The parallel Berlekamp algorithm involves

- Parallel formation of the $(n \times n)$ matrix Q−I [10].

- Parallel triangularization of Q−I to produce a basis of its null space.

- Parallel extraction of factors with greatest common divisor (gcd) computations.

The dimension of the null space of Q−I is r, the number of irreducible factors mod p. Because $r \geq t$, $U(x)$ is irreducible over $\mathbf{Z}$ if $r = 1$. If this is the case for any prime used, then all other parallel activities are aborted and the entire algorithm terminates.

After the factors are obtained for several different primes in parallel, the results can be put through a *degree compatibility* analysis which can infer irreducibility and deduce grouping of extraneous factors.

2.4 Parallel Implementation of PFACTOR

PFACTOR consists of eight modules written in the C language with parallel extensions, system and library calls on the SMP used. Two input parameters are important in controlling the parallel activities of PFACTOR.

- *procs*: the total number of parallel processes to use.

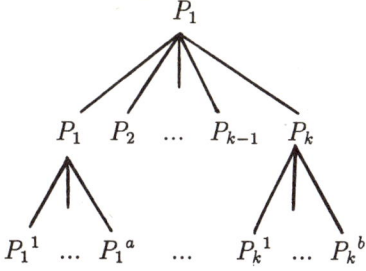

Figure 2: Parallel Process Hierarchies

- k: the total number of primes to use.

For example $procs = 9, k = 3$ means "factor $U(x)$ mod three different primes, all in parallel with nine processes". The primes to use can be specified in the input or generated by PFACTOR. For simultaneous execution of the processes to take place, the parameter $procs$ is limited by the number of actual processing elements available to the user. If $procs = 1$ then sequential processing is forced which is useful for comparative timing and debugging purposes. The following cases are considered.

1. If $procs = k$ then $procs$ factorizations are performed in parallel each with one process and a different prime.

2. If $procs < k$ then the first $procs$ factorizations are performed in parallel each with one process; then k is set to $k - procs$. In this case k must be an integral multiple of $procs$.

3. If $procs > k$ then all k factorizations are carried out in parallel each with one or more processes (Fig. 2).

Let us consider case 3 further. If $k = 1$ then all processes are used for the parallel Berkekamp algorithm with the given prime. If $k > 1$, the number of processes assigned to each finite field factorization is made proportional to the amount of work required in the Berlekamp algorithm which is roughly $p_i n^2 \log n + n^3$. Thus, the number of processes ps_i used to carry out factoring mod p_i is set to the maximum of 1 and

$$\text{round}\left(\frac{(n+p_i)\ procs}{k\,n + \sum_{i=1}^{k} p_i \,\log n}\right) \qquad (2)$$

for all but the largest prime which gets all the remaining processes. For example, distributing 11 processes for the four primes 7, 11, 23, and 37, with $n = 8$ under this scheme results in 1, 2, 3, and 5 processes for each prime factoring respectively.

2.5 Finding Factors in Parallel

In the parallel Berlekamp algorithm, we first form $Q - I$ and obtain a basis for its null space in parallel. This is followed by the parallel extraction of factors by gcd operations. It is this last operation that we will discuss in some detail.

Coming into this part of the computation are a prime p, the polynomial $u(x) = U(x) \bmod p$ of degree n, ps the number of processes to use, the dimension r of the null space which is the number of factors to be found. If $r = 1$ all parallel processes will terminate.

At this stage we have a set of $r > 1$ basis polynomials $v_i(x)$, $1 \leq i \leq r$, in increasing degree with $v_1 = 1$ and we are ready to perform the gcd computations

$$\gcd(f(x), v_j(x) - s) \qquad (3)$$

for $f(x)$ a divisor of $u(x)$, all $v_j(x)$, $1 < j \leq r$ and all $0 \leq s < p$. Such computations are performed until the r irreducible factors of $u(x)$ are found. There are two ways to parallelize computations for (3).

In the *dynamic scheduling* scheme, each process can take an $f(x)$ and a $v_j(x)$ and perform all the gcd computations for the different s values. In the beginning, one process takes on $f(x) = u(x)$ and $v_2(x)$ and breaks up $u(x)$ into two factors: a gcd $g(x)$ and a quotient $h(x)$. The task $[g(x), v_3(x)]$ is put on a shared *task queue* to be picked up by a second process while the first process continues with gcd operations on $h(x)$. When a process is finished with its task, it goes back to pick up another on the task queue. If the task queue is empty, the process has to wait. The job is done when all r factors are found. This scheme works pretty well when there are many factors to find. The only draw back is that not enough parallelism is applied in the beginning. It degrades to a sequential algorithm if $u(x)$ has only two factors.

Alternatively, the computations required by (3) can be computed by employing all ps processes for the prime p all the time. In this parallel scheme two lists, *facs* and *nfacs*, of factors of $u(x)$ are kept in shared memory. Initially *facs* contains only $u(x)$ and *nfacs* is empty. For each basis polynomial $v_j, j > 1$ the following is done.

One factor, called the *current factor*, is removed from *facs*. Each of the ps processes computes gcd's of the current factor (initially $u(x)$) with the current $v_j(x) - s$ for a distinct subset of s values in parallel. The union of the subsets covers all possible s values. Any factors found are deposited in the shared list *nfacs* until either the current factor is reduced to 1 or all ps processes are finished. By the end of this procedure, one or more factors whose product is equal to the current factor will have been put on *nfacs*. Now if *facs* is not empty then a new current factor is removed from *facs* and the procedure repeats. Otherwise, if *facs* is empty, then the values of *facs* and *nfacs* are interchanged and used with the next $v_j(x)$. The entire process is repeated until r factors are found.

To further illustrate this parallel procedure, we set forth the essential parts of the parallel C program in the following pseudo code. The code is executed in parallel by each of the ps processes. Every process has a unique integer *process ID*, $0 \leq$ pid $<$ ps. Variables in all upper case letters are shared.

```
par_findfacs(u(x),v1(x),v2(x),...,vr(x),r,pid,ps)
    NFACS=(u(x));
    FACS=();
    foreach v in (v1 ... vr)
    {   if (all r factors found) then
                break out of foreach loop;
        interchange(FACS,NFACS);
        par_gcd(FACS,NFACS,v,r,pid,ps);
    }
    return(concatenate(FACS,NFACS));

par_gcd(FACS,NFACS,v,r,p,id,ps)
    while (FACS not empty)
    {      if ( all r factors found ) then return;
           cf = remove first factor from FACS;
           n = deg(cf);    NDEG = 0;
           if (cf linear) then { put cf on NFACS; NDEG = NDEG +1; }
           else
           {   s = p - pid - 1;
```

```
            while(s >= 0)
            {   if (NDEG == n) break out of while loop;
                g = gcd(cf,v - s);
                if (g != 1) then
                {   put g on NFACS; NDEG = NDEG + deg(g);
                    if (NDEG == n) break out of while loop;
                    cf = cf/g;
                }
                s = s - ps;
            }   /* end of inner while */
        }   /* end of else */
    }
```

The simplified pseudo code does not show the synchronization or mutual exclusion necessary in a working program. The roles of the shared variables FACS and NFACS are clear. The shared variable NDEG keeps a running total of the degrees of factors inserted onto NFACS. When NDEG is equal to n, the original degree of cf, then the current factor is finished and it is time to process a new cf.

2.6 Performance of PFACTOR

To test the performance of PFACTOR, the degree 40 polynomial, $f_{40}(x)$, in SIGSAM problem 7 is used [9]. Over $\mathbf{Z}$, $f_{40}(x)$ has four irreducible factors

$$a_1(x) = 8192\,x^{10} + 20480\,x^9 + 58368\,x^8 - 161792\,x^7 + 198656\,x^6$$
$$+199680\,x^5 - 414848\,x^4 - 4160\,x^3 + 171816\,x^2 - 48556\,x + 469$$
$$a_2(x) = 8192\,x^{10} + 12288\,x^9 + 66560\,x^8 - 22528\,x^7 - 138240\,x^6$$
$$+572928\,x^5 - 90496\,x^4 - 356032\,x^3 + 113032\,x^2 + 23420\,x - 8179$$
$$a_3(x) = 4096\,x^{10} + 8192\,x^9 + 1600\,x^8 - 20608\,x^7 + 20032\,x^6$$
$$+87360\,x^5 - 105904\,x^4 + 18544\,x^3 + 11888\,x^2 - 3416\,x + 1$$
$$a_4(x) = 4096\,x^{10} + 8192\,x^9 - 3008\,x^8 - 30848\,x^7 + 21056\,x^6$$
$$+146496\,x^5 - 221360\,x^4 + 1232\,x^3 + 144464\,x^2 - 78488\,x + 11993$$

Table 1 and 2 show the timing results obtained by factoring polynomials of increasing degrees using different number of primes and processes on the Sequent Balance with 26 processors. (See [16] for Encore timings.)

In Table 1 $f_{20} = a_1(x) \, a_2(x)$, $f_{30} = a_1(x) \, a_2(x) \, a_3(x)$. Factoring $a_1(x)$ mod 11 and 13 yields its irreducibility over **Z** through degree reconciliation. The primes used are automatically selected by PFACTOR.

TABLE 1: PFACTOR Timing Results

Polynomial	Degree	No. factors	Primes	No. processes	Time (secs.)
$a_1(x)$	10	1	11,13	1	0.733075
	10	1	11,13	2	0.537024
	10	1	11,13	4	0.532023
	10	1	11,13	8	0.616446
$f_{20}(x)$	20	4 (11)	11,13,17	1	4.123983
	20	4 (11)	11,13,17	3	1.957521
	20	4 (11)	11,13,17	4	1.447737
	20	4 (11)	11,13,17	5	1.323721
	20	4 (11)	11,13,17	7	1.236876
	20	4 (11)	11,13,17	8	1.183241
	20	4 (11)	11,13,17	9	1.273457

The effect of additional processes on the speed depends on the size of n, the prime, and the way a particular problem yields factors in the gcd process. Because of the overhead of creating and managing parallel processes together with associated shared memory the speed gain for small problems is negligible or even negative. Table 2 shows that as the problem gets larger, the effect of additional parallel processes becomes considerable. But, because of the large grain size and the available parallelism in the factoring problem, as programmed, a point is soon reached beyond which adding more processes will not help much or even slow down the solution. In the timing tables the number of factors and the prime returned by PFACTOR are indicated.

TABLE 2: PFACTOR Timing Results

Polynomial	Degree	No. factors	Primes	No. processes	Time (secs.)
$f_{30}(x)$	30	4 (19)	11,13,17,19	2	8.667184
	30	4 (19)	11,13,17,19	4	4.907284
	30	4 (19)	11,13,17,19	6	4.076474
	30	4 (19)	11,13,17,19	8	3.475885
	30	4 (19)	11,13,17,19	9	3.304873
	30	4 (19)	11,13,17,19	12	2.837887
	30	4 (19)	11,13,17,19	16	2.421841
	30	4 (19)	11,13,17,19	20	2.359714
	30	4 (19)	11,13,17,19	23	2.242413
$f_{40}(x)$	40	5 (19)	11,19,29,83	4	24.733351
	40	5 (19)	11,19,29,83	8	12.573750
	40	5 (19)	11,19,29,83	10	9.283978
	40	5 (19)	11,19,29,83	15	6.081470
	40	5 (19)	11,19,29,83	16	6.152311

PFACTOR can also be used to simply supply a parallel Berlekamp algorithm on a single prime by simply specifying the prime and the number of processes to use. TABLE 3 shows the timings of factoring f_{40} mod (83).

TABLE 3: Parallel Berlekamp Performance

Polynomial	Degree	No. factors	Prime	No. processes	Time (secs.)
$f_{40}(x)$	40	13	83	1	23.161704
	40	13	83	2	13.516763
	40	13	83	3	10.212376
	40	13	83	4	7.960593
	40	13	83	5	6.577850
	40	13	83	10	4.474641
	40	13	83	15	3.831011
	40	13	83	20	3.795774
	40	13	83	21	3.877265

3. Symbolic Generation of Parallel Programs

Having examined how parallel programs can help speed up polynomial factoring, one of the central computations in symbolic and algebraic computation, we now turn our attention to the topic of how symbolic systems can help create parallel software through automatic program generation.

3.1 Background

Computer scientists and engineers at Kent State and Akron Universities have been involved in an interdisciplinary investigation of advanced computing techniques for engineering applications. A major focus of this collaboration has been finite element analysis (FEA) which, of course, has many applications.

Symbolic computation is employed to derive formulas used in FEA. The derived formulas can be automatically fabricated into numeric codes which are readily combined with existing FEA packages such as NFAP [4] and NASTRAN [5]. The objectives are to reduce routine but tedious formula manipulations, to avoid mistakes in manual computations, and to provide flexibility in situations where new formulations, new materials or new solution procedures are required. The techniques developed however is general and can be applied to generate programs in many other areas.

An area of great promise is the development of techniques to exploit parallelism in engineering computations. For the well-defined area of FEA, our approach to employ parallelism is to automatically generate the desired parallel programs based on the problem formulation. This approach can make parallel software much easier to create for many specific areas in science and engineering. By building the expertise needed to take advantage of parallelism into a software system, it is hoped that the powers of advanced parallel computers can be brought to a larger number of engineers and scientists.

Extending our efforts in the automatic generation of sequential FEA codes, a system can be built to map key FEA computations onto a given parallel architecture and generate efficient parallel routines for these computations. For our investigations, we have experimented with the Warp systolic array computer as well as the SMPs. The availability of these computers at Kent made our research much easier.

Because many FEA problems in practice require super-computing speeds, we have also extended our investigations to generating Cray Fortran codes to take advantage of the vectorization and parallel processing capabilities of the multiprocessor Cray computers. A free-standing code generator, GENCRAY, has been constructed to take derived formulas and render them into correct CFT77 codes. The GENCRAY system defines an input language that also allows the specification of parallel executions.

3.2 Generating Parallel FEA Codes

We have access to different types of parallel computers: the Warp [1] systolic array computer, the SMPs, and the 8-processor CRAY-YMP. We are investigating parallel FEA on all these machines. Here we will focus on work done on the Warp.

The Warp

The Warp is a high-performance systolic array computer designed for compute-intensive applications such as those involving substantial matrix computations. A systolic array architecture is characterized by a regular array of processing elements that have a nearest neighbor interconnection pattern. The Warp we used consists of a SUN-3 host connected, through an interface *cluster processor*, to a linear systolic array of 10 identical *cells*, each of which is a programmable processor capable of performing 10 million floating-point-operations per second (10 MFLOPS). A 10-cell Warp, therefore, has a peak performance of 100 MFLOPS. The Sun-3 host runs under UNIX and provides a parallel operating and debugging environment [3] for the Warp array. A Pascal-like high-level language called W2 [3] is used to program Warp. The language is supported by an optimizing compiler.

All cells can execute the same program (homogeneous) or different programs (heterogeneous). Aside from the per-cell instructions, a cell program also specifies the inter-cell communication through the use of the *send* and *receive* primitives. A *send* statement outputs a 32-bit word to the next cell while a *receive* statement inputs a 32-bit word from the previous cell. There are two I/O channels X and Y between each pair of neighboring cells. The first cell can use *receive* to obtain parameters passed by the host program and the last cell can use *send* to return results to the host program. An overview of the Warp system is shown in Fig. 3.

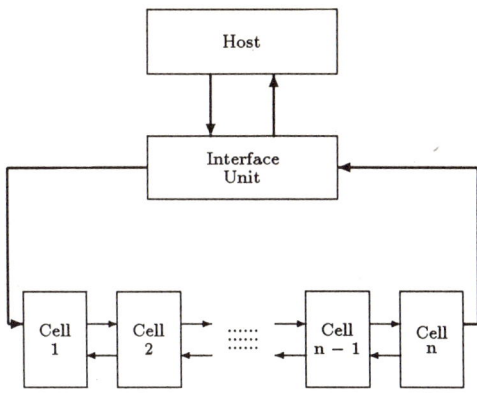

Figure 3: Overview of Warp System

Finite Element Analysis on the Warp

We can map key portions of finite element computations onto the Warp array. The generated cellprograms run under the control of a C program that is also generated. At run time, the C program initiates Warp executions when requested by a generated f77 code module that is invoked by a large existing finite element analysis package, NFAP. We have ported NFAP to run under the SUN-3. The generated f77 module prepares input data that are passed to the cellprograms through the C program. Results computed by the cellprograms are passed back through the C program as well. Fig. 4 shows the relations between these program modules.

Finite element analysis is compute-intensive. It involves repetitions of the same algorithm for all the elements covering a given problem domain. Major computational tasks include discretization of the problem domain into many finite elements, computing the strain-displacement matrix and the stiffness matrix for each element, assembling the global stiffness matrix and its subsequent solution. We have selected the strain-displacement and the stiffness computations as our first targets for parallelization on the Warp.

Given the Warp architecture, we examined various parallel algorithms to compute the strain-displacement and the stiffness matrices. The required W2 code is generated together with the necessary f77 module and the C module to control cellprogram execution. A software system P-FINGER, a parallel extension of FINGER, is constructed to derive

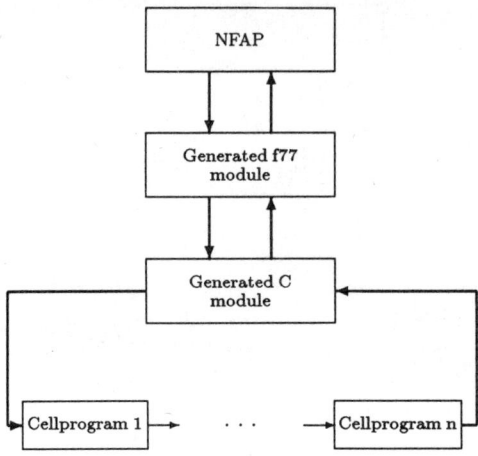

Figure 4: Program Interfaces

the necessary sequential and parallel code modules. An extension to GENTRAN [7], GENW2 [13], is also made to fabricate W2 codes. Generated cell programs may involve declarations, I/O statements, flow control, data distribution, subroutines, functions and macros.

Timing Experiments on the Warp

Two timing tables are presented here. Each row entry represents a complete stiffness computation involving Two-D Four-node elements in the isoparametric formulation. Each run involves a number of Warp invocations. For our timing experiment, each invocation processes only 100 elements. Thus, for example, the 2000-element entry involves 20 Warp invocations. The total time for all Warp invocations is accumulated using a timing mechanism written in C. The sequential timing is obtained by using one Warp cell to run the equivalent sequential code. Times given are in seconds and do not include times used on the Sun-3 host.

TABLE 4: Homogeneous Parallel Processing
Timings for actual Warp Executions
Two Dimensional Four-Node Elements

No. of Elements	Sequential	SIMD WARP Monitor	Speed Up	Efficiency
100	2.36	0.60	3.9	39
300	7.10	1.56	4.6	46
500	11.64	2.72	4.3	43
1000	22.64	4.67	4.8	48
2000	45.16	8.86	5.0	50
3000	68.20	14.14	4.8	48
4000	89.17	18.79	4.8	48
5000	116.12	24.52	4.8	48

TABLE 5: Heterogeneous Parallel Processing
Timings for actual Warp Executions
Two Dimensional Four-Node Elements

No. of Elements	Sequential	MIMD WARP Monitor	Speed Up	Efficiency
100	2.36	0.64	3.7	37
300	7.10	1.42	5.0	50
500	11.64	2.10	5.5	55
1000	22.64	4.14	5.4	54
2000	45.16	7.38	6.1	61
3000	68.20	11.60	5.8	58
4000	89.17	14.82	6.0	60
5000	116.12	18.38	6.3	63

3.3 A CFT77 Code Generator for the CRAY

Many compute-intensive scientific and engineering problems require supercomputing speeds. Thus, it is also important to generate programs to run on a Cray. We have implemented a new code translator/generator called GENCRAY. The output of GENCRAY is f77 or Cray Fortran-77 (CFT77) code with vectorization and parallel features. CFT77 is a superset of f77 and is the standard Fortran available on Cray supercomputers.

One of the outstanding features of GENCRAY is to allow parallel specifications in the input and to generate codes that take advantage of the vectorization and parallel features on multi-processor Cray systems

The C language is used to implement GENCRAY so that it is readily portable to any computer systems with a standard C compiler. GENCRAY also defines its own input language so it can interface with formulas and procedures derived by any symbolic system.

3.4 Generating Vectorizable/Parallel Code in CFT77

The Cray CFT77 compiler is a vectorizing compiler. Much computing power can be derived from vectorization if the loops in the program are written so that they are *vectorizable*. Properties such as data dependencies across iterations, breaks in flow control (exiting the loop prematurely), and so on, can prevent vectorization. Also the CFT77 compiler only attempts to vectorize the innermost loop. It is up to the programmer to analyze the structure of nested loops and to arrange them so that vectorizing the innermost loop reaps the most benefit.

To make it easier to produce vectorizable code, GENCRAY provides several high-level vectorization *macros* for matrix/vector computations:

- `mmult` - matrix multiplication

- `madd` - matrix addition

- `msub` - matrix subtraction.

In the generated code these macros expand inline to do loops that are vectorizable and optimal for the natural algorithms used. For example, consider the matrix multiplication macro:

(mmult a b c 100 400 250)

The code generated for this is:

```
c *** BEGIN GENERATED CODE ***
      integer m0
      integer m1
      integer m2
c ** BEGIN MATRIX MACRO EXPANSION **
      do 1001 m0=1,250
        do 1002 m1=1,100
          c(m1,m0)=a(m1,1)*b(1,m0)
 1002   continue
 1001 continue
c
      do 1003 m0=1,250
        do 1004 m1=1,100
          do 1005 m2=2,400
            c(m1,m0)=c(m1,m0)+(a(m1,m2)*b(m2,m0))
 1005     continue
 1004   continue
 1003 continue
c ** END MATRIX MACRO EXPANSION **
c *** END GENERATED CODE ***
```

The Cray YMP is a family of shared memory parallel computers. Each processor is basically a Cray processor. For instance, the Cray YMP at the Ohio Supercomputer Center is an eight-processor system. It is, therefore, important for GENCRAY to also provide easy-to-use facilities for generating CFT77 programs that take advantage of the parallelism offered by multiple processors. Thus, in addition to vectorization macros, GENCRAY provides several high-level parallel constructs for generating parallel programs that use the multiple processors.

The idea is to provide access to the Cray multitasking library primitives through a set of very high level statements that are much easier to use for specifying a number of useful parallel executions. GENCRAY can translate these high-level statement into multitasked programs for the Cray. The following capabilities are provided:

1. Multitasking: The **pexec** macro is used to specify the parallel execution of several tasks. Logically, when control flow reaches **pexec**, it splits into several independently running threads each to execute one of the parallel tasks. When all of its

parallel tasks are done then `pexec` is finished. The `pexec` macro is suitable for actions of relatively coarse granularity due to the overhead involved in setting up and synchronizing the tasks. The macro can be used, for example, to call several subroutines in parallel. GENCRAY does not check for data dependencies in the tasks which can invalidate the parallel execution. It is the user's responsibility to ensure that no such dependencies exist.

2. Pipelining: The macro `pipe` specifies a coarse-grain pipeline program that organizes multiple processors into an assembly line. It provides a simple way to specify the stages of a computation and the data transfer from one stage to the next. For example, `pipe` can be used to specify a pipeline of forward FFT, element-wise multiplication, and then inverse FFT. GENCRAY translates the `pipe` macro and generates CFT77 codes for each stage of the pipeline with correct data transfer and synchronization.

3. parallel do loop: Also supported by GENCRAY is the macro `doall`. The different statements in a `doall` are executed independently and simultaneously. The `doall` can be used to specify parallel tasks with a finer granularity than that in the `pexec` construct. Doall is best used in nested loops so that the innermost loop can be vectorized while the outer loop iterations are executed in parallel.

4. On-going and Future Work

Parallel polynomial factorization work on the SMPs is continuing at Kent. Strategy details are being ironed out and parallel C codes are being written for the lifting and the true-factors phases. A package called BigNum [11] developed in France is used to supply the extended precision integer arithmetic required in lifting. Parallel polynomial arithmetic routines are also implemented to allow additional speed up in the right situations. The new codes will be combined with PFACTOR to serve as the base for future work on parallel multivariate factorization.

Another focus of our on-going research is to parallelize many key FEA computations on SMPs and automatically generate such parallel programs. We will not only extend our work on the Warp to the SMP but also look into the parallel solution of the global matrix.

Element-by-element (EBE) iterative schemes using preconditioned conjugate gradient are promising on SMPs. The EBE scheme works well for many cases in linear analysis. On the other hand, it encounters difficulties in other cases especially for nonlinear analysis. When it is applicable, the EBE scheme can be a very efficient parallel method.

A software package is also being developed to generate parallel FEA codes for the SMPs [12]. This package will feature a way for the engineer to specify basic computations using familiar notations. These basic numeric computations can be mapped onto a particular parallel architecture and executed in parallel. The load balancing and synchronization details will be handled by the derived code.

5. Conclusions

Parallel computers are here to stay and to provide important speed up for many different kinds of computations. As more people apply parallel programs to solve problems, the gap between the highly developed parallel architectures and the primitive parallel programming tools and operating environments becomes increasingly clear. We are at a point in parallel software development that sequential programming was before FORTRAN. Much work lay ahead in the parallel software area.

1. High-level parallel programming languages and tools to make parallel software much easer to write and test.

2. Program portability to make a parallel program usable across a set of parallel computers.

3. Parallel language features to better accommodate the needs of parallel algorithm designers.

4. Closer collaboration among language, operating system, and architecture specialists to develop machine features to support the development and execution of parallel software.

5. Closer collaboration between computer professionals and applications people to target parallel features for practical use.

It is hoped that the mutually beneficial relations between symbolic computation and parallel software continue to develop and strengthen, and will play an important part in the overall advancement of parallel computation.

References

[1] Annaratone, M., Arnould, E., Gross, T., Kung, H. T., Lam, M. S., Menzilcioglu, O., and Webb, J. A., "The Warp Machine: Architecture, Implementation and Performance," IEEE Trans. on Computers, Vol. C-36, No. 12, Dec. 1987, pp. 1523-1538.

[2] Berlekamp, E. R., "Factoring Polynomials over Finite Fields," Bell System Tech. J., V. 46, 1967, pp. 1853-1859.

[3] Bruegge, B., "Warp Programming Environment : User Manual," Department of Computer Science, Carnegie Mellon University, Pittsburgh, PA, 1984.

[4] Chang, T. Y., "NFAP- A Nonlinear Finite Element Program, Vol. 2 - Technical Report," College of Engineering, University of Akron, OH, 1980.

[5] "COSMIC NASTRAN USER'S Manual," Computer Services, University of Georgia, Athens, GA, 1985.

[6] Dora D. J. and Fitch, J. ed., *Computer Algebra and Parallelism*, Academic Press, San Diego, CA 92101.

[7] Gates, B. L., "A Numerical Code Generation Facility for REDUCE," Proceedings, ACM SYMSAC'86, Waterloo, Ontario, July 1986, pp. 94-99.

[8] Gross, T. and Lam, M., "A Brief Description of W2", Department of Computer Science, Carnegie Mellon University, Pittsburgh, PA, 1985.

[9] Johnson, S. C. and Graham, R. L., "SIGSAM Problem #7", ACM SIGSAM Bulletin, Feb. 1974, page 4.

[10] Knuth, D. E., *The Art of Computer Programming*, Vol. 2:*Seminumerical Algorithms*, 2nd ed., Addison-Wesley, Reading, Mass., USA, 1980.

[11] Serpette, B., Vuillemin, J., and Hervé, J.C., "BigNum: A Portable and Efficient Package for Arbitrary-Precision Arithmetic," Digital Equipment Corp., Paris Research Laboratory, 85, Av. Victor Hugo. 92563 Rueil-Malmaison Cedex, France.

[12] Sharma, N. and Wang, P. S., "Generating Finite Element Programs for Shared Memory Multiprocessors," *Symbolic Computations and Their Impact on Mechanics*, PVP-Vo. 205, American Society of Mechanical Engineers, pp. 63-79, Nov. 1990.

[13] Tan, T. and Wang, P. S., "Automatic Generation of Parallel Code for the Warp Computer," Proceedings, 1st International Workshop on Computer Algebra and Parallelism, June 1988, Grenoble, France, *Computer Algebra and Parallelism*, pp. 91-117, Academic Press, Oct. 1989.

[14] Wang, P. S. and Trager, B. M., "New Algorithms for Polynomial Square-free Decomposition over the Integers," SIAM J. Computing, Vol. 8, No. 3, Aug. 1979, pp. 300-305.

[15] Wang, P. S., "Parallel p-adic Constructions in the Univariate Polynomial Factoring Algorithm," Proceedings, MACSYMA Users' Conference 1979, Cambridge, MA, MIT pp. 310-318.

[16] Wang, P. S., "Parallel Univariate Polynomial Factorization on Shared-Memory Multiprocessors," Proceedings of the ISSAC'90, Addison-Wesley (ISBN 0-201-54892-5), Aug. 1990, pp. 145-151.

[17] Wang, P. S., "Applying Advanced Computing Techniques in Finite Element Analysis," *Symbolic Computations and Their Impact on Mechanics*, PVP-Vo. 205, American Society of Mechanical Engineers, pp. 189-203, Nov. 1990.

[18] Wang, P. S. and Weber, K., "Guide to Parallel Programming on the Encore Multimax," Technical Report (CS-8901-03), Dept. Math and C.S., Kent State University, Kent, OH, 44242 USA.

On the Parallelization of Characteristic-Set-Based Algorithms

DONGMING WANG

Research Institute for Symbolic Computation, Joh Kepler University, A-4040 Linz, Austria
Mathematics-Mechanization Research Center, Academia Sinica, Beijing 100080, China

Abstract

This paper presents a parallelized version of algorithms for computing characteristic sets, characteristic series and irreducible characteristic series of sets of multivariate polynomials, decomposing algebraic varieties into irreducible components and proving theorems mechanically in elementary geometries. These algorithms have been implemented with up to 12 processors in MAPLE system by utilizing distributed workstations connected by a local network. The timing statistics on a set of test problems with remarks is given. The encountered problems of using parallelism for these algorithms are discussed.

1. Introduction

The method of characteristic sets [3, 4, 8, 9] provides algorithms for computing the triangularized set and various zero decompositions of any set of multivariate polynomials. On the basis of this method, a number of efficient algorithms have been designed for different application purposes. It appears that all these algorithms are still unable to attack many large problems within a reasonable time limit; therefore, further improvements from different aspects remain necessary. Our attempt here is to speed up these algorithms by parallel processing, a potential way of improving sequential algorithms for solving large problems. As an initial investigation, we present in this paper a parallelized version of some basic algorithms and report our current experiments with up to 12 parallel processors based on the MIMD model. Our results have demonstrated significant gains of using parallelism for these characteristic-set-based algorithms and indicated meanwhile that at the level of realization new issues and problems like data communication and practical complexity analysis arise and have to be carefully studied in order to achieve ideal performance. The results presented in this paper may be taken into account for considering an implementation of the algorithms with multiprocessors on parallel machines.

The parallelized algorithms studied in the later sections include those for computing characteristic sets, characteristic series and irreducible characteristic series of sets of multivariate polynomials, decomposing algebraic varieties into irreducible components and proving theorems mechanically in elementary geometries. In order to make clear locations where parallel features can be introduced, we supply as Appendix A a sequential version of considered algorithms (which aims mainly to reflect the algorithmic features and principles, and on which many modifications and extensions can be made at the implementation level). We shall discuss which part of the sequential algorithms can be parallelized and describe a parallelized version for each. We have implemented the parallelized algorithms in MAPLE system for research purpose utilizing several distributed

---

This work is supported by the Austrian Ministry of Science and Research under ESPRIT Basic Research Action 3125 (MEDLAR) and Project "Parallel Computation on Workstation Networks".

workstations connected by a local network. The data communication is realized via a simple mechanism, namely, via the network and the reading and writing of data files. This is feasible because MAPLE provides an efficient means for reading and writing files from/to the disc in an internal form. A brief description of our implementation and timing statistics on some test problems with remarks are given. The encountered problems of using parallelism for these algorithms are also discussed.

The reader of this paper is assumed to be familiar with notions including leading variable, initial, rank, reduced, ascending set, pseudo-remainder, basic set, characteristic set and the reducibility of an ascending set in the theory and method of characteristic sets and some basic notions concerning algebraic variety. For full details, we refer to [2-5, 8, 9]. In the description of algorithms the following abbreviations will be used

$cls(F)$	— class of F	$nonc(AS)$	— AS is non-contradictory
$lvar(F)$	— leading variable of F	$irr(AS)$	— AS is irreducible
$ini(F)$	— initial of F	$prem(F, AS)$	— pseudo-remainder of G wrt AS
wrt	— with respect to		

We shall make distinction between for each $\cdots$ do and for all $\cdots$ do in parallel in the repetition statements of algorithm description. The former means that the specified statements are executed sequentially, whereas the latter means to execute these statements simultaneously using multiple parallel processors. In all algorithms, the execution terminates until the last line or until stop occurs, and the state values of the output variables are returned.

All experimental results shown in this paper are obtained by using author's implementation of a characteristic sets package [7] running with MAPLE 4.3 on Apollo DN3500/4000/ 4500 workstations under a UNIX operating system. The timings are recorded in CPU seconds and include those for garbage collection.

2. Characteristic Sets

The sequential algorithm for computing the characteristic set CS, a certain triangular form, of any given polynomial set PS is described as CharSet in Appendix A. It is the main subalgorithm of all other characteristic-set-based algorithms. In this algorithm, two natural parallel variants can be made. The first is the formation of RS which is most time-consuming if the occurring polynomials become large. The second is the formation of QS in the subalgorithm BasicSet which is relatively cheaper. The parallel processing has advantages only if the date communication and waiting cost much less time. In the first case, i.e., to form the pseudo-remainders simultaneously with multiprocessors, we have a straightforward parallelized version of CharSet as follows

```
P-CharSet(Input: PS; Output: CS)
  QS := PS; RS := PS
  while RS ≠ φ do
      CS := BasicSet(QS); RS := φ
      if nonc(CS) then
          for all Q ∈ QS − CS do in parallel
              R := prem(Q, CS)
              if R ≠ 0 then RS := RS ∪ {R}
          QS := QS ∪ RS
```

Table 1 in Section 6 presents the time comparison between this algorithm and CharSet for six test examples.

3. Geometry Theorem Proving

Wu's method [8-10] is now known to be efficient for proving a large number of nontrivial theorems in geometries. To present his basic decision algorithm, let us suppose that the hypothesis and conclusion of a (geometric) theorem have been algebraized as sets of polynomial equations $HYP = 0$ and $CON = 0$. The problem of proving the theorem is reduced to finding first some non-degenerate conditions $\Delta \neq 0$ and determining then whether the conclusion is a formal consequence of the hypothesis under these conditions. The latter is done by determining for each polynomial $G \in CON$ whether any zero of HYP which is such that $\Delta \neq 0$ is a zero of G. The sequential algorithm of this procedure is given as TheoremProver in Appendix A which is essentially the version described in [8, 9].

In the implementation of TheoremProver several techniques may be taken into account for the sake of efficiency. Some strategies used in author's implementation are described in [6]. The algorithm TheoremProver computes first the characteristic set CS of HYP and then the remainders of conclusion-polynomials in CON with respect to CS. In addition to use the parallelized algorithm for computing CS, several further parallel variants can be made. The first variant is to compute the remainders of all polynomials in CON with respect to CS simultaneously instead of the sequential formation of RS, and the second is to split some intermediate remainder, which is got from the successive pseudodivision of a certain $G \in CON$ by some polynomials in CS, into several polynomials, say $H_1, \ldots, H_h$, and compute then the further remainders of all H_j with respect to the remaining polynomials in CS synchronously. The second technique which was introduced by Wu [8, 10] for proving difficult theorems on small computers via sequential computation is rather powerful. Let us describe this split technique in the algorithmic form

Sprem(Input: $G, CS = \{C_1, \ldots, C_r\}$; Output: R)
$GS := \{G\}$; $RS := \phi$; $ind := false$
while $GS \neq \phi$ do
$R :=$ an element of GS; $GS := GS - \{R\}$
for i from r step -1 to 1 do
$RS :=$ Split(R); $R :=$ an element of RS
if RS contains more than one element then
$GS := GS \cup (RS - \{R\})$; $ind := true$
$R := prem(R, C_i)$
if $R \neq 0$ and ind then
$R := prem(G, CS)$; stop

where the subalgorithm Split is written as

Split(Input: R; Output: RS)
$VS :=$ set of all variables occurring in R whose order precedes $lvar(R)$
if $VS = \phi$ then $RS := \{R\}$ else $RS :=$ set of all monomials of R wrt variables in VS

Then, the parallel feature for the while-loop in Sprem can be introduced obviously.

Finally, if the remainder of some G with respect to the characteristic set CS is non-zero while CS is reducible, the proof of the theorem requires an irreducible decomposition of the hypothesis-polynomial set. Then, the parallel processing for the while-loop in TheoremProver becomes possible. This is similar to the parallelization of computing irreducible characteristic series as will be discussed in detail in the next section.

Taking these variants into account we present now a parallelized version of the algorithm TheoremProver.

P-TheoremProver(Input: HYP, CON; Output: Δ, Yes, No or SC)
$\quad \Psi := \{[HYP, 0]\}; \Delta := \phi; dd := -1; ind := false$
$\quad$ while $\Psi \neq \phi$ do
$\quad\quad$ for all $[PS, D] \in \Psi$ do in parallel
$\quad\quad\quad CS := $ P-CharSet(PS)
$\quad\quad\quad$ if $nonc(CS)$ then
$\quad\quad\quad\quad d := $ number of parameters in CS
$\quad\quad\quad\quad$ if $d < dd$ then $\Delta := \Delta \cup \{D\}$
$\quad\quad\quad\quad$ else
$\quad\quad\quad\quad\quad$ if $dd = -1$ then $dd := d$
$\quad\quad\quad\quad\quad RS := \phi$
$\quad\quad\quad\quad\quad$ for all $G \in CON$ do in parallel
$\quad\quad\quad\quad\quad\quad R := $ P-Sprem(G, CS)
$\quad\quad\quad\quad\quad\quad$ if $R \neq 0$ then $RS := RS \cup \{R\}$
$\quad\quad\quad\quad\quad$ if $RS = \phi$ then $\Delta := \Delta \cup \{ini(C)|\ C \in CS\}; ind := true$
$\quad\quad\quad\quad\quad$ else
$\quad\quad\quad\quad\quad\quad$ if $irr(CS)$ then $\Delta := \Delta \cup \{ini(C)|\ C \in CS\}$; stop [No]
$\quad\quad\quad\quad\quad\quad$ else
$\quad\quad\quad\quad\quad\quad\quad$ factorize certain C_k in CS into $G_1, \ldots, G_h$
$\quad\quad\quad\quad\quad\quad\quad \Psi := \Psi \cup \{[PS \cup \{I\}, I]|\ I = ini(C), C \in CS, cls(C) < cls(C_k),$
$\quad\quad\quad\quad\quad\quad\quad\quad cls(I) > 0\} \cup \{[PS \cup \{G_j\}, G_j]|\ 1 \leq j \leq h\}$
if ind then [Yes] else [SC]

P-Sprem(Input: $G, CS = \{C_1, \ldots, C_r\}$; Output: R)
$\quad GS := \{G\}; RS := \phi$
$\quad$ while $GS \neq \phi$ do
$\quad\quad$ for all $T \in GS$ do in parallel
$\quad\quad\quad GS_T := \phi; R := T$
$\quad\quad\quad$ for i from r step -1 to 1 do
$\quad\quad\quad\quad RS:=$Split$(R); R:=$an element of RS
$\quad\quad\quad\quad GS_T := GS_T \cup (RS - \{R\})$
$\quad\quad\quad\quad R := prem(R, C_i)$
$\quad\quad\quad$ if $R \neq 0$ then $R := prem(G, CS)$; stop
$\quad\quad GS := \bigcup_{T \in GS} GS_T$

---

where Yes, No and SC indicate respectively that the theorem is true under the subsidiary conditions $\Delta \neq 0$, it is not true under the conditions $\Delta \neq 0$ and its hypotheses are self-contradictory.

As our current attention of mechanical theorem proving is mainly paid to confirm theorems, the computation of characteristic set of the hypothesis-polynomial set requires rather less time and the irreducible decomposition is generally unnecessary. The most time-consuming process is the formation of successive remainders of the conclusion-polynomials with respect to the characteristic set. The parallel computing can benefit basically from this part. Thus more polynomials CON contains, more parallel processors can be used. If only one polynomial is contained in CON, the parallel processing becomes possible only if the split happens. As argued in [6], it is of reason to consider the case *CON* contains more polynomials, and the split can be made possible for most examples.

If we turn our attention to prove theorems including all degenerate cases, or to find simplest non-degenerate conditions, or to disprove theorems, the further (irreducible) decomposition must be considered. In that case, parallel computation should be much better suited. We shall be concerned with this issue in our further research.

The timings of six test examples given in Table 2 show the parallel performance versus sequential computation for mechanical theorem proving in geometry. More examples can be found in [6].

4. Characteristic Series and Irreducible Characteristic Series

If a polynomial set *PS* has a zero decomposition of the form

$$Zero(PS) = \bigcup_{i=1}^{e} Zero(CS_i/J_i),$$

where CS_i is an ascending set, J_i is the product of initials of polynomials in CS_i for each i, $Zero(PS)$ denotes the set of all common zeros of polynomials in *PS*, and $Zero(CS_i/J_i) = Zero(CS_i) - Zero(J_i)$, then the sequence of ascending sets $CS_1, \ldots, CS_e$ will be called a *characteristic series* of *PS*. If all ascending sets CS_i in the decomposition are irreducible, then $CS_1, \ldots, CS_e$ will be called an irreducible characteristic series of *PS*.

The sequential algorithms CharSer and IrrCharSer in Appendix A compute respectively the characteristic series and irreducible characteristic series Ψ of any given polynomial set *PS*. Both algorithms can be structured as a multi-branch decomposition tree with the polynomial set *PS* at the root. Each son-node associates with an enlarged polynomial set produced by adjoining a polynomial, which is either an initial, or a previously removed factor or a factor of some factorized polynomial, into the polynomial set associated with its father-node. The algorithms consist mainly in computing the characteristic sets of all polynomial sets associated with the nodes. For large problems, especially those with number of variables much bigger than the number of polynomials in *PS*, the set Φ of enlarged polynomial sets expands rapidly due to the recursive generation of initials. This may produce unfortunately thousand branches of the tree and leads to a need of computing thousand characteristic sets. The work of Chou and Gao [1] and our past work were basically devoted to reduce branches of the decomposition tree. Even so the remaining ones are still of hundreds more and the computing time is frequently beyond the reasonable limit. A natural observation has been made that the decomposition tree can be more efficiently computed by parallelization. Namely, one computes different branches simultaneously using parallel processors. This introduces an obvious parallelization of all algorithms for computing characteristic series and irreducible characteristic series. The following is a parallelized version of the algorithms CharSer and IrrCharSer.

```
P-CharSer(Input: PS; Output: Ψ)
    Φ := {PS}; Ψ := φ;
    while Φ ≠ φ do
        for all QS ∈ Φ do in parallel
            CS := P-CharSet(QS)
            if nonc(CS) then
                Ψ := Ψ ∪ {CS}
                Γ_QS := {QS ∪ {I}| I = ini(C), C ∈ CS, cls(I) > 0}
        Φ := ⋃_{QS∈Φ} Γ_QS
```

P-IrrCharSer(Input: PS; Output: Ψ)

$\Phi := \{PS\}; \Psi := \phi$
while $\Phi \neq \phi$ do
    for all $QS \in \Phi$ do in parallel
        $CS := \text{P-CharSet}(QS)$
        if $nonc(CS)$ then
            if $irr(CS)$ then
                $\Psi := \Psi \cup \{CS\}$
                $\Gamma_{QS} := \{QS \cup \{I\}|\ I = ini(C), C \in CS, cls(I) > 0\}$
            else
                factorize certain C_k in CS into $G_1, \ldots, G_h$
                $\Gamma_{QS} := \{QS \cup \{I\}|\ I = ini(C), C \in CS, cls(C) < cls(C_k),$
                            $cls(I) > 0\} \cup \{QS \cup \{G_j\}|\ 1 \leq j \leq h\}$
    $\Phi := \bigcup_{QS \in \Phi} \Gamma_{QS}$

The timing statistics on six test problems for these two algorithms in comparison with their sequential version is given as Tables 3 and 4 in Section 6.

5. Irreducible Decomposition of Algebraic Varieties

The existing algorithms for decomposing an algebraic variety into irreducible components are difficult to be practically used due to their high sequential time complexity. There was even no complete implementation of those algorithms until one based on the computation of characteristic sets and Gröbner bases was made recently by the author. See Appendix A for a description of our used algorithm IrrVarDec, where the input PS is the defining set of a given variety to be decomposed and the output $\Psi = \{GS_1, \ldots, GS_k\}$ is a list of polynomial sets such that

$$Zero(PS) = \bigcup_{i=1}^{k} Zero(GS_i),$$

while each GS_i defines an irreducible algebraic variety.

The parallelization of this algorithm is rather straightforward and its advantage seems evident, for the algorithm contains mainly the computation of the irreducible characteristic series of the given defining set and a Gröbner basis for each ascending set in the series.

P-IrrVarDec(Input: PS; Output: Ψ)

$\Phi := \text{P-IrrCharSer}(PS); \Psi := \phi$
for all $CS \in \Phi$ do in parallel
    $r :=$ number of polynomials in CS
    $I_i =$ initial of the ith polynomial in CS
    $QS := CS \cup \{z_i I_i - 1|\ 1 \leq i \leq r\}$
    $GB :=$ Gröbner basis of QS with lexcial order $x_1 \prec \cdots \prec x_n \prec z_1 \prec \cdots \prec z_r$
    $GS := \{G|\ G \in GB, G \in \mathbf{K}[x_1, \ldots, x_n]\}$
    $\Psi := \Psi \cup \{GS\}$
while $\exists GS, GS' \in \Psi$ such that $\{R|\ R = prem(G, CS), G \in GS', R \neq 0\} = \phi$ do
    $\Psi := \Psi - \{GS\}$

Note that for the computation of Gröbner bases and the while-loop further parallel variants can be introduced, for which the detailed discussions are beyond the scope of this paper.

6. Implementation and Experimental Results

We have implemented all algorithms described in the previous sections with up to 12 parallel processors[1] in MAPLE system by utilizing several workstations for research purpose. These workstations are connected by a local area network (LAN) which is on the basis of ETHERNET with DECnet and TCP/IP as protocols. The data communication is realized via this network and a simple use of the MAPLE functions save and read which provide efficient means for writing and reading data to/from the disc files in an internal form. In our implementation we introduced six global variables for message passing, of which one controls the state of processing and the others coordinate the data. A few time-consuming functions with which the remember tables are associated such as those for factorizing polynomials over algebraic number fields are also passed along. The master processor executes the main program and dominates the whole processing on one machine while the slave processors execute their own subprograms on other machines and remain waiting status at the beginning. The creation and cancellation of remote processors are realized via a UNIX shell script. While parallel processing becomes possible in our algorithms, the master distributes about half of the jobs to the second processor. The second processor starts to perform the computation after receiving jobs and sends the results back to the master as soon as they are completed. If 4 processors are specified, the master and the second processor distribute further half of the jobs, respectively, to the third and fourth processors, and accordingly, if 8 or 12 processors are specified, the first 4 processors distribute half or one third of the jobs to each of the other processors while further parallel processing becomes possible.

Below we present five tables to show the timings and speed-up on six test problems (see Appendix B) for each parallelized algorithm in comparison with the sequential one. The experiments were made in MAPLE 4.3 running on Apollo DN3500/4000/4500 workstations under a UNIX operating system. Note that we used some variant of the described algorithms. For example, the so-called nearly characteristic sets are used instead of basic sets (see [5, 7]) and some characteristic sets are computed in weak sense. The timings are given in CPU seconds without exclusion of those for garbage collection, where the garbage collection occurs approximately after every 100,000 words (= 400,000 bytes) used. The case that the successively multiplied processors all remain free, i.e., the proposed algorithm makes none of the multiplied processors busy for that problem, is indicated by "—", and "Pr #" stands for the Problem Number. For Problem 9 in Table 5, the set HYP is considered as input polynomial set.

Table 1. Timings for CharSet and P-CharSet

Pr #	Serial time	2 Processors		4 Processors		8 Processors		12 Processors	
		time	speedup	time	speedup	time	speedup	time	speedup
1	9.53	9.63	0.99	9.00	1.06	12.13	0.79	12.25	0.78
2	11.07	9.63	1.15	10.58	1.05	11.03	1.00	9.93	1.11
3	44.98	41.50	1.08	36.40	1.24	33.58	1.34	35.57	1.26
4	85.05	75.78	1.12	77.62	1.10	76.80	1.11	—	—
5	1757.32	1000.57	1.76	887.22	1.98	791.23	2.22	718.60	2.45
6	3537.70	2364.60	1.50	1897.35	1.86	—	—	—	—

---

[1] Instead of 16, this number is chosen due to the limitation of available Apollo workstations in our institute.

Table 2. Timings for TheoremProver and P-TheoremProver

Pr #	Serial time	2 Processors time	speedup	4 Processors time	speedup	8 Processors time	speedup	12 Processors time	speedup
9	8.90	4.52	1.97	—	—	—	—	—	—
10	25.08	15.82	1.59	10.52	2.38	7.20	3.48	—	—
11	43.35	28.12	1.54	21.02	2.06	24.63	1.76	20.12	2.15
12	282.97	231.42	1.22	159.77	1.77	120.33	2.35	80.57	3.51
13	379.53	290.10	1.31	158.77	2.39	113.18	3.35	68.68	5.53
14	382.23	259.38	1.47	177.42	2.15	105.93	3.61	72.03	5.31

Table 3. Timings for CharSer and P-CharSer

Pr #	Serial time	2 Processors time	speedup	4 Processors time	speedup	8 Processors time	speedup	12 Processors time	speedup
1	202.53	184.03	1.10	111.43	1.82	73.32	2.76	59.90	3.38
7	321.07	219.93	1.46	210.05	1.53	157.42	2.04	102.75	3.12
2	332.57	224.00	1.48	104.78	3.17	66.60	4.99	78.92	4.21
3	562.35	254.78	2.21	173.62	3.24	127.32	4.42	123.80	4.54
8	856.02	506.98	1.69	323.28	2.65	303.77	2.82	115.32	7.42
4	6525.87	4047.70	1.61	1554.77	4.20	1296.50	5.03	611.15	10.68

Table 4. Timings for IrrCharSer and P-IrrCharSer

Pr #	Serial time	2 Processors time	speedup	4 Processors time	speedup	8 Processors time	speedup	12 Processors time	speedup
7	431.13	172.65	2.50	150.38	2.87	89.15	4.84	72.45	5.95
1	630.45	415.00	1.52	293.03	2.15	184.18	3.42	155.80	4.05
2	670.32	383.37	1.75	440.48	1.52	184.08	3.64	150.57	4.45
3	682.30	499.37	1.37	375.30	1.82	223.95	3.05	162.62	4.20
8	1208.03	678.30	1.78	298.90	4.04	327.15	3.69	172.57	7.00
4	6441.22	4135.78	1.56	2676.53	2.41	782.62	8.23	593.15	10.86

Table 5. Timings for IrrVarDec and P-IrrVarDec

Pr #	Serial time	2 Processors time	speedup	4 Processors time	speedup	8 Processors time	speedup	12 Processors time	speedup
7	450.97	420.55	1.07	185.42	2.43	137.45	3.28	106.25	4.24
3	656.32	425.02	1.54	419.32	1.57	231.28	2.84	175.57	3.74
1	862.05	590.47	1.46	532.92	1.62	208.85	4.13	202.92	4.25
8	986.23	717.25	1.34	313.22	3.15	169.33	5.82	200.33	4.92
9	4289.90	2263.12	1.90	1797.57	2.34	1549.25	2.78	809.48	5.23
4	6494.02	3290.37	1.97	1624.40	4.00	962.15	6.75	666.70	9.74

7. Encountered Problems and Concluding Remarks

From the tables given in the preceding section one sees that the parallelized algorithms give a significant speed-up for most test problems. The algorithm P-CharSet results in a little slow-down for one small problem, since the computation of every individual step is rather cheap while the data communication is relatively frequent and expensive in that case. However, this algorithm does reduce a certain amount of time for two larger problems too. To confirm the remainder set *RS* to be empty at the last step in CharSet for Problem 6, much time is needed for computing the remainders of 3 polynomials with respect to the last basic set. In this case, the parallel processing with both 2 and 4 processors yields a good performance. As the input set of this problem consists of only 4 polynomials, 8 and 12 processors do not lead to further speed-up. For other parallelized algorithms, 2, 4, 8 and 12 processors speed up respectively the computation 1.60, 2.49, 3.87 and 5.39 times at average. This speed-up is quite encouraging but still somewhat less ideal than what the author expected. In our investigation so far, we have encountered several problems on using parallelism, of which some can be mentioned as follows.

Unfull use of parallelism. The parallel features of our discussed algorithms have not been fully utilized and implemented. For example, both in P-IrrCharSer and in P-IrrVarDec, we need to check and remove some redundant polynomial sets from the decomposition. This process is often time-consuming and its parallelization has not yet been well handled. The parallelization of Gröbner bases and polynomial factorization over algebraic number fileds which are expensive in general have not been taken into account.

Data Communication. As mentioned already, the data communication in our current implementation relies on a local network and the reading/writing of MAPLE's internal files. This is not serious if the communication is not too frequent. But in any case it costs a certain amount of time.

Practical Complexity Analysis. The problem of optimal partition of jobs is a common problem encountered in all our experiments on parallelized algorithms. Without a good understanding of the practical complexity of each algorithm, we have difficulties to distribute jobs from the master to each individual slave. In our present implementation the distribution of jobs is essentially random. It happens very often that one processor is busy while all others remain fully free. Accordingly, the master needs often to spend much time to wait for results from its slaves. This is also one of the major reasons which lead to the rate of speed-up to be different form each other.

Loss of Sequential Strategies. In the sequential computation of characteristic series, irreducible characteristic series and irreducible decomposition of polynomial sets, we have used various strategies and techniques for cutting down redundant branches of the decomposition tree and for verifying the reducibility of polynomials and ascending sets at proper stages. This is very critical for reducing many unnecessary computations. In the parallelization, we have difficulties to parallelize these strategies and techniques. If we do parallelize, it may cause much communication while the waiting expenses seem to be high.

There are other two problems which are irrelevant to parallel processing but affect the accuracy of our comparison. First, in the computation of both characteristic series and irreducible characteristic series the time can vary very much with respect to the order in choosing the polynomial set QS from Φ as we used strategies to remove some redundant branches. A branch that is hard to compute may be removed for one order but not for the other. Therefore, if the unlucky case happens with more processors, the computing time in that case may be even more than that in the case of having fewer processors. Problem 8 in Tables 4 and 5 constitutes such a case. The second problem is caused by MAPLE's internal representation. In MAPLE system, some expressions are represented internally in a rather random form. The elements of a same set of polynomials may have different order at different time and the execution of a set of operations may thus have different order at different time as well. On the other hand, the characteristic series and irreducible characteristic series are all not unique. Then, using the same program with the same input at different time, the computation can produce different output and take thus different computing time. This fact may affect the accuracy of timings given in our tables.

In conclusion, we can draw the following remarks. The parallelization of the characteristic-set-based algorithms presented in this paper is natural and quite obvious. Our experiments have demonstrated significant gains of using parallelism for these algorithms. Up to this point, we are able to speed up the sequential computation more than 5 times at average by 12 processors for non-trivial test cases. In realizing parallelism many new issues and problems have been encountered as discussed partially in this section. The natural parallelization may not naturally speed up the computation in some cases. Further research is needed, in particular, for dealing with the encountered problems. It turns out to be worthwhile to improve, experiment and implement the described algorithms with multiprocessors on parallel machines. We believe that the power of characteristic-set-based algorithms can be considerably enhanced by means of parallelization.

References

[1] Chou, S. C. and Gao, X. S., *Techniques for Ritt-Wu's Decomposition Algorithm*, Technical Report TR-90-2, Department of Computer Sciences, University of Texas at Austin, 1990.

[2] Hodge W. V. D. and Pedoe, D., *Methods of Algebraic Geometry*, Vol. I, II, Cambridge University Press, Cambridge, 1947/1952.

[3] Ritt, J. F., *Differential Equations from the Algebraic Standpoint*, Amer. Math. Soc., New York, 1932.

[4] Ritt, J. F., *Differential Algebra*, Amer. Math. Soc., New York, 1950.

[5] Wang, D. M., *Characteristic Sets and Zero Structure of Polynomial Sets*, Lecture Notes, RISC-LINZ, Johannes Kepler University, Austria, 1989.

[6] Wang, D. M., *Some Notes on Algebraic Methods for Geometry Theorem Proving*, Preprint, RISC-LINZ, Johannes Kepler University, November 1990.

[7] Wang, D. M., *An Implementation of Characteristic Sets Method in* MAPLE, RISC-Linz Series no. 91-25.0, Johannes Kepler University, Austria, May 1991.

[8] Wu, W. T., *Basic Principles of Mechanical Theorem Proving in Elementary Geometries*, J. Sys. Sci. & Math. Scis., 4(1984), 207-235; J. Automated Reasoning, 2(1986), 221-252.

[9] Wu, W. T., *Basic Principles of Mechanical Theorem Proving in Geometries (Part on elementary geometries, in Chinese)*, Science Press, Beijing, 1984.

[10] Wu, W. T., *Some Recent Advances in Mechanical Theorem-Proving of Geometries*, Automated Theorem Proving: After 25 years, Contemp. Math., 29(1984), AMS, 235-242.

Appendix A. Sequential Algorithms

```
CharSet(Input: PS; Output: CS)
    QS := PS; RS := PS
    while RS ≠ φ do
        CS := BasicSet(QS); RS := φ
        if nonc(CS) then
            for each Q ∈ QS − CS do
                R := prem(Q, CS)
                if R ≠ 0 then RS := RS ∪ {R}
        QS := QS ∪ RS
```

BasicSet(Input: PS; Output: BS)

$QS := PS$; $BS := \phi$
while $QS \neq \phi$ do
    $B :=$ an element of QS with lowest rank; $BS := BS \cup \{B\}$
    if $cls(B) = 0$ then $QS := \phi$ else
        $QS := \{F \in QS - \{B\} \mid F \text{ is reduced wrt } B\}$

TheoremProver(Input: HYP, CON; Output: Δ, Yes, No or SC)

$\Psi := \{[HYP, 0]\}$; $\Delta := \phi$; $dd := -1$; $ind := false$
while $\Psi \neq \phi$ do
    $[PS, D] :=$ an element of Ψ; $\Psi := \Psi - \{[PS, D]\}$
    $CS :=$ CharSet(PS)
    if $nonc(CS)$ then
        $d :=$ number of parameters in CS
        if $d < dd$ then $\Delta := \Delta \cup \{D\}$
        else
            if $dd = -1$ then $dd := d$
            $RS := \phi$
            for each $G \in CON$ while $RS = \phi$ do
                $R := prem(G, CS)$
                if $R \neq 0$ then $RS := RS \cup \{R\}$
            if $RS = \phi$ then $\Delta := \Delta \cup \{ini(C) \mid C \in CS\}$; $ind := true$
            else
                if $irr(CS)$ then $\Delta := \Delta \cup \{ini(C) \mid C \in CS\}$; stop $[No]$
                else
                    factorize certain C_k in CS into $G_1, \ldots, G_h$
                    $\Psi := \Psi \cup \{[PS \cup \{I\}, I] \mid I = ini(C), C \in CS, cls(C) < cls(C_k),$
                      $cls(I) > 0\} \cup \{[PS \cup \{G_j\}, G_j] \mid 1 \leq j \leq h\}$
if ind then $[Yes]$ else $[SC]$

CharSer(Input: PS; Output: Ψ)

$\Phi := \{PS\}$; $\Psi := \phi$
while $\Phi \neq \phi$ do
    $QS :=$ an element of Φ; $\Phi := \Phi - \{QS\}$
    $CS :=$ CharSet(QS)
    if $nonc(CS)$ then
        $\Psi := \Psi \cup \{CS\}$
        $\Phi := \Phi \cup \{QS \cup \{I\} \mid I = ini(C), C \in CS, cls(I) > 0\}$

IrrCharSer(Input: PS; Output: Ψ)

$\Phi := \{PS\}$; $\Psi := \phi$
while $\Phi \neq \phi$ do
    $QS :=$ an element of Φ; $\Phi := \Phi - \{QS\}$
    $CS :=$ CharSet(QS)
    if $nonc(CS)$ then
        if $irr(CS)$ then
            $\Psi := \Psi \cup \{CS\}$
            $\Phi := \Phi \cup \{QS \cup \{I\} \mid I = ini(C), C \in CS, cls(I) > 0\}$
        else
            factorize certain C_k in CS into $G_1, \ldots, G_h$
            $\Phi := \Phi \cup \{QS \cup \{I\} \mid I = ini(C), C \in CS, cls(C) < cls(C_k),$
                $cls(I) > 0\} \cup \{QS \cup \{G_j\} \mid 1 \leq j \leq h\}$

```
IrrVarDec(Input: PS; Output: Ψ)
  Φ := IrrCharSer(PS); Ψ := ϕ
  for each CS ∈ Φ do
    r := number of polynomials in CS
    I_i = initial of the ith polynomial in CS
    QS := CS ∪ {z_i I_i − 1| 1 ≤ i ≤ r}
    GB := Gröbner basis of QS with lexical order x_1 ≺ ··· ≺ x_n ≺ z_1 ≺ ··· ≺ z_r
    GS := {G| G ∈ GB, G ∈ K[x_1,...,x_n]}
    Ψ := Ψ ∪ {GS}
  while ∃GS, GS' ∈ Ψ such that {R| R = prem(G, CS), G ∈ GS', R ≠ 0} = ϕ do
    Ψ := Ψ − {GS}
```

Appendix B. Source of Test Problems

This appendix indicates the source of our test problems which were chosen on a quite random basis. MM stands for the *Mathematics-Mechanization Research Preprints (1987-1990)* edited by the MM Research Center, Academia Sinica, China, from which 2 examples of Wu are taken. BGK stands for the paper by Boege, Gebauer and Kredel published in *J. Symbolic Computation*, 1(1986), 83-98, from which two examples of Hairer, one example of Butcher, one example of Katsura and one example of Gerdt *et al.* are taken. Three examples are taken from the collection by Kutzler and Stifter available as RISC-Linz Series no. 86-12.0, 1986, which is abbreviated as KS.

Problem 1. Example 3 on Page 6 in MM (No. 2) with variable ordering $x22 \prec x21 \prec x23 \prec x12 \prec x13 \prec x11 \prec x101 \prec x102 \prec x103 \prec x10$.

Problem 2. Example 2 on Page 87 in BGK with variable ordering $C2 \prec C3 \prec C4 \prec B4 \prec B3 \prec A43 \prec A32 \prec A42 \prec B2 \prec A21 \prec A41 \prec A31 \prec B1$.

Problem 3. Example 1 on Pages 92-93 in BGK with variable ordering $L1 \prec \cdots \prec L7$.

Problem 4. Example 4 on Pages 91-92 in BGK with variable ordering $U0 \prec \cdots \prec U4$.

Problem 5. Example 3 on Page 87 in BGK with variable ordering $C5 \prec C3 \prec C2 \prec C4 \prec A54 \prec A53 \prec A52 \prec A43 \prec A42 \prec A32 \prec B5 \prec B4 \prec B3 \prec B2$.

Problem 6. The polynomial set PS'' on Pages 30-31 in MM (No. 4) with variable ordering $X_{71} \prec X_{72} \prec X_{73} \prec X_{80}$.

Problem 7. Example 5 on Page 90 in BGK with variable ordering $B \prec C2 \prec C3 \prec A \prec B3 \prec B2 \prec A32 \prec B1$.

Problem 8. Example 2 on Page 87 in BGK with variable ordering $C2 \prec C3 \prec C4 \prec B4 \prec B3 \prec B2 \prec B1 \prec A21 \prec A31 \prec A32 \prec A41 \prec A42 \prec A43$.

Problem 9. An example on Pages 22-23 in author's Ph.D thesis (Academia Sinica, 1987) with variable ordering $u1 \prec \cdots \prec u6 \prec x7 \prec \cdots \prec x17$.

Problem 10. Example 043 in KS with variable ordering $y_2 \prec \cdots \prec y_{23}$.

Problem 11. An algebraic formulation of Gauss-Point Theorem. The hypothesis- and conclusion-polynomial sets consist of 24 and 3 polynomials, respectively, in 30 variables.

Problem 12. Pascal-Conic Theorem on Page 237 in Wu (Contemp. Math., **29**(1984), 235-241) with variable ordering $x_1 \prec x_2 \prec \cdots \prec x_{25}$.

Problem 13. Example 038 in KS with variable ordering $y_9 \prec y_{10} \prec y_{12} \prec y_{13} \prec y_{15} \prec y_{16} \prec y_{11} \prec y_{14} \prec y_{17} \prec y_{18} \prec y_{19} \prec y_{20}$.

Problem 14. Example 039 in KS with variable ordering $y_9 \prec y_{10} \prec y_{15} \prec y_{16} \prec y_{11} \prec y_{17} \prec y_{18} \prec y_{12} \prec y_{19} \prec y_{20} \prec y_{13} \prec y_{21} \prec y_{22} \prec y_{14} \prec y_{23} \prec y_{24} \prec y_{25} \prec y_{26}$.

Multiplication As Parallel As Possible

P.Lippitsch, K.C.Posch, R.Posch

Department of Applied Information Processing and Communications Technology,
Graz University of Technology, Klosterwiesgasse 32/I, A-8010 Graz, Austria.

Abstract

Public key encryption/decryption with modulus arithmetic is used in a variety of cryptographic applications. A tough computational problem arises due to the very long integer arithmetic needed. Usually serial-parallel multiplication is employed, which slows down speed to the order of $k = log_2(n)$, where n is the modulus. This paper describes a possible implementation of a method using parallel multiplication schemes at the order of $log(k)$ in combination with incomplete modulus reduction. As many partial products as possible are implemented in parallel (As Parallel As Possible, APAP). This leads to a mixture of linear and logarithmic time complexity. This paper describes a hardware solution for the APAP-multiplier with optimized dynamic adder cells without storage elements. Additional available silicon area can be traded against speedup in a smooth way. The underlying method is described and proved in [Posch90]. Using 664 bit long operands, a $40mm^2$ chip manufactured in 1.2 micron CMOS technology can reach an RSA encryption/decryption rate of 240 kbits/second.

Keywords: public key cryptosystems, cryptography, hardware algorithms, VLSI, parallel multiplier, high speed multiplier.

1 Encryption and fast multiplication

Long integer modulo multiplications constitute the main computational activity in public-key cryptosystems. Although this is true for several encryption methods, such as RSA [RSA78] or Dickson polynomials [Postl88], this paper concentrates on the RSA algorithm only. RSA encryption and decryption are characterized by the continued modulo multiplication

$$c \equiv C^x \pmod{n}$$

with c the plain text, and C the cipher text, or vice versa; x stands for the encryption or decryption key e or d, respectively. The number of binary digits is k. To meet security demands, key lengths of at least 664 bits are called for [Rivest84]. A usual assumption for the number of bits for x is $k/2$. These assumptions are sufficient for realistic cases and do not put any constraints on the security of the RSA scheme.

With $l = k/2$,

$$c \equiv C^x = C^{x_0} \cdot C^{2x_1} \cdot \ldots \cdot C^{2^{l-1}x_{l-1}} \pmod{n}, \quad x_i \in \{0,1\}.$$

Computation of c can be done with two multiplication pipes, one with l multiplications to obtain $C^2, C^4, \ldots, C^{2^l}$, plus another one with $l/2$ multiplications to compute c. To avoid excessive long operand, all multiplications are computed modulo n. With the use of two multiplication pipes, the encryption/decryption amounts to 3/4 modulo multiplications per bit [Posch90].

Considering technology standards of the early 90's, a 1-micron CMOS technology with one million transistors per chip and a clock rate of 60 MHz, the implementation of a fully parallel operating multiplier with an operand length of $k = 664$ bits is still not possible. Weak implementations of logic schematics deducted from the Wallace-tree multiplication scheme [Wallace64] lead to at least $k \cdot k = 440\,000$ full adders, each consisting of approximately 20 transistors. Even if one would neglect all storage elements and interconnecting problems, this is well beyond technology borders. On top of this, a carry-free adding scheme has to be employed for high speed operation. Roughly speaking, this would square the amount of full-adders, and thus lead to an even more unrealistic version of the multiplier. Even with a sophisticated implementation of the adders, as shown later in this paper, a parallel version of the multipliers would still amount to an area of $4000 mm^2$.

In contrast to this, a serial-parallel multiplier is by far too slow. It needs $2k$ time steps for multiplication and approximately another $2k$ steps for modulo reduction [Posch90]. With a clock rate of 60 MHz, a speed of only some 22 000 modulo multiplications per second can be reached. Most reported implementations of the RSA encryption scheme are in fact variations of a serial-parallel multiplier and show equivalent results [Orton87].

As an alternative, a reduced parallel multiplication scheme is proposed in [Posch90]. According to the available silicon area, as many partial products as possible are implemented on the chip in parallel. With this mixture of parallel and serial multiplication, any given (extra) chip area can be converted into (additional) rows of partial products. In this way, area consumption can be traded against time consumption rather smoothly.

Figure 1 gives an example with the multiplication of $149 \cdot (100 + 49)$, shown through all its subsequent steps. For the sake of clarity, only 1-Bits are identified, all the empty boxes represent 0-Bits. All $2k$ $(= 20)$ partial products are reduced to only 10 with the method described in figure 7. As the multiplier can only hold 6 partial products at a time, the remaining 4 are taken into account in junks of $b = 2$ in period 2 and 3. After finishing the linear part of the multiplication process in period 3, periods 4 and 5 serve for reduction of the partial products to the product, represented as a pair of numbers.

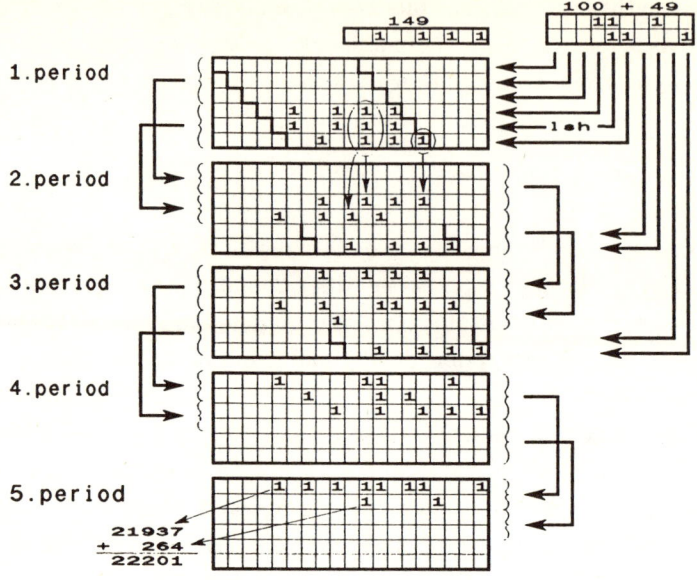

Figure 1: A reduced parallel multiplication scheme [Posch90].

Reduction to the modulus is computed after a full multiplication and can be reduced to the addition of approximately $2k$ extra partial products. The corresponding theorem is proved in [Posch90] and states the following result:

With
$$2^{k-1} < n < 2^k, \quad a < 2^{k+2}, \quad b < 2^{k+2},$$
the relaxed modulo multiplication
$$r' = a \cdot b \pmod{n} + p \cdot n, \quad \text{with} \quad p \in \{0, 1, 2\},$$
can be obtained by computing
$$r' = a \cdot b - \lfloor \lfloor a \cdot b \cdot 2^{-(k-1)} \rfloor \cdot \lfloor n^{-1} \cdot 2^{2k+4} \rfloor \cdot 2^{-(k+5)} \rfloor \cdot n$$

The truncation operations are simple bit extractions and do not cost time. The shifted versions of n^{-1} and $-n$ can be precomputed, as they change very rarely. In a symbolic register transfer language, modulo multiplication with this *relaxed residuum method* can be described the following way:

```
(A)    X[2k+4]     <=   a[k+2]     * b[k+2];
(B)    Q[2k+10]    <=   N1[k+5]    * [k+5]X;
(C)    NegR[2k+7]  <=   NegN[k+2]  * [k+5]Q;
(D)    x[k+2]      <=   NegR[k+2]  + X[k+2];
```

NegN holds a binary representation of $-n$, and N1 stores a binary representation of $\lfloor (1/n) \cdot 2^{2k+4} \rfloor$. $[j]y$ denotes the j leftmost bits of y, and $y[j]$ denotes the j rightmost bits of y. Line (A) of the algorithm costs the addition of $2k+4$ partial products. Lines (B) and (C) add another $k+5$ and $k+2$ partial products. Finally, one addition is added in line (D).

2 Complementary domino twin-adder

This chapter describes a possible implementation of the APAP-multiplier with dynamic adder cells and an interconnecting scheme for the twin-adders. The method shown in figure 1 reduces $3b$ partial products to $2b$ in one clock cycle. Thus, with every clock cycle b positions are available to be fed with new partial products. After $\lceil 2k/b \rceil$ clock cycles all partial products have been considered. Another $log_{3/2}(3b)$ steps are needed for completion of the multiplication. Modulo reduction adds approximately another $2 \cdot (k/b + log_{3/2}(3b))$ time steps.

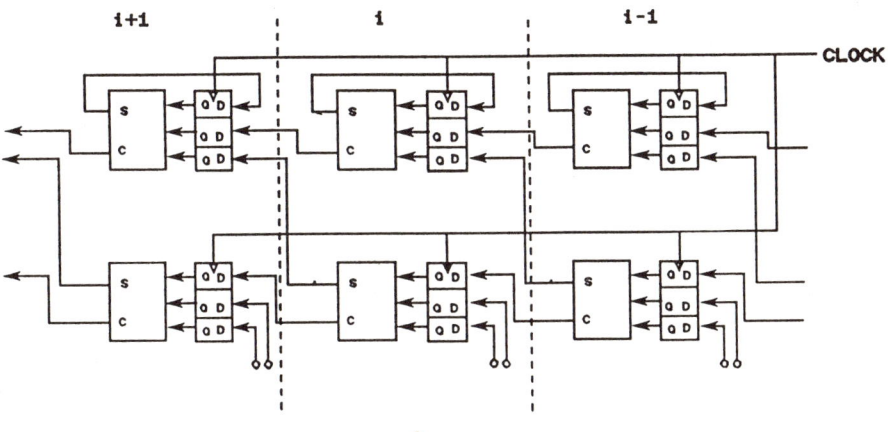

Figure 2: Implementation with logic modules

Figure 2 shows part of a possible implementation of a cluster of basic cells of the multiplier. Two rows of full adders lead to two free positions per bit in each clock cycle. This basic scheme would amount to 2 full adders and 6 storage elements per bit for 6 partial products in parallel. Simple logic implementations lead to at least 70 transistors per bit for 6 partial products. Employing dynamic logic techniques, a modified domino logic version yields far better results. Figure 3 shows a full adder in modified domino logic, using alternating p- and n-blocks. An equivalent logic schematic is shown in figure 4.

Two clocks, CLK1 and CLK2, control alternating discharge/precharge phases and evaluation phases. Input signals x and y must be valid during CLK1, $\bar{z}$ must be valid during CLK2. The outputs s and c are valid during the low phase of CLK2. Obviously,

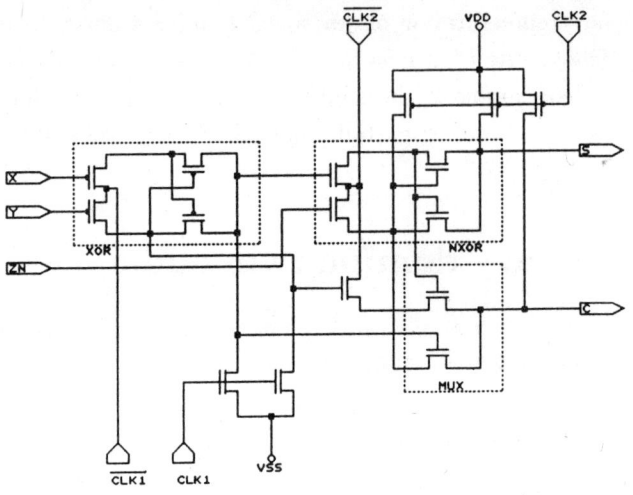

Figure 3: Circuit diagram of modified domino full adder

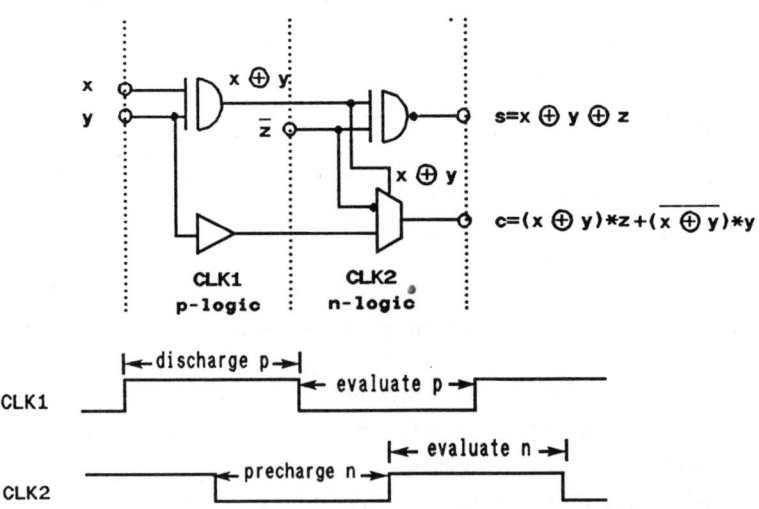

Figure 4: Logic diagram of modified domino full adder

this is the wrong time slot to feed s and/or c back to the input of the block. As shown in figure 5, adding a second full adder with an inverted time behavior yields a 4 phase clocking scheme. This twin-adder has time-compatible inputs and outputs.

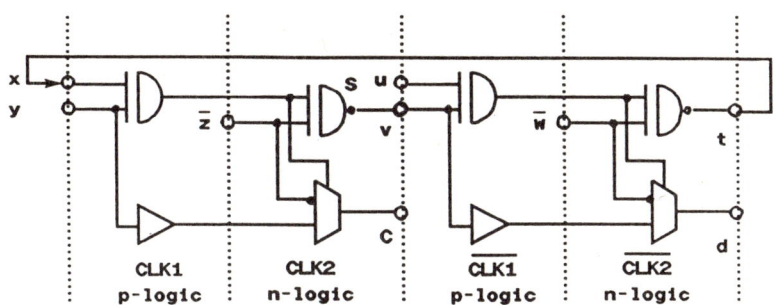

Figure 5: Twin-adder

With each full clock period, the two inputs $\bar{z}$ and $\bar{w}$ can be fed with two new partial products. In this way, a compression of 6 to 4 partial products is achieved in an analogous way as shown in figure 2. But, instead of approximately 70 transistors, now only 30 transistors are sufficient.

A second identical row can be added to this, if it produces outputs at the very moment they are needed. This is achieved with starting the second row 1/4 of a period earlier than the first one. Figure 6 shows four rows of double-adders, each one starting a 1/4 period earlier with computation. Sum-outputs proceed to the next available input at the same i^{th} position. Carry-outputs advance to the $(i+1)^{st}$ bit position. Figure 6 must be seen 3-dimensional, with the missing dimension being interpreted as the bit position i running from 0 to $k-1$.

As long as silicon space is available, twin-adder rows can be added, with each row adding another two free inputs per clock cycle for partial products.

For the following discussion, 4 rows are assumed to fit on one chip. Then, 8 free partial products are available at each cycle, or more precisely, two per quarter-cycle.

3 The APAP-multiplier

In terms of complexity all parallel multiplier schemes are equivalent [Takagi85] [Wallace64] [Dadda65]. All these schemes operate at the order of $log(k)$. The remaining questions concern the complexity of the bit adders as well as the regularity in the interconnections. We concentrate on the Wallace-tree which needs $log_{3/2}(k)$ operations for the result. The

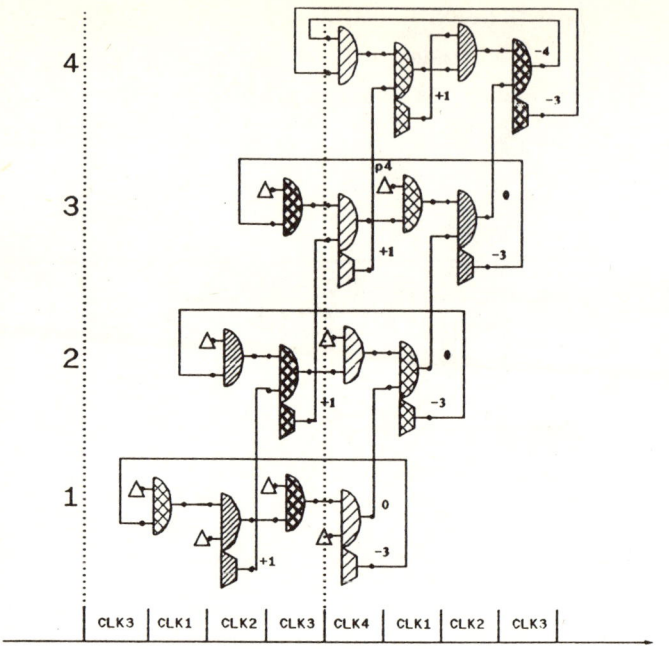

Figure 6: Connection of 4 rows of twin-adders

Wallace-tree involves a redundant number representation; it therefore needs $2k$ bits for a k bit number. The representation of the number x may be seen as $x = x_1 + x_2$, where x_1 and x_2 are conventional binary numbers. For continuous multiplication this representation can be used, but results in four times as many partial products since $x \cdot y = (x_1 + x_2) \cdot (y_1 + y_2) = x_1 \cdot y_1 + x_1 \cdot y_2 + x_2 \cdot y_1 + x_2 \cdot y_2$.

$4k$ partial products can be reduced to $2k$ by adding a mechanism that either uses the partial product as it is, or shifts it to the left by one bit position. The according decision is easy to compute. Figure 7 shows this by using an AND-gate and an EXOR-gate for each partial product.

Beginning from the low order end of the multiplicator b, each succeeding partial product must be shifted left by one position. As a more efficient alternative, one could also insert all partial produces at the same position, and shift all previous results to the right. In each clock cycle 4 bit positions from b are multiplied by $a1$ and $a2$. The resulting 8 partial products are inserted in the available inputs of the twin-adder block. Thus, in the same row all results must be shifted right by four or three positions respectively. This can be accomplished by a corresponding interconnecting network of wires.

As a result, the connection of the sum-output t, the carry-outputs c and d, and insertion of new partial products need 10 horizontal tracks in row 1, 4 horizontal tracks in row 2, 4 horizontal tracks in row 3, and 8 horizontal tracks in row 4.

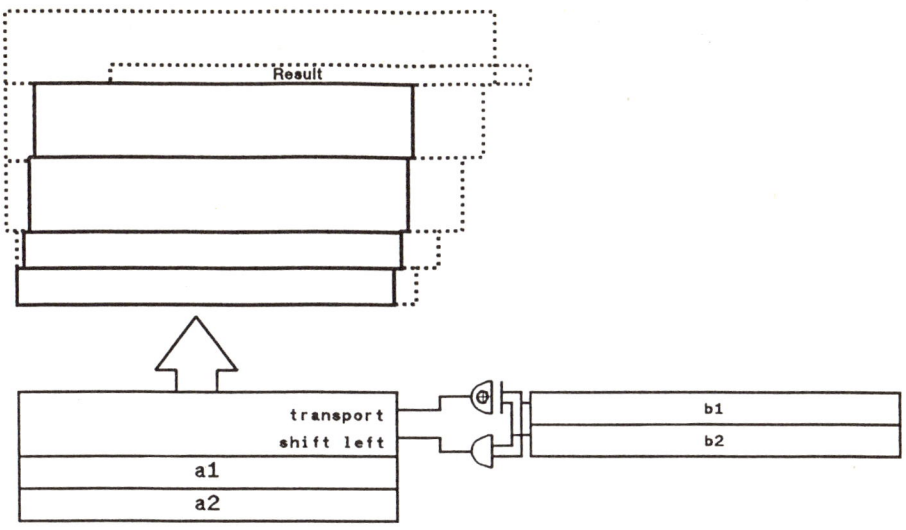

Figure 7: APAP-multiplier

One bit slice of the APAP-multiplier consists of 4 twin-adders, 8 multiplexers to feed the inputs, and 4 register cells for $a1$, $a2$, $b1$ and $b2$. 664 slices are stapled and result in a rather long thin layout. To get a better aspect ratio, it is broken down it into shorter pieces, and laid out in a snake-like way. Finally, clock drivers and signal drivers have to be added at appropriate places. A finite state machine controls the overall procedure.

4 Conclusion

The regular structure of the APAP-multiplier cuts down layout design time enormously. One has only to design a couple of tiles representing twin-adders in their various differently clocked versions. In addition to this, domino register structures and a few more basic logic structures with the same pitch width as the twin-adders are needed.

In 1.2 micron CMOS double metal technology, one bit slice of the described version of the APAP-multiplier amounts to a size of approximately $1000 \mu m \cdot 60 \mu m$, including all registers and multiplexers. In total, a 664 bit multiplier with modulo reduction can be implemented on a size of $40 mm^2$.

Approximately $4k = 2656$ partial products have to be summed up. These are loaded in junks of 8, resulting in 332 clock cycles. The logarithmic reductions add another $3 \cdot 5 = 15$ clock cycles. Assuming a clock rate of 60 MHz, about 180 000 modulo multiplications can be performed per second. According to [Posch90], RSA encryption can be computed at a speed of 3/4 modulo multiplications per bit. This amounts to an encryption/decryption rate of 240 kbits per second.

There is still a couple of open questions. Would the use of a different adder be more efficient? The twin-adder was the obvious solution to the underlying clocking scheme. But there are quite a few alternatives fitting the same 4-phase-clock. A 5-to-3-adder and a 7-to-3-adder were taken into account by the authors, but were not evaluated up to now. As the layout is very regular, a layout generator program with the parameters k, aspect ratio, area or time constraints, and clock rate seems to be of great interest as well.

References

[Orton87]   Orton G.A. et.al.: VLSI implementation of public-key encryption algorithms; Proceedings of Advances in Cryptology - CRYPTO '86, Springer-Verlag, (Berlin, 1987), pp 277-301.

[Posch90]   Posch K.C., Posch R.: Approaching encryption at ISDN speed using partial parallel modulus multiplication; Microprocessing and Microprogramming 29 (1990) 177-184.

[Postl88]   Postl H.: Fast Evaluation of Dickson Polynomials; Contributions to General Algebra 6, B.G. Teubner-Verlag, (1988).

[RSA78]   Rivest R., A. Shamir, L. Adlemann: A Method for Obtaining Digital Signatures and Public-Key Cryptosystems; Comm. of the ACM (Feb.1978), pp 120-126.

[Rivest84] Rivest R. L.: RSA Chips (Past/Present/Future); Proceedings of Advances in Cryptology, EUROCRYPT '84, Springer-Verlag, (Berlin, 1985), pp. 159-165.

[Takagi85] Takagi N. et al.: High-Speed VLSI Multiplication Algorithm with a Redundant Binary Addition Tree; IEEE Transactions on Computers, Vol C-34, No. 9, 1985.

[Wallace64] Wallace C. S.: A suggestion for a fast multiplier; IEEE Transactions on Electronic Computers, Vol. EC-13, Feb. 1964, pp. 14-17.

ON THE EXISTENCE OF AN EFFICIENT PARALLEL ALGORITHM FOR A GRAPH THEORETIC PROBLEM

Janez Žerovnik [1]
Inštitut za matematiko, fiziko in mehaniko
Jadranska 19, 61111 Ljubljana
Slovenia, Yugoslavia

Abstract

The problem of computing the relation Θ among edges of a graph is an important step in algorithms for several graph theoretic problems such as embedding graphs in Cartesian products, decomposing a graph into a product or deciding whether a graph is a binary Hamming graph. By an efficient parallel algorithm we mean one that takes polylogarithmic time using a polynomial number of processors. In this paper we show that there are efficient parallel algorithms for computing the relation Θ, for computing the equivalence classes of its transitive closure Θ̂ and for deciding whether a graph is a binary Hamming graph.

1 Introduction

The problem of computing the relation Θ among edges of a graph is an important step in algorithms for several graph theoretic problems such as embedding graphs in Cartesian products, decomposing a graph into a product or deciding whether a graph is a binary Hamming graph. Some of these problems, in particular the later one, have applications in coding and in communications theory.

A number of polynomial sequential algorithms for the problems mentioned were found recently. In this paper we show that some of these problems have efficient parallel

---

[1] On leave from Inštitut Jožef Stefan, Ljubljana. This work was done while the author was visiting the Institut für Mathematik und Angewandte Geometrie at the Montanuniversität Leoben, Austria, supported by the Research Council of Slovenia.

algorithms. By an efficient parallel algorithm we mean one that takes polylogarithmic time using a polynomial number of processors. A polylogarithmic time algorithm takes $O(\log^k n)$ parallel time for some constant integer k, where n is the problem size. Problems which can be solved within these constraints are universally regarded as having efficient parallel solutions and are said to belong to the class NC.

A subclass of problems of particular interest are those which have optimal parallel algorithms. An optimal parallel algorithm is an algorithm for which the product of the parallel time t with the number of processors p used is equal to the computation time of the optimal sequential algorithm for the problem.

We cannot expect an efficient solution for a problem with no known sequential polynomial time algorithm. Finding an efficient parallel solution for a problem with a polynomial time sequential algorithm, i.e. a problem of class P, seems more likely. There are, however, many such problems which do not seem to admit parallelization readily. These problems form the class of so called P–complete problems.

The rest of the paper is organized as follows. In the next section we briefly introduce the model of computation used. In the third section relevant graph theoretic definitions are given. Efficient parallel algorithms for the problem of computing the relation $\hat{\Theta}$ and for an application, the problem of deciding whether a graph is binary Hamming graph, are then outlined. The last section summarizes conclusions.

2 Model of Computation

Many formal models of parallel computation appear in the literature. There is no general consensus as to which of these is the best. Here we follow the suggestions of Gibbons and Rytter in the book [4], which shall be used as a reference for a number of parallel graph algorithms in the sequel. The idealized parallel computer known as P-RAM (parallel random access machine) is used. This model essentially neglects any hardware constraints which a highly specified architecture would impose. In this respect the model gives free rein in the presentation of algorithms by not admitting limitations which might be imposed by specific hardware. This implies that in any realization of a P-RAM model there will be all possible links between processors and memory locations. This complexity of linkages is not physically realizable in present-day hardware. On the other hand there are methods of simulating such an idealized computer on more reasonable networks (usually fixed networks of processors with the number of linkages from any processor being bounded). Moreover, this simulation only takes polylogaritmic time.

The P-RAM is a shared memory model. There are a number of processors working synchronously and communicating through the common random-access memory. Each processor is a uniform-cost random-access machine (RAM) with usual operations and instructions. The cost of arithmetical operations (addition, subtraction, equality predicate, etc.) is constant. The processors are indexed by the natural numbers $P_1, P_2, \ldots$ and they synchronously execute the same program (through the central main control). In one step each processor can access (either reading from it or writing to it) one memory location. We use the following natural convention for the P-RAM:

- Any number of processors can simultaneously read from the same memory location.

- No two processors may write simultaneously to the same memory location.

For this reason the model is sometimes called CREW P-RAM (concurrent read exclusive write P-RAM).

We describe the algorithms in a general style which needs no formal definition for the reader experienced in sequential programming. The admission of parallelism into algorithmic descriptions will be only through the use of the following type of statement:

for all $x \in X$ in parallel do $instruction(x)$

Here x is an element of the set X and execution of the statement consists of

(a) assigning a processor to each element $x \in X$

(b) executing, in parallel and by the assigned processors, all those operations specified by $instruction(x)$.

The execution stops when all the processors involved complete their (individual) computations. Two points need to be clarified, namely how the processors are assigned and how the processors are activated.

- (i) Assigning processors. We require that the elements of X are distinct integers or can be encoded by distinct integers. Then with every x we associate a processor $P_{code(x)}$ where $code(x)$ is the integer corresponding to x. We assume that the finite control directs processor i to work for $x = code^{-1}(i)$ in constant time.

- (ii) Activating processors. We presume that there is an initial threshold time of $\log p$ to activate p processors at the beginnning of any computation.

3 The Problem

A (finite simple undirected) graph G is defined by the pair (V, E) where $V = V(G)$ is the set of vertices and $E = E(G) \subset V \times V$ is the set of edges. Complexity of the input graph will be usually expressed in terms of $n = |V|$ and $m = |E|$. A path from x to y is a sequence of vertices $P = x_0, x_1, \ldots, x_l$ such that each pair x_i, x_{i+1} is connected by an edge and $x_0 = x$ and $x_l = y$. The length of the path is the number of edges, $|P| = l$. For any pair of vertices x, y we define the distance $d(x, y)$ to be the length of the shortest path between x and y. If there is no (finite) path, we define $d(x, y) = \infty$. A graph G is connected, if $d(x, y) < \infty$ for any pair of vertices x, y. As input for algorithms, a graph G is usually given in terms of the adjacency matrix A, which is defined as follows

$$A(x, y) = \begin{cases} 1 & (x, y) \in E(G) \\ 0 & (x, y) \notin E(G) \end{cases}$$

A relation Θ (first introduced by Djoković) among edges of G is defined as follows [7]: Let $e = (x, y), e' = (x', y') \in E$. Then $e\Theta e'$ if and only if

$$d(x, x') + d(y, y') \neq d(x, y') + d(x', y) \tag{1}$$

It is easy to see that Θ is reflexive and symmetric, but, in general, not transitive. By $\hat{\Theta}$ we shall denote the transitive closure of Θ, which is clearly an equivalence relation among edges of G.

The problem we will consider is computing the equivalence classes of the relation $\hat{\Theta}$. Computing the relation $\hat{\Theta}$ is a step in several graph algorithms. For example, this information is sufficient for constructing the canonical isometric embedding of G into a Cartesian product. If this embedding is surjective, it also gives a prime factorization of G with respect to the Cartesian product. Computing the relation $\hat{\Theta}$ is also a step in a polynomial (sequential) algorithm for factoring a graph [7]. In section 5 we shall discuss an application to the problem of deciding whether a graph is a binary Hamming graph. For definitions pertaining to embeddings into Cartesian products we refer to [5].

4 Computing Equivalence Classes of Θ

In this section an efficient parallel algorithm for computing the equivalence classes of the relation Θ is discussed. We follow a straightforward approach of [7], which does not give an optimal sequential algorithm (for the best known sequential algorithm see [2]), but is easily parallelizable. The sequential algorithm of Winkler is as follows:

1. Compute the distance matrix.

2. Test each pair of edges for the relation Θ.

3. Compute the equivalence classes of the transitive closure $\hat{\Theta}$ of Θ.

In the following subsections we shall show that each of these tasks has an efficient parallel algorithm.

4.1 Computing the Distance Matrix

It is easy to see that this task has an efficient solution. The algorithm we give needs $O(\log^2 n)$ time and uses $O(n^3/\log n)$ processors. This is not optimal since better than $O(n^3)$ time sequential algorithms are known. In comparison with the parallel algorithm of Kučera [4, page 25], which needs $O(\log^2 n)$ time on $O(n^3)$ processors and uses $O(n^3)$ space, our algorithm uses less space and less processors within the same time complexity.

Let us first define a sequence of distance functions d_j, $j = 2^i$ for $i \in \mathbb{N}$

$$d_1(x,y) = \begin{cases} 0 & x = y \\ 1 & \{x,y\} \in E(G) \\ \infty & \text{otherwise} \end{cases} \qquad (2)$$

and

$$d_{2j} = \min_{z \in V(G)} \{d_j(x,z) + d_j(z,y)\} \qquad (3)$$

The d_j's are distance functions, with the same values as the distance function d on the pairs of vertices, which are close enough. On the other hand, d_j ignores distances which are bigger than j, and has infinite value for such pairs of vertices. More formally

Lemma 1

$$d_j(x,y) = \begin{cases} d(x,y) & d(x,y) \leq j \\ \infty & \text{otherwise} \end{cases} \qquad (4)$$

Proof: We prove the assertion by induction. Clearly the statement is true for d_1.

Now assume the assertion is true for $i \leq j$. Consider first the case $d(x,y) \leq 2j$. This implies that there is a path P connecting x and y of length $\leq 2j$. Then there is a vertex on P, say z, such that $d(x,z) \leq j$ and $d(z,y) \leq j$. Hence,

$$d_{2j}(x,y) \leq d(x,z) + d(z,y) = d(x,y) \leq 2j \qquad (5)$$

This implies $d(x,y) = d_{2j}(x,y)$ since $d(x,y) > d_{2j}(x,y)$ would lead to contradiction.

In the second case let us assume $d(x,y) > 2j$, i.e. any path from x to y has length at least $2j + 1$. If

$$d_{2j}(x,y) \leq 2j$$

then there has to be a z such that

$$d_{2j}(x,y) = d_j(x,z) + d_j(z,y)$$

Since, by induction $d_j(x,z) = d(x,z) \leq j$ and $d_j(z,y) = d(z,y) \leq j$, there is a path from x to y through z of length $\leq 2j$, which implies $d(x,y) \leq 2j$, a contradiction. Q.E.D.

Since $\max d(x,y) \leq n-1$ for any connected graph G, we have $d_j = d$ for $j \geq n-1$.

Remark: With essentially the same reasoning one could prove that a similar lemma holds in the case of weighted graphs where the length of a path is defined as the sum of weights of its edges and the distance between two vertices is defined as the length of a minimal path. In this case any path consisting of less than $2j$ edges can be obtained by concatenating two paths consisting of no more than j edges.

The following algorithm computes the distance matrix $d(x, y)$.

for $i = 1$ **to** $\lceil \log n \rceil$ **do** compute d_{2i} using d_i

where computing d_{2i} from d_i is the following procedure

for all $x, y \in V(G)$ **in parallel do** $d_{2i} = \min_{z \in V(G)}(d_i(x, z) + d_i(z, y))$

Only two 'distance' matrices are needed in the same time, therefore space complexity of the algorithm is $O(n^2)$.

Since min can be computed in $O(\log n)$ time using $O(n/\log n)$ processors [4, page 12] the overall time complexity of the algorithm is $O(\log^2 n)$ and the algorithm uses $O(n^3/\log n)$ processors. This is not optimal, since there are $O(n^3)$ (and better) time sequential algorithms. For example, a run of the breadth-first search algorithm from any vertex would work in $O(nm) = O(n^3)$ time. According to [6, page 95] an $O(n^3(\log \log n/\log n)^{1/3})$ algorithm was found by Fredman. Another approach is to quickly compute the powers A^2, A^4, ... of the adjacency matrix using the Strassen's method which gives an $O(n^{\log 7} \log n)$ time sequential algorithm.

4.2 Computing the Relation Θ

For showing that this task has an efficient solution we can use the straightforward algorithm of Winkler [7]. The solution is not optimal since the amount of work needed for the best known sequential algorithm known is of order $O(mn)$ [2], while the amount of work needed for Winkler's algorithm is $O(m^2)$. On the other hand, the approach of Winkler is convenient for parallel implementation. We may independently check each pair of edges for being in relation Θ which gives a constant time algorithm even on the CREW P-RAM model. (Associate a processor to each pair of edges, i.e. to each entry of a matrix which represents the relation Θ.)

for all $x = (x_1, x_2), y = (y_1, y_2) \in E(G)$ **in parallel do**
   if $d(x_1, y_1) + d(x_2, y_2) \neq d(x_1, y_2) + d(x_2, y_1)$
    then $\Theta(x, y) := 1$
    else $\Theta(x, y) := 0$

The space needed for this algorithm is $O(m^2)$. It uses $O(m^2)$ processors and has constant time complexity.

4.3 Computing the Transitive Closure of a Relation

It is easy to see that computing the equivalence classes of a reflexive and symmetric relation is essentially equivalent to computing the connected components of the graph which corresponds to the relation in a natural way. More formally, let H be a graph with vertices $V(H) = E(G)$ (vertices of H are the edges of G) and two vertices of H, $e, f \in E(G)$ are connected if $e\Theta f$. $((e,f) \in E(H) \iff e\Theta f)$. The transitive closure of Θ then corresponds to a graph $\hat{H}$ in which every connected component (of H) is extended to a complete graph.

It is known that the connected components of a graph with m vertices are computable in $O(\log^2 m)$ time with $O(m^2/\log^2 m)$ processors by the algorithm of Chin, Lam and Chen, which is efficient and even optimal [4, page 32].

5 An Application - Recognizing Binary Hamming Graphs

A graph G is called binary Hamming graph if each vertex of G can be assigned a binary address of fixed length such that the Hamming distance between two addresses equals the length of a shortest path in G between the corresponding vertices.

The problem of recognizing and labeling binary Hamming graphs first arose in coding theory and in communications theory. This application was probably one of the reasons for early interest in embedding graphs into products of complete graphs [8].

In this section we show that the problem has an efficient parallel algorithm. The algorithm is based on the following theorems, which we give in the form as they appear in [3]. Let Q_r denote a hypercube graph of dimension r, $V(Q_r) = \{0,1\}^r$ and two vertices are connected if they differ in exactly one coordinate.

Theorem 1 (Graham,Polak) *G is a binary Hamming graph if and only if G is an isometric subgraph of Q_r for some r.*

Theorem 2 (Winkler) *G is an isometric subgraph of some Q_r iff G is bipartite and the relation Θ is transitive.*

A straightforward approach is to

1. Check bipartiteness of G.

2. Compute the relation Θ.

3. Check whether Θ is transitive.

It is known that this approach is not optimal in sequential model of computation since $O(mn)$ time sequential algorithm is known [3].

We already know that task 2 has an efficient parallel algorithm (see 4.2). In this section we show that also task 1 and task 3 admit efficient parallel solutions.

5.1 Checking whether G is Bipartite

We believe it is likely that there are known efficient algorithms for checking whether a graph is bipartite, but, since we do not have a reference, we include a proof.

First we define the relation β as follows: Any pair of vertices of distance 2 in G is in relation β, i.e.
$$d_G(u,v) = 2 \iff u\beta v$$

Now consider the following algorithm:

1. compute $G_1, G_2, \ldots, G_k$, the connected components of G
2. **for** all connected components G_i **do in parallel**
    2.1. compute the relation β on G_i
    2.2. compute the transitive closure of β on G_i
    2.3. **if** the transitive closure of β has exactly 2 equivalence classes **then** G_i is bipartite
3. **if** all G_i are bipartite **then** G is bipartite **else** G is not bipartite

We claim that the algorithm is efficient and that it is correct. First recall from section 4.3 that computing a transitive closure of a relation is equivalent to computing the connected components of an auxiliary graph and there is an efficient algorithm for the later problem. Computing the relation β is straightforward (for example using the second power of the adjacency matrix) and is highly parallel. For deciding the condition in statement 3, at most $O(\log k)$ ($k < n$) time is sufficient for collecting the partial results.

For correctness we argue as follows:

Lemma 2 *Assume G is connected. Then the transitive closure of β has two equivalence classes if and only if G is bipartite.*

Proof: Fix any vertex v of G. All the vertices of even distance from v have to be of the same class. The vertices of odd distance are clearly elements of the same class as the neighbours of v are. Hence, there are at most two distinct equivalence classes of β in a connected graph G.

It is well known that a graph is bipartite exactly when there is no odd cycle in G. Now assume there is an odd cycle C in G. From definition of β immediately follows that all the vertices on C belong to the same equivalence class. Let v be any vertex on C. There are also some neighbours of v on C, hence the two possible classes are a single class.

For the other direction assume there is only one equivalence class on G. Then for any vertex v there must be a pair of vertices such that one, say u, is of odd distance from v and the other, say w is of even distance from u and $d_G(u,w)$ is even. But then we have an odd cycle in G and G is not bipartite. **Q.E.D.**

Since a graph is bipartite exactly if each of its connected components is bipartite, we conclude that

Lemma 3 *Deciding whether a graph is bipartite has an efficient parallel solution.*

5.2 Checking $\Theta = \hat{\Theta}$

There is a sequential algorithm for this task which uses only $O(mn)$ time when the underlying graph G is bipartite [3]. In general a straightforward $O(m^2)$ time algorithm works as follows: compute the connected components of Θ (i.e. the equivalence classes of $\hat{\Theta}$) in $O(m^2)$ time and check on the way whether the new edge is connected (i.e. is in relation Θ) to every other edge already in the current connected component.

To prove that checking whether $\Theta = \hat{\Theta}$ has an efficient parallel solution we use a trivial algorithm, which for all triples checks if the transitivity rule is violated. The correctness of this algorithm follows readily from the definition of transitivity. Furthermore, it is easy to see that for any given triple of pairwise distinct elements x, y, z and any symmetric relation R the implication $xRy \& yRz \Rightarrow xRz$ does not hold if and only if exactly two of the relations xRy, yRz and xRz are true (i.e. =1) and exactly one is false (i.e. =0). Therefore, the following statement checks the transitivity of a symmetric relation Θ:

for all $x, y, z \in E(G)$ **in parallel do**
    if $\Theta(x,y) + \Theta(y,z) + \Theta(x,z) = 2$ **then** send('NOT transitive')

The algorithm is obviously highly parallel. The testing can be done in constant time on $O(m^3)$ processors using $O(m^2)$ space. For collecting the result a factor of $O(\log m)$ is sufficient on CREW P-RAM model.

6 Conclusions

We showed that the two problems related to computing the relation Θ among edges of a graph have efficient parallel algorithms. In particular, efficient parallel computation of the relation Θ enables us to efficiently find canonical embeddings of graphs into Cartesian products and to efficiently decide whether a graph is a binary Hamming graph. W. Imrich conjectured that the problem of factoring a graph with respect to the Cartesian product is also efficiently parallelizable. The conjecture was recently proved [9].

We focused on questions, whether the tasks considered are efficiently parallelizable. In most cases we did not try to find the optimal solution. A natural extension of the present work is to find optimal parallelizations for the problems mentioned in this paper, or to show that optimal parallel algorithms do not exist. A small step in this direction is the algorithm for computing the distance matrix, which is computed with the same time complexity while using fewer processors and less space than the algorithm of Kučera.

Acknowledgment: This work was done while the I was visiting Wilfried Imrich at the Montanuniversität Leoben. I want to thank him for his hospitality and interesting discussions. Special thanks are due to Johann Hagauer, who found a counterexample to an earlier proof of Lemma 3.

References

[1] A.V.Aho, J.E.Hopcroft, J.D.Ullman: The Design and Analysis of Computer Algorithms, Addison-Wesley, Reading, Mass. 1974

[2] F.Aurenhammer, J.Hagauer: Computing Equivalence Classes among the Edges of a Graph with Applications, (to appear in Discrete Mathematics)

[3] F. Aurenhammer, J.Hagauer: Recognizing Binary Hamming Graphs in $O(|V||E|)$ time, (to appear in Discrete Mathematics)

[4] A.Gibbons, W.Rytter: Efficient Parallel Algorithms, Cambridge University Press 1988

[5] W.Imrich: Embedding Graphs into Cartesian Products, Graph Theory and Applications: East and West, Annals of the New York Academy of Sciences, vol. 576, (1989) 266- 274

[6] R.E.Tarjan: Data Structures and Network Algorithms, CMBS-NSF Regional Conference Series in Applied Mathematics, SIAM, Philadelphia 1983

[7] P.M.Winkler: Factoring a graph in polynomial time, European Journal of Combinatorics 8 (1987) 209-212

[8] P.M.Winkler: Isometric Embeddings in Products of Complete Graphs, Discrete Applied Mathematics 7 (1984) 221-225

[9] J.Žerovnik: A Simple Algorithm for Factoring a Cartesian-Product Graph, Arbeitsbericht 5/1991, Institut für Mathematik und Angewandte Geometrie, Montauniversität Leoben

On the Multi-Threaded Computation of Modular Polynomial Greatest Common Divisors*

Wolfgang Küchlin
Department of Computer and Information Science
The Ohio State University
Columbus, OH 43210-1277, U.S.A.
⟨Kuechlin@cis.ohio-state.edu⟩

Abstract

We present a parallelization of the Brown-Collins algorithm in the PARSAC-2 Computer Algebra system, and we describe the design of our *S-threads* parallelization environment. PARSAC-2 is a parallel extension of SAC-2 built upon multiple *threads of control* provided by S-threads. The Brown-Collins algorithm computes the g.c.d. and its co-factors of two polynomials in $Z_p[x_1, \ldots, x_r]$, $r \geq 2$, by first reducing the problem to multiple g.c.d. calculations of modular homomorphic images (MHI) in $Z_p[x_2, \ldots, x_r]$, and then recovering the result by interpolation. After studying timings of the SAC-2 implementation, we first parallelize the interpolation algorithm, and then we parallelize the main MHI loop by executing the modular g.c.d. computations concurrently. We determine speed-up's and speed-up efficiencies over a wide range of polynomials.

1 Introduction

1.1 Overview

This paper makes contributions in the two areas of programming environments for parallel symbolic computation, and parallel algebraic algorithms. It constitutes a progress report on both the development of the *S-threads* parallelization environment [Küc90b], and the parallelization of the Brown-Collins algorithm [Bro71] for the computation of greatest common divisors (g.c.d.'s) of multivariate modular polynomials.

This work is part of our effort to create PARSAC-2 [Küc90a], a parallel extension of the SAC-2 Computer Algebra System [CL]. The main goal in the construction of PARSAC-2 is to explore the practicality and effectiveness of a parallel Computer Algebra system built on light-weight processes or *threads of control*[1]. Symbolic computation suffers from extreme data-dependence, i.e. unpredictability of control-flow, so that a design based on light-weight processes is especially attractive. On shared-memory multiprocessors, such as the Encore Multimax used in our experiments, the operating system can

---

*This material is based upon work supported by the National Science Foundation under Award No. CCR-9009396.

[1] For an introduction to the concept of threads see e.g. [AG89, p. 272], or [CD88].

map light-weight processes to processors at run-time with little overhead[2]. Threads can therefore be *forked* and *joined* according to the dynamic structure of the computation, and independent of the hardware.

PARSAC-2 contains three major bodies of software: the *S-threads* system provides threads of control for parallel *symbolic* computation; SAC-2 algorithms[3], executing unmodified on single threads, form the algebraic kernel; finally, there is a growing number of multi-threaded, parallel algorithms, such as the modular polynomial g.c.d. algorithm presented here.

The S-threads environment is currently implemented on top of C Threads [CD88], as provided by the Mach operating system [ABB+86]. The organization and user interface of Release 1 of S-threads has previously been described in [Küc90b]. In this paper we present two new *fork* constructs, one very light-weight and one heavy-weight, and we describe the principles of threads-based mark-and-sweep garbage collection now incorporated in Release 2. We also sketch how the environment can be extended by heavy-weight processes so that it can utilize networks of multi-processor workstations.

For the algorithmic contribution of this paper, we present a parallelization of the modular case of the Brown-Collins algorithm (algorithm **P** in [Bro71, p. 494]), starting with Collins' SAC-2 implementation **MPGCDC**. The algorithm obtains the g.c.d. and cofactors of two polynomials in $Z_p[x_1, \ldots, x_r]$ by recursively computing, in parallel, k g.c.d.'s, and their cofactors, of homomorphic evaluation images in $Z_p[e_i, x_2, \ldots, x_r]$, $1 \leq i \leq k$, followed by parallel interpolation based on the Chinese Remainder Algorithm.

The Brown-Collins algorithm in $Z[x_1, \ldots, x_r]$ (algorithm M in [Bro71, p. 491] or algorithm **IPGCDC** in SAC-2) is inherently parallel on several levels: First, there is a top-level *coefficient MHI scheme*, which generates multiple modular polynomial g.c.d. computations in $Z_p[x_1, \ldots, x_r]$, deriving the parallelism from the length of the coefficients of the input polynomials. A multi-threaded implementation of this part is presented in a companion paper [Küc91a]. Second, for each multivariate g.c.d. computation in $Z_p[x_1, \ldots, x_r]$, there is a *variable MHI scheme*, which generates multiple recursive g.c.d. computations in $Z_p[x_2, \ldots, x_r]$, deriving the parallelism from the number of variables and the degree of the g.c.d. in each variable. This part is the subject of the present work. Both implementations can be easily combined in PARSAC-2.

In the following, we shall first briefly review other work in this area. Then, in Section 2, we describe Release 2 of the S-threads system. In Section 3 we present the parallelization of **MPGCDC** in several steps: after sketching the sequential algorithm in Section 3.1, we carefully time its main MHI loop in Section 3.2. Based on these timings, we then proceed to parallelize the polynomial interpolation algorithm in Section 3.3, and finally we parallelize the main MHI loop in Section 3.4. Our experiments are summarized in Figures 2, 3, and 4.

---

[2] We measured 5% overhead when executing a parallel integer multiplication algorithm with 243 threads on a single processor Sun SLC [KLN91].

[3] SAC-2 was translated to C from its native ALDES [Loo76], using software written by Hoon Hong.

1.2 Other Work

The building of parallel Computer Algebra systems was studied in the Ph.D. theses of Watt [Wat86], Ponder [Pon88c], Roch [Roc89], and Seitz [Sei90]. Ponder discussed several parallel algorithms [Pon89] and also conducted a survey of parallel algorithms and systems [Pon88a, Pon88b]. A collection of several approaches can also be found in the proceedings of the workshop CAP'88 [DDF89]. To date, no system except PARSAC-2 seems to have been built for a threads environment.

An overview of approaches to sequential and parallel algorithms for the computation of polynomial g.c.d.'s can be found in [Wat86]. Among the sequential algorithms, we mention the modular method of Brown and Collins [Bro71], the p-adic EZ-GCD of Moses and Yun [MY73], and the heuristic GCDHEU by Char et al. [CGG84]. Wang's EEZ-GCD algorithm [Wan80] improves the p-adic method. Zippel has improved the modular [Zip79] and the p-adic method [Zip81] for sparse polynomials by probabilistic means.

Parallel polynomial g.c.d. algorithms were given e.g. by Borodin et al. [BvzGH82] and Kaltofen [Kal85, Kal89]. Davenport and Robert [DR85] design a parallel g.c.d. algorithm for univariate polynomials over Z_p (for small p of at most 10 bits or so), using a systolic array to exploit fine-grained parallelism in Euclid's algorithm. Watt [Wat86] presents a parallel version of Zippel's sparse g.c.d. algorithm. Char [Cha90] reports on executing Watt's algorithm on three Maple processes connected by Linda [CG89]. Weber [Web91] outlines methods for the parallelization of GCDHEU.

The Brown-Collins algorithm is still state-of-the-art for dense polynomials, although it is exponential in the number of variables. Zippel's improvement makes the algorithm tractable for sparse polynomials in many variables by replacing nearly all dense polynomial interpolations by sparse ones. The sparse g.c.d. algorithm still follows the main Brown-Collins design, and still uses some dense interpolations to guess the term structure of the result polynomials. Our present results will therefore still be useful in a parallelization of Zippel's algorithm, which is left for future work.

2 The S-threads Parallelization Environment

The S-threads system [Küc90b] contains a *threads subsystem* providing threads of control, and a *space subsystem* providing list memory handling. The system has been left open on purpose: Synchronization primitives are not covered and list handling only provides a list cell allocation function. The general assumption is that the threads subsystem will be implemented on top of some parallel computation substrate that also provides synchronization, and that an existing sequential list processing system will be imported into the space subsystem to support a particular application. Our current implementation of S-threads is connected to C Threads and to the list processing package of SAC-2.

Every S-thread is an extension grafted onto a substrate C thread, which makes the S-thread about 25% "heavier" (i.e. slower to fork and join) than the substrate. S-threads are thus largely compatible with C Threads. Pure C threads can be used alongside with S-threads to perform computations which may manipulate, but do not allocate, list cells. S-threads can also be synchronized with the mutex and condition handling primitives of the C Threads environment.

Under S-threads, global heap memory is divided into *pages*, which are then dynamically allocated by threads as local page-sets (paged heap segments). We thus have a global page-pool with a free-list of pages, and each S-thread owns a local page-set, constituting its private segment of list memory, with a local unlocked available cell list. Allocating cells by pages alleviates the bottleneck problem through decreased demand for the allocation lock, and by amortizing page allocation cost over many list cells.

We have the following basic mechanisms for passing a list structure L, stored on page-set P, from thread A to thread B:

1. *By reference:* a reference to L is passed.

2. *By transfer:* (a reference to L is passed and) P is transferred from A to B.

3. *By copy and transfer:* L is first copied to L' on a new page-set P'; then L' is passed by transfer.

These three mechanisms for passing list parameters give rise to the following four modes for parallel procedure calls in S-threads:

1. *Reference in—transfer out:* List input parameters are passed by reference from parent to child, while list output parameters are transferred back on the entire page-set M owned by the child upon termination.

2. *Reference in—copy transfer out:* Input parameters are passed by reference; output parameters are passed by copy and transfer.

3. *Copy transfer in—transfer out:* List input parameters are passed by copy and transfer; output parameters are passed by transfer.

4. *Copy transfer in—copy transfer out:* Both input and output list parameters are passed by copy and transfer.

The most critical issue in choosing a mode is that of list *lifetime:* if a thread creates a list cell whose lifetime is longer than that of the thread, then the page containing the cell must be transferred to a thread with a longer lifetime (e.g. the parent). In functional programs, this affects only the output parameters, whose preservation is supported in all modes. In case a thread updates a global data-structure such as a symbol table, its entire page-set may have to be saved in order to protect the cells with longer lifetime. Modes 1 and 3 extend the lifetime of all list cells beyond that of the child, and therefore enable global list updates. However, we suggest the use of dedicated monitor threads to construct and maintain a global structure in their local heap segment.

If we assume a functional programming style, the only important issues are garbage collection support and parallel grainsize. The main problem with garbage collecting parallel processes is that pointers between different memory segments *(cross references)* lead to synchronization requirements (cf. [Küc91b]). If the processes form logical *tasks* without cross references, their memories can be garbage collected by running any sequential algorithm concurrently on the different memories.

In S-threads, functions called in modes 1 and 2 form threads of control in shared memory, because their input is a reference into the parent's memory. Functions called in modes 3 and 4 effectively form *tasks* with private memory, as long as all their children are also forked in these modes. A task can now garbage collect independently. A task can also be executed on a remote processor in a network if page transfer is implemented by message passing instead of by reference (cf. [KS88]). Modes 2 and 4 result in *preventive garbage collection* of the child thread or task. Preventive garbage collection lets every process clean up after itself, and thus closely, and more predictably, attributes garbage collection cost to the cell consuming algorithms.

Our heap design thus suggests two new techniques for parallel garbage collection:

1. *Preventive GC:* Upon thread exit, we copy list output parameters to new pages, thus implicitly compacting them, and subsequently return the private heap segment to the pool of free pages.

2. *Thread independent GC:* We run a traditional sequential GC algorithm independently on each thread which does not have external references into its heap segment.

S-threads provides three different fork constructs, which support parallel procedure calls of different parallel grain-sizes and different garbage collection ability:

1. *Pseudo fork:* A very light-weight fork, interpreted as a procedure call unless there is hardware support; uses parameter passing mode 1 or 2.

2. *Thread fork:* A light-weight fork, interpreted as a C thread fork; uses mode 1 or 2.

3. *Task fork:* A heavy-weight fork, interpreted as a C thread fork on shared-memory machines; it may be interpreted as a process fork, a Linda "eval" [CG89], or a remote procedure call on distributed architectures. It uses mode 3 or 4.

All forks are syntactically very similar and can easily be exchanged for one another. This is useful for adapting software to a different hardware with a different parallel grainsize, or for controlling the number of parallel processes. For example, a run-time load balancer could dynamically replace thread-forks by pseudo-forks.

The level of support for garbage collection depends on the grainsize of the process. Light-weight procedures, which do not use many list cells, can use preventive GC alone. (The pseudo fork construct, in mode 2, supports preventive garbage collection in sequential programs.) Procedures which do use very many list cells, such as high-level sequential SAC-2 algorithms, are necessarily heavy-weight. Hence they can be forked as tasks with insignificant additional overhead, and can then perform garbage collections of their local heap segments independent of all other processing.

A more thorough treatment of garbage collection in S-threads can be found in [KN91]; other parallel GC algorithms are discussed in [Küc91b].

3 Modular Polynomial G.C.D. Computation

For an introduction to modular methods of g.c.d. calculation see [DST88, ch. 4]. An elementary introduction to the univariate cases of the *multiple homomorphic image* (MHI) schemes used is given in Lipson's excellent book [Lip81, ch. 8, especially section 3.2].

```
                    MPgcdc(r,p,A,B,C_,A_,B_)
/* [Modular polynomial greatest common divisor and cofactors.
 * p is a prime BETA-integer.
 * A and B are polynomials in r>0 variables over Z_p.
 * Then C=gcd(A,B). If C is non-zero then A_=A/C and B_=B/C.
 * Otherwise A_=0 and B_=0.] */
(1)   [Initialize.]
(2)   [Main Loop of MHI Scheme: Map, Evaluate, Lift.]
   (2.1) [Map: apply evaluation homomorphism.]
      (2.1.1) [Obtain next evaluation element e.]
      (2.1.2) [Map normalization factor.]
      (2.1.3) [Map normalized A and B.]
   (2.2) [Evaluate: Recursively compute modular g.c.d. (by MPGCDC)]
   (2.3) [Lift: Apply Chinese Remainder Interpolation Algorithm.]
      (2.3.1) [Trivial case: constant g.c.d?]
      (2.3.2) [Initialize Chinese Remainder interpolation process?]
      (2.3.3) [Test for unlucky evaluation element.]
      (2.3.4) [Apply Chinese Remainder Interpolation Algorithm (MPINT).]
         (2.3.4.1) [Initialize: compute M^{-1} (mod x-e).]
         (2.3.4.2) [Lift modular cofactor A_.]
         (2.3.4.3) [Lift modular cofactor B_.]
         (2.3.4.4) [Lift modular g.c.d..]
      (2.3.5) [Update big modulus.]
   (2.4) [Loop control: Test for completion.]
      (2.4.1) [1st test: Normal re-iteration of main MHI loop?]
      (2.4.2) [2nd test: Check with factor degree bound.]
(3)   [Finalize.]
```

Figure 1: Algorithm MPGCDC.

3.1 The Modular Brown-Collins Algorithm

This algorithm was developed independently by W. S. Brown and G. E. Collins. It computes not only the g.c.d. C of two modular polynomials A and B in $\mathsf{F}[\vec{x}] = Z_p[x_1, \ldots, x_r]$, but also its co-factors $\bar{A} = A/C$ and $\bar{B} = B/C$. The degrees of the co-factors are used to detect termination without performing trial divisions. Brown's version is presented in [Bro71, p. 494] as algorithm P. Collins' implementation in SAC-2 (algorithm **MPGCDC** in the PG subsystem) contains some computational optimizations, especially evaluation in the base variable instead of the main variable; an outline is given in Figure 1.

MPGCDC uses the Euclidean algorithm in the base case of univariate polynomials. For multi-variate polynomials it uses an MHI scheme [Lip81, p. 273] of k_d evaluations in the base variable and k_d recursive **MPGCDC** calculations in $Z_p[e_i, x_2, \ldots, x_r]$, $1 \leq i \leq k_d$, followed by polynomial interpolation [Lip81, p. 263] (algorithm **MPINT**) to lift the modular results back to $Z_p[x_1, \ldots, x_r]$.

The number k_d of necessary iterations in the MHI scheme is determined by a method that is part static and part dynamic. Ultimately, a degree bound is used together with the degrees of the current g.c.d. and its co-factors in the MHI loop to terminate the scheme dynamically. However, first an estimate g is precomputed (cf. $\bar{\nu}$ in step 5 of **P**), such that g is greater than, or equal to, the degree of any factor. The MHI loop is performed until the degree of the accumulated modulus $M = \prod(x_1 - e_i)$ reaches g. Then the degree of the current g.c.d. and its co-factors are examined to determine whether extra iterations are necessary in light of the degree bound.

3.2 Timing Analysis of MPGCDC

Since parallel programming may be surprisingly intricate, we would like to predict which algorithms will be worth parallelizing. Since we find it practically hopeless to guess the effects of parallelization, precise sequential timings are essential.

Our experiments were performed on a 12 processor Encore Multimax 320 (12×2 MIPS) with 64MB, running Encore Mach Version 1.0 or 1.1a (Alpha). All times were taken from the Encore's microsecond wall clock and are reported in milliseconds. With the microsecond timer, individual procedure calls can be timed precisely just by dereferencing a time variable twice; all our times therefore reflect only a single run of the algorithm.

MPGCDC was run in its (unoptimized) C form, using the portable SAC-2 procedures DPR and DQR for multiplication and division of β-digits.[4] Figure 2 samples the run-time of the main components of the MHI loop in step (2) of **MPGCDC**. In both examples we chose the inputs $A = \bar{A} \cdot C$ and $B = \bar{B} \cdot C$ such that the g.c.d. C and the co-factors $\bar{A}$ and $\bar{B}$ would all be dense polynomials of degree d in v variables. In Example 1, $d = 11$ and $v = 2$, and in Example 2, $d = 5$ and $v = 3$.

The diagrams on the left show the time spent in each of the components *Map*, *Evaluate*, *Sum-INT*, *Max-INT*, and *Rest*, during each cycle of the MHI loop. *Map* is the cost of computing, in step (2.1), the homomorphic images $\Phi_{x_1-e_i}(\hat{A})$, $\Phi_{x_1-e_i}(\hat{B})$ of the primitive parts of A and B. *Evaluate* is the time spent, in step (2.2), by the recursive g.c.d. computation in $Z_p[e_i, x_2, \ldots, x_r]$. *Sum-INT* is the sum, and *Max-INT* is the maximum, of the times of interpolating, in steps (2.3.4.2)–(2.3.4.4), the g.c.d. and its two co-factors.[5] *Rest* is the time spent in the remainder of the loop, most notably in computing the modular inverse $M^{-1} \bmod (x_1 - e_i)$ in step (2.3.4.1), and in updating the modulus $M = \prod(x_1 - e_i)$ in step (2.3.5).

We can see how dramatically the picture will change if the times for *Map* and *Evaluate* are reduced to 1/12 by parallelization. In Example 1, the contribution of *Rest* suddenly becomes as important as those of *Map* and *Evaluate*. Accurately analyzing, and possibly removing, these serial components is a big challenge when parallelizing in practice. Naturally, the problem increases as the number of processors grows. Parallelizing on only four processors would not yet make *Rest* greater than *Map* or *Evaluate*.

---

[4]DPR and DQR typically become 3–7 times faster on CISC machines, and up to 20 times faster on RISC machines, when rewritten in assembler (cf. [KLN91])

[5]The anomalies in *Sum-INT* (at steps 13 and 24, respectively 7 and 12), indicate that, after the first break, the value of C remains stable, and after the second break C, $\bar{A}$, and $\bar{B}$, all remain stable.

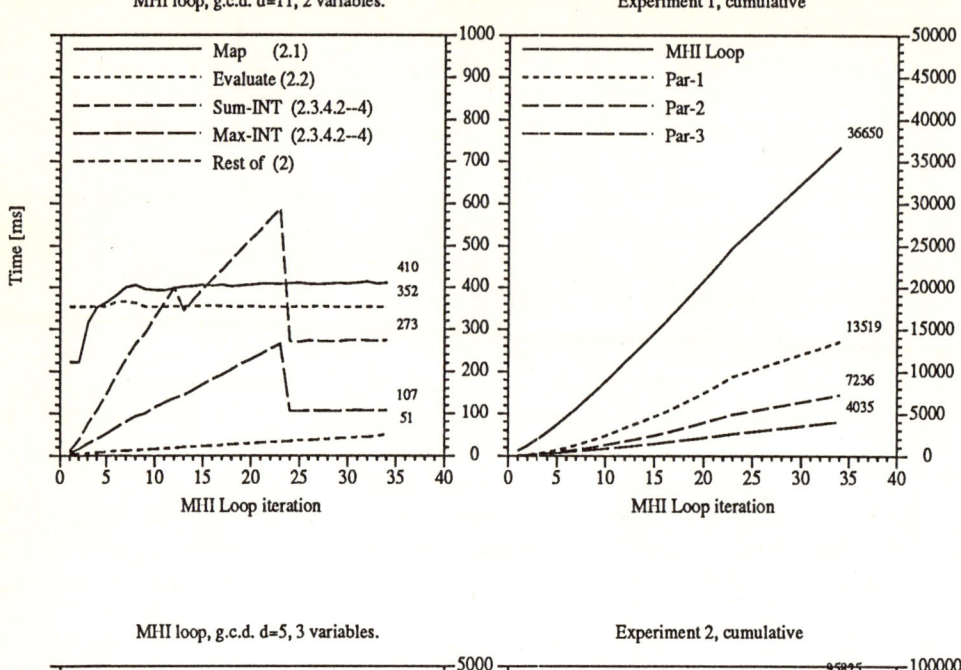
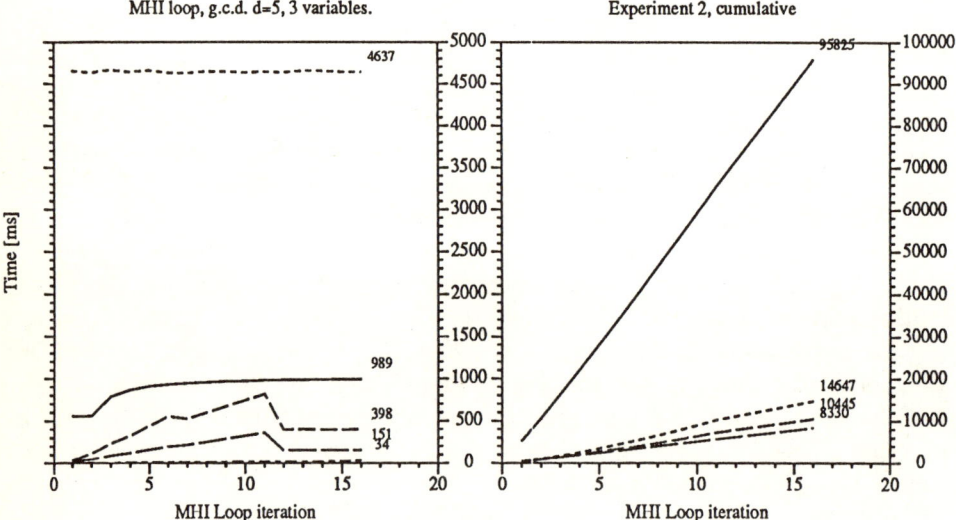

Figure 2: Parallelization prognosis for the MHI loop in MPGCDC.

The diagrams on the right attempt to predict the cumulative cost of the MHI loop iterations under different parallelization scenarios using 12 processors. *MHI Loop* $= \sum_{i=1}^{i=k} Loop(i)$ is the sequential time. *Par-1* is an estimate of the run-time when we perform all *Map* and *Evaluate* computations in parallel, assuming that now *Loop* = (*Map+Evaluate*)/12+*Sum-INT*+*Rest*. In *Par-2* we assume that we also execute the interpolation steps (2.3.4.2)–(2.3.4.4) in parallel, so that *Loop* = (*Map+Evaluate*)/12+*Max-INT*+*Rest*. In *Par-3*, we assume that, additionally, we also parallelize interpolation (algorithm **MPINT**) so that *Loop* = (*Map+Evaluate*)/12+*Max-INT*/4+*Rest*.

Our assumptions of speed-up are of course overly simplistic, but the model still provides valuable guidance. If parallelization is sometimes tricky, then interpretation of the speed-up's is even more complex: Is a speed-up efficiency of 75% good or bad? What is the reason for a disappointing speed-up? Is it intrinsic to the algorithm? Is it due to insufficient parallelization? Are there sequential bottlenecks in S-threads, in C Threads, in Mach kernel threads, or in the architecture? We will now at least be able to view the final timings with the multi-threaded **p_MPgcdc** in light of the predicted optimum.

It also turns out that *Par-1*, *Par-2*, and *Par-3*, roughly reflect a parallelization at grain-sizes of seconds, tenths of seconds, and hundredths of seconds, respectively. Thus it also give an indication of potential performance in a distributed environment, a shared memory environment using heavy-weight processes (Mach tasks), and a shared memory environment using light-weight processes (C threads).

Figure 2 indicates that parallelizing **MPINT** promises significant speed-up over the easily implemented scenario *Par-2*. For Experiment 1, we get speed-up's and speed-up efficiencies of respectively 2.71 (22.5%), 5.06 (42.2%), and 9.1 (75.7%). For Experiment 2, we get 6.5 (54.1%), 9.1 (75.8%), and 11.4 (95%). We see that, while *Par-1* causes the biggest absolute drop in run-time, *Par-3* is still substantially better than *Par-2* for smaller problems. Therefore we now turn to the parallelization of **MPINT**.

3.3 Parallel Polynomial Interpolation

SAC-2's interpolation algorithm **MPINT** is an implementation of Newton's method (cf. [Lip81, p. 264]), extended to the multivariate case $\mathsf{F}[x_1,\ldots,x_r]$. In this case, we have n *value polynomials* $u_i(x_2,\ldots,x_r)$, $0 \leq i \leq n-1$, associated with n evaluation points e_i, and we are computing the unique *interpolation polynomial* $U \in \mathsf{F}[x_1,\ldots,x_r]$ of degree $d_{x_1} < n$ such that $U(e_i, x_2,\ldots,x_r) \equiv u_i(x_2,\ldots,x_r)$ for $0 \leq i \leq n-1$.

Since SAC-2 uses a recursive representation of $\mathsf{F}[x_1,\ldots,x_r]$ as $\mathsf{F}[x_1,\ldots,x_{r-1}][x_r]$, it is advantageous to evaluate and interpolate in the base variable x_1 rather than in the main variable x_r, because this only affects the coefficients. The algorithm is thus readily parallelized by performing the interpolation concurrently on all coefficients $c_{i_j}(x_1,\ldots,x_{r-1})$. This argument then applies recursively to the coefficients of c_{i_j}. The base case is formed by Newton's method in $\mathsf{F}[x]$, using values $e_i \in \mathsf{F}$.

While it is comparatively easy, using S-threads, to write the parallel code which forks the coefficient operations as threads, it is very laborious to make the resulting algorithm robust for all inputs. The main problem is to not fork computations which are below the grainsize of S-threads. In **MPINT**, this occurs in two forms: first, as we descend recursively, we may descend below the parallel grainsize for all our tasks; second, if either

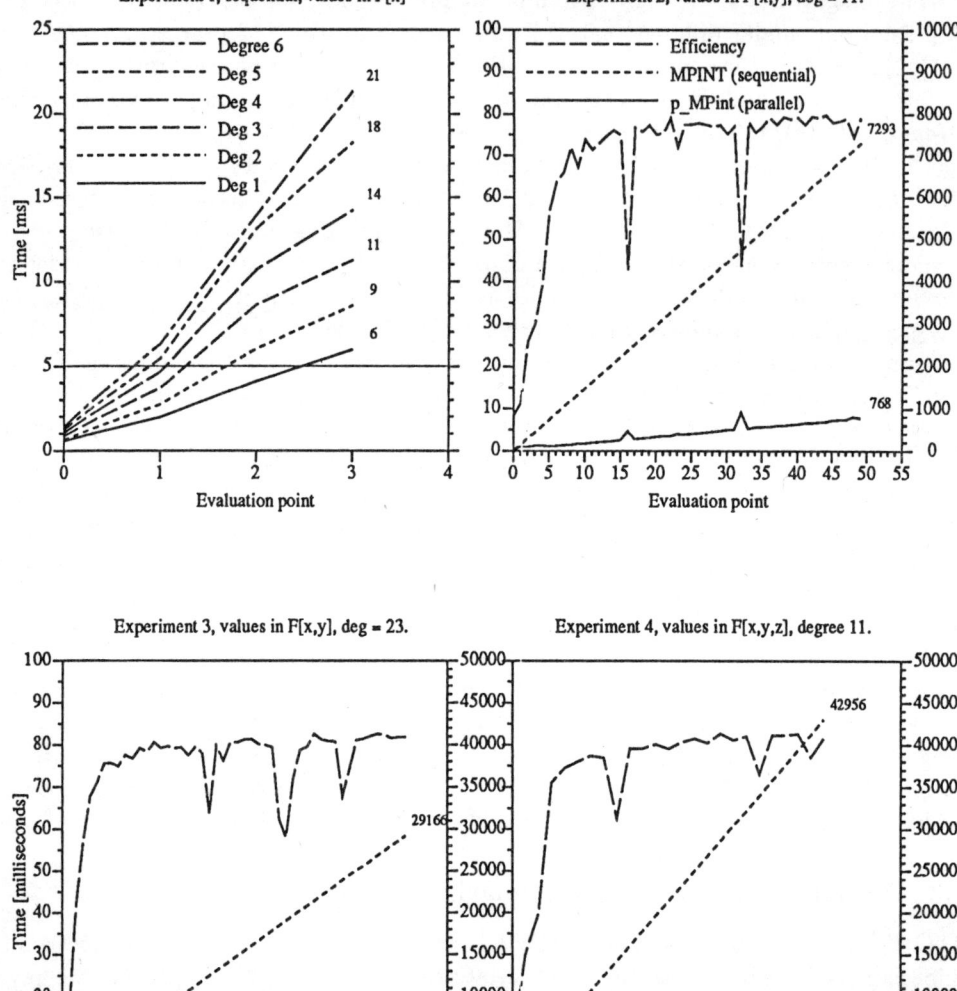

Figure 3: Sequential and parallel Polynomial Interpolation.

of the interpolation polynomial or the value polynomial is sparse, we may fall below the grainsize for a coefficient interpolation subproblem even at high levels of the recursion.

The first problem can be solved relatively easily, by determining a uniform parallel cut-off point beyond which recursive subproblems will not be forked in parallel any more. The second problem is harder, because it means that at high levels of recursion we will have a mix of subproblems, some sequential, to be computed by procedure calls, and some parallel, to be computed by threads, and it has to be decided dynamically into which of the two classes a coefficient interpolation falls. This suggests to use the concept of *futures* developed for Multi-Lisp [Hal85], which do not yet exist in S-threads.

In our implementation of S-threads, the fork/join overhead of a warm-started system is about 300–500μs. To achieve stability even under sequential emulation, we set the *effective* grain-size at $5ms$, or about 10 times the *minimal* one. For the purpose of this work, we circumvented the second problem by using only dense polynomials in our g.c.d. calculations. For the first problem, we assumed that MPINT would be above the effective grainsize for practically all cases of bivariate interpolation polynomials. This is verified in Example 1 of Figure 3, where we interpolated over 4 points ($x_1 = 0, \ldots, 3$) with univariate value polynomials ranging in degree from 1 to 6. From the diagram we can now obtain the combination of degree and evaluation points for which we are under the grainsize. Since those combinations are few, and none actually gets us below the minimal grainsize, we can keep our software simple by still forking off all bivariate evaluation problems and cutting off parallelism at the univariate case.

In Experiments 2–4 we measure the speed-up efficiency of the parallel algorithm p_MPint versus the sequential algorithm on one thread. In Experiment 2, we work with dense random bivariate value polynomials of degree 11 in each variable, while in Experiment 3 the degree is 23 in each variable. In Experiment 4, we have 3 variables and degree 11 in each. Peak speed-up's and speed-up efficiencies are 9.66 (80.48%) for Experiment 2, 9.89 (82.39%) for Experiment 3, and 9.94 (82.80%) for Experiment 4. We are currently investigating possible causes for the efficiency drops. Note that we use all 12 processors of our Encore, so we may get interference from the operating system. Another possible cause lies in dynamic memory allocation by the kernel.

3.4 Parallel Modular Polynomial G.C.D. Computation

We changed SAC-2's MPGCDC (Modular Polynomial G.C.D. and Co-factors) in three ways to arrive at our parallel p_MPgcdc. First, we concurrently evaluated all[6] modular g.c.d.'s and co-factors in step (2.2); secondly, we concurrently lifted the 3 results by executing steps (2.3.4.2)–(2.3.4.4) in parallel; and thirdly, we called the parallel p_MPint of Section 3.3 in each of these 3 steps[7]. p_MPgcdc still contains a substantial serial component outside of the MHI loop, due to steps (1) and (3), which we did not parallelize.

At the beginning of the MHI loop, we now fork k_d Map-Eval threads, each of which performs steps (2.1.2), (2.1.3), and (2.2). Since the number of MPGCDC calculations

---

[6] A production version of p_MPgcdc would first execute one recursive modular MPGCDC call to detect the frequent case of relatively prime inputs. For simplicity, we did not do this here.

[7] It is of great importance in system building that parallel algorithms can be plugged into each other just as sequential algorithms, without reprogramming or reorganizing the system.

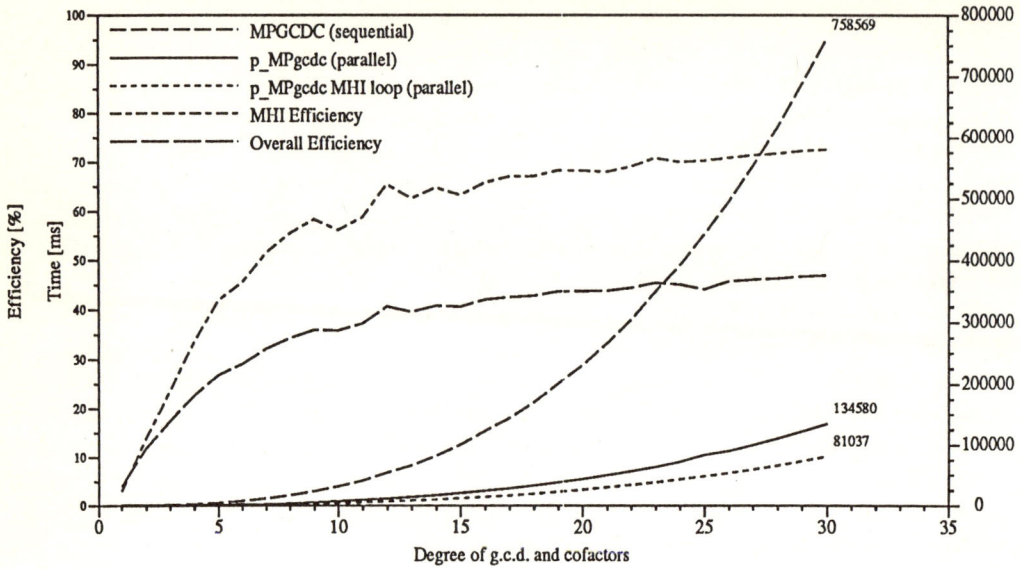
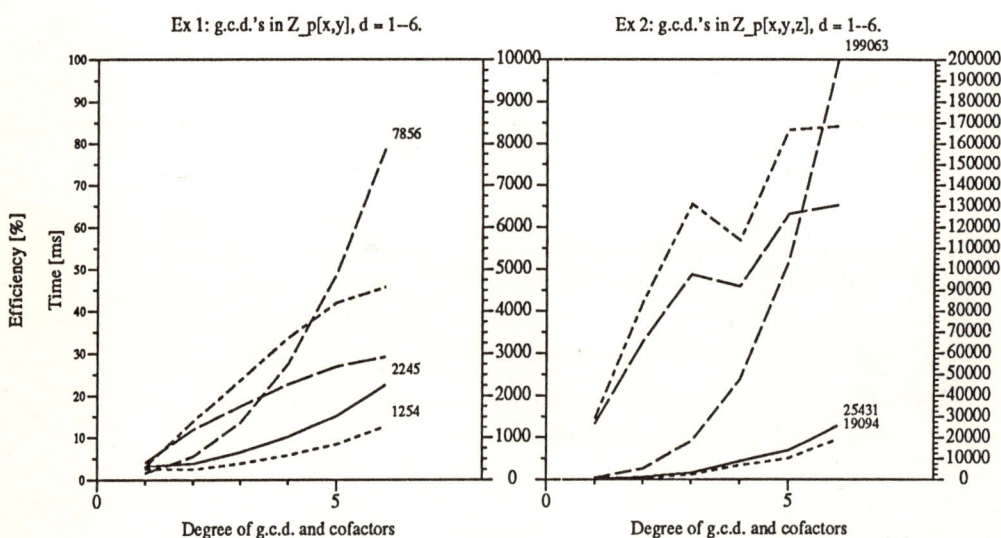

Figure 4: Performance of the parallel polynomial g.c.d. algorithm.

grows exponentially in the number of variables, we only exploited the parallelism of the top-level MHI scheme, and called the sequential algorithm in $Z_p[e_i, x_2, \ldots, x_r]$. After that, in each iteration of the MHI loop we join a *Map-Eval* thread, and fork three p_MPint threads which perform steps (2.3.4.2)–(2.3.4.4) concurrently. In Figure 4, we present the cost of running **MPGCDC** (on one thread) as well as **p_MPgcdc**, and the resulting speed-up's and efficiencies. We also present the cost of the MHI loops proper, and speed-up's and efficiencies of the MHI computations.

In Experiment 1 of Figure 4, we show parallel performance on bivariate polynomials $A = \bar{A} \cdot C$ and $B = \bar{B} \cdot C$ with equal sized, dense random $\bar{A}$, $\bar{B}$, and C. The top graph presents the overall performance, where $\bar{A}$, $\bar{B}$, and C range from degree 1, in increments of 1, to degree 30. The number k_d of independent modular evaluations increases from 4, at degree 1, over 13, at degree 4, up to 91, at degree 30. Peak MHI loop speed-up is 8.70 (72.5%) for degree 30. These tests were run with 4,000,000 list cells to avoid garbage collections in **MPGCDC**.

In the bottom graphs of Figure 4, we compare timings on dense bivariate and trivariate g.c.d.'s of degree 1–6 in each variable. On the bottom left is a magnification of the top graph for degrees 1–6. Sequential and parallel MHI loop performance for degree 11 is $37,643ms$ and $5,339ms$, for a speed-up of 7.05 and 58.75% efficiency, vs. our earlier prognosis of 9.1 (75.7%). On the bottom right we show the performance of g.c.d. computation on trivariate polynomials. We limited parallelism to the top level MHI loop, i.e. recursive calls are to **MPGCDC** rather than to **p_MPgcdc**. Peak MHI loop speed-up is 10.09 for 84.11% efficiency at degree 6. Sequential and parallel MHI loop performance for degree 5 is $99,852ms$ and $9990ms$, for a speed-up of 9.99 and 83.29% efficiency, vs. our earlier prognosis of 11.4 (95%). The efficiency drop at degree 4 may have a cause similar to those discussed in Section 3.3. These tests were run with 1,500,000 list cells.

4 Conclusion

We have studied the parallelization of SAC-2 algorithm **MPGCDC** for the computation of multivariate modular polynomial g.c.d.'s, and we have presented the design of the underlying S-threads parallelization environment. Both subjects were treated together because we hold that, on the one hand, a programming environment is only as good as the applications that it supports in practice, and that, on the other hand, a parallel algorithm implementation is more significant if it is supported by a well defined environment that is easy to use, portable, and stable under heavy loads. This work is part of our effort to build PARSAC-2, a parallel computer algebra system employing the concept of lightweight processes (threads of control).

This work is analogous to our previous parallelization [Küc91a] of SAC-2 algorithm **IPGCDC** for g.c.d. computation in $Z[x_1, \ldots, x_r]$ by the concurrent execution of several calls to **MPGCDC** for the g.c.d. computation of homomorphic images in $Z_{p_i}[x_1, \ldots, x_r]$. It confirms our expectation that **MPGCDC**, like **IPGCDC** before, can also be parallelized with good speed-up efficiency. These efforts are complementary in the sense that the source of parallelism in the top-level case of **IPGCDC** lies in the length of the coefficients, while in the present case it lies in the degree of the polynomials in their minor variables. Both parallel algorithms can be readily combined in PARSAC-2.

Both algorithms create extremely heavy-weight **MPGCDC** tasks which would allow their parallelization even in distributed environments. PARSAC-2, which is based on light-weight processes, allowed us in addition to parallelize also the Chinese Remaindering algorithm **IPCRA** in the coefficient scheme, and the polynomial interpolation algorithm **MPINT** of the variable scheme.

In Section 3.2, we analyzed the sources of parallelism in **MPGCDC** and their grainsizes. Figure 2 indicates that parallel polynomial interpolation is important in order to achieve good speed-up on small problems. We parallelized **MPINT** in Section 3.3 with speed-up efficiencies of around 80% on a broad range of problems. In Section 3.4 we parallelized the overall algorithm, achieving speed-up efficiencies of up to 72% on problems of two variables, and up to 84% on three variables. Our findings are summarized in Figures 2, 3, and 4.

In this paper we limited our experiments to dense polynomials. Further work will be needed to explore and compare alternative methods for polynomial g.c.d. computation, such as Wang's EEZ-GCD algorithm [Wan80] and Zippel's sparse modular method [Zip79], which are better suited for sparse problems. Apart from determining how well Zippel's sparse interpolation algorithm parallelizes in practice, it will be necessary to establish the take-over point between the two interpolation methods in terms of the sparseness of the polynomials. We note, however, that Zippel's algorithm still contains the entire modular Brown-Collins method, so that our parallelization will still be useful for sparse g.c.d. computation.

Acknowledgements

I wish to thank George Collins and Jeremy Johnson for many discussions and explanations, and my student Nick Nevin for helping to build the current S-threads environment. I am grateful to John Mudd for always supporting the latest Mach on our Encore.

References

[ABB+86] Mike Accetta, Robert Baron, William Bolosky, David Golub, Richard Rashid, Avadis Tevanian, and Michael Young. Mach: A new kernel foundation for UNIX development. In *Proc. Summer USENIX Conference*, July 1986.

[AG89] George Almasi and Alan Gottlieb. *Highly Parallel Computing*. Benjamin/Cummings Publishing Company, 1989.

[Bro71] W. S. Brown. On Euclid's algorithm and the computation of polynomial greatest common divisors. *Journal of the ACM*, 18(4):478–504, October 1971.

[BvzGH82] Alan Borodin, Joachim von zur Gathen, and John Hopcroft. Fast parallel matrix and GCD computations. *Information and Control*, 52:241–256, 1982.

[CD88] Eric C. Cooper and Richard P. Draves. C threads. Technical Report CMU-CS-88-154, Computer Science Department, Carnegie Mellon University, Pittsburgh, PA 15213, June 1988.

[CG89] Nicholas Carriero and David Gelernter. Linda in context. *Communications of the ACM*, 32(4), April 1989.

[CGG84]   Bruce Char, Keith Geddes, and Gaston Gonnet. GCDHEU: Heuristic polynomial GCD algorithm based on integer GCD computation. In John Fitch, editor, *International Symposium on Symbolic and Algebraic Computation*, volume 174 of *LNCS*, pages 285–296, Cambridge, England, July 1984. Springer-Verlag. (Proc. EUROSAM'84).

[Cha90]   Bruce Char. Progress report on a system for general-purpose parallel symbolic algebraic computation. In Shunro Watanabe and Morio Nagata, editors, *Proc. ISSAC'90*, pages 96–103, Tokyo, Japan, August 1990. ACM-SIGSAM, ACM Press.

[CL]   G. E. Collins and R. G. K. Loos. SAC-2 system documentation. On-line documentation and program documentation. In Europe available from: Prof. R. Loos, Universität Tübingen, Informatik, D-7400 Tübingen, W-Germany. In the U.S.A. available from: Prof. G. E. Collins, Ohio State University, Computer Science, Columbus, OH 43210.

[DDF89]   J. Della Dora and J. Fitch, editors. *Computer Algebra and Parallelism*. Computational Mathematics and Applications. Academic Press, London, 1989. (Proc. CAP'88, Grenoble, France, June 1988).

[DR85]   J.H. Davenport and Y. Robert. VLSI and Computer Algebra: the g.c.d. example. In *Dynamical Systems and Cellular Automata*, pages 359–367. Academic Press, London-New York, 1985.

[DST88]   J.H. Davenport, Y. Siret, and E. Tournier. *Computer Algebra, Systems and Algorithms for Algebraic Computation*. Academic Press, 1988.

[Hal85]   Robert H. Halstead. Multilisp: A language for concurrent symbolic computation. *ACM Transactions on Programming Languages and Systems*, 7(4):501–538, October 1985.

[Kal85]   Erich Kaltofen. Computing with polynomials given by straight-line programs I: Greatest common divisors. In *Proc. 17th ACM STOC*, pages 131–142. Providence, RI, May 1985.

[Kal89]   Erich Kaltofen. Parallel algebraic algorithm design. Technical report, Department of Computer Science, Rensselaer Polytechnic Institute, November 1989.

[KLN91]   Wolfgang W. Küchlin, David Lutz, and Nicholas J. Nevin. Integer multiplication in PARSAC-2 on stock microprocessors. In *AAECC-9: Ninth Int. Symp. on Applied Algebra, Algebraic Algorithms, and Error-Correcting Codes*, LNCS, New Orleans, LA, October 1991. Springer-Verlag. (To appear).

[KN91]   Wolfgang W. Küchlin and Nicholas J. Nevin. On multi-threaded list-processing and garbage collection. Technical Report OSU-CISRC-3/91-TR11, Computer and Information Science Research Center, The Ohio State University, Columbus, OH 43210-1277, March 1991.

[KR88]   Brian W. Kernighan and Dennis M. Ritchie. *The C Programming Language*. Prentice-Hall, Englewood Cliffs, New Jersey, 2nd edition, 1988. (Based on the Draft ANSI C.).

[KS88]   L. V. Kalé and Wennie Shu. The Chare-Kernel language for parallel programming: A perspective. Report UIUCDCS-R-88-1451, Department of Computer Science, University of Illinois at Urbana-Champaign, Urbana, IL, August 1988.

[Küc90a]   Wolfgang W. Küchlin. PARSAC-2: A parallel SAC-2 based on threads. In *AAECC-8: Eighths Int. Symp. on Applied Algebra, Algebraic Algorithms, and Error-Correcting Codes*, volume 508 of *LNCS*, Tokyo, Japan, August 1990. Springer-Verlag.

[Küc90b]   Wolfgang W. Küchlin. The S-threads environment for parallel symbolic computation. In Richard Zippel, editor, *Computer Algebra and Parallelism*, Ithaca, NY, May 1990. To appear.

[Küc91a]   Wolfgang W. Küchlin. On the multi-threaded computation of integral polynomial greatest common divisors. In *Proc. ISSAC'91: Internatl. Symp. on Symbolic and Algebraic Computation*, Bonn, Germany, July 1991. ACM Press. (To appear. Also Tech. Report OSU-CISRC-1/91-TR2).

[Küc91b]   Wolfgang W. Küchlin. A space-efficient parallel garbage compaction algorithm. In *Proc. Fifth ACM International Conference on Supercomputing*, Cologne, Germany, June 1991. ACM Press. (To appear).

[Lip81]   John D. Lipson. *Elements of Algebra and Algebraic Computing*. Benjamin/Cummings, 1981.

[Loo76]   R. G. K. Loos. The algorithm description language ALDES (Report). *ACM SIGSAM Bull.*, 10(1):15–39, 1976.

[MY73]   J. Moses and D. Yun. The EZ-GCD algorithm. In *Proc. of the ACM Annual Conference*, pages 159–166, Atlanta, GA, 1973.

[Pon88a]   Carl G. Ponder. *Evaluation of "Performance Enhancements" in Algebraic Manipulation Systems*. PhD thesis, Computer Science Division, University of California, Berkeley, CA 94720, U.S.A., August 1988.

[Pon88b]   Carl G. Ponder. Parallel processors and systems for algebraic manipulation: Current work. *ACM SIGSAM Bull.*, 22(3):15–21, July 1988.

[Pon88c]   Carl G. Ponder. Parallelism and algorithms for algebraic manipulation: Current work. *ACM SIGSAM Bull.*, 22(3):7–14, July 1988.

[Pon89]   Carl G. Ponder. Evaluation of "performance enhancements" in algebraic manipulation systems. In Della Dora and Fitch [DDF89], pages 51–73. (Proc. CAP'88, Grenoble, France, June 1988).

[Roc89]   Jean-Louis Roch. *L'Architecture du Systeme PAC et son Arithmetique Rationnelle*. PhD thesis, Institut National Polytechnique de Grenoble, Grenoble, France, December 1989.

[Sei90]   Steffen Seitz. *Verteiltes Rechnen in SAC-2*. PhD thesis, Universität Tübingen, 1990.

[Wan80]   Paul S. Wang. The EEZ-GCD algorithm. *SIGSAM Bulletin*, 14(2):50–60, 1980.

[Wat86]   Stephen M. Watt. *Bounded Parallelism in Computer Algebra*. PhD thesis, University of Waterloo, Waterloo, Canada, 1986. Also Technical Report CS-86-12.

[Web91]   Ken Weber. A heuristic parallel algorithm to compute univariate polynomial GCD's. Preprint, February 1991.

[Zip79]   Richard Zippel. Probabilistic algorithms for sparse polynomials. In Edward W. Ng, editor, *Symbolic and Algebraic Computation*, volume 72 of *LNCS*, pages 216–226, Marseille, France, June 1979. Springer-Verlag. (Proc. EUROSAM'79).

[Zip81]   Richard Zippel. Newton's iteration and the sparse Hensel algorithm. In Paul Wang, editor, *Proc. SYMSAC'81*, pages 68–72, 1981.

A Buchberger Algorithm for Distributed Memory Multi-Processors

David J. Hawley
Institute for New Generation Computer Technology
1-4-28 Mita, Minato-ku, Tokyo 108 Japan.
hawley%icot.jp@relay.cs.net

Abstract

Gröbner Bases are a mathematical tool that has received considerable attention in recent years. Since the Buchberger Algorithm for computing these objects is expensive in both space and time, several attempts at parallelization have been made, with good results for shared-memory multi-processors, but not for distributed memory machines. We present an algorithm that delivers substantial speedups on distributed memory multi-processors, and an incremental version of the algorithm which is suitable for use as the solver in a constraint logic language.

1 Introduction

Recently, there have been several attempts made to parallelize the Buchberger algorithm, with generally disappointing results[6, 7], except for shared-memory machines[10, 3]. Parallelization has been tackled at two levels: a coarse-grain parallel rewriting of the S-polynomials and/or testing for subsumption and critical pairs, and a fine-grain rewriting of single S-polynomials. The feasibility of the latter seems restricted to shared-memory architectures. An interesting concurrent logic programming (data-flow) approach implemented on Transputers was reported by Siegl [8], with good speedups on the small examples shown, but absolute performance was only fair.

We are interested in using Gröbner Bases as the core of constraint solvers for concurrent constraint programming languages.[1] In this application, the input set of polynomials is not given at the start of the computation, but is generated concurrently by some other process, possibly depending on the intermediate sets of basis polynomials. In this paper, we give distributed algorithms suitable for two abstractions of this application: the *static* case in which the complete set of input polynomials is available at the start of the Gröbner Base calculation, and the *dynamic* case, in which the input polynomials are sent at arbitrary intervals from some processor(s).

We begin by reviewing some terminology. The standard definitions are augmented by some useful definitions from the term-rewriting systems literature. Let there be a certain ordering among monomials and let a system of polynomial equations be given. An equation can be considered a rewrite rule which rewrites the greatest monomial in the equation to the polynomial consisting of the remaining monomials. For example, if the ordering is lexicographic, a polynomial equation, $Z - X + B = A$, can be considered as a rewrite rule, $Z \rightarrow X - B + A$. Two rewrite rules $L_1 \rightarrow R_1$ and $L_2 \rightarrow R_2$, of which L_1 and L_2 are not mutually prime, are termed a *critical pair*, since the least common multiple of their left-hand sides can be rewritten in two different ways. The S-polynomial of such a pair is

$$\text{S-poly}(L_1, L_2) = R_1 \frac{\text{lcm}(L_1, L_2)}{L_2} - R_2 \frac{\text{lcm}(L_1, L_2)}{L_1}$$

---
[1]One such language, GDCC[4], is under development by the constraint logic programming group at ICOT.

A rule $L_1 \to R_1$ is said to subsume rule $L_2 \to R_2$ if L_2 is a multiple of L_1. Finally, Gröbner Bases can be characterized by the property that for all pairs (P,Q) in the given set of equations, S-poly(P,Q) rewrites to zero.

There are two main sources of polynomial-level parallelism in the Buchberger Algorithm, the parallel reduction of a set of polynomials, and the parallel checking for subsumption and critical pairs of a new rule against the other rules. Since the latter is inexpensive, we must concentrate on parallelizing the coarse-grained reduction component for shared-memory architectures. However, since the convergence rate of the Buchberger Algorithm is very sensitive to the order in which polynomials are converted into rules, an implementation must be careful to select "small" polynomials early for inclusion in the developing basis. The key idea underlying the algorithms in this paper is that of sorting a distributed set of polynomials, and we will use the "asynchronous enumeration sort" [1, pp. 178-181] as our point of departure.

2 The Algorithm

We begin by considering the "asynchronous enumeration sort" algorithm, which is suitable for distributed memory machines. In the sort algorithm, each processor has a complete set of the input items, and a copy of the *ownership* function which is a many-to-one function from items to processors. Each processor independently compares the items it owns to all the other items in order to determine the items' ranks in the sorted sequence. The method for outputting the items in sorted sequence chosen, because of its applicability to the Buchberger algorithm, is that each processor listens to the output of all the other processors, and outputs its equations when the count reaches the respective ranks.

The sorting algorithm is adapted as follows. Each processor contains a complete set of basis polynomials (called *rules*) and non-basis polynomials, and a load-distribution function which logically partitions the polynomials by specifying which processor "owns" what polynomials. The position in the output (rule) sequence of each polynomial is calculated by its owning processor based on an associated key (for example, the leading power product) which is identical in every processor, and does not change during reduction. Each polynomial is output when it becomes the smallest one remaining. The critical-pairs and subsumptions are calculated independently by each processor, so that the processors' sets of polynomials stay synchronized. As a background task, each processor rewrites the polynomials it owns, starting with those lowest in the sorted order. Termination of the algorithm is detected independently by each engine, when the input equation stream is closed, and there are no non-basis polynomials remaining.

The dynamic problem requires more complex control, in order to prevent the arrival of input polynomials at different times at each processor from causing processors to have inconsistent views about the set of non-basis polynomials and possibly about the output (rule) sequence. Figure 1 shows the algorithm for the dynamic case. This version requires additional information about the basis and non-basis sets of each engine to be made known, eventually, to every other engine.

A serious drawback to the algorithm is that it cannot take advantage of "magic polynomials". That is, since the key which determines the output position of a polynomial is fixed before reduction begins, the key is only a rough approximation of the actual preferability of a polynomial after reduction. A possible refinement is to resort the set of polynomials within each processor inside the same "output slots" owned by that processor.

Since the result for the static algorithm is straightforward, and a special case of the result for the dynamic algorithm, we will only prove correctness for the dynamic version. We would like to show that the processors have the same view of the output (rule) sequence.

Lemma 2.1 *For every $t \geq 0$, exactly one processor outputs to Channel[t].*
Proof by induction on t. Assume $t = 0$. Since B_i is updated exactly when t is incremented, we have $B_i = \mathcal{B}_i = 0$ and $P_i = K_i$. We call a processor i synchronized if $S_i = K_i$; only synchronized processors can output (line 12). By definition, $S_i \subseteq \bigcap_j K_j$, and so for all synchronized processors

```
        comment
            S = stream of polynomials.
            S_i = subset of S that engine i knows has been received by every engine.
            B_i = subset of B_i that engine i knows has been received by every engine.
            Code to maintain S_i and B_i is omitted.

(1)     do i=1, N
(2)         spawn engine(i,S,Channel) on processor i

(3)     engine(I,S,Channel)
(4)         S_i := P_i := K_i := ∅
(5)         B_i := B_i := ∅; t := 0
(6)         do forever
(7)             choose
(8)                 guard       receive X from S
(9)                             B_i = B_i
(10)                do          K_i := K_i ∪ {X}, P_i := P_i ∪ {X}
(11)                guard       (p := min(P_i)) is irreducible w.r.t. B_i
(12)                            ω(p) = i, S_i = K_i
(13)                do          output p to Channel[t++]
(14)                            P_i := P_i ∪ {spoly(p,q) | q ∈ B_i} − {p}
(15)                            B_i := B_i ∪ {p}
(16)                guard       receive p from Channel[t++]
(17)                do          P_i := P_i ∪ {spoly(p,q) | q ∈ B_i} − {p}
(18)                            B_i := B_i ∪ {p}
(19)                guard       (L := {q | q ∈ P_i, ω(q) = i, p is reducible by B_i}) ≠ ∅
(20)                do          Rewrite L by B_i
(21)                guard       P_i = ∅, S is closed
(22)                do          output B_i to Channel[t]
(23)                            stop
(24)            endchoose
(25)        enddo
```

---

[a] The **choose** (guard Cond do Action)* **endchoose** construct specifies a non-deterministic guarded choice. Execution will suspend until at least one of the conditions obtains, and then the action corresponding to one of the guards whose condition obtains will be executed; the testing of guard conditions has no observable effect until an associated action is chosen.

[b] The algorithm for the static problem is obtained by changing all references to the stream S to the set of input polynomials P, replacing line(4) with "$P_i := P$", and deleting the framed code.

Figure 1: Algorithm for Dynamic Problem

$K_i = K = \bigcap_j K_j$. Therefore there is a unique minimum $p \in P_i$. Let $m = \omega(p)$. If processor m is synchronized, then it outputs p as soon as p has been fully rewritten, otherwise it waits until synchronization (which will eventually occur, if S is finite). In either case, t is incremented. After output, K_m will not change until $\mathcal{B}_m = B_m$ (line 9), which also freezes the value of K. We are then guaranteed that no (other) engine can output until receiving p, and incrementing t.

Assume $t = t_1 > 0$. Now $P_i - K_i$ are the identical sets of critical pairs from the first t_1 rules. We argue similarly to the base case to obtain the required result.

Corollary 2.1 *Each processor receives the same sequence of rules.*

Theorem 2.1 *For all $p, q \in S$, S-poly(p,q) rewrites to zero.*
The proof follows easily from the above corollary.

3 Implementation and Results

The dynamic algorithm was implemented on the Multi-PSI, a distributed-memory multi-processor designed as a development platform for operating systems and applications based on concurrent logic programming concepts. The user-level language, KL1[9, 5], is a data-flow language that executes at 128 K reductions/second on a single Multi-PSI node.

The central data structure in the implementation is a sorted list of items of work, comprising input polynomials, critical pairs, and requests to simplify rules. Priorities correspond to the key associated with each polynomial. In the current implementation for rules and input polynomials we use the largest power product as the key, and for S-polynomials we use the largest power product after canceling the largest power product of each of the two parent polynomials. The complete execution of one piece of work is broken down into stages; for example, a critical pair is first converted to a S-polynomial, rewritten, and finally normalized. Based on this breakdown, we pipeline the execution of the entire list, giving us maximum overlap between communication and local computation. Although this implementation only deletes critical pairs arising from subsumed rules, a full implementation of Buchberger's criteria for filtering useless critical pairs should also be possible.

The implementation of the $\mathcal{S}$ and $\mathcal{B}$ variables in the dynamic algorithm is based on ACK (acknowledgment) messages. However, the additional latency introduced applies only to the acceptance of new input polynomials, and the number of $\mathcal{B}$ related ACK messages can be decreased by updating the $\mathcal{B}$ variables less frequently. Information about processor load is piggybacked onto the ACK messages, in order to construct the ω load-distribution function dynamically (being careful to build it identically on each processor).

Finally, the calculation of the coefficients of non-basis polynomials is improved by delaying until a rule to rewrite the associated power product has been found. At that point, the coefficient expression is evaluated using divide-and-conquer, and compared to zero. This strategy results in several fold speed improvements in some examples.

Example	1 PE	2 PE	4 PE	6 PE	8 PE	12 PE	16 PE
Runge-Kutta 1	2.335	1.841	1.493	1.704	1.334	1.514	1.751
Katsura 3	8.854	5.008	3.748	3.359	3.369	3.297	3.463
Little Trinks	49.710	23.592	22.096	14.897	12.351	14.469	15.682
Big Trinks	188.641	94.428	84.328	67.630	46.512	45.070	45.106
Katsura 4	2000.056	1520.289	725.004	377.047	301.324	243.900	209.529

Table 1: Absolute Performance of Dynamic Algorithm (sec)

The benchmarks presented here are from Boege et. al.[2], with Katsura 4 modified to use total degree reverse lexicographic ordering, as do all the others. Except for Katsura 4, the speedup curve (Figure 2) eventually becomes flat, reflecting the limits of polynomial-level parallelism in these examples. The absolute performance of the algorithm is only fair. However, reimplementing the polynomial and rational arithmetic in a standard von Neumann language should bring about a 1-2 order of magnitude performance improvement in the bulk of the computation (measured at over 90%), without affecting the parallelism. Although reimplementation would change the ratio between computation time and communication time/ latency, we conjecture a significant improvement in overall performance.

4 Conclusion

This contribution of this work is the parallelization of the Buchberger Algorithm on a distributed memory machine exhibiting substantial speedups and reasonable performance. Reimplementation of the low-level routines in a von Neumann language should substantially improve the latter. The algorithm uses broadcast messages exclusively, and it would be interesting to investigate its performance on a hardware and software platform that supports broadcasting efficiently.

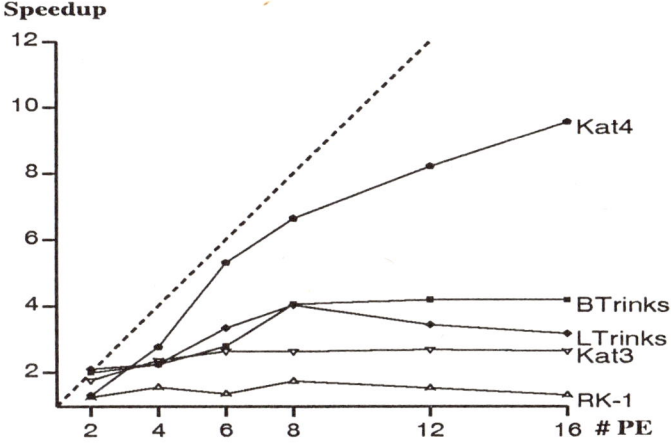

Figure 2: Speedup of Dynamic Algorithm

References

[1] S. G. Akl. *Parallel Sorting Algorithms*. Notes and Reports in Computer Science and Applied Mathematics. Academic Press, 1985.

[2] W. Boege, R. Gebauer, and H. Kredel. Some examples for solving systems of algebraic equations by calculating groebner bases. *J. Symbolic Computation*, 2(1):83–98, 1986.

[3] E. M. Clarke, D. E. Long, S. Michaylov, S. A. Schwab, J. P. Vidal, and S. Kimura. Parallel Symbolic Computation Algorithms. Technical Report CMU-CS-90-182, Computer Science Department, Carnegie Mellon University, Oct. 1990.

[4] D. Hawley and A. Aiba. Guarded Definite Clauses with Constraints - A Preliminary Report. Japan-Italy-Sweden Workshop on Logic Programming and Parallel Processing, Stockholm, Sweden, Aug. 1990.

[5] K. Nakajima, Y. Inamura, N. Ichiyoshi, K. Rokusawa, and T. Chikayama. Distributed implementation of KL1 on the Multi-PSI/V2. In *Proceedings of ICLP'89*, pages 436–451, 1989.

[6] C. G. Ponder. Evaluation of 'Performance Enhancements' in algebraic manipulation systems. In J. D. Dora and J. Fitch, editors, *Computer Algebra and Parallelism*, pages 51–74. Academic Press, 1990.

[7] P. Senechaud. Implementation of a parallel algorithm to compute a Gröbner basis on Boolean polynomials. In J. D. Dora and J. Fitch, editors, *Computer Algebra and Parallelism*, pages 159–166. Academic Press, 1990.

[8] K. Siegl. Gröbner Bases Computation in STRAND: A Case Study for Concurrent Symbolic Computation in Logic Programming Languages. Master's thesis, CAMP-LINZ, Nov. 1990.

[9] K. Ueda and T. Chikayama. Design of the kernel language for the parallel inference machine. *Computer Journal*, December 1990. To appear.

[10] J. P. Vidal. The Computation of Gröbner bases on a shared memory multi-processor. Technical Report CMU-CS-90-163, Computer Science Department, Carnegie Mellon University, Aug. 1990.

Computational Biology on Massively Parallel Machines

Klaus Schulten
Beckman-Institute and Department of Physics
University of Illinois
Urbana, IL 61801, USA

1 Introduction

Computational Methods have long been developed into useful tools in Science and Engineering. The complex nature of living systems has delayed such development in the life sciences; however, during the past decade Biomedical Research and Technology has seen an influx of computational methods equal to that in the physical sciences. An example is the widespread use of computer imaging techniques in medical diagnostics. Another example is the application of computational methods for drug design and structure refinement in Molecular Biology and Medicine. A third example is the emergence of the field of Computational Neural Science which attempts to understand the principles of development and functional cooperation of the neurons in the brain, using computer simulations as a main tool. There have been many reasons for the proliferation of computational techniques in Biology and Medicine, not the least of which has been the rapid development of the computer itself which became increasingly better adapted to the complex data processing tasks required in Biology and Medicine.

Hurdles in Computational Biology: Three Examples

The available computer power and the algorithms of Computational Biology are, in many cases, still inadequate. In Molecular Biology, for example, the numerical simulation of a protein of a few thousand atoms, over the time span of one μs, would require about 100 years even on a Cray 2. Simulations of biopolymers in natural surroundings, e.g., in a membrane and water, would involve 10^6 atoms and, presently, are still very difficult to achieve, even for very brief time spans.
The description of brain activity as observed, for example, through voltage-sensitive dyes in a cortical area of a few mm^2 involves 10^5 neurons with 10^8 synaptic connections. The simulation of the evolution of the connectivity scheme of brain areas with 10^8 dynamic variables, e.g., connections between the retinas of the eye and the striate cortex, requires the fastest modern computers, if possible at all.
Diagnostic techniques, e.g., Magnetic Resonance Imaging (MRI), are based on physical processes which need to be understood if the diagnostic method is to be developed further. The ultimate level of understanding is reached if the measuring process for a sample can be simulated in its entirety, a task which, in case of MRI, requires one to monitor the nuclear spin precession of 10^6 diffusing water molecules over many precession periods. Again, such simulation presently runs many days on the fastest computers.

Opportunities Through Massively Parallel Computers

The five years 1991-1995 will be the first period in the history of computing that experiences an increase in speed by three orders of magnitude in such a short time. This development, of course, is due to the emergence of massively parallel computers. To describe this development let us begin with a look at the state of the art in supercomputing by comparing the Gflop performance of this year's and next year's high end machines. For this purpose, we compare in Table 1 the performance of machines of four vendors running today (1991) and expected to be shipped next year (1992). Certainly, the performance for next year can be estimated only very crudely. (Performance figures for the new (1992) model of the Connection machine were left blank, but should be available by the time of the lecture.)

Table 1 shows several trends. First, the machines compared show a speed-up by a factor of 4 to 6 between 1991 and 1992. This speed up is achieved through use of a new processor, in case of the Transputer-based Parsytec machines (the T800 of the SC-400 is replaced by the T9000 of the GC-2), due to redesign of the machine in case of the Connection Machine CM-5, and due to increased processor numbers in case of Intel's Sigma Touchstone based on the i860 processor.

The manufacturers of the machines listed in Table 1 are expected to push the performance of their respective machines into the Teraflop range. This speed-up, evidently, will be realized both through new chip technologies as well as (and mainly) through increased processor numbers. Because of the latter aspect the first Teraflop machines will be prohibitively expensive and only very few installations, i.e., much fewer than the present numbers of Gigaflop performers, can be expected to be available to Computational Scientists.

A second feature shown in Table 1 is the considerable gap between peak and sustained performance. This gap is small for the 'mature' Cray for which optimizing compilers and considerable programming experience exists. In case of the Transputer-based machines the small gap is due to the scalar character of the FPU of the Transputer T800. The vector processing characteristics of the FPU on the i860 and a bottleneck regarding memory access makes it more difficult, even for a single processor, to achieve a sustained performance close to the peak value. In case of the present version of the CM-2 the limitation is due to the fact that the FPU's (Weitek) actually serve 32 processors and transfer of floating point data between memory and FPU's is less than optimal. Table 1 indicates then that the gap between peak performance and sustained performance is very much a matter of efficient programming of single processors. This is certainly the case, however, the data hide the fact that good performance of massively parallel machines working on a specific problem can only be achieved if the corresponding algorithms exploit the machines parallelism to the fullest extent. In fact, performance data for parallel machines are given for algorithms which work perfect in parallel, but most likely have nothing in common with the algorithms required for a problem of interest. A computational scientist who approaches a parallel computer with a given problem and with a program written for conventonal serial machines must expect to achieve much poorer performance, to the extreme that only a single processor among thousands of processors works on his problem. Only the Computational Scientist literate in parallel programming concepts and algorithms and willing to invest considerable effort in developing new programs can expect to harness the enourmeous increase in power which massively parallel computers promise.

In this respect, the problem of optimal employment of parallel machines appears to be compounded by the fact that the machines available today differ in the programming model they support, i.e., SIMD and MIMD machines with distributed and shared memory and with different data paths between processors. Fortunately, it appears that the parallel machines develop towards a more common ground, namely supporting mainly the MIMD concept through relatively coarse-grained architectures involving 64 bit processors with 4-16 Mbyte DRAM and also using hierarchical nets and efficient routing schemes. The latter features imply that programmers need to differentiate memory only in two classes, fast on-processor and slower off-processor memory, the difference in access times for the latter memory residing on various parts of the machine being relatively small. As long as the band width of the net linking processors is not challenged, e.g., through the 'wicked' task of transposing a matrix across the whole machine, the future parallel computers will behave very close to shared memory machines, even though memory is physically distributed. Of course, Computer Science and manufacturers will support the user through various tools, well developed programming environments on hosts machines, vectorizing and, as far as this is possible, parallelizing compilers, debuggers and performance monitors.

However, to exploit the speed-up furnished by massively parallel machines, Computational Scientists cannot rely solely on such tools, but must spend intense programming efforts to fully exploit machine capacities. In my lecture I will describe such efforts in three areas of Computational Biology, namely Structural Biology, Computational Neural Science and Magetic Resonance Imaging.

Supercomputer Perfomance (in GFLOPS) 1991/1992					
1991			1992 (expected values)		
machine	peak	sustained	machine	peak	sustained
Cray Y-MP (4 processors)	2.7	1–2	Cray Y-MP (16 processors)	12	6–8
SC-400 Parsytec (400 processors)	1	1	GC-2 Parsytec (~256 processors)	6	5
Delta Touchstone (512 processors)	32	3–5	Sigma Touchstone (~2000 processors)	100–200	10–20
CM-2 (32,000 processors)	13.6	2–3	CM-5		

At this point it might also be mentioned that the optimism expressed above about the impending rapid development of computational resources is shared by many, in particular, also by Science Policy makers. Presently, the US (see, e.g., *Grand Challenges: High Performance Computation and Communication Initiative*, Report by the Committee on Physical, Mathematical and Engineering Sciences, National Science Foundation) and the Commission of European Communities (see, e.g., *Report of the EEC Working Group on High-Performance Computing*, Geneva, 1990) plan a large increase in funding of computational equipment, much of it for massively parallel machines, e.g., Teraflop computers. Computational Science needs to prepare itself to take advantage of the opportunities developing. This will require familiarity with concurrent computing and will require also investments in machines which are small versions of large production engines. For example, presently the fastest available computer for U.S. researchers is the 512 processor Delta Touchstone (see table above) at CalTech, whose smaller cousin, the Gamma Touchstone serves at various sites for code development and testing. Similarly, the next generation Connection Machine, the present CM-200 version of which matches the Delta Touchstone closely, is likely to be available in versions of different size. In Europe Parsytec plans a Teraflop computer based on the Transputer T9000 processor which, in keeping with the general concept behind the Transputer, will also be available at very different scales.

Opportunities Through Concurrent Computation Across Networks

The development of the high performance hardware described above can distract from the extremely important fact that massively parallel computation can be realized also on machines emerging from the low performance sector of computer technology. In fact, the advent of massively parallel computers coincides with the proliferation and rapid improvement of low cost computer workstations. Today

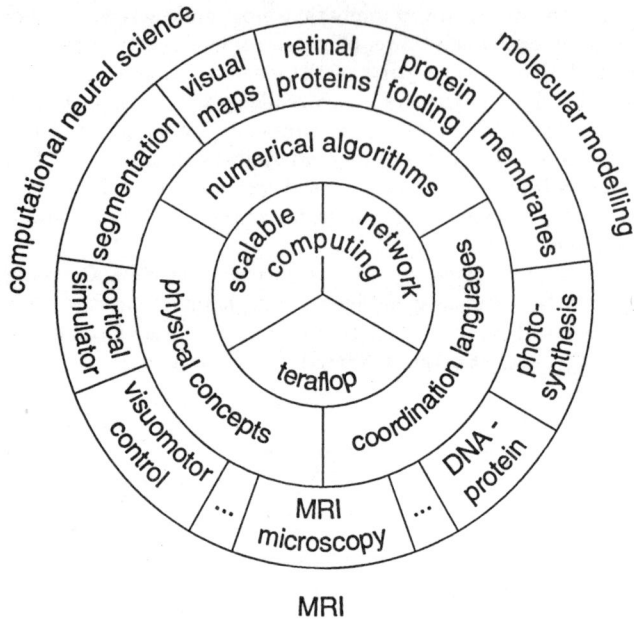

Figure 1: Schematic view of the activities of the Theoretical Biophysics Group at the Beckman Institute of the University of Illinois. The core of the diagram denotes the hardware used, the first layer the algorithm development and the outer layer the various applications for massively parallel computing pursued by the group.

a desktop workstation with 2 Mflops performance costs only about $5,000 (e.g., a NeXTstation) and can easily be configured within a wide network. *Coordination languages* for organizing computation across a massively parallel computer can be employed also over a network, and tasks which require only moderate message passing between processors can obtain Cray YMP processor speed through about 100 such workstations. This estimate suggests that enormous computational resources can be harvested from existing computational equipment. It is also apparent that concurrent computing across networks opens interesting alternatives to installations of single, large scale computers. Again, this capacity will only be available to computational scientists if efforts are spent on adapting algorithms to concurrent computation and to coordination languages.

2 Concurrent Computation in Biology and Medicine – An Overview

Figure 1 presents an overview of the author's efforts to employ parallel computation to solve problems in Biology and Medicine. The efforts can be described as structured in two layers surrounding a core. The core consists of three sectors, corresponding to the three different types of hardware employed. The inner layer describes algorithm development and the outer layer the various biological and medical areas addressed by means of concurrent computation.

Hardware

Let us begin describing the hardware component of Figure 1. The sector "teraflop" symbolizes very large scale parallel machines, i.e., presently a 32K processor Connection Machine CM-2 and a 512 processor Touchstone Delta, which are used by the author's group for research in Structural Biology and Computational Neural Science. Such machines are available at National Centers and computer time is available either through competitive proposals or through contractual agreements. The National Centers are expected to furnish during the next years the fastest and largests machines available to be used for the most demanding and most relevant Science and Engineering projects. Presently, the author's group uses machines at National Centers to describe the reaction mechanism of proteins, in particular, those of the class of visual receptors, and to simulate the formation of so-called brain maps, in particular, the representation of visual images in the optical cortex. The machines are programmed in C and parallel extension of this language.

The second core sector, "scalable computing", denotes parallel computers which are scalable, essentially from single processor to multi-processor machines. Presently, the author's group operates in this category Transputer-based machines of various types: a self-designed and self-built 60 processor machine which began operation (as a 12 processor version) in August 1988, an 18 processor twin machine, and commercially available VME-bus boards with 4 and 6 processors, respectively, connected to a Sun-4 and Silicon Graphics workstation. These machines are programmed in Occam II as well as in C (Par.C). The machines are used for very large scale simulation of biopolymers, e.g., water–DNA–drug systems, membrane–protein systems and protein complexes. For such computations the 60 processor machine achieves the speed of about a single Cray 2 processor as judged by comparision with commercial programs (Charmm of Polygen, Inc.) running on the Cray 2. The Transputer-based machines are also employed for simulations of Magnetic Resonance Imaging, in particular, regarding the application of this method to microscopy with about 10 μm resolution.

The third core sector "network computing" describes the use of Sun workstations for parallel computation employing the "Linda" coordination language. This system was used to simulate medium-sized proteins. Presently, the author's group extends these calculations to networked Silicon Graphics workstations and to networked NeXT workstations.

Benchmarks

Benchmarks of the various computers employed are provided in Fig. 2. On all computers has been carried out a molecular dynamics simulation of the protein lysozyme. The benchmark test measured how many integration steps, each 0.5 fs long, were performed on the various machines. The calculations employed the program MD written in C, except were stated (Xplor written in Fortran on the Cray 2, EGO written in Occam II on the Transputer-based machine). The performance has been measured relative to that of MD running on the Silicon Graphics 320 VGX.

The test calculations showed that 60 Transputers T800 can match about the performance of a Cray 2 processor, demonstrating the suitability and the good cost/performance ratio of the Transputer-based machine (parts cost of our machine with 60 processors and 240 Mbyte DRAM were at 1988, 1989 prices $60,000). One should keep in mind that the Transputer is very scalable and a machine like ours, which is available from vendors in similar configurations, can grow incrementally according to need and budgetary possibilities.

The most exciting entry in Fig. 2 is the (estimated, explicit runs have been completed sofar only on a network of Sun workstations) performance of a network of 16 NeXT workstations. Such network

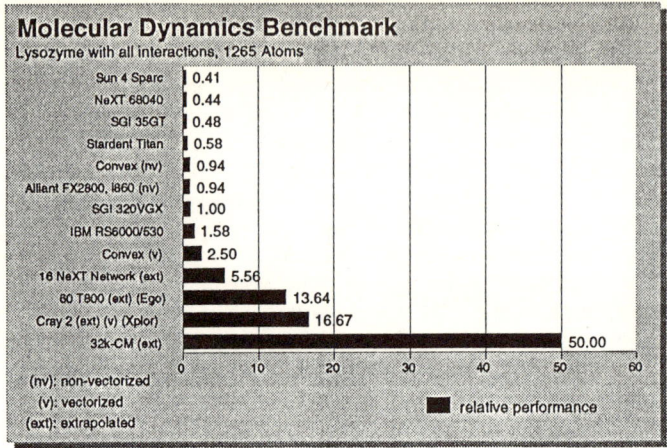

Figure 2: Performance on a number of different platforms. All calculations were made using the program MD, except those made with X-PLOR on the Cray-2 and EGO on the Transputer system. The result for the NeXT-network was extrapolated assuming an 80% efficiency. The CM-2 performance was extrapolated from an 8 K-configuration because of the small size of the molecule lysozyme. For larger molecules the CM-2 performance would be even better than indicated. Additionally, an improvement by a factor of 3–5 can be achieved on the CM-200 by taking advantage of the new slice-wise architecture. (Figure provided by Andreas Windemuth)

is available for under $100,000 and obviously provides a very flexible, multi-purpose solution with a good pice/performance ratio, in particular, in case that existing networks can be utilized.
Another interesting entry is the Connection Machine CM-2 with 32,000 procesors. The tests show that this machine can be utilized well for the simulations. In this respect it should be pointed out that the program, in this case, actually runs on the Sun front end of the Connection Machine, only the (most time consuming) evaluation of non-bonding pair forces being evaluated on the CM-2.

3 Projects

We continue the discussion of Fig. 1, namely, of the outer layer describing various Computational Biology projects being carried out on the various parallel machines mentioned above. In the lecture only a subset of these projects will be described in some detail. These projects are connected with the study of biological vision.

Molecular Dynamics of a Retinal Protein

Retinal proteins act as the receptors of light in the eyes of all animals. The protein resides in a membrane of a receptor cell and through absorption of light is very rapidly switched to a state which, after a series of biochemical amplificaton steps, alters the intracellular potential of the receptor cell and, thereby, transmits an electrical signal to the brain. We have actually investigated a retinal protein

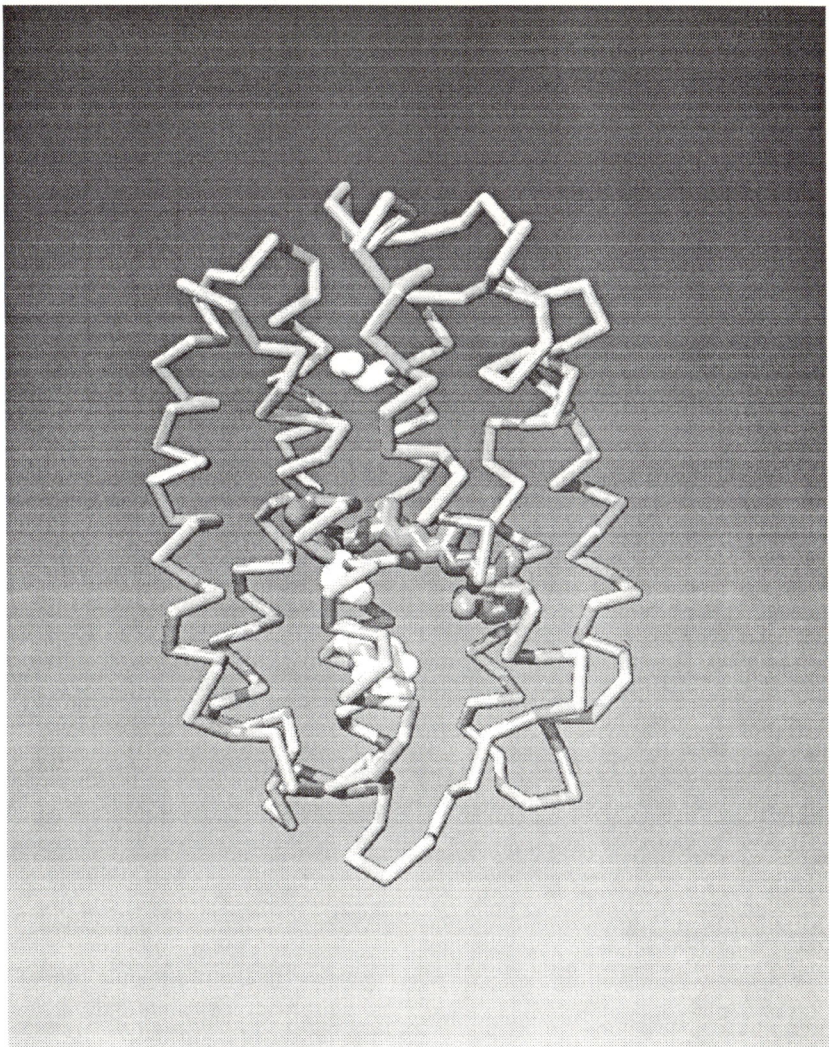

Figure 3: Schematic view of the protein bacteriorhodopsin. Shown is the backbone of peptide bonds together with some important amino acid side groups and with the prosthetic group retinal. Retinal (the large molecular moiety in the center of the protein) absorbs sun light and transforms itself within about 10^{-13} s into a new isomer. The back-reaction of retinal to the initial isomeric state is coupled to transfer of a protein from one side (top) of the protein to the other side (bottom) generating, thereby, a cellular electrical potential. The simulatons on the Connection machine CM-2 completed and refined the structure of the protein as well as identified the nature of the initial photoreaction. (Figure courtesy of A. Windemuth)

in a bacterial cell, namely bacteriorhodopsin, simulating the very fast reaction triggered by light and the subsequent thermal reaction steps. The novelty of the investigation, which utilized our program MD running on the Connection machine CM-2, has been that the structure of the protein had been available only partially and at poor (3.5Å) resolution. Hence, we needed to complete the structure and improve structural defects. Such efforts in structure completion and structure refinement will become commonplace in the near future, in particular, in connection with structure determination through 2-dimensional NMR spectra. Such calculations require very large computational resources as provided by massively parallel computers or through concurrent computation across networks. In the lecture I will also briefly describe molecular dynamics simulations of biological membranes

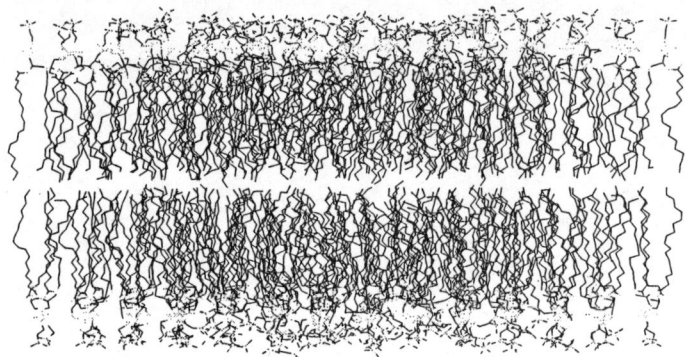

Figure 4: View of the lipid bilayer from the side. The structure has been equilibrated for about 20 ps. (Figure courtesy of H. Heller)

and of the interaction of drugs with DNA. These latter simulatons were carried out were carried out on our self-built Transputer-based computers. Figure 4 shows the structure of water and lipids assumed by a lipid bilayer after about 20 ps of simulation. The figure mainly documents that the Transputer-based machine is capable of simulating systems made up of 25,000 atoms.

Visual Maps in the Optical Cortex

In the lecture we will also report on a second project which is concerned with the representation of visual images in the brain. Such representation is achieved through an ordered connection between cells of the brain's visual cortex and receptor cells of the retinas of the two eyes. Through a technique, called 'voltage sensitive dye technique' much detail is known about this representation from laboratory investigations of monkeys and cats. In fact, one knows well the filter function (receptive fields) of cells in a whole array of the visual cortex, the brain area concerned with primary vision. The distribution of receptive field properties is called the 'visual map'. Most interestingly, these maps are established during the postnatal phase of an animal's life and development is driven through visual experience, i.e., the maps are individually 'learned'. We have studied the rules which underly this learning process.

A few numbers are relevant here. A brain area of a few mm^2 entails about 10^5 neurons which each have about 1,000 connections to the retinas of the two eyes, i.e., a 1 mm^2 patch of the brain is endowed with about 10^8 connections (synapses). Actually a modification of these synapses is the basis of the formation of the visual maps. To simulate the map formation one needs to deal then with dynamical systems of about 10^8 time-dependent variables. Such investigations, presently, can

  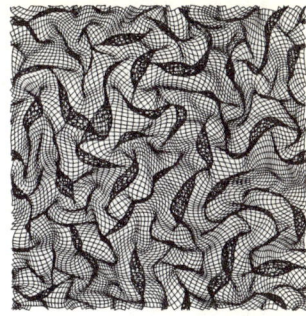

Figure 5: Visual maps simulated on the Connection machine CM-2: orientation preference (left), ocular diminance (center) and locations of receptive field centers (right) in a small area (about 1 mm^2 of the visual cortex). (Figure courtesy of K. Obermayer)

only be carried out routinely on massively parallel machines. We have employed for this purpose the Connection Machine CM-2. Figure 5 shows a mature visual map as generated in a simulation on the CM-2. The simulation run at a computing level of 2.5 Gflops which lies well within the range of optimal sustained performances of a 32,000 processor CM-2 (see Table 1).

The visual map in Fig. 5 (left) presents , the so-called orientation preference map, which codes in shades of gray, the orientation sensitivity of the cortical cells, covering the orientation interval [0°, 180°]. Since black codes for 180° orientation and white codes for 0° orientation, the orinetation around these values appear discontinuous in the map, but actually are continuous. The white points in the map correspond to zones where brain cells are actually insensitive to orientation. Near these zones the visual cortex stablishes cells which are sensitive to texture (granularity of the surfaces in the field of view) and sensitive to color.

Figure 5 (center) presents the same neurons as on the left hand side of the figure showing, however, the sensitivity to input either from the left (black) or right (white) eye, the so-called ocular dominance. This part of the figure, the so-called ocularity map, demonstrates that the cells are also transmitting stereo information to the brain. The right hand side of Fig. 5 presents the so-called retinotopic map for the same cells as the two other parts of the figure. The figure shows how the mesh of a net seen by one of the eyes would be represented in the brain (actually, the figure shows the inverse of the situation just described). One can recognize that such net is orderly represented except for some wrinkles. These wrinkles are unavoidable since the map represents also orientation information. One can show, however, that in some sense the brain tries to keep the wrinkles of the mesh at a minimum. All three parts of Fig. 5 taken together explain then how visual images are actually presented in the brain: the brain processes the retinal images on its way to the brain such that several attributes are compressed into a single brain representation: (1) position in the field of view, (2) orientation of local edges, (3) ocularity, (4) texture, and (5) color. Another important result of the simulation, which we cannot explain here in any detail, is that a small set of rather simple principle suffices to generate the visual maps through visual experience of an individual animal.

Visuo-Motor Control of an Industrial Robot

The brain is an organ the ultimate function of which is to allow an organism to react to sensory information. We have shown in our work that the principles involved in the development of visual maps in young animals can be applied also to other capacities of the brain, for example, to motion

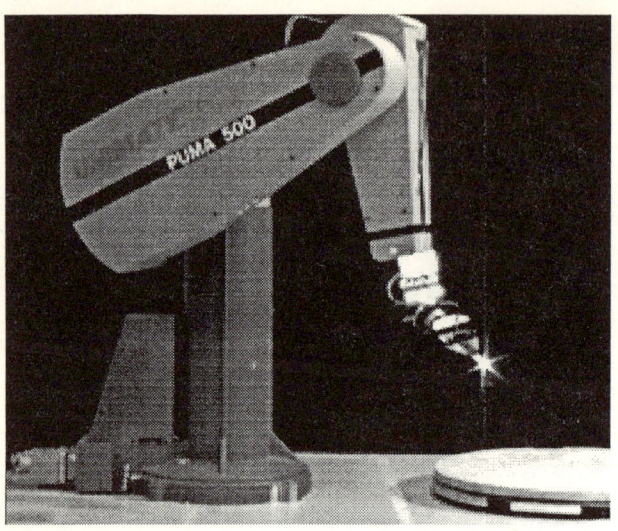
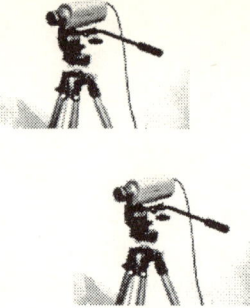

Figure 6: Presentation of the robot–camera system which, endowed with a computer program simulating the principles of neural developmental processes in biological organisms, learns to movethe robot's end effector (light blinking at the end of the robot arm) to any place in the work space. (Figure e of J. Walter)

control. In order to demonstrate that the principles assumed and translated into computer programs provide a basis for the acquisition of proper motion control in an animal, we have employed our programs to a system of two stereo cameras and an industrial robot arm. Such system is shown in Fig. 6. We have demonstrated that the developmental principles postulated by us can serve to teach a robot–camera system to move properly and accurately. For example, the industrial robot Puma 560 can learn after about 2,000 trial movements to point its end effector with a high degree of precion anywhere in the robot's work space. This is achieved by the system through learning first to present the work space in an orderly fashion in a neural net structure which exists as a data structure in a Sun 4 driving the system. The system can then recognize visually its errors in moving the end effector and through a simple learning rule adapts itself to move properly. The map which connects the back planes of the camera to the neural network presented in the computer has many similarities to the map presented in Fig. 5. The signals which drive the motors at the joint of the robot arm are presented as simple vectorial and tensorial data stored at the nodes of the neural network structure.

4 References

Some of the material presented in the lecture can be found in the forcecoming textbook *Neural Computation and Self-Organizing Maps: An Introduction* by Th. Martinetz, H. Ritter, and K. Schulten (Addison&Wesley, New York, 1991). Other publications covering material mentioned in the lecture can be obtained from the author upon request.

TIME-PARALLEL MULTIGRID IN AN EXTRAPOLATION METHOD FOR TIME-DEPENDENT PARTIAL DIFFERENTIAL EQUATIONS

Graham Horton and Ralf Knirsch
Institut für Mathematische Maschinen und Datenverarbeitung
Universität Erlangen-Nürnberg
Martensstr. 3
D-8520 Erlangen

Abstract. *We consider the parallel solution of unsteady partial differential equations with the two-dimensional heat equation as a model problem. Conventional implicit integration methods for the solution of this type of equation proceed by solving a sequence of problems iteratively. It is shown that despite the sequential nature of this process, several processors may be employed to solve at several time-steps simultaneously. The accuracy of an integration method such as backward Euler may be enhanced by embedding it in an extrapolation method which itself contains algorithmic parallelism. A solution procedure based on the multigrid method is presented which utilizes both kinds of parallelism. The efficiencies obtained on a message-passing multiprocessor prove the suitability of the method for this type of problem.*

1. Introduction

The parallel solution of ordinary differential equations (o.d.e.s) has received comparatively little attention in the literature. This is especially surprising considering the importance of the equations in scientific and technical computation. Systems of o.d.e.s, which arise from the discretization of unsteady partial differential equations form some of the most computationally intensive problems currently encountered on supercomputers and multiprocessors. The scarcity of publications on this topic is probably due to the fact that time is a one-way dimension, i.e. the dependencies between variables at successive time-steps seem to enforce sequential computation.

The most well-known application of parallelism in solving systems of o.d.e.s is by splitting up the problem at each time-step. In the case of partial differential equations this corresponds to a grid partitioning or domain decomposition type approach. Such methods retain, however, the sequential nature of the time integration.

The only well-known integration method for o.d.e.s that contains obvious parallelism is the extrapolation method, in which several independent integrations are performed, the solutions of which are then combined to obtain a better approximation to the continuous solution. This type of algorithmic parallelism is exploited by Burrage and Plowman in [5]. The method presented there suffers however from two disadvantages stemming from the use of an explicit integration formula: firstly the method is unsuitable for stiff problems, and secondly there is a low upper bound on the obtainable algorithmic speedup (i.e. ignoring communication and synchronization time), which is caused by the strongly unbalanced load. Bemmerl, Graf and Knödlseder [2] have also considered a parallelization of the extrapolation method, whereby individual processors are assigned multiple integrations such that the total computational load per processor is equal. This approach has only a limited degree of parallelism, and moreover is restricted to special choices of the time-step ratios. The method presented in this paper avoids these difficulties by using an implicit integration method and by increasing the number of processors used to solve the problems with smaller time-steps using a time-parallel method. In addition, it is applicable to any set of time-steps.

The time-parallel approach presented in this paper is based on the parabolic multigrid method suggested by Hackbusch [6], in which the solutions at several successive time-steps may be computed simultaneously. Convergence results for the method applied to a simple model problem have been given by Burmeister [3]. Experimental results have been published by Bastian, Burmeister and Horton [1] for the heat equation and by Burmeister and Horton [4] for the Navier-Stokes equations. A similar approach has also been considered by Womble [10].

In the following section the extrapolation method is presented. As this is a standard procedure, however, the description is relatively brief. In the next section the parabolic multigrid method is given and it is shown how it may be implemented in a time-parallel sense. Section 4 then describes the implementation of the extrapolation method on a transputer-based multiprocessor.

The experimental results obtained by the parallel implementation are presented in Section 5. The behaviour of the method for various parameters is discussed, identifying the causes of the efficiency losses experienced. In the final section the conclusions are presented, together with suggestions for further work and fields of application.

2. Extrapolation methods

We consider the ordinary differential equation

$$\frac{du}{dt} = f(u,t) \tag{1}$$

with the solution function $u(t)$. The discrete variables to be computed are denoted by u_K, $K = 0, \ldots, Kmax$. In the case of a system of o.d.e.s such as is obtained by semi-discretizing unsteady partial differential equations, u will represent a vector.

Extrapolation methods are based on the assumption that the exact solution $u(t_K)$ of the differential equation (1) at time t_K is related to the computed solution u_K with stepsize Δt by the following asymptotic formula :

$$u_K = u(t_K) + a_1 \Delta t + a_2 \Delta t^2 + \cdots + O(\Delta t^N) \tag{2}$$
$$\text{for } \Delta t \to 0$$

When this is the case, and this property can be shown for a range of integration formulae, then the interval from t_K to t_{K+1} may be separately integrated using different step sizes Δt_j, $j = 1, \ldots, m$ to compute the approximations $\tilde{u}_j$, $j = 1, \ldots, m$ at time t_{K+1}. Performing a suitable linear combination of the $\tilde{u}_j$ - in order to eliminate terms from Eq. (2) - then produces an improved approximation u_{K+1} to the exact solution $u(t_{K+1})$. Typical choices for the stepsizes Δt_j are $\Delta t_1 = t_{K+1} - t_K$ and $s_j \Delta t_j = \Delta t_1$ with $s_j = (2, 4, 8, 16, \ldots)$ or $s_j = (2, 4, 6, 8, \ldots)$. In this paper the former choice is used.

Extrapolation methods obtain the improved solution from these m approximations by computing the following tableau :

$$\begin{array}{cccc} Q_{1,1} & & & \\ Q_{2,1} & Q_{2,2} & & \\ Q_{3,1} & Q_{3,2} & Q_{3,3} & \\ \vdots & \vdots & \vdots & \ddots \\ Q_{m,1} & Q_{m,2} & Q_{m,3} & \cdots & Q_{m,m} \end{array} \qquad (3)$$

whereby the $Q_{j,1}$ are the results $\tilde{u}_j$ of the integration with stepsize Δt_j and the $Q_{j,j}$ are the improved approximations where successive terms from Eq. (2) have been eliminated. The $Q_{i,j}$, $j = 2, \ldots, m$ are computed by the following algorithm due to Neville:

$$Q_{i,j} = Q_{i,j-1} + \frac{Q_{i,j-1} - Q_{i-1,j-1}}{\frac{\Delta t_{i-j+1}}{\Delta t_i} - 1} \quad . \qquad (4)$$

The above algorithm allows the extrapolation to be performed without making explicit use of the coefficients a_i in Eq. (2).

Details of extrapolation methods may be found in many standard textbooks on ordinary differential equations, for example Lambert [9].

3. Time-parallel Multigrid Method

We consider as a model problem the unsteady heat equation

$$\frac{\partial u}{\partial t} - \frac{\partial^2 u}{\partial x^2} - \frac{\partial^2 u}{\partial y^2} = q(x, y, t) \quad . \qquad (5)$$

Discretizing the space derivatives with standard central differences using an equidistant grid of meshsize h we obtain a system of ordinary differential equations corresponding to Eq. (1). Choosing Backward Euler with stepsize Δt as the integration method for the time derivative we then obtain at each grid point a discrete equation.

In order to solve the system described by Eq. (6) with a multigrid method we define a hierarchy of grids indicated by a level $l \in \{0, \ldots, lmax\}$. Let $u_{l,k}$ and $q_{l,k}$ now denote grid functions defined on a grid at level l with mesh size h_l at time t_k. The time interval $[t_K, t_{K+1}]$ which the extrapolation method requires to be integrated is divided into n discrete sub-intervals $[t_k, t_{k+1}], \ldots, [t_{k+n-1}, t_{k+n}]$ where $t_k = t_K$ and $t_{k+n} = t_{K+1}$.

The discrete parabolic problem for level l is given by the block bidiagonal system $A\underline{u} = \underline{q}$ (Eq. 6), where I_l denotes the identity matrix on level l, and A_l is the pentadiagonal matrix containing the space coefficients obtained by a lexicographic ordering of the grid points at each time-step.

$$\begin{bmatrix} \frac{1}{\Delta t}I_l + A_l & & & 0 \\ -\frac{1}{\Delta t}I_l & \frac{1}{\Delta t}I_l + A_l & & \\ & \ddots & \ddots & \\ 0 & & -\frac{1}{\Delta t}I_l & \frac{1}{\Delta t}I_l + A_l \end{bmatrix} \begin{bmatrix} u_{l,k+1} \\ u_{l,k+2} \\ \vdots \\ u_{l,k+n} \end{bmatrix} = \begin{bmatrix} q_{l,k+1} + \frac{1}{\Delta t}I_l u_{l,k} \\ q_{l,k+2} \\ \vdots \\ q_{l,k+n} \end{bmatrix} \quad (6)$$

Since there is no forward dependency in the time direction, the usual solution procedure is to calculate the unknown grid functions $u_{l,k+1}, u_{l,k+2}, \ldots$ in a sequential manner. Multigrid methods can be successfully applied to the problem at each successive time-step, because the arising linear systems can be interpreted as discrete elliptic problems [5]. Standard multiprocessor solution methods derive their parallelism from a decomposition of the solution vector u_k at each time-step t_k. The sequential nature of the time integration process is, however, retained, i.e. the rows of the block-structured system shown in Eq. (6) are processed one by one. By contrast, Hackbusch [6] proposed a multigrid approach in which the system is treated as a whole and whereby furthermore individual time-steps may be allocated to different processors and solved simultaneously. In the following a short description of the method for the two-grid case is given, beginning with the smoother, which is based on an incomplete decomposition.

Incomplete decomposition (ILU) methods are a popular class of iterative methods for the solution of elliptic equation systems as they are known to be both efficient and robust. Thus it is desirable to find a suitable incomplete decomposition for the time-parallel case.

Consider the block-bidiagonal matrix A of Eq. (6), where the matrices on the block-diagonal have pentadiagonal form and the block-subdiagonal is a diagonal matrix. This matrix may be approximately factorized pointwise by the lower triangular matrix L and the upper triangular matrix U, which are defined as follows:

$$A = LU + R \quad (7)$$
$$patt(A) \subseteq patt(L) \cup patt(U) \quad (8)$$
$$A_{i,j} \neq 0 \Rightarrow (LU)_{i,j} = A_{i,j} \quad (9)$$
$$diag(U) = I \quad (10)$$

where $A_{i,j}$ denotes the entry at row i, column j of the matrix A and the remainder matrix is denoted by R. The pattern of non-zero entries of the matrix A is denoted by $patt(A)$. The decomposition used in this work is the so-called zero-order ILU, where the equality holds in Eq. (8). Using the temporary storage vectors v and δ, and denoting the rows of the block system (6) by the subscript $k+j$, the smoothing procedure consists of the following steps:

1. Compute $r_{k+j} = q_{k+j} - A_{k+j} u_{k+j}$ $j = 1, \ldots, n$
2. Solve $L_{k+j} v_{k+j} = r_{k+j}$ $j = 1, \ldots, n$
3. Solve $U_{k+j} \delta_{k+j} = v_{k+j}$ $j = 1, \ldots, n$
4. Compute $u_{k+j} = u_{k+j} + \delta_{k+j}$ $j = 1, \ldots, n$

Steps 1,3 and 4 may be performed in parallel without communication between the different time-steps. Note that the solution of the L equation at time-step $k+j$ requires values of v from the preceding time-step $k+j-1$. Thus step 2 above, whilst being parallelizable in a pipeline fashion, transfers a large amount of data at a fine level of granularity. We therefore also consider a smoothing variant in which the correction at the preceding time-step is assumed to be zero, thus decoupling the computations at successive time-steps. The updated values are then transferred at the end of the iteration. The first technique, where values from the preceding time-step and the same iteration are used corresponds to a block Gauß-Seidel-like iteration, whilst the latter version corresponds to a block Jacobi-like method.

Let the i-th iterate of the multigrid iteration be denoted by $u_{l,k+j}^{(i)}$, $j=1,\ldots,n$. Let S_l be a time-parallel smoothing procedure, for which we choose an incomplete decompostion method (ILU), as it is known to be both efficient and robust. We assume standard prolongation and restriction operators p and r to be given. The application of S_l ν times is denoted by S_l^ν. For an introduction to multigrid methods and terminology refer to Hackbusch [7].

The linear parabolic two-grid method is given by the following algorithm:

Time-parallel two-grid algorithm

Pre-Smoothing

$$u_{l,k+j}^{(i+\frac{1}{3})} = S_l^{\nu_1}\left(u_{l,k+j}^{(i)}, A_l, u_{l,k+j-1}^{(i)}\right), \quad j=1,\ldots,n\;.$$

Calculate the defect

$$d_{l,k+j} = \left(\frac{1}{\Delta t}I_l + A_l\right)u_{l,k+j}^{(i+\frac{1}{3})} - q_{l,k+j} - \frac{1}{\Delta t}I_l u_{l,k+j-1}^{(i+\frac{1}{3})}, \quad j=1,\ldots,n\;.$$

Restriction

$$d_{l-1,k+j} = r d_{l,k+j}, \quad j=1,\ldots,n\;.$$

Solve coarse grid equation

$$\left(\frac{1}{\Delta t}I_{l-1} + A_{l-1}\right)u_{l-1,k+j} = d_{l-1,k+j} + \frac{1}{\Delta t}I_{l-1}u_{l-1,k+j-1}, \quad j=1,\ldots,n\;.$$

Prolongation and correction

$$u_{l,k+j}^{(i+\frac{2}{3})} = u_{l,k+j}^{(i+\frac{1}{3})} - p u_{l-1,k+j}, \quad j=1,\ldots,n\;.$$

Post-Smoothing

$$u_{l,k+j}^{(i+1)} = S_l^{\nu_2}\left(u_{l,k+j}^{(i+\frac{2}{3})}, A_l, u_{l,k+j-1}^{(i+\frac{2}{3})}\right), \quad j=1,\ldots,n\;.$$

The algorithm can be extended to a multigrid version by replacing the exact solution on the coarse grid by a recursive call to the two-grid algorithm at level $l - 1$. Note that all components of the multigrid algorithm can be computed independently, and therefore in parallel in different time-steps.

A time-parallel Full Approximation Storage (FAS) method may be defined in an analogous fashion, in order to obtain a solution procedure for non-linear problems. The time-parallel full multigrid V-cycle method (FMG-V) is defined in the standard way as the application of one time-parallel V-Cycle to provide initial approximations on successively finer grids. It is well known that the FMG method obtains a solution of discretization accuracy, assuming that the error reduction at each grid level is sufficient. Experiments have shown that this is also the case for the time-parallel FMG method.

Many of the multigrid components, such as prolongation, restriction and residual computation are easily vectorizable; in addition, vectorizable smoothing procedures such as ADI, Jacobi or Red-Black Gauss-Seidel may be used. One common experience when using a standard parallelization approach is the decrease in performance of the vector unit due to the partitioning of the computational grid, which results in a reduction in vector length. This phenomenon is, however, not encountered in the time-parallel case, as each processor is assigned a complete grid.

The time-parallel approach for the solution of an unsteady partial differential equation differs completely from that of conventional grid partitioning methods. Whereas the latter proceed by dividing a given problem amongst the processors, thus obtaining their speedup by increasing the effective performance of the machine, the parallelization in time can be interpreted as a parallelization of the sequential algorithm itself. Additional processors are not used to solve subproblems of decreasing size but to begin processing data which would otherwise have been computed at a later time. The speedup is thus due to a reduction of the effective number of iterations needed to perform the integration, rather than by increasing the computation speed of the unchanged algorithm. The time-parallel idea may, however, be applied to standard space-parallel techniques in order to considerably increase the number of processors effectively usable.

4. Implementation

The implementation employs two kinds of parallelism: the algorithmic parallelism contained explicitly in the extrapolation method, whereby the time interval may be simultaneously integrated with different step sizes, and time-parallelism, where problems with smaller step sizes are solved with a larger number of processors spread across the time dimension using the time-parallel multigrid method of the previous section. The third possibility of space parallelism via grid partitioning or domain decomposition is well known and therefore not considered here. Processors are assigned according to Fig. 1. Firstly, the number of processor groups is chosen equal to the number m of rows of the extrapolation tableau (3) to be computed. Each group j, $j = 1,\ldots,m$ contains a number p_j of processors in accordance with the associated step size to satisfy $p_j \Delta t_j = \Delta t_1$. The total number p of processors used is thus $2^m - 1$. Each group j is then allocated to the

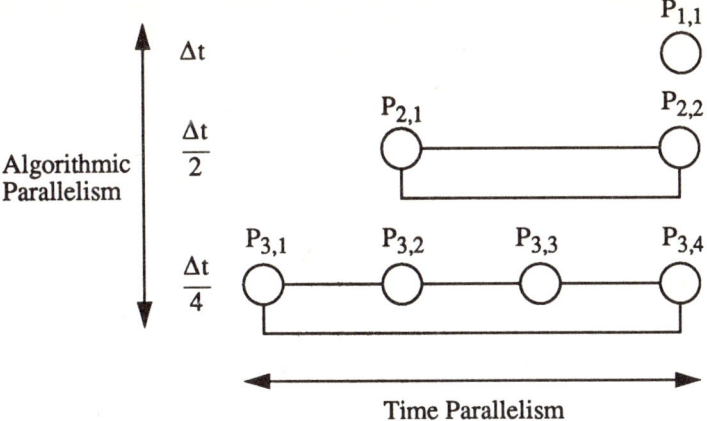

Figure 1: Division of work on the parallel machine

computation of the intermediate solution $\tilde{u}_j$ using the time-parallel multigrid algorithm of the preceding section. In order to satisfy the communication requirements of the time-parallel method, where each time-step depends on data from its predecessor, the required topology for each group is a ring. In addition, the last processor P_{j,p_j} of each group must send the intermediate solutions $\tilde{u}_j$ to processor $P_{1,1}$, which then performs the extrapolation and broadcasts the improved approximation u_{K+1} to each processor group as the initial value for the next integration step.

The above strategy corresponds to the original application of the extrapolation method by Gragg, where a new initial-value problem is defined by the extrapolation at intermediate time-steps. Since, however, the extrapolation process requires both communication and a serial computation stage, it represents an inhibiting factor for the parallel efficiency. It may thus be desirable to delay the extrapolation phase for a number of integration steps, in order to reduce the serial overhead. We therefore introduce the blocking parameter b, $b \geq 1$, which defines the number of time-steps over which the integration is performed between extrapolations. Thus, in the limit case, the extrapolation may be performed only once, at the end of the integration interval.

The time-parallel integration is performed using the parabolic multigrid method from the preceding section. The implementation of the method is based on that of Knirsch [8]. After each iteration a convergence test is performed at each individual time-step. We require that time-steps may only converge in order of increasing t. When one or more processors have computed a converged solution they are immediately allocated new time-steps and the integration proceeds in a cyclic fashion. We consider the situation for the four processors $P_{3,i}$, $i = 1, \ldots, 4$, which are initially allocated time-steps t_{k+i}, $i = 1, \ldots, 4$. After the iteration at t_{k+1} has converged, processor $P_{3,1}$ begins the first iteration on the new time-step t_{k+5}. The cyclic process is complete when processor $P_{3,4}$ has computed the intermediate solution at time t_{K+b}.

5. Results

The implementation of the time-parallel method described in the previous section was carried out on a Transputer system using the C programming language. The ring topology required for each processor group was hard wired for maximum communication efficiency. We chose as a model equation the unsteady heat equation (5) in the unit square and the time interval $(t_0, t_{max}]$. Two model solutions were used :

$$(MS1) \quad u(x,y,t) = \sin(2t) + x^2 + y^2 ,$$
$$(MS2) \quad u(x,y,t) = \sin(t)x(1-x)y(1-y) .$$

These solutions were chosen to be exactly representable by central differences in x and y, so that the effect of the extrapolation of the time derivative is not swamped by the discretization error in the space directions.

We use the standard measures for the effectiveness of a parallel method, the Speedup $S(p)$ and the Efficiency $E(p)$, defined as follows:

$$S(p) = \frac{T(1)}{T(p)} , \quad E(p) = \frac{S(p)}{p}$$

where $T(p)$ represents the computation time for the solution on p processors. Speedup measures the increase in computing speed, i.e. the factor by which computation time is reduced, while the Efficiency, which normalizes the Speedup to a value between 0 and 1 represents the effectiveness of the parallel method.

For the first numerical experiment, where the time-parallel V-cycles were applied to $MS1$, the discretization parameter Δt_1 was set to 0.1 and the finest space grid was equidistant with meshsize $\frac{1}{32}$. A total of 8 time-steps was integrated, i.e. $Kmax = 8$. In addition we used one pre-smoothing step ($\nu_1 = 1$) and no post-smoothing in the multigrid algorithm. The block Jacobi-like method was used as the smoothing procedure and a convergence criterion of $1.0E-9$ for the residual was stipulated for the multigrid iteration.

Table 1 shows the dependency of computation time on the number m of processor groups (lines of the extrapolation tableau) used. The table also gives the total number of multigrid iterations required by the last group of processors in each calculation.

For this computation, which represents an integration over 8 time-steps ($Kmax = 8$), a blocking factor b equal to 8 was used, i.e. the extrapolation was performed once only. The discretization error $\epsilon = \|u(t_{max}) - u_{Kmax}\|_2$ of the method compared to the known continuous solution is seen to decrease as more lines of the extrapolation tableau are computed. An increase in the computation time by a factor of approximately 1.4 with 31 processors is needed to decrease the error by 6 orders of magnitude.

Note that the number of iterations needed by the various groups decreases with increasing m. This is due to the fact that the diagonal dominance of the matrices A_l is successively enhanced owing to the growing $\frac{1}{\Delta t}$ term on the main diagonal. The parallel method takes advantage of this fact by using the decrease in the number of iterations to partially offset the increased communication overhead when more processors are used.

				Standard Problem			Increased Load		
m	p	#Iter	ϵ	$T(p)$	$S(p)$	$E(p)$	$T(p)$	$S(p)$	$E(p)$
1	1	174	$2.89E-05$	29.4	1.00	1.00	77.6	1.00	1.00
2	3	173	$8.59E-06$	32.4	2.71	0.90	80.5	2.86	0.95
3	7	165	$5.46E-08$	34.4	5.81	0.83	80.5	6.49	0.93
4	15	160	$3.35E-10$	36.1	11.4	0.76	81.9	13.2	0.88
5	31	156	$2.52E-11$	41.1	19.8	0.64	84.5	25.3	0.81

Table 1: Dependency of Computation Time on Number of Processor Groups

m	1	2	3	4	5
p	1	3	7	15	31
$T(p)$	43.6	48.8	55.1	55.6	64.1
$E(p)$	1.00	0.87	0.78	0.77	0.67
ϵ_{par}	$1.37E-5$	$1.86E-7$	$3.38E-8$	$2.03E-10$	$6.0E-12$
ϵ_{seq}	$1.37E-5$	$1.86E-7$	$3.38E-8$	$2.03E-10$	$1.9E-12$

Table 2: Accuracy and efficiency of the time-parallel FMG method

The drop in efficiency experienced when the number m of lines of the extrapolation tableau is increased is primarily due to the comparatively large communication overhead incurred by the algorithm - within each iteration the complete solution grid on each multigrid level must be transferred to a neighbouring processor three times. In addition, the amount of arithmetic computation per grid point is relatively small, owing to the simplicity of the model problem.

In order to simulate the solution of more complex problems, the computational load on the processors was increased artificially by requiring nine additional (superfluous) defect calculations within the multigrid cycle. This corresponds to an increase in computational load by a factor of almost three. The results are also given in Table 1, where the computation corresponds in all other respects to that of the standard algorithm. The improvement in efficiency can be clearly seen, in particular in the 31 processor case, where the efficiency obtained increases from 64% to 81%.

Table 2 shows the results obtained by the application of the time-parallel FMG method to $MS2$. The parameters of the multigrid iteration were : $\nu_1 = 3$, $\nu_2 = 1$, $b = 8$ and $\Delta t_1 = 1.0$. The computation times and discretization errors both of the sequential time-stepping method and of the parallel scheme are given. It can be seen that the accuracy of the parallel algorithm is equal to that of the classic time-stepping method, with the exception of the case $m = 5$, where a slight loss is observed. The parallel efficiency drops to 67% on 31 processors, which again is due to the considerable communication requirement and the small computational load of the method.

		\multicolumn{8}{c}{m (p)}

		\multicolumn{2}{c	}{2 (3)}	\multicolumn{2}{c	}{3 (7)}	\multicolumn{2}{c	}{4 (15)}	\multicolumn{2}{c	}{5 (31)}
		ϵ	$T(p)$	ϵ	$T(p)$	ϵ	$T(p)$	ϵ	$T(p)$
b	1	$2.30E-7$	50.4	$4.66E-8$	57.2	$6.59E-10$	58.5	$4.35E-11$	67.5
	2	$1.85E-7$	49.5	$3.37E-8$	56.0	$2.24E-10$	56.8	$7.32E-12$	65.0
	4	$1.86E-7$	49.1	$3.38E-8$	55.4	$2.03E-10$	56.0	$6.00E-12$	64.1
	8	$1.86E-7$	48.8	$3.38E-8$	55.1	$2.03E-10$	55.6	$6.00E-12$	64.0

Table 3: Dependency of computation time and accuracy on b

Table 3 shows the dependency of computation time $T(p)$ on the blocking factor b, i.e. the number of time-steps integrated between extrapolation steps, showing clearly the decrease in computation time with increasing blocking factor b. This is due to the decreased number of extrapolations needed, saving both communication and non-parallel arithmetic. The error in the solution varies slightly with b, but since the change is only slight, we conclude that the reduction in the frequency of the extrapolations is a valid technique to decrease the serial overhead of the method.

6. Conclusions and Outlook

The method presented in this paper for the solution of parabolic p.d.e.s utilizes two kinds of parallelism: the algorithmic parallelism inherent in the extrapolation method, and the time parallelism contained in the parabolic multigrid method of Hackbusch. The third, and most well known type of parallelism for this type of problem is the space parallelism obtained for example by grid partitioning type methods, which, however, is not considered here.

The time-parallel multigrid method was tested both in a V-cycle mode with iteration to convergence as well as in an FMG scheme. The results obtained by both implementations show that the method is capable of achieving high efficiencies (> 75%) for up to 15 processors when applied to the linear model problem. In the general case, where the method would be combined with a standard space partitioning approach, this would enable an effective increase in parallelism by a factor of 15. When more complex problems with a higher computational load per grid point are considered, the results can be expected to improve, as the efficiency of the basic time-parallel method will be higher. The assumption is strengthened by the results obtained for an artificial test case. High parallel efficiencies for a time-parallel multigrid method have been obtained for the Navier-Stokes equations by Burmeister and Horton in [4].

The successive computation of the columns of the extrapolation tableau (3) also contains a certain amount of parallelism, as each entry may be computed independently of the others. Because of the relatively small amount of computational work involved in performing the extrapolation steps, and the increased volume of communication which would be necessary, this possibility was not used in the implementation.

In order to improve the time accuracy of the method, one obvious modification is to replace the implicit Euler integrator by the Trapezoidal (Crank-Nicholson) rule. This method is also implicit, and thus retains the superior stability properties compared to explicit schemes and it would increase accuracy for two reasons. Firstly the Trapezoidal rule has order two, compared to the first order Euler method, and secondly the asymptotic expansion Eq. (2) contains only even powers of Δt, so that for a given number of lines of the extrapolation tableau (3), the first non-zero term in the asymptotic formula for the extrapolated solution will be much smaller.

By using a space-parallel multigrid method within each time-step, a solution procedure combining all three parallelization techniques could be achieved. The degree of parallelism of the combined method is then obtained as the product of that of the grid partitioning method and the number of processors used by the extrapolation/time-parallel method presented in this paper.

Acknowledgement

This work was supported in part by the Stiftung Volkswagenwerk within its program "Entwicklung von Berechnungsverfahren für Probleme der Strömungstechnik" and by the Bundesministerium für Forschung und Technologie within its "PARAWAN" project. The parallel Transputer system used for the test calculations was financed in part by a grant from the Commission of the European Community within its ESPRIT program.

References

[1] Bastian, P., Burmeister, J., Horton, G.: *Implementation of a parallel multigrid method for parabolic partial differential equations.* Proceedings of the 6th GAMM Seminar, Vieweg, 1990.

[2] Bemmerl, T., Graf, U., Knödlseder, R., *Experiences in parallelizing an existing CFD algorithm.* Distributed Memory Computing, Ed. A. Bode, LNCS 487, Springer, 1991.

[3] Burmeister, J.: *Paralleles Lösen diskreter parabolischer Probleme mit Mehrgittertechniken.* Diplom thesis, Universität Kiel, 1985.

[4] Burmeister, J., Horton, G.: *Time-Parallel Solution of the Navier-Stokes Equations.* Proceedings of the 3rd European Multigrid Conference, Bonn 1990, Birkhäuser Verlag, 1991.

[5] Burrage, K., Plowman, S.: *The Numerical Solution of ODE IVPs in a Transputer Environment.* Transputer Applications 90, Southampton, 1990.

[6] Hackbusch, W.: *Parabolic Multi-grid Methods.* In Glowinski, R., Lions, J.-R.(eds.): Computing Methods in Applied Sciences and Engineering, VI. Proceedings of the 6th International Symposium on Computing Methods in Applied Sciences and Engineering. Versailles, France, December 12-16, 1983. North Holland 1984.

[7] Hackbusch, W.: *Multi-grid Methods and Applications.* Heidelberg: Springer-Verlag 1985.

[8] Knirsch, R.: *Implementierung eines parallelen Mehrgitterverfahrens zur Lösung instationärer partieller Differentialgleichungen.* Diplom thesis, IMMD 3, Universität Erlangen-Nürnberg, 1990.

[9] Lambert, J.D.: *Computational Methods in Ordinary Differential Equations.* John Wiley, 1983.

[10] Womble, D.E.: *A Time-Stepping Algorithm for Parallel Computers.* SIAM J. Sci. Stat. Comput., Vol 11, No 5, pp 824-837.

Parallelization of Simulation Tasks:
Methodology - Implementation - Application

F. Breitenecker, G. Schuster
Dept. Simulation Techniques
E-Mail: fbreiten@email.tuwien.ac.at

I. Husinsky, J. Fritscher
Computer Center
E-Mail: husinsky@edvz.tuwien.ac.at

Technical University of Vienna
Wiedner Hauptstr. 8-10, A - 1040 Vienna, Austria

Abstract

After a short discussion on the parallelization of simulation software the so-called MME-structure (model - method - experiment) for simulation tasks is introduced. This study extends the well known structure of model frame and experimental frame by a third frame of methods. The structure of the methods is a hierarchical one, being the base for the parallelization of simulation tasks. Starting at a medium hierarchical level a parallelization can be realized in a model-independent manner. Examples are parameter variation, linearization at different points, model comparison, where also analytical procedures can be used. The concept was implemented within the Simulation System PARALLEL_HYBSYS on a PC based transputer system (T800).

1. Introduction

Simulation of especially continuous systems is very often a number-crunching task, so one tries to accelerate the simulation of a system using special hardware with suitable software: vector processors, parallel processors or special purpose simulation processors play an important role in today's simulation.

Fast computers range from supercomputers (CRAY, VP 50) over minisupercomputers (CONVEX) to smaller computers with parallel features (parallel processors with shared or distributed memory, for instance transputer systems). The advantage of this type of computers is their general purpose, they can be used for different tasks.

Another way of accelerating simulation tasks is the use of special purpose simulation processors, which do number crunching very quickly. There usually a host is extended by a fast (signal) processor (examples are the very powerful AD-100 system with VAX as host, or at the low end the XANALOG-system which uses a signal processor with vector- and pipeline- features and a PC as host).

Although there exists a lot of suitable hardware, there is a lack of software for parallel simulation and also for parallel or vectorized computing.

This contribution tries to analyze different simulation tasks concerning parallel structures at higher levels, which can be implemented on parallel processors.

2. Parallelization of Simulation Software

In principle there exist two kinds of software parallelization on different hierarchical levels:

- functional parallelization (partitioning)
- data parallelization (partitioning)

In case of simulation software both kinds on different levels may be specialized - resulting in model-dependent or model-independent parallel structures.

2.1 Procedure level parallelization

In case of a simulation task the code of the simulation system together with the (usually compiled) model has to be parallelized or vectorized by an appropriate vector compiler or parallel compiler. On this basic level one may either use automatic parallelization features of the compiler or one may analyze the structure of the code manually (data partitioning).

The next step of parallelization is for instance using integration algorithms suitable for parallel computation. This way yields better results, for instance in parallelizing or vectorizing complex integration schemes (data partitioning or functional partitioning) [6].

The disadvantage of this method is that the acceleration of the simulation depends on the code and on the model to be implemented. Furthermore, the resulting acceleration is more suitable for vector- and pipeline-features and shared memory architectures.

2.2 Parallelization at a higher level

2.2.1 Model dependent parallelization

In case of simulation the data to be parallelized are the models to be investigated - one tries to "evaluate" the model in a parallel manner.

A lot of research work has been done in this area [5, 7]. Usually the state variables are the base of parallelization:

$$dx_1/dt = f_1(x_1,x_2,x_3,...x_n)$$
$$dx_2/dt = f_2(x_1,x_2,x_3,...x_n)$$
$$dx_3/dt = f_3(x_1,x_2,x_3,...x_n)$$
$$\dots\dots\dots\dots$$
$$dx_n/dt = f_n(x_1,x_2,x_3,...x_n)$$

Integration algorithms have to evaluate each component of the system equations several times, consequently parallelization of this evaluation accelerates the time domain analysis.

Using a parallel processor system, each processor calculates within an evaluation a component $dx_i/dt = f_i$ of the state equations, while a master processor controls the integration algorithm. Each processor has to communicate with others, if auxiliary variables are to be calculated, - and auxiliary variables are often necessary in order to combine complex multiple calculations (in this case some of the processors calculate auxiliary variables y_j, which need the other processors for calculating the derivatives f_i). This communication has to be controlled by the master processor, the overhead depends on the structure of the memory of the processors (shared memory or distributed memory).

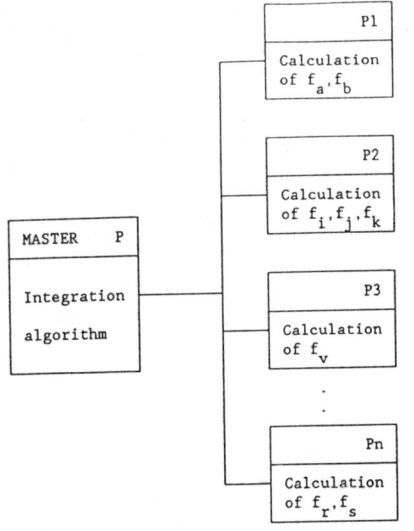

Fig.1: Parallelization of the model with dynamic balancing

New problems arise in case the number of equations is greater than the number of processors, which very often happens. Now each processor has to calculate more than one derivative f_i (or auxiliary variable y_j). The time required for these computations has to be balanced well between the processors (either a priori with static balancing or at runtime with dynamic balancing, which is much more complicated).

Figure 1 shows a dynamic balance of parallelized evaluations of state equations.

This type of parallelization (data partitioning) has been investigated and developed very intensively, but it has one disadvantage: the parallelization is dependent on the model [5,7].

2.2.2 Model independent parallelization

Models are analyzed by certain analytical or numerical algorithms. Within time domain analysis numerical integration algorithms, for instance, can be vectorized or parallelized (for pipeline processors, vector processors, or parallel processors). But this type of parallelization results in a parallelization of the code - with all advantages and disadvantages [6].

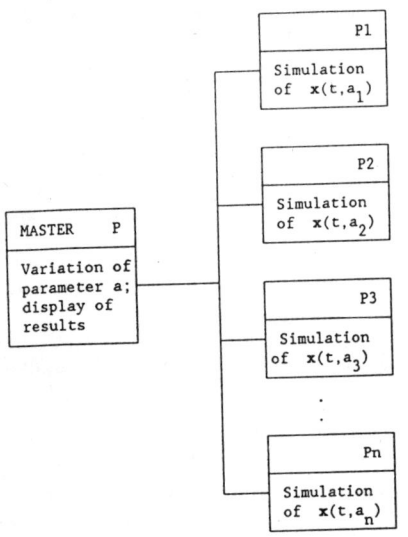

Fig. 2: Parallelization in the parameter sphere

Several investigations try to find parallelizations being independent of the integration algorithm and of the model [6,7].

First attempts were made to investigate parallel structures on the experiment level. In simulation software one distinguishes between the model frame (the model description) and the experimental frame (experiment description, "runtime interpreter") - consequently a search for parallel structures at the experiment level is evident.

It turned out that the simplest parallelization on this higher level is a parallelization in the parameter sphere [7].

If a time domain analysis for different values of a model parameter has to be performed, each processor can calculate the whole time course for one parameter value. Denoting $x(t,a)$ the simulation results of the model $dx/dt = f(x)$ (bold letters indicating vectors), then the first processor could calculate $x(t,a_1)$, the second $x(t,a_2)$, the third $x(t,a_3)$, etc. (figure 2).

This type of parallelization is simple, but very effective, because there exists no overhead caused by communications among the processors. Furthermore, the parallelization does not depend on the model - which is very advantageous. Consequently within the research project of a simulation system described later this type of parallelization will be implemented.

The outlined principles of parallelization belong to different levels of the examined structure of languages (model frame - experimental frame).

But soon it becomes clear that this usual structure (model frame and experimental frame) is not sufficient, also for the parallelization of tasks - which on a higher level are independent of a model.

3. The Methodology of Models - Methods - Experiments

System theory and system technique are the base of simulation. System theory offers quite different theories to analyze, to examine, and to validate systems, usually by means of models.

The classical simulation usually uses only one theory, the time domain analysis (calculus of differential equations). Sometimes simulation languages offer also frequency domain analysis, another theory.

But there exist more theories which may be used for analyzing a system - sensitivity analysis, structure analysis, etc.

Up to now within simulation languages a third level characterizing these different analyzing methods is missing. Using such a higher level, one may try to parallelize tasks on this level - independent of the model.

One very interesting concept of a new structure is the concept of frames by Zeigler [9]. This concept is based on the separation of model frame, experimental frame, and execution control (being another level). The execution control selects and controls a set of experiments, which are defined as a "function" of a certain model frame and a certain experimental frame. This concept seems to be the first modern one, because it introduces an experiment as a function of a model frame and of an experimental frame. There model definition and experimental frame specification are on the same hierarchy level, while the experiment and the execution control build up other levels of hierarchy.

The natural way now is to generalize this three-frames concept.

3.1 Structure of Models - Methods - Experiments (MME-structure)

Up to now the terms *model, experiment, experimental frame, execution control, model base, algorithm*, etc. build up a veritable tower of Babylon. In the following terms are defined, together with the new term "methods" (being the new third level in simulation software):
- A model (MO) is the description of a real system using a mathematical formulation and a certain language.
- A method (ME) is an algorithm which does anything with the model.
- An experiment (E) is the application of a certain method on a certain model.

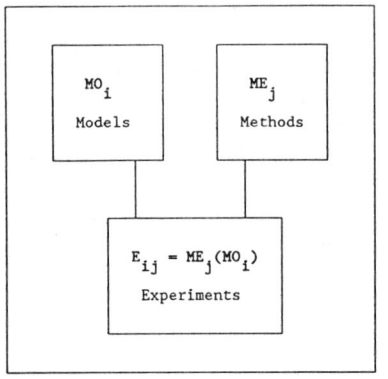

Fig.3: *Structure of models - methods - experiments*

A basic method, for instance, is the simulation run (the integration of the system governing differential equations), the corresponding experiment is the performance of a simulation run with a certain model. Another basic method is the parameter change (accessing the model data base with data input), the corresponding experiment is the change of a certain parameter of a certain model. A complex method is (parameter) optimization.

The basic idea of this concept is to consider an experiment E as application of a certain method ME on a certain model MO, where method and model are strictly independent of each other. Figure 3 sketches this concept, first outlined in [1].

A *model* MO may formally be defined as specification of states and of state interactions of the system to be investigated. The model MO is stored in a more or less structured model data base. A model MO has to be independent of methods and of experiments. Submodels and model libraries can be supported.

A *method* ME is formally to be defined as an algorithm which is to be applied on a model using qualitative and quantitative model data. A method ME has to be independent of models and of experiments, has to support method libraries, and has to be expandable.

Consequently, an *experiment* E is defined as application of a certain method ME on a certain model MO. An experiment is dependent on the method and dependent on the model.

3.2 Hierarchical structure of methods

Analyzing the concept of methods in more detail shows a more or less hierarchical structure.

One may distinguish between methods *reading, writing* and *evaluating* directly the model data base and other more complex methods which use these basic methods. Such basic methods are defined as root methods, usually placed in the kernel of a simulation system.

Within the more complex methods there is a difference between so-called common methods (invoking root methods or other common methods, also in a recursive manner) and user methods (allowing special shells generating other runtime systems). Figure 4 shows this hierarchical structure of the method concept.

Fig. 4: *Different types of methods*

Root methods (RME) are basic methods using no other method. These methods may be summarized as writing, reading, and evaluating the model data base.

Common methods (CME) build up the usual interface level to the runtime interpreter. A common method is invoked by a simple experiment call and consists of root methods and common methods themselves. Examples are: simulation run, display, plot, optimization. Usually the commands of the runtime interpreter of a simulation language correspond to a common method defined here.

User methods (UME) are extensions of any kind, either offered by the system or implemented by the user: special experiment environment, automatic model generation, etc.

3.3 Common methods

All simulation languages support time domain analysis and some also support frequency domain analysis. Figure 5 gives an overview about features of time domain analysis and frequency domain analysis.

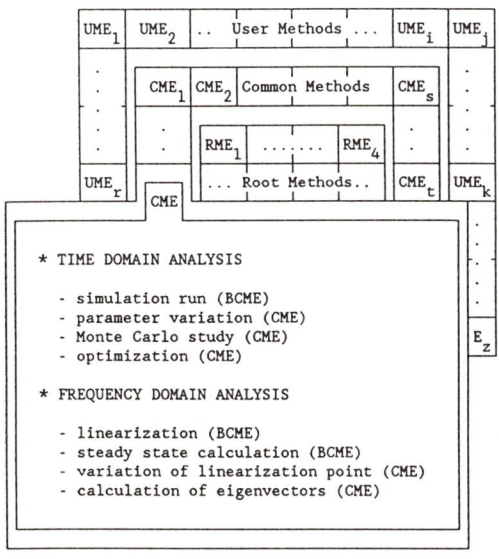

Fig.5 Common methods

Time domain analysis is based on the integration of the system governing differential equations (one simulation run). Frequency domain analysis is based on the calculation of steady states and on the linearization at a certain point (for instance the steady state).

Consequently a simulation run (in the case of time domain analysis) and the calculation of steady states or the linearization at a certain point (in the case of frequency domain analysis) may be classified as *basic common methods* (BCME).

In terms of system technique at this method level different theories for analyzing models can be used. Time domain analysis and frequency domain analysis are two representatives. There exist a lot of other theories that could be used for analyzing models: sensitivity analysis, structural analysis, stability analysis, etc.

At the moment simulation languages realize sensitivity analysis as parameter variations, but for the future symbolic algorithms could be used. For all theories one or more basic common methods can be defined.

4. Parallelization and the MME-structure

The MME-structure allows an interesting insight into parallelization of simulation tasks. Using the terms of MME-structure the parallelization with respects to the states is a parallelization at the level of root methods.

As outlined in section 2.2.2 a parameter study can be parallelized in a model-independent manner (figure 2). In the view of the MME-structure the method *parameter variation* is a sequence of the basic common method (BCME) of the time domain analysis.

The basic common method *simulation run* can be parallelized only in a model dependent way (section 2.2.1) while the parallelization of the common method *parameter variation* can be parallelized in a model independent manner.

Therefore in general a basic common method (BCME) cannot be parallelized in a model independent way. Consequently a model independent parallelization has to be based on the level of common methods excluding basic common methods.

In case of time domain analysis methods similar to the method *parameter variation* can be parallelized in a model independent way: Monte-Carlo-studies, sensitivity analysis based on parameter variation, optimization.

This parallelization approach can also be applied to other system theories.

Time domain analysis is very important in simulation but frequency domain analysis as well. The question arises which analysis method in the frequency domain can be parallelized independent of the model.

Base of all investigations in the frequency domain is the linearization of the (usually) nonlinear model. The nonlinear system $dx/dt = f(x)$ has to be approximated by a linear system $dx_l/dt = A \cdot x_l$, which behaves like the nonlinear system in the surroundings of a certain state x_s:

$$dx_{1,l}/dt = a_{11}x_{1,l} + a_{12}x_{2,l} + ... a_{1n}x_{n,l}$$
$$dx_{2,l}/dt = a_{21}x_{1,l} + a_{22}x_{2,l} + ... a_{2n}x_{n,l}$$
$$d_{x3,l}/dt = a_{31}x_{1,l} + a_{32}x_{2,l} + ... a_{3n}x_{n,l}$$
$$................$$
$$dx_{n,l}/dt = a_{n1}x_{1,l} + a_{n2}x_{2,l} + ... a_{nn}x_{n,l}$$

Here the matrix $A = (a_{ij})$ is the Jacobian matrix evaluated at a certain state x_s. The Jacobian matrix consists of the derivatives of the system equations with respect to the state variables:

$$a_{ij} = df_i/dx_j \mid x = x_s$$

Up to now most simulation systems calculate numerically the Jacobian matrix, the differential quotient df_i/dx_j is replaced by a (central) difference quotient:

$$df_i/dx_j = (f_i(..,x_j+h,..) - f_i(..,x_j-h,..))/2h$$

The calculation of the Jacobian matrix requires several times the evaluation of the perturbed components of the system equations - which could be parallelized model-dependently as discussed before. In the view of the MME-structure this type of parallelization is a parallelization at the level of root methods.

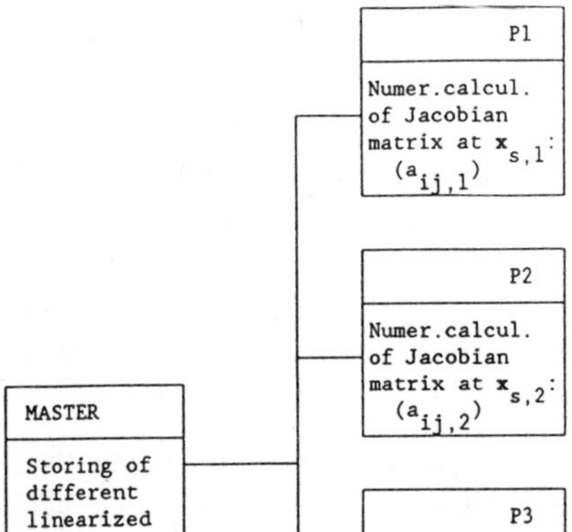

Another idea is to parallelize the calculation of the Jacobian matrix. This type of parallelization is model dependent too. In the view of the MME-structure the calculation of whole Jacobian matrices is the basic common method (BCME) of that theory. The second basic common method is the calculation of a steady state x_s, very often used as perturbation point for linearization.

Fig.6: Parallelization in the numerical linearization procedure

But the linearization depends on the actual state x_s, and consequently frequency domain analysis of a nonlinear system requires more than one linearized model. Therefore the linearization procedure has to be performed for several points $x_{s,k}$:

$$a_{ij,1} = df_i/dx_j \,|\, x = x_{s,1}, \quad a_{ij,2} = df_i/dx_j \,|\, x = x_{s,2}, \ldots$$

In this view the calculation of different linearizations is a special parameter variation of the linearization procedure.

Now the generic way for a model-independent parallelization in the frequency domain becomes clear: each processor calculates the linearization (the Jacobian matrix), but each with a different actual state $x_{s,k}$ (figure 6).

5. Implementation within the Simulation System PARALLEL_HYBSYS

The simulation language HYBSYS has been developed at the Technical University of Vienna as hybrid simulation language. HYBSYS is based on a model data base and is interpreter-oriented.

In 1988 a concept for a digital Simulation System HYBSYS was developed, which is based on the MME-concept (see section 3). The development of the Simulation System HYBSYS is a project supported by the Austrian "Fonds zur Förderung der Wissenschaftlichen Forschung".

On the one side the Simulation System HYBSYS obeys to the CSSL-standard for continuous simulation languages [8], on the other side it is based on the MME-structure presented in section 3.1. The model description is based either on a block-oriented level (37 block types) or on an equation-oriented level. HYBSYS also supports submodels (e.g. submodel blocks).

Due to different data types the model which is stored in an "intelligent" model data base needs not be structured into sections or regions respectively. The data type of the variable (state, derivative, auxiliary variable, output, control, table, parameter, constant) decides which region the statement belongs to.

HYBSYS offers methods to analyze a model (or models). These methods are stored in the data base as blocks of type *method*.

On experiment level (interactive or batch) HYBSYS uses a mathematical type of description.

Let X and DX denote two variables and A a parameter. The command

$$DX(X)$$

displays a phase plot of the variables - where implicitly the method (BCME) *simulation run* with the actual model is performed.

The command

$$X(A=1,10,0.2)$$

displays the terminal values of variable X against the varying parameter A (46 simulation runs).

The command

$$A=1,10,0.2\,!\,X$$

displays the variable X against time for all 46 variations of the parameter A (also 46 simulation runs).

HYBSYS also offers sensitivity analysis, optimization, linearization, etc. For instance, the command

$$\text{ZERO } X, DX \text{ BY } A$$

minimizes the terminal values of X and DX with respect to A. The method ZERO (CME) performs the method *simulation run* (BCME) several times.

HYBSYS uses extensively table functions, not only at model level but also at experiment level. A table function may store results from a simulation run. The stored results can be used for the next simulation runs, or for postprocessing [2].

For instance, the command

$$F=X$$

(F one-dimensional table function) performs a simulation run where the sampled data of variable X are stored into the table function F.

The command

$$F=X(A=1,10,0.2)$$

stores the terminal values of variable X versus the varying parameter A into the table function F.

If also the time history of X is of interest, a two-dimensional table function G may store x(t) for different values of the parameter A:

$$G=X(T;A=1,10,0.2).$$

Table functions may also be used for simulating partial differential equations (discretized by the method of lines).

HYBSYS is written in C, it may be extended by arbitrary C-programs (which can be implemented as additional features), for instance special user shells, automatic model generation, statistical analysis (for instance of table functions), etc.

The Simulation System HYBSYS is available for PC-ATs with coprocessor (beta release April 1991); releases for workstation are being developed (beta release for DEC-station 3100 in July 1991), for more information see for instance [3].

Further developments (second project 1990-1992) regard the following features: data analysis, statistical methods, analytical methods (symbolic computation), user methods (shells for special models), advanced analyzing methods, graphical model representation (block oriented description), generalization of the model data base for static, discrete and stochastic models, submodels, object oriented approach. The main goal of the development is the implementation of the above mentioned features as parallelized common methods (PARALLEL_HYBSYS). First studies are published in [4].

PARALLEL_HYBSYS works with the same experiment environment, the kernel of this system (developed in ANSI-C) uses other structures (for data bases, etc.) with respect to parallelization.

5.1 Parallelization of common methods

As outlined in sections 3 and 4 the MME-concept represents in a generic way different parallel structures of simulation tasks.

PARALLEL_HYBSYS parallelizes simulation tasks in model independent manner. The parallelization starts at the level of common methods while basic common methods remain in a sequential form.

This project is based on a transputer system consisting of four T800 transputers with 2 MB distributed RAM each, on transputer acts additionally as master, a PC AT acts as front-end.

Figure 7 shows the structure of the chosen topology where the dashed lines indicate further extensions (tries).

5.2 Parallelization in the time domain analysis

The simplest model independent parallelization is the parallelization in the parameter sphere. Denoting x(t,a) the simulation results of the model dx/dt = f(x) (x and f vectors), then the first processor calculates $x(t,a_1)$, the second $x(t,a_2)$, the third $x(t,a_3)$, etc. (figure 2).

PARALLEL_HYBSYS could distribute the tasks with the different parameters values automatically depending on the number of variations.

The PARALLEL_HYBSYS command

A = 1,25,3!PLOT X

requires nine simulation runs with different values of the parameter A. The system could distribute the first n tasks to the n transputers; with four transputers available this task would need three cycles, where in the last cycle three transputers are idle (static balance).

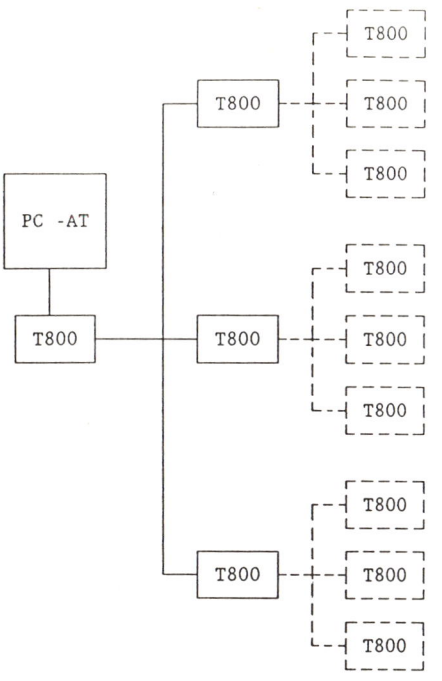

Fig. 7: PARALLEL_HYBSYS hardware structure

Usually each transputer should need the same time for its task - but only if an integration algorithm with fixed step size and without error control is used.

In case of a more sophisticated integration algorithm one processor may spend much more time. Consequently the processors should be balanced dynamically. First each processor gets its task (with different parameter value), the remaining tasks are balanced dynamically: the first idle processor gets the next task, etc. This procedure is more complicated, but it prevents busy waits. PARALLEL_HYBSYS will implement a dynamic load balancing in this case.

A lot of other methods can be represented by special parameter variations. One class of methods are Monte-Carlo-studies, which vary parameters stochastically. PARALLEL_HYBSYS will implement Monte-Carlo-studies as stochastic parameter loops in the fore-mentioned parallel manner. Base is the more general loop command with non-equidistant parameter values:

A={1,5,5.7,1E3,0.001,3.4E-7}!X

PARALLEL_HYBSYS is designed not only for simulation but also for validation and identification of dynamic models. Validation of a model is a very crucial task. A typical validation procedure for engineering tasks is the check of simulation results with respect to different integration algorithms and different integration stepsizes.

This special validation procedure can be implemented immediately in PARALLEL_HYBSYS by parameter variation. Each method is controlled by method parameters, which can be accessed as parameters.

The method *simulation run* is controlled by several parameters, depending on the integration algorithm chosen. The most important method parameter of the method *simulation run* is RUN_ALG which chooses the algorithm:

RUN_ALG = 1,2,3,4,5,6 ..... Runge-Kutta 1st,2nd, 3rd,4th,6th,7th order
= 7 .... Runge-Kutta-Fehlberg,
= 8 .... Adams-Moulton
= 9 .... Gear,
= 10 .... Special Gear

The following command checks the stability of simulation results with respect to algorithms:

RUN_ALG={4,8,9,2,3,6}!X

Figure 8 shows a probable distribution of the tasks to the four parallel processes. The four processes start calculating the variable X with the algorithms RUN_ALG = {4,8,9,2} in a cyclic distribution. Results are $x(t,ALG_4)$, $x(t,ALG_8)$, $x(t,ALG_9)$, and $x(t,ALG_2)$. The fourth process becomes idle first (it integrates with the simplest algorithm), it continues integration with the Runge-Kutta 3rd order yielding $x(t,ALG_3)$; then probably the first process becomes idle, it finishes this parameter loops by calculating $x(t,ALG_6)$.

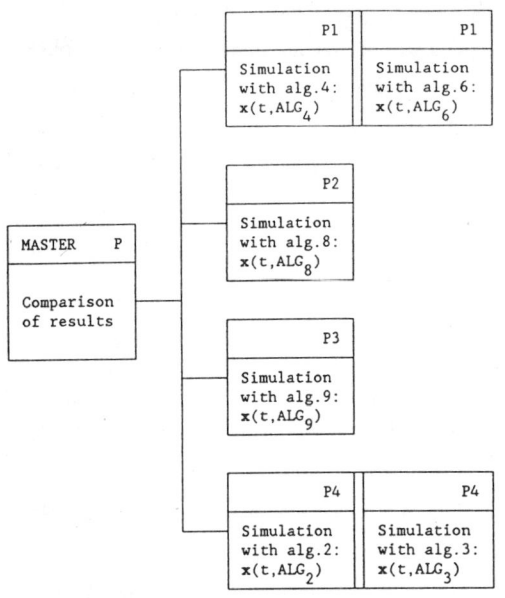

Fig.8: Check of integration algorithms as parallel processes

PARALLEL_HYBSYS offers dynamic optimization features. If the model of a dynamic system is extended by goal functions, model parameters can be optimized (minimized) with respect to these goal functions.

The PARALLEL_HYBSYS method ZERO provides minimization of a defined goal function with different optimization procedures.

Let, for instance, Y and DY denote two variables with initial values Y0 and DY0; if periodic solutions are to be found, the difference between terminal values and initial values of both variables (E, ED) have to be minimized with respect to the initial values. The following ZERO command calculates the periodic solutions - depending on an additional parameter variation:

A=1,5,0.5!{ZERO E,ED BY Y0,DY0;DY(Y)}

For optimization only the terminal values of a simulation run (yielding the values of the goal functions) are of interest in order to calculate new parameter values. The algorithms implemented are perturbing the parameter values depending on the previous values of the goal functions. The number of perturbations within one iteration depends on the number of parameters and on the algorithm used.

The command mentioned above varies additionally a parameter, so that two hierarchical levels of parallelization exist. In this case the system will either parallelize the optimization (with "serial" parameter variation) or only the parameter variation (each process calculates the "full" optimization).

5.3 Parallelization in the frequency domain analysis

In section 4 the calculation of the Jacobian matrix turned out to be a basic common method of frequency domain analysis. Variation of the linearization point is the counterpart to parameter variation in time domain analysis. The implementation of the parallelization (figure 6) is similar to the parameter variation.

The investigations up to now were based on a numerical linearization of the model. Linearization is calculation of the Jacobian matrix - which is an analytical procedure. The derivatives of the system governing equations with respect to the state variables are calculated symbolically - then the symbolic Jacobian matrix is evaluated at the linearization point.

Modern simulation systems should offer symbolic computation, too; PARALLEL_HYBSYS offers as a method symbolic derivation with respect to any variable and any parameter. Consequently in case of linearization PARALLEL_HYBSYS will be able to calculate the Jacobian matrix also symbolically. The results are algebraic equations for each coefficient of the matrix:

$$A(x_1,..,x_n) = (a_{ij}(x_1,..,x_n))$$

PARALLEL_HYBSYS is able to store these algebraic equations as model, so that the model is extended by an algebraic (sub)model describing the Jacobian matrix.

For frequency analysis with certain methods (root locus, pole placement, etc.) now only the Jacobian matrix has to be evaluated at different linearization points, because the Jacobian matrix is known symbolically. This task can be parallelized like the case of numerical linearization: each task evaluates the Jacobian matrix at a certain state (figure 9).

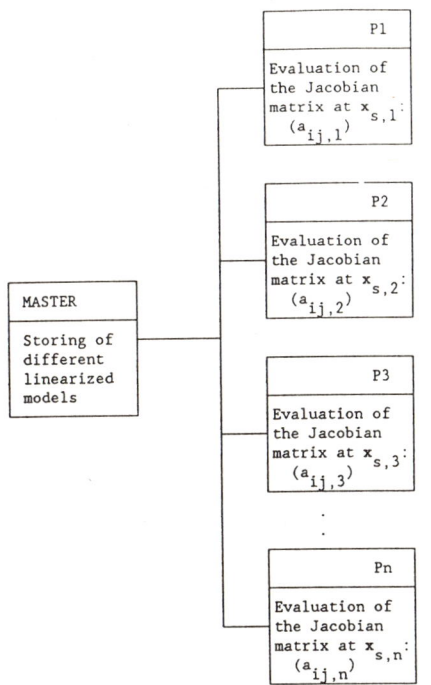

Fig.9: Parallelization in the symbolic linearization procedure

5.4 Parallelization of special methods

Frequency domain analysis offers different linear models approximating the nonlinear model. Of interest are comparisons of these models in the time domain.

PARALLEL_HYBSYS calculates different Jacobian matrices A_{lk}, which can be stored as separate models in the data base, where $x_{l,1}$ denotes the state variable vector of the linearization at the point x_1, etc.:

$$dx_{l,1}/dt = A_{l1}x_{l,1}$$
$$dx_{l,2}/dt = A_{l2}x_{l,2}$$
$$dx_{l,3}/dt = A_{l3}x_{l,3}$$
$$..........$$
$$dx_{l,k}/dt = A_{lk}x_{l,k}$$

This comparison can be parallelized on the base of the time domain simulation of different models.

Figure 10 shows the parallelization of this comparison: the first process calculates the simulation results x(t) of the nonlinear model, the second the results $x_{l,1}(t)$ of the linearization at $x_{s,1}$, the third the results $x_{l,2}$ of linearization at $x_{s,2}$, etc.

5.5 Parallelization of sensitivity analyis

Up to now parallelization of methods allowed a strictly hierarchical organisation of the distributed processes, no communication between the processes was necessary. In this last section a symbolic method for sensitivity analysis is discussed, which requires communication at a low level.

Sensitivity analysis may be performed by parameter variation - but the analytical method is the investigation of the so-called sensitivity equations.

Let $dx/dt = f(x,t;a,b,c,..)$ describe a nonlinear system with significant parameters a, b, c, etc. Then the theory allows to establish systems describing the sensitivity of the state x with respect to a parameter by calculating $x_a(t) = dx(t)/da$, $x_b(t) = dx/db$, $x_c(t) = dx(t)/dc$, etc.

For each sensitivity variable an additional system of differential equations has to be solved (simulated):

$$dx(t)/dt = f(x(t),t;a,b,c,..)$$
$$dx_a(t)/dt = g_a(x_a(t),t;x(t);a,b,c,..)$$
$$dx_b(t)/dt = g_b(x_b(t),t;x(t);a,b,c,..)$$
$$dx_c(t)/dt = g_c(x_c(t),t;x(t);a,b,c,..)$$

The calculation of the sensitivity equations can now be parallelized: the master process calculates the system dynamics, the others calculate the sensitivity equations (figure 11).

This parallelization has to provide data communication from the master process to the others (providing the time course x(t)). The communication could be synchronized for instance with the communication interval of the simulation.

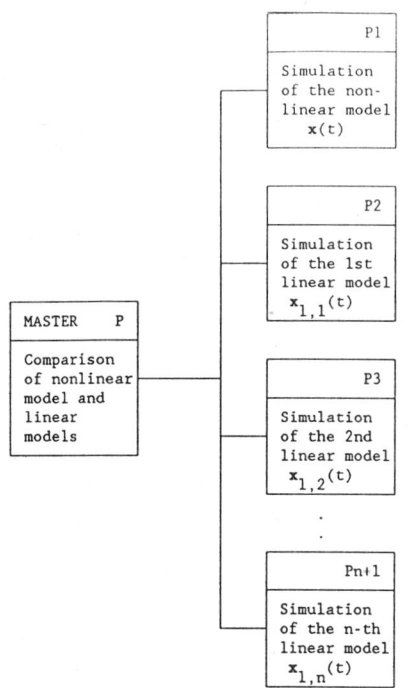

Fig.10: Parallelization of model comparison

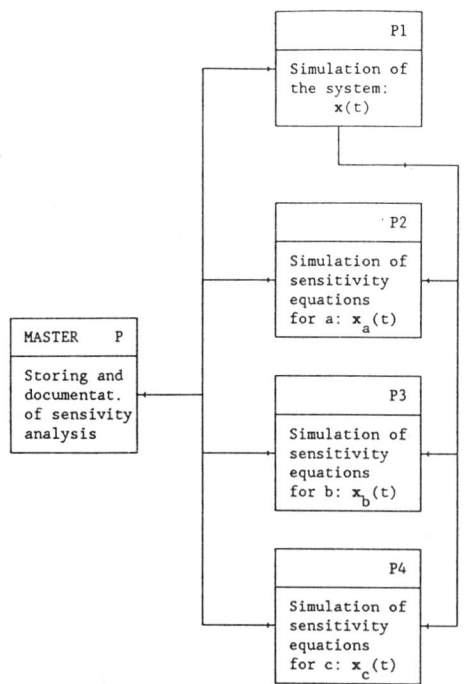

Fig.11: Parallelization of calculation of sensitivity equations

6. Conclusions

The main goal of the investigations was to realize a model independent parallelization of simulation tasks in order to achieve a linear speed-up in the performance of simulation tasks with respect to the number of processors. The chosen topology requires additional communication when using more than four transputers.

References

/1/ Breitenecker F., Solar D.: Models, methods, experiments - modern aspects of simulation languages. Proc. 2nd European Simulation Congress., Antwerp, Publ. SCS San Diego (1986), 195-199.

/2/ Breitenecker F., Solar D., Husinsky I.: A concept for extended table functions in simulation languages and its implementation into the simulation system HYBSYS. Proc. European Simulation Multiconference, Rome, Publ. SCS (1989), 17-20.

/3/ Breitencker F., Solar D., Husinsky I.: HYBSYS - a new simulation system. Proc. 3rd European Simulation Congress, Edinburgh, Publ. SCS (1989), 275-281.

/4/ I.Husinsky, J. Fritscher, G.Schuster, F.Breitenecker: Principles of parallelization of algorithms for analyzing simulation models - implementation in the Simulation System HYBSYS. Proc. Vol. 2 IMACS-MCTS-Symposium, Lille, (1991), 109-114.

/5/ Kerckhoffs E.J.H., Brok S.W.: The Delft Parallel Processor DPP81: Properties and untilization in simulation and related fields. In: System Analysis, Modelling and Simulation (Journal of Mathematical Modelling and Simulation in Systems Analysis). Akademie-Verlag, Berlin, vol.2 (1985), 175-208.

/6/ Kerckhoffs E.J.H.: Parallel Processing and Advanced Environments in Continuous Simulation. PhD-Thesis, University of Ghent, 1986.

/7/ Ruzicka R.: Methoden der Simulation auf Parallelrechnern unter SIMUL_R. Proc. 6. Symposium Simulationstechnik, Fortschritte in der Simulationstechnik Bd.1, Vieweg 1990, 412-416.

/8/ Strauss J.C. et al.: The SCI continuous simulation language. Simulation 9 (1967), 281-303.

/9/ Zeigler P.: A methodology for simulation programs. IMACS TC3 - Simulation Software Committee Newsletter no.10, 1981.

PARALLEL ALGORITHMS FOR STRESS ANALYSIS ON SHARED-MEMORY MULTIPROCESSORS

Hojjat Adeli and Osama Kamal

Department of Civil Engineering, The Ohio State University
470 Hitchcock Hall, 2070 Neil Avenue, Columbus, Ohio 43210-1275

Introduction

Parallel algorithms have been developed for stress analysis of large structures on shared memory multiprocessor computers. Parallelism is achieved through the notion of cheap concurrency and the concept of threads (Adeli and Kamal, 1989). A thread is a unit of execution that is independent of other similar units (threads), yet it can execute concurrently with them. We note how concurrency is implemented in this work. In each step, a certain number of sets is automatically generated by the program. This number is equal to the number of the prescribed processors. Each set is automatically mapped onto a thread. Thus, the number of threads created is equal to the number of prescribed processors. The parallel algorithms have been developed in C on an Encore Multimax shared memory multiprocessor computer (Adeli and Vishnubhotla, 1991).

A Substructuring Algorithm for Concurrent Analysis of Structures

A substructuring algorithm has been developed for automatic partitioning of framed structures. The underlying concept is to pre-process the input data in such a manner that subsequent analysis steps are carried out efficiently on multiprocessor computers. We choose to partition the domain into a number of subdomains equal to the number of the prescribed processors. The partitioning is achieved through a 3-stage algorithm: initial partitioning, intermediate partitioning, and final partitioning (Figure 1).

The initial partitioning stage generates subdomains with a balanced number of elements. The underlying concept is to start at one end of the structure and propagate through it based on connectivity. The algorithm starts at a node with minimum weight (the weight of each node is defined as the number of elements attached to it) which usually resides at one corner or end of the structure. In addition, it goes through the structure based on connectivity and not on the pattern of numbering. This results in a partitioning scheme which is independent of the pattern of numbering of the structure. Furthermore, it helps handling irregular domains and results in subdomains with contiguous elements, thus reducing the number of interface nodes and alleviating the bottleneck situation that arises during the solution of the interface linear equations.

The balance of elements attained in this stage is favorable to the steps of assemblying the structure stiffness matrix and evaluation of the element forces and stresses. On the other hand, the algorithm presented so far has the shortcoming of not maintaining a balance of internal nodes among the processors. In the intermediate partitioning stage, the algorithm attempts to increase the overall number of internal nodes attained in the initial partitioning stage (or decrease the number of interface nodes). The underlying concept is to scan all the interface nodes and attempt to "close" any of them. An interface node is switched to an internal node through a process of exchange of elements between subdomains only if during this process no internal node is switched to an interface node. In essence, this stage attempts to furnish a better starting point for the final partitioning stage: a point with a larger number of internal nodes to be balanced among the processors and a fewer number of interface nodes. This is done in a manner that causes a minimum disturbance (if any) to the features achieved in the initial partitioning stage.

The main purpose of the final partitioning stage is to balance the number of internal nodes within the subdomains. This step is crucial since its goal is to achieve a load balance among the processors for a major portion of the analysis and design calculations. The key concept is to sweep the subdomains several times,

STAGES OF PARTITIONING

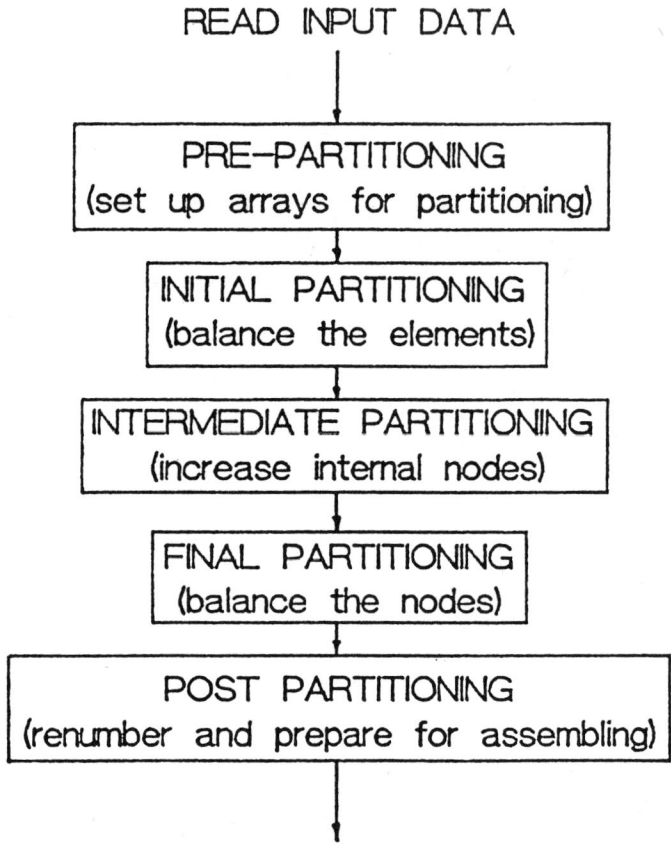

Figure 1

each time with a designated strategy for achieving the desirable balance (Kamal and Adeli, 1990).

The number of sweeps represents the number of times the final partitioning takes place. In the first sweep, the subdomains are scanned forward to allow those subdomains with a number of internal nodes less than their "fair" share to solicit elements from adjacent subdomains with a number of internal nodes greater than their "fair" share. Yet, the soliciting process does not terminate when the soliciting subdomain meets its "fair" share. Rather, the transaction of elements will continue as long as any of the adjacent subdomains has more than its "fair" share. This helps propagate the excess of internal nodes through the structure from one locality to the other, thus providing remote subdomains with a defficiency in the internal nodes with a better chance of being balanced.

Parallel Structural Analysis

The full details of parallel algorithms for stress analysis of structures will be presented in a forthcoming paper (Adeli and Kamal, 1991). In this paper, we present the overall strategies devised and implemented. In each step, a number of threads equal to the number of processors specified by the user is created. The computational task involved within each step is automatically decomposed into a number of subtasks equal to the number of threads. Each subtask is mapped onto a thread. For some of the tasks, a racing condition is inevitable and synchronization of the threads is required (Adeli and Vishnubhotla, 1987, Adeli and Kamal, 1989). Whenever such a situation is encountered, extra storage locations are used to avoid simultaneous updating of shared memory locations. These locations are updated concurrently in a subsequent step.

After the input data is read in, automatic partitioning of the structure takes place. The purpose of this step is to achieve a workload balance among the threads throughout major steps of the solution process and to maximize the amount of calculations that can be performed concurrently without the need for excessive creation of threads.

Seven steps constituting the structural analysis phase follow the

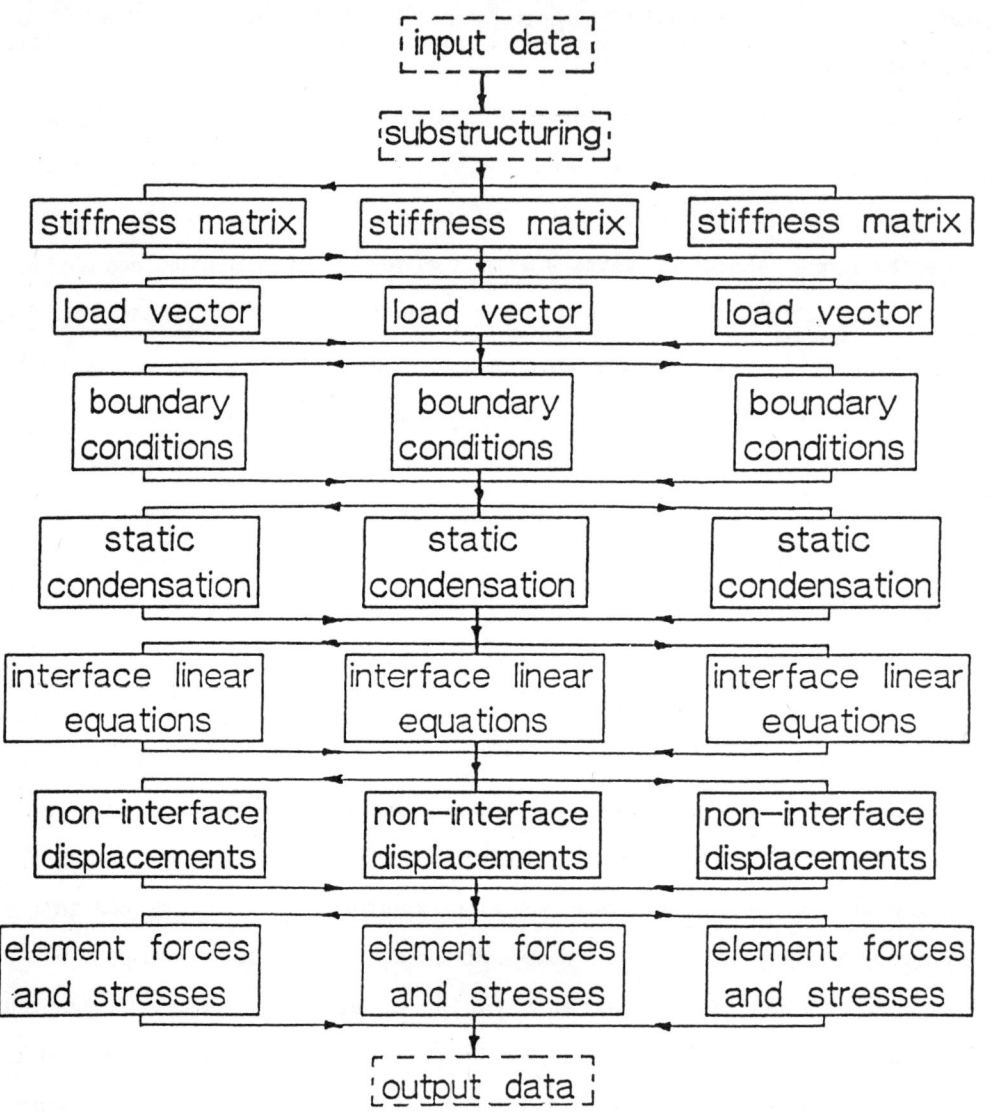

Figure 2

partitioning of the structure. They are: assemblying the structure stiffness matrix, setting up the load vector, applying the boundary conditions, static condensation, solution of the interface linear equations, retrieving the non-interface displacements, and evaluation of element forces and stresses (Figure 2). In the assembly step, the threads concurrently calculate the stiffness matrices of their assigned elements and then assemble them into the structure stiffness matrix. During the assembly process, a racing condition is avoided using the aforementioned strategy. The balance of elements achieved at the end of the initial partitioning stage is used in this step. This balance is also used in assembling the part of the load vector resulting from the initial stresses. Synchronization is required in this case. The balance of nodes is used for assembling the part of the load vector resulting from the point (concentrated) loads acting at the nodes. Synchronization is not required in this case.

The balance of internal nodes attained at the end of the final partitioning stage is used in the static condensation step (i.e. each of the final subdomains is mapped onto a thread). The threads concurrently factorize the subdomains matrices, reduce subdomains load vectors and the matrices coupling the subdomains with the interface, and update the interface load vector and the interface stiffness matrix. Synchronization is required only during the updating stage. Appropriate strategies are used for balancing the workload during each of the three stages of solution of the interface equations, namely, transforming the interface stiffness matrix to an upper triangular matrix, and forward and backward substitutions. A set of threads is created to update the rows below each pivoting element in the interface stiffness matrix. Also, one set of threads is required for updating each element in the interface load vector and another set for finding each of the interface displacements in the stages of forward and backward substitutions, respectively.

The balance of internal nodes achieved at the end of the final partitioning stage is also used for retrieving the non-interface displacements while the balance of elements achieved at the end of the initial partitioning stage is used for evaluating the element forces and stresses. The entire analysis stage is done

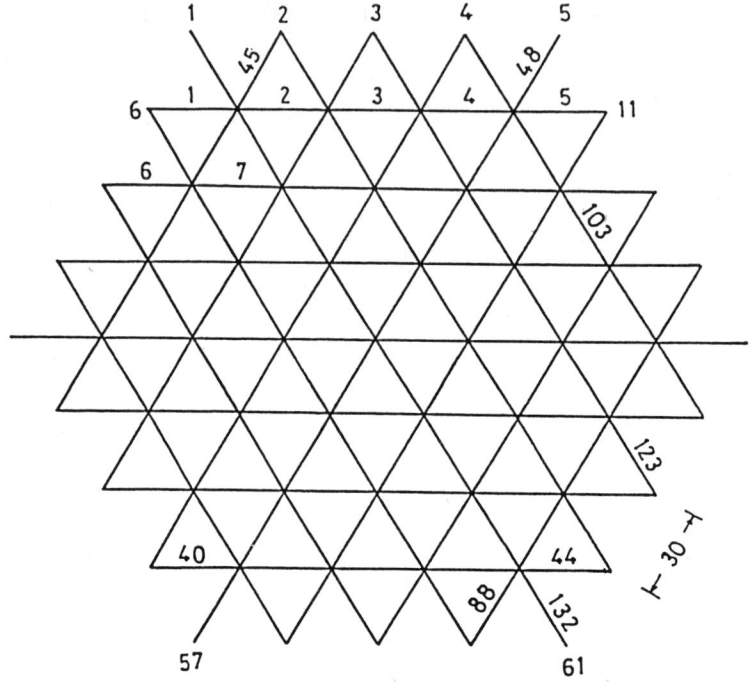

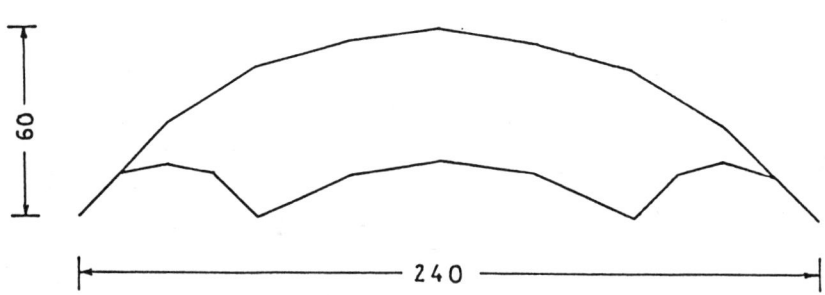

Figure 3

in the context of special storage scheme to allow for the large problems to be handled effectively.

Applications

The parallel structural analysis algorithms developed in this work have been applied to several different types and sizes of the structure on the Encore Multimax shared memory machine. A minimum of nine elements per subdomain is prescribed as a precondition for the initial partitioning stage. Similarly, a minimum of three internal nodes per subdomain is prescribed as a precondition for the final partitioning stage. When any of the preconditions is not satisfied, execution is automatically terminated.

Speedup results for three examples are presented: a Geodesic dome space truss (Figure 3), a 200-bar plane truss (Figure 4), and a 760-element highrise frame (Figure 5). We define the speedup attained for a specified number of processors as the time spent on executing the sequential code to the time spent on executing the concurrent code, when the specified number of processors is in use. The workload balance is defined as the speedup attained when the overhead time required for creating the threads is neglected. This is useful in assessing the effectiveness of the workload balancing strategies developed in this work.

Figure 6 presents the speedup curves for the Geodesic dome space structure, the 200-bar plane truss, and the 760-element plane frame using the final partitioning stage. This figure clearly demonstrates that better speedups are achieved for larger structures. On one hand, this is due to the fact that the overhead time required for creating a thread tends to be insignificant compared to the time required for the thread to execute its task as the size of the task assigned to each thread increases. On the other hand, the percentage of the time consumed in the fine-grained parallelism step (solution of the linear interface equations) tends to be less significant compared to the overall execution time as the size of the problem increases.

Figure 7 shows the overall workload balance for the three structures using the final partitioning stage. The offset of the curves in this figure from the

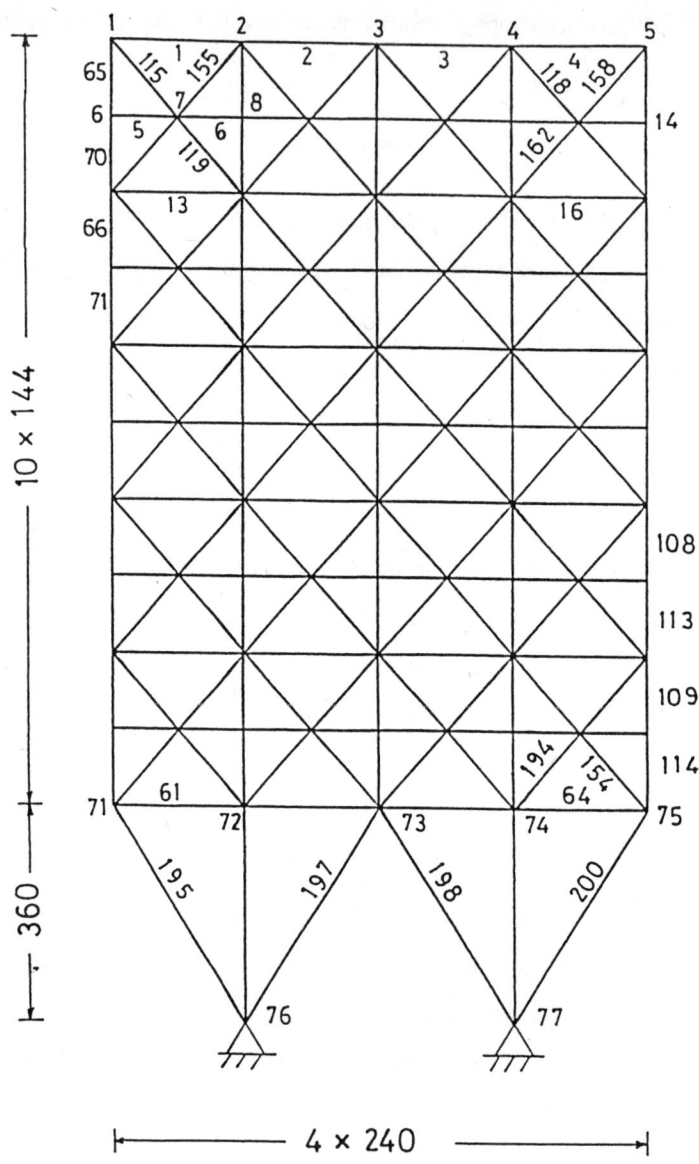

Figure 4

Figure 5

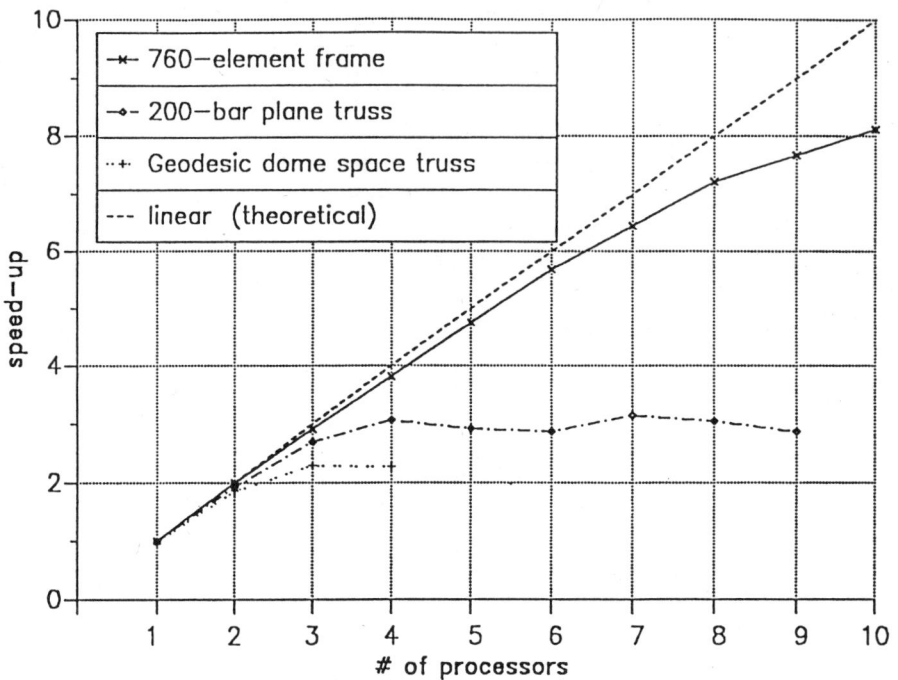

Figure 6 Overall speedups using the final subdomains and different processors

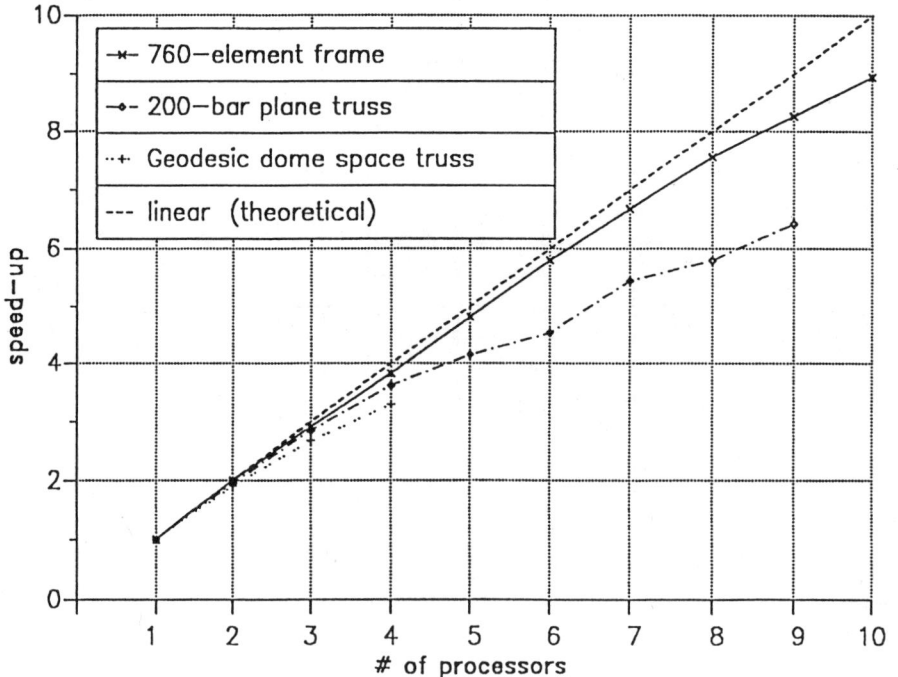

Figure 7 Overall workload balance using the final subdomains and different processors

theoretical linear speedup is due to the imbalance of the workload. The effect of this imbalance becomes more significant as the number of threads (and processors) increases and consequently the task assigned to each thread becomes smaller.

References

Adeli, H. and Kamal, O. (1989), "Parallel Structural Analysis Using Threads", Microcomputers in Civil Engineering, Vol. 4, No. 2, pp. 133-147.

Adeli, H. and Kamal, O. (1991), "Concurrent Analysis of Large Structures - Part I - Algorithms", Computers and Structures (to appear).

Adeli, H. and P. Vishnubhotla, P. (1987), "Parallel Processing", Microcomputers in Civil Engineering, Vol. 2, No. 3, pp. 257-269:1987.

Adeli, H. and P. Vishnubhotla, P. (1991), "Parallel Machines", in Adeli, H., Ed., <u>Parallel Processing in Computational Mechanics</u>, Marcel Dekker, Inc., New York, pp. 1-20.

Kamal, O. and Adeli, H. (1990), "Automatic Partitioning of Frame Structures for Concurrent Processing", Microcomputers in Civil Engineering, Vol. 5, No. 4, pp. 269-283.

Elastic load-balancing for image processing algorithms [1]

Serge MIGUET and Yves ROBERT
Laboratoire de l'Informatique du Parallélisme LIP-IMAG
Ecole Normale Supérieure de Lyon
46 allée d'Italie, 69364 Lyon Cedex 07, France
e-mail: yrobert@ensl.ens-lyon.fr, yrobert@frensl61.bitnet

Abstract : In this paper, we introduce a data redistribution algorithm which aims at dynamically balancing the workload of image processing algorithms on distributed memory processors. First we briefly review state-of-the-art techniques for load balancing application-specific algorithms. Then we describe the data redistribution technique, which we term "elastic load balancing" in a general framework. We demonstrate the usefulness of our redistribution strategy by comparing the efficiency obtained with and without the elastic algorithm for a thinning algorithm which aims at extracting the skeleton of a binary image. We report experimental results obtained with a Supernode machine, based upon reconfigurable networks of 32 Transputers [Nic]. We obtain a speedup of up to 28 over the sequential algorithm, using a Mandelbrot set as a test image. Note that the speedup with a static allocation of the picture was limited to 17 with the same test image, due to the load imbalance among the processors.

Key-words : load balancing, data partitioning, data redistribution, dynamic allocation, image processing algorithms, distributed memory processors.

1. Introduction

The problem of load balancing is central to parallel computing. It determines the speedup for any application. Load balancing can be done statically or dynamically at run time.

---

[1] This work has been supported by the Project C3 of the French Council for Research CNRS, and by the ESPRIT Basic Research Action 3280 "NANA" of the European Economic Community

In static load balancing the work done by a processor is allocated statically so as to optimize the final time and load balance. Many general techniques which take task graphs as input and decide the mapping of tasks to processors are known. Static load balancing has the advantage of low overhead at run time. However, for some applications the time for the different tasks may depend on the inputs in a non trivial way. In such situations, the only solution is to balance the load at run time. This technique is called dynamic load balancing. However, this method may involve a lot of overhead, and its usefulness is often application specific.

In this paper we describe a simple technique for dynamically balancing the workload of image processing algorithms on distributed memory processors. The technique is based upon data redistributions between the processors during the execution of the algorithm. The paper is organized as follows: first we briefly review state-of-the-art techniques for load balancing application-specific algorithms. Then we describe the data redistribution technique, which we term "elastic load balancing" in a general framework. We demonstrate the usefulness of our redistribution strategy by comparing the efficiency obtained with and without the elastic algorithm for a thinning algorithm which aims at extracting the skeleton of a binary image. We report experimental results obtained with a Supernode machine, based upon reconfigurable networks of 32 Transputers [Nic]. We obtain a speedup of up to 28 over the sequential algorithm, using a Mandelbrot set as a test image. Note that the speedup with a static allocation of the picture was limited to 17 with the same test image, due to the load imbalance among the processors.

2. Load balancing application-specific algorithms

In this paper we consider iterative algorithms that operate on regular data structures such as arrays of data points (matrices or images). Typically, the processors are organized so as to form a ring or a 2D-torus, and they are assigned rows (or columns) or sub-rectangles of the data. At each step, they exchange data along their borders with their neighbors, and then they perform independent computations. Such algorithms include many image processing algorithms such as 2D convolution and correlation, thinning, ... and iterative numerical solution techniques such as finite difference analysis.

Effectively executing these algorithms on distributed memory parallel computers requires good mappings of the array of data points onto the processors. The metrics of quality for mappings are that they (1) reduce the communications associated with points in one partition communicating with points in another partition and (2) balance the load across processors.

A first class of methods is based upon the partitioning of the data array to the processors. This partitioning is performed statically under the assumption that roughly the same amount of work is to be done at each point of the array. Hence distributing the same amount of data to each of the processors will equally distribute the workload. Together with the goal of equally distributing the data is the goal of minimizing interprocessor communication. The idea is to have for each processor P_q the ratio = $\frac{\text{number of interior points}}{\text{number of exterior points}}$ as high as possible, where interior points are those points whose neighbors are all in P_q, thereby requiring no communication, and exterior points are points with at least a neighbor not allocated to P_q. This ratio is called the "bulk" of the allocation by Snyder and Socha [SSo], who survey classical partitioning strategies such as 1D-slicing, 2D-slicing, binary decomposition or scattered decomposition and then introduce a near-rectangular decomposition (see also [EJ]). An interesting feature of such static partitioning strategies is that compilers can automatically take these decompositions into account [RW].

In many situations, however, no a priori estimates of load distribution are possible. It is only during program execution that it becomes apparent how much work is being assigned to processors. In such situations, dynamic load balancing techniques must be introduced. In a general context, many heuristic for implementing progress migration are known [BBo, Bok, XH].

Dynamic load balancing for spatial domains can take the regularity of the data structure into account. Strategies for recursive partitions [BBa] or iterative partitions [Hin] have been proposed. Again, the objective of the redistribution of data to processors is twofold: minimizing the communications (recursive partitioning can increase the number of neighbors [SE]) and equally distributing the workload. The global workload is not known to the processors, which only have a local estimate of their own load. Techniques based upon the exchange of local information [Cyb, Hin] have been derived.

In this paper, we present a technique that falls into the class of dynamic load balancing. The idea is to assume the simplest topology, namely the ring (rings can be embedded in more powerful interconnection networks [SSc1]). We consider iterative algorithms that operate on data arrays such as matrices or images. We redistribute data on the fly at each iteration so as to equally balance the workload. The redistribution preserves the ordering, so as to guarantee the locality of the communications that may require exterior points. Hence the name "elastic" given to the redistribution algorithm, which we explain now.

3. The elastic load-balancing algorithm

We describe in this section the elastic load-balancing algorithm in a general framework. We delay the description of a realistic application until next section.

The goal is that the processors perform a data redistribution based upon a global workload analysis. We assume that there are p processors numbered from 0 to p-1, and that the interconnection topology enables to interconnect them into a ring. In other words, we assume that the ring is a sub-topology of the interconnection network. The whole data set consists of a collection of n data items called rows, numbered from 0 to n-1. Each processor P_q, $0 \leq q < p$, initially holds the rows of index belonging to the segment $[r_1(q), r_2(q)]$, where
$$r_1(0) = 0, r_1(q+1) = r_2(q) + 1 \text{ for } 0 \leq q \leq p-2, r_2(p-1) = n-1$$

After the redistribution, Processor P_q should hold rows of another segment $[s_1(q), s_2(q)]$ with the same conditions
$$s_1(0) = 0, s_1(q+1) = s_2(q) + 1 \text{ for } 0 \leq q < p-2, s_2(p-1) = n-1$$
In other words, the global ordering of the rows is not modified: segments are shifted through the processors, but rows that were consecutive remain consecutive. Hence the name "elastic" given to the redistribution. This property is very important for algorithms which require processor interchanges of boundary rows to perform the computation. See figure 1 for an example.

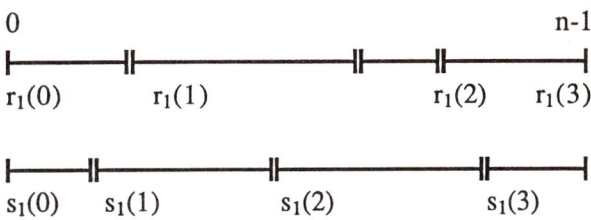

Figure 1: Redistribution example with p=4 processors

Each row i has a computational cost $W(i)$, $0 \leq i < n$. We assume that each processor knows the cost $W(i)$ of all the rows in its segment $[r_1(q), r_2(q)]$ before the redistribution (in many iterative algorithms this information will come for free, see next section).

We make a short digression to motivate our assumption that the computational cost of the rows is data dependent and hence not known a priori. We give two examples. First consider an algorithm that processes a binary image made of 0-pixels (the ground) and 1-pixels (the image itself). Usually, the processing of 0-pixels is considerably shorter than that of 1-pixels, hence the workload is strongly data-dependent, even though each processor is assigned the same number of rows (i.e. the same volume of data). Another example is from sparse matrix computations where the load is directly proportional to the number of non-zero elements. This number can be data-dependent and dynamically evolves as the algorithm iterates.

The redistribution is based upon the simple idea of re-balancing the total load among the processors. There are three main steps:
Step 1   distributed computation of the workload histogram
Step 2   distributed computation of new indices $s_1(q)$ and $s_2(q)$ for $0 \leq q < p$
Step 3   redistribution of the rows among the processors

3.1. Distributed computation of the workload histogram

The objective is that each processor P_q computes for each of its rows $i \in [r_1(q), r_2(q)]$ the cumulative load $CW(i)$ of all the preceding rows:
$$CW(i) = \sum_{j=0}^{i} W(j)$$
This is done very simply by each processor P_q as follows:
- P_q computes its local cumulated workload
$$LCW(i) = \sum_{j=r_1}^{i} W(j)$$
- P_q knows its own workload
$$WL(q) = LCW(r_2)$$
- P_q ($q \neq 0$) receives from its predecessor P_{q-1} the sum of the workloads of the processors that are before itself:
$$S(q) = \sum_{k=0}^{q-1} WL(k)$$
- P_q ($q \neq p-1$) sends to its successor P_{q+1} the sum of $S(q)$ and $WL(q)$, that is
$$S(q+1) = S(q) + WL(q)$$

- P_q adds $S(q)$ to the local cumulated load of each of its row to get the global cumulated workload:
$$CW(i) = LCW(i) + S(q)$$

This operation can be viewed as a left-to-right propagation of information on the linear array. The communication cost is clearly proportional to p.

After this operation, the last processor P_{p-1} knows the total load
$$\text{total\_load} = CW(r_2(p-1)).$$
It broadcasts it to all the processors (right-to-left propagation), again for a cost proportional to p. Now each processor can compute the elementary load per processor
$$\text{elem\_load} = \frac{\text{total\_load}}{p}$$
The value of elem_load is the only thing that P_q needs to know for computing the destination processor dest_proc(i) of all the rows $i \in [r_1(q), r_2(q)]$:

$$\text{dest\_proc}(i) = \left\lceil \frac{CW(i)}{\text{elem\_load}} \right\rceil - 1$$

See figure 2 for an illustration of the histogram.

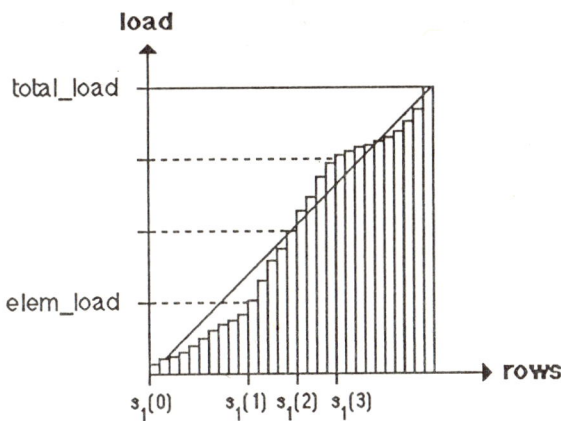

Figure 2 : Histogram with p=4 processors

3.2. Distributed computation of the new indices

The objective in this step is that each processor P_q computes the new index $s_1(q)$ (note that $s_1(0) = 0$). When this is done, each processor P_q but the last one will receive from its successor P_{q+1} the value $s_1(q+1)$ and will deduce that $s_2(q) = s_1(q+1) -1$ (note that $s_2(p-1) = n-1$).

In fact, the characterization of row indices i such that $i = s_1(q)$ for some q>0 is that dest_proc(i) = dest_proc(i-1) + 1. Let us call threshold indices such index values. Each processor P_q, q>0, has already received $S(q) = CW(r_2(q-1))$ during step 1, and hence can compute dest_proc($r_2(q-1)$). Scanning its rows, P_q can determine all the threshold indices i such that $i \in [r_1(q), r_2(q)]$, together with their destination processors dest_proc(i).

Including the threshold index $0 = s_1(0)$, there are p threshold indices that are computed by the processors. Some processors can find several threshold indices, some can have none. But the total number is p in all cases. A naive solution is to use a total-exchange algorithm to redistribute the threshold indices in such a way that each processor P_q knows its own threshold index $s_1(q)$. For instance we can use a left-to-right communication process where each processor but P_0 receives a message from P_{q-1}, appends the threshold indices that is has computed and (exept if it is P_{p-1}) sends the whole thing to P_{q+1}. At the end, P_{p-1} knows all the p indices and initiates a backward process. Clearly, this naive solution has a communication cost which is proportional to p^2, since there are p indices to gather and then broadcast. A more efficient solution will be described later.

3.3. Elastic redistribution of the rows among the processors

Now each processor P_q knows the old indices $(r_1(q), r_2(q))$ and the new ones $(s_1(q), s_2(q))$. See figure 3 for a case analysis of the different situation that may occur.

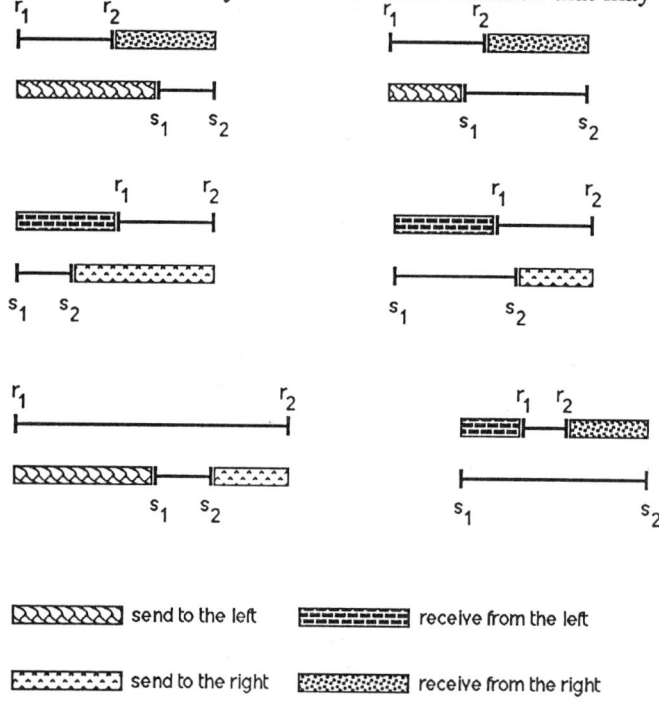

Figure 3: Case analysis for the data redistribution

Consider for instance the first case, where $r_1 < r_2 < s_1 < s_2$ (we suppress the index q because no confusion can be made here). The new rows of P_q will come from the right. P_{q+1} will send them, regardless of the fact that it already hold all these rows, some of them or none: the only thing we know is that these rows are currently held by consecutive processors $P_{q+a}, P_{q+a+1}, ..., P_{q+b}$, where a and b are positive integers with a ≤ b. How many rows will P_q receive form the right ? Clearly, the answer is $s_2 - r_2$, because P_q needs row s_2 and therefore will receive the whole segment $[r_2+1, s_2]$. From this segment, it will keep only the last part, that is rows $[s_1, s_2]$. The first part $[r_2+1, s_1-1]$ is propagated leftwards to P_{q-1} (and perhaps will progress further to the left). On the other hand, P_q has to send rows $[r_1, r_2]$ to the left in addition to those that it transmits from P_{q+1}. To summarize, P_q receives $s_2 - r_2$ rows (whose indices are increasing) from the right and sends $s_1 - r_1$ rows to the left (same remark). If we adopt a strategy where rows are communicated one by one rather than by packets, then P_q can receive and send in parallel $\min(s_2 - r_2, s_1 - r_1)$ rows. It will then continue its communications by sending (if $s_1 - r_1 > s_2 - r_2$, as in the figure) or by receiving (if $s_1 - r_1 < s_2 - r_2$).

The general case can be deduced from this analysis. Communications are best summarized by the following table, according to the values of the parameters s_1-r_1 and s_2-r_2:

	> 0	< 0
s1 - r1	send s1 - r1 rows to the left	receive r1 - s1 rows from the left
s2 - r2	receive s2 - r2 rows from the right	send r2 - s2 rows to the right

Table 1 : Communications to be made by the processors

The redistribution algorithm is then the following:

Program of processor P_q
1. determine $s_1(q)$ and $s_2(q)$ as previously stated
2. compute
$$\begin{cases} \delta = \min(\mid s_1(q) - r_1(q) \mid, \mid s_2(q) - r_2(q) \mid) \\ \Delta = \max(\mid s_1(q) - r_1(q) \mid, \mid s_2(q) - r_2(q) \mid) \end{cases}$$
3. perform δ communications with both neighbors P_{q-1} and P_{q+1} in parallel (whether these communications are sends or receives is known from Table 1)
4. perform $\Delta - \delta$ communications with a single neighbor (which neighbor and which direction is known form Table 1)

The fact that the redistribution algorithm is correct needs to be proven: it could happen that some processors could be blocked while requiring a communication with a neighbor. In fact the redistribution algorithm requires that each processor holds at least one row at the beginning (we discuss such a case below). Under this hypothesis we can prove the correctness as follows.

Let us call pivot rows those rows that belong to the same processor before and after the redistribution. Note that row 0 and row n-1 are always pivot rows. These pivot rows act as barriers that separate the redistribution into disjoint fields. Because of the elasticity of the redistribution, communications involving rows to the left and to the right of a given pivot row are fully independent. See figure 4 for an example. In the interval inside two consecutive pivot rows, all the communication is unidirectional (in the example from right to left), otherwise there would be another pivot row. This ensures the correctness of the algorithm.

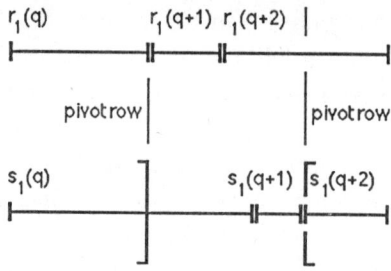

Figure 4 : Elastic redistribution between two consecutive pivot rows
(involving 3 processors)

Note that if one processor has no row at the beginning, it must perform a single receive before entering phase 3 (with the total number of communications being reduced by 1). This situation is not very likely to happen with rows. But coming back to step 2, namely the redistribution of threshold indices, we see that in fact we have another example of elastic redistribution, where some processors can have no data item at the beginning. So we can use this (modified) version of the elastic algorithm for redistributing indices.

As usually assumed in the literature, let $\beta + L\tau$ be the cost for the communication of a message of size L between two neighbor processors, where β is a start-up and τ is the elemental communication time [Dun, MV, Rob, SSc1, SSc2]. Assume that all rows are of same size L. In particular, this assumption is fulfilled in the case when a matrix or an image is distributed to the processors. The cost of the elastic algorithm is clearly data-dependent. We have let

$$\Delta = \max_{0 \leq q < p-1} \{ \mid s_1(q) - r_1(q) \mid, \mid s_2(q) - r_2(q) \mid \}$$

The time needed to redistribute the data is equal to $\Delta (\beta + L\tau)$. In other words, the time is related to the longest distance that a row may travel before reaching its destination processor. In many practical situations, only a few rows will be shifted from one processor to another, which in most cases will be a direct neighbor, and the elastic algorithm will execute very rapidly.

3.4. Minimizing the memory requirement

As the number of data items allocated to each processor will evolve dynamically, it is necessary to use a flexible data structure. The simplest solution would be that each processor P_q allocates enough space for storing the whole array in its memory, say an array A[0..n-1] of rows. The two indices $r_1(q)$ and $r_2(q)$ would be used to address the rows currently stored by P_q. However, this solution requires a lot of memory.

We have adopted a more flexible data structure to minimize the memory requirement while avoiding copies of buffers. The idea is to maintain a circular list A[0..M-1] of rows, where M is a constant specified by the user: see figure 5.

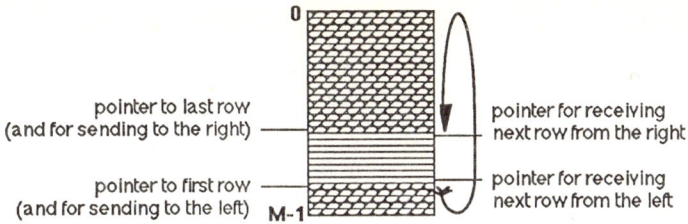

Figure 5 : Internal structure for storage
(all pointers are taken modulo M)

The constant M should be chosen carefully. Without any information on the application, almost all the rows could be sent to the same processor, requiring a memory storage as large as with the first simple solution. Nevertheless, for some applications like the thinning of a binary image illustrated in the next section, bounds on memory storage can be derived by examining the worst case.

4. Application to the thinning of a binary image

Thinning of binary pictures is a cost-intensive problem, and has been widely studied by many authors, in the sequential case as well as in the parallel case (see for instance [BT,GH,LMR,Ols,ON,Ube]). A thinning algorithm takes as input a binary picture consisting of objets (the d_8-connected black pixels) and background (the d_4-connected white pixels). It produces as output a skeleton of the objects, which preserves their shape, their connectivity and their number of holes, but which is one pixel thin. We test the algorithm with pictures of the Mandelbrot set with different resolutions. Figure 6 below presents such an image and the corresponding skeleton. There are two different approaches used to skeletonize a picture, namely the "contour peeling" approach and the mask-based approach. The first one is more efficient for objects whose contour is regular, but it is more difficult to parallelize. The experiments with our elastic load-balancing technique were performed with an algorithm of the second class of methods.

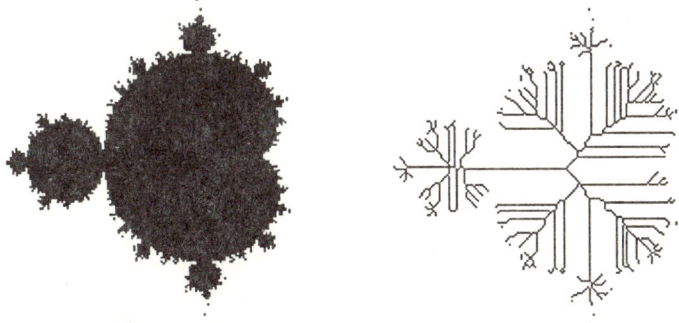

Figure 6 : Mandelbrot set and its skeleton

We use the algorithm of Olsewski [Ols] which performs successive iterations on the picture by deleting pixels which do not belong to the skeleton. A deletion condition is computed according to the 3x3 window centered in the pixel. The execution is completed when no pixel is deleted during a whole iteration. The processing of white pixels is immediate since they are just skipped during the scan. On the other hand, a black pixel is much longer to process, since we have to compute a survival condition depending of its 8 nearest neighbors. (see [Ols] for a complete description on the survival condition).

In our experiments, run on a 32-Transputer Supernode machine [Nic], we compare the static allocation of the rows with the dynamic elastic redistribution. As explained before, the computation of the workload histogram is very easy to perform : we estimate the computational cost of a row at an iteration to be equivalent to the processing time of that row at the previous iteration. This approximation is good since only a few pixels of each row are deleted at each iteration, and the processing time of a row does not evolve dramatically between two successive iterations. Figures 7a and 7b, are 3D-plots of the workload as a function of the iteration number for each of the 32 processors, when processing an image of size 560x560 (respectively without and with redistribution). In figure 7a, we see that the workload is very poorly balanced among the processors. "Central" processors have much more black pixels than "border" processors. Since processors exchange their frontier rows after each iteration, they synchronize themselves, and the duration of an iteration is the time spent by the slowest. In figure 7b, one can see that after the first iteration, which has the same load imbalance as in figure 7a, all the processors have approximately the same workload. It is interesting to point out that after the first redistribution is done, the elastic redistribution is limited to the exchange of very few rows, and is therefore very cheap.

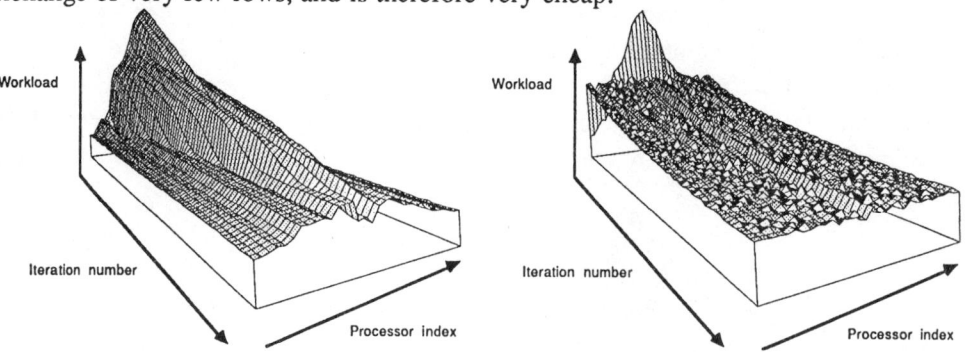

7a : Static allocation   7b : Dynamic redistribution
Figure 7 : workload of the processors as a function of the iteration number

In the next experiment (see figure 8), we plot the speedup of the parallel algorithm as a function of the number of processors, when processing an image of size 560x560. The "elastic" speedup is close to the linear speedup, whereas the "static" one is much less. We reach a speedup of 28 with 32 processors whereas the static approach is limited to 17.

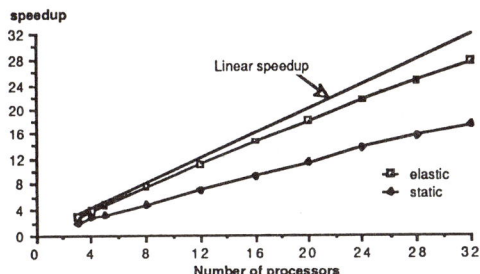

Figure 8 : Speedup as a function of the number of processors

In the last experiment (figure 9 below), we fix the number of processors to 32 and let the size of the picture vary. We see that the efficiency of the algorithm (defined as the speedup divided by the number of processors) is increasing with the size of the picture, since the influence of the communications for large pictures is less important as compared to the computations. The communication complexity is $O(n)$ whereas the computation complexity is $O(n^2)$, where n denotes the size of the picture.

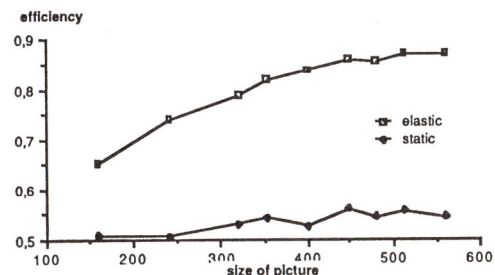

Figure 9 : Efficiency as a function of the size of the picture

5. Conclusion

In this paper we have described a very efficient technique for dynamically balancing the workload of image processing algorithms on distributed memory processors. The technique is based upon on-the-fly data redistributions between the processors during the execution of the algorithm. We have demonstrated the usefulness of our "elastic" redistribution strategy by comparing the efficiency obtained with and without the elastic algorithm for a thinning algorithm which aims at extracting the skeleton of a binary image.

We believe that the elastic redistribution technique can be applied to a wide class of problems. Most favorable are those situations where the histogram computation can come for free, as a by-product of other computations. Concerning iterative algorithms, an interesting extension would be to redistribute the workload only every k iterations, and to determine the best k as a trade-off between the cost of redistribution and the cost of load imbalance.

References

[BBa] Belkhale K.P., Banerjee P., "Recursive partitions on multiprocessors", in *The Fifth Distributed Memory Conference,* D.W. Walker et al. eds., IEEE Computer Society Press (1990), 930-938

[BBo] Berger M.J., Bokhari S.H., "A partitioning strategy for nonuniform problems on multiprocessors", IEEE Trans. Computers 36, 5 (1987), 570-580

[Bok] Bokhari S.H., "Partitioning problems in parallel, pipelined and distributed computing", IEEE Trans. Computers 37, 1 (1988), 48-57

[BT] Baek J.H., Teath K.A., "Parallel thinning on a distributed memory machine", in *The Fifth Distributed Memory Conference,* D.W. Walker et al. eds., IEEE Computer Society Press (1990), 72-75

[Cyb] Cybenko G., "Dynamic load balancing for distributed memory multiprocessors", J. Parallel Distributed Computing 7 (1989), 279-301

[Dun] Dunigan, T.H., "Hypercube performance", in *Hypercube Multiprocessors 1987,* H.T. Heath ed., SIAM Press (1987), 178-192

[EJ] Embrechts H., Jones J.P., "An input/output algorithm for M-dimensional decompositions on N-dimensional hypercubes multicomputers", in *The Fifth Distributed Memory Conference,* D.W. Walker et al. eds., IEEE Computer Society Press (1990), 876-882

[GH] Guo Z., Hall R.W., "Parallel thinning with two subiteration algorithms", C.A.C.M. 32, 3 (1989), 359-373

[Hin] Hinz D.Y., "A run-time load balancing strategy for highly parallel systems", in *The Fifth Distributed Memory Conference,* D.W. Walker et al. eds., IEEE Computer Society Press (1990), 951-961

[LMR] J. J. Li, S.Miguet, Y. Robert, S. Ubeda. "Image processing algorithms on distributed memory machines", in *Parallelism in image Processing*. J.C. Simon ed. North Holland, to appear.

[MV] MacBryan O.A. , Van de Velde E.F., "Hypercube algorithms and implementations", *SIAM J. Sci. Stat. Comput.* 8, 2 (1987), s227-s287

[Nic] Nicole D. A., "Esprit Project 1085, Reconfigurable Transputer Processor Architecture", in *CONPAR 88*, C. R. Jesshope et al. eds., Cambridge University Press (1989), 81-89.

[Ols] Olszewski J., "A flexible thinning algorithm allowing parallel, sequential and distributed application," Technical report, Unviversität des Saarlandes, Saarbrücken, Germany (1990), to appear in ACM Trans. Math. Software

[Rob] Robert Y, *The impact of vector and parallel architectures on the Gaussian elimination algorithm,* Manchester University Press and John Wiley (1990)

[RW] Rosing M., Weaver R.P., "Mapping data to processors in distributed memory computations", in *The Fifth Distributed Memory Conference,* D.W. Walker et al. eds., IEEE Computer Society Press (1990), 884-893

[SE] Sadayappan P., Ercal F., "Nearest-neighbor mappings of finite element graphs onto processor meshes", *IEEE Trans. Computers* 36, 12 (1987), 1408-1424

[SSc1] Saad, Y., & Schultz, M.H., "Topological properties of hypercubes", *IEEE Trans. Computers* 37, 7 (1988), 867-872

[SSc2] Saad, Y. & Schultz, M.H., "Data communication in parallel architectures", *Parallel Computing* 11 (1989), 131-150

[SSo] Snyder L., Socha D.G., "An algorithm producing balanced partitionings of data arrays", in *The Fifth Distributed Memory Conference,* D.W. Walker et al. eds., IEEE Computer Society Press (1990), 867-875

[Ube] Ubeda S., "Comparison of thinning algorithm on distributed memory machines". Technical report LIP-IMAG 90-29 (1990). Submitted for publication

[XH] Xu J., Hwang K., "Heuristic methods for dynamic load balancing in a message-passing supercomputer", in *Supercomputing'90*, IEEE Computer Society Press (1990), 888-897

Lecture Notes in Computer Science

For information about Vols. 1–504
please contact your bookseller or Springer-Verlag

Vol. 505: E. H. L. Aarts, J. van Leeuwen, M. Rem (Eds.), PARLE '91. Parallel Architectures and Languages Europe, Volume I. Proceedings, 1991. XV, 423 pages. 1991.

Vol. 506: E. H. L. Aarts, J. van Leeuwen, M. Rem (Eds.), PARLE '91. Parallel Architectures and Languages Europe, Volume II. Proceedings, 1991. XV, 489 pages. 1991.

Vol. 507: N. A. Sherwani, E. de Doncker, J. A. Kapenga (Eds.), Computing in the 90's. Proceedings, 1989. XIII, 441 pages. 1991.

Vol. 508: S. Sakata (Ed.), Applied Algebra, Algebraic Algorithms and Error-Correcting Codes. Proceedings, 1990. IX, 390 pages. 1991.

Vol. 509: A. Endres, H. Weber (Eds.), Software Development Environments and CASE Technology. Proceedings, 1991. VIII, 286 pages. 1991.

Vol. 510: J. Leach Albert, B. Monien, M. Rodríguez (Eds.), Automata, Languages and Programming. Proceedings, 1991. XII, 763 pages. 1991.

Vol. 511: A. C. F. Colchester, D.J. Hawkes (Eds.), Information Processing in Medical Imaging. Proceedings, 1991. XI, 512

Vol. 512: P. America (Ed.), ECOOP '91. European Conference on Object-Oriented Programming. Proceedings, 1991. X, 396 pages. 1991.

Vol. 513: N. M. Mattos, An Approach to Knowledge Base Management. IX, 247 pages. 1991. (Subseries LNAI).

Vol. 514: G. Cohen, P. Charpin (Eds.), EUROCODE '90. Proceedings, 1990. XI, 392 pages. 1991.

Vol. 515: J. P. Martins, M. Reinfrank (Eds.), Truth Maintenance Systems. Proceedings, 1990. VII, 177 pages. 1991. (Subseries LNAI).

Vol. 516: S. Kaplan, M. Okada (Eds.), Conditional and Typed Rewriting Systems. Proceedings, 1990. IX, 461 pages. 1991.

Vol. 517: K. Nökel, Temporally Distributed Symptoms in Technical Diagnosis. IX, 164 pages. 1991. (Subseries LNAI).

Vol. 518: J. G. Williams, Instantiation Theory. VIII, 133 pages. 1991. (Subseries LNAI).

Vol. 519: F. Dehne, J.-R. Sack, N. Santoro (Eds.), Algorithms and Data Structures. Proceedings, 1991. X, 496 pages. 1991.

Vol. 520: A. Tarlecki (Ed.), Mathematical Foundations of Computer Science 1991. Proceedings, 1991. XI, 435 pages. 1991.

Vol. 521: B. Bouchon-Meunier, R. R. Yager, L. A. Zadeh (Eds.), Uncertainty in Knowledge-Bases. Proceedings, 1990. X, 609 pages. 1991.

Vol. 522: J. Hertzberg (Ed.), European Workshop on Planning. Proceedings, 1991. VII, 121 pages. 1991. (Subseries LNAI).

Vol. 523: J. Hughes (Ed.), Functional Programming Languages and Computer Architecture. Proceedings, 1991. VIII, 666 pages. 1991.

Vol. 524: G. Rozenberg (Ed.), Advances in Petri Nets 1991. VIII, 572 pages. 1991.

Vol. 525: O. Günther, H.-J. Schek (Eds.), Advances in Spatial Databases. Proceedings, 1991. XI, 471 pages. 1991.

Vol. 526: T. Ito, A. R. Meyer (Eds.), Theoretical Aspects of Computer Software. Proceedings, 1991. X, 772 pages. 1991.

Vol. 527: J.C.M. Baeten, J. F. Groote (Eds.), CONCUR '91. Proceedings, 1991. VIII, 541 pages. 1991.

Vol. 528: J. Maluszynski, M. Wirsing (Eds.), Programming Language Implementation and Logic Programming. Proceedings, 1991. XI, 433 pages. 1991.

Vol. 529: L. Budach (Ed.), Fundamentals of Computation Theory. Proceedings, 1991. XII, 426 pages. 1991.

Vol. 530: D. H. Pitt, P.-L. Curien, S. Abramsky, A. M. Pitts, A. Poigné, D. E. Rydeheard (Eds.), Category Theory and Computer Science. Proceedings, 1991. VII, 301 pages. 1991.

Vol. 531: E. M. Clarke, R. P. Kurshan (Eds.), Computer-Aided Verification. Proceedings, 1990. XIII, 372 pages. 1991.

Vol. 532: H. Ehrig, H.-J. Kreowski, G. Rozenberg (Eds.), Graph Grammars and Their Application to Computer Science. Proceedings, 1990. X, 703 pages. 1991.

Vol. 533: E. Börger, H. Kleine Büning, M. M. Richter, W. Schönfeld (Eds.), Computer Science Logic. Proceedings, 1990. VIII, 399 pages. 1991.

Vol. 534: H. Ehrig, K. P. Jantke, F. Orejas, H. Reichel (Eds.), Recent Trends in Data Type Specification. Proceedings, 1990. VIII, 379 pages. 1991.

Vol. 535: P. Jorrand, J. Kelemen (Eds.), Fundamentals of Artificial Intelligence Research. Proceedings, 1991. VIII, 255 pages. 1991. (Subseries LNAI).

Vol. 536: J. E. Tomayko, Software Engineering Education. Proceedings, 1991. VIII, 296 pages. 1991.

Vol. 537: A. J. Menezes, S. A. Vanstone (Eds.), Advances in Cryptology – CRYPTO '90. Proceedings. XIII, 644 pages. 1991.

Vol. 538: M. Kojima, N. Megiddo, T. Noma, A. Yoshise, A Unified Approach to Interior Point Algorithms for Linear Complementarity Problems. VIII, 108 pages. 1991.

Vol. 539: H. F. Mattson, T. Mora, T. R. N. Rao (Eds.), Applied Algebra, Algebraic Algorithms and Error-Correcting Codes. Proceedings, 1991. XI, 489 pages. 1991.

Vol. 540: A. Prieto (Ed.), Artificial Neural Networks. Proceedings, 1991. XIII, 476 pages. 1991.

Vol. 541: P. Barahona, L. Moniz Pereira, A. Porto (Eds.), EPIA '91. Proceedings, 1991. VIII, 292 pages. 1991. (Subseries LNAI).

Vol. 542: Z. W. Ras, M. Zemankova (Eds.), Methodologies for Intelligent Systems. Proceedings, 1991. X, 644 pages. 1991. (Subseries LNAI).

Vol. 543: J. Dix, K. P. Jantke, P. H. Schmitt (Eds.), Nonmonotonic and Inductive Logic. Proceedings, 1990. X, 243 pages. 1991. (Subseries LNAI).

Vol. 544: M. Broy, M. Wirsing (Eds.), Methods of Programming. XII, 268 pages. 1991.

Vol. 545: H. Alblas, B. Melichar (Eds.), Attribute Grammars, Applications and Systems. Proceedings, 1991. IX, 513 pages. 1991.

Vol. 546: O. Herzog, C.-R. Rollinger (Eds.), Text Understanding in LILOG. XI, 738 pages. 1991. (Subseries LNAI).

Vol. 547: D. W. Davies (Ed.), Advances in Cryptology – EUROCRYPT '91. Proceedings, 1991. XII, 556 pages. 1991.

Vol. 548: R. Kruse, P. Siegel (Eds.), Symbolic and Quantitative Approaches to Uncertainty. Proceedings, 1991. XI, 362 pages. 1991.

Vol. 549: E. Ardizzone, S. Gaglio, F. Sorbello (Eds.), Trends in Artificial Intelligence. Proceedings, 1991. XIV, 479 pages. 1991. (Subseries LNAI).

Vol. 550: A. van Lamsweerde, A. Fugetta (Eds.), ESEC '91. Proceedings, 1991. XII, 515 pages. 1991.

Vol. 551: S. Prehn, W. J. Toetenel (Eds.), VDM '91. Formal Software Development Methods. Volume 1. Proceedings, 1991. XIII, 699 pages. 1991.

Vol. 552: S. Prehn, W. J. Toetenel (Eds.), VDM '91. Formal Software Development Methods. Volume 2. Proceedings, 1991. XIV, 430 pages. 1991.

Vol. 553: H. Bieri, H. Noltemeier (Eds.), Computational Geometry - Methods, Algorithms and Applications '91. Proceedings, 1991. VIII, 320 pages. 1991.

Vol. 554: G. Grahne, The Problem of Incomplete Information in Relational Databases. VIII, 156 pages. 1991.

Vol. 555: H. Maurer (Ed.), New Results and New Trends in Computer Science. Proceedings, 1991. VIII, 403 pages. 1991.

Vol. 556: J.-M. Jacquet, Conclog: A Methodological Approach to Concurrent Logic Programming. XII, 781 pages. 1991.

Vol. 557: W. L. Hsu, R. C. T. Lee (Eds.), ISA '91 Algorithms. Proceedings, 1991. X, 396 pages. 1991.

Vol. 558: J. Hooman, Specification and Compositional Verification of Real-Time Systems. VIII, 235 pages. 1991.

Vol. 559: G. Butler, Fundamental Algorithms for Permutation Groups. XII, 238 pages. 1991.

Vol. 560: S. Biswas, K. V. Nori (Eds.), Foundations of Software Technology and Theoretical Computer Science. Proceedings, 1991. X, 420 pages. 1991.

Vol. 561: C. Ding, G. Xiao, W. Shan, The Stability Theory of Stream Ciphers. IX, 187 pages. 1991.

Vol. 562: R. Breu, Algebraic Specification Techniques in Object Oriented Programming Environments. XI, 228 pages. 1991.

Vol. 563: A. Karshmer, J. Nehmer (Eds.), Operating Systems of the 90s and Beyond. Proceedings, 1991. X, 285 pages. 1991.

Vol. 564: I. Herman, The Use of Projective Geometry in Computer Graphics. VIII, 146 pages. 1992.

Vol. 565: J. D. Becker, I. Eisele, F. W. Mündemann (Eds.), Parallelism, Learning, Evolution. Proceedings, 1989. VIII, 525 pages. 1991. (Subseries LNAI).

Vol. 566: C. Delobel, M. Kifer, Y. Masunaga (Eds.), Deductive and Object-Oriented Databases. Proceedings, 1991. XV, 581 pages. 1991.

Vol. 567: H. Boley, M. M. Richter (Eds.), Processing Declarative Kowledge. Proceedings, 1991. XII, 427 pages. 1991. (Subseries LNAI).

Vol. 568: H.-J. Bürckert, A Resolution Principle for a Logic with Restricted Quantifiers. X, 116 pages. 1991. (Subseries LNAI).

Vol. 569: A. Beaumont, G. Gupta (Eds.), Parallel Execution of Logic Programs. Proceedings, 1991. VII, 195 pages. 1991.

Vol. 570: R. Berghammer, G. Schmidt (Eds.), Graph-Theoretic Concepts in Computer Science. Proceedings, 1991. VIII, 253 pages. 1992.

Vol. 571: J. Vytopil (Ed.), Formal Techniques in Real-Time and Fault-Tolerant Systems. Proceedings, 1992. IX, 620 pages. 1991.

Vol. 572: K. U. Schulz (Ed.), Word Equations and Related Topics. Proceedings, 1990. VII, 256 pages. 1992.

Vol. 573: G. Cohen, S. N. Litsyn, A. Lobstein, G. Zémor (Eds.), Algebraic Coding. Proceedings, 1991. X, 158 pages. 1992.

Vol. 574: J. P. Banâtre, D. Le Métayer (Eds.), Research Directions in High-Level Parallel Programming Languages. Proceedings, 1991. VIII, 387 pages. 1992.

Vol. 575: K. G. Larsen, A. Skou (Eds.), Computer Aided Verification. Proceedings, 1991. X, 487 pages. 1992.

Vol. 576: J. Feigenbaum (Ed.), Advances in Cryptology - CRYPTO '91. Proceedings. X, 485 pages. 1992.

Vol. 577: A. Finkel, M. Jantzen (Eds.), STACS 92. Proceedings, 1992. XIV, 621 pages. 1992.

Vol. 578: Th. Beth, M. Frisch, G. J. Simmons (Eds.), Public-Key Cryptography: State of the Art and Future Directions. XI, 97 pages. 1992.

Vol. 579: S. Toueg, P. G. Spirakis, L. Kirousis (Eds.), Distributed Algorithms. Proceedings, 1991. X, 319 pages. 1992.

Vol. 580: A. Pirotte, C. Delobel, G. Gottlob (Eds.), Advances in Database Technology – EDBT '92. Proceedings. XII, 551 pages. 1992.

Vol. 581: J.-C. Raoult (Ed.), CAAP '92. Proceedings. VIII, 361 pages. 1992.

Vol. 582: B. Krieg-Brückner (Ed.), ESOP '92. Proceedings. VIII, 491 pages. 1992.

Vol. 583: I. Simon (Ed.), LATIN '92. Proceedings. IX, 545 pages. 1992.

Vol. 584: R. E. Zippel (Ed.), Computer Algebra and Parallelism. Proceedings, 1990. IX, 114 pages. 1992.

Vol. 585: F. Pichler, R. Moreno Díaz (Eds.), Computer Aided System Theory – EUROCAST '91. Proceedings. X, 761 pages. 1992.

Vol. 586: A. Cheese, Parallel Execution of Parlog. IX, 184 pages. 1992.

Vol. 587: R. Dale, E. Hovy, D. Rösner, O. Stock (Eds.), Aspects of Automated Natural Language Generation. Proceedings, 1992. VIII, 311 pages. 1992. (Subseries LNAI).

Vol. 588: G. Sandini (Ed.), Computer Vision – ECCV '92. Proceedings. XV, 909 pages. 1992.

Vol. 589: U. Banerjee, D. Gelernter, A. Nicolau, D. Padua (Eds.), Languages and Compilers for Parallel Computing. Proceedings, 1991. IX, 419 pages. 1992.

Vol. 590: B. Fronhöfer, G. Wrightson (Eds.), Parallelization in Inference Systems. Proceedings, 1990. VIII, 372 pages. 1992. (Subseries LNAI).

Vol. 591: H. P. Zima (Ed.), Parallel Computation. Proceedings, 1991. IX, 451 pages. 1992.